Knowledge Management for Librarians

Knowledge Management for Librarians

Dr. Anil Kumar Dhiman
Information Scientist
Gurukul Kangri University
Haridwar (UK)
and
Dr. Hemant Sharma
Reader & Head
SOS in Library Science
Jiwaji University, Gwalior (MP)

Ess Ess Publications

4837/24, Ansari Road, Darya Ganj,
New Delhi-110002
✆: 23260807, 41563444
Fax: 011-41563334
E-mail: info@essessreference.com
url:http://www.essessreference.com

First Published 2009

Published by SUMIT SETHI
for Ess Ess Publications
4837/24, Ansari Road, Darya Ganj,
New Delhi - 110 002
Ph. : 23260807, 41563444
Fax : 011-41563334
E-mail: info@essessreference.com
url:http://www.essessreference.com

Price : Rs. 1675/-

Laser Typesetting:
Mukesh Graphics
T-1264, Mangolpuri, New Delhi
Ph. : 9899079035, 20106135
E-mail:mukeshgraphics29@yahoo.com

Printed at :
Print Line

Contents

Preface

Knowledge Management is emerging as a new concept in the management field. Though the concept is for business organizations but it is also attracting Library Professionals to participate and make use of it in managing library and information centres. This book on *Knowledge Management for Librarians* is written to make aware the working librarians about knowledge management and its possible uses in the library and information centres.

The book is divided into 12 chapters. First chapter is Introduction about knowledge and knowledge management. Next chapter describes origin of the Knowledge Management and its Developmental History. Knowledge creation and its dissemination are two very important tasks or the activities of knowledge management. Next two chapters discuss the ways and means of creation of knowledge, its capturing and codification. Once the knowledge is created and codified, its dissemination is important. Unless the knowledge is not disseminated, it is of no use, so its transfer and sharing with others is important. Next chapter discusses and describes knowledge transfer and its sharing for various purposes. Tools used for Knowledge Management are described in next chapter. Artificial Intelligence and networks plays important roles in knowledge management. Neural Networks and Value Networks are discussed in next chapter.

Data Mining and Web Mining are important steps to find out knowledge from the universe of knowledge. Both play a crucial role in managing knowledge. Various ways of mining data in traditional mode and web environment and models with their impact on the society have been discussed in next chapter. For successful implementation of any programme, an effective leadership is very essential and so is the case with knowledge management. Next chapter describes leadership role and implementation of knowledge management. It also gives a general idea about formulation of strategies and road map for implementation of Knowledge Management. Knowledge management is emerging as an effective way of managing knowledge in the era of information and communication technologies, but on the other hand it is also posing some of the social and legal issues in front of knowledge managers. A chapter on Ethical and Legal Issues in Knowledge Management is retained in the book describing some of the important aspects of social, ethical and legal issues for knowledge management. As the book is written primarily for the librarians and working professionals, next chapter on Knowledge Management in Libraries, describes the role of knowledge management in libraries, typology of knowledge management in libraries and possible uses of knowledge management in academic, public and special libraries. Some of the barriers for migrating librarians into knowledge managers are also discussed along with state of art of knowledge management in the libraries in this chapter. The last chapter of the book *Epilogue* is devoted to the latest development in the field of Knowledge Management, where its prospects are also described in brief.

The book is appended with two appendices on *Alternative Schemes for Structuring Knowledge Management System and Software Tools for Knowledge Management.*

The book is written primarily for the working librarians and library professionals so that they could adopt this management technique in the library and information centres, but it is believed that this book will also be equally useful for those who are interested to know the mystery of knowledge management in the field of library science. The students and the teachers will also be benefited with this book to enhance their knowledge in the emerging field of Knowledge Management.

In preparing this book, the help of various sources and books have been taken. We would like to thank all the authorities whose works have been consulted during the preparation of this book. *Dr. Dhiman* is indebted to his parents *Shri Ramlal Dhiman* and *Smt. Kamla Devi* for their blessings and moral encouragement. He is also thankful to his son *Aman*, to whom like his other works, he could not pay much attention, which he deserved while writing the book. He is also thankful to his wife *Smt. Yashoda Rani*, the co-authoress of many books with him in Library Science, who has always been a source of inspiration to enable him to complete this work. *Dr. Sharma* is also thankful to his family members, especially to his wife *Smt. Ranjana Sharma* who made him free from every type of home responsibilities while working on the manuscript of this book.

Lastly but not least, our thanks are also due to the *Shri Sumit Sethi*, the owner of Ess Ess Publications, New Delhi, for beautiful, nice and timely publication of the book with in a short span of time.

May 2009

Dr. Anil Kumar Dhiman
Information Scientist
Gurukul Kangri University
Haridwar (UK)
and
Dr. Hemant Sharma
Reader & Head
SOS in Library Science
Jiwaji University, Gwalior (MP)

1

Introduction

Knowledge management might be "hot" as of today, but successful managers have always realized its value. Long before terms such as *expert systems, core competencies, best practices, learning organization and corporate memory* were in vogue, these managers knew that their company's key asset was not its buildings, its market share, or its products, but it lay in its people, their knowledge, and skills. After having tried everything else — from the greatest products and the best technology to virtual monopolies — in their respective markets, more businesses have finally come to the realization that the only sustainable source of competitive advantage is their knowledge.

Knowledge and knowledge management are lofty concepts — debated by academics and managers and even doubted by some analysis — one that only a few businesses have mastered. Knowledge is fluid mix of framed experience, values, contextual information, expert insight and grounded intuition that provides an environment and framework for evaluating and incorporating new experiences and information. It originates and is applied in the minds of knowers. In organizations, it often becomes embedded not only in documents or repositories but also in organizational routines, processes, practices and norms.

The Knowledge management can be extended to

"management of organizational knowledge for creating business value and generating a competitive advantage." Knowledge management enables the creation, communication and application of knowledge of all kinds to achieve business goals. Kirk Klasson elucidates, "Knowledge management is the ability to create and retain greater value from core business competencies." Knowledge management addresses business problems particular to your business — whether it is creating and delivering innovative products or services; managing and enhancing relationships with existing and new customers, partners and suppliers or administering and improving work practices and processes.

Knowledge management is a framework within which the organization views its processes as knowledge processes. In this view, all business processes involve creation, dissmination, renewal and application of knowledge toward organizational sustenance and survival.

The term of yester years was Information Management. This term came about when people realized that information is a resource that can and needs to be managed to be useful in an organization. When Ranganathan wrote that 'the Universe of subjects is synonymous to Universe of Knowledge, he became the first to identify knowledge management in libraries. Though claims may be there, from various other quarters of contributors, for the introduction of the term in library management, there cannot be any doubt about Ranaganathan's originality of the claim. From this, the ideas of Information Analysis and Information Planning came about. Organizations are now starting to look at Knowledge as a resource as well. This requires ways for managing the knowledge in libraries of organizations.

Information and Management (IM) and Knowledge Management (KM) – both concepts refer to managing (handling, directing, governing, controlling, coordinating, planning, organizing) processes and the products of those processes. In addition, since knowledge is a form of information, it follows that KM is a form of IM. More specifically, KM is a more robust form of IM that provides managment of activities not necessary in specifying the concept of information management.

One difference between basic IM and KM is that basic IM focuses on managing how information is produced and integrated into the enterprise, while KM does the same with respect to knowledge. A second difference between basic IM and KM is that basic IM focuses on managing a more narrrow set of activities than KM. The two information processes managed by an organization are information production and information integration. The two basic knowledge processes are knowledge production and knowledge integration.

Knowledge production includes (a) knowledge claim formulation, (b) individual and group learning, and (c) information acquisition and (d) knowledge claim evaluation activity. Knowledge integration includes (a) knowledge broadcasting, (b) searching/retrieving), (c) teaching, and (d) knowledge sharing. The two knowledge processes, once again may be viewed as part of the KLC, a knowledge "value network". The knowledge life cycle or KLC and the interaction of the two knowledge processes are illustrated in Figure 1.1. The major task clusters within knowledge production and knowledge integration are also illustrated in Figure 1.1.

Basic information processes are different from knowledge production and integration processes in that they lack knowledge claim evaluation and therefore fail to distinguish between knowledge claims that are surviving, falsified, or otherwise. Information Prodcution includes information acquisition, individual and group learning, even knowledge claim formulation, but excludes knowledge claim evaluation. So the information "life cycle" or value network is incomplete in comparison with the knowledge life cycle. Similarly, information integration includes broadcasting, searching/retrieving, teaching and sharing but what is being broadcasted, searched for, retrieved, taught and shared is information rather than knowledge.

IM activities can be defined in analogy to KM activities. There are three categories of IM activities in the information management process: interpersonal behaviour; information processing behaviour; and decision making.

- Interpersonal IM behaviour includes:
- figurehead

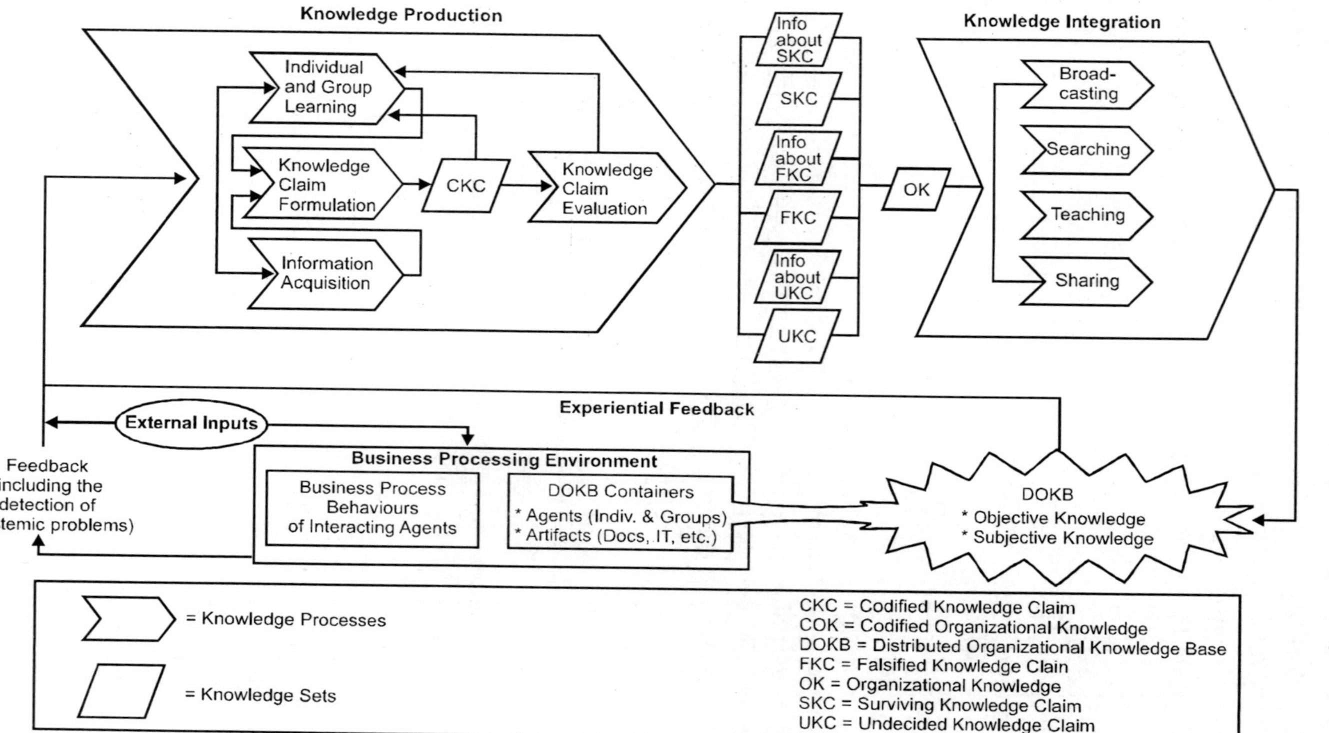

Fig. 1.1. Knowledge Life Cycle

- leadership
- external relationship-building activity

Information processing behaviour includes:

- IM information production (no knowledge claim evaluation)
- IM information integration (only broadcasting, searching/ retrieving, teaching or sharing information, but not knowledge)

Decision making includes:

- changing information processing rules
- crists handling
- allocating IM resources
- negotiating agreements with representatives of other business process

The difference between information processes at the IM level and knowledge processes at the KM level therefore arise from the absence of knowledge claim evaluation activity in IM. As a result, broadcasting, searching/retrieving, teaching and sharing at the IM level are all focused on information and not on knowledge.

Knowledge Management depends upon the resources of a well articulated library. The generation and the application of knowledge management cannot be independent of a library information system.

1.1. KNOWLEDGE FRAMEWORK

Data, Information and Knowledge are three often-encountered words that belong closely together, seem to have slightly different meanings. Sometimes, they are interchangeably used also. Yet, a clarity in their meanings is quite essential to understand the gamut of knowledge management.

Data is the plural form of Datum. Data are the uninterpreated signals that reach the human senses every minute by zillions. Computers are full of data– signals consisting of strings of numbers, characters, and other symbols that are blindly and mechanically handled in large quantities.

Information is data equipped with meaning. Processed data are called information. Data are the input for information processing.

While information provides an understanding of the relations between data, it generally does not provide a foundation for what, why and how of the data. Information has a tendency to be relatively static in time and linear in nature. Information is a relationship between data and, quite simply, is what it is, with great dependence on context for its meaning and with little implication for the future.

Knowledge is derived from information but it is richer and more meaningful than information. It includes familiarity, awareness and understanding gained through experience or study, and results from making comparisons, indentifying consequences, and making connections.

Traditionally, knowledge has been all the core of philosophical considerations. Philosophy has striven for a common and accepted definition or conceptualization of knowledge for centuries with great philosophers contributing to the subject. Here is presented a brief and far from comprehensive survey of definitions offered by writers and researchers in knowledge management.

Knowledge is :

- "Justified true belief": This is the venerable definition of many philosophers, especially of empiricists who believe knowledge claims can be justified by facts. It also is the definition adopted by Nonaka and Takeuchi.
- "Information in context": This is a definition that may have its roots in Cartesian rationalist epistemology. In that conceptual framework, its import is that a knowledge claim is valid if it fits without contradiction and adds to the systematic coherence of a larger framework of knowledge. That is, the rationalist view that knowledge is information in context and that context is what makes it knowledge derives from the more complete idea that information is justified as knowledge when it is coherent with a larger deductive system within which it fits. In this formulation, the validity criterion and the theory of truth are the same. They form a coherence theory of truth and validation, where coherence means that a knowledge claim is consistent with its broader context. In

other words, according to the Cartesian rationalist version of the information in context view, information is knowledge when and if (because) it is validated by consistency with its context.

The rationalist view of knowledge as information in context is only one variant of that view. A second is the pragmatist idea that information that is useful in a situational context of decision and action is knowledge. This view does not focus on logical consistency with other knowledge claims in a system. Instead, it focuses on how instrumental a piece of information is as a tool for action. A further variant of the pragmatist view results from those who do not believe that mere information, our linguistic expressions recorded in documents, information systems, or other cultural products can ever be knowledge. This variant views knowledge as belief and suggests that the utility of information in context is determined by the belief knowledge that exposure to the information produces.

- "Knowledge is understanding based on experience": This is an idea that is central to modern pragmatism and its associated epistemology. It is also a standard definition found in English language dictionaries. Since it refers to "understanding," it is clearly a definition of knowledge focused on belief.
- "Knowledge is experience or information that can be communicated or shared.": Even though Allec refers to experience here, her emphasis is clearly on sharable information and community,' not beliefs. "Knowledge, while made up of data and information, can be thought of as much greater understanding of a situation, relationships, causal phenomena, and the theories and rules (both explicit and implicit) that underlie a given domain or problem." Here Bennet and Bennet refer to knowledge as "understanding" of situations, relationships, and causal phenomena but associate data, information, theories, and rules, and also "understanding" of them with knowledge.
- "Knowledge can be thought of as the body of understandings,

generalizations, and abstractions that we carry with us on a permanent or semi-permanent basis and apply to interpret and manage the world around us ... we will consider knowledge to be the collection of mental units of all kinds that provides us with understanding and insights." Wiig clearly defines knowledge as a form of belief.

- "The most essential definition of knowledge is that it is composed of and grounded solely in potential acts and in those signs that refer to them". This is another definition originating in pragmatism and specifically in the work of Charles S. Peirce. A definition offered in the same spirit is "knowledge is social acts," provided by Ralph Stacey.
- "Knowledge is the capacity for effective action." This definition is the one favoured by the organizational learning community.
- "Knowledge is a fluid mix of framed experience, values, contextual information, and expert insight that provides a framework for evaluating and incorporating new experiences and information. It originates and is applied in the minds of knowers. In organizations it often becomes embedded not only in documents or repositories but also in organizational routines, processes, practices, and norms".

Lets have a look on the knowledge framework. We distinguish three types of knowledge:

- World 1 knowledge—encoded structures in physical systems– such as genetic encoding in DNA, that allow those objects to adapt to an environment;
- World 2 knowledge—beliefs and belief predispositions as in minds, about the world, the beautiful, and the right that we believe have survived our tests, evaluations, and experience;
- World 3 knowledge—sharable linguistic formulations, knowledge claims about the world, the beautiful, and the right, that have survived testing and evaluation by the agent–individual, group, community, team, organization, society, etc. for acquiring, formulating, and testing and evaluating the knowledge claims.

All three types of knowledge are about encoded structures in one kind of system or another that arguably help those systems to adapt. The World 1, World 2, and World 3 distinctions were introduced by Proper and Eccles. Popper also defined the distinction between World 2 and World 3 knowledge. But he did not define either type of knowledge in precisely the terms we have used.

It is comparatively easy to accept Popper's distinction between the World I material and World 2 mental objects that underlies the distinction between World 1 and World 2 knowledge. It is much harder however, to accept the reality of World 3 objects and therefore World 3 knowledge. Following Popper, it is proposed that there are things that affect our behavior which (1) are not part of World 1 or World 2, (2) are made by intelligent beings, (3) are sharable among us in that they provide sharable content for those exposed to them, and (4) are partly autonomous once created by us. World 3 objects include theories, arguments, problems, works of art, symphonies, constitutions, public policy statements, and all the cultural objects that express content.

While Popper called these objects "World 3," he was quick to recognize that such objects come in many varieties and indicated that he thought that World 3 had many different regions. He had no strong feelings about whether these regions should all be called World 3 products or whether we should break things out into a number of distinct worlds based on the differences among art, science, music, law, truth, beauty, justice, and other cultural products. One can agree with his views and also think that it makes little difference how we label the different World 3 regions as long as we recognize that all are cultural products, that humans create them, and that their function is to help us adapt.

Among World 3 products, problems and knowledge claims as key objects have already been named. Thus, knowledge claims exist within any organization or social system and are among its World 3 products. Among World 2 objects beliefs and belief predispositions of various kinds are distinguished.

So in World 2 we have beliefs and belief predispositions, and in World 3 linguistic expressions in the form of knowledge claims. Where, then, is knowledge? As indicated earlier, knowledge is found in both World 2 and World 3 in those beliefs, beliefs predispositions, and knowledge claims that have best survived our attempts to test and evaluate them against competitors. Thus, knowledge is a term applied to the best performing beliefs, belief predispositions, and knowledge claims of an agent—that is, the individual or group that holds the belief or belief predisposition, or expresses the knowledge claims in question—in the course of the agent assessing the performance of those claims.

The definitions of Worlds 2 and 3 knowledge do not require that knowledge be true. In fact, our position is that knowledge claims are fallible and that while a particular knowledge claim may be true, and that its function is to state what is true, even those that we call "knowledge" may prove false in the future if they fail to survive our tests. If knowledge need not be true, then clearly it cannot be called objective on grounds that it is true.

Further, World 2 belief knowledge, even though it has survived individual tests and evaluations, since it is fallible, also has the problem that it is not sharable among agents. Thus, such knowledge is personal and psychological, and the beliefs that constitute it do not exist outside the knowing subject that holds them. In exactly this sense, World 2 belief knowledge is subjective.

On the other hand, World 3 knowledge claims, once created, do exist outside the knowing subjects that created them, do not die with these subjects, and, in addition, are sharable among these knowing subjects and others that may not encounter them until years after their creation. Further, the track record of testing and evaluating knowledge claims also exists outside the knowing subjects involved in creating it and is sharable among knowing subjects interested in the knowledge claims. So this sharability of knowledge claims and their track records makes them "objective" in a way that beliefs and belief predispositions are not.

If knowledge claims are "objective," what may be said about the objectivity of World 3 knowledge itself? It is already defined that World 3 knowledge is composed of the best surviving knowledge claims of an agent. But this notion implies that knowledge is the product of a classification decision by the agent producing that knowledge. So what, exactly, is "objective" about this classification decision that may well be dependent on ideological or political criteria that are biased and therefore essentially subjective in nature? The answer is that in the general case there is nothing necessarily "objective" about such decisions, nor need there be to ensure that the knowledge produced by the decision is "objective."

The reason for this is that the classification decision need not be correct for the resulting "knowledge" to be objective. Nor need it follow a decision procedure that conforms to any recognizable notion of rationality. Though the knowledge that emerges from it would certainly be higher quality if it did, and therefore an "objective" decision procedure is certainly preferable to one that is not objective.

Rather, the objectivity of the knowledge produced lies in the sharable nature of the knowledge claims that have been classified as knowledge and the metaclaims constituting the track record of testing and evaluation. The sharable nature of these claims always makes the decision to classify a knowledge claim as knowledge subject to review. Thus, it has no effect on the objectivity of knowledge that the classification decision is made by one particular agent rather than another, because the designation "knowledge" for a particular knowledge claim carries no greater connotation of "objectivity" than the objectivity that inheres in the unclassified knowledge claims themselves.

The distinction between World 2 and World 3 knowledge, and particularly the use of the term "knowledge" for World 3, is frequently-hard to accept.

World 3 expressions of knowledge are not the same as knowledge in the World 2 sense because they are expressions of knowledge, not knowledge. They are vestiges of knowledge. To call them knowledge is a little bit like calling a person's shadow a form of "person" because it expresses the shape of a person whose very essence can be deciphered from a study of the shadow. Therefore, shadows are "objective" people.

This argument, though trenchant and attractive, has many problems. First, it can not be said that World 3 knowledge claims are the same as World 2 knowledge. World 2 knowledge is belief knowledge; most of it is not even reducible to language; most of it is predispositional in character and is not even conscious. And all of it is subjective in the sense that it cannot be shared with other agents. Second, World 3 knowledge claims are not expressions of belief knowledge as claimed just above.

It is a fallacy to think that we can faithfully express or copy our belief knowledge except in the most superficial sense. Rather than being expressions of belief knowledge, knowledge claims are simply products that we create in an effort to help us solve problems. They are one type of linguistic expression. What do they express? What the claims say, not what the authors believe. We do not know the correspondence between what the authors say and what they believe. Nor does the truth of the expressions—the knowledge claims—have anything to do with the truth of a person's beliefs. Truth as a coherent philosophical construct is a relationship between linguistic entities and facts. It is not a relationship between beliefs and facts. It is not even clear what the analogous relationship between beliefs and facts is, but it is not truth.

Third, World 3 knowledge claims are not "vestiges of knowledge." They are not because they are a resultant of belief knowledge, situational forces, cultural and social structural influence, and individual creativity expressed in the creation of World 3 objects. So, much more goes into creating them than just belief knowledge.

They are also not vestiges because as linguistic objects, they have an entirely different character than beliefs and are in no sense a "leftover" or "vestige" of them. They are also not vestiges because while beliefs cannot be shared with others, these knowledge claims can be shared, and this sharability characteristic makes them more testable, more open to evaluation, more open to gradual refinement over time, and more useful in both solving problems and in generating new problems that can lead to further progress than beliefs can.

Finally, in the passage: "To call them knowledge is a little bit like calling a person's shadow or a form of 'person' because it expresses the shape of a person whose very essence can be deciphered from a study of the shadow. Therefore, shadows are "objective people," such ideas express an entirely false analogy. In the analogy, the person is the reality and the shadow is the representation of it we use to try to divine its essence. But in the World 2/World 3 contrast, reality is the system and environment within which we have to act, and our problem is to understand that reality so that we can achieve our goals in that context. At any given time, our belief knowledge is the "shadow" of reality present in our minds, and our problem is to refine this shadow, this understanding, so that we can use it to act more successfully. How do we do that?

We do it by combining with others to create linguistic expressions, cultural products that are representations of reality themselves, more shadows. But there are differences between these shadows and the belief shadows. First, unlike belief shadows, with these knowledge claim-based shadows, we can at least formulate the idea of truth correspondence coherently. Second, we can test and evaluate these knowledge claims in collaboration with other people, so that we can create organizational knowledge. Third, we can share these shadows with others in order to refine them and to test them against alternative shadows, so that eventually we can arrive at a shadow that has performed better in the face of our tests. Fourth, when our construction of our knowledge claim shadows is, for the time being, complete, we can use these shadows to reshape our belief shadows, so that these "belief shadows" that we must rely upon to make decisions, provide us with better results.

This last point is of paramount importance. Following Popper's account, evolution begins within World 1. When biological creatures evolve, they first achieve their goals through limited adaptive and learning capabilities. They have brains but do not have minds. Minds evolve as control mechanisms for the brain. And as we have seen, minds allow agents to develop belief "shadows" for tracking reality and enhancing adaptation. However, the shadows created by mind alone cannot incorporate an objective shared perspective on reality. Therefore their fit with external conditions is less than ideal.

So evolution proceeds further. It creates creatures that not only have brain, mind, and consciousness, but also creatures that have language and culture. These creatures can use language and culture to create "shadows" that do incorporate a sharable perspective on reality, and this perspective, in turn, with continued inquiry, can produce "shadows" that benefit from this shared perspective and that can even correspond closely with reality. In other words, the creation of language and culture creates more objective "shadows" or knowledge claims that place constraints on the personal, subjective "shadows" or beliefs of the mind. These subjective shadows, in turn, help it to better understand reality, which it must do if it is to fulfill its role as the controller of behaviour.

This brings the end of attempt to introduce a knowledge framework but we note that in many organizations, there is little concern with World 1 knowledge, and with the beautiful, and only slightly greater concern with the right, so we are left with Worlds 2 and 3 knowledge of reality as the outcomes of knowledge processes that are of primary concern to knowledge management. Let us now consider some of the definitions of knowledge in the light of their internal difficulties and the World 2/World 3 distinction.

World 2 Definitions

The definition of knowledge as "justified true belief" has the difficulty that we cannot know for certain that any knowledge belief, no matter how well validated, is true. Yet some knowledge claims, the well validated ones, are what we mean by knowledge. It also has the additional difficulty that "justification" of knowledge claims cannot be accomplished through the testing and evaluation processes that comprise validation, because no finite amount of evidence can provide a warrant for inferring that a knowledge claim is true. And nether can a finite amount of evidence force one to accept the conclusion that a knowledge claim is false. In short, the problem with justified true belief as a definition of knowledge is that we can neither "justify" knowledge claims nor ever know for certain whether they are true. So, if knowledge is justified true belief, we are led to the conclusion that there is no knowledge, a conclusion that is unacceptable as a foundation for knowledge management.

The definition of World 2 knowledge provided earlier implies that knowledge is not the same thing as "understanding" whether qualified by experience, or greater understanding, or insight. Understanding, for one thing, is conscious. When we understand something, we are aware of our understanding in consciousness. Knowledge in World 2, on the other hand, can refer to unconscious predispositions of various kinds that we cannot make conscious. Further, we may hold beliefs that we have not tested and evaluated, understand those beliefs completely, but not believe that those beliefs are knowledge because they have not been tested and evaluated. For at least these two reasons, "understanding" is not a sufficient condition of knowledge, and therefore the pragmatist definitions are put into question.

Nor is World 2 knowledge the same thing as experience we can share. Some tacit knowledge, as characterized by Polanyi is inexpressible. We know it but cannot tell it. This kind of World 2 knowledge is impossible to share. So if we accept Polanyi's idea of personal, tacit knowledge, on those grounds alone we must also accept that knowledge is not always experience we can share. Even beyond such tacit knowledge, however, there is an even more important reason why World 2 knowledge is not the same thing as experience we can share, and that is that World 2 knowledge whether tacit or not is internal to our minds and ultimately private. Since no one has direct access to the mind of another; there is no way to directly share the experience of another.

Other than through ostensive demonstration, which does not share personal experience, the way we attempt to share experiences with others is primarily by using language-based communication, visuals, and art, in other words, World 3 knowledge claims, to describe our experiences to others. But clearly neither our descriptions of our experiences, nor our demonstrations, are the same as our subjective experiences. There is an irreducible epistemic gap between these external things and our inner experience. What we are sharing with others is not our World 2 beliefs, but our World 3 expressions of knowledge claims resulting from these beliefs, or our expressions of these World 2 beliefs, or our demonstrations comprised of actions reflecting our beliefs.

So the above definitions of World 2 knowledge have serious difficulties as accounts of it. It is viewed, World 2 knowledge is belief that the agent holding it has "justified" by subjecting it to the agent's testing and evaluation process. But it need not be true, and it cannot be "justified" by logical rules of whatever kind. World 2 knowledge is an immediate precursor of our decisions, and we use it to make them. Such knowledge is "subjective" in the sense that it is agent-specific and cannot be directly shared with others.

World 2 knowledge exists at levels above the individual, as well as at the individual level of analysis. That is, an "agent" "holding" World 2 knowledge can be a group, a team, an organization, even a nation, as well as an individual. Much research on culture suggests that group cognitive predispositions including belief and knowledge predispositions, are a useful concept in accounting for group behaviour. If we do not recognize the existence of such predispositions, we restrict World 2 knowledge to the level of the individual. Such individual World 2 knowledge is "personal," in the sense that other individuals do not have direct access to one's own knowledge in full detail, and therefore cannot "know" it as their own belief.

World 3 Definitions

Some of the earlier surveyed knowledge definitions may be viewed as World 3 definitions. These are knowledge as "information in context,"knowledge as "a potential act," knowledge as "social acts," knowledge is the "capacity for effective action," and knowledge is "a fluid mix of framed experience, values .... All these definitions have severe problems.

First, the idea that knowledge is information in context suggests that knowledge is linguistic in character because the term "information" is almost never used to characterize belief and World 2 objects. But this definition does not distinguish knowledge from information, because information can have every bit as much context as knowledge.

What distinguishes knowledge from information from the viewpoint of the agents distinguishing one from the other is the content of the validation contexts of knowledge and the extent to which it tests and evaluates competing knowledge claims. The history of an organization's tests of knowledge claims and their competitive performance determines the validity of such claims. So the validation context is the aspect of context that is all-important in distinguishing knowledge from information, and if we wish to use the information in context idea to define knowledge, it would be much closer to the mark to define knowledge as information in its validation context, rather than simply as information in context.

Second, World 3 knowledge is also not the same thing as a "potential act" and "those signs that refer to them," or as "social acts." To see this, first note that potential acts are not beliefs, but abstractions, forecasts that are World 3 objects themselves. And we express such potential acts, as Peirce indicated, with the signs that refer to them.

However, not every potential or social act is a knowledge claim, much less a tested or evaluated knowledge claim. Though every potential act may either be or imply a knowledge claim relating the act to its anticipated consequences, unless we already have validated the knowledge claim implied by the potential act, it is just information, no different than any alternative potential knowledge claim act. So the definition of knowledge as a potential act raises the question of how potential acts that are knowledge claims are tested and evaluated.

Third, the definition of knowledge as "social acts" raises the same concerns as we just expressed for knowledge construed as potential acts. Social acts are also not beliefs but are either material as World 1, in character, or insofar as they are potential social acts, they are, as we have said, World 3 objects. And as World 3 objects we must address the question of whether they are knowledge claims, and if they are, whether they have been tested and evaluated and whether they have survived better than competitive alternatives.

Fourth, "knowledge is the capacity for effective action" is a World 3 definition in so far as the capacity referred to is the possession of sharable knowledge resources such as problems, theories, models arguments, information systems, policies, programs, etc. This definition of knowledge has the political scientist's problem. That is, knowledge may be a necessary condition for effective action, but it is not sufficient. Effective action also requires (a) the intention to use one's knowledge, and (b) the capability or power to take those effective actions.

Fifth World 3 definition is Davenport and Prusak's:

Knowledge is a fluid mix of framed experience, values, contextual information, and expert insight that provides a framework for evaluating and incorporating new experiences and information. It originates and is applied in the minds of knowers. In organizations it often becomes embedded not only in documents or repositories but also in organizational routines, processes, practices, and norms.

This definition, with its reference to "framed experience," "contextual information," "framework," and "embedding in documents," etc., is squarely in the World 3 rather than the belief camp. But as with the other definitions reviewed it ignores the role of testing and evaluating knowledge claims in distinguishing knowledge from information.

Instead of any of the above definitions, it is thought that World 3 knowledge consists of models, theories, arguments, descriptions, problem statements, etc., that have survived our tests and evaluations. It consists of linguistic formulations or expressions. It is not psychological in nature or even sociological, though it is made by intelligent agents. We talk about the truth, or nearness to the truth of such World 3 objects, and of knowledge defined as descriptions, models, theories, or arguments that are closer to the truth than their competitors.

This kind of knowledge is not an immediate precursor to decisions. It impacts decisions only through the impact it has on (World 2) beliefs. These beliefs, in turn, immediately impact decisions. This kind of knowledge (World 3 objects), further, is "objective."

It is objective in the sense that it is not agent specific and is shared among agents as an object whether or not they believe in it. It is also not "personal," because (a) all agents in the organization have access to it, and (b) it emerges from the interaction of a number of agents. Finally, it is objective because, since it is sharable, we can sensibly talk about its organizational validation. To understand the essence of World 3 knowledge we can do no better than to quote Karl Popper who first formulated this idea of "objective knowledge," on the objective knowledge content in books:

"A man who reads a book with understanding is a rare creature. But even if he were more common, there would always be plenty of misunderstandings and misinterpretations; and it is not the actual and somewhat accidental avoidance of misunderstandings which turns black spots on white paper into a book or an instance of knowledge in the objective sense. Rather; it is something more abstract. It is its possibility or potentiality of being understood, its dispositional character of being understood or interpreted, or misunderstood or misinterpreted, which makes a thing a book. And this potentiality or disposition may exist without ever being actualized or realized.

To see this more clearly we may imagine that after the human race has perished, some books or libraries may be found by some civilized successors of ours (no matter whether these are terrestrial animals that have become civilized, or some visitors from outer space). These books may be deciphered. They may be those logarithm tables never read before, for argument's sake. This makes it quite clear that neither its composition by thinking animals nor the fact that it has not been actually read or understood is essential for making a thing a book, and that it is sufficient that it might be deciphered.

Thus, I do admit that in order to belong to the third world of objective knowledge, a book should—in principle or virtually—be capable of being grasped by somebody. But I do not admit more."

Thus, the distinction between World 2 and World 3 knowledge raises the issue of which type of knowledge should be the object of Knowledge Management.

Many writers have addressed the distinctions among data, information, and knowledge. This version will provide a necessary background to taking up future issues on the distinctions between data management and knowledge management, and information management and knowledge management. What are the differences among data, information, and knowledge in human organizations?

That depends on whether we are talking about World 3 or World 2 phenomena. Let us consider World 3 first.

World 3 Data, Information, Knowledge, and Wisdom

What are the differences among World 3 data, information, and knowledge in human organizations? Data, information, and knowledge all emerge from the social process. They are global properties of an organization, or its constituent agents, depending on the organizational level that is the focus of analysis. They are inter-subjective constructs, not personal data, information, or knowledge. Organizational data, information, and knowledge are World 3 objects.

A datum is the value of an observable, measurable, or calculable attribute. Data are more than one such attribute value. Is a datum (or are data) information? Information is always provided by a datum, or by data, because data are always specified in some conceptual context. And, it is important to note, the conceptual context is one that expresses data in a structured format. Without that structured format we would not call it "data." So data are a type of information. They are a type of information whose conceptual context provides the data with structure and whose purpose is to represent observation.

Information, in more general terms, is data plus conceptual commitments and interpretations, or such commitments and interpretations alone. Information is frequently data extracted, filtered or formatted in some way.

Organizational knowledge is a subset of organizational information, not a superset. But it is a subset that has been extracted, filtered, formatted—that is, processed, in a very special way. It is information that has been subjected to and that has passed tests and evaluations aimed at eliminating errors and seeking the truth. It is information that has been enhanced by the record and experience provided by the validation process. Ideally, this enhanced information is that which is most truthlike.

This brings us to the Case of the Misconceived Pyramid (see Fig. 1.2). In treating the distinctions among data, information, and knowledge, it is often assumed that these are arranged in a pyramid with data, the most plentiful type, at the bottom; information produced from data above it; knowledge produced from information through the hard work of refining, or "mining," above it, and wisdom produced from knowledge, the rarest of all, at the top. This makes a nice picture. But if data and knowledge are also information, what happens to the pyramid?

Fig. 1.3 presents a new picture. In it, information is not made from data. Data and knowledge are made from preexisting information. That is. "just information," data, knowledge, and problems are used in the knowledge life cycle to produce more information, including new knowledge. In effect this figure is saying, "Get rid of the pyramid; get on to the cycle."

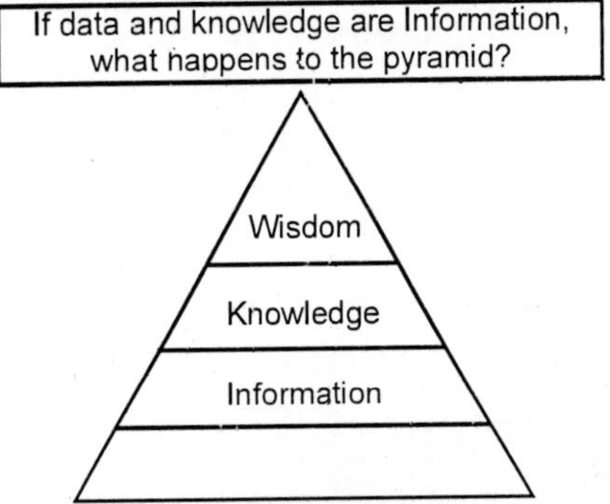

Fig. 1.2. Case of Misconceived Pyramid

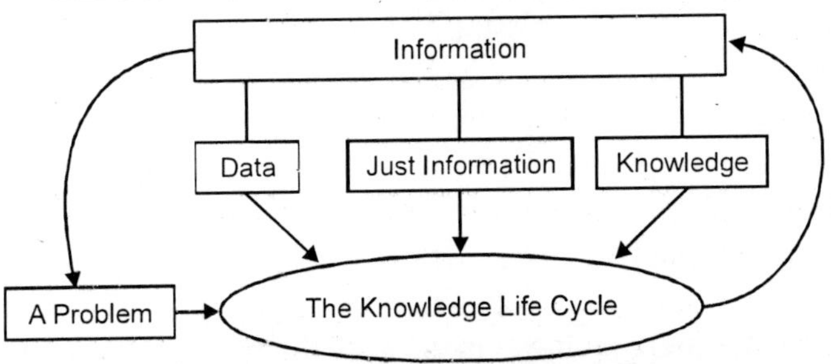

Fig. 1.3. Get Rid of the Pyramid, Get On the Cycle

What has happened to wisdom in this new image? Wisdom is knowledge of what is true or right coupled with "just" and judgment about action to achieve what is right. Another definition is the application of knowledge expressed in principles to arrive at prudent, sagacious decisions about conflict situations. Both these definitions are consistent with the parable of Solomon, but they suggest that wisdom is ambiguous. It is either (a) a form of knowledge (i.e., also information) about doing what is right or (b) a kind of decision (in which case it is not information, but a type of action in a business process). That is, depending on how it is defined, wisdom may not be the same kind of thing as data, information, or knowledge.

World 2 Data, Information and Knowledge

Earlier, we defined World 2 knowledge as beliefs about the world, the beautiful, and the right that have survived our tests and evaluations. What if the beliefs do not survive or we cannot decide if they have or nor? Then we have information. Are surviving beliefs "information," as well as knowledge? They are nonrandom structures, and as such fit Shannon's definition of information. So, there is no reason to deny knowledge the appellation information, as well.

Where do data come into this picture? "World 2 data" must refer to beliefs about observational experiences. These beliefs are like other beliefs in that we view them as validated, unvalidated, or invalidated by our experience, and also they fit into and relate to the general structure of the rest of our beliefs. So they, like World 2 knowledge and information, are also information.

What about the pyramid? Does the pyramid image (see Figure 1.2) make sense for World 2 data, information, and knowledge? Again, the experience argues against it. Data are not the foundation from which we produce information, from which we produce knowledge, from which we produce wisdom. Instead, we are born with geneti-cally encoded knowledge (World 1 knowledge) that enables us to interact with the external world and to learn. This knowledge is more plentiful in quantity than all of the knowl-edge we will acquire through learning for the rest of our lives. We use it to approach the world with predispositions and beliefs. With these we create and structure experience, and from the process of doing this we produce new data, information, and knowledge continuously but in no particular order.

1.2. KNOWLEDGE ATTRIBUTES

Regardless of what definition of knowledge one adopts and regardless of which knowledge resource is being considered, it is useful to appreciate various attributes of knowledge. An attribute is a dimension along which different instances of knowledge can vary. An attribute dimension may comprise a range of values (e.g.. knowledge age) or may be categorical (e.g.. tacit vs. explicit). The categories may take the form of multilevel taxonomies. Taken together, several attributes of interest form the axes of an attribute space. A particular instance of knowledge will have some location in that space at any given time, and may assume new locations over time. Its location will determine what kind of processors can operate on it and the kind of processing to which it can be subjected.

An appreciation of multiple knowledge attributes enriches one's understanding of knowledge resources and their processing. Several attribute dimensions for knowledge are described in the ensuing sections. These are summarized in Table 1.1. The list is not necessarily exhaustive, but does give a sense of the characteristics a knowledge worker may want to consider in dealing with a knowledge portfolio. These attributes are suggestive of variables that a knowledge management researcher may want to investigate. They also highlight facets of knowledge that a manager might consider in designing and overseeing a knowledge management initiative.

A commonly employed attribute dimension when discussing knowledge is its mode. Following Polanyi, a distinction is made between knowledge that is tacit and knowledge that is explicit. In the former case, the knowledge is inconvenient or difficult to formalize and communicate. It is not articulated, at least not yet. Typical examples include a person's mental models, perspectives, intuitions, experiences and know-how. Explicit knowledge is conveyed in formal, systematic representations that are readily

Table 1.1 Representative Knowledge Attributes

Attribute	Nature of Dimension
Mode	Tacit vs. explicit knowledge
Type	Descriptive vs. procedural vs. reasoning knowledge
Domain	Subject area or problem domain where knowledge is used (e.g., marketing, engineering, policy, manufacturing)
Orientation	Domain vs. relational vs. self knowledge
Applicability	Range from local to global
Management level	Operational vs. control vs. strategic
Usage	Practical vs. intellectual vs. recreational vs. spiritual vs. unwanted
Accessibility	Range from public to private
Utility	Progresssion of levels from a clear representation to one that is meaningful to one that is relevant to one that is important.
Validity	Degree of accuracy or certainty about knowledge
Proficiency	Degree expertise embodied in knowledge
Source	Origin of knowledge
Immediacy	Latent versus currently actionable
Age	Range from new to established to old knowledge
Perishability	Shelf-life of knowledge
Volatility	Degree of which knowledge is subject to change.
Location	Position of knowledge (e.g., ontological, organizational, geographic locus)
Abstraction	Range from concrete to abstract
Conceptual level	Automatic vs. pragmatic vs. systematic vs. idealistic
Resolution	Range from superficial to deep
Programmability	Degree to which knowledge is transferable and easy to use
Measurability	Degree to which knowledge its processing can be measured
Recursion	Knowledge vs. meta-knowledge vs. meta-meta-knowledge

communicated. It is articulated, as in knowledge artifacts such as reports, books, and speech; or it is codified as in a database, software library, or set of rules that can be used by a computer-based processor.

Three primary knowledge types are the categories of descriptives, procedural, and reasoning knowledge. Categories of secondary, derivative types of knowledge have also been identified;

these include linguuistic, assimilative, and presentation knowledge. Knowledge belonging to any of the primary types can be tacit. Knowledge of any of these types can be explicit, to the point of being computerized.

Descriptive knowledge characterizes the state of some world, be it actual, predicted, or speculative. This type of knowledge includes descriptions of objects, of concepts, of past, present, future and hypothetical situations. Data and information are descriptive in nature. Thus, they can be regarded as descriptive knowledge that is of limited utiility; or, from a kvi perspective, they are precursors of descriptive knowledge. In either case, they can be lead to or be interpreted in light of other descriptive knowledge such as forecasts, expectations, problems, solutions, insights, judgements, blueprints, goals, decisions, definitions, schemes, taxonomies, and so forth.

Descriptive knowledge can be acquired from external souces (e.g., by observation, by purchase). It can be selected from internal repositories (e.g., extraction, assembly). It may be generated by derivation (e.g., results of analyses) or discovery (e.g., recognizing a pattern, creative intution). Descriptive knowledge can be internalized (e.g., stored or disseminated internally) or externalized.

This knowledge is sometimes called declarative knowledge. That is, a description can be thought of as a declaration about some world. Descriptive knowledge has also been called environmental knowledge; the world being described is an environment for the processor of that knowledge.

Philosophers have long recognized a type of knowledge that is fundamentally different from descriptive knowledge. Russell explains that "there is knowledge which may be described as 'mirroring,' and knowledge which consists in capacity to handle." In mirroring the state of some world of interest, the former is descriptive knowledge. Very different from this is knowledge about how to do something or how something occurs. This knowledge, consisting of step-by-step procedures for handling various tasks or explaining various happenings, is called procedural knowledge.

Examples of procedural knowledge include algorithms, strategies, action plans, programs, and methods. Like descriptive knowledge, procedural knowledge can be in a tacit mode (e.g., a mental representation) or an explicit mode (e.g., written or digital representation). Also, like descriptive knowledge, it can be acquired, selected, generated, internalized, and externalized. However, the means for performing these manipulations and the skills required for doing so may be very different for procedural versus descriptive knowledge. For instance, generating a forecast, blueprint, or goal may well require different skills and processing than generating an action plan or programme. Interestingly, procedural knowledge can be applied to descriptive knowledge to derive new descriptive knowledge.

A third major type of knowledge is for reasoning. An instance of reasoning knowledge specifies what conclusion is valid or what action can be taken when a particular situation exists. The connection between the situation and the conclusion/action could be based on logic, correlation, analogy, or causality. This type of knowledge is quite distinct from the description of a situation or the specification of a procedure. Examples may include a rule, policy, code of conduct, regulation, principle, and the case.

Reasoning knowledge can be tacit or explicit. It can be acquired, selected, generated, internalized, or externalized by an organization's knowledge processors; however, the processor capabilities needed to do so can differ from those that work for descriptive or procedural knowledge. Like procedural knowledge, reasoning knowledge can be applied to generate new knowledge. For example, for a given description of a situation and a goal, instances of reasoning knowledge may be put together to reach logical conclusions. These conclusions may take the form of procedural knowledge indicating how to reach that goal. Or, they may take the form of descriptive knowledge (e.g., characterizing a diagnosis or expectation). The use of reasoning knowledge to reach such conclusions is referred to as inference.

Instances of the three types of knowledge can be applied in the generation of new knowledge. Descriptive knowledge, in the sense of data and information, does not by itself yield new knowledge, aside from rearranging (i.e., assembling, relating, packaging it in novel ways). This may be why some observers are inclined to exclude it from being called "knowledge," reserving that term for procedural and reasoning knowledge. It is when a processor is able to manipulate procedural and/or reasoning knowledge in the processing of descriptive knowledge that its "hidden" potential is released in the guise of generating new knowledge. The value of an interplay among the three primary knowledge types has long been recognized in the building of decision support systems.

1.3. CLASSIFYING KNOWLEDGE

Knowledge — whether it is about your customers, your company's own markers, its products and services, its competitors, its processes,its employee skills, regulatory environments, or methods — can be classified along four key dimensions, as shown in Fig. 1.4. These four dimensions are :

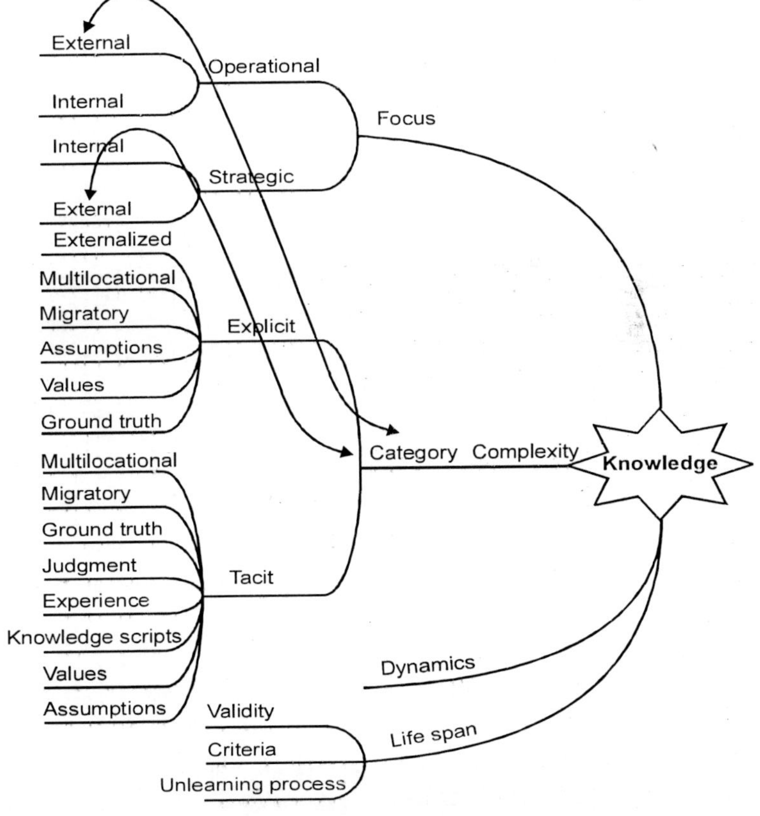

Fig. 1.4. A Map of Some Key Facets of Knowledge

- Complexity, which includes categories and types, and specifies the degree of context needed to give it meaning and make it useful.
- Life span
- Dynamics
- Focus : operational or strategic

As figure 1.4 only partially illustrates, the compliexity of knowledge is closely related to other dimensions. One way of looking at knowledge from a pragmatic viewpoint is to consider one key subdimension, category of complexity.

Table 1.2 Summary of Knowledge Classifications

Knowledge Classifications		**Definition**
Knowledge versus	Data	Primary level, derived from transactions: building blocks for information.
Data and Information	Information	Secondary level, derived from processing data or transforming knowledge into information. Information has meaning to the recipient.
	Knowledge	High level, derived from experience and processing information for example.
Levels of Knowledge	Knowledge as an object	Knowledge is an object that can be manipulated and transferred independent of people.
	Knowledge with in an individual	Knowledge resides within individual and is not always understood or even known by that individual.
	Knowledge within a group/community	Knowledge resides within a group or community through shared experiences, discussions, discoveries; it is not within one single individual.
	Knowledge within an organization	Knowledge resides within an organization through culture, processes, and experiences; it is not within one single individual or group.
	Public Knowledge	Knowledge resides within public, it is well known to everyone; it is not knowledge that resides with one individual organization,group or individual.

Types of Knowledge	Explicit Knowledge	Explicit knowledge is easily coded (e.g., documented, identified, articulated). Some argue that explicit knowledge does not exist independently of tacit knowledge; others argue that explicit knowledge, independent of tacit knowledge, is simply information.
	Tacit Knowledge	Tacit Knowledge is extremely difficult to code (e.g., identify, articulate, document). Some consider this true knowledge and tacit knowledge may not be fully known by the individual who has the tacit knowledge.
Knowledge Processes I	Externalization	The translation of explicit knowledge into tacit knowledge.
	Internalization	The translation of explicit knowledge into tacit knowledge.
	Combination	The creation of new explicit knowledge through combining existing explicit knowledge.
	Socialization	The transfer of tacit knowledge through mentoring.
Knowledge Processes II (i.e., Business process)	Knowledge Generation	The creation of new knowledge, either through creating it in-house, or through acquiring it from external sources.
	Knowledge Codification	Codification of knowledge into diagrams, documents, knowledge maps etc.
	Knowledge Transfer	The sharing of knowledge between one individual to another (or between groups, etc).
	Knowledge Use	The application of knowledge to business practices (e.g., problem solving).
Knowledge Management Business Practices	KM Systems	Information systems and technology to assist in codification and transfer of knowledge (e.g., intranets, Lotus Notes, Knowledge maps, executive support systems, artificial intelligence, neural nets, documents management systems).
	Documentation	Organizational documents assist in codification and transfer of knowledge.

Communities of practice	Communities of practice are groups (communities) of professionals or individuals with the same interest and goals. They are volunteer based communities in which knowledge is created, and transferred.
Mentoring	Mentoring is a practice, which is best for the transfer of knowledge from an expert to a novice individual, through illustration, instruction, and active learning.
Story telling	Story telling is a practice in which tacit knowledge is transferred through its illustration in context-rich stories.
Serendipitous/Water cooler discussion	This is the business practice in which knowledge is created, and transferred through accidents/ casual conversations between individuals.

As far as Categories of Knowledge, are concerned, Knowledge can be classified into two broad categories-tacit and explicit. These categories can be subdivided into types. Further, each category consists of various components such as intutition, experience, ground truth, judgement, values, assumptions, beliefs and intelligence, which must be supported.

- ***Tacit knowledge*** is personal, context-specific knowledge that is difficult to formalize, record or articulate:- it is stored in the heads of people. The tacit component is mainly developed through a process of trial and error encountered in practice.
- ***Explicit knowledge*** is that component of knowledge that can be codified and transmitted in a systematic and formal language:- documents, databases, webs, e-mails, charts, etc.

A widely recognized distinction in knowledge management circles is Polanyi's distinction between tacit, personal knowledge and explicit, codified knowledge. By tacit knowledge, Polyani meant "committed belief" that is contextual in character and difficult to express. Infact, he characterized some tacit knowledge as inexpressible, or "ineffable," and stated that "we can know more than we can tell." He also saw knowledge as inhering in mental models that provide the knower with a gestlat. Moreover, the context of the gestalt provides one way in which we can understand the tacit component of knowledge. In a gestalt, we can distinguish the portions we focus attention on from the background context that helps to establish the pattern of the gestalt, or that is used as a tool to integrate the focal portions into a more comprehensive whole. The "focal" knowledge in the pattern receives our attention and notice. The "tacit" or background knowledge, on the other hand, while much more extensive and absolutely necessary to the pattern, is not noticed and remains unarticulated.

The importance of the tacit/explicit distinction for knowledge management is emphasized in Nonaka and Takeuchi's account of The Knowledge Creating Company. They assume that knowledge is created through the interaction between tacit and explicit knowledge, and they postulate four different modes of knowledge conversion :

- from tacit to tacit (called socialization);
- from tacit to explicit (externalization);
- from explicit to explicit (combination); and
- from explicit to tacit (internalization).

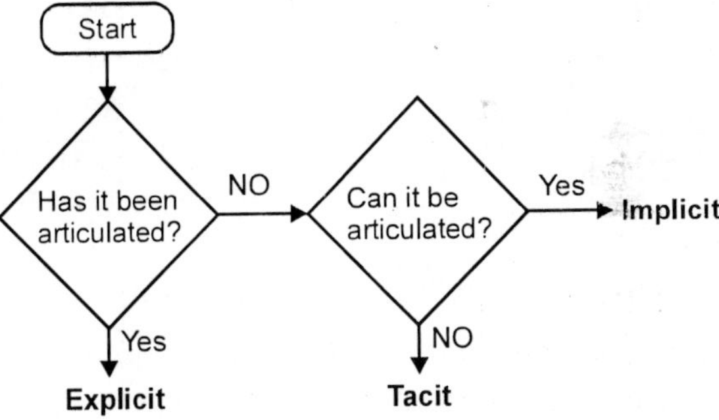

Fig. 1.5. Explicit, Implicit and Tacit Knowledge

1.3.1. Implicit Knowledge

Knowledge that can be articulated but has not, is called implicit knowledge. Its existence is implied by or inferred from observable behaviour or performance. This is the kind of knowledge that can often be teased out of a competent performer by a task analyst, knowledge engineer or other person skilled in identifying the kind of knowledge that can be articulated but has not. In analyzing the task in which underwriters at an insurance company processed applications, for instance, it quickly became clear that the range of outcomes for the underwriters' work took three basic fdrms: (1) they could approve the policy application, (2) they could deny it or (3) they could counter offer. Yet, not one of the underwriters articulated these as boundaries on their work at the outset of the analysis. Once these outcomes were identified, it was a comparatively simple matter to identify the criteria used to determine the response to a given application. In so doing, implicit knowledge became explicit knowledge.

1.3.2. Declarative, Procedural and Strategic Knowledge

The explicit, implicit, tacit categories of knowledge are not the only ones in use. Cognitive psychologists sort knowledge into two categories: declarative and procedural. Some add strategic as a third category. As before, we will use a diagram to aid in sorting out matters (see Figure 1.6).

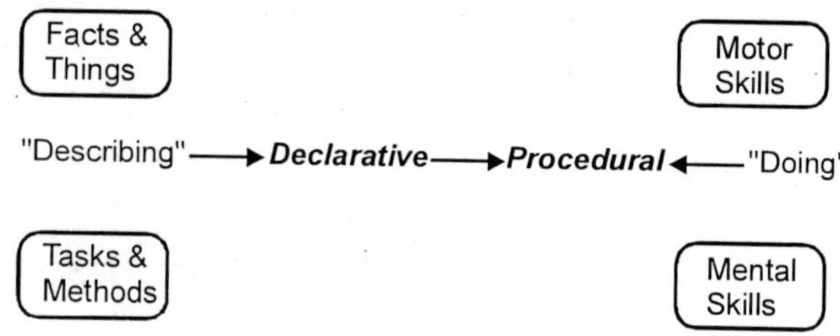

Fig. 1.6. Declarative and Procedural Knowledge

Declarative knowledge has much in common with explicit knowledge in that declarative knowledge consists of descriptions of facts and things or of methods and procedures. The person most closely associated with the distinction between declarative and procedural knowledge is John Anderson of Carnegie-Mellon University. He has been writing about these two notions for almost 25 years. Being able to state the cut off date for accepting applications is an example of declarative knowledge. It is also an instance of explicit knowledge. For most practical purposes, declarative knowledge and explicit knowledge may be treated as synonmys.This is because all declarative knowledge is explicit knowledge, that is, it is knowledge that can be and has been articulated.

Procedural Knowledge is an area where important differences of opinion exist. One view of procedural knowledge is that it is knowledge that manifests itself in the doing of something. As such it is reflected in motor or manual skills and in cognitive or mental skills. We think, we reason, we decide, we dance, we play the piano, we ride bicycles, we read customers' faces and moods and our bosses' as well, yet we cannot reduce to mere words that which we obviously know or know how to do. Attempts to do so are often recognized as little more than after-the-fact rationalizations. This knowing-is-in-the-doing view of procedural knowledge is basically the view of John Anderson, the Carnegie-Mellon professor mentioned earlier.

Another view of procedural knowledge is that it is knowledge about how to do something. This view of procedural knowledge accepts a description of the steps of a task or procedure as procedural knowledge. The obvious shortcoming of this view is that it is no different from declarative knowledge except that tasks or methods are being described instead of facts or things.

Pending the resolution of this disparity, we are left to resolve this for ourselves. We have chosen to acknowledge that some people refer to descriptions of tasks, methods and procedures as declarative knowledge and others refer to them as procedural knowledge. However, we choose to classify all descriptions of knowledge as declarative and reserve procedural for application to situations in which the knowing may be said to be in the doing. Indeed, as the diagram in Figure 1.6 shows, declarative knowledge ties to "describing" and procedural knowledge ties to "doing." Thus, for our purposes, we may able to comfortably view all procedural knowledge as tacit just as all declarative knowledge is explicit.

Some reading this will immediately say, "Whoa there. If all procedural knowledge is tacit, that means we can not articulate it. In turn, that means we can not make it explicit, that is, we can not articulate and capture it in the form of books, tables, diagrams and so on." That is exactly what we mean. When we describe a task, step by step, or when we draw a flowchart representing a process, these are representations. Describing what we do or how we do it yields declarative knowledge. A description of an act is not the act just as the map is not the territory.

Strategic knowledge is a term used by some to refer to what might be termed know-when and know-why. Although it seems reasonable to conceive of these as aspects of doing, it is difficult to envision them as being separate from that doing. In other words, we can separate out strategic knowledge only in the describing, not the doing. Consequently, strategic knowledge is probably best thought of as a subset of declarative knowledge instead of its own category.

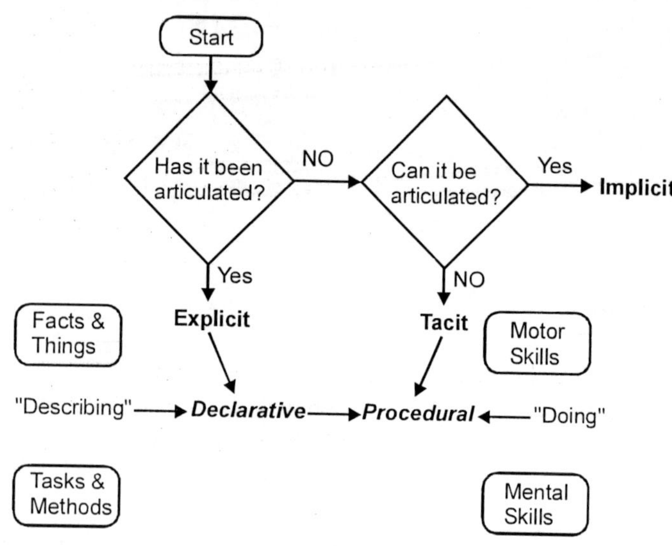

Fig. 1.7. Integration

Fig. 1.7 integrates the diagrams from Figures 1.5 and 1.6 and illustrates the "fit" between and among explicit, implicit, tacit, declarative and procedural knowledge. These relationships are reasonably clear and, with two exceptions, warrant no further discussion.

The arrow connecting declarative and procedural indicates that we often develop procedural knowledge or the ability to do something as a result of starting with declarative knowledge. In other words, we often "know about" before we "know how."

The arrows connecting explicit with declarative and tacit with procedural are meant to indicate the strong relationships that exist between these terms.

Polanyi indicates that much tacit knowledge can be made explicit, and that there is some that remains ineffable and can never be expressed. Further, he even distinguishes "implicit beliefs," suggesting a third category of knowledge: implicit beliefs, defined as those "held in the form of our conceptual framework, as expressed in our language".

In short, Polanyi identifies tacit knowledge that can not be expressed, tacit knowledge that can be made explicit, and implicit knowledge as defined above. So, we believe that the Nonaka and Takeuchi interpretation of Polanyi's work is too simple. If we agree that tacit knowledge is sometimes composed of beliefs we cannot express, and that explicit knowledge is made of expressed beliefs, then that leaves a third category: those cognitions or beliefs that, while not focal or explicit, are expressible, given the environmental conditions effective in eliciting them. We call this category implicit knowledge, while recognizing that it contains not only those nonfocal or assumed portions of our conceptual frameworks, but any nonfocal beliefs that can be brought into focus and made explicit. So now we have a three-way distinction relevant to the study of knowledge conversion: explicit, implicit, and tacit. It is also useful to view this three-way classification from the point of view of Popper's distinction between World 2 and World 3. That is, Popper's objective knowledge (World 3) is obviously all explicit and codified, and involves the expression of Polanyi's "focal knowledge." To the extent that we can think of "implicit knowledge" in the World 3 sense, its character is very different from World 2 implicit knowledge. The latter is based on a psychological association with focal knowledge that is part of a gestalt. World 3 implicit knowledge, in contrast, is knowledge that is logically implicit in explicit knowledge (in linguistic formulations), in the sense that it can be derived from such knowledge.

On the other hand, some of Popper's World 2 mental phenomena are obviously personal and "tacit" in the sense that they may represent mental objects that cannot be focused in expressible psychological orientations. Other World 2 mental phenomena represent objects that can be focused in such orientations and are therefore implicit. Finally, there are still other World 2 phenomena that represent explicit, focal beliefs, situational orientations that express explicit linguistic knowledge in the mind. Such tacit, implicit, and explicit phenomena in the mind are all unob-servable abstractions or "hidden variables." They are hypothetical constructs whose characteristics must be inferred using measurement instruments, models, surveys, observation, etc.

Note, also, that all explicit statements are not about World 3 objects and all personal, tacit knowledge is nor about World 2. Thus, if we say that we know that the "many-worlds" interpretation of quantum theory is true, this explicit statement is about our belief that the many-worlds interpretation is true. It is an explicit statement about a World 2 object. It converts our implicit knowledge into an explicit knowledge claim about our belief. It is not a direct statement about the (World 3) many-worlds model. It also does not convert our implicit knowledge orientation into explicit linguistic knowledge in the sense that we have fully and faithfully transformed our implicit psychological orientation into an explicit, codified form. That cannot be done because our implicit belief is not a linguistic formulation, and the epistemic gap between internal, non-linguistic psychological connections and internal or external linguistic formulations is irreducible.

On the other hand, if we say that the many worlds interpretation of quantum theory is true, this explicit statement is about quantum theory, the linguistic formulation, itself. It is about a World 3 object, not our World 2 belief. It is a description of the relationship that we claim exists between quantum theory and reality and is in no way a claim about what we believe.

On the other hand, we can also hold subjective knowledge (beliefs) about either subjective states or about World 1 or World 3 objects. Our procedural knowledge about how to make lamb stew is about World 1, for example, because it is made up of World 2 belief predispositions about how to act (World 1) to manipulate the (World 1) components to make the stew. So subjective knowledge is in no way restricted to knowledge about World 2 objects.

Lkujiro Nonaka, in his cornerstone book – The Knowledge Creating Company, indicated that the essence of knowledge creation is the substantite distinction between the age-old concepts of tacit and explicit knowledge.

Knowledge creation processes can be thought of as those activities that surrounded the conversion of subjective tacit knowledge (based on experience) to objective explicit knowledge, also called externalization. The problem with this process is that tacit knowledge based on experience is often difficult to articulate, formalize and encode.

For example, when you drive on an interstate, you make a complex set of decisions based on traffic patterns, your position relative to other vehicles ahead of and behind you, trafic speed, local speed limits etc. Using experience, you can subconsciously make these decisions in split seconds, often without fatal errors. However, it would be extremely difficult you were to codify this series of decisions processes or transfer them to another person.

The process of externalization results in the conversion from a tacit, unarticulated form to an explicit form of representation which is easier to move across communication networks. Externalization is often driven by metaphores and analogy. Seeing how a new project in your company is similar to another unrelated project that your company undertook in the past is an example of such analogy.

1.4. TYPES OF KNOWLEDGE

Tacit and explicit knowledge interact in these types :

1.4.1. Externalized Knowledge

Knowledge is complex and initially tacit; however, it can be externalized and embedded in a company's products and processes. One of the aspects of tacit knowledge is the cognitive dimension that comprises beliefs, ideals, values, schemata, and mental models that are deeply ingrained in participants, often taken for granted by the prossessors. While this cognitive component, like any other aspect of tacit knowledge, is difficult to articulate, it shapes the perception of the participants. This cognitive component should be extracted to retain context and fullness of the captured exlicit knowledge.

1.4.2. Multilocational Knowledge

Knowledge might be resident both within the organization and outside it. Knowledge management encompasses activities surrounding the integration of this knowledge from different sources in different forms and maintaining it. Knowledge management creates value by actively leveraging the know-how, experience, and judgement resident within and outside an or organization. The initial key to knowledge creation thus lies in mobilazation and conversion of this tacit knowledge into a form of explicit knowledge.

1.4.3. Migratory Knowledge

Migratory Knowledge is knowledge that is independent of its owner or creator. As knowledge becomes more and extensively codified, its capacity to move increases. Codification implies some kind of capture — in documents, databases, picutres, illustrations, spreadsheets on a disk, e-mails, video tapes, or on a Web pages on the corporate intranet. Codification however does not imply that capture has to be electronic. It could be on paper, on tape, or on film. Converting these to an electronic format that is more amenable to easy transfer is rarely a challenge these days. When we talk about the movement of knowledge, we are talking about our ability to transfer knowledge from one person or organization to another without losing its context and meaning.

Above discussion so far has highlighted a number of different definitions and conceptions of knowledge. Some of these have been rejected as confused, ambiguous, vague, or contradictory and others have been distinguished as identifying different types of knowledge. Table 1.3 summarizes the discussion so far and adds some more information. Its categorization is based on the following distinctions:

- Worlds 1 (material), 2 (mental) and 3 (artifact-based) knowledge
- Situational knowledge and knowledge predispositions
- Tacit, implicit, and explicit knowledge
- Psychologically implicit knowledge and logically implicit knowledge.

This table provides a framework that is a proposal for solving the knowledge conundrum. The types defined there are World 1 knowledge; World 2 situational, tacit, implicit, or explicit knowledge; World 2 predispositional knowledge; World 3 types of explicit knowledge; and by implication World 3 implicit knowledge.

Table 1.3 at least provides a much better foundation for knowledge management than has existed previously. It resolves the conflict between those who believe in mental knowledge and those who believe in knowledge embedded in artifacts by pointing out that these are different types of knowledge, and that they in turn differ from knowledge embedded in biological organims or other agents in the material world. It intoruduces the important distinction in the area of mental knowledge between predispositional knowledge and situational knowledge, a distinction that has been largely ignored in knowledge management in all of the hubbub surrounding among the discussion of belief knowledge. It recognizes the distinctions among tacit, explicit, and implicit knowledge. And finally, it recognizes that implicit beliefs and knowledge claims implied by preexisting explicit knowledge are two different things.

1.5. FROM DATA TO INFORMATION TO KNOWLEDGE AND FROM KNOWLEDGE TO WISDOM

Information, Knowledge and wisdom are more than simply collections. Rather the whole represents more than the sum of its parts and has a synergy of its own. It begins with data, which is the raw material and input for information processing.

A data is a set of particular and objective facts about an event or simply the structured record of a transaction. The event might be the purchase of your favourite beer at the grocery store or a change in the stock price of the stock you might be betting your life's savings on. Such figures in themselves, do not say anything meaningful. A transaction at a grocery store, for example, does not tell you whether the brand of beer you bought is selling more than the others today— in this store or nationwide — and whether it did so yesterday. In a similar fashion stock prices do not tell you whether the company is doing better than it was doing yesterday, or whether you would have reaped a windfall had you sold your stock this morning. Such meaning comes to these raw facts and figures once they are

17. Semiformal language utilities
18. Meta-knowledge claims
19. Planning knowledge claims
20. Descriptive knowledge claims
21. Factual knowledge claim measurement of abstractions
22. Knowledge claims about imact, cause, and effect
23. Predictive knowledge claims
24. Assessment knowledge claims

converred into some form of information. Though raw data in itself has purpose, it might have little or no relevance.

While there are firms and organizations whose very survival rests solely on their effectiveness and efficiency in handling and keeping this raw data. Thomas Davenport calls these "data cultures", or cultures whose lifeblood is keeping records. The Internal Revenue Service (IRS), the Social Security Administration (SSA), the Census Bureau are examples of organization with strong data cultures.

The terms knowledge, data and organizational learning are subject to varied interpretion and use. Davenport and Prusak suggest that data should not be stored per se into a system for managing knowledge; instead, it should be stored as value-added information— by the addition of historical context.

Information as Peter Drucker describes it, "*is data endowed with relevance and purpose*." Information has its root in *inform*, which means something that changes or shapes the person who gets it. It is the recipient of this information who decides whether it is truly information or purely noise. If someone told you that Microsoft stock went up by two dollars, and in fact you do own some of it, that information shapes your idea of how well Microsoft is probably doing, However, if someone told you that the Hong Kong stock exchange took a downward plunge, it might have little meaning for you sitting in the United States without a stake in the Hong Kong market, and you might consider that noise rather than information. On the other hand, a person running a company in Hong Kong might find the same message very relevant and will not perceive it as noise. What qualifies as useful information in different situations is a subjective judgement. Fig 1.8 illustrates the conversion process. And that is where the entire problem of generating useful information, information that can help a manager run a businesss better, make effective decisions and change things in the right direction, comes into the picture.

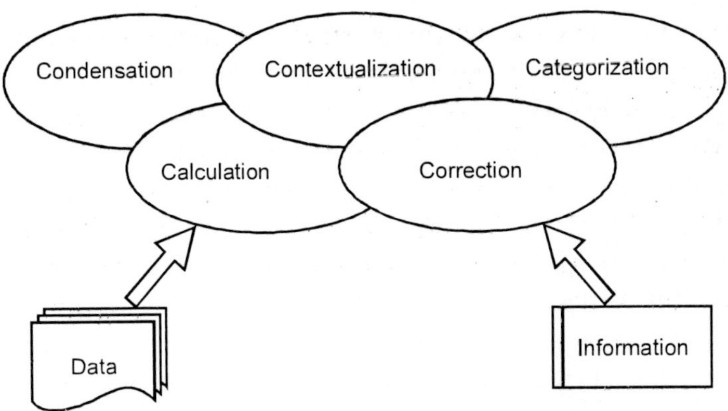

Fig. 1.8. Five C's that differentiate Data from Information.

Information moves arround both in electronic and hand format, through electronic net works and social networks. As the volume of information that flows through our desks grows, we approach the same problem that we once had with data: information overload. This means that there is more relevant and irrelevant information arround us than we want to have to deal with. Having too much information is, in some respects, better than having too little, since we can then figure out how to focus only on the information that is relevant and currently applicable. On the other hand, having an overwhelming amount of information that makes it difficult to make sense of it is often no better than having none at all.

Table 1.4 shows different ways in which meaning can be added to data to transform it into information.

Table 1.4. Different Ways of Creating Information by Adding Meaning to Data: The Fice C's

Addition of Data	Result
Condensed	Data is summarized in more conscise form and unnecessary depth is eliminated
Contextualized	We know why the data was collected
Calculated	Analyzed data, similar to condensation of data
Categorized	The unit of analysis is known
Corrected	Errors have been removed, missing "data holes" have been accounted for

Look at your checkbook. How frequently do you update its balance register? If you are like most of us, you use the balance register quite frequently. But how frequently do you use it to actually make changes in your spending patterns. Rarely? This is exactly is the problem with many organizations and businesses. They tend to collect a lot of data, hoping that it will give them that imaginary esoteric notion of the fountainehead of competitive advantage that any firm yearns for.

At every swipe that each product at your local grocery goes through and before it ends up in your refrigerator, there is a wealth of captured data. The (UPC) and the accompanying bar code scanner tell the store about the product, its date of manufacture, the time and date the sale was made, who sold it, how it was charged etc. Although it is exciting to see how much data is captured in one swipe, the threat comes from that very ability: the collection of too data is captured in one swipe, the threat comes from that very ability: the collection of too much data all too easily. As firms overcome their inability to gether data by using pieces of technology, they often begin to make an overkill in the amounts of data and information that they capture. The result is that firms end up with overwhelming volumes of data-so overwhelming that they have a hard time figuring out just what do with it.

Examples of the data-hoarding mentality are not just seen in large businesses. Government-run census data contains invaluable information, much of which is never extracted. Companies running surveys often collect very iota of information, just hoping that each additional piece of data collected might be useful for something later on. The meaning and purpose of much of the collected data are not clear to the firms that collect it.

Not being able to make sense of a good chunk of data that firms collect is the underlying reason why they try to desperately make sense of it through data mining and similar techniques. The hope driving that is just a two-sided question:

- Can this help us run our business any better?
- Does this tell us what, if anything, is wrong with what we are doing?

The advantage that a firm gains is not from its data riches but from its knowledge riches.

The same piece of data that might represent a piece of useful information to one person might represent nothing more than a meaningless element of data to another. Very often, when data is shared and distributed among people within a firm, it starts to become increasingly userful as some people perceive it as useful, as illustrated in Fig. 1.9.

Most managers readily recognize that getting knowledge to move arround in a company can be difficult. But, often, as several studies have found, after being convinced by tool vendors and for other reasons, they, very inaccurately reduce this problem to an issue of information flow. As a result, a number of companies have invested in intranets with great hopes. Intranets do have their own benefits and, beyond a doubt, add value to the organization. But the value added is that due to the improved information flow, not knowledge flow. While technology has pushed us beyond the point where information flow is not a problem, as people begin to use this information, act upon it, and rely on it for making decisions, it makes a form that resembles actionable information — information that leads to knowledge. Merely making information flow smoothly does not guarantee that it will actually be used. The idea of retrieving locally developed knowledge for use elsewhere does not address the whole issue. Intranets, by themselves, can only help ensure that this information flows.

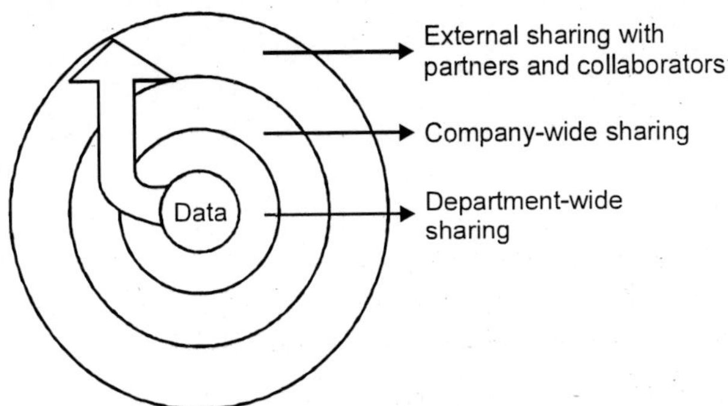

Fig. 1.9. Data becomes increasingly useful as it is shared within the Department, throughout the Company, and beyond the Organisational boundaries with Suppliers and Partners.

Restricted search and retrieval paths are a significant issue but are not the only issue. Bringing locally created knowledge, say, from a specific department, into view is only the first step toward making that knowledge useful elsewhere. For example, if a company thinks that making its sales figures for its PDA available to its engineering and product development department is covering a lot of ground in sharing knowledge, that company is unfortunately mistaken.

A good case in point is Hewlett-Packard (HP), which pursued a strategy of making its best practices available throughout the company. Although HP was quite successful in identifying its best practices, it was not successful in moving them from one location to another.

When an intranet, for example, moves the knowledge without the practice, what actually gets moved is the know-what without the know-how. What does not move this way is the the warranting mechanisms and standards of judgement on which people distinguish the valid and the worthwhile from the useless pieces of "knowledge".

The fundamental mistake that companies repeatedly make is that of equating information and knowledge. While the former can be handled well by information technology tools such as intranets alone, the latter is not.

Wisdom arises when one understands the foundational principles responsible for the patterns representing knowledge.

And *wisdom,* even more so than knowledge, *tends to create its own context.*

In summary the following associations can reasonbly be made:

- Information relates to description, definition or perspective (what, who, when, where).
- Knowledge comprises strategy, practice, method or approach (how).
- Wisdom embodies principle, insight, moral or archetype (why).

The patterns of relations of data and information have the

capacity to represent knowledge. For the representation to be of any utility it must be understood. When understood the representation is information or knowledge to the one that understands.

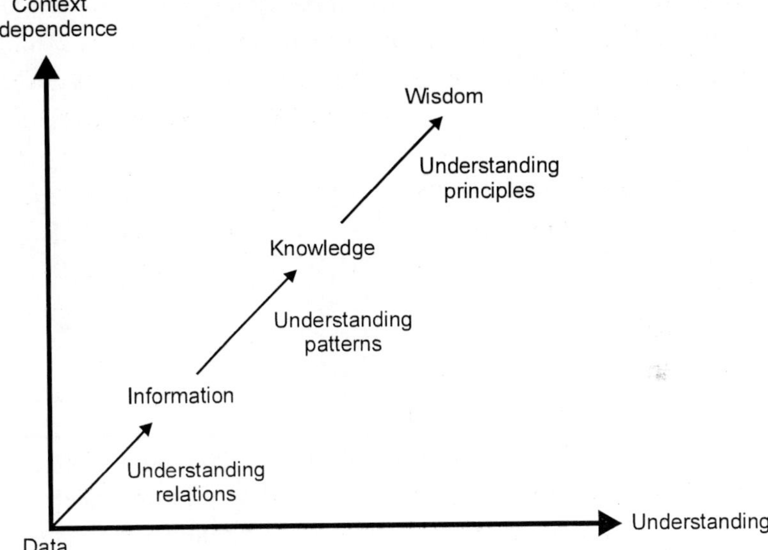

Fig. 1.10. Pattern of Relation of Data and Information

1.6. INTEGRATION OF KNOWLEDGE SOURCES

So what are the primary feeds to a knowledge management system? Where does knowledge come into the system from? A quick roundup of the sources from which knowledge comes is presented in Table 1.5.

Table 1.5. Sources of Knowledge that Feed a Knowledge Management System

Source	Explicit/ Condificable	Tacit/Needs Explication
Employee knowledge, skills and competencies	✓	✓
Experiential knowledge (both at an individual and group level)	✓	✓
Team-based collaborative skills	✓	✓

Informal shared knowledge	✓	✓
Values	✓	✓
Norms	✓	✓
Beliefs	✓	✓
Task-based knowledge	✓	✓
Knowledge embedded in physical systems	✓	✓
Human capital	✓	✓
Knowledge embedded in internal structures	✓	✓
Knowledge embedded in external structures	✓	✓
Customer capital	✓	✓
Experiences of the employee	✓	✓
Customer relationships	✓	✓

Although the list in Table 1.5 is a partial one, it is clear that much of the knowledge can be explicated, put into systems, and reused. However, some critical pieces of tacit knowledge are extremely difficult, if not impossible, to externalize in such a manner.

1.7. THE THREE FUNDAMENTAL STEPS

Three basic steps are involved in the knowledge and learning process. Taking a closer look at these three basic steps, which many researchers like Nonaka and Takeuchi have expanded, will give us a better feel for what type of information technology functionality will support this effort. These three fundamental steps, illustrated in Fig. 1.11.

- Knowledge acquisition
- Knowledge sharing
- Knowledge utilization

An important aspect in these stages is that they need not be in a sequence. They can and often do, run in parallel.

1.7.1. Knowledge Acquisition

Knowledge acquisition is not to be confused with information acquisition. Knowledge acquisition is the process of development and creation of insights, skills, and relationships. For example, when an experienced stockbroker can see the trend line on a computer monitor and tell which way the market is headed — that is an example of intuition or acquired knowledge. It is the type of knowledge in which information technology components surrounding this process need to focus. Data-capture tools with filtering abilities, intelligent databases, keyboard sanners, CrossPad type note-capture tools and electronic white boards are examples of information technology components that can support knowledge acquisition.

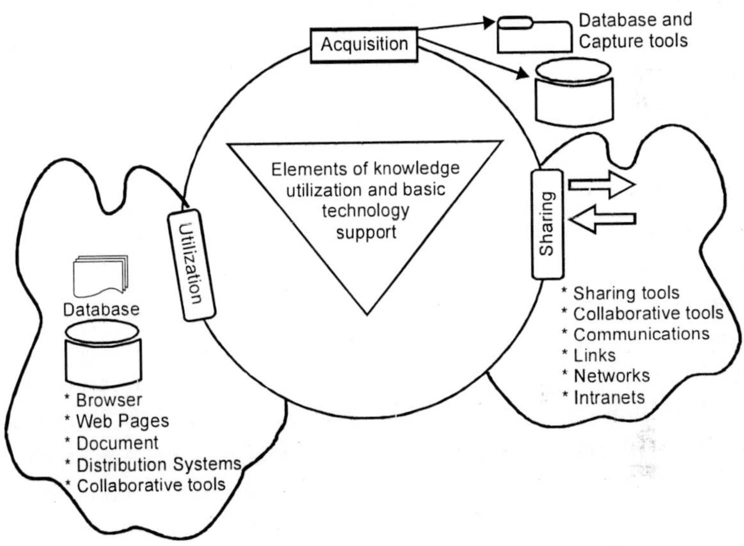

Fig. 1.11. Basic Elements of Knowledge utilization and Typical Technology Tools that can be used to Each Stage

James Brian Quinn and his colleagues describe intellect and knowledge in an organization on four bases or levels in their landmark 1996 hardvard Business Review article. A company's knowledge, in the order of importance, can be viewed at four levels. Not all these stages stand to benefit from a knowledge management system. An understanding and appreciation of technology's limitations will help your team place reasonable expectations on your knowledge management system. Lack of support by the knowledge management system does not mean that the knowledge management strategy cannot support those levels. The four levels of professional intellect, in the decreasing order of momentousness are, care-why, know-why, know-how, and know-what.

1. Care-why : Care-why represents self-motivated creatively that exists in a company. This happens to be the only level that cannot be supported by a knowledge management system. Care-why explains why highly motivated, creative, and energetic groups and companies outperform larger corporations with more money and resources. This level of knowledge exists in a company's culture, and after we have done all we can to provide technology support for the other three levels, we must give this one our best shot, since technology is of little or no help at this level. Beliefs, in some respects, fall into this category — hence the difficulty in comprehensively supporting beliefs with a knowledge management system.

2. Know-why : A system's understanding represents the know-why aspect of knowledge. It is the deep knowledge of the complex slush of cause-and-effect relationships that underlie an employee's range of responsibilities. This knowledge enables individuals to move a step above know-how and create extraordinary leverage by using knowledge, bringing in the ability to deal with unknown interactions and unseen situations. Examples include a stockbroker who intuitively knows just when to sell and buy, or a baseball player who knows the perfect moment to hit.

Most companies are at one stage below this level of understanding — the know-how stage, where they can use known rules and apply them well. But the knowledge economy demands more than just that ability. To be able to move knowledge workers from the know-how level, a knowledge management system must support extensive discussion and conversion so that the participants and employees get a feel for the problems rather than simply apply well-known rules that have worked in most situations. Conversation is stressed in meetings and brainstorming sessions, but an alarmingly small number of firms support the same types of conversations in systems intending to leverage their corporate knowledge.

Perhaps, we have bought into the concept of expert systems and conventional decision support systems a little too much. Value creation from knowledge is enhanced if experimentation in the course of problem solving increases know-why and if incentive structures stimulate care-why, rather than solely focusing on know-how.

3. Know-how : Know-how represents the ability to translate bookish knowledge into real world results. Marketing departments, for example, know that advertising during the Superbowl is expensive, but the payoffs are huge. This is a general rule that can be applied very well by a marketer. Being able to compete beyond these rules, which might be common knowledge, requires a shift from a know-how information-oriented environment to know-why, that is, knowledge orientation. Professional know-how is developed most rapidly through reopened exposure to real-world, complex problems. Any networking or knowledge support system that intends to move workers from this level to the know-why level must enable extensive exposures to problem solving.

4. Know-what : This represents cognitive knowledge. This is an essential but insufficient basis for competing. An analogy would be the kind of detailed knowledge a college graduate might have when he graduates with a degree in his discipline. He might know what should be done but might not have ever done it in real life.

1.7.2. Knowledge Sharing

Knowledge sharing is the next component. As figure 1.11 shows, this stage comprises disseminating and making available what is already known. An expert system that helps a novice technical support person answer tech support calls at the help desks of Microsoft is a good example of knowledge that is being shared with that person.

One characteristic that distinguishes a firm's knowledge from its information assets is the foundation on which knowledge is primarily built. Collaborative problem solving, conversations, and teamwork generate a significant proportion of the knowledge assets that exist within a firm.

In today's dynamic environments and industries, even the knowledge about the process of doing things is incomplete at the outset and develops gradually over time, through various kinds of learning. These processes, as Macro Iansiti demonstrates with Netscape's case, consist of a series of interdependent solutions, each of which adds something to what a firm knows.

Knowledge involved in deliberation on alternative decisions that could have been made is typically lost in the process, once the job is done. Knowledge utilization is inherently a colaborative process, and neither within-firm nor cross-firm utilization and transfer of knowledge can succeed without effectively supporting collaboration. This focus on collaboration and collaborative support is perhaps one of the primary distinguishing factors that differentiates knowledge support systems from information systems. A simple question such as "Has anyone seen something like this before?" Can perhaps generate an amazingly rich array of responses, all but one of which will soon be forgotten once the problem is solved. Fortunately, this happens to be one of the easiest avenues for capturing knowledge electronically. Inclusion of learning allows deliberate actions before relevant processes are completed.

1.7.3. Knowledge Utilization

Knowledge utilization comes into the picture when learning is integrated into the organization. Whatever is broadly available throughout the company can be generalized and applied, at least in part, to new situations. The example of the tech support guy at Microsoft is a perfect case of this: Sharing and utilization are taking place simultaneously. Any computer-supported facility on enhance these functions, in part or as a whole, will have to keep these three broad concepts in clear view before successful implementation can begin.

When we begin thinking of technology support for knowledge management, the first technology that comes to the minds of most managers is their interanet. But what often is forgotten is a device as common as their coffeepot and arguably more useful than their Palm Pilot: the telephone.The telephone represents the best set of characteristics that one could wish for in a system that supports knowledge flow effectively. As you speak into the telephone, you can convey context, meaning, an attitude, and tone, along with information and data.

The telephone, the fax, and the newspaper are successful devices not because they carry information but because they are deeply embedded in the communities within a company. For this reason, the telephone is perhaps the best role model for a knowledge management system. Any successful knowledge management system will have to possess the characterisitcs and communication richness of a telephone; as it is embedded in the organization, its use is almost transparent, rarely formal, natural and hesitation free. The telephone provides us with a laundry list of basic characteristics that any system supporting knowledge must possess:

- The system should be well accepted in the community that will actually use it, not just the community that creates it.
- The system should allow and support rich communication.
- Context, meaning, opinions, tone, and biases should have a way to move through the system.
- The user should not feel as if she were using something she would not use it given a choice.
- The system should support informal communication and multiple ways of expressing ideas, thoughts and communication.
- The system should be transparent to the user. A good example of a relatively powerful too that has emerged recently is the CrossPad. The CrossPad is a digital device that resembles a clipboard on which the user can place a regular legal scratch pad and takes notes just as he normally would. The pen that he uses digitally captures everything he writes on the page. This data can then he transferred to a personal computer.
- A transparent technology must allow the user to do things the way he would normally do them, such as taking notes on an OfficeMax® yellow legal pad. A technology that requires the legal-pad-loving user to key in all the notes that he takes during a meeting is unlikely to be accepted easily because it

requires a fundamental shift in the way the user had been trained to do things — the way he is comfortable doing them.

- The system should support the informal *slang* used in the company or department. The informal language that people use to communicate with colleagues is often very different from the formal language used in presentations to senior management or clients. The system needs to support that and ensure that the users are comfortable using it on the system. The telephone, for the most part, offers a certain degree of confidentiality that makes people comfortable using this "slang". This is an imperative to prevent the system from decaying into a formality that no one actually cares to use — but still uses it because it is mandated.

Supporting Informal Knowledge : Knowledge sharing and utilization necessitate support for informal technology: something that most information technolgoy is not designed to handle. The demand for formality made by technlogists and their technologies often disrupts the more productive informal relations between knowledge workers. Search engines and electonic library catalogues are a good example of how formality constricts and severely limits our ability to either capture or support retrrieval of informal knowledge. You can use keywords, for searching but if a document, Web page, or book does not closely match the keywords they might never show up in your results. Narrowing down searches is fine, but then a lot remains to be easily missed. In terms of retrieval in the context of knowledge management, intelligent agents, look very promising. But they will not help if you cannot capture informal knowledge. The problem with information systems today is that the user must know where to look, what to ask for it, and how to ask. Information overload is probably more descriptive of this situation than information abundance: Iterative keyword searching, for example, is frustrating and often ends up retrieving too much noise. Too much information is about as dangerous as too little. In stark contrast with how much an information system can help you find, say, a book in a library, a knowledgeable librarian would perhaps be a better bet.

Perils of Excessive Formalization : Excessive formalization prevents people from behaving in ways other than those that are negotiated ahead of time and constrained by technology. In a research study involving a major personal digital assistant accessories manufacturer, a colleague and we found that the same idea described as an optimized design by an engineer in the company was described very differently by a marketing manager, even though they meant exactly the samethings: a good product that the consumer liked. Excessive focus on formal knowledge leaves little room for informal, tacit, and socially embadded knowledge, which is where the know-why lies and the most significant work gets accomplished.

The definition and details of the term knowledge as presented here describes the persperctive of knowledge management. As the goals of this work are to investigate concepts and scenarios for the application of knowledge management system or KMS as part of knowledge management intitatives, thid definition needs further operationalization. This is a difficult task as the discussion of certain aspects of the definition or certain entities that deal with or hold knowledge–individuals, organizations or even documents, will necessarily challenge the definition. Figure 1.12. summarizes the discussion and gives an overview of the specifics of the term knowledge. The figure shows a selection of seven paired types of knowledge which helps to study the possibilities a selection of seven paired types of knowledge which help to study the possibilities to support the handling of knowledge by KMS. Interviews with knowledge managers in the empirical study suggest that these are the most important types of knowledge that require distinctive treatment in KMS. The implications of KMS support for the various types of knowledge, the medium to which knowledge is bound as well as *knowledge content*, are as under.

Source : The dimension source distinguishes between organization-internal and organization-external knowledge. Even though organizational boundaries are increasingly blurry in a time of virtual or project organizations, cooperations, mergers and acquisitions, just to name a few, the organization as a legal or social institution remains a focal point for the distinction of internal and external knowledge. Internal knowledge is knowledge that originates from within the organization either from members of the organization or in the form of e.g., organizational routines or documented experiences. Organization-external knowledge is brought into the organization, e.g., personally by newly recruited employees, consultants, partners, suppliers or customers or in documented form with the help of studies and reports, benchmarking reports, accessibility.

Accessibility : This dimension distinguishes between electronically accessible versus electronically inaccessible knowledge. Knowledge that is published e.g., on an organization's Intranet or in a document management system can be accessed by all members of the organization that have access to these systems whereas documented knowledge that is stored on the individual hard disc of one employee cannot be found by interested knowledge seekers. Additionally, it refers to access to experts that hold knowledge about a specific topic. If KMS support the identification of experts, his or her knowledge is thus implicitly accessible by knowledge seekers. If nobody knows about the skills of the expert, he or she cannot be asked for the knowledge.

Security : The dimension security distinguishes secured from unsecured knowledge. The current trend in many organizations is towards more transparency of knowledge, a trend from implicit to explicit knowledge. The higher visibility of experts, knowledge, networks and structures increases the risk that important knowledge flows to competitors and threatens an organization's competitive advantages. Thus, security is an important issue at hand. It refers to legal mechanisms such as patents and licenses, copyrights and trade secrets as well as organizational mechanisms such as incentives to employees, employee conduct rules or job design to secure knowledge. In addition to these measures, KMS have to be designed so that the access to knowledge allows for protection of knowledge through disaggregation. There is also the whole range of information technology security issues, e.g., threats from hackers, that have to be considered.

Organizational level : The organizational level comprises individual and collective knowledge. A central element of most of the organizational level theories and approaches is the hypothesis that organizations have a collective body of knowledge that their individual members share: collective knowledge, collective practice or organizational knowledge. Collective knowledge is materialized in organizational routines no matter whether explicit in e.g., bureaucratic rules, role expectations or implicit in the norms, values and shared understanding of the organizational culture. It is separated from individual knowledge held by each individual member of the organization.

Formality : This dimension distinguishes between formal, institutionalized, approved and informal, unapproved knowledge and reflects the degree of institutionalization of knowledge in an organization. As today's business organization more or less rely on the hierarchy, rules, roles and standard operating procedures, there is a host of institutionalized knowledge which is applied by the organization's members. This knowledge evolves as the person or collective responsible for a certain area of the organization formally approves new knowledge as being part of the standard procedures in the organization. In addition to this type of knowledge, employees develop and apply knowledge independently of the formal approval system and might also share it within their community. This important part of the organization's knowledge base is less transparent than the formally approved one and thus needs special treatment when one considers the implementation of a KMS.

Externalization : Externalization turns tacit knowledge into explicit knowledge. Ever since Polanyi postulated that "we know more than we can tell", the tacit dimension has been a popular distinction used in the KM literature, although not in Polanyi's originally intended way. Many authors distinguish between tacit and explicit knowledge, whereas Polanyi postulated that every knowledge has got a tacit dimension. In the knowledge management literature, tacit knowledge is subconsciously understood and applied, difficult to articulate, developed from direct experience and usually shared through highly interactive conversation and shared experience like socialization, apprenticeship. Explicit knowledge can be formally articulated and shared through meetings, conversations, mathematical formulas, models or even documents and the like. If explicit knowledge is documented, it is removed from

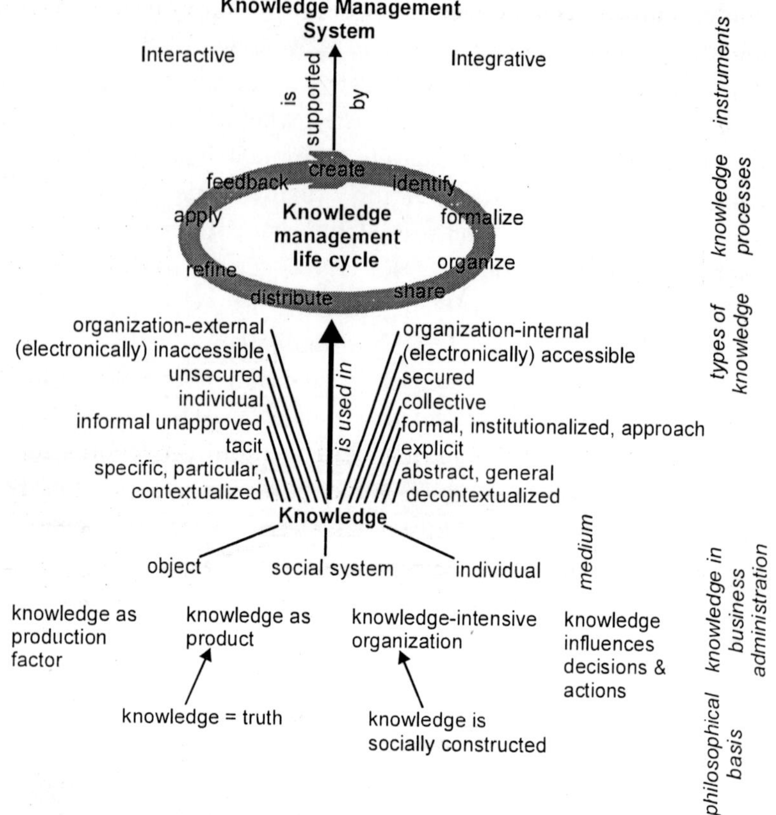

Fig. 1.12. Knowledge and its Application in Knowledge Management

its original context of creation or use. KMS can help receivers of explicit knowledge to reconstruct its context.

Nonaka calls the process of turning implicit into explicit knowledge externalization and the reverse process of turning explicit into implicit knowledge internalization. Not any knowledge that is explicable is actually explicated in an organization. There might also be in appropriately explicated knowledge. According to Polanyi, there will always remain a tacit dimension to all knowledge, even the explicated one. The distinction between tacit or the implicit and explicit knowledge helps to postulate different KM activities and different systems to support these activities.

Generalization : The level of context of knowledge defines another continuum which extends from specific, particular, contextualized knowledge describing one particular episode or event e.g., in a story to abstract knowledge, general, decontextualized knowledge captured e.g., in a mathematical formula. Before knowledge is distributed to a larger group of people, particular experiences can be generalized to lessons learned e.g., by extracting the factors that might have influenced the outcome, aggregating similar experiences to describe a practice – good or best practice. The degree of generalization has to be considered when KMS are used to support the transfer of knowledge. The more specific a knowledge element is, the more context has to be provided in order for the knowledge seeker to be able to understand, learn and reuse the knowledge.

Medium : The medium on which knowledge resides can be an object, an individual or a social system. Many authors make a distinction between knowledge as a product and knowledge as a process, especially those who use the definition of the term knowledge for a subsequent analysis of the suitability of information communication technology to support corresponding organizational processes . Knowledge as an object is independent of a holder whereas knowledge as a process can be viewed as a process of simultaneously knowing and acting by applying expertise.

Knowledge as a product comprises documented experiences. A couple of terms were coined in the practitioner-oriented literature to underline the higher value of documented knowledge as opposed to data or documented information. Examples are lessons learned, best practices, experience data bases, benchmarks, customized reports or context-enriched documents. In this perspective, knowledge is basically seen as information plus context, as networked information. The distinction between information and knowledge is a gradual one, a continuum. The common denominator of this perspective is that knowledge used in organizations can be explicated and externalized and as a consequence untied from its creator and made available for "easy" reuse by other members of the organization. In this objective perspective, a knowledge unit or knowledge element can be viewed as "a formally defined, atomic packet of knowledge content that can be labeled, indexed, stored, retrieved, and manipulated. The format, size and content of knowledge units may vary, depending on the type of explicit knowledge being stored and the context of its use". Examples for knowledge elements are : concepts, categories and definitions (declarative knowledge), processes, actions and sequences of events (procedural knowledge), rationale for actions or conclusions (causal knowledge), circumstances and intentions of knowledge development and application of specific contextual knowledge. Non-objectified knowledge can also be distinguished according to the organizational level in individual knowledge and collective knowledge, that is knowledge bound to a social system. However crude and pragmatic this distinction is, it helps to understand why the term KMS is used, what is required for the design and implementation of KMS and what the differences to other information and communication systems are.

Content : In addition to the generalized types of knowledge as discussed so far, organizational knowledge can be divided according to the main organizational area in which it is applied or in which it has been generated: knowledge about products and processes can be attributed regularly to the production division of an organization whereas knowledge about customers and competitors is usually gained in the market-oriented divisions of an organization-marketing, sales, customer service. Examples for contents that can be distinguished in KMS are product knowledge versus market versus expert versus leadership knowledge, leadership knowledge.

These different types of knowledge are systematically handled by the tasks of the KM life cycle which in turn is supported by KMS. The design and implementation of KMS therefore depends on the KM initiative's perspective on knowledge.

1.8. KNOWLEDGE MANAGEMENT

Knowledge management is knowledge process management; that is, the management of knowledge production, knowledge integration, the knowledge life cycle and their immediate outcomes can be defined as "the harnessing of a company's collective expertise wherever it resides and the distribution of that expertise to the right people at the right time. It is not a product but a process — the process of gathering, managing and sharing employees' knowledge capital."

In practice, knowledge management often encompasses identifying and mapping intellectual assets within the organization, generating new knowledge for competitive advantage within the organization, making vast amounts of corporate information accessible, sharing of best practices, and technology that enables all of the above — including groupware and intranets knowledge management includes

- management strategies
- methods, and
- technology for leveraging intellectual capital and
- know-how to achieve gains in human performance and competitiveness.

"Knowledge management involves efficiently connecting those who know with those who need to know and converting personal knowledge into organisational knowledge." A range of definitions has been provided at Yogesh Malhotra's well known website (www.brint.com) and a variety of views beginning with Malhotra's own definition.

Malhotra (1998) : Knowledge Management caters to the critical issues of organizational adaptation, survival and competence in the face of increasingly discontinuous environmental change ... Essentially, it embodies organizational processes that seek synergistic combination of data and information processing capacity of information technologies, and the creative and innovative capacity of human beings.

He looks at KM as a synthesis of IT and human innovation! While information generated by computer systems is not a very rich carrier of human interpretation for potential action, knowledge resides in the user's subjective context of action based on that information. Hence, it may not be incorrect to suggest that knowledge resides in the user and not in the collection of information, a point made two decades ago by West Churchman, the leading information systems philosopher.

In this definition, it is not clear what management is? Or what knowledge is? It is not clear what information is? If knowledge is personal, does that mean that Malhotra rules out organizational knowledge? And why is information, as well as knowledge, not personal? Does Malhotra think there is something about personal information that automatically makes it valid and therefore "knowledge"? Is everything we believe "knowledge" just by virtue of our believing it? If so, this is a highly subjectivist view of knowledge and derivatively of knowledge management.

Sveiby (1998) : ... Both among KM-vendors (researchers and consultants) and KM-users (read short descriptions of what companies and other practitioners are doing) there seem to be two tracks of activities—and two levels. Track KM = Management of Information. Researchers and practitioners in this held tend to have their education in computer and/or information science. They are involved in construction of information management systems, AI, engineering, groupware, etc. To them, knowledge = objects that can be identified and handled in information systems. This track is new and crowing very fast at the moment, assisted by new developments in information technology.

This definition begs the question of defining KM. It does not define "management" or "knowledge." And it does not distinguish knowledge from information, or knowledge management from information management.

Track KM = Management of People. Researchers and practitioners in this held tend to have their education in philosophy, psychology, sociology or business/management. They are primarily involved in assessing, changing and improving human individual skills and/or behaviour. To them Knowledge = Processes, a complex set of dynamic skills, know-how, etc., constantly changing. They are traditionally involved in learning managing these competencies individually—like psychologists— or on an organisational level— like philosophers, sociologists or organisational theorists. This track is very old, and is not growing so fast.

"Knowledge" is clearly not a process. "Learning," "KM," and "knowing" are processes, but knowledge itself, the outcome of processes such as learning and knowing, is not a process.

Sveiby's two alternative "definitions" of KM are presented by him as originating with others, identifying two schools of thought. But knowledge management should be interpreted as directed at the views stated without the implication that Sveiby subscribes to them. We note, however, that his statement of them declines to offer a critique of either, and that he prefers to remain above the fray.

Ellen Knapp (1998) : Knowledge management is defined as "the art of transforming information and intellectual assets into enduring value for an organization's clients and its people."

Knapp thinks it is more important to tell us that KM is an "art" than it is to tell us what management is and what exactly it is we are managing. "Intellectual assets" is far too vague a construct to define the scope of KM. "Transforming" is not managing, and things other than knowledge can have "enduring value." In other words, this definition confuses acting upon information with managing knowledge and knowledge processing with knowledge management. It is a characteristic error, committed again and again in knowledge management circles.

University of Kentucky (1998) : Knowledge is a vital organization resource. It is the raw material, work-in-process, and finished good of decision making. Distinct types of knowledge used by decision makers include information, procedures, and heuristics, among others.... A variety of computer-based techniques for managing knowledge (i.e., representing and processing it) have been and will continue to be devised to supplement innate human knowledge management skills. As a field of study, knowledge management is concerned with the invention, improvement, integration, usage, administration, evaluation, and impacts of such techniques.

Rather than being the "finished good of decision making", knowledge is the finished good for decision making. In any event, it is hard to see the distinction between information and procedures and heuristics, since these appear to be information also. Moreover, this definition limits KM to "computer-based techniques," a limitation neither acceptable to the KM community in general, nor justified by the common concept of management, which encompasses far more than computer techniques.

Karl Wiig (1998) : He states that Knowledge Management in organizations must be considered from three perspectives with different horizons and purposes:

Business Perspective—focusing on why, where, and to what extent the organization must invest in or exploit knowledge. Strategics, products -and services, alliances, acquisitions, or divestments should be considered from knowledge-related points of view.

Management Perspective—focusing on determining, organizing, directing, facilitating, and monitoring knowledge-related practices and activities required to achieve the desired business strategies and objectives.

Hands-On Operational Perspective—focusing on applying the expertise to conduct explicit knowledge-related work and tasks.

Karl Wiig, one of the more systematic thinkers in the field of knowledge management today, is the closest so far on the management side. The business perspective focuses attention on resource allocation, certainly a managerial activity. The management perspective identifies a number of management activities. The "hands-on" perspective recognizes that knowledge managers must also do knowledge processing. But Wiig's definition of knowledge as "understandings" and "mental units" is highly debatable and clearly falls entirely on the World 2 side of things. So his definition of KM does not orient us towards managing, producing, and/or intergrating World 3 knowledge, or toward managing how either World 2 or World 3 information is validated and hence becomes "knowledge."

R. Gregory Wenig (1998) : "Knowledge Management consists of activities focused on the organization gaining knowledge from its own experience and from the experience of others, and on the judicious application of that knowledge to fulfill the mission of the organization....."

Currently, there is no consensus on what knowledge is ... . The definition that is found most useful when building systems is as follows: knowledge is understanding the cognitive system possesses. It is a construct that is not directly observable. It is specific to and not residing outside the cognitive system that created it. Information, NOT knowledge, is communicated among cognitive systems. A cognitive system can be a human, a group, an organization, a computer, or some combination.

Wenig's definition is strong on many of aspects of World 2 knowledge, especially on the distinction between individual knowledge and collective knowledge, and on the idea that it is a kind of information (World 3 knowledge) and not World 2 knowledge that is communicated among cognitive systems. But Wenig's definition is weak on the activities comprising KM and how they are distinguished from knowledge processing activities.

Philip C. Murray (1998) : "The perspective at Knowledge Transfer International or KTI is that knowledge is information transformed into capabilities for effective action. In effect, knowledge is action...."

For KTI, knowledge management is a strategy that turns an organization's intellectual assets—both recorded information and the talents of its members—into greater productivity, new value, and increased competitiveness. It teaches corporations, from managers to employees, how to produce and optimize skills as a collective entity.

If knowledge were action, we would not need two words. In fact, there is a great gap between knowledge and action and even between knowledge and the capability for action. As we have seen knowledge is a necessary condition for effective action, but it is not sufficient by itself. Not only knowledge, but also power and other resources are required for effective action to occur, as is the will to take such action. Also, let us not forget that information combined with capability and intention is also sufficient for action, but not for success. Finally, KM is a process and not a strategy as specified in Murray's view.

Tom Davenport (1998) : Knowledge is: "information with value, from the human mind and KM is: "processes of capturing, distributing, and effectively using knowledge".

"Information with value" is getting close to knowledge. But what kind of value? Information can have value for producing knowledge and yet not be knowledge itself. Thus, in producing knowledge, one may select from among a number of competing models. All may be of value in providing the context for an assessment which validates only one of them as knowledge, but that doesn't change the fact that all but one are just information.

This specific definition of KM, further, does not cover the interpersonal and decision-making aspects of KM. Moreover, why are "capturing," "distributing," and "using" knowledge, distinctively knowledge management, as opposed to knowledge processing, which consists of activities that all knowledge workers as well as knowledge managers engage in? Here, then, is another case of someone confusing knowledge processing with knowledge management.

Most definitions of KM suffer from the lack of careful treatment of both "management" and "knowledge." It's almost as if KM experts think that "knowledge management" is not a form of "management" and therefore does not have to be defined or characterized in a manner consistent with well established meanings of that term.

The above definitions are striking in that they tell us so little. Why do KM definitions tell us so little about (a) the activities that are part of KM and (b) the target of those activities?

The situation with respect to "KM" is very similar to what we have already found with regard to "knowledge." There is no consensus on definition and attempts to define KM are relatively superficial. It is a case of another key concept in KM being defined so vaguely and ambiguously that research and writing on KM is weighed down with conceptual baggage and difficulties in communication, inhibiting both the search for KM knowledge and effective KM decision making. Here the attempt to solve the problem of definition begins with consideration of the differences between information management and knowledge management.

Thus, we can say, *KM is a management discipline that seeks to enhance organizational knowledge processing.* KM is also human activity that is part of the interaction constituting the Knowledge Management Process (KMP) of an agent or collective.

This last definition reduces KM to the definition of the KMP. *The KMP is an ongoing, persistent, purposeful interaction among human-based agents through which the participating agents manage (handle, direct, govern, control, coordinate, plan, organize, facilitate, enable, and empower) other agents, components, and activities participating in basic knowledge processing (knowledge production and knowledge integration), with the purpose of contributing to the creation and maintenance of an organic, unified whole system, producing, maintaining, enhancing, acquiring, and transmitting the enterprise's knowledge base.*

This definition in effect defines the KMP as a process aimed at the management of knowledge processes and their outcomes. But this is only the beginning in specifying the character of KM. We need now to specify KM by providing a classification based on a multidimensional view of KM activities.

We can distinguish among organizations along five important KM dimensions, thereby providing the basis of a useful classification. These are:

- the number of levels of knowledge management interaction an organization has implemented;
- the breadth of knowledge management activities it has implemented at each level;
- the target(s) of knowledge management activity;
- whether a knowledge management intervention is a social process intervention or a technology intervention; and
- whether the intervention is a policy or program intervention.

1.9. LEVELS OF KNOWLEDGE MANAGEMENT

We mean to distinguish multiple levels of KM process activity arranged in a hierarchy by levels of knowledge management interaction. In principle, and, at least with respect to knowledge production, the hierarchy has an infinite number of levels. The hierarchy is generated by considerations similar to those specified by Behxand Russell in his theory of types, and Gregory Bateson in his theory of learning and communication.

Knowledge processes occur at the same level of agent

interaction as other business processes, even though they are about those processes. Let us call this business process level of interaction Level Zero of enterprise Complex Adaptive System (CAS) interaction.

At this level, preexisting knowledge is used by business processes and by knowledge processes to implement activity. And in addition, knowledge processes produce and integrate knowledge about business processes using (a) previously produced knowledge about how to implement these knowledge processes, (b) infrastructure, (c) staff, and (d) technology, whose purpose is to provide the foundation for knowledge production and knowledge integration at Level Zero. But from where does this infrastructure, staff, knowledge, and technology come? Who manages them, and how are they changed?

They do not come from, by, and through the Level Zero knowledge processes—these only produce and integrate knowledge about business processes such as sales, marketing, or manufacturing processes. Rather, this is where Level One of CAS interaction, the lowest level of knowledge management, comes in.

This Level One KM process interaction is responsible for producing and integrating knowledge about Level Zero knowledge production and integration processes to knowledge workers at Level Zero. It is this knowledge that is used at both Level Zero and Level One to implement knowledge processes and KM knowledge and information processing. Let us call this Level One knowledge the Enterprise Knowledge Management (EKM) model.

The KM process and EKM model at Level One are also responsible for providing the knowledge infrastructure, staff, and technology necessary for implementing knowledge processes at Level Zero. In turn, knowledge processes at Level Zero use this infrastructure, staff, and technology to produce and integrate the knowledge used by the business processes. The relationships between Level One KM and Level Zero knowledge and business processes are illustrated in Figure 1.13.

Knowledge about Level Zero knowledge processes, as well as infrastructure, staff, and technology, change when Level One KM process interactions introduce changes. That is, changes occur:

when the Level Or KM process produces and integrates new knowledge about how to implement Level Zero knowledge processes; and when it adds or subtracts from the existing infrastructure, staff, and technology based on new knowledge it produces. There are two possible sources of these changes.

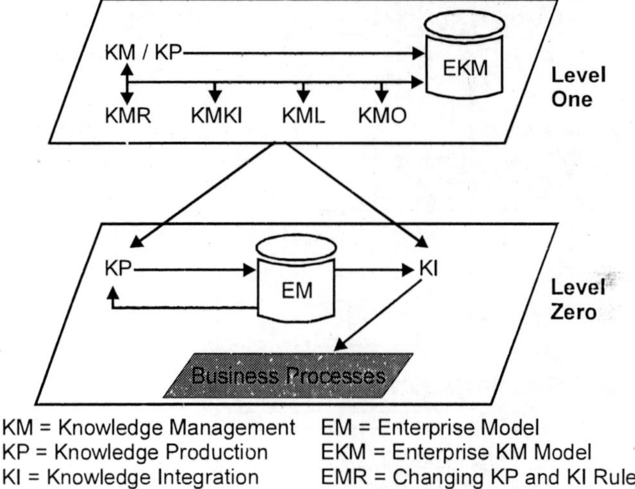

Fig. 1.13. Relationships between Level One Knowledge Management and Level Zero Knowledge and Business Processes

First, knowledge production at Level One can change the EKM model, which, in turn, impacts on : (a) knowledge about how to produce or integrate knowledge about (Level Zero) business processes, (b) knowledge about how to acquire information or integrate knowledge about Level One information acquisition or integration processes (c) staffing, (d) infrastructure, and (e) technology. This type of change, then, originates in the KM Level One process interaction itself.

Second, knowledge expressed in the EKM model about how to produce Level One knowledge may change. This knowledge, however, is only used in arriving at the Level One EKM model. It is not explained or accounted for by it. It is determined, instead, by a KM Level Two process and is accounted for in a Level Two EKM model produced by this interaction. Figure 1.14 adds the KM Level Two process to the process relationships previously shown in Fig. 1.13.

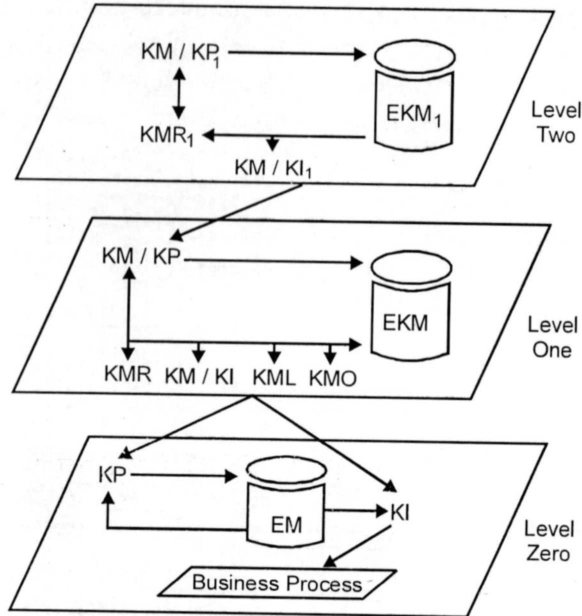

Fig. 1.14. Adding Knowledge Management Level Two to the Relationshop

Instead of labeling the three levels of processes discussed so far as Level Zero Level One, and Level Tiro, it is more descriptive to think of them as the knowledge process level, the KM or metaknowledge process level, and the meta-KM or Metaprise level of process interaction, respectively. There is no end, in principle, to the hierarchy of levels of process interaction and accompanying EKM models. The number of levels we choose to model and to describe, are to be determined by how complete an explanation of knowledge management activity we need in order to accomplish our purposes.

The knowledge process level produces knowledge about business processes and uses knowledge about how to produce and how to innovate knowledge about business processes. This level cannot change knowledge about how to produce knowledge. But it can change knowledge about business processes.

The KM (metaknowledge) process level produces knowledge about how to produce knowledge about business processes, i.e., knowledge processing knowledge. The KM level also uses knowledge about how to produce KM level knowledge about how to produce knowledge about business processes. This level can change knowledge about how to produce knowledge but cannot change knowledge about how to produce KM-level knowledge.

The meta-KM, or first Metaprise level (i.e., Level Two), produces: (a) knowledge about how to produce knowledge about KM knowledge processes at Level One, and (b) knowledge about how to produce KM level knowledge (again, at Level One) about how to produce knowledge about knowledge processes for use at Level Zero. It uses knowledge about how to produce meta-KM level knowledge about how to produce knowledge about KM knowledge processes. This level can change knowledge about how to produce KM-level knowledge but cannot change knowledge about how to produce meta-KM level knowledge.

Level Three, the meta-meta-KM process, or second Metaprise level of interaction, produces knowledge about how to produce meta-KM level-produced knowledge about how to produce knowledge about KM knowledge processes, and uses meta-meta-KM level-produced knowledge about how to produce knowledge about meta-KM level knowledge processes. This level can change knowledge about how to produce meta-KM level knowledge, but cannot change knowledge about how to produce meta-meta-KM level knowledge.

Level Two, the first Metaprise level, then, seems to be the minimum number of levels needed for a view of KM allowing one to change or accelerate the rate of change in KM level knowledge. And in some situations, where we need even more leverage over our knowledge about how to arrive at knowledge about KM processes, we may even need to go to levels higher than Level Two.

Keeping in mind the above distinctions among enterprises according to the level of knowledge management practiced in them, let us talk about KM, meta-KM, meta-meta-KM level enterprises, and so on. It should be possible to usefully characterize the successful twenty-first century intelligent enterprise, at least on a business-domain specific basis, as a Level X Metaprise, when we have more empirical evidence on how many KM levels are needed for competitiveness in any business domain.

Thus, the relative effectiveness of enterprises -practicing different levels of KM is an empirical question, not something we should assume as given. While it is very likely that effectiveness will increase as enterprises move from the KM level to higher levels, there may be a point at which diminishing returns set in. Or there may even be a point at which movement up the ladder of levels leads to negative returns relative to the investment required to add a KM level, or leads to fewer returns than alternative investments in other areas.

1.10. KNOWLEDGE MANAGEMENT — RESOURCES

Knowledge Management is a discipline that promotes an integrated approach to identifying, managing and sharing all of an enterprise's information assets. These information assets may include.

- database
- documents
- policies and procedures, and
- previously unarticulated and experience resident in individual workers.

1.11. PROCESSES AND FUNCTIONS OF KNOWLEDGE MANAGEMENT

Knowledge management issues include developing, implementing and maintaining the appropriate technical and organizational infrastructures to enable knowledge sharing and selecting specific contributing technologies and vendors.

Knowledge management requires technology, business strategy, and people. It is the process of capturing the collective knowledge of the organization, analyzing it and transforming it into easily recognizable forms for mass consumption, and communicating the results to the organization by means of a readily accessible vehicle.

1.12. KNOWLEDGE MANAGEMENT - RELATED SUBJECT DOMAINS

Knowledge management draws from a wide range of disciplines and technologies.

- *Cognitive science* : Insights from how we learn and know will certainly improve tools and techniques for gathering and transferring knowledge.
- *Expert systems (ES), artificial intelligence (AI) and knowledge base management systems (KBMS)* : Artificial Intelligence and related technologies have acquired an undeserved reputation of having failed to meet their own — and the marketplace's — high expectations. In fact, these technologies continue to be applied widely, and the lessons practitioners have learned are directly applicable to knowledge management.
- *Computer-supported collaborative work (Groupware)* : In Europe, knowledge management is almost synonymous with Groupware Sharing and collaboration are clearly vital to organizational knowledge management — with or without supporting technology.
- *Library and information science* : One can find that card catalogues in libraries will help to find the right book when needed. The body of research and practice in classification and knowledge organization that makes libraries work will be even more vital as inundated by information in business. Tools for thesaurus construction and controlled vocabularies are already helping to manage knowledge.
- *Technical writing* : Also under-appreciated — as a professional activity, technical writing or technical communication forms a body of theory and practice that is directly relevant to effective representation and transfer of knowledge.
- *Document management* : Originally concerned primarily with managing the accessibility of images, document management has moved on to making content accessible and re-usable at the component level. Early recognition of the

need to associate "meta information" with each document object prefigures document management technology's growing role in knowledge management activities.

- *Decision support systems* : Daniel J. Power states, "Researchers working on Decision Support Systems have brought together insights from the fields of cognitive sciences, management sciences, computer sciences, operations research, and systems engineering in order to produce both computerised artifacts for helping knowledge workers in their performance of cognitive tasks, and to integrate such artifacts within the decision-making processes of modern organisations." That already sounds a lot like knowledge management, but in practice the emphasis has been on quantitative analysis rather than qualitative analysis, and on tools for managers rather than everyone in the organization.
- *Semantic networks* : Semantic networks are formed from ideas and typed relationships among them — sort of "hypertext without the content," but with far more systematic structure according to meaning. Often applied in such arcane tasks as textual analysis, semantic nets are now in use in mainstream professional applications, including medicine, to represent domain knowledge in an explicit way that can be shared.
- *Relational and object databases* : Although relational databases are currently used primarily as tools for managing "structured" data — and object-oriented databases are considered more appropriate for "unstructured" content — we have only begun to apply the models on which they are founded to representing and managing knowledge resources.
- *Simulation* : Knowledge Management expert Karl-Erik Sveiby suggests "simulation" as a component technology of knowledge management, referring to "computer simulations, manual simulations as well as role plays and micro arenas for testing out skills."
- *Organizational science* : The science of managing

organizations increasingly deals with the need to manage knowledge — often explicitly. It's not a surprise that the American Management Association's APQC has sponsored major knowledge management events.

Other technologies include : object-oriented information modeling; electronic publishing technology; hypertext and the World Wide Web; help-desk technology; full-text search and retrieval; and performance support systems.

1.13. BASIC ACTIVITIES OF KNOWLEDGE MANAGEMENT

It is the breadth of knowledge management processes, we mean the extent to which all of the major KM activities are implemented at any specified KM level of the enterprise. So what are these major KM activities? Here is a conceptual framework that begins to specify them.

Enterprise KM activities may be usefully categorized according to a scheme of task clusters which, with some additions and changes, generally follows Mintzberg. We use Mintzberg's categorization of activities because it was developed from an extensive empirical study of managerial behaviour. These include:

- changing knowledge processing rules
- crisis handling
- allocating KM resources
- negotiating agreement with representatives of other business processes

We are specifying these areas of KM activity under following headings.

1.13.1. Interpersonal Behavior

Figurehead or Ceremonial Representation KM Activity

This activity focuses on performing formal KM acts such as signing contracts, attending public functions on behalf of the enterprise's KM process, and representing the KM process to dignitaries visiting the enterprise. Such symbolic representation is an aspect of all managerial activity. Managers have authority, part of what maintains that authority is the symbolism used and manipulated by them to express the legitimacy of their authority and to claim it.

Figurehead activity in the KM area is similar to that in other areas of executive activity. Methods such as personal networking, meet-ings, public appearances, Web-enabled representing, and infrastructure such as intranet facilities used for figurehead activity, conference and presentation rooms, fax, telephone facilities, etc., are also similar. What is perhaps different is the focus of figurehead activity on conferences, meetings, and events where knowledge processing and knowledge management are the primary topics of interest.

Leadership

This includes setting policy, hiring, training, motivating, monitoring, and evaluating KM and some knowledge processing staff. It also includes persuading non-KM agents within the enterprise of the validity of KM process activities. That is, KM leadership activity includes building political support for KM programmes, projects, and knowledge processes within the enterprise and influencing the climate and norms within which knowledge processing will occur, so that knowledge production will be enabled. Finally, leadership activities cut across all the other categories of KM activities. That is, leadership is an aspect of each of the classes of KM activities.

That leadership activities are central to KM is axiomatic. Leadership is a key management activity in any business process, and knowledge and KM processes are business processes. Again, what is different here is the focus on leadership of knowledge production and integration activities and on changing knowledge processing rules such as those impacting knowledge claim evaluation. And in the area of resource allocation, the focus on allocating software applications supporting knowledge production, integration, and management is different.

Building Relationships with Individuals and Organizations External to the Enterprise

This is another political activity designed to build status for KM and to cultivate sources of support for KM external to the enterprise. To build new external relationships requires joining professional associations, serving on committees, attending and presenting at conferences, visiting colleagues and allies, forming strategic alliances and partnerships, and networking individual contacts. There is no magic here, just the need to design and implement a systematic program to generate alliances and close relationships with individuals. These personal relationships are essential for information acquisition at the KM level. Some information can only be acquired through personal networks. Building external relationships means performing those activities intended to produce friendships, alliances, and "partnerships" with decision makers external to one's own company. These relationships are essential tor providing "role models" for knowledge managers.

1.13.2. Knowledge and Information Processing

Knowledge Production is a KM as Well as a Knowledge Process

KM knowledge production is different in that it is here that the "rules," frameworks, perspectives, and methodologies for knowledge production used at the level of knowledge processes are specified.'

Keep in mind that knowledge production at this level involves planning, descriptive, cause-and-effect, predictive, and assessment knowledge about the two fundamental Level Zero knowledge processes, as well as these categories of knowledge about Level One interpersonal, knowledge integration, and decision-making KM activities. The only knowledge not produced by Level One knowledge production is knowledge about how to accomplish knowledge production at Level One. Once again, the rules, perspectives, etc., constituting this last type of knowledge are produced at Level Two.

KM Knowledge Integration

KM knowledge integration is affected by KM knowledge production and also affects knowledge production activities by stimulating new ones. KM knowledge integration at any KM level also plays the critical role of diffusing "how-to" knowledge to lower KM and knowledge process levels. But the essential character of knowledge integration at the KM level is unchanged from that at the basic KLC at Level Zero.

1.13.3. Decision-Making Activities

Changing Knowledge Processing Rules

The task clusters of information acquisition, individual and group learning, knowledge claim formulation, knowledge claim evaluation, broadcasting, searching/retrieving, teaching, and sharing are all com-posed of tasks. Knowledge workers execute these tasks, and knowledge managers produce the processing "rules" contributing to the execution of the tasks. Knowledge managers also change the rules once they produce new knowledge about them. Essentially this involves making the decision to change knowledge processing rules and causing both the new rules and the mandate to use them to be transferred to the lower level. The term "rules" here should be interpreted liberally, as signifying perspectives, customs, frameworks, etc., as well as rules. It is not claiming that Rules produced by knowledge managers necessarily govern, or should govern, all or even most knowledge production. On the contrary, rules govern most knowledge production in business process DECs. But knowledge is frequently produced through the use of novel perspectives and frameworks as well as rules in knowledge life cycles.

Crisis Handling

Crisis handling involves such things as meeting CEO requests for new competitive intelligence in an area of high strategic interest for an enterprise and directing rapid development of a KM support infrastructure in response to requests from high level executives. Crisis handling does not occur in KM as frequently as it does in other management processes. But when it does occur, it is a significant KM activity.

Allocating Resources

Allocating resources for KM support infrastructures, training, professional conferences, salaries for KM staff, funds for new KM programs, etc., is also an important KM activity. KM software implementation also falls into this category.

Negotiating Agreements

Negotiating agreements with representatives of business processes over levels of effort for KM, the shape of KM programs, the ROI expected from KM activities, etc., is another important area of KM activity. Once again, this activity is not unique to KM. But its lack of distinctiveness makes it no less essential to the practice of KM.

1.14. TARGETS OF KNOWLEDGE MANAGEMENT

Knowledge management manages knowledge processes and their outcomes. Thus, these, rather than business processes and business outcomes, are the targets of knowledge management. This relationship is expressed in Figures 1.15 and 1.16. In Figure 1.17, we list the 10 most generalized targets of KM, the KLC subprocesses and their outcomes. This 10-category taxonomy is highly expandable, since each of the subprocesses may be broken down further into task clusters and patterns.

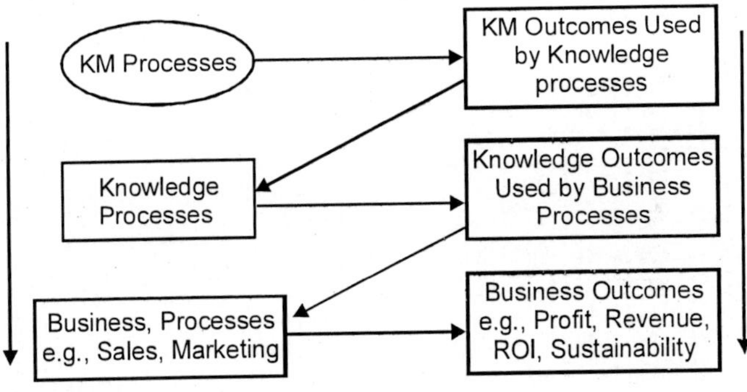

Fig. 1.15. From Knowledge Management Processes to Business Outcomes

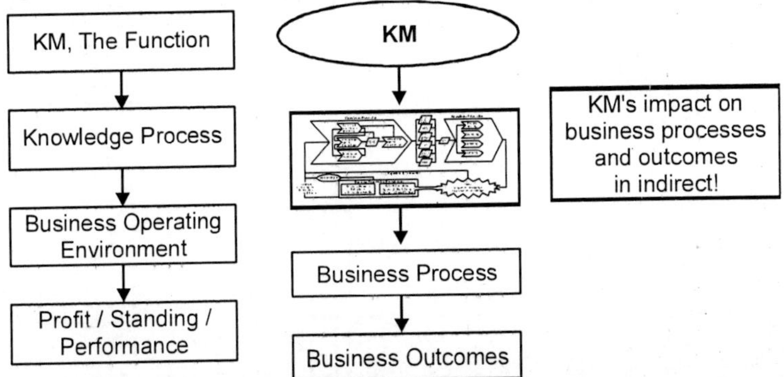

Fig. 1.16. Reference Model for Knowledge Management

1.15. SOCIAL AND TECHNOLOGICAL & POLICY AND PROGRAM INTERVENTIONS

The social dimension of KM interventions deals with people and processes using a variety of tools and methods including recruiting, communities of practice, knowledge cafes, social process redesign and many others. The technological dimension, of course, deals with technology-based interventions, such as enterprise knowledge portals, community support software, text-mining software, and other KM-related applications. Figure 1.18 provides examples of KM interventions classified by the social versus

•Information Acquisition •Individual and Group •Learning •Knowledge Claim •Formulation •Knowledge Claim •Evaluation •Organizational Knowledge	•Broadcasting •Searching/Retrieving •Teaching •Sharing •Distributed •Organizational •Knowledge Base
	To enhance the KLC

And KM business processes are composed of tasks which, in turn, are comprised of Mintzberg activities

Fig. 1.17. Knowledge Management Business Processes–Different Purposes and Targets

	Demand-Side KM	Supply-Side KM
Social Dimension (People and Process)	• Individual Learning • Group Learning • Innovation & IC Mgmt • Communities of Inquiry • KAIZEN Events in Mfg • Think Tanks • Management Planning	• Training Programs • Communities of Practice (CoP) • Knowledge Capture • Storytelling • KM Cultural Initiatives • Operations Mgmt
Technology Dimension (IT)	• Knowledge Portals • Innovation Mgmt Tools • Groupware - Collaboration Apps - Virtual Teaming Tools - E-mail • Listserv Discuss'n Grps	• Information Portals • Intranets • Information Mgmt • Work Product Mgmt • Content Mgmt • Imaging • Groupware

Fig. 1.18. Examples of Common Knowledge Management Initiatives

technology and demand-side (knowledge production) versus supply-side (knowledge integration) dichotomies. In the classification we are forming here, the demand-and supply-side categories are further broken down into KLC subprocesses and outcomes.

Policy and program KM interventions differ, of course, in their intent and generality. Policies are supposed to be highly general and may require several programs to implement. Programs are more specific in their focus on social and technological targets. Here are two examples:

Policy : Employees shall have meaningful opportunities to engage in self-directed learning.

Program : 3M's Fifteen Percent Rule – Employees may spend up to 15% of their time on self-chosen, self-managed learning, with full management support.

Thus, we can see that when we add the policy versus program dimensions to the demand- versus supply-side and social versus technology intervention matrix, we get an even richer framework for categorizing KM strategies and intervention types.

1.16. CLASSIFICATION OF KM ACTIVITIES

This classification of nine KM categories or task clusters can not be said complete. There are likely other task clusters and patterns but this classification of activities is specific enough to (along with the level, target, social/technological, and policy/program dimensions) provide the capability to define many types of KM interventions which may then be analyzed for impact and effectiveness. If we assume only two KM levels on the Metaprise dimension, the 9 KM activity categories, the 10 target categories, the two social/technological, and the two policy/program categories, then the KM taxonomy that results specifies a 720-category classification of KM interventions. And this is only the beginning of differentiation, since further category segmentation can easily be developed in both the KM activity and target dimensions and perhaps almost as easily in the social/technological and policy/program dimensions as well.

But basically 9 – KM activity is said to be sufficient for knowledge management.

1.17. NEED FOR KNOWLEDGE MANAGEMENT

Why do we need to manage knowledge? Macintosh of the Artificial Intelligence Applications Institute University of Edinburgh, has written a "Position Paper on Knowledge Asset Management". According to this, the need for knowledge management is as follows:

- Any work is information and knowledge based.
- Organizations compete on the basis of knowledge.
- Lack of time to experience and acquire knowledge.
- Need to manage increasing complexity.
- Need for life-long learning is an inevitable reality.
- To remain aligned with the dynamically changing needs of the environment.

The underlying premise is that 'best practices' of yesterday may not be taken tor granted as 'best practices' of today or tomorrow. Hence, double loop learning, unlearning and releaming processes need to be designed into the organizational business processes.

Knowledge management is necessary for organizations because what worked yesterday may or may not work tomorrow.

To remain aligned with the dynamically changing needs of the business environment, organizations need to continuously assess their internal theories of business for ongoing effectiveness. That is the only viable means for ensuring that today's 'core competencies' do not become 'core rigidities' of tomorrow.

Tiwana (2001) has summarized following reasons for knowledge management.

1. Companies are becoming knowledge intensive, not capital intensive : Knowledge is rapidly displacing capital, monetary process, natural resources, and labour as the quintessential economic resource. Knowledge is the only input that can help your company cope with radical change and ask the right questions before you attempt to find the answers, for without this knowledge you might never even realize how your industry's competitive environment is changing until it is a little too late. It is this knowledge that brings quality into any company's product and service offerings. Further, product life cycles and service time-to-market can be accelerated in unprecedented ways through knowledge. Knowledge management is the only way to reach and apply this knowledge in time.

2. Unstable markets necessitate "organized abandonment : "Your target markets might under- go radical shifts, leaving your company in a disastrous position of being with the wrong producer, at the wrong time, and in the wrong place. The impact of these forces is witnessed most prominently in high-technology environments and financial markets, and increasingly in other markets as well. KM lets you undertake what Drucker calls organized abandonment reshape products, get out of projects and product lines that can pull your business down, and get into others that maximize growth potential.

National Semiconductors, an excellent example, closed down its division Cyrix Corporation, the well-known manufacturer of low-end Intel-clone microprocessors in 1999 when it realized that it was pulling the entire company down as it tried to withstand price based assaults from mighty Intel, which had pockets deeper than those of National.

3. KM lets you lead change so change does not lead you : KM is no longer needed by service based businesses and consultants alone. Even conventional retailers like Wal-Mart consider then competence in logistics management- a knowledge-intensive activity—to be their primary driver of business success. Drucker warns that no industry or company has a natural advantage or disadvantage; the only advantage it out possess is the ability to exploit universally available knowledge. He describes knowledge as "*the window of opportunity.*" After all, the next critical piece of critical information could take any form—an evolving social trend affecting customer preferences, a new management practice, a nascent technology, or a political or economic development in a remote manufacturing location. You cannot manage this change, Drucker reminds. You can only lead change, and stay ahead of it.

In a data-obsessed business environment where only 2 percent of grocery store scanner data collected is ever analyzed, knowledge management can help you determine those points and see opportunities through these "windows" in processes where change needs to be led, before your competitors do.

4. Only the knowledgeable survive : "The survival of the fittest firm" is an outmoded thought in the knowledge-based economy. The ability to survive and thrive comes only from a firm's ability to create, acquire, process, maintain, and retain old and new knowledge in the face of complexity, uncertainty, and rapid change. It becomes deterministic in the firm's long-term survival. Drucker points out that knowledge is productive only if it is applied to make a difference and suggests that it is this productivity that is going to be the deterministic factor in the competitive position of any company, or industry. Knowledge management can make that a reality.

When your company can apply its past experience for accelerating future work, why should you start every project with a blank sheet and then work feverishly, sometimes even desperately, to make the deadline on budget? Yet companies do it all the time, Connie Moore notes that mass stupidity lies the opportunity to differentiate your company's processes.

5. Cross-industry amalgamation is breeding complexity: Drucker warns us that complexity, uncer tainty, and ambiguity are the hallmarks of todays production and business systems irrespective of the nature of business or type of industry. Knowledge management has allowed many companies such as Bay Networks to turn this complexity to their advantage.

6. Knowledge can drive decision support like no other: Providing effective decision support by making knowledge about past projects, initiatives, failures, successes, and efforts readily available and accessible can make a significant contribution toward convalescing this process. Drucker lists four diagnostic tools for decision making that we will focus on: foundation, productivity, competence, and resource allocation knowledge. KM solutions that are capable of effectively supporting collaboration and knowledge sharing enable individual knowledge workers, teams, and communities to collaboratively make better decisions faster—and act on those decisions to create more economic value for their company.

7. Knowledge requires sharing : KM requires a strong culture of sharing that information systems do nor inherently support, In the United Stares, Tom Davenport has been feverishly supporting the idea of figuratively creating "water cooler cultures" in the same way as the Europeans have been demanding "coffee machine cultures" environment that allow and systems that support social informality. Knowledge, as any witness to artificial intelligence research knows, "is not about machines, but about culture." Principles that have traditionally driven information technology design, though with moderate success, no longer apply in designing KM systems.

8. Tacit knowledge is mobile : Too often when someone leaves your firm, his or her experience leaves too. This knowledge, skills, competencies, understanding, and insight then often go to work for a competitor. Knowledge management can save your company from losing critical capabilities when that happens.

9. Competitors are no longer just on the West Coast: We are becoming increasingly global, Drucker notes, keeping up with developments and ensuing threats or opportunities in other countries is a tedious, time-consuming, and difficult process. Knowledge management technology, when given the right source feeds, can deliver relevant and timely knowledge.

As companies shift from a product-centric form to a knowledge-centric form, it becomes essential to support various dimensions of this knowledge as a critical asset. Companies—big or small—cannot afford to underinvest in using, reusing, and not losing knowledge that they already have. Knowledge management is therefore an imperative for companies that do not operate in purely cost-driven markets anymore.

Thus, we see that here have been many attempts to define KM, but remarkably few attempting to specify the activities or processes comprising it. This is one of the mysteries of KM literature. It is as though KM theoreticians have gone from KM abstractions to stories, case studies, tools, software, and the rest of the diversity we see in KM without developing further the core concept of the field, and thereby leaving a huge gap (see figure 1.19) between core definitions and the more concrete objects named above.

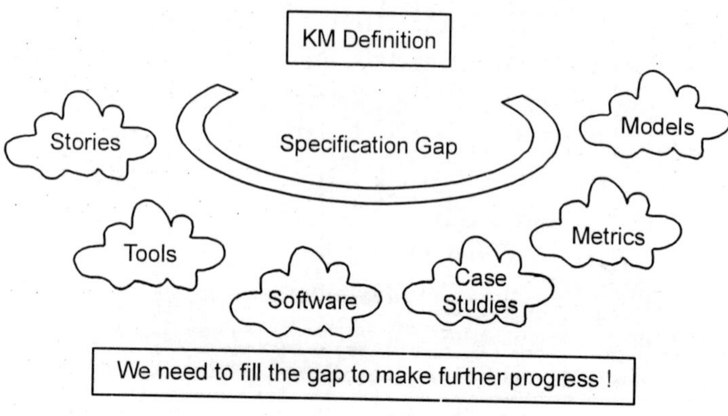

Fig. 1.19. A Specification Gap

In brief, knowledge and information have become the medium in which problems occur. As a result, managing knowledge represents the primary opportunity for achieving substantial savings, significant improvements in human performance, and competitive advantage.

Knowledge management is the harnessing of a company's or organization's collective expertize wherever it resides and the distribution of that expertise to the right people at the right time. It is not a product but a process—the process of gathering, rnanaging and sharing employees' knowledge capital.

2

Origin and Development of Knowledge Management

The progress of humanity over the past 30,000 years has been predominantly due to the effectiveness of the organizations used to achieve human goals. For example, religious goals have been achieved through organizational structures developed by the world's major religions. Economic progress throughout history has been driven by commerce and business organizations. Political organizations have both provided stability and been the catalyst for change.

Organizational systems have internal structures that mediate roles and relationships among people working towards some identifiable objectives. These internal structures, together with cultural, leadership, and management characteristics, provide the ability to effectively interact with their environment and achieve desired goals.

2.1. INTRODUCTIONAL HISTORY

Organizations have a much longer history than is usually understood. While a study of evolution demonstrates the ubiquitous role of interactions and relationships among all life, the beginnings of structure, function, and dedicated efforts to meet objectives through intention, planned action, and individual roles had to wait until man reached the hunter gatherer/agriculture transition.

Since the early hunter gatherer, circa 35,000 B.C., the success of small bands of humans gathering berries, leaves, and grubs and occasionally hunting larger animals is clear from the world-wide distribution of archeological sites where human colonies lived. Environmental forces demanded specific actions for survival, leading to the development of culture via the need and propensity to cooperate. Thus began the first attempts at structure and organization, driven by the same forces that drive organizations 37,000 years later – threats and opportunities in the environment and a strong desire to survive and achieve goals.

As demonstrated in this human activity, organizations usually existed through a successful balance between the forces in their environment and their own creativity and adaptivity. The boundary between the organization and its environment is almost always porous, flexible, and foggy. This frequently unpredictable external environment is driven by physical, political, sociological, economic, natural, and technological forces.

Organizations, a product of man's superb cognitive and linguistic capabilities, have always made use of knowledge and one of its offspring, technology, to survive during their hour on the stage of history. An early example of this occurs during the eighteenth through twentieth Egyptian dynasties (1550 to 1069 B.C.). The Overseer of All the King's Works - a man of science, an architect, and the authority figure - directed the massive labour force required to build a pyramid. "His palette and papyrus scrolls were the symbols of the authority of knowledge, and bureaucratic lists and registers were the tools of political and economic power."Knowledge, demonstrated by writing, provided the authority, and the use of technology, in the form of pulleys, levers and wheels, provided the means.

The success of the Taizong dynasty (626-49 A.D.) was a direct result of Taizong's strong leadership and management approaches built on a solid cultural and military base. While building and stocking the latest instruments of war, Taizong used literature to spread manners and guide customs. He instituted a system of state schools and colleges and gave the highest positions in the government to those who passed literary exams. Thus, Taizong not only recognized the value of learning and knowledge, but also used it to expand the Imperial family's influence throughout the empire.

Throughout history, the environment has become increasingly complex, dynamic, and technologically sophisticated. In response, organizations have become more complex, more flexible, and more egalitarian, with success very much dependent on making optimum use of all available information, experience and insight.

The technology revolution of the late 1700s began with the invention of the steam engine and ultimately brought about factories and mass production. With the emergence of the tycoons of oil, railroads, steel, and automobiles came the rise of the modern bureaucracy and the great test of its precepts of specialists and rigid rules. While economically successful, it took a large toll on human freedom. Specialization, limited learning and initiative, and assembly lines made mechanical robots out of workers. As new technology was developed, it was frequently misunderstood or misapplied and ended up restricting employees rather than liberating their potential.

2.2. THE BUREAUCRATIC ORGANIZATION

Max Weber (1864-1920) developed the formal theory recognized today as the bureaucratic model. Weber, a lawyer familiar with power politics, economics, and religion, migrated to sociology through his attempt to understand how capitalism came into existence. His world of ideas was multidimensional.

The bureaucratic framework created by Max Weber in the late 1800s called for a hierarchical structure, clear division of labour, rule and process orientation, impersonal administration, rewards based on merit, decisions and rules in writing, and management separated from ownership. The bureaucratic model was built on management power over workers in what Weber called "imperative control." The key success factors of Weber's bureaucracy rested on authority and its acceptance by workers, and on the design and management of processes and rigid rules and procedures.

He linked knowledge with power. He believed that "Every bureaucracy seeks to increase the superiority of the professionally informed by keeping their knowledge and intentions secret." Because the pure interest of the bureaucracy is power, secrecy would grow with the increase of bureaucracy. We still live with the legacy of this intent.

With the rise of large corporations in the early twentieth century came a strong interest in research in fields such as leadership, management, organizational theory and capitalism. Frederick Taylor, Henry Fayol, Mary Parker Follet, Chester Bernard, Adam Smith, Herbert Simon. Abraham Maslow. etc., all contributed to the foundational research and set of organizational concepts of the early twentieth century. This era created the formal foundation of management and organizational theory. Although the origins lay in Weber's bureaucracy, church and state autocracy and military leadership, these were all modified by the social, political, and capitalistic drives in the free world after World War II. The new theories and concepts such as Theory X, Theory Y, Theory Z, Charismatic and Transformational Leadership. General Systems Theory, and Organizational Linking Pins, became popular and a noticeable shift occurred from bureaucracy toward a more benign and malleable organizational structure. Tools such as Management by Exception, Span of Control, Kurt Lewin's Force Field Analysis and Taichi Ohno's Toyota Production Line techniques helped both managers and workers implement change throughout their organizations. While some changes occurred, most organizations continued to be hierarchical. Knowledge and information were held close by supervisors and managers and protected as knowledge and information represented personal power and authority. Economic progress was relatively steady and, until the 1970s. fairly predictable. During this post-bureaucratic era, the key factors were a combination of Tayloristic time and motion management and participative management slowly bringing some of the workforce into the arena of worker responsibiliy and empowerment.

As the affluence, mobility and expectations of the workforce in developed countries continued to rise, coupled with the explosive growth of information and communication technologies and the creation of knowledge, organizations found themselves in situations of restructure or collapse. The old mechanical metaphor would no longer serve in the nonlinear, dynamic, complex global web of the mid 1990s. Many organizations failed, some were acquired, and the best set about seeking the popular vision of the "world-class" corporation. The stage was now set for the rise of information and knowledge organizations, with the information organizations taking the lead via computers and communications technology in the early 1980s and 1990s and the knowledge organizations, currently in their developing form, focusing on networking and knowledge creation, sharing, and application.

Knowledge is built on data and information and created within the individual. Knowledge, of course, has many levels and is usually related to a given domain of interest. In its strongest form, knowledge represents understanding of the context, insights into the relationships within a system, and the ability to identify leverage points and weaknesses and to understand future implications of actions taken to resolve problems. Thus knowledge represents a richer and more meaningful awareness and understanding that resonates with how the "knower" views the world. Knowledge is frequently considered actionable.

2.3. ORGANIZATIONS OF THE YEAR 2000

Time accelerates. Distance shrinks. Networks expand. Interdependencies grow geometrically. Uncertainty dominates. Complexity overwhelms. Such is the environment and the context within which current organizations must survive and thrive.

This situation is a result of many years of evolution driven by a number of major factors. Of significance is the increasing economic affluence of the worker in the developed countries coupled with their increased education level, resulting in a strong demand by workers to be recognized, respected, and allowed to participate and have determination in their work. Economics and technology provide both the means and pressures for mobility, thereby giving workers the freedom to leave their jobs for other, more challenging positions. While the last 50 years have seen many ups and downs in terms of employment, productivity, interest rates, investments, etc., the recent decades have provided increasing wealth and economic success.

Consistent with this history, every organization lives at the pleasure of its environment - economic, sociological, scientific, technological, and political. Technology plays a dominant role in determining both the landscape of competition and the cultural and educational needs of the workforce. It is arguably true that technology has played the strongest role in creating the present environment within which organizations must adapt and learn how to excel compared to their competitors. For example, tremendous increases in processing speed, communication bandwidth, miniaturization of technology and the development of complex algorithms and application programs have spawned the rapidly changing pace of society and the increasing need and capability for communication, collaboration, and networking, both virtual and real. The phenomenal rise of the Internet, coupled with the spin-offs of intranets, extranets, portals, etc., have created a networking potential that drives all of society and corporations in terms of speed, interdependencies, global markets, and the creation and spread of memes instantaneously throughout the world. Memes are ideas that become a part of the culture. Those organizations that have found ways to compete successfully within this nonlinear, complex, and dynamic environment may dominate their competitors by as much as twenty-five percent in growth rate and profitability relative to the average in their industry.

Specific characteristics of these "world class" organizations are key to their success. While most of today's organizations are far from this world class region, many are working hard to improve their performance, that is, efficiency, effectiveness and sustained competitive advantage, in order to improve their competitive status and in some cases prevent being acquired or going into bankruptcy.

Often the tools, methods, structures, and principles that the best organizations have found to drive high performance are neither new nor, in many cases, unique. For example, many of the ideas that Toyota created in the late 1940s and early 1950s relative to lean manufacturing in the automobile industry 'although refined and improved' are still considered world class, and, in fact, Toyota is considered by many to be the leader throughout the world in automobile manufacturing Taichi Ohno created the Toyota production system just after World War II as a response to potential bankruptcy and changing consumer demands. The system eventually included just-in-time supply parts delivery, floor workers in the factory taking responsibility for product quality and having authority to stop the production line, and teams of workers solving problems on the factory floor and learning cross-functional jobs to insure continuous production line flows. Recognize that it took Toyota more than twenty years to create its present system, and it is still being improved. Approximately fifty years later many of these early ideas are still considered best practices and used by manufacturing organizations worldwide. They represent a significant departure from the bureaucratic hierarchy chain of command and minimum freedom of the worker.

In *Built to Last*, Collins and Porras did a six-year study of eighteen companies that had outstanding performance over time periods between fifty and two hundred years. Reviewing their results, together with other research on long-lived world-class companies, the following factors are offered as representative of long-term, highly successful organizations:

- Continuous striving to improve themselves and doing better tomorrow than what they did today, always remaining sensitive to their customers and their environment.
- Not focusing on profitability alone, but balancing their efforts to include employee quality of life, community relations, environmental concerns, customer satisfaction and stakeholder return.
- A willingness to take risks with an insistence that they be prudent and have an overall balanced risk portfolio. In general, they were financially conservative.
- A strong feeling about their core ideology, changing it seldom, if ever. Their core values form a solid foundation and, while each company's individual values were unique, once created, they were not allowed to drift with the fashions of the day. This core value molded their culture, and created a strong sense of identity.
- Relative to their employees, these companies demanded a

strong "fit" with their culture and their standards. Thus, employees either felt the organization was a great place to work and flourished or they were likely short-term. At the same time, they were tolerant of individuals on the margins who experimented and tested for possibilities.

Many current top organizations have made significant changes in the way they do business in the past decade and have been able to create performance through change management and deliberately develop the fundamental characteristics needed for success. These characteristics must provide those responses necessary to excel in today's environment. For example, time to market or the ability to quickly develop new products is a key factor in many industries because of the decreased production time created through technology, concurrent engineering, and agile manufacturing techniques. The use of simulation, integrated product teams and world-wide subject matter experts operating virtually have been instrumental in bringing new knowledge and ideas together to rapidly produce products desired by a sophisticated and demanding market. Examples of this capability are: (1) mass customization where economic order quantities of one are being pursued and (2) agility, the ability of an organization to move rapidly in response to changing and unique customer needs. Creativity and innovation have come to the forefront as key success factors with organizations striving to develop and unleash these capacities throughout their workforce, using a combination of management, workers, customers, and the ability to pull collaborative teams together as a situation or problem dictates.

Employee involvement has now been accepted and understood by world class organizations and many "hope to be's." Examples are Wal-Mart, Hewlett-Packard, IBM, Texas Instruments, Motorola, and the Chaparral Steel Company. These world-class organizational structures have moved significantly away from bureaucratic decision making, and have modified their hierarchies to include team-based organizations and horizontal structures with minimum "white space." These firms encourage cross-communication by all employees, supported by technology such as e-Mail and groupware and reward employees who play a strong role in influencing organizational direction and decision-making.

These same organizations, working predominantly in the fast-moving world of information and knowledge application, recognize the value of decisions made at the lowest qualified level and the payoff from smart workers who know their jobs. However, for employees at all levels to use their knowledge to make effective decisions, they must understand the context within which those decisions are made. This context is provided through shared vision, clear values, and strong organizational direction and purpose, combined with open communication. As described by Peter Senge in the *Fifth Discipline*, smart companies put significant effort into transferring their vision, purpose, and goals to all employees. Good employee decision-making stems from understanding their work in terms of its impact on adjacent areas of the organization, as well as its direct impact on the customer. This requires effective empowerment and systems thinking and customer orientation and focus. Note how far we have departed from Weber's description of bureaucracy and its relative impotency in the current world context.

Nurtured by Total Quality Management (TQM) and Total Quality Leadership, the transfer of better business practices has recently become a hallmark of high-performing organizations. Many tools are continuing to be developed to help organizations create environments that make maximum use of employee knowledge and creativity. These practices include benchmarking, business process reengineering, lean production, value chain analysis, agility, integrated product teams, balanced score card, and, most recently, knowledge management.

The birth of knowledge management (KM), occurring in the early 1990s, grew from a recognition of the difficulty of dealing with complexity and with ever increasing competition spurred by technology and the demands of sophisticated customers. First came an awareness of the importance of information and knowledge, followed by a constant search for ways to create, store, integrate, tailor, share, and make available the right knowledge to the right people at the right time. Fundamental to this picture was a growing appreciation for the knowledge level of employees. Although still in its infancy, as indicated by the large number of meanings and uses of the words knowledge and KM, the field has pushed many organizations far from the classical Weberian bureaucracy. For example :

- The knowledge organization's focus on flexibility and customer response compared to bureaucracy's focus on organizational stability and the accuracy and repetitiveness of internal processes.
- Current practices that emphasize using the ideas and capabilities of employees to improve decision-making and organizational effectiveness. Bureaucracies utilize autocratic decision making by senior leadership with unquestioned execution by the workforce.
- Current efforts to bring technology into the organization to support and liberate employee involvement and effectiveness. Classical bureaucracies use technology to improve efficiency and expect employees to adapt.
- Current actions to eliminate waste and unnecessary processes while maximizing value added. Bureaucracy seeks to establish fixed processes to ensure precision and stability with little concern for value.
- Current organizational emphasis on the use of teams to achieve better and more balanced decision-making and to share knowledge and learning. The axiom is "knowledge shared is power." Bureaucracies minimize the use of teams to maintain strong control and ensure knowledge is kept at the managerial and senior levels. The axiom is "personal knowledge is power."

As valuable as the above ideas are, their implementation continues to be a challenge to all organizations. Although many of these tools were originally touted as silver bullets, after they become popular, and as companies try them without fully understanding the difficulties of their implementation, they frequently achieve less than anticipated results. Michael Hammer, co-creator of Business Process Reengineering, has defined business process reengineering (BPR) as "the fundamental rethinking and radical redesign of business processes to achieve dramatic improvements

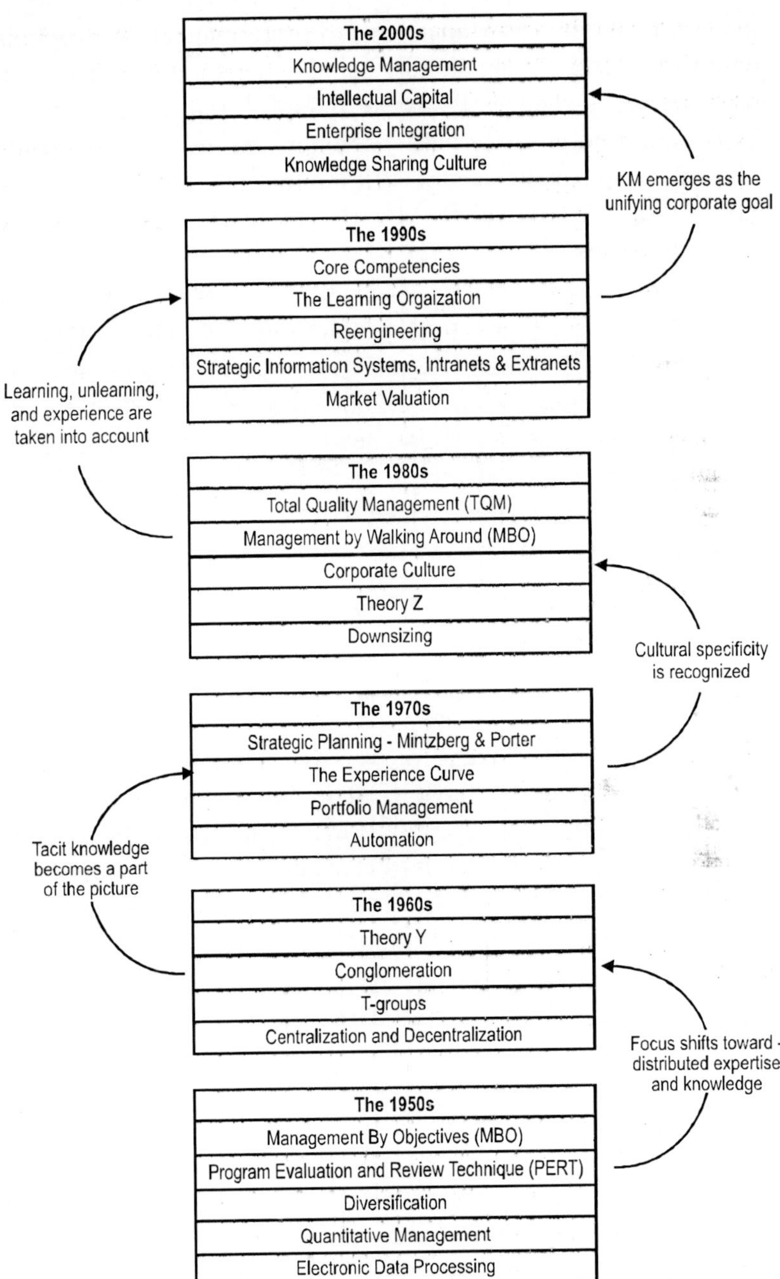

Fig. 2.1. Manager's Tool through the decades: Knowledge Management has been coming since the 1950s.

in critical contemporary measures of performance". We find that ten years later, BPR is just now being understood well enough to provide a good chance of success, if applied to the right situation by experienced professionals. The unproven perception was that as many as seventy percent of BPR implementations failed to meet expectations. Many feel TQM suffered the same difficulties. As time progresses and more organizations learn how to successfully implement these tools, they are becoming more and more useful and contributing significantly to organizational improvement.

Figure 2.1. shows the darling tools of managers as they evolved from the 1950s to the 2000s. Some of these died much anticipated deaths as fads, and some live today. Notably, a pervasive thread runs through all these — about leveraging experience, intellectual assets, and their management. And this consistent thread has led businesses to what we now call knowledge management.

2.4. GENERATIONS OF KNOWLEDGE MANAGEMENT

The practices associated with managing knowledge have their roots in a variety of disciplines and domains. An overarching theory of knowledge management is yet to emerge. A number of management theorists have contributed to the evolution of knowledge management. Among them such notables as Peter Drucker, Paul Strassmann, and Peter Senge in the United States. Drucker and Strassmann have stressed the growing importance and explicit knowledge as organizational resources.

One account, by Mark Koenig, sees KM as a field that was originally driven by information technology, the Internet, best practices, later lessons learned, and most important, knowledge sharing. This theory sees a second stage of KM as about human factors, organizational learning, and knowledge creation viewed as the conversions among tacit and explicit knowledge. The third stage of KM is the stage of the arrangement and management of content through taxonomy construction and use and like the first is also heavily biased toward information technology.

The second view of change, by David Snowden, is a bit more subtle than the first. According to this theory, the first age of knowledge management is one in which the word knowledge itself was not at first "problematic," and in which the focus was on distributing information to decision makers for timely use in decisions. The second age replaced the information technology focus with one on tacit/explicit knowledge conversion inspired by Nonaka's SECI model. It is just ending. Snowden contends that the third age will be one in which: knowledge is viewed paradoxically as a thing and a flow; context, narrative, and content management will be central to our view of KM; there will be an understanding of organizations as engaged in sense making through utilization of complex adaptive systems phenomena constrained by human acts of free will attempting to order them; and finally, the use of the insights and practices of scientific management will be restricted to appropriate contexts, while "insights and learnings" from theories of chaos and complexity will supplement them in contexts where these new insights are relevant.

The third view of change, first presented by Mark W. McElroy based on work hosted by the Knowledge Management Consortium International (KMCI) and continuing partly under its auspices since then, views first-generation KM, also called "supply-side KM," as primarily about integrating ("supplying") previously created knowledge through knowledge distribution, sharing and other integrative activities. It is typically associated with two well-known phrases that serve as the mantras for advocates of the "knowledge sharing" side of KM: (1) It is all about capturing, codifying, and sharing valuable knowledge, and (2) It is all about getting the right information to the right people at the right time. The third view sees second-generation KM as first appearing in the mid-1990s and as being focused not only on "supply-side" knowledge processing such as knowledge sharing, but also on "demand-side" knowledge processing, or "knowledge-making" in response to problem-induced demands. This combined focus on knowledge integration and knowledge production is the defining characteristic of Second Generation KM (SGKM), or alternatively, The New Knowledge Management (TNKM). But an important aspect of it is also the recognition that organizations are permeated with complex adaptive systems phenomena and that knowledge management in them is about using KM to enable or reinforce self-organization in knowledge processing for the purpose of achieving accelerated sustainable innovation in support of organizational adaptation.

2.4.1. The Three Stages of Knowledge Management

Mark Koenig viewed that "The initial stage of KM was driven primarily by information technology. That stage has been described ... as *by the Internet out of intellectual capital.*"

By this, Koenig means that the development of the Internet and the use of its technology to implement intranets provided the enterprise with an unprecedented tool for knowledge sharing and transfer. Knowledge management was the name introduced to describe the management activity concerned with implementing such solutions, in order to gain competitive advantage and increase productivity and effectiveness.

Further, this activity could be rationalized by its proponents including large consulting organizations selling their own newly developed expertise in implementing such solutions, in terms of increasing the value of an enterprise's Intellectual Capital (IC). The notion of IC had appeared a few years earlier to account for the increasing disparity between the market value of real world enterprises and their book value as computed using measurable financial indicators and conventional formulae for computing company valuations. In addition to the above, the first stage of KM was also characterized by a focus on "best practices," later revised to a focus on "lessons learned." But it is not clear from Koenig's account what "best practices" and "lessons learned" in KM have to do with the IT or information technology focus supposedly dominant in stage one.

So for Koenig, the first stage of KM was about applying technology to accomplish knowledge sharing and coordination across the enterprise. The second stage, on the other hand, was primarily a recognition that KM was not all about applying technology, but rather had also to include a focus on human and cultural factors as essential in implementing KM applications, if failures were to be avoided. Koenig calls attention to the work of

Senge on organizational learning and Nonaka and Takeuchi on the SECI model and its applications as essential to phase two. Koenig also calls attention to the focus of these works on organizational learning and knowledge creation, but not on systems thinking, which was an important element in Senge's treatment and in the rising popularity of stage two activities. Koenig also mentions the importance of communities of practice in stage two, but neglects to make the connection between the communities of practice emphasis and the thinking of Senge and Nonaka and Takeuchi, or for that matter, between communities of practice and knowledge creation and innovation.

Koenig thinks that the third stage of KM "is the awareness of the importance of content—and, in particular, an awareness of the importance of the retrievability and therefore of the arrangement, description, and structure of that content." In particular, the third stage is about finding relevant content and about taxonomy development and content management to facilitate this goal.

2.4.2. Difficulties with the Three-Stages View

There are a number of difficulties in Koenig's account of the development of knowledge management. First, the dates in his account of development are unclear. His theory is one of the onset of new KM stages which then exist along with the old. If such a stage theory of KM development is to be applied we need either clear dates to distinguish the beginning of each successive stage, or a clear period of transition in which the previous stage is gradually supplemented by the features of the new stage. Without these criteria it is very hard to characterize a particular period as stage one rather than stage two and to confirm that analysis. Specifically, Koenig claims that stage one precedes stage two and that stage one is about applying IT, while stage two is about the human element in KM. Yet Senge's book, identified, as a stage two milestone was written in 1990 much before the trend toward intranets and knowledge sharing applications, supposedly characteristic of stage one, gained momentum. Karl Wiig's work introducing KM as a field was also written much before the widespread adoption of Internet-based technology in enterprises, and even before Senge's book. And then Wiig wrote three books from 1993 to 1995, looking at KM comprehensively. Even Nonaka and Takeuchi dates from 1995, a date that surely preceded the heyday of so-called stage one KM with its emphasis on intranet-based knowledge sharing and coordination applications.

The same difficulty applies to the supposed transition from stage two to stage three KM. If we are to believe Koenig, it was not until 2001 that content management and taxonomy development became important for KM. However, the 1998 combined KM World/AIIM conference held in Chicago had a major content management element. In fact, attendees were frequently heard by these authors to complain that content management was dominating the conference and that such applications were not KM applications, and that claims to the contrary were merely "vendor speak" hiding the fact that vendors had very few KM applications to offer.

Following that conference, moreover, the conference circuit began to see an explosion of content management and portal conferences. These were frequently closely associated with so-called KM applications. Both types of conferences included sessions on tools for taxonomy development and for increasingly efficient retrieval of information through application of search technology.

While there is no question that the interest in content management and taxonomy development continues to increase, there is no reason to claim that this trend is either later than the second stage or even that such activities are new and go beyond the concerns of the second stage. After all, the concern with taxonomy and content management is about more efficiently retrieving knowledge or information that already exists. Thus, its core motivating concern is not different from Koenig's stage one. That is, taxonomy development and content management are primarily about coordinating and sharing already existing knowledge and only secondarily about aiding knowledge making. So there is a good argument for asserting that Koenig's stage 3 is really just an extension of his stage 1.

Second, another difficulty with Koenig's account is the ad hoc character of its classification of the three stages of KM, apparently based on anecdote and personal observation. There is no underlying conceptual framework organizing the analysis of change. KM supposedly begins as an IT field. Then suddenly, under the influence of Senge and Nonaka, it begins to incorporate the human element, and this element is apparently either discontinuous with what has gone before, or a response to the perceived failure of the IT applications implemented in the first age. It is presented as if it is a mere adaptation to a problem, the problem of getting organizations to accept IT interventions defined as KM projects. Further, a similar ad hoc adaptation is viewed as triggering the move from stage 2 to stage 3. That is, Koenig seems to think that we have a new stage of KM because people realize that they can neither share nor create knowledge without good Web-based navigation to help them "find" it.

The third difficulty with Koenig's view is that its lack of a conceptual framework provides only limited guidance for the further development of KM. He points to the fact that his view suggests that librarians may have an important part to play in taxonomy development as a positive reason for taking it seriously. But what does his analysis imply about knowledge management activities or policies more generally, or about knowledge production, organizational learning, sustainable innovation, intellectual capital, KM metrics, methodologies and IT requirements for KM applications? That is, once you understand his account, what can you do with it? The answer is very little. Unless one is interested in content management and taxonomy development, there is little of interest in it, or of general significance for the further development of KM. Thus it provides both an inadequate analysis of the past and fails to provide a road map for the future.

In brief, it is believed that Koenig's approach to the analysis of stages of KM is much too ad hoc in character, focusing on tools and techniques and not on the broad purposes of KM. As a result, his typology only records shifting fashions, not fundamental shifts in disciplinary concerns. Thus, he cannot recognize that both IT applications in support of KM and taxonomy/content management concerns are not about central issues of knowledge management orientation, but rather are about techniques and tools for supporting such KM orientations. The development of these techniques and tools, however, is driven by the basic orientations and purposes themselves.

So, current content management, taxonomy, and portal application concerns are about supporting knowledge coordination and transfer applications. They are not yet about supporting knowledge making, production and creation. This is true because first generation KM is still dominant, while Second Generation Knowledge Management (SGKM) 'originating as a coherent orientation toward the subject somewhere in the period 1995-1999' is still in the process of taking hold.

2.4.3. The Two Ages of Knowledge Management (with a Third Yet to Come)

Snowden mentions that the first age of KM, prior to 1995, was about "the appropriate structuring and flow of information to decision makers and the computerisation of major business applications leading to a technology enabled revolution dominated by the perceived efficiencies of process engineering."

He calls this age "information for decision support." And his characterization of it, as the above quote implies, does not distinguish it from Business Process Reengineering (BPR). In fact, for Snowden, KM in the first age seems to be a species of BPR, which proceeded without recognition of knowledge gained through experience or person-to-person processes of knowledge transfer. Since it ignored these aspects of knowledge, Snowden thinks that the word knowledge itself became problematic in knowledge management by the end of the first age.

He further contends that the second age of knowledge management began in 1995 with "the popularisation of the SECI Model" after the publication of Nonaka and Takeuchi's, The Knowledge Creating Company. But he also says that "to all intents and purposes knowledge management started circa 1995" with the publication of this book. That statement, combined with his characterization of the first age as one of information for decision support, raises the question of why there is a first age in his change framework at all, or more properly, why his second age of knowledge management is not his first age.

The second age of KM, in Snowden's view, is characterized by a focus on the SECI model's four processes describing the conversion of knowledge from: explicit to tacit (socialization) tacit to explicit (externalization), explicit to explicit (combination), and tacit to tacit (internalization). He goes on to comment about the misunderstanding of Polanyi's views on the nature of the relationship between tacit and explicit knowledge that is prevalent in the second age, specifically that it was "dualistic, rather than dialectical," in contrast with both Polanyi's and Nonaka's understanding of the relationship. But he says little else about the second age, leaving the impression that there was little else to this age of KM.

2.4.4. Difficulties with the Two-Ages View

The description of the first two ages of KM of Snowden's characterization leaves a lot of open questions. First, was there really no more to the first age of KM than "information for decision support"? If so, then why was the term KM used at all? After all, the field of business intelligence provides information for decision support. So do data warehousing and data mining. So does the still broader category of Decision Support Systems (DSS). So what was the term KM supposed to signify that those other terms do not?

Second, if there was no more than information for decision support to the first age, then what were the attempts to distinguish data, information, knowledge and wisdom about? What was the development of Xerox's community of practice for the exchange of knowledge among technicians about? What was knowledge sharing at Buckman Laboratories in 1987 and 1992 about? Where does Hubert St. Onge's work on the relationship of customer capital to the learning organization fit? Or Senge's (1990) work on systems thinking? Or Karl Wiig's early introductions to KM.

Snowden's characterization of the first age of KM as focused on providing information for decision support and implementing BPR schemes in brief, suggests much too heavy an emphasis on KM as primarily composed of IT applications to reflect the full reality of the first age. In fact, his failure to take account of the human side of KM during the first age suggests a desire for the same kind of neat distinction we find in Koenig's analysis. In effect, Snowden, like Koenig, seems to want to say that the first age was about technology and the second age was about the role of people in Nonaka's four modes of conversion.

Third, in describing the second age of KM, Snowden's account is, once again, far too spare in its characterization. No doubt the Nonaka and Takeuchi book has had an important and substantial impact on knowledge management, but the period since 1995 has seen important work done in many areas nor explicitly concerned with knowledge conversion.

These areas include semantic network analysis, the role of complex adaptive systems theory in knowledge management, systems thinking, intellectual capital, value network analysis, organizational learning, communities of practice, content management, knowledge sharing, intellectual capital, conceptual frameworks for knowledge processing and knowledge management, knowledge management metrics, enterprise information portals, knowledge management methodology, and innovation, to name some, but far from all, areas in which important work has been done. Finally, as indicated by the title of Nonaka and Takeuchi's book, their concern, and a central concern of second generation KM as we shall see shortly, is about "knowledge creation," or knowledge production. It is only secondarily about knowledge conversion.

Nonaka mistakenly identified knowledge creation wholly with knowledge conversion. However, knowledge conversion only produces belief or psychological knowledge. In the area of producing organizational knowledge as a cultural product, the role of knowledge conversion is focused on only one subprocess in knowledge production – the subprocess of knowledge claim formulation. It does not address knowledge claim evaluation or validation, a critical subprocess in the creation of explicit, shared, culturally based knowledge.

Snowden's account of the coming third age of knowledge management is developed much more carefully in his work than his account of the other two ages. It will be much easier to develop, understand, and critique his forecast of a third age if we provide the third view of change in knowledge management first, and along with it some additional comments on both the Snowden and Koenig interpretations of generations.

2.4.5. The Two Generations of Knowledge Management

The third perspective on the evolution of KM distinguishes between two "generations": first and second generation KM which first was developed in McElroy. According to this view, a distinction can be made between "supply-side" knowledge management, in which interventions are aimed at knowledge integration, or sharing, and demand-side KM, which is focused, instead, on knowledge production, or making. In the first case, the practice of KM is predicated on the assumption that valuable knowledge already exists; the purpose of KM, then, is to capture, codify and share it. In the second, no such assumption is made. Before knowledge can be shared, much less captured and codified, it has to first be produced. Thus, supply-side KM focuses on enhancing the "supply" of existing knowledge to workers who need it, whereas demand-side KM seeks to enhance our capacity to satisfy our "demands" for new knowledge.

First generation KM, according to this view, was supply-side only in its orientation. Second generation practice, however, is both supply- and demand-side oriented. Of crucial importance to this view of KM, then, is the contention that knowledge is not only something we share, but is also something we make. Indeed, we can only share knowledge that exists, and knowledge can exist only after it is created—by people.

A cyclical view of knowledge making and sharing—or, more generally, production and integration—therefore comes sharply into focus as a consequence of this third perspective. Rather than assume, as first generation thinkers do, that valuable knowledge already exists and that the sole task of KM is merely to enhance its distribution, second generation thinkers contend, as well, with the problem of knowledge production. It is because of this that second generation KM is more closely aligned with the fields of organizational learning and innovation management than the second age envisioned by Snowden.

Of additional foundational importance to this third view of KM is the distinction it makes between knowledge processing and knowledge management. This rather fundamental distinction is not made in either the Koenig or Snowden accounts of the evolution of KM. Knowledge processing is precisely the cycle referred to above, through which people in organizations, in response to problems arising in business processes, collectively engage in knowledge production and integration. Knowledge processes, therefore, are social processes through which organizations make and share their knowledge.

Knowledge management, on the other hand, is a management activity that seeks to enhance knowledge processing. Not all organizations support formal knowledge management functions, but all organizations do engage in knowledge processing. The purpose of KM according to this view is to enhance an organization's ability to perform knowledge processing and ultimately by improving it to enhance the quality of its business process behaviour and its ability to adapt to its environment.

Also central to the generational view of KM is the position that knowledge processing in human social systems is a self-organizing affair. That is, people in organizations tend to self-organize in emergent, pattern-like ways around the production and integration of knowledge. We can generally describe the shapes of these patterns using terms like problem detection, intrinsically motivated learning, group and community formation, communities of inquiry or practice, problem solving, knowledge evaluation and adoption, knowledge sharing, and so forth. That these activities are selt-organizing and pattern-like in their appearance is explained with the aid of complexity and complex adaptive systems theories in the generational view of KM. Indeed, SGKM is deeply rooted in the application of complex adaptive systems theory to knowledge processing in human social systems, a perspective it applies backwards and forwards in its characterization of how KM has evolved over the years.

While the generational view of KM does point to two distinct bodies of practice that are supply-side on the one hand and demand-side on the other, it does not suggest that the second one started only after the first one ended. Rather, the two streams of practice are concurrent in use and will probably carry on in this way for some time to come.

Consider, for example, the field of Organizational Learning (OL), which is arguably focused on nothing if not demand-side knowledge processing. This is a field that clearly started long before the term KM came into fashion in the mid-1990s. The same can be said for the fields of Innovation Management (IM), Organizational Development (OD), and even Human Resources Development (HRD), which has always been concerned with the transfer of knowledge in the form of training and other knowledge sharing programs.

What we have, then, according to the generational view of KM, is two distinct bodies of practice that are separate in content but not necessarily in time. That said, the first generation of KM arguably began quite some time ago, even as early as the late nineteenth/early twentieth centuries with the work of Frederick Taylor, whose scientific management system explicitly called for the capture, codification, and use of what we today would refer to as "best practices." This was supply-side KM in action, since its intent was to enhance knowledge capture and sharing. Later on in the twentieth century, work related to enhancing knowledge production began to appear. This took many forms, including the evolution of R&D and its various methodologies and management schemes, innovation management, organizational learning, and institutionalized science, which has always been concerned with the production of new knowledge. From this perspective, supply- and demand-side KM is more than 100 years old.

Despite this, the term "KM" is considerably younger in age. Its initial appearance in the mid-1990s was clearly tied to supply-side KM, and it was not until 1999 that the formal distinction between that sense of the term and the new, or second, sense was introduced using the supply-side/demand-side language. Indeed, it was not until McElroy and his colleagues at KMCI began to think of differences in KM practice as being somehow related to the separate and distinct notion of social knowledge processing that the combined form of supply- and demand-side KM was viewed as adding up to a new and unique body of practice (SGKM) deserving of special recognition.

So even though we can say that both supply- and demand-side KM were theoretically being practiced in various forms prior to the advent of "KM" as such in the 1990s; they were clearly not being practiced, much less compared to one another, in these terms. Nor were they being tied to a formal conceptual distinction between knowledge processing and KM. That dates from the end of the 1990s, following the advent of KM in the mid-1990s in its supply-side form.

Comparing this third view to the other two, we can see important differences. The Koenig view, as is said, presents an ad hoc classification scheme in which the three "stages" of KM are based more on anecdote and personal observation than on any sort of underlying conceptual framework related to knowledge processing and how it is practiced. The third, generational view, by contrast, relies explicitly on a vision of social knowledge processing, against which all forms of practice in KM can be seen and understood. Indeed, it is SGKM that is associated with a formal articulation of this vision for just this purpose. That articulation is the knowledge life cycle framework, or KLC, as developed and refined by Firestone and other members of the Knowledge Management Consortium International (KMCI) over the past four years. The KLC framework is illustrated again in Fig. 2.2.

Next, because the scope of the KLC is comprehensive in its representation of knowledge processing in human social systems, all forms of KM practice, both current and future ones, can be related to it. Everything we do in KM is designed to have impact on one or more elements of the KLC. A generation of KM, therefore, should not, according to SGKM, be defined in terms of a Koenig-like focus on practice types, tools, or trends. Indeed, such a definition risks losing sight of the central purpose of KM interventions and tools. The appearance and/or departure of different kinds or styles of interventions need not—and should not—have anything to do with our attempts to make sense of them in terms of what their basic purpose is.

What is of more fundamental relevance to analysis of the

evolution of KM is what its practitioners are trying to do, not what their tools and methods are. Of course, we must be interested in tools and methods, too, but only after we've settled on a purpose, and used it to define the basic thrust of KM. Different flavors of tools come and go, but the purpose of KM is always to enhance knowledge processing.

SGKM's conceptual framework for knowledge processing gives rise to another important distinction between it and the Koenig view of stages. As stated earlier, the Koenig view seems to begin and end with an appreciation of the importance of taxonomy development and content management. Under this logic, the very next issue to pop up on the KM landscape would give rise to a fourth stage, a fifth one after that, and so forth. This is what happens when we define evolution from the perspective of tools and styles of interventions-each stage becomes too narrow, too tightly bounded, with nowhere else to go, driven by short-term problems and adaptations. Such a specification of stages is ad hoc and lacks depth of insight into what KM is ultimately trying to achieve or have impact on that is, to enhance knowledge processing.

By contrast, the third, generational view of KM is relatively free of bias toward intervention types or styles. According to the generational view, new tools and methods are constantly being created and tested, and there is nothing wrong with that. But what should not change along the way, except very infrequently, is the intended target of their use. Why? Because tools are used in the service of theory, and until such time as theory changes, no fundamental shift in thinking can be said to have occurred. That, and not fluctuations in tool sets or methods, must be the standard of evaluation. Practitioners of KM either seek to have an impact on knowledge production, knowledge integration, or both. Variations in the tools we use do not change such basic objectives.

In comparing the third, generational view of KM to that of Snowden's, the generational perspective can help us add to our earlier critique of his account of the first two ages of KM. First, his account seems to suffer from the same lack of an underlying conceptual framework used to organize his analysis of change.

In the first age, we are encouraged to envision individuals at

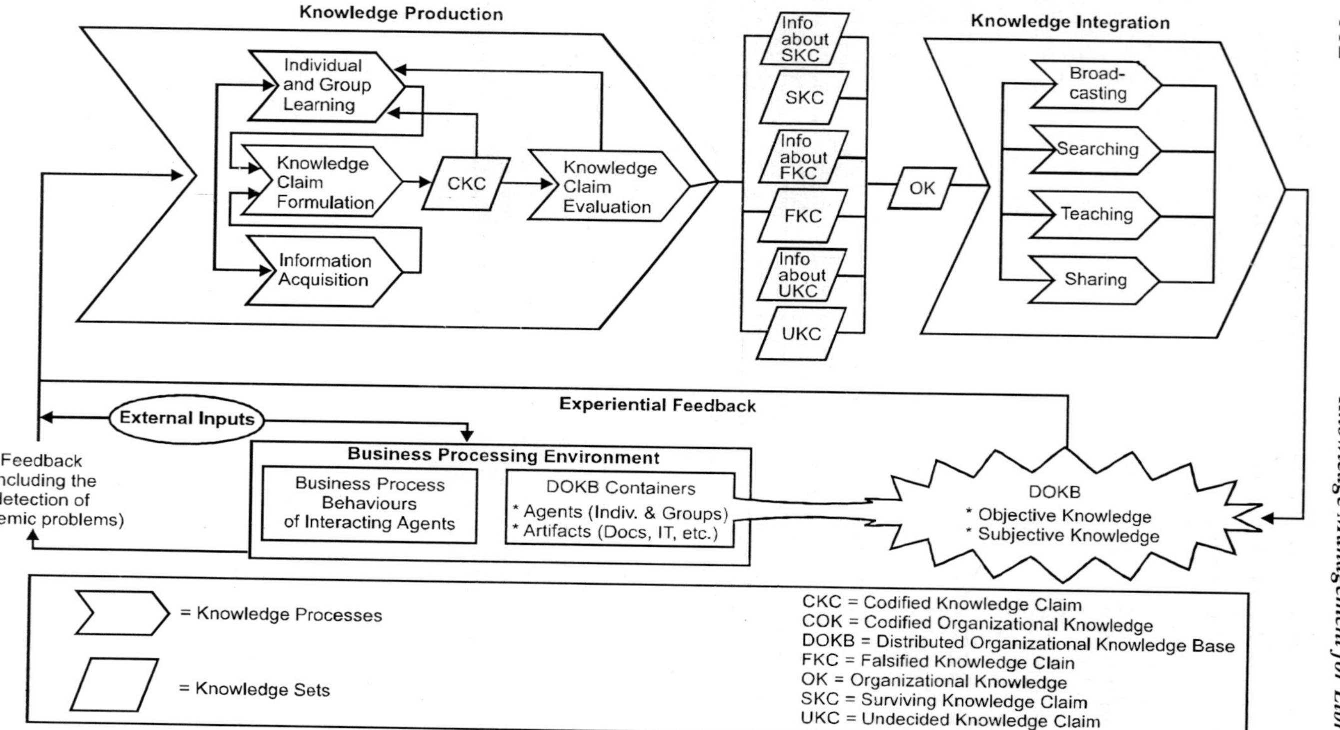

Fig. 2.2. The Knowledge Life Cycle (KLC)

work whose momentary needs from time-to-time require informational support. Then KM comes to the rescue (or is it information management or IM?), delivers the information, and declares victory. In this view, there is no social system, only individuals. And in this view, there is only the momentary and discrete decision transaction that frames the backdrop for KM, thus failing to distinguish KM, as is pointed out earlier, from data warehousing, business intelligence, or DSS. From the perspective of the third generation view of KM, however, this is an act of knowledge integration (supply-side KM). But this only makes sense in the context of a more comprehensive knowledge processing framework that can help us to distinguish knowledge integration from knowledge use. It is a distinction that Snowden does not make, but that is fundamental to first generation, supply-side KM.

In Snowden's second age we are suddenly thrust into the realm of knowledge conversion using Nonaka's SECI model as a reference. This is indeed an improvement over his first age, since his account of the second age characterization at least employs a conceptual framework—some vision of knowledge processing, which arguably goes on between individuals and other individuals, and between groups and individuals and other groups. Nonetheless, we are still left with a fairly narrow frame of reference and a failure to place the Nonaka model into a broader context of knowledge processing or a framework of KM concepts and practice.

This narrow frame of reference, of course, is determined by the scope of the SECI model that Snowden has selected to conceptualize the second age. In the SECI model, knowledge processing is reduced to four kinds of transactions—the "knowledge conversion" transactions. In using this model as the basis of his second age, Snowden reduces all of KM practice between the years of 1995 and today to a concerted effort on the part of KM professionals to get these four transactions to work better.

Never mind the much broader scope of KM activity observable since 1995. Never mind that he takes us from "information delivery" in the first age to "knowledge conversion" in the second, without explaining the difference between information and knowledge in the transition, or why the SECI model is only about knowledge and not information.' And never mind, for that matter, that the SECI model, since it, too, does not address this question, could just as easily be seen as a way of converting "misinformation" or "falsified knowledge" from one party to another. Or that it could be seen as a model for generating unvalidated knowledge claims rather than knowledge. Or that it fails to make the distinction among tacit, explicit, and implicit knowledge and not just between tacit and explicit knowledge.

Regarding the term "knowledge," Snowden tells us that it was not problematic at the beginning of the first age, but became so at its end because the first age did not recognize the character of knowledge that was embedded in social interaction and in minds. In the first age. then, we can infer that Snowden thinks that the terms "information" and "knowledge" were used loosely relative to one another, if not interchangeably. Knowledge in the second age, however, took on some special meaning, although he never really tells us what that is. Its special meaning is somehow tied in with the SECI model, the touchstone of the second age. Still, none of this would seem to support the assignment of "age" status to either period in Snowden's account. Why? Because even if we can agree to include the pre-1995 period in which he describes the handling of information and not knowledge at all, these distinctions, from a generational point of view are, like Koenig's ideas, nothing more than "a story" about evolution in tools and methods. They do not point to evolution in the underlying conceptual or analytical frameworks of KM and knowledge processing.

The generational view, on the other hand, has a much easier time of accommodating the phenomena just mentioned without having to resort to the declaration of new ages, stages, or generations. Indeed, they are all mainly about information and/or knowledge transfer or integration. You can add them a long list of other techniques aimed at enhancing knowledge sharing or transfer, but you are still left with one stream of practice: supply-side KM. Thus the generational view comprises a much broader framework than the SECI model, in that it incorporates all of the varied activities of KM practice listed earlier in this paper as occurring since 1995. In fact, SGKM is broad enough to include much, perhaps most, of the aspects that are supposed to distinguish Snowden's third age from SGKM itself.

2.5. SNOWDEN'S FORECAST? A THIRD AGE OF KM

Snowden contends that the third age will be one in which:

- knowledge is viewed paradoxically as a thing and a flow;
- context, narrative, and content management will be central to our view of KM;
- there will be an understanding of organizations as engaged in sense making through utilization of complex adaptive systems phenomena constrained by human acts of free will attempting to order them; and
- scientific management with its mechanistic models will be applied to carefully selected targets where it is appropriate, while the outlooks of chaos and complexity theory will be applied to other targets and situations where they are appropriate.

We can interpret that Koeing and Snowden basically take a storytelling approach to analyzing changes in the KM evolutionary change on the KLC knowledge processing framework and the distinction between knowledge processing and KM.

Koenig takes an IT approach to KM and basically tells a story starts by noting that the first stage of KM was about using the Internet for knowledge sharing and transfer. The second stage was a reaction to the failure of the first to live up to its promise by failing to take account of human factors essential to make IT applications successful, and the third stage is about improving the IT side by making it easier for humans ro navigate to the information or knowledge they want or need.

This story of changes occurring in response to a desire to make IT-based KM solutions successful does not specify a conceptual framework based on concepts of knowledge, KM, business processing and outcomes. Lacking such a framework, Koenig has no tool to compare the three stages of KM in order to evaluate the comprehensiveness of change in its key elements. That is why his analysis seems ad hoc and questionable from the standpoint of whether the changes he records are really so fundamental as to suggest new stages in the KM evolutionary process.

The situation is little better with Snowden's approach. Boiled down to its essentials, he almost seems to be saying:

- the first age was about applying the BPR notions of Hammer and Champy on a foundation of Taylor;
- the second age was about applying the vision expressed in Nonaka and Takeuchi;
- the coming third age will be about applying the vision coupled with the paradoxical character of knowledge, and expanded through its synthesis.

So, Snowden's story of change is not guided by a conceptual framework providing us categories setting a context for describing change, but rather is a claim that KM proceeds from vision to vision expressed in great books and/or articles. His view provides no guide about what the next fundamental change in KM will bring, because how can we know what the rest of a story might be?

McElroy's (1999) approach to change uses the conceptual framework of the Knowledge Life Cycle (KLC) to analyze the change in KM that he believes suggests there have been two and only two generations so far.

2.6. PERSPECTIVES ON KNOWLEDGE MANAGEMENT

Although early writings on knowledge management were dominated by an emphasis on tools and techniques, now the 'field' - referring here to the, now large, literature on the subject - appears to have diverged. Currently, and broadly speaking, at least two main perspectives and approaches seem to dominate behind the meaning of 'knowledge management' with the latter strengthening and gathering ground largely as a result of a critique of the former.

Consciously polarizing these perspectives in order to highlight their different orientations, the first can be described as 'knowledge management as technology' camp. This has been labeled, variously, as the Engineering perspective, the Cognitive perspective or the Codification strategy. This perspective is grounded in seminal work from library and information studies —

that informed the development of internet search engine technologies as well as in a strong tradition of knowledge engineering research among artificial intelligence and computer science experts — that has formed the development of knowledge-based systems development. It has also informed attempts among Information Systems experts to develop IT-based tools (e.g., intranets, data warehouses data exchange tools) aimed at the capture, storage, retrieval and sharing of knowledge.

Proponents of the engineering school often comment that knowledge management is not simply about developing computer systems. However, following this initial caveat and some hints of discomfort with the technologically deterministic view, the focus frequently then narrows to an emphasis on using IT-based systems and methodologies to capture, codify and store knowledge so that it can be exploited more effectively in the organization. Thus, comments as: "some might say that cultural problems are insurmountable using knowledge technology is disagreed. It is believed that with further modification and adaptation our techniques and tools can be used to capture the ways in which behavioural, cultural and organizational change takes place, and how it can be managed best". Such beliefs in the power of technology are rarely as honestly or openly stated, but nonetheless appear to underpin much of what is written in the 'knowledge management as technology' perspective.

This approach, then, emphasizes the cognitive aspects of knowledge - knowledge is seen as something that resides predominantly in peoples' heads and that can be extracted, codified, stored, and transferred in order to improve the information processing capability of the organization. As with information processors, the main problems associated with knowledge management are to do with the capacity and heuristic capabilities of the tools and systems involved - including the human systems' limited capacity to use knowledge management tools. The basic assumptions of this perspective, then, are:

– knowledge can be codified, stored and distributed.
– knowledge management is about managing/fitting together pieces of intellectual capital.

- knowledge is as an objective 'stock' or entity, with characteristics in its own right.
- the purpose of knowledge management is the explification of knowledge - the conversion of tacit to explicit and explicit to explicit.
- knowledge can be captured and transferred via IT systems. 'Weak ties' are also important; and
- the outcomes of knowledge management are reuse.

Its conclusions are, then, that knowledge is able to be abstracted from context and transferred from place to place and therefore using IT systems is essential for knowledge management. The main strategy for knowledge management could be described as codification.

More recently an alternative perspective on knowledge management has emerged in the literature. This can be described broadly as the 'knowledge management as people camp' and has been labeled variously as the 'cultivation' perspective, the 'community' perspective and the 'personalization' strategy. This perspective dominates in the fields of organization studies particularly in organizational learning and strategic management, and has emerged in part as a backlash to the failure of knowledge management systems and the obvious limits of technology in codifying relevant organizational knowledge. Hence comments such as: "There is much more to KM than technology alone: KM is a business process ...KM is not seen as a matter of building a large electronic library but as one of connecting people so they can think together", emphasize the cognitive but also the social and relational nature of knowledge. For example, knowledge is seen as developing through and within social relationships and 'learning communities' or 'communities of practice'. Moreover, the exploitation of intellectual capital is seen as developing through the development of social capital and networks. Here, technology is seen as possibly enabling the development of such communities, but not an essential component of knowledge management. The major assumptions of this perspective, then, are:

- the development of knowledge is closely linked to the

development of social relationships, networks and communities of practice.

- sharing tacit knowledge is critical but much valuable knowledge remains tacit - hence there are limits of codification.
- knowledge is seen as (i) in peoples' heads but also (ii) situated in social communities, the purpose of knowledge management is the sharing of tacit knowledge.
- knowledge flows through networks and communities that connect people. 'Strong ties' are important for sharing tacit knowledge.
- the outcomes of knowledge management are to exploit and create new knowledge.

Its conclusions are, then, knowledge is social in nature - inextricable from the communities that create it. Thus, while IT may enable knowledge management by linking people, it is secondary. The strategy for knowledge management could be described as personalization.

This latter wave of debate in knowledge management stresses that knowledge is social in nature and that social relationships are dependent on context (e.g., organizational, institutional), there is a need to understand knowledge as contextually embedded and situated in practice and action. As noted, the perspectives outlined above are consciously stylized in order to demonstrate the different waves of thinking in relation to knowledge management. Of course, the distinction between the two 'camps" is not clean cut. For example, whilst the community perspective may pay closer attention to socialization and internalization processes, it would not dismiss combination and externalization as important for the creation of knowledge. The difference is one of emphasis rather than type. Moreover, some common assumptions - and critiques - can be noted in connection with both perspectives, especially in terms of their treatment of social relations and action.

2.7. APPROACHES TO KNOWLEDGE MANAGEMENT

There are three approaches to knowledge management :

- Mechanistic approaches
- Cultural/behaviouristic approaches, and
- Systematic approaches to knowledge management.

2.7.1. Mechanistic Approaches

Mechanistic approaches to knowledge management are characterized by the application of technology and resources to do more of the same better. The main assumptions of the mechanistic approach include:

- Better accessibility to information is a key, including enhanced methods of acces and -reuse of documents (hypertext linking, databases, full-text search, etc.)
- Networking technology in general (especially intranets), and groupware in particular, will be key solutions.
- In general, technology and sheer volume of information will make it work.

2.7.2. Cultural/Behavioristic Approaches

Cultural/behaviouristic approaches, with substantial roots in process re-engineering and change management, tend to view the "knowledge problem" as a management issue.

Technology — though ultimately essential for managing explicit knowledge resources — is not the solution. These approaches tend to focus more on innovation and creativity (the "learning organization") than on leveraging existing explicit resources or making the working knowledge explicit.

Cultural/behaviouristic approaches are based on the following assumptions :

- Organizational behaviors and culture need to be changed dramatically. In our information-intensive environments, organizations become dysfunctional relative to business objectives.
- Organizational behaviours and culture can be changed, but traditional technology and methods of attempting to solve the "knowledge problem" have reached their limits of effectiveness. A "holistic" view is required. Theories of behaviour of large-scale systems are often invoked.

- It is the processes that matter, not the technology.
- Nothing happens or changes unless a manager makes it happen.

2.7.3. Systematic Approaches

Systematic approaches to knowledge management retain the traditional faith in rational analysis of the knowledge problem: the problem can be solved, but new thinking of many kinds is required. Some basic assumptions are:

- KM's sustainable results are vital in order to identify the right process.
- A resource cannot be managed unless it is modeled. Many aspects of the organization's knowledge can be modelled as an explicit resource.
- Traditional methods of analysis can be used to re-examine the nature of knowledge work and to solve the knowledge problem.
- Cultural issues are important but they too must be evaluated systematically. Employees may or may not have to be "changed." but policies and work practices must certainly be changed, and technology can be applied successfully to business knowledge problems themselves.
- Knowledge management has an important management component, but it is not an activity or discipline that belongs exclusively to managers.

These are some of the approaches to knowledge management. Lets have a role on some basic activities of knowledge management.

2.8. KNOWLEDGE MANAGEMENT – BASIC ACTIVITIES

Knowledge management encompasses three major activities namely

— Knowledge creation

— Knowledge transfer and

— Knowledge storage

2.8.1. Knowledge Creation

The process of creating new knowledge requires that organisational members acknowledge the existence of useful data and information. They should then transform it, through some form of process, into insights. New knowledge is created through a continuous dialogue between tacit and explicit knowledge. The business provides the infrastructural support to creative individuals or provides the context for such individuals to create knowledge.

It is argued that knowledge will be facilitated by the development of a culture based on appropriate incentives and management leadership. A number of enabling conditions for the creation of knowledge such as incentive schemes, training programmes, project debriefs and social events can be identified.

The creation of new organisational knowledge has been identified as providing the basis for organizational sustainable competitive advantage. In this context firms must create knowledge that can be used in the development of new products and services. Knowledge creation can be specified as consisting of five phases:

- sharing of knowledge among team members
- creation of new service concepts
- justification of these concepts (e.g. via market research)
- buiiding a prototype, and
- leveraging the knowledge, concepts and prototypes.

Top management create the analytical environment in which innovations take place. This framework is built by– cultivating particular skills; encouraging an innovative mindset; and sponsoring on-going experiments and linkages among those experiments.

Learning is critical to new product success and identifies three different forms of team learning –

- within-team learning (e.g. exchange of knowledge amongst team members).
- cross-team learning (e.g. transfer of knowledge gained by one team to another team).
- market learning (e.g. knowledge gained from competitors, suppliers and customers).

Market learning is especially critical when developing new products for new markets.

2.8.2. Knowledge Transfer

Knowledge transfer is about exchanging good ideas, research results, experiences and skills between universities, other research organisations, business, the public sector and the wider community to enable innovative new products and policies to be developed.

Knowledge transfer can involve a range of methods - from seminars to media relations, from placements to partnerships - fundamentally it is a two-way process. By creating more of a dialogue between researchers and research users, the results of research are more likely to be applied in policy and practice.

It is important to transfer knowledge between different members and areas of the organisation so that knowledge can be fully exploited. Knowledge is recognisably created, codified and transferred embodying the experience and know-how that task group members.

Knowledge can be transferred formally (e.g. via training) or informally (e.g. on-the-job learning). Face-to-face communication can transmit much "richer" information (e.g. facial clues, language variety, personalisation) than more formal document based methods.

Knowledge transfer is aided by the :

- transfer of personnel,
- the use of multifunctional teams or
- the introduction of specialised knowledge intermediaries which includes interaction and collaboration.

In general, it is argued that internal communication is important for new service development as it reduces the amount of uncertainty with regard to user needs, the competition and technology.

2.8.3. Knowledge Storage

Once knowledge has been created, to be of long-term value to the organisation it must be stored for subsequent use by people in different parts of the organisation. However, knowledge storage is more than simply codifying knowledge and storing in databases, documents and the like. It is the embodiment of tacit knowledge into processes, practices, materials and culture. The process of storing knowledge for subsequent use may be similar to a type of organisational memory. Organisational memory becomes more powerful when it, and its context, are stored in a form that makes it easily retrievable by staff and management who have need of it.

The most likely storage locations for organisational memory are posited to be individual memories, organisational culture, transformations – the guidelines by which work processes are managed, organisational structure and the physical structure of workplaces. Four categories of a business memory base have been identified:

- brainware (knowledge in peoples minds),
- hardware (e.g. prototypes, production processes, R&D equipment),
- groupware (knowledge shared by people e.g. rules of thumb, procedures), and
- documentware (paper-based or IT based information systems).

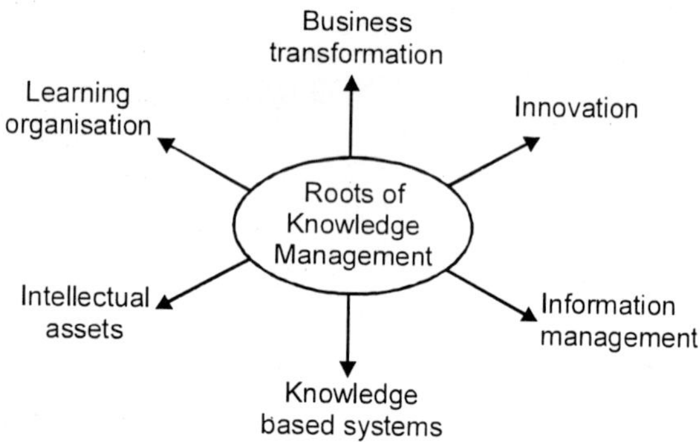

Fig. 2.3. Roots of Knowledge Management

Once information has been codified and transposed from individual brains into documents or physical objects it can be diffused quite rapidly. However, in reducing complexity, some of the original value of the idea may be lost.

If an organisation conforms to the required norms and can

be termed as a learning organisation, then it becomes one of the starting points of knowledge management.

The systems that are evolved in an organization to facilitate the smooth functioning of the organization should facilitate harnessing the existing knowledge in the organization. These systems could be a basis of knowledge management.

2.9. KNOWLEDGE MANAGEMENT: IN SEARCH OF A NEW IDENTITY

Senge has focused on the "learning organization," a cultural dimension of managing knowledge. Chris Argyris, Christoper Bartlett, and Dorothy Leonard-Barton of Harvard Business School have examined various facets of managing knowledge. In fact, Leonard-Barton's well-known case study of Chaparral Steel, a company which has had an effective knowledge management strategy in place since the mid-1970s, inspired the research documented in her Wellsprings of Knowledge — Building and Sustaining Sources of innovation.

Everett Rogers' work at Stanford in the diffusion of innovation and Thomas Allen's research at MIT in information and technology transfer, both of which date from the late 1970s, have also contributed to our understanding of how knowledge is produced, used, and diffused within organizations. By the mid-1980s, the importance of knowledge and its expression in professional competence, as a competitive asset was apparent, even though classical economic theory ignores knowledge as an asset and most organizations still lack strategies and methods for managing it.

Recognition of the growing importance of organizational knowledge was accompanied by concern over how to deal with exponential increases in the amount of available knowledge and increasingly complex products and processes. The computer technology that contributed so heavily to superabundance of information started to become part of the solution, in a variety of domains.

Doug Enqelbart's Augment (for "augmenting human intelligence"), introduced in 1978, was an early hypertext/

groupware application capable of interfacing with other applications and systems. Rob Acksyn's and Don McCracken's Knowledge Management System (KMS), an open distributed hypermedia tool, is another notable example and one that predates the World Wide Web by a decade.

2.10.1. Expert System and Artificial Intelligence (ES & AI)

The 1980s also saw the development of systems for managing knowledge that relied on work done in artificial intelligence and expert systems, giving us such concepts as "knowledge acquisition," "knowledge engineering," "knowledge-base systems" and "computer-based ontologies".

2.10.2. Initiative for Managing Knowledge Assets

The phrase "knowledge management" entered the lexicon in earnest. To provide a technological base for managing knowledge, a consortium of U.S. companies started the Initiative for Managing Knowledge Assets in 1989.

Knowledge management-related articles began appearing in journals like Sloan Management Review, Organizational Science, Harvard Business Review, and others, and the first books on organizational learning and knowledge management were published. For example, Senge's The Fifth Discipline and Sakaiya's The Knowledge Value Revolution.

By 1990, a number of management consulting firms had begun in-house knowledge management programs and several well known U.S., European, and Japanese firms had instituted focused knowledge management programs. Knowledge management was introduced in the popular press in 1991, when Tom Stewart published "Brainpower" in Fortune magazine. Perhaps the most widely read work to date is Ikujiro Nonaka's and Hirotaka Takeuchi's, The Knowledge-Creating Company: How Japanese Companies Create the Dynamics of Innovation.

By the mid-1990s, knowledge management initiatives were flourishing, thanks in part to the Internet. The International Knowledge Management Network (IKMN), begun in Europe in 1989, went online in 1994 and was soon joined by the U.S. based Knowledge Management Forum and other KM-related groups and publications. The number of knowledge management-conferences and seminars is growing as organizations focus on managing and leveraging explicit and tacit knowledge resources to achieve competitive advantage. In 1994 the IKMN published the results of a knowledge management survey conducted among European firms, and the European Community began offering funding for KM-related projects through the ESPRIT program in 1995.

2.10.3. Recent Trends

Since its visible emergence onto the management scene in 1995, knowledge management has evolved through several overlapping phases:

- *Emergence Phase (circa 1995-1997)* : Knowledge management was featured at conferences and gained attention on management agendas. The end of this period saw a wave of many new books on the subject. In reality, only a small number of companies had formal programmes, mostly just in one or a few divisions. These tended to be organizations in sectors that are heavily knowledge-based and/or globally dispersed: oil, chemicals, pharmaceutical, and high technology. The geographic bias was clearly North American and Northern European.
- *Discovery and Relabelling (1997-1999)* : Knowledge management was actively promoted as strategic, particularly by the large management consultancies, which used their own internal KM programmes as exemplars. As a consequence many software and service suppliers relabeled their products and services as 'KM solutions'. A growing number of large companies created formal KM posts, such as Chief Knowledge Officers, created new knowledge initiatives and brought several existing programmes, which originally were designated under other labels, such as 'business transformation' or 'the learning organization', under the KM umbrella.
- *Growth and Consolidation (1998 – 2000)* : Knowledge management became a mainstream activity in many large organizations. For example, a Conference Report survey

showed that 80 per cent of large organizations had KM projects in place. In addition, there was growing adoption in all business functions, in many more geographic regions and in different sectors, such as the public sector. KM also became recognized as a distinct academic discipline, stimulating several new university courses, such as the UK's Open University MBA course module – Managing Knowledge. However, its overall status varied from being an important high-level initiative to just another project. Some companies dispersed their central KM teams into business units, while in other organizations KM initiatives faltered.

- *Redefinition (2000 onwards)* : Many companies are still embarking on formal KM programmes for the first time. With KM's growing maturity, there is increased questioning as to its distinctive essence. After all, knowledge is very pervasive, and many enterprise initiatives - such as innovation, e-commerce and customer relationship management - have a heavy knowledge emphasis. Significantly, many providers of 'KM solutions' have reinvented their products as content management, portal or enterprise information solutions!

Now a question-mark as to how KM will evolve. One argument is that as KM becomes so embedded in an organization's everyday business practices, then the need for a special focus disappears, and it will merge into many other practices under different names. Several Chief Knowledge Officers have openly said that their mission will be completed within two or three years. On the other hand, others point out that KM still has a long way to go and needs continued focus if companies are fully to exploit its potential. For example, KPMG has classified companies against a KM maturity model. Its 1999 survey showed that only 43 per cent of organizations were at the first of five stages (knowledge chaotic), with only ten per cent at either of the two most advanced stages– knowledge managed and knowledge-centric.

To gain a better appreciation of likely developments, here is a review of the top 10 trends identified from a content analysis of mainstream management literature during the period 1999-2000, undertaken by Trend Monitor International.

Significant trends

- *Real → virtual → real* : In the move to get online many companies are now realizing the loss of rich knowledge previously provided by human contact and are making efforts to look more closely at social interaction and adding a human element to websites e.g. through online communities.
- *Content → context* : More emphasis is being given to the context of information and knowledge - its applicability, usefulness and user experiences.
- *Growth → consolidation* : An increased emphasis on integration within the enterprise.
- *Learning → doing* : Learning resources are accessed when needed and less as part of a formal training session. This is 'knowledge for action' and 'on-the-job learning'.
- *Producing → co-creating* : The two-way benefit of knowledge flow is important. Customers are increasingly involved in new product and service creation.

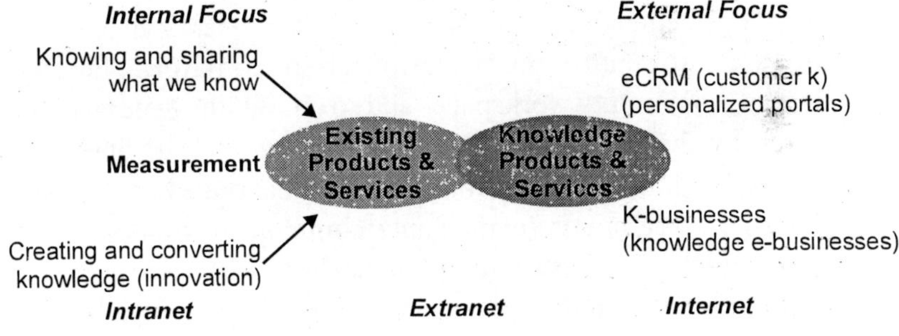

Fig. 2.4. Overall Trends in Knowledge Management

Emergent trends

- *Knowledge → experience* : Personal experience is more valuable than bland information. Techniques like storytelling are in the ascendant.
- *Measurement → contribution* : Although there is growing interest in measuring intangibles, such as the use of

intellectual capital measurement, companies are recognizing that they must understand and make more explicit the causal link from knowledge to its contribution to business objectives and the bottom line.

- *Mechanistic → inspirational* : However systematized knowledge processes are, many breakthroughs and innovations come from creative thinking and charismatic champions.
- *Tools → services* : The emergence of the ASP (Application Service Provider) model will make it impact on the KM scene. For example, organizations use collaboration services such a ProjectPlace.com, rather than installing their own team collaboration software.
- *Sharing → trading* : While there is much talk of the 'free flow of knowledge', every transaction has a cost. Therefore people trade, often in a social network on a reciprocity basis. However, as micro-payment systems evolve, more will be on a financial transaction basis.

Additionally, there are many trends in the growth of specific practices – After Action Reviews, storytelling, knowledge audits, knowledge centers etc., and of specific IT tool sets - visualization software, automatic classification engines, natural language retrieval, community workspaces and so on. But the general picture offered by this analysis is that of a rich panoply of knowledge activities and the countervailing tensions that have been a feature of business for many years. Some common tensions are those between technology-based and human-based processes, between organizational standardization and local flexibility, between innovation and consolidation, between centralization and decentralization, between systematization and informality. These tensions will continue to challenge knowledge managers as they embed knowledge management more deeply within their organizations. They also provide contextual background for the challenge of commercialization.

Returning to the bigger picture, the attention given to sharing internal knowledge in the early days of KM has been shifting gradually to a more outward looking focus exempted by developments in e-commerce and CRM (customer relatioinship management) systems. The emphasis of new initiative will increasingly consider how to make money from knowledge, not just as an adjunct to physical products and services, but in creating knowledge products and services in their own right.

Summing up, we can say knowledge management provides an excellent foundation for any organization in number of ways. As the new technologies grow and knowledge management becomes establihsed, it seems the natural follow on to successful initiative.

3

KNOWLEDGE CREATION

Knowledge management in organizations is concerned with creating, mobilizing, and applying knowledge for competitive advantage. The ultimate goal of knowledge management (KM) initiatives is also to "make the right knowledge available to the right processors (human or computer) at the right times in the right presentation for the right costs". Often times, the "right" knowledge is new knowledge: it does not exist within the organization and it is too expensive, too revealing, too slow, or outright impossible to acquire it from external sources. Therefore, knowledge creation is an essential part of the conduct of knowledge management within an organization. The relationship between knowledge creation and knowledge manipulation activities is evident in the collaboratively built ontology of KM conduct.

There are five basic kinds of knowledge activities; knowledge can flow among these activities, and the activities can be arranged in various configurations and can be performed by various processors. Knowledge acquisition occurs when knowledge in the external environment is identified and possibly transformed (e.g., filtered, restructured), for use within the organization. Knowledge selection describes the identification and possible transformation, of knowledge from among an organization's internal knowledge asset base. Knowledge internalization is the activity of taking knowledge that has been acquired, selected, or generated and distributing or storing it within the organization.

Knowledge externalization is the activity of embedding

knowledge in outputs (e.g., products, services) for release into the external environment. Knowledge generation entails the production of new knowledge from existing knowledge and it can take the forms of discovery or derivation.

Although some authors include both acquistion and generation as being knowledge creation, knowledge creation in the sense of generation is an active and ongoing relationship between knowledge generation, on the one hand, and the other knowledge manipulation activities. That is, a KM episode that creates new knowledge may involve not only knowledge generation, but also acquisition, selection and internalization that enable the generation activity to happen.

3.1. KNOWLEDGE MANAGEMENT TASKS OR ACTIVITIES

Generally, there are a lot of approaches that view KM as a life cycle of knowledge tasks or a complex organizational "function" that designs, implements and evaluates a set of knowledge management tasks. Goal of knowledge management is to improve these tasks in the sense of organizational effectiveness and performance. The list of tasks provided in the literature comprises a large number of knowledge-related tasks. Examples are:

- creation, building, anticipation or generation;
- acquisition, appropriation or adoption;
- identification, capture, articulation or extraction;
- collection, gathering or accumulation;
- securing (legally);
- evaluation or validation;
- conversion;
- organization, linking and embedding;
- formalization; and storage;
- refinement or development;
- distribution, diffusion, transfer or sharing;
- presentation or formatting;
- application, deploying or exploiting;
- review, revision or evolution of knowledge.

A subset of these tasks is described here that deals with, involves or is supported by knowledge management system and, at least at the current state of practice, is carried out by a person or a collective.

Knowledge Identification : The main goal of knowledge identification is to make the organization's knowledge assets visible. These are, for example the employee's skills, networks of experts, organizational competencies, but also the knowledge sources, such as data and document bases. Knowledge identification not necessarily stops at organizational boundaries and thus might also comprise the identification of industry best practices, competencies of experts and consultants outside the organization, on-line data bases as well as literature, such as books, magazines, studies and reports and thus provides the basis for knowledge acquisition. Once knowledge is identified, it can be organized, published and distributed in order to be applied wherever it is useful. Knowledge identification is a permanent task as skills and competencies evolve. A knowledge management initiative might also start with an effort to identify the organization's core competencies and thus provide an initial knowledge structure that evolves as it is used to organize knowledge. Some authors use the term capturing of knowledge which reflects knowledge identification as well as documentation or codification and storage. This task is basically supported by knowledge modeling and mapping technologies.

Knowledge Acquisition : Knowledge is acquired from outside the organization. There are numerous alternatives for this task that mainly fall into three categories.

The first category contains the permanent or temporary engagement of experts, e.g., the hiring of talent and experts, the engagement of professional services firms, the development of joint ventures, strategic alliances, virtual organizations, the merger with or the acquisition of companies that hold competencies required.

The second category of alternatives is to gain access to documented knowledge, e.g., in the form of scientific and practitioner literature, e.g., patents, licenses, books, journals, reports, access to on-line data bases of professional information service organizations.

The third category is the *participation in knowledge-related events and processes,* e.g., conferences, workshops, meetings, fairs, exhibitions, research projects, benchmarking groups, industry organizations or industry best-practice groups, etc.

Whereas the first category is predominantly either a matter of strategy and corporate planning or a matter of human resource management, the second and third categories are targeted and organized systematically by the knowledge management initiative in many organizations.

Knowledge Creation : Complementary to *knowledge acquisition* knowledge is created within the organization which provides e.g., new skills, ideas and improved organizational processes and competencies. Knowledge creation is also called *knowledge construction.* Knowledge is primarily created due to processes of individual and collective learning that cannot be "managed" but supported not only with the help of specialized R&D units and projects, but also with instruments that support creativity, e.g., by providing room for ideas and interaction and tolerate errors throughout the organization, and last but not least a creativity-supporting organizational culture. Examples for ICT supporting knowledge creation are creativity support systems provided in Groupware.

Knowledge Organization : Once a knowledge element is created, it can be linked to other knowledge elements. Knowledge is valued by individuals or by collectives, e.g., communities and thus selected for documentation and storage. The main product is an organizational knowledge structure, an ontology, a knowledge map or a set of these instruments. After the initial set up of a knowledge structure which is part of a concerted effort of knowledge identification, it is updated or extended each time a new knowledge element requires an alteration of the structure. The knowledge structure is visualized with the help of knowledge mapping technologies. Thus, knowledge elements can be classified and integrated into the existing knowledge structure, linked to other knowledge elements etc.

Knowledge Publication : The process of publishing knowledge that can then be distributed to knowledge seekers using push and pull technologies is one of the most widely researched area of knowledge management. Knowledge publication involves the *codification of knowledge,* i.e., in a general sense, putting knowledge in various forms that can be stored and thus retained, leveraged and transferred. In Nonaka's terms knowledge publication is a form of *articulation* or *externalization* . This can be documentation and formalization of knowledge using artificial intelligence or more traditional technologies, but also structuring and organizing it. As with most tasks in knowledge management, knowledge can be published in various degrees of centralization such as entirely centrally e.g., by a knowledge management department or a group of knowledge brokers or decentrally directly by the participants or both. In the latter case, the *release of knowledge elements*—the formal approval of institutionalization—is an important step in the publication process. In this case, knowledge documents are submitted to an expert or a group of experts in order to be reviewed so that quality and organization is maintained. Knowledge publication is supported e.g., by content management systems or Web publishing systems.

Knowledge Distribution : Knowledge distribution is also called knowledge diffusion, dissemination or transfer. It comprises of the systematic processes of bringing knowledge to the employees who need it (knowledge push) as opposed to knowledge search and retrieval that comprises knowledge being searched for by the employees (knowledge pull). Both knowledge tasks together primarily support *internalization* of knowledge at the receiving end of the push and pull processes. Another alternative forum for knowledge distribution applied widely by large organizations, such as Ernst & Young, Siemens and Daimler-Chrysler, is a so-called organization-wide *knowledge fair.* In this fair, all groups, teams and communities that work on knowledge management-related projects can exhibit their work. All employees interested in knowledge management can visit the fair, collect material, network, meet experts and thus knowledge is distributed. Technologically, knowledge distribution is not only supported by knowledge push technologies such as Listservers or information subscriptions, but also by the whole set of learning support technologies– e-learning platforms and learning management systems.

Knowledge Search and Retrieval : Search and retrieval is initiated by the participants (knowledge pull). The boundaries are not clear-cut, though, because it is also the participants' initiative that is required to start information subscriptions e.g., by providing an interest profile or sending an email to a listserver. In most cases, participants will search for knowledge on their own. However, there might also be roles (e.g., knowledge broker) that are specialized in professionally searching the organization's and external knowledge assets and thus provide a value-added search service. Knowledge search and retrieval can be supported by knowledge maps which are the results of the task knowledge organization, by recommendations and comments of other participants and experts and by search engines.

Knowledge Application : Application or the usage of knowledge is the ultimate goal of knowledge management. Knowledge that is created or acquired and then organized, published or otherwise distributed should be reused wherever it is useful. Knowledge is applied, e.g., in projects or business processes. However, a number of barriers prevent participants from applying knowledge not created within their organizational unit, most of which are psychological factors, such as fear from lowered own status of expertise, resistance to change, cultural and language barriers. Organizational instruments have to be applied in order to lower these barriers and create incentives for the reuse of knowledge not invented in the respective organizational unit. The application of knowledge also provides feedback for knowledge evolution. All knowledge management technologies ultimately aim at a support of the application of knowledge, especially search and retrieval systems and all visualization systems that provide context for a translation of the knowledge into the current application situation.

Knowledge Evolution : Knowledge evolution comprises all tasks that aim at an improvement of already existing knowledge. Participants might comment existing knowledge in order to assess its usefulness or in order to report experiences with its application. Subject matter specialists might refine knowledge, translate it, summarize it, provide additional context, explain terms and definitions or repackage it for the use by different groups of users, e.g., novices as opposed to experts or functional departments as opposed to information technology. Also, knowledge decentrally published by participants might be evaluated by knowledge quality management that assures the quality of the content and the documentation. Another important task assures that the knowledge is timely, relevant and actualized. Knowledge evolution can be supported e.g., by workflow management functionality and by automatic checks of links and document expiration dates.

Knowledge Deletion and Archiving : Irrelevant or outdated knowledge has to be systematically removed from the organization's active knowledge base, such as outdated reports, dead links or obsolete themes and topics. The selection of the knowledge to be deleted or archived is an important task as otherwise the organizational knowledge base is cluttered with outdated or even wrong documents, links or structures making it less efficient for employees to retrieve the knowledge needed. As deletion and archiving can be viewed as special forms of knowledge evolution, it can be supported by the ICT technologies.

Knowledge Selling : Knowledge selling is the counterpart of knowledge acquisition. In many organizations knowledge products and knowledge services can be offered on the market. Examples are patents, licensing, consulting services, reports and studies. More recently, especially professional services firms also demand fees for access to their knowledge management system and knowledge bases. The task knowledge selling comprises securing results of organizational R & D as well as the management of appropriability of profits which can be subject to bargaining, e.g., with business partners, such as customers, suppliers or distributors, and the employees.

Collaboration : Collaboration aims at a transfer and joint application of knowledge by direct interaction within a collective of participants. It is closely related to socialization. Collaboration is primarily supported by interactive knowledge management system and maps of skills and experts, yellow pages, skills directories, expert finder, generally by synchronous communication and collaboration tools and Groupware.

Knowledge (management) processes in the sense of service processes for core business processes in a process-oriented organizational design require the combination of several of these knowledge management tasks and their embedding in or connection to the organization's business processes various activities are summarized in Table 3.1.

An examination of the activities reveals considerable variation. No one view subsumes the others. This suggests there is a need for a generic ontology that describes knowledge manipulation activities clearly and completely, and also identifies their possible interrelationships. Here, the focus is on elemental activities (and their subactivities) rather than higher-level, composite ones. The focus is on activities that directly manipulate knowledge and produce knowledge flows within a KM episode, rather than activities that start or control the episode.The manipulation activities in this ontology are not dependent on any particular attribute of knowledge is; nor do they stem from a focus on any particular attribute of knowledge such as its mode (tacit versus explicit), its type (descriptive versus procedural versus reasoning), or its orientation or domain.

Above activities as the tasks can better be explained and understood through knowledge chain Model or KCM.

3.2. KNOWLEDGE CHAIN MODEL

The knowledge chain model is based on a descriptive KM ontology developed via a Delphi-study involving an international panel of prominent KM practitioners and academicians. This ontology identifies five major knowledge manipulation activities that occur in various patterns within KM episodes. It also identifies four major managerial influences on the conduct of knowledge management. Respectively, these form the five primary and four secondary KM activities in the knowledge chain model. The model asserts that these activities yield organizational learning – i.e., changes in an organization's state of knowledge; and projections– i.e., organizational resources being released into the environment. A basic premise of the knowledge chain model is that how well an organization learns and how well it projects are important

Table 3.1. Summary of Knowledge Management Activities

Author	Knowledge Management Activities
Alavi,1997	1. Acquisition (knowledge creation and content development); 2. Indexing; 3. Filtering; 4. Linking involves screening, classification, cataloguing, integrating and interconnecting internal and external sources); 5. Distributing (packaging and delivery of knowledge in the form of Web pages); 6. Application (using knowledge).
Arthur Anderson and APOC, 1996	1. Share; 2. Create; 3. Identify; 4. Collect; 5. Adapt; 6. Organize; 7. Apply.
Choo, 1996	1. Sensemaking (includes "information interpretation"); 2. Knowledge creation (includes "information transformation"); 3. Decision making (includes "information processing").
Holsappieand Whinston, 1987	1. Procure; 2. Organize; 3. Store; 4. Maintain; 5. Analyze; 6. Create; 7. Present: 8. Distribute; 9. Apply.
Leonard-Barton, 1995	1. Shared and creative problem solving; 2. Importing and absorbing technological knowledge from the outside of the firm; 3. Experimenting prototyping; 4. Implementing and integrating new methodologies and tools.
Nonaka,1996	1. Socialize (convert tacit knowledge to tacit knowledge); 2. Internalize (convert explicit knowledge to tacit knowledge); 3. Combine (convert explicit knowledge to explicit knowledge); 4. Externalize (convert tacit knowledge to explicit knowledge).
Szulanksi, 1996	1. Initiation (recognize knowledge need and satisfy that need); 2. Implementation (knowledge transfer takes place); 3. Ramp-up (use the transferred knowledge); 4. Integration (internalize the knowledge).
Van der spek and Spijkervet, 1997	In the Act Process 1. Develop; 2. Distribute; 3. Combine; 4. Hold.
Wiig, 1993	1. Creation; 2. Manifestation; 3. Use; 4. Transfer.

determinants of the organization's viability and success in a competitive environment.

The model's set of interrelated knowledge activities appears to be common across diverse organizations. It asserts that these are major activities with which a chief knowledge officer needs to be concerned. KM skills of an organization's participants need to be cultivated, harnessed, and organized in the performance of these activities. Thus, will an organization's knowledge resources lead to enhanced competitiveness through the learning and projections it produces.

The primary activities that an organization's knowledge processors perform in manipulating knowledge resources are summarized in Table3.2. When a particular instance of a knowledge manipulation activity occurs in an organization, it is performed by one or more processors. Some processors are human and others may be computer-based. Many processors may be capable of performing a given type of primary activity. Conversely, multiple types of primary activities may be performed by a given processor. Moreover, each primary activity involves sub-activities.

An organization may possess the best knowledge resources and the best knowledge manipulation skills, but they are of no use until they are effectively applied during the conduct of knowledge management. The Delphi study identified three major kinds of forces that conspire to influence how the conduct of knowledge

Table 3.2. Primary Activities in the Knowledge Chain Model

Knowledge Acquisition	Acquiring knowledge from external sources and making it suitable for subsequent use.
Knowledge Selection	Selecting needed knowledge from internal sources and making it suitable for subsequent use.
Knowledge Generation	Producing knowledge by either discovery or derivation from existing knowledge.
Knowledge Internalization	Altering the state of an organization's knowledge resources by distributing and storing acquired, selected or generated knowledge.
Knowledge Externalization	Embedding knowledge into organizational outputs for release into the environment.

management ultimately unfolds in an organization – managerial influences, resource influences, and environmental influences. Because the managerial influences denote meta activities that impact or determine the deployment of resources and patterns of manipulation activities, they are included as secondary activities in the knowledge chain model. Table 3.3 summarizes these secondary KM activities that support and guide the performance of primary KM activities. There is also an interplay among the secondary activities; one may support or guide the performance of another.

Table 3.3 Secondary Activities in the Knowledge Chain Model

Knowledge Leadership	Establishing conditions that enable and facilitate fruitful conduct of KM.
Knowledge Coordination	Managing dependencies among KM activities to ensure that proper processes and resources are brought to bear adequately at appropriate times.
Knowledge Control	Ensuring that needed knowledge processors and resources are available in sufficient quality and quality, subject to security requirements.
Knowledge Measurement	Assessing values of knowledge resources, knowledge processors and their deployment.

As management scholars have pointed out, "espoused theory" tells us little about real behaviour; we need to study "theory in practice" i.e., view the actions that reflect managerial conduct. Some of the evidence involves use of technology to better perform a KM activity; some is not technology-based. Competitiveness due to KM practices can manifest itself in such ways as increasing profits and bolstering an organization's reputation, employees' creativity, productivity, efficiency, flexibility and innovation. Therefore, it should examine the support for the competitive role of each activity in terms of one or more of the following standpoints: improving productivity (e.g., lower cost, greater speed), enhancing reputation (e.g., better quality, dependability, brand differentiation), enhancing organizational agility (e.g., greater flexibility, rapid responsiveness, change proficiency), and fostering innovation (e.g., new knowledge products, services, processes).

Figure 3.1 identifies the major activities of acquiring, selecting, internalizing, and using knowledge. The latter refers to the activities of externalizing and generating knowledge. Arrows indicate major knowledge flows. For instance, execution and performance of the acquisition activity entails a knowledge flow into that activity from the environment and a consequent flow to the internalizing or using environment, these, are leading and projection respectively.

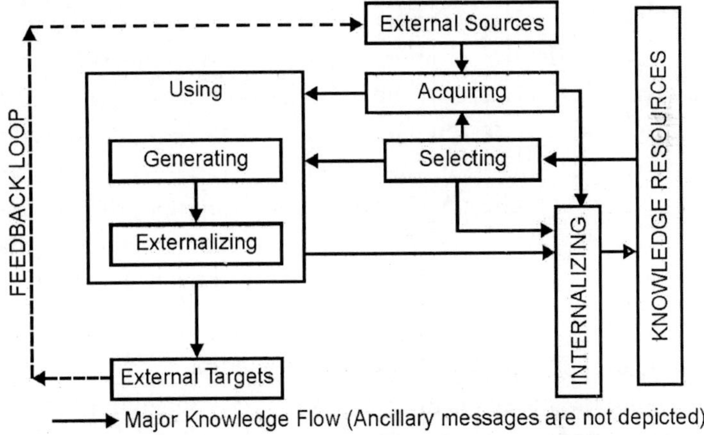

Fig. 3.1. Major Knowledge Manipulation Activities

Aside from the main knowledge flows activites can send messages. An example is a request from one actvity to another (e.g. the generating activity requests a knowledge flow from the selection activity). Requests can range from procedural (specifying how the activity should be carried out) to nonprocedural (merely indicating what is needed). They can range from explicit (e.g., a command) to implicit (e.g involving recognition of a needed responses; others tolerate performance of an activity acknowledges receipt of a knowledge flow or comments on the value the flow that is recieved.

Each instance of knowledge manipulation can be overformed exercise knowledge manipulation skills to perform multiple activities within a knowledge management episode. For instance, a person (or a computer system) may participate in both acquiring and generating knowledge within a single knowledge management episode.

Managerial, resource, and environmental factors affect how the knowledge manipulation skills of an organization's participants are deployed to accomplish the activities. These factors also influence the pattern of activities that occur within a specific KM episode – which are performed and by whom, how many instances are performed, which one is first, which is last, and so forth.

3.3. THREE PREMISES ABOUT KNOWLEDGE

There are three premises on which knowledge is built. First, knowledge exists as both an individual and an organizational phenomenon in explicit and tacit forms. Second, knowledge competition is universal, rather than relating to select groups of firms or market niches. And third, no single competitive advantage is sustainable in today's hypercompetitive environment, no matter how inimitable. So, letting go of old knowledge is as important as creating the new.

3.3.1. Premise 1: The Nature of Knowledge

Knowledge exists in organizations as both an individual and an organizational phenomenon, and in both explicit and tacit forms. Explicit knowledge is knowledge that can be transmitted to others in a relatively straightforward manner. Although it may belong to individuals, it may be transferred to the organizational level in written documents, contracts, and formal presentations, for example, Tacit knowledge is more difficult to articulate, including skills that others may learn by doing and mental models or schemes that others may learn through interaction. It may belong to individuals — when people know more than they can say and exist at the level of organizations— when organizations know more than contracts can say. Examples include the individual and organizational routines and beliefs. Whereas formal and problem- or goal-focused interactions are useful for sharing explicit knowledge in organizations, casual and non-directed interactions among people are more likely to result in the sharing of tacit knowledge.

3.3.2. Premise 2: Knowledge Competition Is Universal

Knowledge competition is often referred to as competition among knowledge-intensive firms (KIFs). The term KIF imitates economists' labeling of firms as capital-intensive or labour-intensive. Labeling a firm as knowledge-intensive implies that knowledge has more importance for it than other inputs.

Because people define knowledge differently, discussions of KIFs may lead to debate about the proper definition of such companies. Adding further fuzziness to the concept is the fact that all organizations are becoming more knowledge-intensive in the service, industrial and governmental sectors because knowledge is rapidly becoming a univeral source of competitiveness. The term is thus losing its specialized meaning. Managing knowledge has become a top priority for all organizations.

3.3.3. Premise 3: Competitive Advantage Is Not Sustainable

Larry Prusak of IBM has concluded that "the only sustainable competitive advantage comes from what you know and how fast you can put it to use". But what you know today may be of little use tomorrow. In fact, core competencies often become core rigidities in highly competitive environments. Hamel and Prahalad suggest periodic reengineering of a company's genetic code for this reason.

It is essential to renew and cannibalize prior capabilities. A complete life cycle for knowledge management must thus not only include the creation, dissemination, and application of knowledge but also its retirement when it has outlived its usefulness. The focus of most knowledge destruction or undoing at the point in time when it has become old or irrelevant or otherwise no longer useful.

3.4. KNOWLEDGE CREATION

Knowledge creation is an important activity for organizations that strive to achieve greater effectiveness and responsiveness in this turbulent global environment. Knowledge creation is important not only for organizational competitiveness and survival, but can have far-reaching societal, national and global consequences. It is known also as knowledge capturing.

Knowledge creation plays a vital role in innovation, a process that is important because it facilitates an organization's ability to keep pace with a dynamic environment. Infact, creating new knowledge for innovation is considered one of the three reasons that organizations are motivated to use information. An innovation has been described as "an idea, practice or object that is perceived as new," to a person or organization. In a knowledge management context, the act of innovation involves the generation of knowledge that is perceived to be new by the organization that does the generating. Innovation can serve many purposes. For instance, it may entail finding new ways to approach questions, solve problems, or reach decisions. It may yield new processes, products or services. Innovations within the same domain. They must respond to or cope with the innovation.

3.4.1. Attribute Dimensions for Knowledge Creation

Knowledge can be thought of as being multi-dimensional, having a variety of attributes. Two fundamental attribute dimensions are the knowledge type and the knowledge mode. The former is concerned with distinctions in the nature of the knowledge itself; each type of knowledge can be created and each type can be used in the creation of knowledge. The latter is concerned with the way the knowledge can be processed in transforming it from one mode to another; knowledge creation can occur for either mode, and perhaps during the transformations between modes.

The first attribute dimension, featuring definiting characteristics, partitions knowledge into three types — descriptive knowledge, procedural knowledge and reasoning knowledge. Each type of knowledge is an integral part of the knowledge creation process. Descriptive knowledge, which can be thought of as "know what", describes the state of a domain, the items that exist in it, the context in which they exist, and the relationships that may exist between the items and different domains. Procedural knowledge, which can be thought of as "know how," is comprised of algorithms such as the steps needed to reach a specified goal. Reasoning knowledge, which can be thought of as "know why," is comprised of logic that specifies what consequences are expected, what conclusions are valid, or what actions are appropriate if a certain situation is given or assumed to exist. Newly created knowledge could be any one of these types. For example, a new forecast is descriptive knowledge, a new plan is procedural knowledge, a new heuristic is reasoning knowledge. A relationship that is particularly notable is that applying existing procedural or reasoning knowledge to existing descriptive knowledge often generates new knowledge, thus jumpstarting the knowledge creation process.

The second attribute dimension stems from the notion that knowledge is the result of a process whereby meaning is attached to it via interpretation and cognitive construction. This dimension recognizes knowledge as existing in two modes - tacit and explicit with the possibility of transforming knowledge existing in one mode into the other and the possibility of transforming (e.g., creating) knowledge within a mode. Gaining an understanding of tacit and explicit knowledge and the relationship between them is helpful in understanding the dynamic nature of knowledge creation processes.

Tacit knowledge is the implicit knowledge that people have developed. Examples of tacit knowledge can be found in formal and informal face-to-face conversations, telephone conversations, and what a person keeps in his/her own mind. *Explicit knowledge* is knowledge that has been put in a form that allows its creator, acquirer, or others to access and use it. Explicit knowledge is found in many familiar forms including journals, magazines, newspapers, business records, databases, email, and Web sites.

Knowledge can become more valuable when it evolves from tacit to explicit. As knowledge loses its tacit quality it often becomes more commonly available although that varies depending on the environment it is acting within. For example, at an educational institution the dissemination of new knowledge is likely to be quite broad and include public venues. Conversely, in a corporate setting, knowledge may be distributed across departments or job sites, but will still be confined to organizational boundaries.

A third mode of knowledge that is primarily associated with organizations is *cultural knowledge.* This knowledge is held in the assumptions, beliefs, and norms of the organization and in a corporate sense could be called corporate culture.

The two attribute dimensions provide different perspectives on the knowledge creation phenomenon, and interaction exists between the dimensions. For example, someone may hold procedural knowledge in a tacit form, which is characterized by the fact that he/she has performed the procedure repeatedly, but there is not yet a way (e.g., shared language) to formally pass this knowledge on to others. The tacit version of some other procedural knowledge may be amenable to being recorded in a manual, thereby being converted into explicit knowledge.

Knowledge creation can result from a serendipitous event or an intentional act. For example, some new knowledge is discovered unintentionally. One example is the discovery of penicillin, which resulted from observing the antibiotic effects of some molds during an unrelated experiment. Other times, knowledge creation begins when a situation reveals a gap in the existing knowledge and the individual or organization reacts to fill it. The gap could be filled by acquiring the desired knowledge from an external source or selecting it from an internal repository.

However, if this is not practical or possible, then new knowledge needs to be created via a generation activity that occurs in the context of- and through the use of - what is already known.

Knowledge in tacit, explicit, and cultural modes and of descriptive, procedural, and reasoning types may be utilized to generate new knowledge through two different means: knowledge discovery or knowledge derivation. *Knowledge discovery* describes finding new knowledge in relation to what is already known, perhaps through a creative insight, analogy, pattern recognition, or synthesis. *Knowledge derivation* applies procedural and/or reasoning knowledge to descriptive knowledge to reach new conclusions, often through analysis and logic.

Examples of how knowledge creation may occur include tapping the skills of the organization's own workers or acquiring knowledge from those outside the group. At the individual level, knowledge is shared through dialogue, discourse and other formal channels with analogies and metaphors being used to share intuitive knowledge. At the organizational level, the organization may view knowledge as a process rather than a product, which suggests that the knowledge creation process may be guided by gatekeepers who regulate information flow and boundary spanners who help link different areas of knowledge.

Similar to the individual level, knowledge creation at the organizational level begins when the organization serendipitously finds new knowledge or when it recognizes that new knowledge is needed. Additionally, there are subactivities associated with knowledge generation. These include monitoring the organization's external environment and its own knowledge resources, evaluating selected and acquired knowledge to determine if it will impact knowledge generation, and using an existing knowledge base to create, synthesize, analyze, and construct new knowledge.

3.4.2. Knowledge Creation in Organisations

A mechanism is required for organisations to tap the most of knowledge acquired, created or existing in the organizations. Such tapping can occur through the organisation's various activities. Organisations stand to benefit more. Strategically, organisations should thrive to ensure that – a knowledge gain is created, or acquired in one unit or by an individual. Simultaneously, it should be also gained by another and ultimately influence the overall performance of the organisation.

Knowledge transfer has been identified as a core factor of a firm's performance. Core competence is facilitated with what the firm knows. It is the leverage by which firms can acquire competitive advantage. Knowledge transfer is , the means by which they can continuously enhance their vision and mission.

It has been suggested that tacit knowledge could be tapped by conversion to explicit form. Such a process would create knowledge. Nonaka and Takeuchi have termed knowledge creation as a "socialization process" that constitutes four components:

- a socialization component where knowledge is transferred when there is social contact as through apprenticeship, or experience-sharing.
- an externalization component as when the experience is documented and hence made explicit thus chances of converting tacit to explicit knowledge exist.

- a combination as and when records, experiences are updated, reviewed, evaluated. Hence knowledge conversion is transferred mainly from explicit to explicit.
- an internalization component enhances the tacit knowledge within an individual hence knowledge is converted from explicit to tacit knowledge.

Knowledge in also created through Intra-organisational and Inter-organisational Knowledge Transfer. Intra mean within an organization or internal. "Inter-organisation" denotes among various organizations, i.e., external. Opportunities for learning between firms exist as firms in the industry do not work in isolation. Inter-organisational knowledge transfer could hence be the solution for

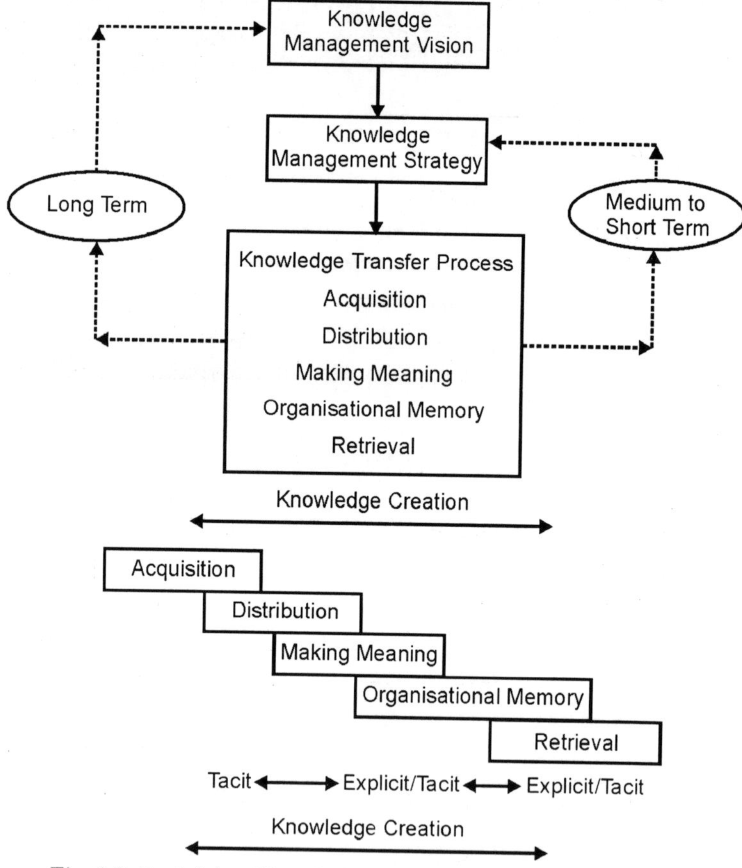

Fig. 3.2. Sustaining Knowledge through Knowledge Transfer

firms to share knowledge and thus enhance capacity. However, the capacity of a firm to absorb knowledge has a significant role to play for it may learn from the external environment. Inter-firm knowledge transfer, knowledge acquisition and creation capabilities of the firms is also essential.

The capacity of a firm depends on its ability to create and acquire knowledge as a pre-requisite in the knowledge transfer process whether it is inter or intra.

Organisations are not simply information and knowledge processing units that solve existing problems and adapt to changing environments. Rather in the course of re-defining problems and solutions and recreating their environment they create knowledge. Creating new knowledge is also not a matter of simply learning on acquiring knowledge from the outside. Knowledge has to build on its own, frequently requiring intensive and laborious interaction among members of the organisation.

Nonaka and Takeuchi's theory of knowledge creation postulates that the process has two interrelated dimensions – an ontological and epistemological.

The former referring to the fact that an organisation cannot by itseif create knowledge but rather this has to occur through individuals. Nonaka and Takeuchi further state that knowledge created within the organisation moves spirally through various levels. Knowledge created by individuals is amplified and crystallizes as a part of the knowledge network of the organisation. This process, they consider crosses intra and inter-organisational levels and boundaries.

As for the epistemology view, knowledge is created through a conversion process of tacit and explicit forms through what they termed as a "socialization process".

Davenport and Prusak taking knowledge generation to be similar to knowledge creation, acknowledge the contribution of Nonaka and Takeuchi on this aspect and come up with their own mode of knowledge generation constituting five features:

- Acquisition
- dedication of resources

- fusion
- adaptation and
- knowledge networking.

Nonaka and Takeuchi in their socialization mode of knowledge creation looked into the interplay of the tacit and explicit form of knowledge during its creation process.

Knowledge creation occurs in organizations through a conversion process of two forms of knowledge, the tacit and explicit form; and that such process occurs as conceptualised in Nonaka and Takeuchi. This is referred to as a "socialization process", which constitutes four modes:

- a socialization,
- an externalization,
- a combination and
- an internalization mode.

Knowledge is created through a socialization process where knowledge conversion occurs between the two forms of knowledge, tacit and explicit knowledge.

Socialization Mode – Tacit to Tacit Knowledge Conversion : The first mode is the socialization mode, where conversion is from *tacit to tacit*. Socialization has been defined as a process of sharing experiences and thereby creating tacit knowledge such as shared mental models and technical skills.

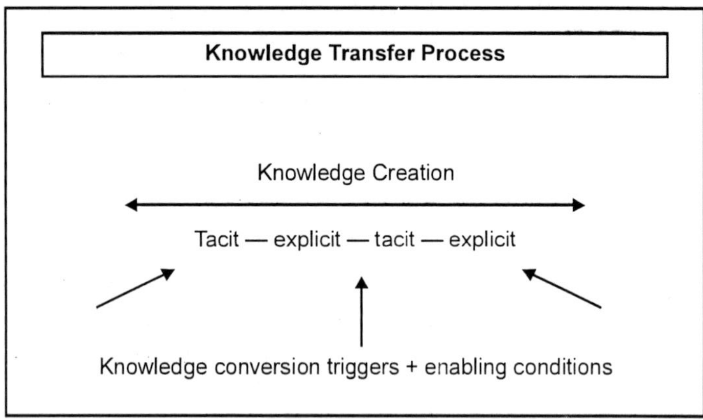

Fig. 3.3. Knowledge Transfer Process

From \ To	Tacit Knowledge	Explicit Knowledge
Tacit Knowledge	Socialization	Externalization
Explicit Knowledge	Internalization	Combination

Fig 3.4. Knowledge Conversion Modes

Socialization in organisations is facilitated in various areas and scenarios. This includes situations such as: in apprentices, where individuals acquire knowledge through observation; imitation and practices; on the job training; working side by side as in peer assist method where informal meetings are held to discuss and solve the difficult problems.

Externalization Mode – Tacit to Explicit Knowledge Conversion : The second mode is externalization mode where conversion is taken from tacit to explicit.

Among the four modes of knowledge conversion, the externalization mode is considered key to knowledge creation. This is taken as key presumably based on the fact that it makes the tacit knowledge that is difficult to access, more accessible. In this mode tacit knowledge is converted to explicit knowledge and may occur through metaphors, analogies, concepts, hypotheses, models, dialogue, collective reflection and articulation of tacit knowledge through codification or verbal means.

Combination – Explicit to Explicit Knowledge : This is the third mode a combination mode where conversion is from explicit to explicit.

This mode presupposes that re-configuration of existing information as in sorting, adding, combining and categorizing of explicit knowledge may create new knowledge. Such mode of knowledge creation is seen for example in formal education through training. In organizations, Nonaka and Takeuchi consider the creation occurs when for instance middle management breaks down and operationalise a corporate vision, business or product concept. They consider for instance when a team forms a concept, this constitutes a combination of existing data as well as knowledge that resides outside the team to create more shareable knowledge. The combination mode makes use of documents, meetings, discussions, telephone conversations, face to face and other forms of communication in knowledge creation. The combination mode is also found in patents, written rules, charts and similar documents of the organization.

Internalization – Explicit to Tacit Knowledge Conversion : Lastly is internalization mode where conversion is from explicit to tacit.

This is a process that has been identified as closely related to "learning by doing", a process whereby explicit knowledge is embodied into tacit knowledge. It occurs when experiences through socialization, externalization and combination are internalised into individuals' tacit knowledge bases in the form of shared mental models or technical know-how.

Such a conversion may be facilitated through verbalisation, use of diagram, documents, manual or sharing experiences such as the telling of success stories.

3.4.3. Triggers of Knowledge Conversion

In emphasizing the significance and the interdependence of two forms knowledge, the tacit and explicit form of knowledge are limited when acting on the own own. For instance, cite the compilation of a financial report, which essentially is explicit knowledge, does not add on to an organisation's knowledge base unless conversion process occurs. Rather they emphasize the dynamic interaction between tacit and explicit knowledge through the four modes of knowledge conversion essential to knowledge creation and identify mechanisms that trigger sub conversion through the various modes. The following summary gives the trigge that facilitate a conversion of the two forms of knowledge.

Table 3.4. Triggers of knowledge

Knowledge conversion mode	Triggers
Socialization mode	Interaction, sharing of experiences
Exlemalization mode	Meaningful dialogue, collective reflection
Combination mode	Networking of knowledge
Internalizalion mode	Learning by doing

As can be noted from the above table, the socialization mode being trigger by building a field of interaction that facilitates the sharing of members experience and mental models.

The externalization mode is triggered by meaningful dialogue or collect reflection. It uses appropriate metaphor or analogy helping team members to articulate hidden tacit knowledge that is otherwise hard to communicate. Combination mode is triggered by networking newly created knowledge and exist knowledge from other sections of the organisation thereby crystallising them into new product, service, or managerial system and finally, learning by doing triggering the internalization mode.

3.4.4. Enabling Conditions for Knowledge Creation

Nonaka and Takeuchi have further more identified five enable conditions for knowledge creation and they include:

- intention,
- autonomy,
- fluctuation and creative chaos,
- redundancy and
- requisite variety.

Intention as an enabler is described as featuring in the form of strategy within the business setting.

Autonomy is explained as a potential for bringing in creativity or introducing unexpected opportunities in the process, creating knowledge whereby it may feature from the individual level to organisational level.

Fluctuation and creative chaos as an enabling feature is seen through the breaking of monotony - as stated, "order without recursiveness". It is understood that evoking a sense of "crisis" by proposing challenging goals may also result in the same. Allowing "interpretative equivocality" to emerge from lower levels of the organization may trigger a change in fundamental ways of thinking and also help to externalize tacit knowledge.

Redundancy being the fourth condition for knowledge creation refers to existence of information that goes beyond the immediate operational requirements of organizational members. The ways of building redundancy into organizations includes: introduction of overlapping approaches such as when different departments work together, having strategic rotation and frequent meetings both on regular and irregular bases, or facilitating formal and informal networks - such as after office drinking sessions.

Requisite variety as a condition for knowledge creation refers to an organisational internal diversity that enables it to deal with the variety and complexity posed by the environment.

The whole knowledge creation process involves five steps:

- Sharing tacit knowledge
- Creating concepts
- Justifying concepts
- Building a prototype
- Cross-leveling knowledge

Knowledge creation process focusses on tacit knowledge and the use of technology in generating or transmitting such knowfedge to others. Using electronic meetings or chat rooms for collaboration, knowledge sharing and transfer are well known in todays knowledge organization.

Despite the advancement of technology, one limitation remains: the ability of technology to support the use of tacit knowledge in face to face meeting and direct interactions. Human knowledge continues to be a valuable resource and technology, is expected to trickle slowly into a human domain where knowledge creation and knowledge transfer can be expedited.

3.5. GROUP KNOWLEDGE CREATION

Knowledge can be created by individuals as well as groups also. Group knowledge creation is a social process. Analysis of research in knowledge creation reveals four groups of processes, which in combination provide a comprehensive representation of knowledge generation. The four groups of process includes :

- Accumulation,
- Interaction,
- Analysis, and
- Integration and Creation.

3.5.1. Accumulation

The first process accumulation, reflects the congress of accumulated individual inputs of knowledge that are theoretically available to the team. The idea of accumulation is extended retrospectively to include the development of knowledge within individual members' originating functional area or community-of-practice.

3.5.2. Interaction

Through extended in-depth interaction and shared practice, members of the same functional area and to a greater extent, community-of-practice have similar experiences and interpret those experiences similarly. These shared experiences lead to the development of shared tacit knowledge bases. The connection of segregated functional areas provides an opportunity for exchange of knowledge that is unique to each area. Unlike sources within an individual's dominant work environment, the weak ties formed in cross-functional teams provide access to novel information and tacit knowledge.

Interaction is the second group process. Within teams, the term is used to describe the use of language and other symbols to develop enriched and shared understanding. The aim of interaction incorporates a desire to evolve deeper and shared understandings, which encompasses and is partly directed by the objective of boundary-spanning. Boundary-spanning reflects the understanding that members with different backgrounds operate from different perspectives underpinned by distinct cognitive structures based on their different work-related experience. Effective interaction relies on and may be thwarted by, the ability to interact across the cognitive boundaries that underlie functional differences.

3.5.3. Analysis

The third process is analysis, during which group members debate points of view, assumptions and the merits of possible solutions. The group's analytical discussion impacts individual analytical processes by highlighting certain pieces of knowledge, drawing attention to faulty logic and presenting arguments in support of particular conclusions. Such reasoning facilitates creative solutions because it allows group members to link their inventory of past experiences to the current situation.

By bringing together members from diverse backgrounds, group analytical reasoning has the potential to result in the application of a broader variety of experiences and knowledge than would be available to individuals operating alone. While the source of information regarding a previous problem or solution is the individual, the invocation, negotiation and manipulation of this information occurs through group interactions. Group analogic reasoning builds on itself as discussion of one member's experiences prompts the introduction and exploration of further experiences from other members.

3.5.4. Integration and Creation

The fourth process is integration and creation. The objective of this phase is the articulation of an agreed position or solution which integrates the best of knowledge available to members and incorporates new knowledge created on the basis of the previous phases. Integration and creation may be described as the externalized construction of problem solutions or decisions, involving the manipulation and integration of knowledge through debate, bargaining and agreement.

In addition, there are three individual processes of new knowledge creation within a team. These processes occur in repeated patterns, with each process capable of stimulating another. Individual as a member of a group may create knowledge and it falls into two types of processes namely – Transmission and Cognition.

Transmission : The first individual process is transmission, which encompasses the development of an explicit representation of what is known and the interpretation of received messages through application of the receiver's tacit knowledge.

In cross-functional groups, this interpretation can be described as a process of analysis in which the meaning of words and phrases is investigated with the aim of converting the decoded message into a meaningful message.

Members' ability to accurately interpret other member's messages is dependent on their ability to successfully apply their own mental models to message content. If an individual with tacit knowledge markedly different to the original knower is asked to interpret knowledge codified by the latter, the process of interpretation may lead to generation of a novel elucidation. Novel elucidation is an important component in the development of creativity.

Cognition : The second process is cognition encompassing accommodation and assimilation. Assimilation occurs as new knowledge is integrated into existing cognitive structures, and accommodation occurs when structures are altered or recreated to more comprehensively reflect new knowledge. The process of cognition also incorporates intuiting, described as the perception of patterns or possibilities in a personal stream of experience. Intuiting occurs during the process of applying tacit knowledge to new experiences and is related to the level and depth of tacit knowledge available.

A highly complex mental model, associated with the development of expertize, facilitates the perceptions of patterns that may not be apparent to novices. Within cross-functional groups, the application of complex mental models to knowledge presented from different functional areas provides an opportunity for new patterns to be recognized.

There is another process that is third process which is task-focused positioning. This involves new pars individual thought processes aimed at deciding strategies and tactics. As their understanding of issues related to the task and others perspectives develops, members prioritize, search for possible alliances and agreements and opportunities to collaborate and/or compromise.

3.6. FACTORS FACILITATING NEW KNOWLEDGE CREATION

The knowledge creation model provides an informative context for understanding how different group dynamics and processes may facilitate or thwart group creativity efforts. These dynamics and processes inform the management of groups as knowledge creating mechanisms. As organizations become expert at manipulating these factors, their knowledge creation capability increases. In addition, as the manipulation of these factors is unlikely to be observable and likely to be socially complex, the ability of competitors to imitate or acquire this capability decreases as expertise increases. In the first step towards verifying the utility of this model, a number of propositions relating to such factors are developed relating to two of the group processes namely accumulation and interaction.

1. Accumulation – Cognitive Diversity and Transactive Memory : The first group process is accumulation. It is based on acquisition of knowledge by groups. Accordingly, the success of the accumulation phase includes the dimensions of cognitive diversity and transactive memory.

Cognitive diversity is defined as the extent to which the group reflects differences in knowledge, including beliefs, preferences and perspectives. If accumulation of diverse knowledge is critical to knowledge creation efforts then cognitive diversity will increase the likelihood of creative new knowledge emerging in groups. Conceptually, this connection is primarily based on the understanding that, through the integration of diverse knowledge, groups have the potential to overcome the factors constraining the development of new knowledge imposed by the social relations. This includes the institutional and task-related pressures identified by institutional theorists, which parallel the paradigmatic boundaries described by path dependency theorists and pragmatic concerns about criticism identified by decision theorists. If new knowledge is developed that extends beyond the parameters of current functionally specific concepts, it is more likely to contribute to the development of group outputs with truly novel features.

Cognitive diversity may also be linked to enhanced knowledge creation efforts through a secondary mechanism. The debating of dissenting issues consequent to different approaches and perceptions associated with cognitive diversity stimulates divergent thinking in individual members, which is closely linked to creativity output.

The process of accumulation theoretically relies not only on the existence of a broad range of information and tacit knowledge, but also on the ability to access this knowledge. Such access relies on members' knowing 'who knows what'.

Transactive memory is described as a team's understanding of who has access to what specialized information within the team. Groups with high transactive memory have good understanding of the knowledge and skills available to each individual member and this has been found to facilitate both access to information and co-ordination. The importance of this to cognitively diverse teams relates to enhancement of group performance through the accurate understanding of the information available to the group and where it is located in terms of member expertise.

2. Interaction - Open-mindedness Norms : The second group process, interaction, is based on a process of communication. It focuses on investigation, reflection and efforts to understand. As such, the interaction process relies on members to actively and openly listen to the information provided by others. Such an approach to communication is encompassed by the notion of open-mindedness norms.

Open-mindedness norms are beliefs relating to the way in which members approach the views and knowledge of others and incorporates the beliefs that others should be free to express their views and that the value of others' knowledge should be recognized.

Researchers have found that open-minded interaction leads to curiousity and information-seeking when members are confronted with an opposing position. In addition, while the majority of research undertaken on open-mindedness norms has focused on conflict and negotiation, much of this has found a strong link with information sharing and enhanced shared understanding.

If effective interaction is critical to 'knowledge creation efforts' then open-mindedness norms will increase the likelihood of 'creative new knowledqe' emerging in groups.

3.7. KNOWLEDGE MATURATION CYCLE

Knowledge is dynamic, it may be regarded as passing through different phases of a cycle. Knowledge creation and its ultimate role in a knowledge economy, can be examined in terms of Shukla's four-stage maturation cycle for knowledge. This cycle is heavily focused on how tacit knowledge affects organizations.

Stage 1: Discovered knowledge : This stage occurs when an idea, need, or possibility leads to knowledge creation. At this stage, knowledge is tacit; it exists in the mind of the discoverer. However, a knowledge management system can provide an important service by offering an e-workspace within which a knowledge discoverer can begin to organize these ideas. Information seeking often accompanies the process of knowledge discovery, because the discoverer is likely to research his/her ideas or at least search for confirmatory information. Knowledge management systems that allow people to easily incorporate this information-seeking into the process will enhance this stage and create greater value within the firm.

Stage 2 : Codified knowledge : The discovered knowledge is translated into a physical form that helps it to survive and become useful. Codification is explicit knowledge because it can be represented by skills, documents, or products. Knowledge management systems should have the capability to handle the different desired representations of codified knowledge.

Stage 3 : Migratory knowledge : When knowledge is codified it gains mobility. This means that knowledge takes on its own identity and is no longer attached to its originator or owner. This is the stage when dissemination begins to take place. This is the area in which knowledge management systems excel and can create added value in the knowledge creation process.

Migratory knowledge creates special challenges. For example, knowledge can exist in more than one place at a time, but depending on the environment it is in, it may not be identified with the same classification terms. Additionally, as knowledge migrates, it generally becomes less scarce, which means that there are more "versions" available. This could lead to the quality of the knowledge degrading, as it is subject to "wear and tear," which could make it less accurate. The challenge then becomes finding and identifying authoritative-versions of the codified knowledge.

Stage 4 : Invisible knowledge : As know ledge spreads, it begins to be viewed as commonplace and is viewed as a public good. This means the knowledge has lost its special character and instead has become so pervasive that it changes the social and business environment. This can happen in a proprietary situation; for example many current-day '"basics" of aerodynamic designs were once carefully guarded migratory knowledge. Knowledge management systems play a role at this stage in several ways including retaining an authoritative version of the knowledge before it became "invisible" and supplying information that allows participants to ascertain the validity of "invisible" knowledge, because this type of pervasive knowledge may also be corrupted.

3.8. ORGANIZATION LEARNING AND KNOWLEDGE CREATION

Organization Learning is a science practiced by all of us and learning extends our capacity to create and generate. The idea that the nature of organizations is changing is not new. Nearly four decades ago, it was noted that organizations were becoming more complex and that the change was occurring at an increasing rate. The environment has changed in two ways – it has become more complex in terms of the numbers, diversity, and interconnectedness of relationships; and it has also become more turbulent because events and their reactions occur more quickly. Thus, learning on the organizational level is dependent, at least in part, on knowledge creation.

Organizational learning requires that the organization have the ability to access its collective knowledge base. Learning organizations are skilled at creating, acquiring and transferring knowledge which is then used to modify the organization's behaviour. This behaviour reflects new knowledge and insights.

In many circumstances, organizational learning is a process of detection of an error, proper diagnosis of its cause and correction of the error so that it can learn from experience and take actions that are favourable for its survival. Often this leads to identifying a need that requires new knowledge to be created to answer the need.

Learning in an organization can be considered to take place in two ways. First Adaptive, or single loop learning, occurs when problems are resolved using standard operating procedures; however, there is no attention to error reduction. Second Generative, or double loop learning, occurs when the organization detects, diagnoses and corrects errors; this is the hallmark of a learning organization. A learning organization is based on five pillars– personal mastery, shared mental models, team learning, shared vision and systems thinking. Organizational Learning is essential because the organization's intelligence is greater than the sum of the knowledge of the individuals within that organization.

Organization learning relies on an environment that encourages learning and that has information processes and systems that promote knowledge creation and use. In this type of organization, knowledge creation is not just the responsibility of a few. Instead, it is a collaborative effort driven by a shared vision. This means that processes are integrated, often through an open network. Organizational Learning is further facilitated by the dissolution of organizational boundaries that isolate groups and block the flow of knowledge.

These requirements mean that an organization must have a structure that encourages communication, interaction and flexibility. What type of structure is needed? Historically, many organizations were structured in a pyramid-like hierarchy. However, the global communications and fast-paced decision making that are hallmarks of the knowledge economy have highlighted the pyramid structure's inability to respond quickly to change. Organizations have sought a way to create a more flexible structure that allows greater responsiveness to environmental change. These flexible structures often involve complicated network relationships and computing/ communication technologies serve as the rope that binds together this vast network of teams.

Johansen and Swigart use the metaphor that these new structures are fishnets. This reflects how the traditional hierarchy has been flattened and how the new structure is more horizontal. This new structure is composed of complex interconnections that allow soft hierarchies-to develop as needed for specific tasks. In an organization of this type, teams are often the key work group. However, because teams can align into informal ad hoc networks as the task demands, they also have a tendency to encourage knowledge creation through knowledge sharing and synergy.

All this comes at a time when the need for faster decision making is in the forefront. And to make decisions, people need knowledge of all three types and all modes. The change in organization structure and the environments they exist in, has led to a need for faster knowledge processing, renewal and creation. This means that knowledge is no longer centralized, but that it can emerge at any point in the environment, and that a system and perhaps people to mediate it, must be in place to receive it.

As organizational learning is encouraged, the organization's knowledge requirements are enlarged. Learning organizations rely not only on external sources of knowledge, but also on their own knowledge capital. Knowledge capital includes the tacit knowledge of its employees and also the knowledge that results from knowledge sharing within the organization.

Four concepts from the discipline of architecture are very useful in creating effective learning organizations:

- Architecture's ultimate test is that it provides utility to the people who have to use it. A learning organization should be configured so that it provides utility to the individuals within the organization including facilitating knowledge creation.
- The best architecture does not have rigid specifications. Organizations benefit from architecture that guides, facilitates and provides a framework for knowledge creation.
- Architecture must meet the immediate needs of the organization, but it must also be capable of reflecting the aspirations of those who use it.
- Architecture cannot be imposed, but must evolve. An

organization represents a large number of people working together toward a shared vision. In a sense, the organizational architecture could be thought of as having a social dimension.

Knowledge management systems can have a vital role in a learning organization. For example, a knowledge management system can be instrumental in helping to assure that the following three components of a learning organization are implemented successfully :

- Supporting leadership processes that facilitate the intent to learn and create.
- Supporting learning mechanisms that encourage knowledge creation and acquisition.
- Supporting structures and processes that facilitate learning activities.

Obviously, learning organizations are very different from the traditional model, and they have many characteristics that are worth noting, including permeable boundaries versus clear boundaries, evolving design versus being predesigned, maximizing skills versus minimizing skills, integrated processes versus segmented tasks, and open, multi-functional networks rather than functional and hierarchical groupings.

Summing up, Knowledge creation is a dynamic activity that can enhance organization success and economic well-being. In addition, it is an important driver of innovation, which can increase organizational agility and improve organizational performance, Knowledge creation is associated with knowledge generation, which is one of the five primary knowledge manipulation activities identified by the ontology for the conduct of knowledge management. Knowledge creation also has a very symbiotic relationship with knowledge acquisition and knowledge selection and often the three activities are closely linked.

Knowledge creation involves a maturation process that begins when knowledge is discovered, is then codified, becomes migratory, and finally invisible. However, this dynamic process still relies on individual processors to share knowledge and transform it. Knowledge sharing relies on strong support from leadership. Sharing can occur in four processes - socialization, externalization, combination, and internalization. On an organizational level, knowledge creation can occur through knowledge conversion, knowledge building, or knowledge linking. Additionally, organizational information seeking or sensemaking can drive knowledge creation as can organizational learning. And knowledge management provides the framework to support knowledge creation by focusing on the relationships between knowledge activities and identifying areas that are essential elements of successful knowledge creation.

4

Knowledge Capturing, Certification and Organization of Knowledge

Knowledge management systems derive their power from the knowledge they use. In knowledge management, the first step is capturing tacit knowledge which resides in the minds of people. Although knowledge may exist at the organizational level, much of the critical knowledge exists not in some theoretical blueprint of activities but in the knowledge, skills and talents of the organization's members. In fact, it is becoming increasingly clear that competitive advantage in resource-or knowledge-based competition depends heavily on the human resources and human resource practices of a firm.

The idiosyncratic nature of knowledge makes it difficult to trade or move across boundaries. Knowledge assets are not only difficult to trade but are accumulated through a number of mechanisms over time and in specific contexts. The underlying knowledge of a firm may be conceptualized as both stocks and flows of knowledge that contribute to the firm's superior performance. Stocks of knowledge are accumulated knowledge assets that are internal to a firm or organization and flows of knowledge are knowledge streams into the firm or various parts of the firm that may be assimilated over the time and developed into stocks of knowledge.

Asset stocks are accumulated over time by choosing appropriate paths for both internal development and tying into external flows over a period of time and converting these flows into knowledge stocks by developing organizational routines, gaining patents, or incorporating these flows into products and services. The bath-tub metaphor illustrates the differences and connections between asset stocks and flows.

At any point in time, the stock of water in a bathtub is indicated by the level of water in the tub. This stock of water is the cumulative result of flows of water into the tub through the tap and out of the tub through leaks. With respect to firm capabilities, the amount of water in the tub may represent the stock of know-how at a particular point in time. Current R&D spending, knowledge acquired through-an ongoing alliance, or a recent acquisition is represented by the water flowing into the tub and the water leaking out illustrates knowledge depreciation over time or knowledge that is simply not retained by conscious choice or because of personnel turnover. Flows like water coming into and leaking out of the tub may be adjusted through the use of such tools as discussed—hybrid structures and mergers and acquisition. Human resource practices that improve the retention of critical knowledge workers or enhance the ability of the firm to protect knowledge from leaking out through alliances can affect the outward flow of knowledge. Over the time these flows can be used to adjust the stock of knowledge that a company retains by embedding the knowledge into procedures, activities, products, patents and other forms. Also over the time the firm's stocks of knowledge can be adjusted if it decides to stop offering certain product lines or services or if patents lapse or are licensed out. A firm's stock of knowledge can be thought of as similar to its available cash balance. Although these balances can be adjusted, they are fixed at any specific point in time.

Knowledge flows may have several sources. Different labs in a single university or in several universities or even several regions and countries may contribute to a flow of knowledge about a specific subject. However, to maintain the water metaphor, it is generally not possible to license the entire river but only the small streams that are the sources of the river. Monitoring these various sources and selecting partners or acquisition targets from among them can pose a significant challenge. As we move forward, we are working on the assumption of a single source of the flow, but in the real world the selection of that source is likely to be a difficult and important challenge.

Although the characteristic of the knowledge being acquired as a stock or a flow has important implications for knowledge acquisition strategies it cannot be considered in isolation. The tacit versus explicit component of the stock or flow of knowledge must also be considered. Important is the amount of learning by doing, close interaction training and observation required to complete the transfer of the knowledge or skill across the organizational boundaries.

By combining these two sets of characteristics, we gain four basic knowledge classes: tacit-stock, explicit-stock, tacit-flow and explicit-flow. These classes form the basis for the first set of decision criteria for the model. Before we move on, let us acknowledge that there are few pure forms and that the decision needs to be based on the predominant characteristics of the knowledge a firm is attempting to acquire.

Explicit-stock knowledge is perhaps the simplest type of knowledge to acquire from outside a firm's boundaries. Examples of this type of knowledge are patented chemical formulas, algorithms, software code and so on. These are easily transferred because they are easily codified—that is, turned into written, executable instructions. It is also fairly easy to judge the quality of knowledge with these characteristics from the start and in general this type of knowledge has strong intellectual property protection. These characteristics make it amenable to simple licensing agreements. More complex processes could be employed, but these processes require investment of greater resources in the management of the process. Therefore, the most appropriate tool for the acquisition of this type of knowledge is a simple licensing agreement.

In contrast, tacit-stock knowledge creates several challenges for an acquiring firm. An example of tacit-stock knowledge might be the artistry of a chef who can prepare stunning cuisine. Although this chef can write out and transmit his recipes, the knowledge of the exact colour of the sauce or the specific taste he is trying to achieve or an eye to select the highest-quality ingredients is not easily translated. The acquisition of his stock of knowledge will require significant direct interaction or perhaps even the acquisition of the chef himself. Acquiring tacit-stock knowledge poses several challenges. First, the transaction will require significant interaction among the parties, and the ultimate success of this transaction will depend on the quality of this interaction. Essentially, acquiring this type of knowledge requires at a minimum a substantial training process, which increases the dependence of the acquiring firm on the other organization. This dependence raises the risks for the acquirer and accordingly, increases the need for a more complicated governance structure for the transaction in order to mitigate those risks. Acquiring tacit-stock knowledge will require at minimum a strategic alliance, but depending on some of the other characteristics it could call for a joint venture or even that the transaction be internalized through an acquisition. These increasingly complex structures place greater demands on the managerial resources of the organization and are much more dependent on the development and maintenance of a strong relationship between the parties.

Explicit-flow knowledge poses a monitoring and access challenge for the firm acquiring it. Although the output of the knowledge flow is easily transferred across boundaries because of its explicit nature, the ongoing development of new knowledge in the flow is of significance to the acquiring firm. An example of explicit-flow knowledge would be the continual development and refinement of a series of software techniques and algorithms to sort through the increasingly large database of gene sequences and proteins. It has important implications and is likely to be protected intellectual property but is easily communicated and monitored because of the explicit nature of the software. Therefore, the acquirer has to monitor the source of the flow continually and maintain access to the knowledge being produced. One possible solution is simply to monitor the flow and as interesting new knowledge is created enter into a license agreement for that specific knowledge. For example, a company might monitor the activities of a bioinformatics lab in a university and enter into licenses for any interesting new algorithms that are discovered This would limit the firm's investment in the stream simply to monitoring the outflow and committing additional resources only when something interesting is developed. However, if the flow has significant strategic value, a more formal long-term contractual arrangement-a strategic alliance-becomes the appropriate governance mechanism. In these circumstances alliances generally allow for provision of resources and funds on the part of the firm attempting to acquire the knowledge in exchange for a contractual right of first refusal to an exclusive license of any products of the knowledge flow, generally a series of patents or intellectual property, but perhaps new information about the workings of a particular process in the human body. Strategic alliances are the preferred choice in these circumstances. They allow a firm to guarantee exclusive rights to a potentially valuable flow, but because it is explicit and easily transferred across boundaries the firm can avoid the expense and resource commitment of an acquisition. It is the next category, tacit-flow knowledge, that poses the greatest challenge for the firm acquiring knowledge.

Tacit-flow knowledge is the most difficult and frequently the most critical type of knowledge to acquire. These types of flows are frequently the leading edge of thought and development in a specific area of science or technology. The quality, value and applications of such knowledge are highly uncertain, but the competitive implications are also potentially very significant, Capturing tacit knowledge requires an extensive time commitment from the domain expert and the special skills of the knowledge developer. At times the expert might loose interest in the project and even feel like quitting. Perhaps the knowledge developer and the expert just never seem to hit it off because the knowledge developer may use the wrong tool or approach. Hence it is vital to know the technical part of capturing knowledge.

4.1. KNOWLEDGE CAPTURE

Knowledge Capture can be defined as the process of capturing the expert's thoughts and experiences. There are many definitions for knowledge capture. Some of them are :

- An applied brain drain.
- A manual craft that depends on the skill and effectiveness of the developer.
- The transfer of problem solving expertise from some knowledge source to the repository or a program.
- The process by which knowledge management system developers discover that knowledge that experts use to perform the task of interest.
- An investigative experimental process involving interviews and protocols analysis in order to build a knowledge management system.

Knowledge capture is a demanding mental process in which a knowledge developer collaborates with the expert to convert expertise into a coded program. Here three important steps are involved:

- using an appropriate tool to elicit information from the expert.
- interpreting the information and inferring the experts underlying knowledge and reasoning process.
- Finally, using the interpretation to construct the necessary rules which can represent the experts reasoning process.

Knowledge is usually captured when the knowledge developer interviews the expert who answers the following questions:

- What do you do as the first step?
- What information do you consider next?
- What constraints do you look for[7]

Those types of questions lead the experts through scenarios or case situations. To capture knowledge used in building complex knowledge management systems, knowledge developers use flow charts, flow diagrams, decision trees, decision tables and other graphic representations.

Knowing how experts know that they know is the bottom line in knowledge capture. Expert knowledge is cognitively complex and tacitly pragmatic. It is not always easy to capture through a traditional interview process. In many cases in which knowledge capture was unsuccessful, the knowledge developer did not quite understand the pragmatic nature of the expertize.

Sometimes experts perceive knowledge developers as domain novices who require patience and who must go through an apprenticeship process that takes them from novice to near expert status during the building of knowledge management system. The following suggestions can be used to improve the knowledge capture process.

- Knowledge developers should focus on how experts approach a problem. They must look beyond the facts or the heuristics.
- Knowing that true expertise takes the form of chunked knowledge, knowledge developers should reevaluate how well they understand the problem domain and how accurately they are modeling it. Can they see patterns and relationships leading to a solution? Can the knowledge developer grasp the complexity of the domain? Conceptual tools provide the developer with a concise, easy way to capture heuristics.
- The quality of human emulation is best captures through episodic knowledge or knowledge based on previous experience. Therefore, a knowledge developer should elicit the expert's knowledge through concrete case situations or scenario.

4.2. KNOWLEDGE CAPTURING - TOOLS

Capturing tacit knowledge and converting it into rules that a computer can use is a costly business. It requires an extensive time, commitment from the domain expert and special skill of the knowledge developer. The important tools for knowledge capturing are

- Expert Evaluation
- Developing Relationship with Experts

- Fuzzy Reasoning & Quality of Knowledge Capture
- Interviewing as a Tacit Knowledge Capture Tool

4.2.1. Expert Evaluation

Tacit knowledge capture requires free access to cooperative and articulate experts. Without a good match of expert and project, the knowledge developer could spend hours questioning someone whose knowledge might be unusable in the proposed system. There are several indicators of expertise such as :

- The expert commands genuine respect.
- The expert is found to be consulted by people in the organization, when some problem arises.
- The expert possess self confidence and he/she has a realistic view of the limitations.
- The expert avoids irrelevant information, uses facts and figures.
- The expert is able to explain properly and he/she can customize his/her presentation according to the level of the audience.
- The expert exhibits his/her depth of the detailed knowledge and his/her quality of explanation is exceptional.
- The expert is not arrogant regarding his/her personal information.

Experts usually exhibit the following qualifications. An Expert should :

- be able to tolerate stress.
- be able to think creatively.
- be able to exhibit self-confidence.
- be able to generate enthusiasm as well as motivation.
- know when to follow hunches and when to make exceptions.
- posses good communication skills.
- maintain credibility.
- operate within a schema-driven/structured orientation.
- share his/her expertise willingly and without hesitation.
- should emulate an ideal teacher's habits.

Experts levels of expertize can be classified as :

- Highly Expert persons
- Moderately Expert Problem Solvers and
- New Experts

Highly expert persons - generally give concise explanations. They assume that the listener has enough knowledge about the problem. Therefore they focus on the key steps often skipping the vital details.

Moderately expert problem solvers - may be more tentative in their explanations, but they tend to provide detailed explanations. They are quicker to give answers than the highly expert persons and more often adapt their description to the level of the knowledge developer.

New experts - are more likely to offer answers that are brief and fragmented which suggest shallow knowledge of the domain.

Capturing Single vs Multiple Experts' Tacit Knowledge : To ensure the reliability and quality of the knowledge management system, a prime consideration is whether to tap one expert or a panel of experts. This decision is based on several factors such as the complexity of the problem, the criticality of the project to the organization, the types of experts available and the funds allocated for building the knowledge management system. Each alternative has advantages and limitations.

Advantages of working with a single expert : These are :

- Ideal for building a simple knowledge management system with only few rules.
- Ideal when the problem lies within a restricted domain.
- The single expert can facilitate the logistics aspects of coordination arrangements for knowledge capture.
- Problem related/personal conflicts are easier to resolve. The single expert tends to share more confidentiality.

Limitations with working with a single expert : These include :

- Often, the experts knowledge is found to be not easy to capture.
- The single expert usually provides a single line of reasoning.

- They are more likely to change meeting schedules.
- The knowledge is often found to be dispersed.

Advantages of working with multiple (team) experts : These are :

- Complex problem domains are usually benefited.
- Stimulates interaction.
- Listening to a multitude of views allows the developer to consider alternative ways of representing knowledge.
- Formal meetings are sometimes better environment for generating thoughtful contributions.

Limitations with working with multiple (team) experts: These include :

- Disagreements can frequently occur.
- Coordinating meeting schedules are more complicated.
- Harder to retain confidentiality.
- Overlapping mental processes of multiple experts can result in a process loss.
- Often requires more than one knowledge developer.

4.2.2. Developing Relationship with Experts

A better understanding is essential between the expert and the developer. This will promote a perfect knowledge creation. To achieve this, the developer should develop a cordial relationship with the expert who knows the subject very well.

Working with experts can be a complicated one. Perception plays an important role in the early phase of the building process. From the experts view, the knowledge developer is building a knowledge management system in an area about which he/she knows little. The expert may have a poor perception of what the knowledge developer can do. To reverse this perception the knowledge developer must learn quickly and use psychology, commonsense, marketing and technical skills to gain the experts attention and respect. The following are the check points :

- Creating the right impression
- Understanding of the expert's style of expression
- Preparation for the session

- Deciding the location for the session
- Approaching multiple experts
- Small groups approach

Creating the right impression: The knowledge developer must learn to use psychology, common sense, technical as well as marketing skills to attract the experts respect and attention.

Understanding of the expert's style of expression : Experts are usually found to use one of the following styles of expression:

- *Procedure type* : These type of experts are found to be logical, verbal and always procedural.
- *Storyteller type* : These type of experts are found to be focused on the content of the domain at the expense of the solution.
- *Godfather type* : These type of experts are found to be compulsive to take over.
- *Salesperson type* : These type of experts are found to spend most of the time dancing around the topic, explaining why his/her solution is the best.

Preparation for the session

- Before making the first appointment, the knowledge developer must acquire some knowledge about the problem and the expert.
- Initial sessions can be most challenging/critical.
- The knowledge developer must build the trust.
- The knowledge developer must be familiar with project terminology he/she must review the existing documents.
- The knowledge developer should be able to make a quick rapport with the expert.

Deciding the location for the session

- Protocol calls for the expert to decide the location.
- The expert is usually more comfortable in having his/her necessary tools and information available close to him/her.

– The meeting place should be quiet and free of interruptions.

Approaching multiple experts

– *Individual approach* : The knowledge developer holds sessions with one expert at a time.

– *Approach using primary and secondary experts*: The knowledge developer hold sessions with the senior expert early in the knowledge capture program for the clarification of the plan.

– For a detailed probing, he/she may ask for other experts' knowledge.

Small groups approach

– Experts gather together in one place, discuss the problem domain, and usually provide a pool of information.

– Experts' responses are monitored and the functionality of each expert is tested against the expertise of the others.

– This approach requires experience in assessing tapped knowledge, as well as cognition skills.

– The knowledge developer must deal with the issue of power and its effect on expert's opinion.

4.2.3. Fuzzy Reasoning & Quality of Knowledge Capture

Fuzzy reasoning is concerned with decisions on uncertain conditions. People reason with words not numbers which can lead to a problem commonly encountered in interviewing. Experts are not always easy to understand. Because the problem domain is likely to be technical or complex, decision making often involves rules with many shades of meaning that may be fuzzy to the non expert.

- Sometimes, the information gathered from the experts via interviewing is not precise and it involves fuzziness and uncertainty.
- The fuzziness may increase the difficulty of translating the expert's notions into applicable rules.

- *Analogies/Uncertainties*: These include :
  - In the course of explaining events, experts can use analogies comparing a problem with a similar problem which has been encountered in possibly different settings, months or years ago.
  - An expert's knowledge or expertize represents the ability to gather uncertain information as input and to use a plausible line of reasoning to clarify the fuzzy details.
  - Belief, an aspect of uncertainty, tends to describe the level of credibility.
  - People may use different kinds of words in order to express belief.
  - These words are often paired with qualifiers such as highly, extremely.

  Understanding experience : These are
  - Knowledge developers can benefit from their understanding/knowledge of cognitive psychology.
  - When a question is asked, then an expert operates on certain stored information through deductive, inductive, or other kinds of problem-solving methods.
  - The resulting answer is often found to be the culmination of the processing of stored information.
  - The right question usually evokes the memory of experiences that produced good and appropriate solutions in the past.

Sometimes, how quickly an expert responds to a question depends on the clarity of content, whether the content has been recently used and how well the expert has understood the question.

How well the expert can represent internal processes can vary with their command of the language they are using and the knowledge developer's interviewing skills. The language may be unclear in the following number of ways:

- Comparative words (e.g., better, faster) are sometimes left hanging.

- Specific words or components may be left out of an explanation.
- Absolute words and phrases may be used loosely.
- Some words always seem to have a built-in ambiguity.

4.2.4. Interviewing as a Tacit Knowledge Capture Tool

Interview is a tool that is used commonly in the early stages of tacit knowledge capture. It is the oldest and most often used tool for capturing or verifying tacit knowledge. The knowledge developer need to make special efforts to eliminate interviewer bias that would reduce validity. Often validity of information is reliable if it is freely given. In an interview, the knowledge developer has an opportunity to verify information and observe the experts thought process in action. The interview as a tacit knowledge capturing tool has many advantages:

Advantages of using interviewing as a tacit knowledge capture tool: These are :

- It is a flexible tool.
- It is excellent for evaluating the validity of information.
- It is very effective in case of eliciting information regarding complex matters.
- Often people enjoy being interviewed.
- Interviews can range from the highly unstructured type to highly structured type.

– The *unstructured types* are difficult to conduct and they are used in the case when the knowledge developer really needs to explore an issue.

– The *structured types* are found to be goal-oriented, and they are used in the case when the knowledge developer needs specific information.

– Structured questions can be of the following types:

  * Multiple-choice questions.
  * Dichotomous questions, and
  * Ranking scale questions.

– In *semistructured types*, the knowledge developer asks

predefined questions, but he/she allows the expert some freedom in expressing his/her answer.

Guidelines for successful interviewing: These guidelines comprise of :

- Setting the stage and establishing rapport,
- Phrasing questions,
- Listening closely/avoiding arguments and evaluating the session outcomes.

Reliability of the information gathered from experts: Some uncontrolled sources of error that can reduce the information's reliability:

- Expert's perceptual slant.
- The failure in expert's part to exactly remember what has happened.
- Fear of unknown in the part of expert.
- Problems with communication.
- Role bias.

Errors in part of the knowledge developer: Validity problems are often caused by the interviewer effect (something about the knowledge developer colours the response of the expert). Some of the effects can be as follows:

- Gender effect
- Age effect
- Race effect

Problems encountered during interviewing : Major problems are :

- Response bias.
- Inconsistency.
- Problem with communication.
- Hostile attitude.
- Standardizing the questions.
- Setting the length of the interview.

Process of ending the interview: This has below steps :

- The end of the session should be carefully planned.

- One procedure calls for the knowledge developer to halt the questioning a few minutes before the scheduled ending time and to summarize the key points of the session.
- This allows the expert to comment a schedule a future session.
- Many verbal/nonverbal clues can be used for ending the interview.

Issues: Many issues may arise during the interview and to be prepared for the most important ones, the knowledge developer can consider the following questions:

- How would it be possible to elicit knowledge from the experts who can not say what they mean or can not mean what they say.
- How to set up the problem domain.
- How to deal with uncertain reasoning processes.
- How to deal with the situation of difficult relationships with expert(s).
- How to deal with the situation when the expert does not like the knowledge developer for some reason.

Rapid Prototyping in interviews: Rapid prototyping is an approach to building knowledge management systems, in which knowledge is added with each knowledge capture session.

- This is an iterative approach which allows the expert to verify the rules as they are built during the session.
- This approach can open up communication through its demonstration of the knowledge management system.
- Due to the process of instant feedback and modification, it reduces the risk of failure,
- It allows the knowledge developer to learn each time a change is incorporated in the prototype.
- This approach is highly interactive.
- The prototype can create user expectations which in turn can become obstacles to further development effort.

Some points for Capturing Tacit Knowledge

- — Collect the insights that percolate from work related conversations.
- — Record the best solutions to common problems and issues.
- — Construct an ontology / taxonomy, identify gaps and seek expertise to fill them.
- — Encourage collection, indexing and distribution of best practices and lessons learned.
- — Conduct formal After Action Reviews (AARs), encourage periodic reflections, craft patterns top collect solutions that work from experience.
- — Apply knowledge harvesting techniques using tools such as Infinos or HKc.
- — Perform acquisition using knowledge engineering methods.
- — Use a technique called enumerative description to ask questions and gather key situational diagnostics.
- — Set up a question driven community, e.g. using Organik and mine the insights.
- — Construct 'profiles' and have a space where issues can be discussed and pushed to key decision makers, e.g. using *Vignette dialog.*
- — Mine electronic messages and construct dynamic profiles using products like *Autonomy* or *Tacit* to link people to people via content matching.

4.3. OTHER KNOWLEDGE CAPTURING TECHNIQUES

Like any other professional, the knowledge developer must be well versed in the use of specialized knowledge capture tools. Each tool has a unique purpose, depending upon whether knowledge capture revolves around single expert or multiple experts. They are as follows:

- Brainstorming
- Synetics
- Delphi Technique
- Nominal Group Technique (NGT)
- Heurastic Technique

- Protocol Analysis (Think-Aloud Method)
- Consensus Decision Making
- Repertery Grid
- Concept Mapping
- Blackboarding

4.3.1. Brainstorming

Brainstorming is an unstructured approach towards generating ideas about creative solution of a problem which involves multiple experts in a session.

It was developed by Alex F. Osborn to help to trigger creative ideas in the field of advertising agency. He explained the term as meaning the use of the brain to storm a creative problem — "and to do so in commando fashion, with each stormer audaciously attacking the same objective." In order to obtain the maximum creatively from the group under the brain-storming technique, following points may be kept in mind:

– Ideas can be criticised freely.
– "Free-wheeling" is easier to take down ideas than to think them up.
– Quantity is encouraged. The people should be asked to develop as many ideas as possible.
– Combination and improvement are sought. In addition to contributing ideas of their own, participants should react to the ideas of others so that they can be turned into better ideas; or how two or more ideas can be joined into still another new idea.

Besides these points, there are many other specific procedures that will lead to optimum effectiveness : The sessions need to be recorded to avoid the missing of ideas generated. Problems may be spilit into parts if it is umanageable, etc.

Brainstorming reached the peak of its popularity in the 1950's. However, the study conducted by Thomas S. Bouchard at Yale University in 1958 found that individuals working alone could produce more unique ideas than could a group.

There are several criticisms of brainstorming. It is very time consuming and thus costly; and only superficial ideas are brought out. Unfortunately, as a technique for assisting decision-makers to reach basic, risk-uncertainly decisions, it is very superficial.

4.3.2. Synectics

Synectics not so well known as brainstorming, but of greater value to decision-making is a creative technique developed by William J.J. Gordon in 1944. He termed the technique synectics, a word of Greek derivation which means fitting together different, distinct, novel and irrelevant ideas. Its purpose is to increase the creative output of individuals and groups. The synecitc process involves : (a) making the strange familiar, and (b) making the familier strange.

In this process, the leader has to play a vital role in forcing members to be away from routine and encourage them to offer solutions after analysing the problem. Methods like role playing, anlaogies, paradoxes are employed to generate creative ideas. William J.J. Gordon, however cautions that:

"Although the mechanisms are simple in concept, their application requires great energy output. Infact, synectics does not in anyway make creative activity easier .... The mere string together of metaphors is non-productive. Synetics participants must keep in the back kof their minds the problems as understood so that they can identify those mechanisms which illuminate the problem."

Synectics differs from brainstorming in several important respects. It is much more adaptable to complex decisional problems. Yet, similar to brainstorming, synectics is very time-consuming and exepensive. Overall, synectics seems to have potentially a great deal to offer and might be able to help making basic or risk-uncertainly decisions that requires creative solutions.

4.3.3. Delphi Technique

Although Delphi was first developed by N.C. Dalkey and his associates in 1950 at the Rand Corporations' Think Tank, it has only recently become popularised as a technique to assist in making risk-uncertainly decisions, e.g., long-range forecasting. Today, numerous organizations in business, education, government, health and the military are using Delphi. Norman Delkey an expert of the

Delphi has said that Delphi technique involves the solicitatio and comparison of anonymous judgements on thc topic of interest through a set of sequential questionnaires interspersed with summarized information and feedback of opinions from earlier responses. No decisions technique will ever be able to predict the future completely but the Delphi technique seems to be as good a crystall ball as is currently available.

The technique, named after the oracle at Delphi in ancient Greece, has many variations, but generally it works as follows :

- A panel of experts on the particular problem in question is drawn from both inside and outside the organization.
- Each expert is maked to make anonymous predictions.
- Each panelist then gets a composite feedback of the way the other experts answered he questions.
- Based upon the feedback, new estimates are made and the process is repeated several times.

A major key to the success of the techniques lies in its anonymity. Keeping the responses of panel members anonymous eliminates the problem of 'saving face' and encourages the panel experts to be more flexible and thus to benefit from the estimates of others. In the traditional interacting group-decisions technique, the experts may be more concerned with defending their vested positions than they are with making a good decision. It has the advantage of being able to involve people with special qualifications who are to-face interactions insulates member from the undue influence of others. As rightly pointed out by Bedian and Glueck, the Delphi technique "reduces committee activity, eliminates the band-wagon effect of majority opinion, minimizes influences of face-to-face pressures, and provides each panel member with the time to deliberate and carefully think out responses."

The major objectives of the Delphi process have been summarized by Delbecq Van Deven, and Gustafson are :

- To determine or develop a range of possible programme alternatives.
- To explore or expose underlying assumptions or information leading to different judgements.

- To seek out information which may generate a consensus on the part of the respondent group.
- To correlate informed judgements on a topic spanning a wide range of disciplines.
- To educate the respondent group as to the diverse and interrelated aspects of the topic.

In other words, Delphi can be applied to a wide variety of programme-planning and decision problems in any type of organization.

The major cirticisms of the Delphi technique are : time consumption, cost and effect, and no scientific approach or support.

4.3.4. Nominal Group Technique (NGT)

The Nominal Group Technique follows a highly structured process and tries to intergrate creative thinking through group interaction in order to solve organisational problems in a useful manner. This provides an interface between consensus and brainstorming. Nominal grouping has been used by social psychologists for a couple of decades. A nominal group is simply a "paper group", because no verbal exchange is allowed between the members. In group dynamics research, social psychologists would pit a fully interacting group agianst a nominal group. In terms of number of ideas, uniqueness of ideas and quality of ideas, research has found nominal groups to be superior ro real groups. The general conclusions is that interacting groups inhibit creativity. This, of course, applies only to idea generation because the interactive effects of group members is known to have a significant effect on other variables.

When the nominal grouping approach is used as a specific technique for decision-making in organizations, it has been labelled NGT by Delbeq and Van de Ven. NGT consists of the following steps :

- Silent development of ideas in wirting.
- Rouud-robin feedback from group members to record each idea in a terse phrase on a flip chart.
- Discussion of each recorded idea for clarification and evaluation.

– Individual voting on priority ideas with the group decision being mathematically derived through rank-ordering or rating.

The difference between this approach and Delphi is that the NGT members are usually acquainted with one another, have face to face contact, and communicate directly with each other. Although, research is just starting to emerge on NGT, there is some evidence that the technique leads to many more ideas than traditional interacting groups and may do as well or slightly better than Delphi groups. NGT is an ideawriting technique.

4.3.5. Heuristic Technique

Similar to Delphi and nominal grouping, the heuristic technique has recently come into its own as a decision-making technique. The classic definition of heuristic was given by Polya as follows :

Heuristic, or heuretic, was the name of certain branch of study, not very clearly circumscribed, belonging to logic, or to philosophy, or to psychology, often outline, seldom presented in detail, and as good as forgotten today. The aim of heuristic is to study the methods and rules of discovery and inventing ... Heuristic, as an adjective, means, "serving to discover."

Heuristic can be considered as a sophisticated technique of controlled trial and error. When applied to decision-making, heuristics, John Hutehinson feels, is a wedding of the systems and behavioural approaches because it considers both major variables and the reactions and feelings of people in the system. "In other words, heuristics allows the decision-maker to consider less-than-rational paths and thus preclude frustration when more more preferable alternatives are somehow available."

The major cause of the recent widespread use of heuristics as a decision making technique is its adaptablity to computer programming. The decision making process is a major function of management. The techniques for decision-making have been dominated mainly by quantative models. New effective techniques applicable to thc more basic decisions have not kept pace with the management science techniques. There are only a few creative techniques (brain-storming and synectics), and participative techniques which are not equal to the sophistication of the quantitative models. Yet, it is the basic, uncertain management decisions which are crucial for organisational success.

Creativity techniques do not replace management judgement in the risky process of decision-making. These techniques do have the potential to improve the process by improving the quality and quantity of inputs to those that must make the final decision. Techniques such as Delphi, nominal grouping and heuristics offer some hope, but much more needs to be done in this important but negelected area of management decision-making.

4.3.6. Protocol Analysis (Think-Aloud Method)

In this case, protocols (scenarios) are collected by asking experts to solve the specific problem and verbalize their decision process by stating directly what they think. knowledge developers do not interrupt in the interim. The elicited information is structured later when the knowledge developer analyzes the protocol. Here the term scenario refers to a detailed and somehow complex sequence of events or more precisely, an episode. A scenario can involve individuals and objects; and it is provides a concrete vision of how some specific human activity can be supported by information technology.

4.3.7. Consensus Decision Making

Consensus decision making usually follows brainstorming. It is effective if and only if each expert has been provided with equal and adequate opportunity to present their views. In order to arrive at a consensus, the knowledge developer conducting the exercise tries to rally the experts towards one or two alternatives. The knowledge developer follows a procedure designed to ensure fairness and standardization. This method is democratic in nature and can be sometimes tedious and can take hours.

4.3.8. Repertory Grid

This is another method used for knowledge capturing. Its procedure consist of following steps :

– The grid is used for capturing and evaluating the expert's model.

- Two experts (in the same problem domain) may produce distinct sets of personal and subjective results.
- The grid is a scale (or a bipolar construct) on which elements can be placed within gradations.
- Here the knowledge developer usually elicits the constructs and then asks the domain expert to provide a set of examples called elements. Each element is rated according to the constructs which have been provided.

4.3.9. Concept Mapping

This is a network of concepts technique consisting of nodes and links. Here : a node represents a concept, and a link represents the relationship between concepts. It is designed to transform new concepts/prospositions into the existing conginitive structures related to knowledge capture. Concept mapping is a structured conceptualization. It is an effective way for a group to function without losing their individuality.

There is a Six-step procedure for using a concept map as a tool:

- Preparation.
- Idea generation.
- Statement structuring.
- Representation.
- Interpretation and
- Utilization.

Concept mapping can be done for several reasons:

- To design complex structures.
- To generate ideas.
- To communicate ideas.
- To diagnose misunderstanding.

4.3.10. Blackboarding

In blackboarding case, the experts work together to solve a specific problem using the blackboard as their workspace. Each expert gets equal opportunity to contribute to the solution via the blackboard. It is assumed that all participants are experts, but they might have acquired their individual expertise in situations different from those of the other experts in the group. The process of blackboarding continues till the solution has been reached.

Characteristics of blackboard system: Its important features are :

- Diverse approaches to problem-solving,
- Common language for interaction,
- Efficient storage of information,
- Flexible representation of information,
- Iterative approach to problem-solving, and
- Organized participation.

Components of blackboard system: Various components are :

- *The Knowledge Source (KS)* : Each KS is an independent expert observing the status of the blackboard and trying to contribute a higher level partial solution based on the knowledge it has and how well such knowledge applies to the current blackboard state.
- *The Blackboard* : It is a global memory structure, a database, or a repository that can store all partial solutions and other necessary data that are presently in various stages of completion.
- *A Control Mechanism* : It coordinates the pattern and flow of the problem solution.

The inference engine and the knowledge base are part of the blackboard system. This approach is useful in case of situations involving multiple expertise, diverse knowledge representations, or situations involving uncertain knowledge representation.

4.4. MODEL OF CONTINGENCIES

The modal has three key contingencies: type of the knowledge being acquired (tacit-stock, explicit-stock, tacit-flow, explicit-flow), strategic importance of the knowledge to be acquired, and distance of the knowledge from the firm's current knowledge base. When making a decision about which tool to use to acquire knowledge outside a firm's boundaries, the manager needs to weigh each of these contingencies. In fact, a decision process based on looking at the strategic importance first, followed by considering the distance from the current knowledge base and finally thinking through the type of knowledge that is being acquired will lead to the appropriate choice. Strategic importance needs to be the first decision point because of the risks of getting it wrong. A firm that attempts to access critically important knowledge through an alliance exposes itself to risks of opportunistic action by its partner. This has been a significant problem for small technology ventures dealing with large established firms. Recent research has questioned the benefit of alliances with large firms for technology ventures. These results maybe due to an overreliance on alliances to access critical strategic knowledge, such as marketing or regulatory know-how, that leaves them open to exploitation by opportunistic partners. This is explained in table 4.1.

Once its strategic importance has been determined, then an accurate assessment of the distance of the knowledge from the firm's current knowledge base must be made. The distance of the knowledge affects the firm's ability to judge its quality and to assimilate it, both of which are critical to success. The more distant the knowledge the greater the learning potential but the higher the probability of failure; these are the conditions under which an options-based strategy using alliances will provide the greatest benefit. Finally, the type of knowledge being acquired will have an impact on the structure of the transaction because of its effect on the level of interaction needed to acquire it.

4.5. KNOWLEDGE CODIFICATION

Once the knowledge is captured, the next step is to find a way to codify and organize knowledge into a form so that others may use when needed. Getting the right knowledge to the right people at the right time is the whole idea behind knowledge codification. It is not a mere transfer of what exists in human brains to another agent, but the creation of a truly new knowledge, implying an active creative, complex and costly activity.

Both codified knowledge and codification processes are not mere stocks resulting from an accumulation of information, independent of its holders or its time or location. Codified knowledge has a recurrent and dynamic structure: knowledge requires to be needed to codify as well as to exploit a given piece

Table 4.1. The Model and Contingencies

	Type of Knowledge				Strategic Importance		Distance from Firm's Current Knowledge Base		
	Stock		Flow						
	Tacit	Explicit	Tacit	Explicit	High	Low	Close	Medium	Far
Characteristics of Knowledge	Difficult to judge and transfer—not amenable to pure market transaction.	Easy to judge and transfer—amenable to market transaction.	Difficult to judge and transfer. Requires continual interaction since new knowledge is continually being developed.	Easy to judge and transfer but requires continual interaction since new knowledge is contiually being developed.	Needs to control knowledge-pressure to internalilze in order to avoid risk of opportunism.	Doesn't need to control knowledge-minimal risk of opportunistic action.	Easy to assimilate. Capable of judging quality of target's knowledge base.	Capable of judging quality. Moderate difficulty in assimlating knowledge.	Difficult to judge quality and difficult to asstimate knowledge.
Acquisition Strategy	Acquistion or strategic alliance	License	Exclusive alliance or acquisition, depending on the strategic importance and the source of the flow	Alliance	Acquisition, exclusive license	License, alliance	License or alliance based on type of knowledge	Alliance or acquistion, depending on the strategic importance	Alliance learning opportunity, option strategy.

of codified knowledge. To be able to learn from a model, firms need to engage in a learning process to interpret the model, combine it with local specificities and then create a specific internal knowledge representation.

Knowledge management systems are slowly succeeding in standardizing terminologies and meanings for the end user. As a matter of procedure after knowledge is captured, it is organized and codified in a manner amenable for transfer and effective use. Knowledge codification is organizing and representing knowledge before it is acceded by authorized personnel. The organizing part is usually in the form of a decision tree, a decision table or a frame. Codification must be in a form and a structure that will build the knowledge base. Codification makes knowledge accessible, explicit and easy to access.

From a knowledge management view, codification is converting tacit knowledge to explicit knowledge in a usable form for organizational members. From an information system view, codification is making corporate-specific knowledge – tacit and explicit visible, accessible, and usable for value-added decision-making, no matter what form it may take.

Tacit knowledge such as human expertise is identified and leveraged through a form that delivers the highest return to the business. It may be through knowledge edge-sharing events, organized directories, yellow pages, or other means, that will connect the ones who need the expertise to the source expertise.

Explicit knowledge should be organized, categorized, indexed, and accessed via the company's intranet or some other means to make it visible, accessible and usable. As conceptualized we cultivate new organizational communities and keep them aligned around the company's intranet. This includes the social, interpersonnel, financial, managerial, legal and marketing systems. Such a "constellation" encompasses that make the linkages among the "islands" viable and bind the constellation together.

4.5.1. Codification : Need and Purposes

Codification seems to affect the speeding-up of knowledge creation, innovation and economic change by improving the reliability of information storage and retrieval. By reducing the costs of knowledge acquisition and diffusion, codification may facilitate the emergence of new forms of innovation in a learning organisation. On the other hand, within firms, if knowledge is highly tacit so the underlying structures are not well understood, learning is limited because that knowledge cannot be as systematically applied.

Consequently, deep understanding and long-lasting effective organisational learning may require mechanisms of codification of knowledge and interaction procedures that permit dispossessing employees of their individual improvement ideas to benefit the organization

Codification may therefore be used as a management strategy to structure information and decision-making. It helps to achieve deep understanding of an issue, or to support processes of knowledge diffusion and accumulation.

Nevertheless, despite the fact that codification may be a tool for the production and accumulation of knowledge, it may not lead to the production of radically new knowledge. Hence, firms are likely to be caught in local peaks, with low probabilities of exploring radically diverse organisational arrangements. However, support for codification has been often prescribed to policy-makers to support the diffusion and accumulation of knowledge.

4.5.2. Application Areas of Codification

In codifying knowledge, the resulting knowledge base serves in several important training and decision making areas. The important areas where knowledge base are applied/used are

- Diagnosis
- Instruction/Training
- Interpretation
- Planning/scheduling
- Prediction
- Diagnosis

A diagnostic knowledge management system is given identifiable information through users observation or experience.

The Knowledge base is built with list of identifiable symptoms of specific casual factors.

1. Instruction/Training : Codified knowledge promotes training of junior or entry level personnel based on captured knowledge of senior employees. Most knowledge management systems have explanatory capabilities and display the reasoning behind their solutions. Some systems allow students to pose hypothetical "What if" scenarios enabling them to learn by exploration.

2. Interpretation : Interpretive codified knowledge systems compare as aspects of an operation to preset standards. Typically they use sensor data to infer the status of an on-going process or to a given situation. Much of the reasoning is coupled with confidence factors.

3. Planning/Scheduling : A planning knowledge management systems maps out an entire course of action before any steps are taken. The system creates detailed lists of sequential tasks necessary to achieve two or more specific goals.

Once a plan is completed, the system refines each step to arrive at the optimum schedule. The system rejects any out of line approach that is not within the prescribed constraints.

4. Prediction : Predictive knowledge management systems infer that likely outcome of a given situation and flash a proper warning or suggestions for corrective action. The system evaluates a set of facts or conditions and compares it by analogy to precedence stage stored in memory. Knowledge base contains several patterns on which predictions are based.

5. Criteria for Codification : The identification of knowledge that has to be codified depends on an entrepreneurial or hierarchical strategic decision. Hence, codification will also strongly structure decision-making patterns and performance assessment.

Therefore, codification processes can be vertical, involving attempts to codify knowledge held by other communities, and perhaps take it over, or they can be horizontal, involving efforts to codify knowledge in a way that can be interpreted and used without any restriction by any type of community.

4.5.3. Knowledge Codification - Tools and Procedures

Before starting codification, an organization must focus on the following:

- What organizational goals will the codified knowledge serve. For example if the intend of the Librarian is to improve the use of traditional documents then the knowledge base containing the pull out statistics of the books should be used
- Different goals for a knowledge management project require different perspective. What knowledge exists in the organization that addresses these goals? It means starting with the survey of various aspects of knowledge presence, availability, transfer, use, and so forth. At this stage there is a need to understand the knowledge and work practices of an organization and use these insights to help transform the organization into what it tends to be. Such knowledge must be identified and put into some usable form before sharing it outside the organization.
- How useful is the existing knowledge for codification.
- How would one codify knowledge? That is what medium or tool would be the most appropriate for codification.

Whether it is a Codification or Personalization? The question arises, because there are the two most dominant approaches to deploying a knowledge management application – Codification and Personalisation. The Codification (or "Product-based") approach consolidates reuseable assets into one or more designated repositories. Sophisticated search engines are then used to generate indices for the stored assets as well as to locate them based on, in most cases, a menu and keywords-based input. This approach favours greater emphasis on the use of technology, especially search engines. The Personalisation (or "Process-based") approach, on the other hand, focuses specifically on the people and cultural issues in the establishment of virtual groups or knowledge communities. Technologies are also used to support the sharing of knowledge in such groups and communities but it is deemed to play a secondary role compared to connecting and locating people of common interest. In a very general sense, the codification approach is more suited to situations where work tasks are similar and existing assets can be adapted within reasonable bounds for reuse. In contrast, the personalisation approach is appropriate for situations where the bulk of the critical knowledge in an organisation is tacit, work tasks are fairly unique, and it is difficult to reuse knowledge assets from task to task without significant modifications. The two approaches are complimentary; it is not unusual for organisations to adopt a combination of the two approaches in deploying knowledge management application(s).

Sometimes, debate arises whether it is codification or personalisation that we need? There is no right or wrong approach—both are required in the right balance. The right balance is determined by company's objectives in pursuing knowledge management. For any knowledge management initiative to be successful, both approaches must be present in the knowledge entation of the firm, but hot with equal weightage. If a company decides to use codification as its primary strategy, it should direct, for example, 80 percent of its efforts toward codification and the remaining 20 percent toward personalization.

Table 4.2. Comparison of Codification and Personalization KM Strategies

Business Strategy Question	**Codification**	**Personalization**
What type of business do you think your company is in?	Providing high-quality, reliable, fast, and cost-effecitve services.	Providing creative,rigorous and highly customized services.
How much old material, such as past project data, existing documents, and archived projects, do you reuse as a part of new projects?	You reuse portions of old documents to create new ones. You use existing products to create new ones. You know that you need not begin from scratch to deliver a new product or service.	Every problem has a high chance of being a "one-off" and unique problem. Although cumulative learning is involved highly creative solutions are often called for.
What is the costing model used for your company's products and services?	Price-based competition.	Expertise-based pricing; high prices are not detrimental to business; price-based competition barely (if at all) exists.

What are your firm's typical profit margins?	Very low profit margins; over all revenues need to be maximized to increase net profits.	Very high profit margins.
How best can you describe the role that IT plays in your company's work process?	IT is a primary enabler; the objective is to connect people distributed across the enterprise with codified knowledge (such as reports, documentation, code etc.) that is in some reusable form.	Storage and retrieval are not the primary applications of IT. IT is considered a great enabler for communication applications such as e-mail and video conferencing age considered the most useful applications;conversations, socialization, and exchange of tacit knowledge are considered to be the primary use of IT.
What is your reward structure like?	Employees are rewarded for using and contributing to databases such as Notes discussion databases.	Employees are rewarded for directly sharing their knowledge with colleagues and for assisting colleagues in other locations/offices with their problems.
How is knowledge exchanged and transferred?	Employees refer to a document or best practices database that stores, distributes, and collects codified knowledge.	Knowledge is transferred person to person; intrafirm networking is encouraged to enable sharing of tacit knowledge, insight, experience and intuition.
Where do your company's economies of scale life?	Economics of scale lie in the effective reuse of existing knowledge and experience and applying them to solve new problems and complete new projects.	Economics rest in the sum total to expertise available within the company;experts in various areas of specializtion are considered indispendable.
What are your typical team structure demographics?	Large teams; most members are junior-level employees; a few project managers lead them.	Junior employees are not an inordinate proportion of a typical team's total membership.

The table illustrates, the personalization strategy is more focused on connecting knowledge workers through networks and is better suited to companies that face one-off and unique problems that depend more on tacit knowledge and expertize than on codified knowledge. The codification strategy is more focussed on technology that enables storage, indexing retrieval and reuse. This strategy is better suited to companies that have do deal with similar problems and decisions over and over. And remember, it is foolish to try using both approaches to the same degree. It is equally unsound to use only one. As one would suspect, the incentives needed to make either one work are very different. Focus on those incentives that help you get the *primary* strategy right.

4.6. KNOWLEDGE MAPS & MAPPING OF KNOWLEDGE

Mapping corporate knowledge is an essential part of the codification process. To do the job, the knowledge developer must identify the type of knowledge — rich versus schematic, tacit versus explicit, rule based or frame — based, and so forth.

The knowledge map is a navigation aid to explicit (codified) information and tacit knowledge, showing the importance and the relationships between knowledge stores and dynamics. The knowledge map, an outcome of synthesis, portrays the sources, flows, constrains and sinks of knowledge within an organization.

A knowledge map, generally consists of two parts: a ground layer that represents the context for the mapping, and the individual elements that are mapped within this context. The ground layer typically consists of the mutual context that all employees can understand and relate to. Such a context might be the visualized business model of a company (e.g., the lending business model of a bank), the actual product (e.g.. a vehicle model in the case of a truck company), the competency areas of a company (as in the example of the multimedia company), the value chain of a firm (as in the example of the market research group), or a simple geographic map. The elements that are mapped onto such a shared context range from experts, projects-teams, or communities of practice to more explicit and codified forms of knowledge such as white papers or articles, patents, lessons learned (e.g., after action reviews or project debriefings), events (i.e., meeting protocols), databases or similar applications, such as expert systems or simulations. Knowledge maps group these elements to show their relationships, locations and qualities.

Here, we refer to knowledge maps as graphic directories of knowledge-sources (i.e., experts), -assets (i.e., core competencies),

-structures (i.e., skill domains), -applications (i.e. specific contexts in which knowledge has to be applied, such as a process), or -development stages (phases of knowledge development or learning paths).We focus on these five types of maps as they answer the questions that come up most frequently in action research.

A different, more abstract set of map categories is used by Huff in her anthology on the topic of mapping strategic thought. Her mapping typology focuses on cognitive maps and distinguishes the following map types: text and language analysis maps, classification maps, network maps, conclusive maps, and schematic maps of cognitive structures.

"A knowledge map is a visual display of captured information and relationships, which enables the efficient communication and learning of know ledge by observers with differing backgrounds at multiple levels of detail. The individual items of knowledge included in such a map can be text, stories, graphics, models, or numbers ... Knowledge mapping is defined as the process of associating items of information or knowledge (preferably visually) in such a way that the mapping itself also creates additional knowledge."

While this definition adequately describes the purpose of knowledge mapping, it does not distinguish the various types of knowledge maps that can be used in a corporate context. Below we provide such a distinction with the aforementioned five types of knowledge maps:

1. Knowledge source maps : These maps structure a population of company experts along relevant search criteria, such as their domains of expertise, proximity (for an example of such a knowledge-map, without hypertext links behind the map), seniority, or regional distribution. Knowledge source maps answer questions such as "where can I find somebody who knows how to calculate a company valuation" or "do we have people who have run large e-commerce projects?"

2. Knowledge asset maps : This type of map visually qualifies the existing stock of knowledge of an individual, a team, a unit, or a whole organization. It provides a simplified, graphic 'balance sheet' of a company's intellectual capital. Knowledge asset maps answer questions such as "how many SAP-consultants do we have, and how many SAP-projects have we completed?" or "how many of our software engineers have been with the company for more than five years?"

3. Knowledge structure maps : These maps outline the global architecture of a knowledge domain and how its parts relate to one another. This type of knowledge map assists the manager in comprehending and interpreting an expert domain. Typical questions that can be answered by such a map are "which are the skills needed to run a project, how do they relate to one another, and what are the available courses for every such skill?"

4. Knowledge application maps : These maps show which type of knowledge has to be applied at a certain process stage or in a specific business situation. Usually, these maps also provide pointers to locate that specific knowledge (documents, specialists, databases). Knowledge application maps answer questions of people who are involved in a knowledge-intensive process, such as auditing, consulting, research or product development. They provide answers to questions such as "who do I talk to if the market tests are inconclusive?" or "what are your experiences in moving from a prototype to mass-production?"

5. Knowledge development maps : These diagrams can be used to depict the necessary stages to develop a certain competence, either individually, as a team, or as an organizational entity. These maps can serve as visualized learning or development roadmaps that provide a common corporate vision for organizational learning. They answer questions such as "how do we achieve business excellence for our unit?" or "how can we prepare our unit for the entry into a new market?" We may also used this type of map to visualize the necessary steps to develop e-commerce competence– from mere web designing skills, to community development skills, to secure electronic contracting skills, to inter-business networking skills.

Besides these five types of maps, one can also imagine maps that combine some of the above types into a single map. Typically, a knowledge application map and a (partial) knowledge source map are combined into a single image. In this way, one can not only show what knowledge is relevant at what project stage, but also how to locate that knowledge.

There are numerous visualization techniques that can be used to design such knowledge maps. They include, but are not limited to, the methods identified in Table 4.4.

Table 4.4. Techniques for the Knowledge Map Context

Simple Mapping Techniques	Complex Mapping Techniques
Mind mapping	Concept maps
Clustering	Cause maps
Matrices or portfolio diagrams	Concentric circles or Venn diagrams
Fishbone graphs	Metaphoric maps (e.g., a house, a balance, a compass or a park)
Cartesian and polar co-ordinate systems	Process charts or flow charts
Pyramids	Spider web graphs
Hierarchic trees	Decision trees
Geographic maps	3D-environments (e.g., globes, landscapes)

The choice of one of these techniques depends upon two factors. First, there are requirements of the conceptual framework that provides the base layer for the knowledge map. Flow charts are feasible techniques for knowledge application maps, while concept maps are more apt for knowledge structure maps. Second, there are the technological infrastructure and software available to implement a clickable map. There are numerous software packages that support hypertext mind-maps, concept maps, or interactive flow charts, yet very few products available that support more complex forms of knowledge maps such as metaphoric maps or 3D-environments.

The following section examines a number of examples of how these visualization techniques can be used to design knowledge maps of the five mentioned types.

4.6.1. Intranet Knowledge Map Examples

The following series of knowledge maps is a result of imaginary action research with six partner companies over the course of three years (1998-2001). All examples represent manually generated and designed maps, though they can also generated automatically.

1. Knowledge Source Map : In principle, a knowledge map can be implemented on any technological platform that allows us to combine visualization engines with hypertext capability (i.e., linking sensitive, visual zones to other data points) and database technology. Nevertheless, we have found the intranet to be the most accessible medium to host knowledge map applications. This is especially true because many intranet users are familiar with clickable maps or touch-sensitive visual zones from the Internet. Hence, the user-acceptance of a knowledge map in a browser interface is likely to be higher than in a proprietary application. The first example of an intranet-based knowledge map is taken from a multimedia company that mainly works in the development of web-sites, CD-ROMs, and stand-alone multimedia terminals. One of the company's problems is the adequate staffing of such projects with the right experts.

Thus, a knowledge map was designed to help project leaders and human resources professionals to assess the current state of experts available within the company at its three main locations New York, Berlin and Basel.

The map divides the company's competence into five areas, namely graphic design, animation (*i.e*., Shockwave programming), database design, project management, and technology know-how (*i.e.* server administration). The people within the company apply these skills to the aforementioned three areas of CD-ROM production, stand-alone systems and Web site development (the concentric circles in Fig. 4.1).

The partial view of the actual map reveals that the most expertise resides in the company's headquarter in Kolkata (colour-coded accordingly), especially for the domain of web-site development. It also reveals that there are very few project management or animation specialists within the company. The map reflects the shift in activities away from CD-ROM production to Web development where most experts in the map apply their skills.

The technology behind this map is quite simple and consists of three elements: the actual knowledge map which is drawn in Microsoft Vision and linked to an Access database that holds the expert profiles (expert area, application area, location, phone number, etc.) and a CGI-script that provides a browser interface for the map. The experts update their profiles via a form that they can access through their browser. This form is directly linked to the Access database, which in turn is referenced in the Visio chart.

While this particular map is still in the testing phase, an identical application with the same architecture and map design has already been used for several months in a semiconductor company where it is also used to map specialized communities of practice.

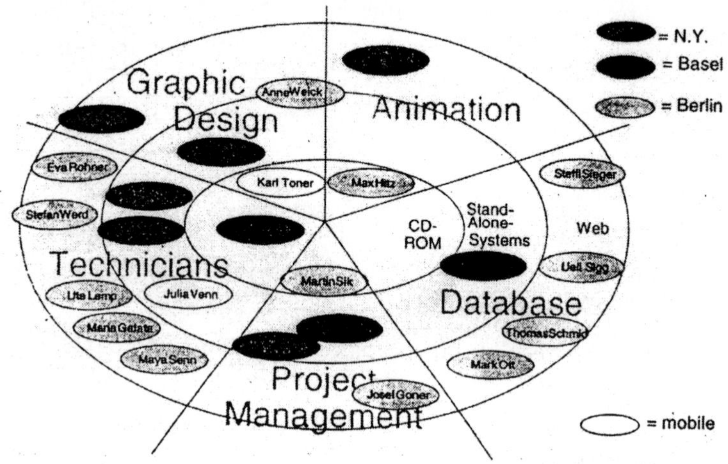

Fig. 4.1. A Knowledge Source Map for a Multimedia Company

2. Knowledge Asset Map : Knowledge asset maps provide a visual balance sheet of a company's capabilities. These capabilities can be represented in the form of a core competency tree or as a visual directory of individual or aggregated skills of the work force. Based on such a map, a company can outline its capability profile bottom-up instead of top-down, as in a core competence tree. The following simple map provides an overview of a consulting team in terms of the competencies of its members. Large blocks represent expert knowledge on the particular topic, small blocks refer to basic knowledge in a particular domain. The domains in which these consultants work are IT – information technology, strategy, mergers and acquisitions (M&A), accounting and marketing.

The knowledge asset map in Figure 4.2 illustrates various properties of the know-how constellation of the consulting staff. The map reveals, for example, that S.K. Singh is a central asset for the company in terms of his skills. He has substantial experience in all five sectors of the consulting activities. The map also reveals that there is a general lack of specialized knowledge in the domain of mergers and acquisitions. Thus, it might be advantageous to drop this consulting service in the future. The map furthermore reveals training and personnel development needs. It shows clearly that P.Gautam has not yet been able to gather an expert status in any of the five domains. The future staffing decisions need to take this fact into account.

Consultants	IT	Strategy	M&A	Accounting	Marketing
Sharma, A	▬	▬	▬		
Arya, C		▬			▬
Gautam, P	▬			▬	
Pal, B					▬
Singh, SK	▬	▬	▬	▬	▬
Negi, PS	▬	▬			▬
....				▬	▬

Fig. 4.2. A Knowledge Asset Map of a Consulting Company

Such a knowledge asset map can be valuable to plan the allocation of staff members or their training needs or assess the overall situation of a company's intellectual assets. By clicking on a name, further information on the consultant is provided such as e-mail, location, special interests, etc. By clicking on a block, the map reveals the projects and courses that the consultant has completed in the particular field.

3. Knowledge Structure Map : As mentioned earlier,

knowledge structure maps divide a skill domain into logical blocks. The map in Fig. 4.3 shows that a Web publisher requires three levels of know-how. First, basic editing knowledge is needed, which consists of layout and sequencing skills, as well as the content selection for an Internet site, plus an adequate vocabulary and writing style for its communication. Secondly, the publisher or editor requires knowledge on how to design the interactive environment for the cages he or she generated. Lastly, the Web site designer needs to know the relevant HTML or Java codes, a Web programming languages to make the site look attractive and implement adequate security measures.

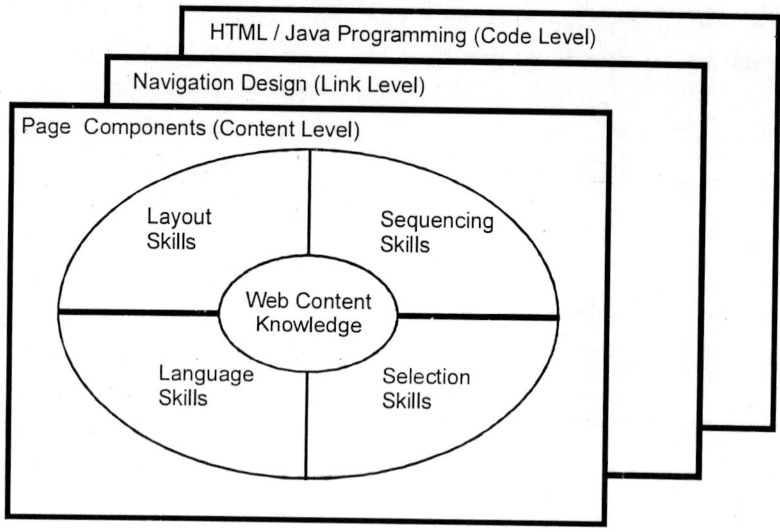

Fig. 4.3. A Knowledge Structure Map for the Internet Authoring Context

Other examples of knowledge structure maps can be found in product development where the various engineering, marketing, and management capabilities are mapped around a product or process and; project management where the various skills that are required to manage a project are mapped in a framework that shows which skills serve what purpose in the course of a project; or financial engineering where the inter-relationship of insurance skills and banking skills are mapped out.

4. Knowledge Application Map : The knowledge application map is probably the most frequently used knowledge mapping format today. It outlines which knowledge is required at a certain process step, e.g., in the value chain of a company. In the example below, the value chain of market research company is divided into four processes: acquiring or generating data, transforming it into information by analyzing it, administrating and archiving this information and transforming it into knowledge by educating its clients about its findings.

In every process step, various IT-based tools and conceptual methods can be applied. If an employee is interested in one of these instruments, he can simply click at the name of a tool or method and a short description of the tool, its application context, functioning and contact person as well as a rating of the tool or method by the corresponding specialist will appear on the screen. Fig. 4.4 shows the actual map (with the exception of the terms translated into English) that may currently be installed in the knowledge portal of the company's intranet. Underlined methods or tools are also sold as products to clients. Every term in the map is linked to an explication- and reference-page for the corresponding tool. This page consists of three columns. The first column outlines the tools title, the second column describes its application context, functioning, experts and their rating of the tool, the third column provides links to related tools or to relevant Internet sites.

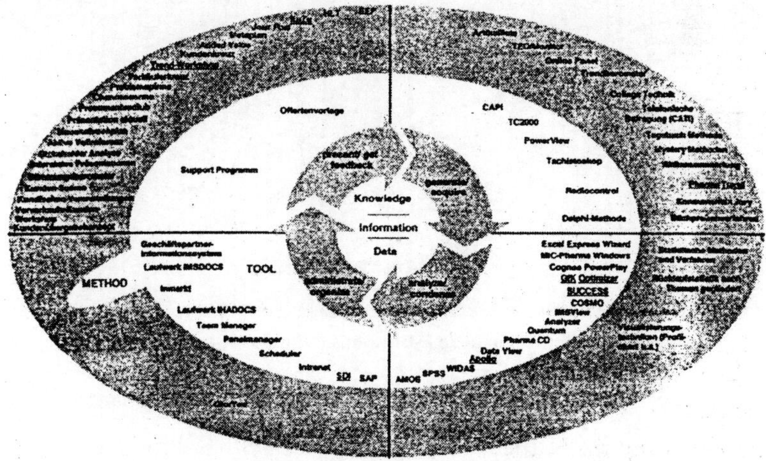

Fig. 4.4. A Knowledge Application Map of a Market Research Company

5. Knowledge Development Map : The last type of knowledge map can be used to visualize the necessary steps to develop a certain type of competence. The relevant knowledge is mapped at various sequential levels. By clicking on a certain level of knowledge, the map reveals further details and describes the necessary activities to acquire or develop that competence. The example shown in Fig. 4.5 is taken from an e-business context.

The map can be used to illustrate the necessary steps to develop competence in e-commerce passing through various stages from a mere web-presence that only provides on-line information, to more complex sites that offer community functionalities (e.g., forums, mailing lists, polls, etc.) or full scale e-business sites that include payment services. The map in its current form is not yet hypertext-based. Hence, the mapped steps cannot be "zoomed in" on the corporate intranet.

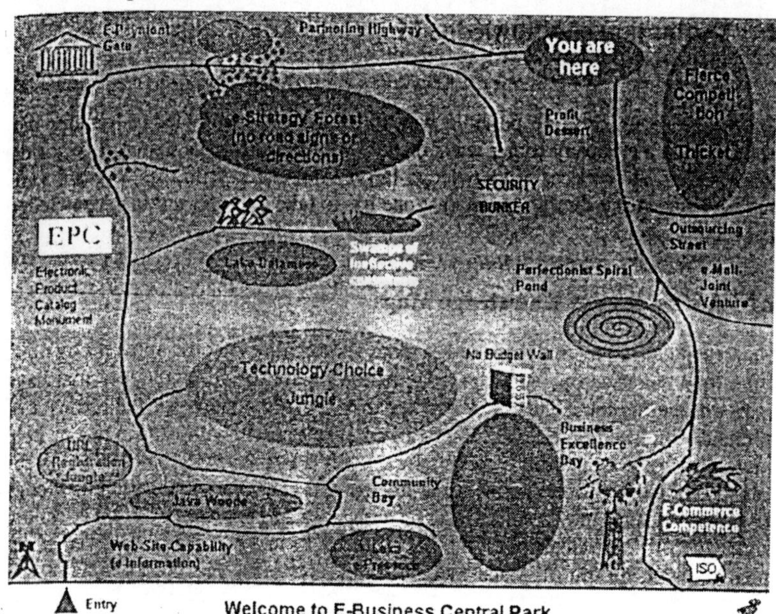

Fig. 4.5. A Knowledge Development Map for E-Business Competence

In summary, these examples illustrate that knowledge maps can serve the following five purposes:

– They increase the visibility of knowledge sources and hence facilitate and accelerate the process of locating relevant expertize or experience.

- They improve the evaluation of intellectual assets and liabilities in a corporation.
- They assist employees in interpreting and evaluating knowledge domains.
- They connect processes with knowledge sources and thus go beyond the mere documentation of a process as found in most quality manuals.
- They sketch the necessary steps for knowledge development in a certain area.

Having outlined the various functions of knowledge maps, we will now examine their possible disadvantages and advantages in more detail.

4.6.2. Evaluation of Knowledge Mapping: Advantages and Disadvantages

Knowledge maps are one possible way to improve the knowledge transfer and utilization in a company or an organization. Associated with this way are various advantages and disadvantages that one has to take into account in a knowledge mapping project.

1. Advantages of Knowledge Maps : The general advantages of knowledge maps should have become apparent by now. First, they render corporate knowledge assets visible for all employees that have access to the Intranet. Thus, they provide a systematic context for the retrieval of reference information. Second, they can connect experts with each other or help novices or rookies identify experts quickly. As a consequence, knowledge maps can speed up the information seeking process and facilitate systematic knowledge development since they connect insights with tasks and problems. Another central advantage of knowledge maps is their potential to make implicit knowledge explicit through the use of visual metaphors and symbols. From marketing point of view, knowledge maps can be used to emphasize and sell the competencies of a company to external groups e.g., potential clients, potential employees, shareholders, analysts etc.

One can say that knowledge maps can help employees and

clients remember, comprehend and relate knowledge domains through the insightful visualization and aggregation of information about the company's experiences, skills, or intellectual resources in general. To clarify this advantage, which is a direct result of the visualization techniques used in knowledge mapping, we can rely on the following explanation by hypertext cartography expert Michael P. Peterson :

"Firstly, a diagram offers a synoptic, global representation of structure or a process and this contributes to the globality and the immediacy of understanding. Secondly, a diagram is an ideal tool for bridging between a conceptual interpretation and the practical expression of a certain reality. A diagram is a synthesis between these two apparently opposed types of representations - the symbolic and the iconic. Diagrams are not, generally, the direct image of a certain reality. It is the figural expression of an already elaborated conceptual structure, like any other symbolic system."

Although a knowledge map uses these two features of a diagram global understanding and conceptual representation of reality — it is more than just a diagrammatic representation. A knowledge map is more than a simple diagram because it offers more dimensions and richer semantics than a diagram. Specifically it offers more elements that are relevant to solve a problem than a diagram, such as time, location, quality levels, relationships, and time aspects. Unlike a diagram, it is not inert and finished but interactive and expandable.

In addition knowledge maps make extensive use of metaphors – such as mountains, layers, routes, or buildings. Finally, a map also shows pathways and options and can relate to other maps e.g., via embedded hypertext links.

A knowledge map is therefore more similar to a geographic map than a diagram. It answers the same basic four questions that a geographic map seeks to answer, namely:

— Where am I, what is my context (environment)?
— Where can I go, what are my options?
— How do I get there quickly, and in the most direct way possible?

— What does it take to get there; what are the required resources?

In consequence, a knowledge map provides systematic orientation in the intellectual territory of a company and helps to find directions, assess situations, or plan resources.

2. Disadvantages of Knowledge Maps : As with geographic maps, which still many people find difficult to comprehend or use, knowledge maps also have certain disadvantages. The disadvantages associated with this method of conveying knowledge are summarized in Table 4.5. It shows that there are several potential drawbacks from knowledge maps for map users and for map designers. The dangers of using a knowledge map may result from the direct legitimate use of a low-quality map, such as misinterpreting it or using an outdated or overloaded map. They may also result from an illegitimate use of the map by headhunters, competitors or competitive intelligence professionals who abuse the map for purposes that were not intended by management. The drawbacks for map designers are mainly the costs of creation, design and maintenance.

These numerous potential disadvantages have to be weighed against the benefits that result from establishing a knowledge map.

Table 4.5. Disadvantages of Knowledge Map

Disadvantages for Map Users	Disadvantages for Map Designers
• The potential harmful effects if the map is seen by illegitimate users (such as map head hunters or competitors)	• The commitment to one other persp-ectives
• The danger of misinterpretation	• The difficult depiction of dynamic processes
• The fixation or 'refication' of one frame of reference (i.e., the layout of the kno-wledge map)	• The relatively high costs for produc-tion and updating
• The danger of information overload if the map represents too many elements or dimensions of a knowledge area	• The missing quantification of inter-dependencies
• The danger of using an outdated map	• The difficult and time-consuming task of ergonomic visualization

Inspite of disadvantages, Knowledge Maps provide a visual orientation for managers or specialists who wish to locate, evaluate or develop knowledge in an organizational context. They condense information about knowledge sources, assets, structures, applications, or development needs in an accessible way.

4.7. KNOWLEDGE MAPPING

What exactly is Knowledge Mapping? It is an ongoing quest within an organization including its supply and customer chain. It is :

- to help to discover the location, ownership, value and use of knowledge artifacts,
- to learn the roles and expertise of people,
- to identify constraints to the flow of knowledge, and
- to highlight opportunities to leverage existing knowledge.

Knowledge mapping is a important practice consisting of survey, audit and synthesis, it aims to track the acquisition and loss of information and knowledge. It explores personal and group competencies and proficiencies. It illustrates or "maps" how knowledge flows throughout an organization. Knowledge mapping helps an organization to appreciate how the loss of staff influences intellectual capital, to assist with the selection of teams, andio match technology to knowledge needs and processes.

What are the key principles of knowledge mapping?

- Understand that knowledge is transient.
- Explain the sanction, establish boundaries, and respect personal disclosures.
- Recognize and locate knowledge in a wide variety of forms: tacit and explicit, formal and informal, codified and personalized, internal and external, short life cycle and permanent.
- Locate knowledge in processes, relationships, policies, people, documents, conversations, links and context, suppliers, competitors and customers.
- Be aware of organizational level and aggregation, cultural issues and reward systems, timeliness, sharing and value,

legal process and protection (patents, trade secrets, trade marks, NDAs).

4.7.1. Need for Mapping Knowledge

What is the need for mapping the knowledge in an organization? Knowledge mapping is practiced in an organization to :

- Encourage re-use and prevent re-invention, saving search time and acquisition costs,
- Highlight islands of expertise and suggest ways to build bridges to increase knowledge sharing,
- Discover effective and emergent communities of practice where learning is happening,
- Provide a baseline for measuring progress with KM projects
- Reduce the burden on experts by helping staff to find critical information quickly. Improve customer response, decision making and problem solving by providing access to applicable information,
- Highlight opportunities for learning and leverage of knowledge,
- Provide an inventory and evaluation of intellectual and intangible assets, and
- Research for designing a knowledge architecture or a corporate memory.

4.7.2. Tools necessary for Knowledge Mapping

Following tools are needed to mapping the knowledge :

- Location, ownership, validity, timeliness, domain, sensitivity, access rights, storage medium, use statistics, medium and channels used,
- Documents, files, systems, policies, directories, competencies, relationships, authorities,
- Boundary objects, knowledge artifacts, stories, heuristics, patterns, events, practices, activities,
- Explicit and tacit knowledge which is closely linked to strategic drivers, core competencies and market intelligence. For good knowledge mapping process the essential sources

are Newsfeeds, contact addresses, network transactions, helpdesks, patent registers, asset and HR databases, warrantee claims, LAN directory structures, library, record archives, process descriptions, push profiles, meta-data directory.

4.7.3. How to collect the information for knowledge mapping?

The collection of information for knowledge mapping include –

- Conduct interviews and ask targeted questions,
- Observe the work in progress,
- Track the boundary objects,
- Obtain the network traffic logs,
- Explore the common and individual file structures,
- Gather policy documents, organizational charts, process documentation,
- Concentrate on formal an informal gatherings, communication and activities,
- Move across multiple levels (individual, group, department, organization), and
- Gather from internal-external sources.

4.7.4. What is to be done with all this information?

Following is to be done after collection of information :

- Compile yellow pages and register of boundary objects and templates,
- Record promising heuristics and best practices,
- Construct a proto ontology,
- Explore re-use opportunities,
- Look for learning points, natural knowledge stewards, gatekeepers, isolated islands, and narrow communication channels,
- Map, flows, sequences, and dependencies,
- Check for network patterns, critical nodes, high traffic, and highly valuable information,
- Write your report providing feedback on the objectives and supporting data in the appendices (interview transcripts,

boundary object register, file structure, concept maps, ontology, knowledge maps), and

- Consider your next move.

Knowledge mapping is often conducted in phases: overview to uncover opportunities, details to drill down to specifics or to cover different department, locations of functional groups.

4.7.5. Knowledge Mapping as a Business Strategy

Various benefits of knowledge mapping as a business strategy may include :

- Knowledge mapping can be offered as training, as an information seminar, as an introductory 'free' service. It is a useful way to get a 'foot in the door'.
- Knowledge mapping helps you to understand the client's needs, gaps, opportunities and competitive leverage at a very fundamental level.
- After completion, you can offer a follow-up survey to chart progress, send the client information on new tools or offer a benchmarking report.
- Knowledge mapping is associated with a major trickle down effect. There are opportunities for further services in architectural and specialized KM practices, implementation and culture change, i.e.,
    - Helpdesk and customer service
    - Data and text mining with data marts, OLAP and other backups\ Intranets
    - Conversation servers
    - GroupWare and workflow
    - Virtual communities, psychographics and e-commerce
    - Corporate intelligence, push and scanning applications
    - Setting up an integrated knowledge architecture (messaging, repository documents, discussion, publishing)
    - Dedicated KM tools, search engines, text and data visualization—Training in systems thinking, creative thinking, on-line facilitation

- Technical documentation to clean and abstract critical documents and presentations

In addition, specialized knowledge engineering services may include corporate memory, heuristics, expert systems, ontology development, concept extraction, knowledge structuring, patterns, communities of practice, customer capital, and IC management.

4.8. DECISION MAKING

Decision-making is "the art of action". Shull and his associates define the decision-making process as ".... a conscious and human process, involving both individual and social phenomena, based upon factual and value premises, which includes a choice of one behavioural activity from among one or more alternatives with the intention of moving toward some desired state of affairs." According to Ishwar Dayal, "Decision is the commitment of the decision-maker to act, thereby committing the personnel, material and financial resources of the organization towards the action objectives." Emory and Niland view a decision as only one step in an intellectual process of differentiating among relevant alternatives. It is ".... the point of selection and commitment .... The decision-maker chooses the preferred purpose the most reasonable task statement or the best course of action." According to Hodge and Johnson, "Decision-making is to solve any obstacle (problem) that stands between decision-maker and the accomplishment of the organization." According to Donald J. Clough : "The decision-making process involves a problem to be solved, a number of conflicting objective to be reconciled, a number of possible alternative courses of action from which the 'best' has to be chosen and some way of measuring the value or pay off of alternative courses of action."

To Felix M. Lopez: "A decision represents a judgement; a final resolution of conflict of needs, means or goals and a committement to action made in the face of uncertainty, complexity and even irrationality." It is only one of the ways in which executives can influences the efficient and effective accomplishment of goals.

W. Brooke Groves, has defined "Decision-making is the

selection from two or more reasonable possibilities of a course that will, at the time and under circumstances, provide the most suitable solution of the problem at hand."

Newmann has indicated distinct stages which can help the Chief Executive in this process.

- *Saturation* : to be familiar with the problem.
- *Deliberation* : to consider alternate solutions and to rearrange them.
- *Incubation* : to let the subconscious mind work on the problem.
- *Illustration* : to get the new ideas and sensing that it may work.
- *Accomodation* : to work out the new ideas so that it is a practical solution to the problem.

Hicks gives the following types of creativity in sound decision-making :

- *Innovative* : Creativity to think totally new ideas.
- *Synthesis* : Creativity to absorb, combine and use ideas from different sources and making it new.
- *Extension* : Creativity to use old or new ideas.
- *Duplication* : Creativity to use the other's successful ideas.

Decisions have been classified differently by different writers, Simon has classified decisions into programmed and non-programmed decisions. According to Simon, "decisions are programmed to the extent that they are repetitive and rontine to the extent that a definite procedure has been worked out for handling them. ... If a particular problem recurs often enough, a routine procedure will usually be worked out for solving it. ... Decisions are non-programmed to the extent that they are novel, unstructured, and consequential. There is no cut and dried method for handling the problem because it has not arisen before or because its prece nature and structure are elusive or complex, or because it is so important that it deserves a custom-tailored treatment.

Drucker classified them into generic and unique decisions. Generic and unique resemble programmed and non-programmed decisions respectively.

Delbecq classifies decision into routine decisions, creative decisions and negotiated decisions.

Gore also classified decisions into routine, adaptive and innovative decisions. In Gore's words, "Routine decisions activate, channel, and terminate hundreds of units of behaviour in such a way that broad goals are implemented through the same activities that meet immediate objects. Since both the conditions under which the goals can be realized and the goals themselves are constantly changing, routinized activities must continually be adopted to, maintain a satisfactory rate of goal achievement. But, since on a broader field, the objects embodied in goals are changed from time to time, the innovative decision exists. The essential rhythm of organizational adjustment is from routine to adaptive to routine; or from routine to adaptive to innovative and back to adaptive and eventually to routine again."

Chester Barnard classifies them into Personal and Organizational decisions. *Personal decisions* cannot ordinarily be delegated to other, whereas *organisational decisions* can often if not always be delegated.

Some have classified decisions as "Policy and Operating Decisions". *Policy decisions* are those which are taken by top management influencing the entire functioning of the organisation while *operating decisions* are those which are taken by the middle management for the purpose of executing policy decisions. There are others who have classified decision as "individual and Group decision". Group decisions are generally preferred as it permits representation of defined interest groups, encourage a feeling of co-operation among those participating in decision-making and leads to a more creative decision as all participants participate effectively. On the other hand, the opponents of group decision-making mention that such decision-making impairs individual initiative, entails high cost and time and induces in managers the habit of shrinking responsibility.

4.8.1. Essentials of Decision-Making

These essentialities are :

1. Need of Capabilities in the Top Executive to take Worthwhile Decisions : The techniques of decision-making are important but more important is the skill and commitment on the part of the top executives. To be successful in developing decision-making skills, decision-makers must go beyond a willingness to accommodate to change; they must want to create change and to control situation surrounding them because they have identified worthwhile things to do and they want to do these things. Men can not develop decision-making skills unless they are action-oriented and want to do worthwhile things.

Louis A. Allen in his book, "Management and Organization", has rightly said that a person is born with the talent for personal leadership but must learn management leadership. There is a need to equip the top executives in the art and science of top management rather than dealing merely with the operative management. Ralph Currier Davis in his book, "The Fundamentals of Top Management", has made a fine distinction between the two. He writes, "Administrative management is chiefly group management. Operative management is chiefly project management. The former is concerned largely with long time projections of the activities of Organizational groups. Operative management is concerned largely with the short time actions in the execution of specific projects." Operative management is like a business mechanic who has learnt his executive trade chiefly in the school of "hard knocks" by the process of trial and error. Administrative management is like a professional executive who is trained in the art and science of management, decision-making and also equipped intermittently, who can adjust the management to maintain internal and external equilibrium and keep the organizational state and efficient.

2. Need of Using Multi-disciplinary Approach : Decision-making is a complex process and is influenced by a number of disciplines —Social Sciences, Physical Sciences, Pure Sciences, Mathematics and Applied Sciences. We can represent the inter-disciplinary frame-work of decision-making with the help of the diagram 4.6 given on the next page.

3. Knowledge of Environment : The decisions affect and are affected by political, economic, social and cultural factors prevailing in the environment. Therefore, decision-making must be suited to the environment. The same decision may not be correct under two different sets of circumstances. "A continuing situation of necessary interaction between an organization and its environment introduces an element of environmental control in the organization."

4. Familarity with the Aspirations of the Clients : Decisions are the means and not the ends. Decisions affect the lives of the people directly or indirectly. Therefore, it is useful to consult the people interested in the decision such as interest groups.

5. Personnel and Organisational Requirements : In a complex organization, there must be genuine goodwill between the superiors and the subordinates. This requires leadership equipped with technical knowledge. Leadership must be innovative. We can sum up in the words of Simon who suggests that the process

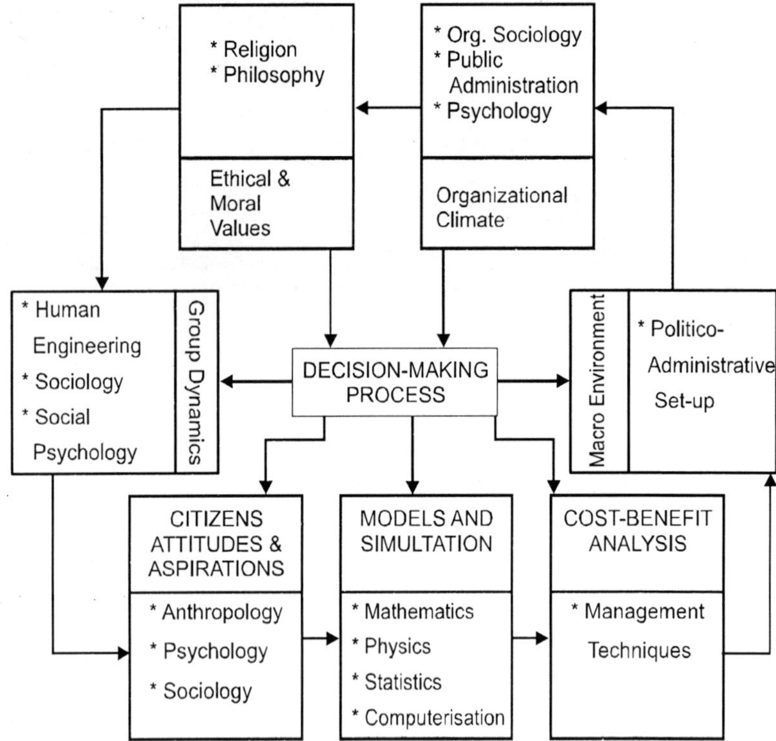

Fig. 4.6. Inter-disciplinary Frame-work of Decision-making

of decision-making includes three identifiable and essential phases. "The first phase of decision-making processes — searching the environment for conditions calling for decision — I shall call intelligence activity (borrowing the military meaning of intelligence). The second phase — inventing, developing and analysing possible courses of action—I shall call design activity. The third phase selection — a particular course of action from those available — I shall call, choice activity."

6. Data Base (Management Information System) : Social, political and economic data are indispensable for decision-making. Information is the most important and crucial ingrediant of the decision-making process. It is now well recognized that the decisions that an executive makes today and the efficiency with which he discharges his functions and responsibilities, depend to a large extent on the quality of information which he is able to obtain, and the manner in which he uses this information. Decision-making in today's complex situation and environment requires scientific basis. With large number of variables, some of them uncontrollable; more and more quantitative information is required to enable the executives to take rational decisions. It is now less of imagination and personnel judgement and more of quantitative analysis which is needed for providing the executives with the different alternative courses of action, clearly bringing out the implications of the following of each course of action, so that the executive may be able to take their decisions after considering all relevant aspects. In order to take right decisions they must get certain information — nothing more or nothing less — in the right form and the right time. The aim of administration is to develop an intellectual climate in which the non-rational elements are reduced to a minimum, therefore, administrative organization as such, becomes less important as a determining factor in decisions and finally in which the logic of the situation narrows the possible choice to one right answer.

7. Knowledge of Management Techniques : There are many management techniques available which can help the executive in taking quick and accurate decisions. The executive must learn these techniques so that the decisions made by them are sound. These techniques wherever applied, have proved useful in good decision-making.

4.8.2. Approaches to Decision-Making

Broadly speaking, there are three widely held approaches towards the process of decision-making :

- Rationalist Approach.
- Humanistic Approach.
- Integrative Approach.

1. Rationalist Approach : This classical approach presupposes that a number of alternatives are available based on mathematical anlaysis and logic. The approach considers reason as a superior source of knowledge and expands the ability of the manager to avoid usought and undesired consequences.

A variant of this theory is the approach of March and Simon in viewing the organization seeking a satisfying solution rather than an optimum one. According to this view, "The central concern of Administrative theory is with the boundary between the rational and the non-rational aspect of human social behaviour. Administrative theory is peculiarly the theory of intended and bounded rationality of the behaviour of human beings who satisfy because they have not the wits to maximize."

The Rationalist approach is recommended by Dror also. He mentioned its five limitations as :

- Too strong dependence on quantifications.
- Impossible to deal with conflicting values.
- Precise criteria indispensable.
- Special characteristics of the political resources.
- Inability to deal with large and complex system.

2. Humanistic Approach : The humanistic process is discussed by Chester Barnard in his book. "Functions of the Executives". He states that the ultimate decision may not be the result of logical processes, but may be determined by an approach developed within a frame-work of social and environmental conditions, past and present. Perceptions and past experience highly influence the decision-making in this approach. The basic elements of the humanistic solution to a problem are :

– The social setting or environment of the decision-making.
– The nature of the decision-making.
– The goals of the decision.
– The social impact of the decision.

3. Integrative Approach : An integrative decision process combines both the rational and humanistic, the economic and social, authoritarian and the autonomous in such a way that all members of the work group feel better. This approach is most successful when decisions are made by those who do the work at the scene of the action rather than by those occupying executive offices, a long way from the firing line – rational, ethical, economic and social considerations must be considered concurrently during the decision-making.

The ultimate purpose of decision-making is to ensure rational, feasible, acceptable and practical decisions. According to Mr. L. Mehl, there are three zones of decisions.

(*a*) *Calculable Zone :* In this zone, the processing of elements is done in a reasonable and precise manner, i.e., in the logic deductive sense. In this zone, large number of technocrats work and their results are often realiable and somewhat quick.

(*b*) *Uncertain Zone :* It suggests a state where the information available is always in an incomplete form. This is a zone mostly dominated by the generalist administrators.

(*c*) *Axiologic Zones :* It is the area of ultimate reality where the decision is taken and made public.

Most of the decisions involve risk, adventure and uncertainties. Therefore, to improve decision-making we must reduce the uncertain zone as far as possible. It is not possible to eliminate the uncertain zone altogether in a democratic form of government. Therefore, the only possiblity is that the calculable zone could be extended to reduce the uncertain zone. In special sciences, value hazards are inherent and no decision-maker can be completely free from the elements of risks and uncertainties but we should see that the rationality component of the decision should be maximized and all efforts should be directed to eliminate value judgements which may enter due to incomplete knowledge and information. This is explained in diagram 4.7 given below.

(c) Axiologic zone	(b) Uncertain zone		(a) Calculable zone
CHOICE	Conflict Choice versus Reason		Reason
(c) Axiologic zone	(b) Reduced Uncertain Zone		(c) Calculable zone
		↑	
		↑	Extended Calculable Zone

Fig. 4.7. Zones of Integrative Approach

4.9. GROUP DECISION

Group decision-making is a must in complex situations dealing with multiple aspects and to deal with such situations, we generally appoint committees, study teams, task forces, review panels, expert committees, etc. Group decision-making is significantly influenced by the climate and culture of oragnizations and the actions profile of its members. Democratization and dispersal of power are the basic ethos for effective group decision-making in an organisation which is predominantly characterised by an authocratic decision-making style."

4.9.1. Advantages of Group Decision-Making

Various advantages or merits of group decision-making may be summarized as below.

1. Establishing Realistic Objectives : Groups possess greater cumulatives knowledge and facts as the members represent different specializations and thus each can contribute from his angle and help in sharpening the decision to be made. The individual may take the decision in a hurry while all the pros and cons are thoroughly examined by the members of the group.

2. Developing Alternatives : Since a group consists of many members, therefore, there is a possibility of many alternatives before a decision is finalized. An individual may be based in favour of one-sided approach while the group examines all the available alternatives before finalizing the decision.

3. Participation and Support from Members : Since the decision is taken with the help of members, therefore, they support it during implementation. They are ready to owe any responsiblity for any lapse, etc. They are more satisfied with the decision and are more likely to support it.

4. Group Cohesion : Members of a group while deciding collectively develop certain common attitudes, beliefs and emotions. These feelings and beliefs, over a period of time, get strengthened and develop group norms.

4.9.2. Disadvantages of Group Decision-Making.

There are some disadvantages also the — group decision is slow process and it needs some compromise also.

Table 4.6 mentions the advantages and disadvantages of group decision-making in a nice way.

Table 4.6. Advantages and Disadvantages of Group Decision-Making

Advantages	Disadvantages
1. A group has more information drawn from diverse fields, can provide more information and knowledge about the problem.	Groups are notorious time-wasters. They may waste a lot of time and energy, clowning arround and getting organized.
2. A group can generate a greater number of alternatives. It can bring to bear a wider experience, a greater variety of opinions and more thorough probing of facts than a single.	Group create pressures toward con-firmity, other infirmities, like group think, force members to compromi-se on the least common denominat-or.
3. Participation in group decisions incre-ases acceptance and commitment on the part of people who now see the	Presence of some group members, who are powerful and influentialy may intimidate and prevent other

	solution as their own and acquire a psychological stake in its success.	members from participating freely. Domination is counter-productive; it puts a damper on the groups best problem-solvers.
4.	People understand the decision better because they saw and heard it develop; thus paying the way for smooth implementation of the decision.	It may be very costly to secure participation from several individuals in the decision-making process.
5.	Interaction between individuals with varied view-points lead to greater creativity.	The group consists of several individuals and hence, it is easy to pass the buck and avoid responsibility.
6.	Groups may also be able to capitalize on individual talents, allowing individuals to work on problems at which they are most adept specialization of labour.	Finally disagreement over arriving at a decision may lead to conflict, resentment and ill-feelings between group members.
7.	Groups can accumulate more knowledge and facts.	Groups often work more slowly than individuals.
8.	Groups have a broader perspective and consider more alternative solutions.	Group decision involves considerable compromise which may lead to less than optimal decisions.
9.	Individuals who participate in decisions are more satisfied with the decision and are more likely to support it.	Groups are often dominated by one individual or a small clique, thereby negating many of the virtues of group procedures.
10.	Group decision processes serve an important comunication function as well as a useful political function.	Over-reliance on group decision-making can inhibit management's ability to act quickly and decisively when necessary.

Once the decisions have been made, they are put to decision tables or decision tree for knowledge codification.

4.10. DECISION TREES

It is also a knowledge codification technique. A decision tree is usually a hierarchically arranged semantic network. It is a flow chart-like tree structure where each internal node denotes a test on an attribute, each branch represents an outcome of the test, and leaf nodes represent classes or class distribution. The top most node in the tree is called root node. Decision trees can be better explained through following example. Let us assume the following discount policy of a publisher.

Bookstores get a trade discount of 25% for orders from libraries and individuals. 5% allowed on orders of 6-19 copies per book title: 10% on orders for 20-49 copies per book title; 15% on orders for 50 copies or more per book title.

A policy statement like this can be time-consuming to describe and confusing to implement. The anlayst needs to use tools to portary the logic of the policy. The first such tool is the decision tree.

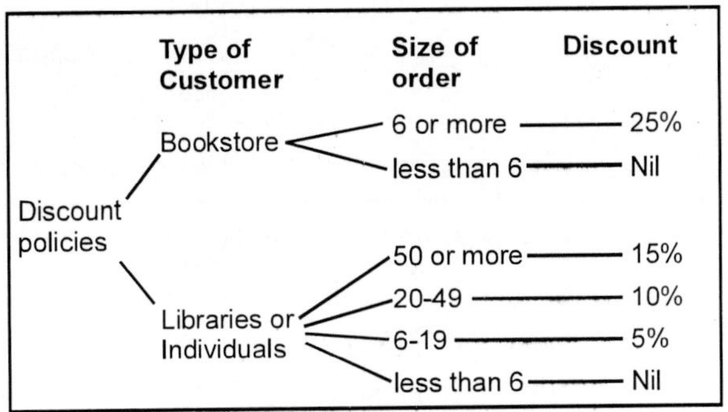

Fig. 4.8. Decision Tree — An Example

As shown in Figure 4.8, a decision tree has as many branches as there are logical alternatives. It simply sketches the logical structure based on the stated policy. In this respect, it is an excellent tool. It is easy to construct, easy to read, and easy to update. It shows only the skeletal aspects of the policy however in the sense that it does not lend itself to calculations or show logic as a set of instruction for action.

Decision trees are used to verify logic and in problems that involve a few complex decisions resulting in a limited number of actions. Decisions trees are the best suited for dealing with complex branching routines such as calculating discounts or sales commissions or inventory control procedures.

4.11. DECISION TABLE

A major drawback of a decision tree is the back of information in its format to tell us what other combinations of conditions to test. This is where the decision table is useful. A decision table is a table of contingencies for defining a problem

Elements	Location	Definition
Condition stub	Upper left quadrant	Sets forth in question form the condition that may exist
Action stub	Lower left quadrant	Outlines in narrative form the action to be taken to meet each condition
Condition entry	Upper right quadrant	Provides answers to questions asked in the condition stub quadrant
Action entry	Lower right quadrant	Indicates the appropriate action resulting from the answers to the conditions in the condition entry quadrant.

Fig. 4.9. Elements and Definitions in a Decision Table

and the actions to be taken. It is a single representation of the relationships between conditions and actions.

A decision table consists of two parts : stub and entry. The stub part is divided into an upper quadrant called the condition stub and a lower quadrant called the action stub. The entry part is also divided into an upper quadrant, called the condition entry and

Condition Stub		**Condition Entry**					
		1	2	3	4	5	6
IF (condition)	Customer is bookstore?	Y	Y	N	N	N	N
	Order-size 6 copies or more?	Y	N	N	N	N	N
	Customer librarian or individual?			Y	Y	Y	Y
	Order-size 50 copies or more?			Y	N	N	N
	Order-size 20-49 copies?				Y	N	N
	Order-size 6-19 copies?					Y	N
THEN (action)	Allow 25% discount	X					
	Allow 15% discount			X			
	Allow 10% discount				X		
	Allow 5% discount					X	
	No discount allowed		X				X
Action Stub		**Action Entry**					

Fig. 4.10. Decision Table — Discount Policy

a lower quadrant called the action entry. The four elements and their definitions are summarized in Figure 4.9.

Note in Fig. 4.10 that the answers are represented by a Y to signify yes, an N to signify no, or a blank to show that the condition involved has not been tested. In the action entry quadrant, an X (or a check mark will do) indicates the response to the answer (s) entered in the condition entry quadrant. Furthermore, each column represents a decision or a rule. For example, rule 1 states :

IF customer is a bookstore and order size is 6 copies or more. THEN allow 25% discount.

So, according to the decision table, we have six decisions and therefore six rules. A look at the table provides each decision (answer) immediately. The following rules should be followed in constructing decision tables :

— A decision should be given a name, shown in the top left of the table.
— The logic of the decision table is independent of the sequence in which the condition rules are written, but the action takes place in the order in which the events occur.
— Standardized language must be used consistently.
— Duplication of terms or meanings should be eliminated, where possible.

4.11.1. Advantagtes of Decision Tables

A decision table have following advantages :

(i) Decision tables are best suited for dealing with complex branching routines such as calculating discounts or sales commissions or inventory control procedures.
(ii) A decision table may be easier to construct than a flowchart.
(iii) It is easy to understand and useful for programmers.
(iv) Table users do not require computer knowledge.
(v) It is very effective for communication between analysis or programmers.
(vi) Direct conversion of decision table into a computer program is possible.
(vii) It provides a framework for a complete and accurate statement of decision logic.

4.11.2. Disadvantages of Decision Tables

As far as disadvantages are concerned, a decision table has following drawbacks.

(i) Decision tables does not show the overall picture as presented by flowchart.

(ii) For the simple logic, flowcharts are more useful than decision tables.

4.12. DECISION FRAMES

A frame is a codification scheme used for organizing knowledge through previous experience. It deals with a combination of declarative and operational knowledge. Key elements of frames are :

– *Slot* : A specific object being described/an attribute of an entity.

– *Facet* : The value of an object/slot.

Marvin Minsky in his book "Computer Vision" proposed frames as a means of representing common sense knowledge. He proposed that knowledge is organized in to small packets called frames. The contents of these frames are certain slots which have values. All frames of a given situation constitute the system Whenever one encounters a situation, a series of related activities are activated and reasoning is done. For example consider a Library with various sections like circulation, serials, reference, periodicals, theses and dissertations, office establishment etc. The image of this Library center is in ones mind. Now consider a situation where the same person has a chance to visit a Library.

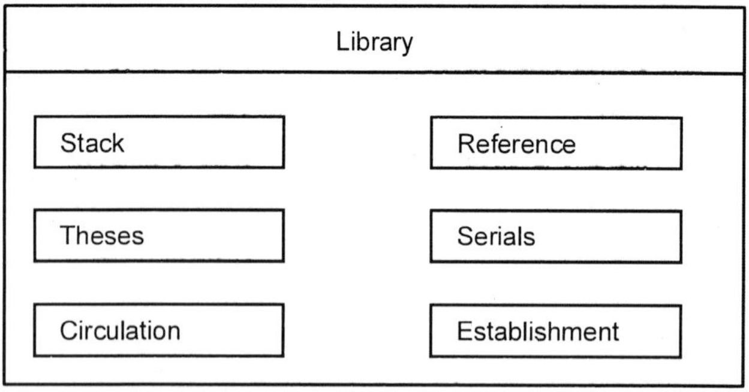

Fig. 4.11. Decision Frames for Library

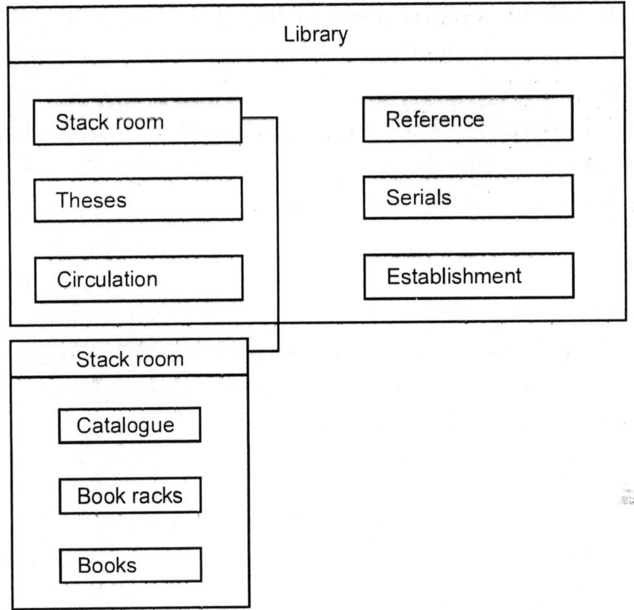

Fig. 4.12. Frame Structures

The mind considers a series of permutations and combinations and the frame of the library in the mind is matched towards the present situation with some slots being added or removed. For every section we see in the library we form a frame. For example the stack room itself can be considered as a frame. A frame can be defined as a data structure that has slots for various objects. A collection of frames consists of expectations for a given situation.

A frame structure provides facilities for describing objects, facts about situations, procedures on what to do when a situation is encountered. Because of these facilities a frame provides, frames are used to represent the two types of knowledge viz., declarative and procedural.

4.12.1. Reasoning Using Frames

Reasoning using frames is done by instantiation. Instantiation begins when given situation is matched with frames that are already in existence. The reasoning process tries to match the frame with the situation and later fills up slots for which values must be assigned. The values assigned to the slots depict a particular situation and by this the reasoning process try to move towards a goal. The reasoning process can be defined as filling frames, slots in frames. Generally if a given slot characteristic is not present, the slot provides a default value for that characteristic.

Reasoning using frames allows one to move from one frame to another to match the current situation. This process builds up a wide network of frames thereby facilitating one to build a knowledge base for representing knowledge about common sense. Frames being a general purpose structure for representing knowledge are slightly modified to give a precise description about a particular eventing.

4.12.2. Production rules

They are conditional statements specifying an action to be taken in case a certain condition is true. They codify knowledge in the form of premise-action pairs. Syntax: IF (premise) THEN (action)

- *Example* : IF membership is 'standard' and returning history is 'good', THEN 'approve home loan'.

In case of knowledge-based systems, rules are based on heuristics or experimental reasoning.

- Rules can incorporate certain levels of uncertainty.
- A certainty factor is synonymous with a confidence level, which is a subjective quantification of an expert's judgment.
- The premise is a Boolean expression that should evaluate to be true for the rule to be applied.
- The action part of the rule is separated from the premise by the keyword THEN.
- The action clause consists of a statement or a series of statements separated by AND's or comma's and is executed if the premise is true.

In case of knowledge-based systems, planning involves:

- Breaking the entire system into manageable modules.
- Considering partial solutions and liking them through rules and procedures to arrive at a final solution.

- Deciding on the programming language(s).
- Deciding on the software package(s).
- Testing and validating the system.
- Developing the user interface.
- Promoting clarity, flexibility and making the rules clear, and
- Reducing unnecessary risk.

Inferencing implies the process of deriving a conclusion based on statement, that only imply that conclusion. Role of inferencing :

- An inference engine is a program that manages the inferencing strategies.
- Reasoning is the process of applying knowledge to arrive at the conclusion.
- Reasoning depends on premise as well as on general knowledge.
- People usually draw informative conclusions.

Thus, knowledge is codified and organized for knowledge management. But a knowledge manager should be trained in the use of various tools and be must know which tool is to be used in what circumstances and where.

5

Knowledge Transfer and Knowledge Sharing

Knowledge transfer in the fields of organizational development and organizational learning, is the practical problem of getting a packet of knowledge from one part of the organization to another parts of the organization.

The fundamental premise underlying a comprehensive examination of knowledge flows or transfer is knowledge enables actions and decisions. All knowledge flows consist of the actions of agents on artifacts. However, not all knowledge flows are the same. Knowledge flows differ in many ways, and when we study their characteristics, we can understand their dynamics and can take the steps necessary to promote those knowledge flows critical to the success of the enterprise.

Critical to any discussion of knowledge flows are three basic concepts – agents, artifacts and transformations. These are related by the fact that agents perform behaviours directed toward some meaningful end.

The concept of being an agent (agency) is one that occurs frequently in the existing literature on knowledge management, information technology, organizational dynamics and other related fields. Within these domains, two general definitions seem to predominate – agents as specialized objects, and agents as specific roles played by people, organizations, societies, automata and so forth. More specifically, within Knowledge Management literature, the dominate theme seems to revolve around computer systems acting as agents.

Over the past fifty years, computer-based technology (CBT) has transformed lives and organizations. One way it has done so has been to transform how knowledge work is done. CBT is fundamentally concerned with digital means for representing and processing knowledge of several types including :

- Descriptive knowledge, in its various gradations from data and information at the low end to problem solutions, designs, and decisions at the high end,
- Procedural knowledge, specifying the steps for performing some task, and
- Reasoning knowledge, specifying what conclusions is valid when a particular situation exists.

As such, CBT has transformed the ways in which both individuals and organizations accomplish knowledge work. It has done so by amplifying, complementing, leveraging, and in some cases improving on innate human knowledge handling capabilities. It has relaxed some of the temporal, cognitive, economic and geographic limits on human knowledge work.

Tracing the evolution of CBT, we see a progression from data processing systems to management information systems to decisions support systems to organizational computing systems to ubiquitous computing. These are summarized in Table 5.1.

The trajectory of the first three phases is into increasing value, revelance and importance for knowledge workers. The next phase builds on the first three, adding the dimension of intra-and inter-organizational knowledge flows and knowledge reuse.

The ubiquitious computing phase builds on all that precede it and is driven by such forces as Moore's Law, Metcalf's Law, and advances in content technologies that allow computers to better represent and process. In the world of ubiquitous computing, the hallmarks are 24 × 7 operations, global connectivity, and everday objects with embedded computers. Such objects 'e.g., vending

Table 5.1. Evolution of CBT

Computer Based Technology	Emerged	Emphasis
Data processing systems	1950s-1960s	Representation of low grade descriptive knowledge Recording transactions Producing transactions
Management information systems	1960s-1970s	Representation of low to descriptive middle grade knowledge Record keeping based on transactions Producing predefined types of reports that organize data into more usable chunks of information.
Decisions support systems	1970s-1980s	Representation of descriptive, procedural and/ or reasoning knowledge Use of knowledge to solve or find problems Delivery of knowledge needed by a decision maker : • in a desired format • possibly, on the spur of the moment • possibly, in response to unanticipated or novel knowledge needs Includes modeling systems, expert systems, online analytical processing, business intelligence systems.
Organizational computing systems	1980s-1990s	Facilitates knowledge flows and reuse among multipleparticipants in some organizational form May involve descirptive, procedural and/ or reasoning knowledge Includes groupware, collaboration systems, workflow systems, enterprise systems, inter organizational systems, adaptive systems.
Ubiquitous computing	1990s-	Universal, non-stop availability of knowledge and knowledge processors Includes Web-based, mobile and embedded computing systems

machines, appliances, drums of chemicals, running shoes, garments, vehicals, houses' will increasingly have the abilities to observe, record experiences, communicate, solve problems and take actions. They can be constantly on, active, "aware" — interacting with their environment, other computers and people.

Bukowitz and Williams point out that "from a knowledge perspective, technology triumphs in its ability to connect more people in more ways than ever before. E-mail, intranets, discussion forums, chat rooms — they alll make the truly networked organization possible .... Advantage comes from conversation, the back and forth questioning, the easier access to expertise and the broadened sense of membership in different communities ..." On the horizon, Bieber et al., describe how a digital library can be augmented with computer-mediated communications, community process support technology, decision support technology, advanced hypermedia features, and conceptual knowledge structures for constructing a collaborative knowledge evolution support system.

CBT for connecting intelligent knowledge processors– 'human and computer' and for collective construction of reusable knowledge bases furnishes a foundation for implementing knowledge-based organizations. This technology is evident in the e-business boom, including the notions of e-commerce, collaborative commerce and mobile commerce. Indeed, e-business can be viewed as a major arena of KM– e-business is concerned with approaches to achieving business goals in which technological means for representing and processing knowledge are used to implement and facilitate activities within and across value chains, as well as supporting decisions that underlie those activities.

So, the idea is that modern knowledge management is inseparable from a consideration of computer-based technology, of CBT users, and of CBT impacts.

The discussions surrounding the general concept of *agency*, especially those dealing with causality are both interesting and relevant in forming our foundations for the practice of Knowledge Management. However, from a practical viewpoint, what the Knowledge Manager and the Knowledge Engineer need is an easily understood framework to discuss, understand and model requirements and characteristics of knowledge-based systems.

In most discussions of this nature, the roles within knowledge-based systems fall into one of three groups – the people, the technology, or the organization. This grouping captures a number of meaningful distinctions that characterize the strengths and limitations of agents within knowledge-based systems.

These groups are referred as *Individual agents*, *automated agents*, and *collective agents*. Individual agent are human, automated agents are non-human, and collective agents are a specific collection of individual and/or automated agents.

The second of the three major concepts associated with knowledge flows is the *knowledge flow artifact*, or simply, the *knowledge artifact*. These are the documents, memories, norms, values, and other things that represent the inputs to, and products of, the knowledge-enabled activities of agents.

"Artifact" is the word we use to describe what we as humans construct, then it should be equally valid as a description of our mental or conceptual constructions. Bardige seized the idea of artifacts resulting from mental or conceptual constructions as the foundation for his theories on the growth and evolution of knowledge. However, to those concerned with knowledge flows, the concept fills a more important role.

In many circles, references to the abstract nature of a given knowledge artifact are made by the use of the terms data, information, knowledge, understanding and wisdom. While these distinctions may still prove helpful in some cases, problems in definition and interpretation often arise from any attempt to maintain rigid lines of demarcation. This, in turn, impacts both their usefulness and scalability when it comes to understanding knowledge flows. These problems can be avoided through the use of the collective term *artifact* (knowledge artifact) without any significant loss in the effectiveness or validity of the framework. As important as the concept of the artifact was to Bardige's work, so it is to our understanding of knowledge flows.

The third essential knowledge flow concept is *transformation*. Transformations are the behaviours that agents perform on artifacts. If we were to address every possible way in which an agent could act upon a knowledge artifact, the list of possible transformations would be too large to support effective modeling. The full range would include such behaviours as inference, logical and deductive reasoning, abstraction, translation, transliteration, assumption, and goal seeking, summation, integration, ordination, aggregation, selection, conversion, separation, confrontation, realization, looking at consequences, introspection, denial, transference, acceptance, faith, trust, belief, awareness of potential, exposure, education, mutation, evolution, compartmentalization. But, we have chosen instead to focus on four major categories of activities that are common to all knowledge-based systems. These are knowledge creation, knowledge retention, knowledge transfer, and knowledge utilization. These four categories have been chosen because each represents a fundamental difference in both policy and process. Knowledge creation includes all those behaviours through which new knowledge enters a knowledge-based system. Knowledge can enter a system in one of two ways. It can either be created within the system or captured from external sources. Knowledge transfer covers those behaviours through which agents share knowledge and knowledge artifacts. Knowledge retention includes all the ways in which we store, maintain, and retrieve previously developed knowledge. The final category, knowledge utilization, actually forms the cornerstone of knowledge-based behaviors. Knowledge utilization addresses the ways in which we use knowledge to further the goals and aims of the enterprise.

Together, the three basic concepts, agents, artifacts, and transformations, form the building blocks of knowledge flows. Precisely stated,

> *knowledge flows are sequences of transformations performed by agents on knowledge artifacts in support of specific actions or decisions.*

Knowledge flows or transfer focus on the enablers for business process tasks rather than on the sequence by which the tasks are associated. One should not confuse the concept of a knowledge flow with the related concepts of business processes and workflows. In general, the idea of a "workflow" relates to the creation of explicit representations of process logic. Methodologies and tools, focus on workflow mapping and analysis, have their greatest application in the computerized control, monitoring, optimizing, and support of business processes. In contrast, knowledge flow analysis and mapping has its greatest application in the engineering of holistic systems that encompass the full spectrum of knowledge-based activities.

5.1. AGENTS OF KNOWLEDGE TRANSFER OR FLOW

To better understand the ramifications and characteristics of knowledge flows or transfer, it is important that we expand our understanding to include their three key elements; agents, artifacts, and transformations. We continue our examination of the elements within knowledge flows with a closer look at knowledge artifacts.

5.1.1. Knowledge Artifacts

For most, exposure to knowledge flows or transfers comes through various knowledge artifacts. Knowledge artifacts are what we deal with every day. We write reports, send e-mail, read books, remember bits and pieces of old thoughts, engage in conversations, and follow procedures. The use of the term "knowledge artifact" does more than just provide us with an effective collective. It also points to the fact that, as with other artifacts, we need to be mindful of the processes associated with retention, establishing provenance, and enabling reusability.

When we speak of a knowledge flow artifact, we are actually making a simultaneous reference to two important entities. First, we are referring to the *cognitive knowledge artifact*, which makes up our awareness and understanding of a particular aspect of our real or meta-physical world. This is commonly referred to simply as "knowledge." Second, we are referring to the *physical knowledge* artifact, which serves as a representation of the associated cognitive knowledge artifact. Understanding both the cognitive and physical characteristics of a knowledge artifact, and how they relate to the unique behavioural characteristics of the individual, automated, and collective agents, is a critical aspect in modeling how knowledge is applied in making decisions and enabling actions.

Understanding the critical aspect improves our ability to engineer knowledge artifacts and knowledge flows that support critical business processes and decisions. All knowledge artifacts contain aspects of the cognitive and the physical and fall somewhere between fully cognitive (tacit) and fully physical (explicit). The degree to which they are predominantly one or the other will have a significant impact on how it relates to other elements of the knowledge flow.

Knowledge artifacts differ one from another in other ways as well. These variations include the way they are codified, the way they are rendered, and their degree of abstraction. Knowledge artifacts also vary in their structure, their content, their intended context, and in how well they are articulated. Individually, knowledge artifacts can be explicit, implicit or tacit. However, most artifacts, depending on how they are used, occur in complex forms that contain a combination of explicit, implicit, and tacit components.

Denham Grey, Tom Finneran, and Robert Seiner are among those who, while agreeing that knowledge artifacts are human constructs (i.e., cognitive) to which we have attributed a degree of reality, would argue that they occupy a much more specific and limited position within a knowledge architecture. Grey views knowledge artifacts as an important new genre of object closely tied to the knowledge economy. He sees knowledge artifacts as one level above what John Seely Brown terms "boundary objects" with greater levels of "invested energy, support rituals, and greater reach." Boundary objects are classifications, conventions, and processes that carry meaning between communities allowing effective exchange and transitions to take place. Boundary objects represent a special group of knowledge objects because they cross organizational boundaries and carry meaning, they serve as both containers and carriers. Boundary objects are also a highly abstract and generalized form of knowledge organization to which we have attributed a degree of reality. If you place people, activities, and relationships in the context of boundary objects with which they are associated, you have a powerful way to portray, arrange and monitor knowledge flows.

Finneran invests knowledge artifacts with a degree of reality that exists independent of any agent. He also seems to agree that knowledge artifacts can be retained, transferred and enable actions and decisions. He, however, limits the overall role and scope of knowledge artifacts when he associates them with an instance of a "knowledge asset."

Grey and Finneran typify those who would limit knowledge artifacts to instances of explicit codification, as is the case when the term is used in association with the field of Artificial Intelligence - and in contrast with the processes associated with human decision making. The limitations imposed by restricting the term to the just the explicit and codified have resulted in the implied exclusion of all knowledge artifacts that cannot be made explicit. To address the full range of artifacts associated with knowledge flows, it is important that we include those artifacts that exist across the full spectrum of articulation, including the explicit, implicit and tacit.

Whether a knowledge artifact is explicit, implicit, or tacit can have a significant effect on how different types of agents are able to interact with them. All agents are not equally qualified to deal with differing forms of codification. Therefore, significant insights can be gained by examining the characteristics of the knowledge artifacts that form the inputs and outputs of agent behaviours.

By far, explicit knowledge artifacts are the most familiar to us. Explicit artifacts are those that have been codified in a way that makes it possible to touch, see, hear, feel and/or manipulate them, e.g., books, reports, data files, newsreels, audio cassettes and other physical forms. Explicit knowledge artifacts can be transferred from one person to another. However, regardless of how well a report is written, or how complete and comprehensive it might be, if it is written – codified, in a language not understood by the agent who will use the report, it will have little value in supporting the associated knowledge flow. For a moment, consider the case of highly detailed listings of computer programs or rule bases that serve to codify complex procedural knowledge. When transformed by a compiler or other suitable automated agent, they can prove to be a highly effective aspect of a larger automated knowledge-based system. However, they may not be nearly as effective if used as an input to the activities of a Board of Directors (a collective agent). Recognition of this fact is one of the primary motivators behind why web site authors offer different "views" and personalization.

Not as well articulated, but just as effective in the right situation, are the implicit knowledge artifacts. These are knowledge artifacts whose meanings are not explicitly captured, but can be inferred. In effect, the codification process is incomplete. Whereas explicit artifacts can be interpreted based on their content, interpreters of implicit artifacts must rely on knowledge from other sources. Even those knowledge artifacts that are well structured and highly codified – explicit, will also contain some element of the implicit. For example, in a highly detailed computer program listing, there could be inferences as to the type of computer on which the program would run, to knowledge of mathematical theorems, to loeical proofs, or to natural limits or conditions in the physical world - such as the implied knowledge that programs written in the early days of business applications need not be concerned with events taking place after 1999.

The potential for ambiguity is one of the characteristics of implied knowledge artifacts. Most readers of the statement, "Sita put on her heavy coat and locked up her classroom," would infer that it is winter and Sita is a teacher. However, there are other inferences that could be made as well. For consistent interpretation, the person making the statement, as well as the person interpreting it, must share some common frame of reference to understand when heavy coats are worn and who locks up classrooms.

The underlying knowledge embedded in processes or process descriptions can also be considered as an implicit artifact. For example, a manual detailing the safe way to handle corrosive materials might include statements such as, "this material should not be used on polished or anodized aluminum surfaces," or, "if swallowed, immediately rinse mouth and drink a glass of milk or water. Do not induce vomiting." The implicit knowledge contained within these warnings, combined with what the reader might recall from high school chemistry, tells the reader that the material is likely to be caustic.

Implicit knowledge artifacts can also be found in process-specific software. In developing the software, the designers had to conceptualize the processes that the software would be supporting. That knowledge will become apparent in the way the software is intended to be used and in the range of behaviours it directly supports. Even if not explicitly apparent, the implicit decisions made by the software designer, such as, which function to implement and how to implement it, can significantly constrain users' actions. This is often referred to as, "implicit policy making by technologists".

When we look to the far end of the scale, we find those artifacts that seem to defy codification. These tacit artifacts may be the most insidious and powerful of the three. The problem of tacit knowledge, its acquisition, and epistemic status has been the focus of considerable philosophical investigation by such people as Ludwig Wittgenstein, Edmund Husserl. Hilary Putnam and, most significantly, Michael Polanyi. Polanyi referred to tacit knowledge as "knowing more than we can say". Tacit artifacts are those that defy expression and codification. However, this is not to say that tacit knowledge artifacts are without influence. In fact, they may be the more prevalent and influential of the three.

5.1.2. Agents

Agents are the active components of knowledge flows. Knowledge artifacts do not perform actions or make decisions. Actions and decisions are performed by agents– people, organizations, societies and/or, technology. Agents carry out all the actions and exhibit all the behaviours within a knowledge flow. While individual agents are an essential element of any knowledge flow, in today's enterprise, they rarely, if ever, operate alone. Computers and other forms of automated agents have clearly established that non-human agents have their place in knowledge flows as well. Besides the individual and automated agents, most knowledge flows involve one or more collective agents. Groups, organizations, companies, societies and trade unions are all examples of collective agents. As a class of agents, collective agents are not limited to just aggregations of individual agents. They can just as well include automated agents and other collective agents. Collective agents can range from the purely organic to the well-engineered, from one with a general social orientation to one geared to a specific organizational need.

In this way, we strengthen our understanding of knowledge flows. Focusing attention on the significant differences in the capabilities of each of these three types of agents, we can better understand how they interact with various types of artifacts. For instance – the individual agent can deal with tacit artifacts, whereas the automated agent cannot. The collective agent can retain knowledge beyond the life of individual agents. Automated agents can perform many types of transformations on explicit artifact much faster and with a greater degree of repeatability than can individual agents.

Individual agents sit at the center of every knowledge flow. For most analysts, the individual serves as the prototypical active force for affecting change. By referring to this category of agents as "individuals," we do not mean to imply that every specific individual is capable of the full range of behaviours attributed to this class of agent, rather, that as a class of agents, we share some general behaviours and capabilities.

As individual agents, we are capable of working with knowledge-and knowledge artifacts in all degrees of abstract articulation. We are limited, however, in our ability to deal with artifacts that are codified in ways that fall outside the range of human perception. As individual agents, we are unique in that we are the one agent type capable of performing all aspects of knowledge development, retention, transfer and utilization without the need for intervention by either of the other two agent types. However, with their help, there are things we can do better.

Automated agents include any human construct that is capable of retaining, transferring, or transforming knowledge artifacts. They are not exclusively computerized processes. For example, a conventional camera that encodes a representation of the visual world through chemical changes to the surface of a film acts as an automated agent, supporting both knowledge creation and capture.

The third category of agents is the *collective agent*. As with all agent types, problems can arise from ascribing a single behavioural model to all collective agents. Nevertheless, there are some basic characteristics that do apply to all collective agents. For instance, collective agents are not homogeneous. The agents that make up the collective agent will differ in their abilities to create, retain, transfer, and make use of knowledge, and to interact with different forms of knowledge artifacts. The collective agent will also manifest characteristics that may not be exhibited by any particular agent within the collective.

One important characteristic that collective agents exhibit is the ability to transcend ontological differences between constituent agents through the formation of shared values and world views.

The ability of organizations and communities to establish value systems that outlive the involvement of specific individuals and the power that these value systems have to influence the behaviour of individuals and groups. However, the principles and practices that make up these value systems are often not codified. In fact, when individuals within the organization attempt to describe an organization's value system, their descriptions are usually incomplete, reflecting either their interpretation of the organization's values or a blending of organizational and individual values. The common use of terms, such as "unwritten rules" and "organizational culture," is a clear reflection of the difficulties involved, and further evidence that collective agents can, and do, act as repositories of tacit knowledge.

The idea that collective agents can retain and act upon tacit knowledge may appear to be entirely logical, but for some, it may also be problematic because it does not offer one specific place where such tacit knowledge would reside. In actuality, this inexpressible knowledge is codified, in part, as a component of the relationships between the members of the collective. Foundations for this position can be traced to work performed in the fields of individual human cognition and individualized knowledge which is consistent with our views of knowledge held by individual and automated agents.

Because of the myriad of knowledge flows occurring within a collective agent, you may be tempted to simplify the model of agents and concentrate on just the individual and automated agents. However, evidence clearly points to the dangers of such a position, and the reader is strongly cautioned against such shortcuts. To eliminate the collective agent from our analysis and understanding is to ignore the effects of cultural norms, organizational paradigms, shared values systems, and almost the entirety of societal impacts. The collective agent, and the knowledge embedded therein, is a source of highly important structural couplings between member agents. These structural couplings are critical factors in agent-to-agent alignments and the availability of much of the content and context within knowledge flows.

5.1.3. Transformations

Now come to the third of the three fundamental elements of knowledgeflows, transformations. Knowledge flows are the medium through which knowledge is made available to enable individuals and organizations to achieve their goals. As is seen, agents are responsible for the actions that transform knowledge artifacts from one form to another in the process of creating, retaining, transferring, and using knowledge. Now, it is time to look at those behaviours through which agents create, change, remove and otherwise transform knowledge artifacts within knowledge flows.

Once the knowledge in acquired, the next question arises is, how it is retained? Like acquistion, knowledge retention can take many forms. The behaviours and transformations asociated with knowledge retention include all activities that preserve knowledge and allow it to remain in the system once introduced. Knowledge retention also includes those activities that maintain the viability of knowledge within the system. To properly understand the dynamics of knowledge retention within knowledge flows, it is necessary to address such issues as :

– How the selection of retention transformations are

constrained by agent capabilities.

- The role of meta-knowledge in knowledge retention.
- The role of context in knowledge retention.
- The role of classification schemes and methodologies.
- The effects of previously retained knowledge on future knowledge retention processess.

- The ramifications of various codification schemes on long-term knowledge viability.

Any time a knowledge flow involves more than a single agent, there will be a need for some type of knowledge transfer behaviour. For this reason, knowledge transfer behaviours are one of the most prevalent types of behaviours within knowledge flows. This includes, but is not limited to, communication, translation, conversion, filtering, and rendering.

When we decide how to render a knowledge artifact for transfer between agents, we are, infact, choosing how we will interpret the meta-physical content of the artifact and represent that interpretation in some explicit form. Each of these two transformations, interpretation, involve selecting certain elements of the artifact supports down-stream transformations, behaviours, and ultimately, the ability to enable the action or decision in question.

A similar problem surfaces when we consider the role of agent-specific ontologies. An agent's ontology is their way of viewing and understanding the world. As such, it comprises such elements as concepts held, taxonomies, syntax (terminology), semantics (meaning), rules, relationships, and constraints. How agents view the world effect what they consider important and significant when it comes to knowledge transfers. The ontology of a sales organization may cause it to place a different importance on product customization than would the accounting department or the production manager. These differences could have significant impacts on the nature of the knowledge artifacts created, retained, and transferred by, and between, these collective agents as they work to achieve the goal, "maintain target gross profit per unit."

This brings us to our fourth class of transformations and

behaviours, the use of knowledge contained within the system to enable those actions and decisions through which we achieve our goals and objectives. When we speak of knowledge utilization behaviours, transformations, and actions directly related to applying knowledge to enable decisions and actions.

5.2. NEED AND PURPOSES

The importance of knowledge transfer with an organization lies in the strategic advantage of knowledge.

First, knowledge that is transferred within the organization increases knowledge diversity. Using diverse knowledge is a necessary condition for innovation. Diverse knowledge is defined as knowledge from various functional areas.

Secondly, using knowledge from different units helps to avoid 'glitches' that are a drawback in project work and thus helps to increase project effectiveness.

Generally, knowledge transfer stresses the fact that there is knowledge elsewehere in the organization that might also be useful for local application. Thus, organisational learning needs as one ingredient heterogeneity or diversity, as it is sometimes called, in knowledge.

Knowledge transfer is the process that makes heterogeneous knowledge available for local use. Different reasons apply to why knowledge sharing is important. The definition of organizational learning hints at developing commonly accepted knowledge.

5.3. FACTORS AFFECTING KNOWLEDGE TRANSFER

The factors influencing knowledge transfer and sharing are :

— Opportunity

— Motivation and

— Ability

5.3.1. Opportunity

It is generally agreed that opportunity for knowledge sharing or transfer is established through appropriate social relationships between members in an organization. Learning is interwined with a social component. Social relationships must satisfy three aspects in creating an opportunity for organizational learning. First, there must exist a connection between people in order to safeguard knowledge transfer. People must have contact with others for gathering new knowledge. Second the type of social relationships should be 'appropriate' for knowledge transfer. Third, knowledge must also be shared in order to realize organizational learning.The three aspects are recognized by theories of social captial. They distinguish between social bridging capital and social bonding capital. Both represent distinct types of social networks that are appropriate for knowledge transfer and sharing, respectively.

5.3.2. Motivation

There are three lines of reasoning on how an individual's motivation to share and transfer knowledge is influenced.

Some conceive motivation as an individual characteristic that can be influenced by an organization's reward system. Other approaches stress the efforts an individual must undertake to share or transfer knowledge as an important variable. Effort is interpreted in two ways : it can take an individual cognitive effort to explain particular knowledge to someone else. Effort is, then, related to cognitive ability and absorptive capacity. It can also take effort to maintain a social relationship. In this case, effort is connected with an individual's position in a social network. It takes much more effort to build up and/maintain a good relationship with somebody who works at a distance or with whom one has irregular contact. Direct relationships are more prone to effective knowledge transfer. A third factor that influences motivation is reputation. Generally, one may assume that knowledge transfer and sharing is facilitated when one's reputation; is improved. Being perceived as an expert enhances the readiness to share and transfer knowledge. Reputation as motivator has, as a precondition, a tight social network through which reputational effects are realized. In sum, the motivation for knowledge sharing is determined by multiple factors. Effort and reputation as motivators for knowledge sharing and transfer, both, presuppose a tight social network. Here, again, it becomes clear how knowledge sharing is related to social networks. Relationships in a network form the ground on which motivational factors can be realized.

5.3.3. Ability

Ability is a third type of factor that influences organizational learning. It could take too much effort to transfer knowledge to a colleague because of his (low) cognitive and absorptive capability. This is often the, case when people from diverse disciplinary backgrounds need to share their knowledge. Successful knowledge transfer only takes place: between people with the same background knowledge and the same experience, in practice. Cognitive similarity is also correlated with social networks as people with tight connections develop 'relation-specific heuristics' that facilitate understandings.

It can be concluded that various factor play a role when actually realizing knowledge transfer and sharing. Social relationships in a network are a necessary condition for knowledge transfer.

For successful knowledge sharing, there should be a 'fit' between opportunity, motivation and ability. Relationships in networks are considered as balanced and without tensions. It is

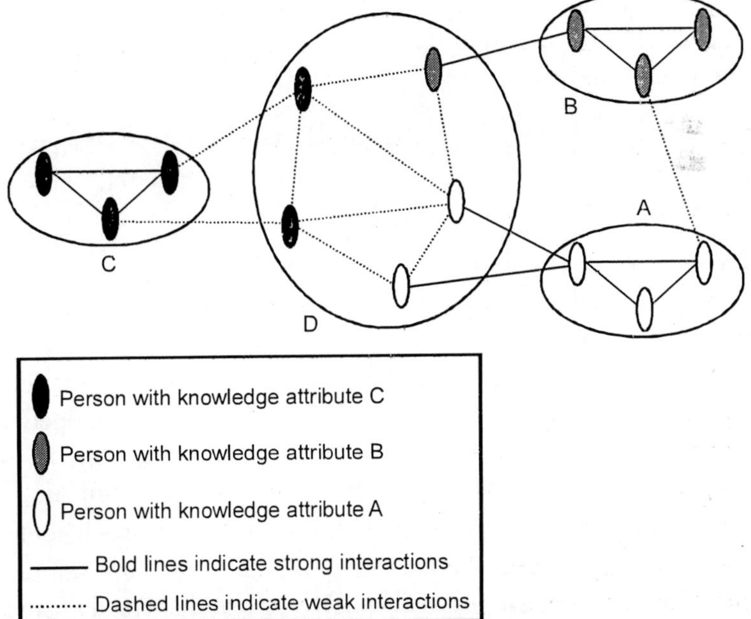

Fig. 5.1. Ideal Network Situation for Knowledge Sharing and Transfer

assumed that the wider network does not have an influence on an individual's learning behaviour in a group i.e., on an individual's motivation or ability. Only the direct relationships are considered important. The sources or motivation and ability are sought in the direct relationships, leaving the wider network condition in creating the opportunity out of considerations.

There is a constant debate going on to discuss whether knowledge creation and transfer are related. In general the two concepts are connected in the sense that in order for someone to transfer his or her knowledge to someone else, the receiver has to understand and create his or her own knowledge base on what the sender has transferred.

In the same way, documented knowledge must be understood by the reader who then creates his or her own interpretation and knowledge in the area in order for a transfer to have taken place. Based on this, it can be argued that creation and transfer of knowledge are inseparable.

Unless knowledge is absorbed, it is not transferred, and merely making knowledge available does not egual its transfer. Therefore the creation of knowledge also involves the transfer of knowledge and vice versa.

5.4. TOOLS FOR TRANSFERRING KNOWLEDGE

There exist various tools for knowledge transfer. These are described below.

5.4.1. Having an Enabling Context

One of the tools identified for transferring knowledge is to create an enabling context. This tool is important, because on the one hand it can be said that it enhances the other tools in the sense that an enabling context encourages interaction between people, and also that the other tools reinforce an enabling context. An enabling context can be fostered in a high-care environment.

Knowledge needs a context to be created and such context can be thought of as a shared space for emerging relationships. It does not have to be a physical space – office, dispersed business space; it can also be virtual (email, teleconference), mental (shared experiences, ideas, ideals), or any combination of thorn and that serves as a foundation for knowledge creation.

Some organizational conditions are more favourable than others when fostering knowledge creation and transfer. The way people in the organisation relate to each other is particularly important. The environment in which the people in the organization relate to each other may be high-care or low-care. Typical characteristics of a low-care environment are untrustworthy behaviour, constant competition, imbalances in giving and receiving information and a "that is not my job" attitude.

According to Krogh, all these characteristics endanger effective sharing of tacit knowledge, since they might decrease the participation and interaction between people, which is often required for the transfer of tacit knowledge. In this kind of environment, the individual will try to capture his/her knowledge rather than sharing it, thus blocking the creation of new knowledge. An enabling context can be seen as a tool that, if it is accomplished, can encourage knowledge transfer.

5.4.2. Shared Experiences

Shared experiences and a common language facilitates knowledge creation and transfer in all four modes. If people lack a common language, it may be difficult to assimilate some knowledge. Shared experiences may facilitate the transfer of tacit knowledge, which cannot always be conveyed in words.

When working in similar areas and receiving the same type of training, the understanding of one another's words and actions increases. This can be referred to this as having a shared stock of knowledge, i.e., that some knowledge cannot be transferred unless sender and receiver have the same basic knowledge.

Specialized groups produce specialized knowledge and the information that circulates easily in one community might have little value for those who lack the background knowledge necessary to make it comprehensible. Related to having a shared experience is the importance of having a common language, since without it, it will be difficult to transfer knowledge even though the experiences are the same.

There is a need for a common language when transferring knowledge. An individual's tacit knowledge must be made explicit in a language known and acceptable to the others in order to be understood.

5.4.3. Knowledge Vision and Focus

The third tool is knowledge vision and focus. It works as an overarching tool, because it shows in which direction the organisation should head in terms of knowledge. It is the most critical element of corporate strategy. The organization should conceptualize a vision about what kind of knowledge should be developed and operationalized.

The knowledge creation and transfer would be facilitated by a knowledge vision, either articulated separately or incorporated in other corporate statements. The vision should not only include what knowledge the company should seek and create in the future, but also how they should work today. The vision should encourage the individual to identify sources of knowledge that can aid other parts of the organization. Furthermore, the organization should identify how it could move towards the knowledge vision.

A good knowledge vision inspires and gains commitment at all levels of the organization, from top-management to frontline personnel, it should be a stable vision that the organization can keep during a longer time period. One way to create this setting is to involve employees from various departments m the creation of a vision. By identifying knowledge activists, i.e. souls of fire, who can energize and maintain the level of commitment to the knowiedge vision, the organization is more likely to be able to spread the message and gain devotion to the vision. These souls of fire can be individuals or a department dedicated to enabling knowledge transfer.

5.4.4. Knowledge Focus

It is important to define what kind of knowledge is the most critical to transfer, i.e., a knowledge focus. This will help the employees know where in the organization knowledge transfer is most critical and also why this kind of knowledge should be transferred. This focus may change or vary with departments; the important thing is that the focus is flexible. In order to create a vision and knowledge focus, the organization needs management support. Management can show their support by communicating the vision, and also by actively inspire to share knowledge, and act as mentors in doing so. The notion that knowledge should be kept away from subordinates as a source of power should be given up. One way to enforce this way of thinking and acting is by evaluating managers and supervisors within projects.

5.4.5. Communication

This tool encompasses dialogue, meetings and collective reflection. The collective name, communication, was chosen because each of the three aspects involves some form of communication. These aspects of communication can be guided and structured to encourage knowledge creation and transfer, wherefore we see it as a suitable tool.

Talking is the key method to share and transfer knowledge. Of course, this can involve any number of informal or formal settings and practices – Water cooler chats, fairs, conferences or any forums with direct face-to-face contact are identified as the most effective.

Through formal group discussions and conversations, people can exchange and reflect upon each other's ideas. By assigning someone who manages the conversations or group discussions, the organization can maintain a certain etiquette and standard of these meetings. This is one of the best ways to share tacit knowledge although it is often overlooked by organizations as a way to create and share knowledge.

5.5.5. Mentors and Social Networks

The reason why mentors and social networks have been put together is that both deal with interaction between people where the main purpose is to gain knowledge from each other.

Mentors are relation that exists between an apprentice and his/her master in organizations today. It is more used by craftsmen. The relation between a mentor and his/her protegees is identified to be similar to that of an apprentice and his/her master. This tool is important because it shows how knowledge within an organization can be shared from experienced employees to less experienced in an informal way.

Having mentoring programs where less experienced colleagues have access to senior members or experts in the organization is a way to access knowledge. The mentors should be responsible "for helping junior members to grow and actualise their full potential in the organization". Mentoring programs must encourage senior members to share their knowledge, which can be difficult, since keeping knowledge to oneself can by some be seen as a way to make oneself hard to replace.

The most important qualifications for participation in a mentoring program are commitment to growth, the ability to listen, trustworthiness and objectivity. Senior managers should be strongly encouraged to become mentors and then evaluated on their success in this role.

Likewise, proteges should be recognized for their initiative to broaden their business knowledge and advance in their profession. It is important to get support from senior management to demonstrate to all employees that the organization stands behind the program. Corporate mentoring programs are meaningful to mentors as well as for the proteges. Another key issue is thoughtful pairing of mentors and proteges.

This can be decisive for the success of a mentoring program. Mentors should have experience in the particular area of interest to their protege, whether it is technical knowledge in a specific area of business or well-developed interpersonal skills. Another purpose with mentoring programs is to create networks. The reason is-that while the proteges gain tacit knowledge from more experienced employees through observations they can at the same time be helped with establishing networks faster.

Social networks can be described as the link between two people, which in turn are linked to additional people. Relationships in a network are symmetric in the sense that no given centre can be identified, with the result that a network's boundaries are determined from the individuals', unit's or organization's perspective. Through the relation between people, new knowledge can be created.

Furthermore, the relationship can be both positive and negative in the sense that it is demanding at the same time as it creates possibilities. Networks are not only used to create contacts outside the organization, but are important for the informal contacts within the organization as well. These networks can be called informal networks and they are important for satisfying different social needs. The foremost used form of communication in informal networks is the informal communication.

Informal communication is more advantageous than formal communication. It is more spontaneous and pleasant and that it can be more informative. Furthermore, it is claimed that it is faster than official communication channels.

5.5.6. IT and Databases

The last tool is information technology or IT and databases. It is better to combine the highlighted factors, namely, documents, documentation and databases, into this tool. The reasoning behind this is that when documenting something it is often stored either in a database or in other IT tools. Consequently, this is, a place where stored knowledge can be found. Theorists have given IT great attention as an enabler for knowledge creation and transfer. IT has made it possible to handle knowledge resource demanding way, through codification and virtual storage. It makes knowledge accessible to people in an organization without it being connected to a specific person. This positive view of IT as a knowledge management tool reflects to a large extent the knowledge management literature, and it is also visible in how organisations use IT.

Table 5.2 provides a list of the categories of knowledge dissemination technologies currently in use, with examples shown in parentheses.

The specific implementations of these technologies can be expected to change in the years ahead, but each of them should continue to be important. In addition, new types of technology will surely be applied.

With perhaps the exception of document management, none of the technologies listed in Table 5.2 were developed with

Table 5.2. Knowledge Dissemination Technologies

Technology	Uses and Example
World Wide Web	For connecting individuals to a repository (search engines, URL's)
On-line access	For real-time sharing (ICQ, Net Meeting, On-line chat rooms)
E-mail	One-to-one and one-to-many dissemination; computer conferences
Groupware	For topic based discussions and collaboration. (LotusNotes); team room software (Groupsystems)
Wireless technology	For stand-alone connecting electronic devices such as laptops, PDA's, cell phones, WAP devices
Video conferencing, teleconferencing	For connecting ad-hoc groups (Microsoft NetMeeting, WebEx, Sharepoint)
Document management systems	To access reports, purchase orders, and other corporate documents; Use of XML.
Intelligent agents	To find knowledge on the Internet or in a knowledge repository
Geographic information systems	To display knowledge in two and multiple dimensions
Information portals	To point to the location of knowledge

knowledge management as the driving force. Many of the dissemination technologies listed in Table 5.2 such as: World Wide Web; Groupware; On-line access and video conferencing; and Document management are used for collaboration, which is a primary function within knowledge management.

Each of above is briefly discussed below.

1. World Wide Web : The predominant search technology for external information is the Internet search engine. Examples are Google, Alta Vista, and Lycos. Some engines, such as Google, hire people to determine the appropriate categories to attach to Web items. Search engines generally use simple Boolean word matching algorithms to find and retrieve results. Searches often result in thousands of matches being returned in response to a query, resulting in information overload for the user. Search engines are being augmented with artificial intelligence, taxonomies, and weighted search patterns to provide more accurate and more focused search results. The World wide Web technology is, of course, also used for intranets and extranets.

A step above search engines are intelligent agent systems. These agents scour the Internet, intranets, and extranets to pull knowledge.

2. On-line Access : On line access is used for synchronous knowledge exchange. It allows both explicit and tacit knowledge to be transferred in text form. The people exchanging knowledge are collaborating while being separated from one another, whether in an office building or around the world. On-line access systems generally have a central directory where users can be register and find one another.

With these systems, users connected via a LAN, WAN, or the Internet. They can initiate chat sessions, collaborate on documents, share applications, and draw on digital whiteboards. Online access is primarily a 'pull' technology, since the user who needs the knowledge initiates the on-line discussion.

Some examples of popular on-line access systems are:

AOL Messenger	*Business Collaborator*	*ERoom*
Excite Messenger	*Facilitate.com*	*HelpMeeting*
HelpOverIP	*ICQ*	*Microsoft NetMeeting*
MSN Messenger	*Netscape Messenger*	*Raindance*
SameTime	*Web-4M*	*Yahoo Messenger*

Fig. 5.2. Some Popular Online Access System

For example, NetMeeting from Microsoft offers an on-line computer conference that includes text chat, audio/video chat, application sharing and computer remote control, and whiteboards. In addition, online real time sharing is available through chat rooms that are available on most major Internet portal sites, such as Yahoo.com.

3. E-Mail : E-mail systems give users the ability to share knowledge with one another asynchronously. Sharing can be one to one, one to many, or many to many. The knowledge may be typed into the e-mail message and/or may be included as a document, audio, or video attachment.

Threaded email discussions – computer conferences, provide a popular forum for discussion. In these discussions, the user can either enter a message on a new topic or add a message to an existing topic. The e-mail system is indexed so that particular discussions and new contributions can be retrieved easily. Discussion capabilities are available both in private systems and in popular Internet services such as Yahoo.

Active Inbox from UDU World, can gather knowledge from a variety of sources including legacy systems, and push the knowledge, via email. Tacit Knowledge-Mail from Tacit Knowledge Systems enables companies to scan their email systems to find the knowledge and skills of its employees. Users can then search for knowledge found by the system, or request to be contacted by a human expert who may have the knowledge that they need. As its title indicates, this system is an initial attempt to transfer tacit knowledge in e-mail into explicit knowledge. Or-ganik from Orbital Software builds individual profiles by analyzing email discussion databases and corporate documents. It's aim is to help users find expert(s) who can help them with a specific problem.

New forms of e-mail, such as audio mail and video mail are being used experimentally since 2001. They can be expected to become ubiquitous in the years ahead as techniques for sharing knowledge.

4. Groupware : Groupware systems facilitate working together and sharing knowledge by providing product suites that facilitate on-line discussions, knowledge retrieval, and collaboration. Groupware include technologies for creating repositories (such as Lotus Notes or its successor, Lotus Domino) and for supporting meetings.

Groupware allows people to share knowledge. It can be considered in terms of the same and different time and place dimensions shown in Figure 5.3. Here the entries indicate groupware technologies used under each condition.

	Same Place	Different Place
Same Time	GroupSystems support for meetings	Distributed meetings supported by audio and videoconferencing, screen sharing, and Group Systems
Different Time	Team rooms	Repositories, computer conferencing, group authoring

Fig. 5.3. Examples of Knowledge Sharing through Groupware

Same time support is provided through group decision support systems such as Group Systems from Ventana Corporation. This software system suitable for both same place and different place meetings, provides a series of tools such as – brain-storming, outliner, topic commenter, categorizer, vote, survey, that people in a meeting use to collaborate. In the case of same place/same time–where all the meeting participants are present, a public screen, typically a computer projection device, shows the current work being done by the team for all to see. In addition, each user has a private screen where they can do their own work and where they can consult the available knowledge repositories. In a distributed meeting, (same time, different place) screen sharing and audio and videoconferencing combine with GroupSystems to allow real-time knowledge sharing.

Collaboration often involves groups working in different times and different places, e.g., a team scattered around the world or consultants working for different clients. Here, the group process involves :

- people putting knowledge into a repository, and
- people taking their own and other people's knowledge out of the repository as they need it.

Lotus Domino/Notes from Lotus Development Corporation is typical of the available groupware used. It provides e-mail, databases, bulletin boards, editing, and other sharing capabilities. It is used for team discussion, retrieving knowledge, tracking projects and for knowledge push. The software replicates its databases at multiple servers. It is a very rich package, but one that requires considerable skill on the part of its users.

5. Wireless Technology : Wireless technologies were initially developed as a way for people to stay connected and productive while on the go. Today, wireless technology satisfies the demand for real-time remote access to knowledge. For example, wireless technologies are used to disseminate knowledge to a workforce to keep them informed and reduce delays involved with decision-making and problem-solving.

Wireless technologies come in three variations:

- Point Device – one-way pager,
- Push/Pull Devices – WAP, 2-way pagers, e-mail forwarding devices, PDA w/wireless access, data capable cellular phones,
- Pull Devices – cellular phone, laptop with cellular modem etc.

Examples of wireless devices used in knowledge dissemination are:

– Cell-phones and cell-phone bridges (which turn cell-phones into modems to be used with other devices such as PDA's and Notebook computers).

– Minstrel Wireless Modem from Novatel Wireless

– BlackBerry wireless email from Research in Motion

- Two-way pagers from Motorola

6. Video and Audio Conferencing : Video conferencing allows individuals and groups to share knowledge. It is similar to using the telephone. The caller, also known as the host, can initiate an immediate call, as with NetMeeting in which case the person being called, the guest, is informed of the incoming call, and he/she can either accept or refuse the call. The caller can also schedule a videoconference for a future time, in which case, the guest will generally be informed of the meeting time via e-mail, and they can join the video-conference at that time.

Video conferencing systems are supplemented by whiteboards, computer access and storage, and video recording to keep a permanent record of the knowledge transferred.

Video conferencing products are made for two markets–one-to-one personal desktop video conferencing, and multi-user group conferencing. There are many products for the personal desktop, such as *NetMeeting* by Microsoft Corporation, *CUseeMe* by Cuseeme Networks, and the *Intel Video Phone software*. In addition, these software applications will work with a host of audio and video camera equipment available for the personal computer market. Some examples are the Intel PC Camera and the Logitech Quickcam. Personal desktop video conferencing systems are used with modems, cable modems. DSL, or on a corporate LAN.

Group conferencing systems provide high-quality audio and TV-quality video, as well as voice tracking camera's. Some examples are *PictureTel* by PictureTel Corporation, and *ViewStation* by Polycom, Inc. Group video conferencing systems utilize ISDN and high-speed data circuits for their connections. Many manufacturers now have product suites to meet the video conferencing needs of desktop users and group conferences. This market is highly competitive and the systems are used for many purposes beyond knowledge transfer.

7. Document and Text Management : Although some assume that knowledge management is document management, document management is really only one technology among many. Documents contain a company's explicit knowledge, be it text, video, voice, and images such as drawings, diagrams and pictures. Documents may be simple i.e., in one location or compound separated in different locations but connected through hypertext. Of the various media in which documents are stored, the vast majority is still on paper.

Electronic document management systems (EDMS) are software used to optimize and/or reorganize workflow, reduce document handling costs and improve both internal decision support and customer support. The technologies used include:

- Document scanners with optical character recognition for input,
- CDs, magnetic disk, or magnetic tape for storage,
- COLD (computer output to laser disk) for distribution,
- Document repository, which is just a large data base,
- Web browsers,

- Workflow engines to automate the process of moving documents, and
- Heavy use of XML.

These components are used to convert the image to searchable/editable documents, to allow indexing for search and retrieval, and version control. Check in/ check out software allows access to the document and shows who is working on it.

Web browser and Internet standards are used to gain access and organize the documents. The Web is not inherent. It is plumbing that recognizes people's browser experience. The Web allows off-site access, which is easier to maintain than client-server technology, and is scalable as the number of documents increases.

Among the unresolved document management issues are:

- Stability of the storage medium. Most optical disks are designed for a 10-year lifetime. Preferred storage media change over time as new ones are invented.
- Required retention time for legal purposes.

Representative document management systems available are:

- *4i Platform by Documentum, Inc.*- An open, scalable, secure platform for document management. Can create, manage, and delivering XML content. Support 50 file formats and integrates with major Enterprise Resource Planning systems such as SAP and PeopleSoft, and with portal systems such as Plumtree, Epicentric, Verity and Autonomy.
- *Document and Content Management Products by Hummingbird Ltd.* - A suite of document management tools with extensive search and retrieval capabilities including scalability, Web-based access, version history and security.
- *BASIS by Open Text Corporation* - Manages document collections consisting of documents and metadata. Web-enabled, with search and security functionality.
- *Panagon Platfom by FileNet Corporation.* -Manages dynamic documents throughout their lifecycle. Secure access, collaboration, creation, delivery, revisions, online publishing, and re-use.

8. Intelligent Agents : Intelligent agents are the products of artificial intelligence research. An intelligent agent is software program that is told what the user wants to retrieve by a questionnaire. Intelligent agents may be passive or active. *Passive agents* monitor incoming and available sources of knowledge (e.g,, the New York Times) for matches with the users preferences. *Active agents* seek out any information that is relevant to the users preferences no matter where the information is located, as long as the information is in a format that can be interpreted by the agent, and the agent can gain physical access to the information. An example of an active intelligent agent is Knowledge Update from Autonomy Inc. This software behaves like a personal assistant. The user can train the agent to do better in future searches by ranking the results returned by the agent.

9. Geographic Information Systems : The term "geographic information systems" (GIS) usually refers to systems for displaying maps and other two-dimensional information on a screen. The concept, however, is much broader. Technically, GIS is based on computer aided design software, where multiple pictures can be overlayed on one another and the user can choose which set of layers to display. Thus, for example, a GIS can display a street map with overlays of real estate lots; demographic information; schools and other public facilities; electricity, sewer, gas, and other utilities. The user can select which information he needs to display. From the point of view of knowledge management, any knowledge that is two-dimensional can be encoded and multiple layers selected.

10. Non-computer-based Knowledge Dissemination : Although knowledge is disseminated or transferred primarily with digital means, non-computer based methods are still in wide use. Three examples– the library, the London Taxi Cab licensing systern, and the team room are discussed here.

Libraries : Paper-based content is still the norm in libraries even though they are being increasingly computerized to increase their knowledge contents and to speed dissemination. The library is known as the repository. The librarian is a classic example of a human who points, telling people where to look for the specific knowledge they seek. The numeration systems (be it Dewey

Decimal or Library of Congress or Colon Scheme) also serve a point function.

London Taxi Cabs : Since 1851, aspirants for a London taxi license need to know, in detail, how to drive between any two points in the 25,000 streets within six miles of the Charing Cross railroad station. To prove their knowledge, they must pass a series of verbal tests. They are first given a 'blue book' called "The Knowledge", containing 400 typical runs, which they must master. They appear for a series of 15-minute interviews over a two to four year period at each of which they are asked 5 questions. The process is both grueling and time consuming. Although there are schools to help to people learn, the transfer of knowledge both from the book and from actually driving the streets requires transfer of explicit knowledge to tacit knowledge or, as some would say, 'from the head to the gut', that is then used to answer questions and then to drive passengers to their destinations. What is intriguing is the vast amount of knowledge involved in a non-computer based system. Fortunately for the taxi driver, streets and locations change slowly. Therefore, the knowledge is mostly static.

Team Rooms : Many firms dedicate rooms for group activities. Known as team rooms, these facilities provide both a place where team members can share knowledge and a place where team members can store knowledge about a project. Team rooms are examples of same place, different time groupware. In an advertising agency, a team room is used by the people who work with a particular client. People go to the team room to interact with others and, often, to see what others have done since they last visited. Sketches of proposed and existing advertising material cover the walls. The files in the room pertain to the particular client. However, all the team members do not have to be present at the same time.

But IT is a common way of sharing explicit knowledge, whereas tacit knowledge is best shared through people. Some forms of databases may function as ways to capture tacit knowledge and this is best achieved by the organization of such databases. One way is to structure the content around best practice and experiences gained within the organization. This kind of knowledge should be presented in short descriptions with contact information of who possess this knowledge within the organization. Another way is to use discussion databases, and the idea is to let employees communicate business gaps and solutions.

5.6. KNOWLEDGE TRANSFER AS A STEP – IN PROCESS

Knowledge transfer is a part of organizational life. It is carried out whether the process is managed or not. It is transmission of knowledge (experience lessons, learned, know - how) and use of transmitted knowledge. It is conveying the knowledge of one source to another source. Merely making knowledge available is not considered to be knowledge transfer. It is transmission plus absorption. The goal, is to promote and facilitate knowledge sharing, collaboration and networking. It is the access to scarce resources, new insights, new expertise, cross fertilization of knowledge, and creating an organizational environment of excellence. Collaboration means the ability to connect diverse assets into unique capabilities in pursuit of new opportunities for personal, group and organizational growth.

Knowledge transfer is done directly by working together, communicating, learning by doing, apprenticing, through face-to-face discussions, or embedding knowledge through procedures, mentoring, or documents exchange. It is not done solely from knowledge bases or repositories. Knowledge can be transferred from repositories to people, from teams to individuals, and between individuals.

To transfer knowledge, one should consider three factors:

- *Source of knowledge transfer* : Knowledge bases, innovations, lessons learned, programs, books, experts, articles, or data warehouses.
- *Media used in knowledge transfer* : Local area networks, wireless transmission, secure versus unsecured lines, or encrypted or plain text.
- *Target of knowledge transfer* : Apprentice, user, another computer, a team, any authorized individual, a manager, a customer, or an automated product maker.

Knowledge transfer facilitates knowledge sharing. The

collective knowledge of an organization is gleaned from the learning of its members as well as its stakeholders and customers. Knowledge transfer enhances knowledge fiows through collaborative technologies, especially the intranet or Internet. Hard, high -tech communications technologies and networks serve as the enablers of knowledge transfer and assure constant availability of knowledge on demand. This is best enforced by support from top management.

There are various requisities for knowledge transfer; these are discussed below :

5.6.1. Prerequisites for Transfer

The terms transfer and share are interrelated. Knowing is considered deeply personal. In one aspect, it asks someone to give something that is her or her own property. Knowledge transfer is a mechanistic term, which provides knowledge for someone else. The term share is an exchange of knowledge between individuals, between or within teams, or between individuals and knowledge bases repositories, and so forth. Knowledge sharing recognizes the personal nature of people's management gained from experience.

5.6.2. Instill an Atmosphere of Trust in the Organization

Trust is the foundation of knowledge transfer. It is psychological state, where people feel confident about sharing ideas, experiences and relationships with others. For decades, people in organizations have learned to hoard knowledge rather than to share it. There is still inherent fear that once knowledge is shared, the knower, the person who has the knowledge, becomes vulnerable.

5.6.3. Fix the Culture to Accommodate the Change

The trust factor has cultural and political implications. An organizational culture that promotes and rewards cooperation and collaboration is a better candidate for knowledge sharing than a competitive culture that drives explores to performance through the fear of punishment – such as layoffs or dismissal. There is the case of a 2006 graduate from a premier MBA school who accepted a 6-digit salary with the fast growing consulting firm. When the recession hit in 2007, the company laid off 40 percent of its staff without notifying anyone.

Early in the year, this graduate sensed things were not on the level. Managers kept information to themselves, and partners were working feverishly to attract new clients. He soon decided to keep to himself his technology - based knowledge required for installing two major projects for fortune 500 clients. That strategy saved him from being axed by the sudden layoffs.

5.6.4. Positive Cultural Values

These cultural values include the following –

- *Leadership* : for example, a leader is a champion who promotes change and one who if highly regarded by the employees.
- *Understanding company mission* : for example, a company can have a clear mission statement regarding knowledge management and how it plans to embed it in the organization.
- *Culturally internalized management practices* : For example, a company can have enthusiastic management that is optimistic about the changing environment.
- *Culturally internalized operational practices* : for example, a company can make decisions and solve problems by using collaboration and teamwork.
- *Culturally driven forces* : for example, employees must trust one another in a shared learning atmosphere. Trust in others generates honesty and fairness for all participants.

The key factors that retard cultural values include the following:

- *Culturally driven forces* : for example, specialists may hoard knowledge or deny that they have sought after knowledge. It is also the attitude of "I do not care" or "It is not my job".
- *Understanding company priorities* : for example, employees and management have a fuzzy understanding of the company's mission, policies, and strategies. Any out-of-the-ordinary ideas or innovations are perceived as unnecessary work.
- *Questionable values* : for example, the company may value money or financial goals as the ultimate goal of the business.

- *Questionable beliefs* : for example, a business may view employees as being replaceable.

5.6.5. Push Reasoning before Process

It never seems to fail that employees undergoing training show greater in process ("how to do ") than the reasoning ("why") behind process. For example in database training using Microsoft access, greater attention is given when trainees learn how to create tables, access data, and enter records than is paid to knowing why a database is designed and why you need a database for decision making. We experience the same situation every time we teach the database management system in school. Students think it is an answer rather than a process.

When people are hired into an organization, supervisors and managers introduce themselves, tell the new comer who they are? what the company philosophy is? and what they hope the new employee will be excepted to achieve? That should be the first thing to provide before employees are shown how to do the job.

5.6.6. Practice is far Better than Talking

Once a philosophy is understood, the next guideline is to teach and train employees as a way of knowing-not merely talking, conceptualizing, and thinking. Learning from doing things together brings up the concept of knowledge transfer via teams. In most of todays consulting firms. For example, junior staff just out of college are assigned to teams with field knowledge to be mentored by senior team members as a step toward more responsibilities in the future.

Teaching explaining and mentoring are the ways of transforming and sharing knowledge. So is doing the work and experimenting with different ways to do a job. Once you do it, you will know. Being involved in the actual process is the best way to learn it.

We live in an era of distance learning, where employees can acquire knowledge by learning on their own. There also jobs that are best learned by firsthand, tangible and physical experience. The traditional way of teaching and learning is for the trainer to stand up, show concepts and procedures through transparencies or slides, and expect people to go back to the job and do something with it. A better way of learning is to form a team with experienced members who show novices why a job is needed and how it is done before they are released to do the job.

5.6.7. Know How the Firm handles Mistakes

Mistakes are bound to be made and they are a cost for the firm to incur. Tolerating and forgiving mistakes in the interest of learning are important. A story is told about a young IBM executive who caused a $10 million mistake in the way he managed a high risk project. When brought before Dr. Watson, the founder of IBM, the young man snapped, "I guess I am here because you will want my resignation". Dr. Watson replied, "You have to be kidding. We just blew $10 million to train you".

There is rarely any "doing" without mistakes. In fact, some of the best learning in business is by trail and error, which implies some failure or taking steps backward to move foreword. The question is in how the firm reacts. Being human, certain mistakes are forgivable as long as the employees owns up to them. Tolerance for mistakes allows room for learning to take place.

Ensure that cooperation and collaboration are not competition of internal rivalry. Today's growing trend is that the best projects are accomplished via teamwork, cooperation, and collaboration of company specialists committed to produce the best product or service against outside competition. The product is based on common effort and shared goals; and the success of each employee depends on joint cooperation and knowledge sharing by everyone in the group. Employees begin to learn from one another build an attitude of a belief that the best, way for them to succeed is if their product competitive in the marketplace.

5.6.8. Identify What Counts and What makes Sense

An organization relies on reports and computer-based information to assets what happens over time. All reports historical events, transactions, or developments. Unfortunately, nothing is represented that analyzes the reasoning behind the information or why the resulting business turned out the way it did. In addition, there seems to be no prioritization of what should be acted on or what changes should be made that make sense to create a better future for the firm.

5.6.9. Take a Close Look at the Managers and how They view Knowledge Transfer

Managers and leaders set the tone for how a department, a division, or the entire firm should perform. Within the framework of knowledge management practices, managers are expected to create a culture or an organizational climate that sets work and norms and values the transfer of knowledge to produce value-added products and services. It is an effective way to bridge the knowledge-action gap.

5.6.10. Assess Employee Job Satisfaction and Stability of the Workplace

The success of knowledge transfer and knowledge sharing depends to get a great extent, on how satisfied employees are on the job and the turnover rate in the workplace. For knowledge transfer to be effective, employees have to work in a culture that accommodates transfer, and they must apply and share transferred knowledge in an environment of trust and trust–worthiness. Regardless of these factors, employees must be satisfied with the *status quo* if they are to cooperate and collaborate with others as a team.

Job satisfaction is derived from the degree of match between an employee's vocational needs and the requirements of job. The major known vocational needs include the following:

Ability Utilization, Acheivement, Activity, Advancement, Authority, Compensation, Creativity, independence, Moral values, Recognition, Responsibility, Security, Status, Supervision - human relations, Supervision–technical, Variety, and the Working conditions.

5.7. TRANSFER STRATEGIES

Knowledge management implies formalized knowledge transfer and requires specific strategies to ensure successful transfer. Knowledge is transferred via documents, an intranet, groupware, databases, knowledge bases, and a lot more. By far, the most effective channel for knowledge transfer is a face-to-face meeting in the business place.

5.8. INHIBITORS OF KNOWLEDGE TRANSFER

There are several organizations and cultural factors that inhibit reliable knowledge transfer. Some inhibitors are easier to correct than others. The following are the key areas where friction occurs and ways to correct it.

5.8.1. Lack of Trust

A major element in the success of any knowledge transfer project is one commonality of language people have with one another. A shared language can only strengthen trust among the participants, whether they are professors, surgeons, attorneys, or night watchmen of a high-rise building. Trust develops after people share proprietary knowledge and feel the reciprocal to be at least intrinsically rewarding. The more people assess one another and have a feel for where they stand, the easier it is to decide how much they can trust one another. Finally, we shall find that cultural, language, status who gives the knowledge, and location mistakes could be "make or break" of trust for successful knowledge transfer.

5.8.2. Lack of Time and Conference Places

People tend to find knowledge nearby or get the closest source, not the best one. To expedite knowledge transfer, people must show interest, take time and find meeting places where they can exchange ideas. The "I do not have time because I am snowed under", excuse is rarely a valid excuse. A volunteering spirit of cooperation, collaboration and coordination is a powerful enabler of knowledge transfer.

5.8.3. Status of the Knower

People decide to act on knowledge or information based on who gives it to them. A senior vice president to attend a union meeting gives an impression that the company cares. Status refers to the individual's position within a group or an organization, compared with those of fellow employees. One attribute that tends to give a person status, for example, is age. If a company does not want age to be given status, it will have promotions and reward policies that favour youth and work against age.

Status and status symbols – title, size of office, office views, types of furniture in the office is located on, the kind of company car assigned, and so forth, are important management factors that affect the behaviour of individuals and groups. We should look at what status can and cannot do for organizations.

People who consider status and still are reluctant to transferred knowledge to good use could have several reasons for feeling that way – not respecting or trusting the knower, not considering the knowledge to be important, pride, and lack risks. When this happens, it does little good to push knowledge transfer for the mere show that knowledge is freely shared.

5.8.4. Quality and Speed of Transfer

When is knowledge is transferred from a reliable, high profile source, it is expected to be of the quality that promotes its use. Unfortunately, that is not always the case. The quality to transfer can be influenced by factors such as mentorship, on the job training, job rotation, and career paths that define the way, timing and duration of job experiences. In contrast, knowledge downloaded form a database or a knowledge base is not a match for the on-site, person-to-person knowledge transfer.

5.9. HOW KNOWLEDGE IS TRANSFERRED

Once the foregoing elements are put into place, knowledge transfer should turn into new action. The question is what types of knowledge can/be transferred. Three main types are as follows:

- Collective sequential transfer,
- Explicit inter–team knowledge transfer, and
- Tacit knowledge transfer.

Each category is explained below. When it comes to design considerations, each type requires a unique design, depending on the recipient, the type of knowledge transferred and the complexity of the project. The goal is to ensure that the delivery mechanism will meet the requirements of the users of the knowledge.

5.9.1. Collective Sequential Transfer

This is one of the easiest and most straight forward types of knowledge transfer. An ongoing team specialized in one specific task moves to other locations and performs the same tasks. For example, in building new homes in the suburbs, septic systems are installed by a team that does nothing else. Based on the local code, a team of three to five members digs up a designated area with a backhoe; installs pipes, feeders, a trap, and so forth; buries them; and reseeds the area to blend with the rest of the landscape. This know-how requires decisions on the size of the pipes, the direction and slope of the flow, and provisions for venting and future repairs. Once the system is completed, the same team reuses the same knowledge; goes to another new home site; and builds the same septic infrastructure, with variations to meet the local codes. The procedure remains the same. Change occurs only if the country or city alters the regulations or the septic codes. What is unique about collective sequential transfer is that knowledge is transferred from one site to another by the same team.

In every team setting, there is a protocol or a way to specify how a team should function. With a focus on collaborative sequential knowledge transfer, where jobs are interdependent and performed in some sequence, each team member is expected to carry a "suitcase" of knowledge. There is also an assumption that each member has vested interest in sharing rather than hogging knowledge. The activity carried out by members is done in fulfilling team goals - completing a project collectively, and effectively.

The unique features of collaborative sequential knowledge transfer include the following:

- Team meetings are usually brief, but are held regularly a time and the occasion permit. Meeting, monitors are understood, based on the way the team has conducted previous meetings. There is usually a facilitator or an informal leader who initiates the meeting, monitors the discussions or exchanges, and makes sure things do not drag unnecessarily. Facilitators are routinely rotated among the members. Some of the questions raised centered around what happened during the job just completed, whether there were any differences that should be discussed, and why things happened the way they did.
- Meetings are held with all participants being equal. There should be no discrimination or hierarchical priorities set as

to who speaks first, how influential one's comments are compared to the rest and the like. With this in mind, team members are expected to be proactive rather than reactive and assertive rather than laid back with no attitude such as "look this was not my job, so I can not comment" my job is to lay pipes, no more no less".

- Whatever takes place in meetings is kept within the team. There is no reporting relationship to the organizations higher-ups. This eliminates that team members begin to understand and trust the circumstances under which they can or cannot share knowledge.
- A unique feature of collaborative sequential knowledge transfer is focus on the project not the person or the personality. The approach, the setting and the seating arrangements are not army, i.e., style one row behind the other, or classroom style. Team members face one another, and anyone can make a comment anytime within reason. The goal is to fine-tune performance, improve quality and assure integrity of the work perfromed by the team.

5.9.2. Explicit Inter–team Transfer

This type of knowledge transfer simply allows team that has done a job on one site to share the experience with another team working on a similar job on another site.

5.9.3. Tacit Knowledge Transfer

This type of knowledge transfer is complex and is used in non-algorithmic projects where knowledge is mentally stored. The team receiving tacit knowledge is different by location by experience, by technology and by cultural norms. This means that what ever is being transferred has to modified in language, tone and content to be usable by the receiving team.

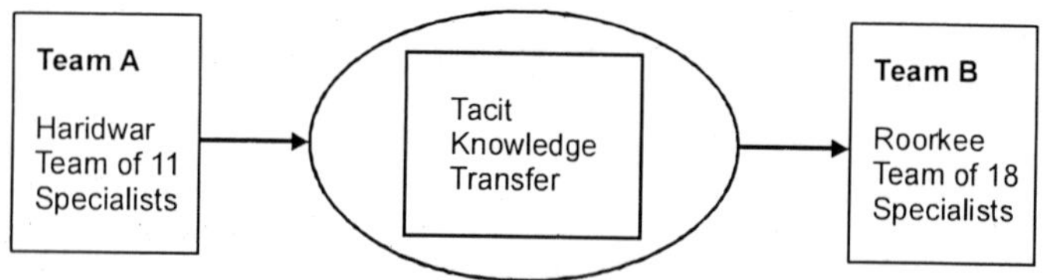

Fig. 5.4. Tacit Knowledge Transfer

5.10. KNOWLEDGE TRANSFER IN E-WORLD

Since 1960, when the first business computer appeared, information technology has changed the way commerce is conducted around the globe. From mainframes to accounting systems the personal computer revolution, local area networks, electronic data interchange, client/server design and enterprise resource planning have all had a hand in shaping today's business organization. The past decade had been the Internet decade, however, when companies worldwide have embraced a change without equal. It is a change that promises to have more impact and be more lasting than anything else we have to seen to date. Technology is setting the place for how a company does business, how it changes knowledge with suppliers, and how it communicates with customers and others in the new marketplace.

The primary technology for this transformation is the internet-global data, information and knowledge network that moves closer and closer to the ubiquity of the telephone with each passing day. What makes the Internet so powerful is that it is more about knowledge exchange and communication than it is about technology. It is a medium and a market. It is virtually unstoppable, forcing all kinds of business to reexamine their practices and their futures.

The Internet began with message communications, but now it is possible to transmit and receive information containing graphics, voice, photos, and even full-motion videos. The part of the Internet that can accomplish these tasks is called the World Wide Web, also known as WWW or the Web. The Internet today offers a variety of services including e-mail, access to remote computers, news, and the quick and easy transmission of information between computers worldwide.

Internet Service Providers : To link rapidly growing commercial Internet landscape, the Internet Service Provider (ISP) industry was born in the mid - 1990s, and it offers a variety of services include the following:

- Linking consumers and business to the Internet (for example, America online, Microsoft Network, and CompuServe),

- Monitoring and maintaining customers websites,
- Network management and system integration,
- Backbone access services for other ISPs such as PSI and UUNET, and
- Payment systems for online purchases.

Almost everything one needs on the internet is free. Among the free services are the following :

- Hotlists, which tell the user what is popular and what is not.
- Comics that focus on entertainment events.
- Software archives that list the latest free software available.
- Weather services that provide free weather forecasts anywhere in the world.
- Magazines and broad casting stations that constantly update the news.
- Searchers that help locate items or subjects on the internet.
- Dictionaries that include thesaurus and "fact" books on almost all subjects, and
- Government services that publicize what is available from them.

Unique Benefits of the Internet : The Internet is the enabler of knowledge transfer and knowledge sharing worldwide. Managers use it to glean intelligence about rivals, monitor sales, and so on.

Among the uses and advantages of the Internet as they relate to knowledge management are the following:

- *Doing business fast*, knowledge transfer is conducted in minutes rather than hour or days, compared to waiting on the phone or meeting as a team. This speed compresses transfer time and promotes the growth of knowledge sharing.
- *Gathering opinions and trying out new ideas*, the Internet is an ideal place for trying out new ideas at low cost. Interactive surveys provide quick feedback. Opinions can be gathered from just about anywhere. Many online opinion polls provide real-time statistics to the user after a computer package analyses the user's response in real time.
- *Leveling the playing field*, when a company advertises its

products or services on the Internet, it is on equal footing with larger companies. The nice feature about the Internet is that it allows your business to appear alongside big-name companies.

Limitations : Like any system, the Internet and the World Wide Web also have unique limitations. The main limitations of Internet use for knowledge of knowledge exchange are – security and privacy. Key questions that are continually asked by online consumers are "How do I know am sharing knowledge on a secure line?", "How do I know the web site assures me privacy for the information I am seeking?"

In addition to fakes and forgeries, there are other threats. Hackers, worms, Trojan horses, viruses, and zombies threaten the security and integrity of any information or knowledge exchange. Viruses are the best-known malicious software. These programs secretly attach themselves to other programs and then infect and reproduce in a manner similar to biological viruses.

5.11. KNOWLEDGE SHARING

Acquiring or creating knowledge is critical for an organization to compete effectively in a knowledge-based economy, but these processes do not guarantee success. For the organization to benefit most from employee's knowledge, their knowledge must be shared. Knowledge sharing promotes the widespread learning and minimizes the likelihood of wasting resources to solve the same problem repeatedly.

Knowledge sharing is a conditional process for, developing homogeneity in organizational member knowledge. The overall result of organizational learning should be an improvement in 'the range of an organization's potential behaviour'. The need for both-heterogeneity and homogeneity in knowledge - for organizational learning is also recognized in the famous distinction between exploitation and exploration. The need for both types of knowledge renders the question of how processes of knowledge transfer (between groups) and knowledge sharing (within a group) are related to each other.

The success of knowledge sharing also relies heavily on

knowledge leadership, because sharing activities are facilitated in an environment that discourages knowledge hoarding and rewards knowledge creation.

Nonaka and Takeuchi outline four processes that explain how knowledge is shared. The first process is *socialization*, where the tacit knowledge of one person is converted through conversation or other personal means into tacit knowledge for another person. An example would be an informal conversation between coworkers in which one shares an insight about a customer with the other. The second process is *externalization*, in which tacit knowledge is converted into explicit knowledge such as when someone writes down what they have learned. An example of this would be writing a memo about a meeting, or creating a manual about a specific process that has not been previously recorded. The third process is *combination*, in which explicit knowledge is converted into another form of explicit knowledge. Some examples of combination include writing a paper that incorporates explicit knowledge or creating a Web site from some form of explicit knowledge. The final process is *internalization*, in which explicit knowledge is converted into tacit knowledge. This is demonstrated when a person reads a manual and can perform the procedure described therein.

In organizational contexts, some of these processes have been integrated into three models of knowledge creation– knowledge conversion, knowledge building and knowledge linking.

Knowledge conversion features conversion between personal, tacit knowledge of the individual and the shared, explicit knowledge of the organization. Once it has become explicit knowledge within the organization, then it is converted back into tacit knowledge as individuals learn about it and assimilate it. This model focuses on an internal knowledge cycle, and requires some special conditions within the organization. The organization must have an "organizational intention" and this vision must be transmitted to individuals so they know what knowledge is valuable to the organization. The individuals must also be allowed to work with autonomy, so they are free to discover new knowledge.

Sharing of tacit knowledge and other ideas needs to be promoted through "information redundancy," which is the idea that it is acceptable for information to be repeated or replicated among individuals and throughout the organization. The organization can also encourage the knowledge conversion process through ''fluctuation and creative chaos" which sets the stage for rethinking and reinventing routines. Finally, the organization's internal diversity must be a good match for the diversity visible in the external environment. This means that an organization must have a sufficient range of resources and processors to address the dimensions of the external environment. For example, an organization that exists in the domain of biotechnology, needs to have a sufficient array of experts and knowledge resources to address the issues that comprise this field.

Knowledge building is a process that relies on the organization creating an environment that nurtures knowledge building activities and increases the core capabilities of the individuals within the organization. These kinds of activities include shared problem solving, experimenting and prototyping, importing knowledge from outside the organization, as well as implementing and integrating new processes and tools.

Knowledge linking features learning alliances with other organizations that allow knowledge to be transferred between them. This model requires examination of and coordination of specialized relationships, work cultures and operating styles.

Each of these three models encourages interaction between individuals and ideas, thereby raising the possibility that any given problem may be tackled from multiple perspectives. Knowledge often takes on different meaning when observed from different viewpoints. This creates the synergy that drives innovation and knowledge creation. But, this also breeds several problems in terms of system design including how to classify and organize knowledge artifacts so that they can be utilized from these multiple perspectives and subject to disparate interpretations.

From the perspective of the socio-cultural rules employed to guide the sharing of knowledge in an organization four types of environments for knowledge sharing can be distinguished.

5.11.1. Law-and-Order Model

In the law-and-order model, power, rights and privileges determine the practice of sharing knowledge. The power system in an organization standardizes the distribution, sharing and handing-on of knowledge. There is a clear distinction between those who are informed and those who are not. As the power system is subject to organizational design, management prescribes the "ideal" form of the organizational knowledge base in the law-and-order-model. Here, power is used to enforce this ideal form.

5.11.2. Family Culture Model

In the family culture model, the sharing of knowledge is determined by interpersonal sympathy and antipathy as well as traditional, and unwritten moral obligations. Solidarity ensures that all members of the "family" share the knowledge. As there is no standardization, a family member is at the mercy of the other family members to share in the family's knowledge. The consequence is that there are all kinds of group relations that lead to informal standardization of knowledge and the way of knowledge sharing specific to groups. This eases sharing within groups and hinders sharing between groups.

5.11.3. Market Model

In this model, knowledge is considered a resource the value of which is determined on the basis of supply and demand. As opposed to the law-and-order model, it is not the flows of knowledge that are designed with respect to their contents, but the framework in which the market transactions take place has to be guaranteed. Thus, organizational "deregulation" replaces traditional principles of organization such as privileges and rewards. *Deregulation* means, for example establishing property rights for knowledge, improving transparency through standardization of knowledge and enforcing standards for the quality of knowledge.

5.11.4. Discourse Model

In the discourse model, the goal is to achieve "objective" truth, material, normative findings as well as to achieve consensus about the valuing of these findings. The process of the development of knowledge is based solely on the power of convincing arguments.

A discursive standardization of the organizational knowledge base thus requires that the members of the organization make their usually divergent mental models explicit, share them and unify them in an ongoing process of exchanging arguments.

These four types reflect social rules of give and take and are the main basis for the cultural dimension of sharing knowledge.

But the truth is knowledge that is available but never applied is of little use. Unless employees apply their knowledge appropriately, investments in knowledge acquisition and knowledge creation will produce little in return. To the extent that knowledge use is an intentional behaviour, employees must not only possess the required knowledge but also recognize that they have the required knowledge, be motivated to use it, and believe that it is feasible to use it.

5.12. IMPLICATIONS FOR KNOWLEDGE MANAGEMENT

Knowledge flow, transfer, or sharing, whether it is face to face, through an electronic knowledge base or is team-base involves management support. Any transfer should be carried out with the larger goals of the organizations in mind. The link between knowledge and goals should be clearly defined and effectively defined and effectively implemented with the framework of the organizations knowledge management strategic plans.

In addition a knowledge management system that accommodates knowledge transfer on an going basis should have a facility to monitor its process, report and promote its benefits to participants, and ensure continuity by the knowledge developer or the chief knowledge officer (CKO). In the final analysis, the process and outcome become a compliance based on choice.

If top management is serious about knowledge management and knowledge transfer, several types steps should be taken to ensure a reliable infrastructure that will serve the organizations, long-term needs. First a candidate department or company division with interest in knowledge sharing should be selected to set the tone for the enterprise. As we do in major projects, a committee representing the entity should be formed to begin strategic thinking about how to build a knowledge management environment and launch knowledge sharing. This might involve changes in policy, procedures, training and retraining, and addressing the cultural and work norms to effect a change from knowledge hoarding to knowledge sharing.

Once a steering committee is in place, the next task is to undertake knowledge assessment evaluating existing knowledge, where it resides, how it is being used, and what apart of it needs to be updated, deleted, and so forth. Following this critical step a procedure should be designed for knowledge transfer and the types of knowledge and how they should be determined. Doing that means looking more closely at existing technology, the company intranet, e-mail technology, and security status. To complete the transfer, receiving individuals or receiving teams must begin to share their knowledge with the right people so that everyone in the division will enrich their experience, improve their productivity and add value to the strategic goals of the organization. In doing so, the organization as an ongoing venture should begin to realize benefits and grow exponentially in the competitive environment in which it operates.

6

KNOWLEDGE MANAGEMENT TOOLS

Knowledge management involves recognizing generating, documenting and distributing, and transferring between persons explicit and tacit knowledge to increase organizational effectiveness. It involves developing a system for collecting and maintaining data, information, experiences and lessons, as well as understanding how to facilitate social interaction so that both explicit and tacit knowledge are developed and exchanged. The former involves information technology or hardware development; the physical arrangement of the work environment, and effective processes for work teams.

Most of the knowledge management efforts emphasize technology— the capture, storage and transfer of codified information such as statistics, presentations and reports using an intranet or other type of computer network or the technology. This emphasis on technology misses a key ingredient of knowledge management–facilitating workplace learning and generating knowledge. However, the three dominant streams of research into Knowledge Management can be identified on the basis of knowledge managment research.

The first stream focusses primarily on research into the theory of knowledge, the knowledge of the firm, organisational culture, measurement of intellectual capital and learning organisations. These researchers tackle the theoretical aspects of knowledge management, developing models for valuing intellectual capital. Some researchers even challenge Nonaka and Takeuchi's framework for the socialisation and externalisation of knowledge.

The second stream is represented by the work on corporate memories (aka organizational memories and organizational memories and organizational memory information (OMIS)) for enhanced decision making. A corporate memory embraces all forms of institutional knowledge, whether formally encoded within the current information systems, or tacit (informal) knowledge used by individuals in professionals practice. This group has a strong focus on knowledge sharing and on practical applications of knowledge management in a enterpirsek-wide perspective.

The third stream, with a strong contribution from computer scientists and artificial intelligence (AI) researchers in particular, tackles the areas of intelligent agents, ontologies or taxonomies, data mining, knowledge modeling and computer-mediated collaborations. As far as tools for knowledge management are concerned, they are stressed over the use of computer's and communication technology.

6.1. CATEGORISATION OF KM TOOLS

Quite logically, most of the commercial knowledge management or KM supports one or both of the above approaches. In order to better understand the origin and the characteristics of these software, it is necessary to reflect upon the major KM research streams stated above. All the research streams in KM, especially the third have spawned the development of tools for supporting various knowledge processes (e.g., capturing, encoding, organising, searching, distributing and measuring) at the individual level and virtual collaborations at the group and organisational levels. Generally speaking, a KM system is any organisational information system that integrates various knowledge processes to solve one or more business problems. In a wider sense, the objectives of developing and deploying a KMS are :

– Capture, create and share knowledge assets

- Locate relevant information knowledge
- Provide an environment for knowledge exchange
- Connect people with relevant interest and/or skills
- Facilitate and/or support intelligent problem solving (e.g., decision making)

One can perceive from the above objectives that, the fields of Artificial Intelligence (AI) and Information Retrieval (IR), among other areas, have a strong influence on the origin and evolution of KM tools. After nearly three decades of research, many of the proven techniques in AI have now evolved into commercial products. Such techniques include, but are not limited to, rule-based reasoning, inexact reasoning, case-based reasoning, data mining, conceptual clustering, natural language processing and generation.

6.2. INTELLIGENCE

The computational part of the ability to achieve goals in the world is intelligence. It involves mechanisms and Artificial Intelligence research that discover how to make computers carry out some of them. If doing a task requires only mechanisms that are well understood today, computer programs can give very impressive performances on these tasks.

Artificial Intelligence (AI) is the science and engineering of making intelligent machines, especially intelligent computer programs. It is related to the similar task of using computers to understand human intelligence, but AI does not have to confine itself to methods that are biologically observable. It is also abbreviated as AI.

There are two ways of Artificial Intelligence –

1. On the one hand, man can learn something about how to make machines solve problems by observing other people or just by observing human methods.
2. On the other hand, AI involves studying the problelms or challenges presented to intelligence instead of studying people or animals.

AI researchers are free to use methods that are not observed in people or that involve much more computing than people can do.

Alan Turing was the first to decide that AI was best researched by programming computers rather than by building machines. By the late 1950s, there were many researchers on AI, and the most of them were basing their work on programming computers. In his article on computing Machinery and Intelligence, he argued that "If the machine could successfully pretend to be human to a knowledgeable observer then certainly it should be considered intelligent."

This test would satisfy most people but not all philosophers. The observer could interact with the machine and a human be teletype (to avoid requiring that the machine imitate the appearance or voice of the person), and the human would try to persuade the observer that it was human and the machine would try to fool the observer.

The turing test is a one-sided test. A machine that passes the test should certainly be considered intelligent, but a machine could still be considered intelligent without knowing enough about humans to imiate a human.

Turning in 1950, published another article in the magazine, which triggered a controversial topic, "Can a machine think?" Here, he proposed an 'limitation game' which was later modified to "Turning Test". In the imitation game, the players are three humans — a male, a female and an interrogator. The interrogator who is shielded from the other two, asks questions to both of them and based on their typewirtten answers determines who is male and who is female. The aim of the male is to imitate the female and deceive the interrogator and the role of the female is to provide replies that would inform the interrogator about the true sex.

Daniel Denett's book *Brain children* has an excellent discussion of the Turing test and the various partial Turing tests that have been implemented, i.e., with restrictions on the observer's knowledge of AI and the subject matter of questioning. It turns out that some people are easily led into believing that a rather dumb program is intelligent.

The ultimate effort is to make computer programs that can solve problems and achieve goals in the world as well as humans.

However, many people involved in particular research areas are much less ambitious. A few people think that human level intelligence can be achieved.

- by writing large numbers of programs and
- assembiling vast knowledge bases of facts in the languages now used for expressing knowledge.

However, most AI researchers believe that new fundamental ideas are required, and therefore it cannot be predicted when human leve intelligence will be achieved.

6.3. COMPUTERS FOR ARTIFICIAL INTELLIGENCE

Scientists have tried two methods for AI. One is designing a special machine and then use a computer to test it. The other one is using the computer itself for AI.

1. *Computers can be programmed to simulate any kind of machine* : Many researchers invented non-computer machines, hoping that they would be intelligent in different ways than the computer programs could be. However, they usually simulate their invented machines on a computer and come to doubt that the new machine is worth building. Because many billions of dollars that have been spent in making computers faster and faster, another kind of machine would have to be very fast to perform better than a program on a computer simulating the machine.
2. *Making a "child machine" that could improve by reading and by learning from experience?* : This idea has been proposed many times, starting in the 1940s. Eventually, it will be made to work. However, AI programs have not yet reached the level of being able to learn much of what a child learns form physical experience. Nor do present programs understand language well enough to learn much by reading.

6.4. APPLICATIONS OF ARTIFICIAL INTELLIGENCE

Artificial Intelligence programmes are applied in many fields. They are :

- Game Playing
- Speech Recognition

- Understanding Natural Language
- Computer Vision
- Expert Systems etc.

Game Playing : One can buy machines that can play master level chess for a few hundred dollars. There is some AI in them, but they play well against people mainly through brute force computation – looking at hundreds of thousands of positions. To beat a world champion by brute force and known reliable heuristics requires being able to book at 200 million positions per second.

Speech Recognition : In the 1990s, computer speech recognition reached a practical level for limited purposes. Thus United Airlines has replaced its keyboard tree for flight information by a system using speech recognition of flight numbers and city names.

It is quite convenient on the other hand, while it is possible to instruct some computers using speech, most users have gone back to the keyboard and the mouse as still more convenient. But now it has become possible to identity the voice as well as the face and other things by the computers; this comes under Biometry.

Understanding Natural Language : Just getting a sequence of words into a computer is not enough. Parsing sentences is not enough either. The computer has to be provided with an understanding of the domain the text is about, and this is presently possible only for very limited domains.

Computer Vision : The world is composed of three-dimensional objects, but the inputs to the human eye and computers' TV cameras are two dimensional. Some useful programs can work solely in two dimensions, but full computer vision requires partial three dimensional information that is not just a set of two-dimensional views. At present there are only limited ways of representing three-dimensional information directly and they are not as good as what humans evidently use.

Expert System : A 'Knowledge engineer' interviews experts in a certain domain and tries to embody their knowledge in a computer program for carrying out some task. These works depend on the intellectual mechanisms required for the task. One of the first expert systems was MYCIN in 1974, which diagnosed bacterial infections of the blood and suggested treatments. It did better than medical students or practicing doctors, provided its limitations were observed.

Its ontology included bacteria, symptoms and treatments and did not include patients, doctors, hospitals, death, recovery, and events occuring in time. Its interactions depended on a single patient being considered. Since the experts consulted by the knowledge engineers knew about patients, doctors, death, recovery, etc., it is clear that the knowledge engineers forced what the experts told them into a predetermined framework. In the present state of AI, this has to be true. The usefulness of current expert systems depends on their users having common sense.

Heuristic Classification is one of the most feasible kinds of expert system is to put some information in one of fixed set of categories using several sources of information. An example is advising whether to accept a proposed credit card purchase. Information is available about the owner of the credit card, his record of payment and also about the item he is buying and about the establishment from which he is buying it, e.g., about whether there have been previous credit card frauds at this establishment.

6.5. TOOLS

However, AI are KM are not the same; they are related but there are also significant differences between these two fields. One should also note that back in the 1980s and 90s, large organisations invested considerably into the development of expert systems. These systems are mostly problem solving, both rule-based and neural-based, in nature and are applicable only in a restricted domain.During the development of these systems, a great deal of decision-making knowledge or so-called "domain expertise" has been acquired and represented in rules and/or decision tables. Compared to today's KM efforts which typically have a "macro" focus on fostering knowledge sharing inside as well as between organisations, AI projects represent a somewhat "micro" focus on KM dwelling on the representation and processing of knowledge structures by computers. The following tool categorizations are increasingly becoming evident in the market focusing on the origin, alignment with business processes, and capabilities of commercial KM software.

6.5.1. Search Engines

Search engines have become a critical component of the internet and corporate intranets because of the vast increase in electronically available information. This information explosion is due to two major influences. First, the general availability of inter-networked databases and information repositories has expanded user's access to information. Second, the rapid acceptance of network access as a standard business and home tool is energizing organizations to add information to online databases.

Search can range from simple keyword match or attribute-based input to context-sensitive search (i.e., taking into consideration the user's interest, role type, and the very activities he or she is conducting just prior to issuing the search). Some tools also make extensive use of a word taxonomy or an ontology.

Some tools also make extensive use of a word taxonomy or an ontology which can either be manually created or automatically discovered with user guidance to navigate the search space so that results are contained and are highly aligned to the user's need(s). More sophisticated tools are emerging and these will, progressively, incorporate collaborative filtering techniques allowing the user to be more selective in controlling the search space and precise in terms of the specificity and format of the information being sought. For example, some of the latest products allow the user to enter a goal statement instead of keywords, as input and the search engine translates the goal to a list of specific search probes on a pre-defined search space, which may include public web sites, intranets, and individual PCs. Collaborative filtering also allows search patterns, results, and work products to be shared and reused among a group of interested parties, typically via a Web-based common collaborative area or shared spaces that can be replicated among all the participants (e.g., Groove). Some of the challenges in conducting searches are to seamlessly integrate the results gathered from inside as well as external to an organisation and to apply a dynamic and effective relevance-ranking mechanism in filtering and ranking the results.

6.5.2. Meta/Web Crawler

Crawlers are Web-based tools that facilitate intelligent searching with extensive use of meta-data and indexing. Data are not limited to texts and numerals, but often involve multimedia formats (i.e., voice, graphics, video, etc.). A common feature of Web crawlers is the ability to place "hooks" on targeted locations on the Web, detect changes in the content, and notify the user of the change either immediately or at pre-set intervals. Among other applications, such tools are especially suited for performing research on the Web and the gathering of market and competitive intelligence. Another characteristic of Web Crawlers is their ability to conduct seemingly parallel searches on other major search sites, combine, prune (i.e., remove duplicates, delete "dead links" or replace "dead links" by cached results), and rank the final results for the user. This feature yields significant time saving for the user as, otherwise without the tool, one needs to re-enter the same search cue multiple times that often sequentially and has to consolidate the results manually.

6.5.3. Process Modeling and Mind Mapping

These tools provide a visual environment for ideas to be captured and shared, both at the individual and group levels. Some of the advanced tools also allow business processes to be defined and modeled. Such tools greatly enhance the conceptualisation of procedural and declarative knowledge. However, up to now nearly all the tools in this category are stand-alone products rather than "plug-in" to other existing information/communication systems.

As a central component of any Personal KM tools, there are two key challenges to future tools in this category. Firstly, the ability to automate the conversion of the defined business processes to operable business objects for presentation and simulation allowing versatile questions to be posed. Some progress has already been made. In particular, a tool called Mind Manager supports the generation of concept maps (called "mind maps") as well as automatically generating documents, presentations, and Web pages from these maps. There is significant progress in the academic research as well. Secondly, set operations (e.g., join, expand, contract, superimpose, conflict resolution) governing the "processing" of concept maps still need to be defined. For instance, there is no reason why email messages, which have been mostly text in nature, cannot be supplemented by concept/mind/knowledge maps so that users can define and communicate visual information in synchronisation with a pre-defined corporate taxonomy, e.g., a base layer of knowledge maps representing terms that are commonly used in an organisation or industry. In fact, some of the personal mind mapping tools are beginning to be used for brainstorming in real time virtual collaborations.

6.5.4. Case-Based Reasoning (CBR)

CBR is an AI technique that enables past cases (i.e., problems and solutions), with appropriate modifications, to be reused in unseen/new situations. Many CBR systems have been developed for help desk (e.g., call centre) and software development applications. In the product development area, organisations are, for example, packaging their "case bases" (which contain product development and product support knowledge) when new products/ services are launched. In some cases, these "case-bases" (a form of "organisational experience") are embedded in a self-help system that is bundled into a new product. With the increasing demand in profiling personalisation in all customer-related activities in service-oriented organisations, CBR tools will continue to play a significant role in the landscape of KM tools.

6.5.5. Data and Text Mining

This category of tools, which enables meaningful patterns and associations of data – words and phrases to be identified from one or more large databases, has been around for more than a decade. They form part of a KM solution as many developers and researchers consider data and text mining to be a type of "micro" knowledge strategies (as opposed to Knowledge Program Management as a suite of "macro" knowledge strategies) for an organisation. Data and text mining systems are being used extensively in business intelligence, direct marketing and customer relationship management applications. As most organisations only have a small group of data miners, it is doubtful that data and text mining tools, though remaining a strong technical component, will be accessed via an enterprise-wide corporate portal. On the other hand, Enterprise Information Systems (EIS), which have a much stronger focus on reporting and forecasting, but less in "discovering" patterns, are becoming readily accessible from corporate intranets to support routine tactical and strategic decision making. In the near future, the output from using such tools will be gradually aligned to support key business processes in organisations, but functionally they are expected to operate independently (apart from the sourcing of data) from other enterprise systems. Business processes can range from data gathering to data mining, encoding of business rules, capturing of decision making criteria, matching of customer profiles to product services, content management and the incorporation of feedback.

6.5.6. Taxonomy/Ontological Tools

A taxonomy can be defined as a collection of terms/keywords that is commonly used in an organization or industry. Very often the relationship(s) between these terms are also captured. Examples of a relationship are 'hierarchical' – where one term is more general hence subsumes another term; 'functional' where terms are indexed based on their functional capabilities, and 'networked' – where they are multiple links between the terms defined in the taxonomy. An ontology can be a far more elaborate framework than a taxonomy. In addition to the definition and linkages between terms (concepts), an ontology also supports deep (refined) representation (for both descriptive and procedural knowledge) of each of the concepts as well as defined domain theory or theories that govern the permissible operations with the concepts in the ontology.

There are at least three ways to develop a taxonomy/ontology-manually constructed (using some kind of building tools), automatically discovered (from a repository of knowledge assets), or purchased off-the-shelf, (e.g., medical ontologies representing injuries, body parts, and clinical information). Taxonomies/Ontologies serve multiple purposes in an organization. They can be used as a corporate glossary holding detail descriptions of every key terms used in an organization or industry. They can also be used to constrain the search space of search engines and prune search results, identify and group people with common interests, and act as a content/knowledge map to improve the compilation and real time navigation of Web pages. Ontologies can also be used to support business process modeling. A niche area in the landscape of KM software, some of the taxonomy/ontological tools also form part of a broad-based KM system (e.g., Autonomy). Industry-specific ontologies as well as stand-alone ontological toolkits (e.g., Semio, Health Language's CyberLE) are now available in the market.

Groupware : This category of software has the strongest representation for two reasons. First, there is a clear alignment of the features/capabilities offered by groupware with the "Personalisation" approach to KM. Second, the advancement of E-Business/Commerce over the past few years has increased the need for virtual collaborations. This is especially the case for distributed and virtual project teams, where team members are from multiple organisations and in dispersed locations. Examples of common features offered by groupware tools are email communications, instant messaging, discussion areas, file area or document repository, information management tools (e.g., calendar, contact lists, meeting agendas and minutes), and search Common platforms/groupware are Intranets, MS Exchange, Novell GroupWise, and Lotus Notes. Detailed comparisons and contrasts of Lotus Notes, Intranet, and other groupware have been widely reported. While intranets are extremely popular, generally more economical and compatible with nearly all of the tools on the market, K-Station, the latest entrant from Lotus, has a very unique feature. By tracking user interest and expertise, K-Station assists in the location of relevant information as well as connecting certain employees in an organisation. Intelligent features like this and others will continue to be introduced by product vendors to gain differentiation and competitive advantage over their competitors. Clearly, one of perceived benefits of groupware is to provide a common virtual space for people of common interest and/or working on the same assignment to collaborate but it remains a challenge for these tools to locate/recommend the needed person(s) in the first instance.

6.5.7. Measurement and Reporting

One of the prominent strategies adopted by organizations that embrace KM is measurement of Intellectual Captial or IC. For these organisations, KM is tackled from a strong human resources focus and criteria are defined to quantify the value of human capital, intellectual assets, and the Return-On-Investment (ROI) for KM-related projects/investments. Established methods include, but are not limited to, monitoring the growth in infrastructural assets (e.g., best practices, process knowledge), tracking the flow and speed of an idea from conception to becoming an intellectual property and surveying "grass-roots" support of the corporate KM environment (e.g., personal adoptions of knowledge communities, portals). Tools are now available to measure, track, and report on the value of intellectual capital (i.e., non-financal assets) in an organisation. Most noticeably, these tools are based on the Balanced Scorecard method or the Intangible Asset Monitor (IAM). Tools for tracking and reporting professional development, online self-paced learning, and perform-ance reviews for employees are also available.

6.5.8. Internet and Intranet Tools

The training and development components of the information technology infrastructure may include distance learning, Web-based training, e-libraries and simulations. These technologically based forms of knowledge management can be highly effective in communicating embedded knowledge, through many types of interactive sessions, to other employees. Also, the structured environment provided by Internet-or intranet-based knowledge management technology helps employees to coordinate their activities. Furthermore, much knowledge work involves self-directed learning such as finding information to complete a project, and learning technologies provide an organized structure that supports such learning.

Distance learning is a powerful tool for knowledge organizations because employees who are physically separated or work at different organizational sites may more efficiently gain competencies and share knowledge. Distance learning is characterized by having an instructor who is physically and technologically remote from the learner, and it can make use of several media, including radio, television and computers. Increased use of the Web has made distance learning over the Internet without an instructor present in "real time" a common, effective tool.

The absence of personalized attention from an instructor who is not physically present limits the types of knowledge that can be shared. But if tacit knowledge exists in one part of an organization, it is more easily shared with geographically remote parts of the organization with distance learning.

As intranets and the Internet are becoming more popular in organizations, Web-Based Training and E-Learning are increasingly being used for sharing and transferring knowledge. Web-based training refers to instructional programs that use the attributes and resources of the World Wide Web to create a learning environment. All instruction is delivered over the Web-trainers may be electronically linked to the students to serve as resource persons but they do not deliver instruction. Its low cost over time and the increased availability of information make Web-based instruction a vehicle for efficient knowledge sharing.

E-Learning is rapidly becoming one of the major forces in KM software as, unlike E-Training which is merely web-enabling Computer-Based Training (CBT) material, E-Learning also stresses on the success and the dynamics of integrating learning and mentoring in the daily workplace. Advances in content management, workload balancing and personalisation techniques have contributed to the market acceptance of E-Learning software, along with perceived cost reductions. The success of E-Learning is closely associated with an organization's quest to become a truly "learning organizations." In the strategy development phase of selecting and deploying E-Learning software, linkages to virtual collaborations (e.g., knowledge communities, instant messaging, video conferencing), knowledge management projects, and the required technical infrastructure are being identified.

Simulations are emerging as a method for distributing tacit knowledge across organizations. Web-based simulations can offer a high level of fidelity to the actual physical or interpersonal work environment with few logistical constraints. In a simulation, the learner responds to a wide range of stimuli that may include tacitile and cognitive information, as well as interpersonal communications. In real time learners see how the environment (for example, equipment, people) reacts to their behaviour.

6.5.9. Portals

The portals are Web-based centers for people to find important and relevant information, and links to other sources of information. Their central benefit is the organization and structured presentation of information from a variety of sources. Portals act as a single point of access to information. There are different types of information, such as – validated archival content (policies, forms) ; current awareness (news, announcements); open source; content (yellow pages); external links; and group messaging (email, chat rooms, Communities of Practice). Each of these information types can also be in unstructured text and multimedia files, or in structured databases. In addition, portals can cover a broad set of topics, such as for a general corporate Intranet, or a specific job function, such as Human Resources. The latter narrowly-focused type of portal is some times referred to as a vortal for its focus on the vertical channels of an organizations's functions.

Portals are becoming popular primarily because of the advance in e-Business models (e.g., cyber-stores, vertical integators, net markets, volume procurement) and Customer Relationship Management (CRM) (e.g., customer knowledge management, measurement of relationship capital, and direct marketing). E-Business has also impacted KM by gradually transitioning it from an internal focus (e.g., a corporate program) to an external focus (e.g., addressing the flow of knowledge between/among suppliers and customers). As a result, many KM tool vendors have re-positioned their product offerings to align with the portal market (e.g., commerce/trading, information, procurement, collaboration, and learning portals) in the last few years. However, it is important to understand that the fundamental technologies underpinning the composition and hosting of portals remain predominantly the same.

One can anticipate the following stages of increased sophistication in future portals based on the forecasts by Delphi Group and Gartner Group on portals.

Stage 1

— Simple

— Information dissemination point

Stage 2

— Core content with pre-defined variations in page delivery

— Expanding set of interactive and informative facilities

— Centralised search facility for organisational content

— Engagement of common business processes

Stage 3

— Advanced search facilities and seamless integration of search results (external and internal)

— Simple expertise locater

— Online knowledge communitites

— Customers an initiate and check transactions

— Ability to perform transactions with suppliers and partners

Stage 4

— Extensive and dynamic personalisation of content for individuals

— Active collection and distribution of knowlede

— Full integration with e-Business systems

— Decision support and problem solving capabilities

Some fo the technical challenges underpinning the success of future portals are Web-access to enterprise application systems (i.e., enterprise applications integration (EAI), automatic categorisation of corporate resources and assets, intelligent and multiple search strategies (e.g., interactive and offline search, sharing of search cues and results), content management, and real time user profiling and personalisation strategies.

Whether the portal is broadly or narrowly focused, the most stringent design constraint for the user interface is the limited available screen space. This space must be carefully used to maximize the amount of information presented without creating a confusing appearance. Most portals use densely filled screens that employ graphics and human factors designs to organize components of the screen into easily perceived sections. The high information density of the screens may seem to contradict design principles that emphasize using white space, but actually has arisen from users' workflow needs to avoid having to switch screens or constantly navigate to different sites to see the variety of information they need for their work. In addition, another industry trend is to allow users to personalize the portal by defining their own interest profiles. These profiles can be used to arrange the portal interface, or to define agents that automatically retrieve information tailored to the user's interests.

A portal must be able to access data from different repositories and across firewalls. Data are typically stored in several formats, such as Lotus Notes databases, relational databases, word processing documents, email systems, and HTML pages. The portal design should have an automated spider to continually access new information and detect changes in previously accessed information. An important concern to address when using spiders is the security of the data repositories. Multi-level security controls should be implemented to restrict people from accessing unauthorized information. User roles with associated access rights can be assigned based on management plans. These roles can be connected to the corporation's central Access Control List and login user profiles to reduce complexity and conform to a central security plan.

The fast paced nature of information creation and use has led to a significant challenge for IT systems to ensure that the most up to date information is delivered to users. This has led away from portal designs using static predefined web pages, to architectures based on dynamic real-time retrieval from databases using a modular structure with general routines written in Cascading

Style Sheets (CSS), ActiveX, Javascript and extensible Markup Language (XML). This modular approach uses style sheets (e.g. CSS. XSL) and data schema (e.g. XML Document Type Description) to separate the data from the code for accessing and presenting it, so that only the information source itself has to be continually updated.

Examples of portals are:

- Plumtree, Plumtree Corp, www.plumtree.com
- K-station, Lotus Corp, www.lotus.com
- SharePoint Portal Server, Microsoft Corp, www.microsoft.com
- Hummingbird EIP, Hummingbird Corp, www.hummingbird.com
- Portal-in-a-box, Autonomy Corp, www.autonomy.com
- XPS Portal, Citrix Corp, www.citrix.com
- Verity K2, Verity Corp, www.verity.com
- Knowledgecenter, KnowledgeTrack Corp, www.knowledgetrack.com

The above categorisation of tools is primarily functional and techniques-based. Other categorisations also exists. For example, Hahn and Subramani provide another framework to classify KMS based on the locus of the knowledge and the a prioristructuring of contents. Holsapple and Joshi present a comparative analysis of various frameworks by focussing on the salient characterisitics of the KM phenomena. Among the commercial research services comapnies, for example, the Delphi Group's classification of KM tools extends to cover Enterprise Resource Planning (ERP), Electronic Document Management (EDM), and Information and Aggregration tools. IDC separates KM software into two groups– infrastructure and access software. KM infrastructure software is the base or platform upon which KM solutions are deployed. Access software operates on the KM infrastructure to provide (groups of) individuals with access to internal and external knowledge repositories. Gartner Group's classification of KM tools tends to focus more on the traditional areas (i.e, document management, information, retrieval, content management, groupware) and treats nearly all of the above types of softwarc as "spccialised" tools. Binney has developed a KM spectrum that maps all kinds of organisational information systems (including transaction processing systems and learning systems) into the following six categories :

- Transactional
- Analytical
- Asset Management
- Process
- Development (i.e., training and learning)
- Innovation and Creation

Binney also identifies the intrinsic relationships and continuity between the each of the above categories as well as highlihting the interplay between organisational change, training and personal adoption for various systems in the spectrum.

6.6. EVALUATION OF KM TOOLS

Irrespective of the "buy versus build versus outsource" decision, here are some useful criteria to apply when performing an overall evaluation of a KM tool :

- Power of the search engine (e.g., intelligent search, meta-crawler, colaborative filtering, efficiency).
- Flexibility and ease in browsing and availability of visualisation tools.
- Automatic classification using a taxonomy/ontology of documents.
- Collaborations and personalisation features (e.g., file sharing, content management, discussions, instant messaging).
- Active collection and distribution of knowledge (i.e.,knowledge pump) and Push/Pull features.
- Repository for document management.
- Ability to handle multiple file formats, media and technical platforms.
- Cater for Personal KM (PKM), as well as Corporate KM (CKM).

- Capture operational statistics and provide analytical tools.
- Security mechanisms and compliance with industry standards.
- Extent and ease of accessing external sources and integration with legacy databases.

Furthermore, one should not expect to find a tool that satisfies all the criteria. In order to derive an exact list of evaluation criteria, one needs to take into consideration the needs of the buying organisation, category that the tool belongs to, the stated features of the tool, scalability issues, and its technical fit with the existing and planned technical infrastructure. It is also common for an organization to pilot test a tool with a small group of users for a short period, typically 10–12 weeks, before making a decision on a full scale implementation/deployment of the tool.

6.7. STRENGTHS AND WEAKNESSES OF THE TOOLS

As a general observations of the KM tools in the market, they are powerful and fast in search and dissemination of explicit knowledge, but Ester and Nelson outline test criteria and benchmarks for evaluating text search engines. Some tools can cope with multi-modal information and most tools can handle files stored in various formats and in a range of platforms. Some tools also, when coupled with other Web/search engines, support simultaneous searches across a range of databases or the sites. Results from searching internal sources (e.g., a corporate intranet or Lotus Notes databases) can be merged with results from external sources (e.g., public Web sites or extranet of a third party organisation) and presented to the user in a structured interface. Tools are especially appealing to professional with a technical background and, on many occasions, have spearheaded the early adoption of a KM system in an organisation — a view that is commonly shared by industry practitioners. However, this can also be a disadvantage for two reasons. First, organisations should always define its KM strategies (or principles) before any tool is adopted, even though a particular tool is considered to be a good "technical fit" to the problem on hand. Second, as in all acquisitions, organisations should always critically assess the "buy versus outsource" proposition before making a decision. Some additional observations of current KM tools are :

- They can be tedious to configure. Integration with legacy systems and operational databases has been reported as a key systems integration and implementation issue.
- Security mechanisms employed in certain tools are ad hoc and fall well short of the expected security level needed for information systems in large organisations. This is especially true for a new entrant that produces a very specialised tool, aims for a niche market and targets the tool for a large organisation in the financial services industry.
- Although there are plenty of virtual collaboration tools, only a very limited number of commercial KM software can locate/discover expertise or assist in connecting people with common interests in an organisation. In fact, the majority of the so-called "people-finder" (or "expertise directory", "yellow pages") systems are custom built bespoke systems or research prototypes. There are two possible explanations for this phenomenon. First, there is no industry-wide taxonomy for classifying expertize or skills. Second, the way that organisational information systems has evolved in the last few years has resulted in the much needed data to establish an expertize directory being not only unstructured but also highly dispersed in an organisation. In reality, these two factors have added a lot of complexity and integration problems to any would-be off the shelf products.
- Nearly all of the interfaces to KM software use text-based input. The application of KM to voice-recognition systems or voice portals is only at the research stage. It is also only recently that access to some KM software is available on PDA and other mobile devices.

Summing up – No one tool supports the full spectrum of KM processes. Most of the tools on the market are search and collaboration tools although, as discussed above, the landscape is changing. Software that supports virtual collaborations, content management, categorisation and E-Learning are rapidly gaining popularity.

7

Networks in Knowledge Management

Organizations or the business enterprises behave as a complex adaptive systems. The networks are the webs of relationships that generate tangible and intangible value through complex dynamic exchanges between two or more individuals groups or organizations.

Networks are the basis for increasing social capital through the resources derived from relationships in the organization. In order to benefit from the knowledge be aware of who knows what. The organization relies on its dispersed elements to collaborate with and adjust to one another. For such behaviour to occur, interpersonal networks must be built on a foundation of trust, familiarity and shared understandings. Knowledge workers rely on their personal networks for many purposes— to develop their competencies, to become personally visible in the organization and aware of opportunities and to be able to operate effectively in the interdependent knowledge system. They derive a sense of professional identity and peer support from their knowledge communities.

Networks can be formally established, built into the work design of the organization. Technical councils and communities of practice can be established as formal work units. Networks may also be built into the core work units of the organization. When people serve on the same temporary and possibly emergent teams or take on liaison roles with other parts of the organization, they remain part of each other's personal networks long after a project has been completed and the team disbanded. If they have a sequence of assignments and team memberships, they develop a network of contacts based on their experience working with each other and becoming aware of each other's competencies. More informally, IT systems such as expert lists and readily accessible project and knowledge files can extend the reach of all employees to each other's knowledge and experience and enable connections throughout the organization. Organizations can plan development activities such as training sessions, business processes such as planning meetings and collective work activities such as peer project reviews and customer visits to expose people to one another and build networks.

An organization can create a web of formal and informal connectivity that matches the saturated interdependency of the system by attending to the network-building aspects of work design. This approach also meets the needs of professional workers to-have networks for various career and work effectiveness purposes. Although much research has described how networks are formed and maintained, there are many unanswered questions. What kinds and density of networks contribute to work effectiveness and employee outcomes in different kinds of knowledge settings? How many active links can employees maintain before they become less productive?

7.1. TYPES OF NETWORKS

There are various networks' concept used, but generally neural networks and value networks are used in knowledge management.

7.2. NEURAL NETWORK

A Neural Network (NN) is an information processing paradigm that is inspired by the way biological nervous systems, such as the brain, process information. The key element of this paradigm is the novel structure of the information processing system. It is composed of a large number of highly interconnected processing elements (neurons) working in union to solve specific problems, ANNs, like people, learn by example.

The first proposal to use an artificial neuron appeared in 1943, but computer usage of neural networks did not actually begin until the 1980s. Neural networks (NN), often referred to as artificial neural networks (ANN) to distinguish them from biological neural networks, are modeled after the workings of the human brain. The NN is actually an information processing system that consists of a graph representing the processing system as well as various algorithms that access that graph. As with the human brain, the NN consist of many connected processing elements. The NN, then, is structured as a directed graph with many nodes (processing elements) and arcs (interconnections) between them. The nodes in the graph are like individual neurons, while the arcs are their interconnections. Each of these processing elements functions independently from the others and uses only local data (input and output to the node) to direct its processing. This features facilitates ths use of NNs in a distributed and/or parallel environment.

7.2.1. Need and Purposes of Neural Networks

Neural networks has different purposes. They —

- have a remarkable ability to derive meaning from complicated or imprecise data, and
- can be used to extract patterns and detect trends that are too complex to be noticed by either humans or other computer techniques.

A trained neural network can be thought of as an "expert" in the category of information it is assigned to analyse. This expert can then be used to provide projections given new situations and answer "what if" questions.

7.2.2. Advantages of Neural Networks

Various advantages of neural networks can be as under.

Adaptive Learning : An ability to learn how to do tasks based on the data given for training or initial experience.

Self-Organisation : An ANN can create its own organisation or representation of the information it receives during learning time.

Real Time Operation : ANN computations may be carried out in parallel and special hardware devices are being designed and manufactured which take advantage of this capability.

Fault Tolerance via Redundant Information Coding : Partial destruction of a network leads to the corresponding degradation of performance. However, some network capabilities may be retained even with major network damage.

7.2.3. Neural Networks versus Conventional Computers

Neural networks take a different approach to problem solving than that of conventional computers.

Neural networks process information in a similar way the human brain does. They have a large number of highly interconnected processing elements working in parallel to solve a specific problem. Neural networks learn by example. They cannot be programmed to perform a specific task. The examples must be selected carefully otherwise useful time is wasted or even worse the network might be functioning incorrectly. The disadvantage is that because the network finds out how to solve the problem by itself, its operation can be unpredictable.

Conventional computers use an algorithmic approach. The computer follows a set of instructions in order to solve a problem.

The specific steps that computer needs to follow should be known. Otherwise the computer cannot solve the problem. That restricts the problem solving capability of conventional computers to problems that we already understand and know how to solve. But computers would be so much more useful if they could do things that we do not exactly know how to do.

On the other hand, conventional computers use a cognitive approach to problem solving. The steps involved are

- the way the problem is to be solved must be known and stated in small unambiguous instructions.
- These istructions are then converted to a high level language program and then into machine code that the computer can understand.

These machines are totally predictable; if anything goes wrong is due to a software or hardware fault.

7.2.4. Interdependence of Computers and Neural Networks

Neural networks and conventinal algorithmic computers complement each other. There are the tasks that are more suited to an algorithmic approach like airthmetic operations and tasks that are more suited to neural networks.

A large number of tasks, require systems that use a combination of the two approaches. Normally a conventional computer is used to supervise the neural network in order to perform at maximum efficiency.

Neural networks do not perform miracles. But if used sensibly they can produce some amazing results.

7.2.5. Applications of Neural Networks

Neural networks have proven to be quite robust in classification problems. For example, suppose that your firm wants to classify new customers into four types–those who are likely to pay their bills on time, those who may take between two and three months to pay, those taking three to six months, and those who are not likely to pay at all. You might design a neural network to try to classify potential customers. The input to the network would be information about the customer and the output would be a classification into one of four groups corresponding to the likely payment categories.

1. Neural Networks in Practice : Neural networks have broad applicability to real world business problems. In fact, they have already been successfully applied in many industries. They are best at identifying patterns or trends in data. So they are well suited for prediction forecasting needs that include–

— Sales forecasting

— Industrial process control

— Customer research

— Data validation

— Risk management, and

— Target marketing

2. How Human Brain Learns : Much is still unknown about how the brain trains itself to process information. There are many theories. Let us see, how human brain learns.

In the human brain :

- a typical neuron collects signals from others through a host of fine structures called dendrites.
- The neuron sends our spikes of electrical activity through a long, thin stand known as an axon, which splits into thousands of branches.
- At the end of each branch, a structure called a synapse converts the activity form the axon into electrical effects.
- This inhibits or excites activity from the axon into electrical effects that inhibit or excite activity in the connected neurones. When a neuron receives excitatory input, it sends a spike of electrical activity down its axon.

Learning occurs by changing the effectiveness of the synapses so that the influence of one neuron on another changes.

7.2.6. Architecture of Neural Networks

In the simplest network, neurons in one layer are connected only to neurons in the next layer. More complex networks feature neurons that are connected within a layer. Probably the most common business uses of neural nets feature feed-forward networks; the neurons in one layer receive inputs from the layer below and send outputs to the layer above. In a feed-forward network the flow of inputs is in one direction, from the input layer, through intermediate layers and finally to the output layer.

There are two kinds of architetures for neural networks. They are

- Feed forward Networks, and
- Feedback Networks

1. Feed-forward Networks : Feed-forward ANNs allow signals to travel one way only; from input to output-there is no feedback (loops) i.e. the output of any layer does not affect that same layer. Feed-forward ANNs tend to be straight forward networks that associate inputs with outputs. They are extensively used in pattern recognition. This type of organisation is also referred to as bottom-up or top-down.

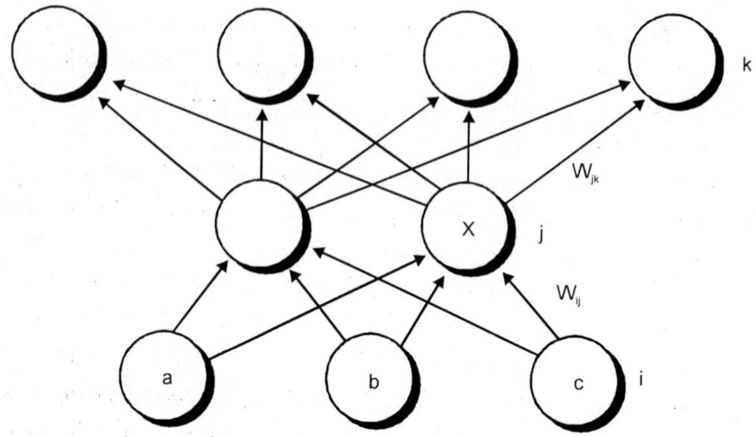

Fig. 7.1. A three-layer neural network

2. Feedback Networks : Feedback networks can have signals travelling in both directions by introducing loops in the network. Feedback networks are :

- very powerful and can get extremely complicated.
- dynamic; their 'state' is changing continuously until they reach an equilibrium point.
- remain at the equilibrium point until the input changes and a new equilibrium needs to be found.

Feedback architectures are also referred to as interactive or recurrent although the latter term is often used to denote feedback connections in single-layer organizations.

7.2.7. Network layers

The most common type of artificial neural network consists of three groups, or layers of units. A layer of "input" unit is connected to a layer of "output" unit throuqh a layer of "hidden" units.

- The activity of the input units represents the raw information that is fed into the network.
- The activity of each hidden unit is determined by the

activities of the input units and the weights on the connections between the input and the hidden units.

There are also single-layer and multi-layer architectures.

The single-layer organization, in which all units are connected to one another, constitutes the most general case. It is of more potential computational power than hierarchically structured multi-layer organizations.

In multi-layer networks, units are often numbered by layer, instead of following a global numbering.

7.2.8. Perceptrons

The most influential work on neural nets in the 60's went under the heading of 'perceptrons[1] a term coined by Frank Rosenblatt. They were mainly used in pattern recognition even though their capabilities extended a lot more.

In 1969 Minsky and Papert wrote a book in which they described the limitations of single layer Perceptrons. The book was very well written and showed mathematically that single layer perceptrons could not do some basic pattern recognition operations. They realized only during 80's, given the appropriate training, multilevel perceptrons can do these operations.

7.2.9. The Learning Process

The memorisation of patterns and the subsequent response of the network can be categorized into two general paradigms:

- Associative mapping
- Regularity detection

Associative Mapping : The network learns to produce a particular pattern on the set of input units. The associative mapping can generally be broken down into two mechanisms:

- auto-association
- hetero-association

(a) ***Auto-association*** **:** It is an input pattern associated with itself and the states of input and output units coincide. This is used to provide pattern completion, i.e. to produce a pattern whenever a portion of it or a distorted pattern is presented. In the second case, the network actually stores pairs of patterns building an association between two sets of patterns.

(b) ***Hetero-association*** **:** It is related to two recall mechanisms. First is– nearest-neighbour recall, where the output pattern is produced corresponds to the input pattern stored, which is closest to the pattern presented, and second is interpolative recall, where the output pattern is a similarity dependent interpolation of the patterns stored corresponding to the pattern presented. Yet another paradigm, which is a variant associative mapping is classification, i.e., when there is a fixed set of categories into which the input patterns are to be classified.

Regularity Detection : The units learn to respond to particular properties of the input patterns. In regularity detection the response of each unit has a particular 'meaning'. This type of learning mechanism is essential for feature discovery and knowledge representation.

Every neural network posseses knowledge which is contained in the values of the connections weights. Modifying the knowledge stored in the network as a function of experience implies a learning rule for changing the values of the weights.

Information is stored in the weight matrix W of a neural network. Learning is the determination of the weights. Following the way learning's performed, we can distinguish two major categories of neural networks:

Fixed networks in which the weights cannot be changed, i.e., $dW/dt = 0$. In such networks, the weights are fixed a priori according to the problem to solve.

Adaptive networks which are able to change their weights, i.e., dW/dt not $= 0$.

All learning methods used for adaptive neural networks can be classified into two major categories.

7.2.10. Learning Process - Types

Learning process falls into two types namely :

— Supervised Learning

— Unsupervised Learning

Supervised Learning : Supervised learning incorporates an external teacher, so that each output unit is told what its desired response to input signals ought to be. During the learning process global information may be required. Paradigms of supervised learning include error-correction learning, reinforcement learning and stochastic learning.

An important issue concerning supervised learning is the problem of error convergence, i.e., the minimisation of error between the desired and computed unit values. The aim is to determine a set of weights which minimizes the error. One well-known method, which is common to many learning paradigms is the least mean square (LMS) convergence.

Unsupervised Learning : Unsupervised learning does not use external teacher and is based upon only local information. It is also referred to as self-organization, in the sense that it self-organizes data presented to the network and detects their emergent collective properties. Paradigms of unsupervised learning are Hebbian lerning and competitive learning.

A neural network learns off-line if the learning phase and the operation phase are distinct.

A neural network learns on-line if it learns and operates at the same time.

Usually, supervised learning is performed off-line, whereas usupervised learning is performed on-line.

7.2.11. Transfer Function

The behaviour of an ANN (Artificial Neural Network) depends on both the weights and the input-output function (transfer function) that is specified for the units. This function typically falls into one of three categories:

- linear
- threshold
- sigmoid

For *linear units*, the output activity is proportional to the total weighted output.

For *threshold units*, the output is set at one of two levels, depending on whether the total input is greater than or less than some threshold value.

For *sigmoid units*, the output varies continuously but not linearly as the input changes. Sigmoid units bear a greater resemblance to real neurones than do linear or threshold units, but all three must be considered rough approximations.

An Example to illustrate the above teaching procedure is given below.

Assume that we want a network to recognize hand-written digits. We might use an array of, say, 256 sensors, each recording the presence or absence of ink in a small area of a single digit. The network would therefore need 256 input units (one for each sensor), 10 output units (one for each kind of digit) and a number of hidden units.

For each kind of digit recorded by the sensors, the network should produce high activity in the appropriate output unit and low activity in the other output units.

To train the network, an image of a digit is presented and compare the actual activity of the 10 output units with the desired activity. We then calculate the error, which is defined as the square of the difference between the actual and the desired activities. Next we change the weight of each connection so as to reduce the error. We repeat this training process for many different images of each different images of each kind of digit until the network classifies every image correctly.

7.2.12. Error Detection

To implement this procedure we need to calculate the error derivative for the weight (EW) in order to change the weight by an amount that is proportional to the rate at which the error changes as the weight is changed.

One way to calculate the EW is to perturb a weight slightly and observe how the error changes. But that method is inefficient because it requires a separate perturbation for each of the many weights.

Another way to calculate the EW is to use the Back-propagation algorithm which is described below, and has become nowadays one of the most important tools for training neural networks. It was developed independently by two teams, one consisting of Fogelman-Soulie, Gallinari and Le Cun in France, the other of Rumelhart, Hinton and Williams in U.S.

7.2.13. The Back-Propagation Algorithm

In order to train a neural network to perform some task, we must adjust the weights of each unit in such a way that the error between the desired output and the actual output is reduced. This process requires that the neural network compute the error derivative of the weights (EW). In other words, it must calculate how the error changes as each weight is increased or decreased slightly. The back propagation algorithm is the most widely used method for determining the EW.

The back-propagation algorithm is easiest to understand if all the units in the network are linear. The algorithm computes each EW by first computing the EA, the rate at which the error changes as the activity level of a unit is changed. For output units, the EA is simply the difference between the actual and the desired output. To compute the EA for a hidden unit in the layer just before the output layer, we first identify all the weights between that hidden unit and the output units to which it is connected. We then multiply those weights by the EAs of those output units and add the products.

7.3. VALUE NETWORKS: SYSTEM APPROACH FOR EVOIVING BUSINESS FORMS

In the fast-moving world of business we are seeing increased attention around new business models and network views of the enterprise such as e-webs and business webs. But business webs are just one type of value network. Virtually any organization or group of organizations can be understood as a value network. A value network is a web of relationships that generates tangible and intangible value through complex dynamic exchanges between two or more individuals, groups, or organizations. A value network perspective can help to explain the dynamics of non-profits, economic clusters and national economies as well. Furthermore, as traditional organizational boundaries become more permeable, organizational hierarchies become flatter and decision making is driven to ever lower levels. Value network principles and dynamics become far more useful than traditional organizational charts, process flow diagrams and performance management tools, when managers are trying to understand their most important functions.

Despite the interest and hype about value networks as the new business model, we have seen little serious work in developing simple and easily accessible business modeling techniques to analyze, develop and manage organizations from a network perspective. Social network analysis, which has been around for over thirty years, is being used to some degree to understand the human interactions within organizations, but does not readily lend itself to business modeling. Some people are applying complex adaptive systems principles to the knowledge focus, including Brian Arthur who identifies the new economic law of increasing returns. More relevant to managers are those who have explored how organizations behave as complex, adaptive systems, providing valuable insights into principles that help people shape and influence business networks. However, most approaches to analyzing and reconfiguring value networks have not taken into account the role of knowledge and intangible value exchange as the foundation for these emerging networked enterprises.

7.3.1. Modeling the Value Network

Most of us know how to model our businesses using flow charts and process maps as the primary view of how work happens. But these tools, while useful, are woefully inadequate for modeling the role of knowledge and other intangibles in the business model. A process view focuses on only one process. Piecing together two or more interdependent processes can be done, but it is tedious and time consuming. This is because the complexities of a dynamic whole system cannot be reduced to process, which is linear and sequential. In complex systems, many things are going on at once and one needs to understand how all the processes are working together.

A whole system view shows how all the processes work together, as well as key dynamics such as feedback, interdependencies, flows and exchanges. One cannot see a whole system from a process view; but a systems view can show not only the key processes, but a whole lot more as well. To successfully understand how intangibles directly contribute to business value, we must move to a different type of modeling tool based on systems thinking principles. The following diagrams utilize the ValueNet Works™ modeling technique, which is an example of emerging methods of business modeling that are proving valuable in the knowledge economy. ValueNet Works™ Analysis is a variation of the HoloMapping™.

Let's use an example of a mythical pharmaceutical company, PharmCo. In this case the sales and marketing group would like to improve its ability to use customer feedback in developing new products. First, we would consider all the groups, both internally and externally, that play key roles in those types of activities. In this case, the four key groups inside the company are Sales and Marketing, Research, Product Development Group, and Manufacturing. Key participants outside the company are Patients, health care Providers such as doctors, Payers such as insurance companies, and Regulators. See Figure 7.2.

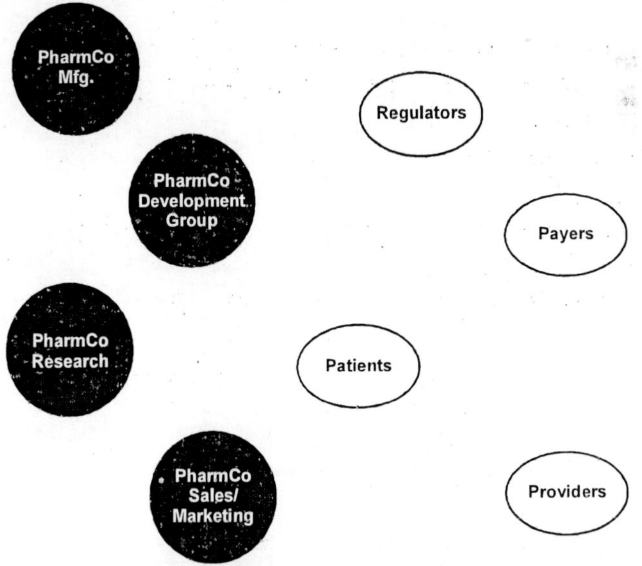

Fig. 7.2. Value Network Participants

Now we are ready to start modeling the real business dynamics. The first things to consider are tangible exchanges. What are the core money-related transactions? What are the tangible deliverables in the system? We can depict these activities with an arrow originating from the group responsible for the deliverable and ending at the participant who receives it. The label on the arrow names the deliverable Now we know who is accountable for the deliverable and who is impacted by it. Figure7.3. shows tangible deliverables such as product candidates, process specifications, claims, payments, orders and so on. In this case the communication channel is considered a tangible deliverable because it consists of data links, Web sites, and call centers that are paid for and hosted by PharmCo as part of the expected customer service support.

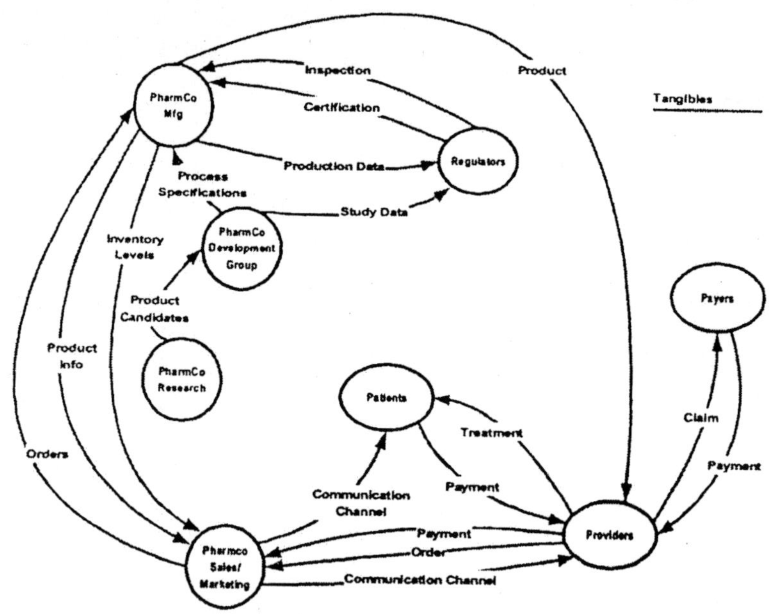

Fig. 7.3. Tangible Deliverables in a Value Network

We can also map intangible exchanges the same way. For PharmCo, intangibles include patient requirements, disease knowledge that PharmCo makes available through publications and its website, informal assurances that Payers make to Providers advising that a new product will be covered and reports of adverse reactions to the Regulators. See Figure7.4 . These are intangible because people do not pay for them directly so they are not contractual or expected. They are extras, offerings extended to another participant that help things work smoothly or that help build relationship.

We now can pull together a whole system view of value creation that shows how both tangibles and intangibles are working in the system, including knowledge. See Figure 7.5. When we diagram all these exchanges and deliverables together we have much truer picture of how the business really operates, compared to more traditional modeling methods.

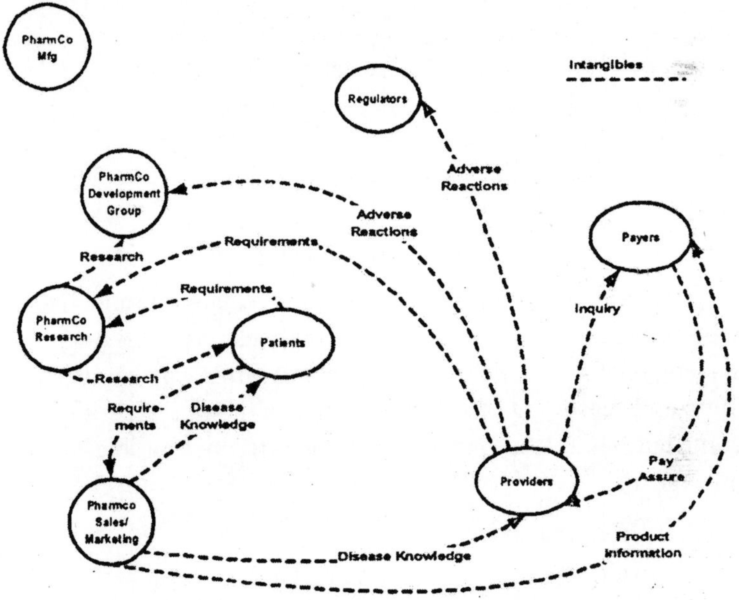

Fig. 7.4. Intangibles in a Value Network

With this view of the enterprise we can begin to more fully understand the role of knowledge in value creation. The modeling process maps the most strategically critical knowledge exchanges, allowing for easy targeting of knowledge value opportunities. The diagramming process is completed by sequencing the deliverables and ordering them into a table. This not only reveals the processes in the system but also allows conducting a very detailed analysis along a variety of dimensions.

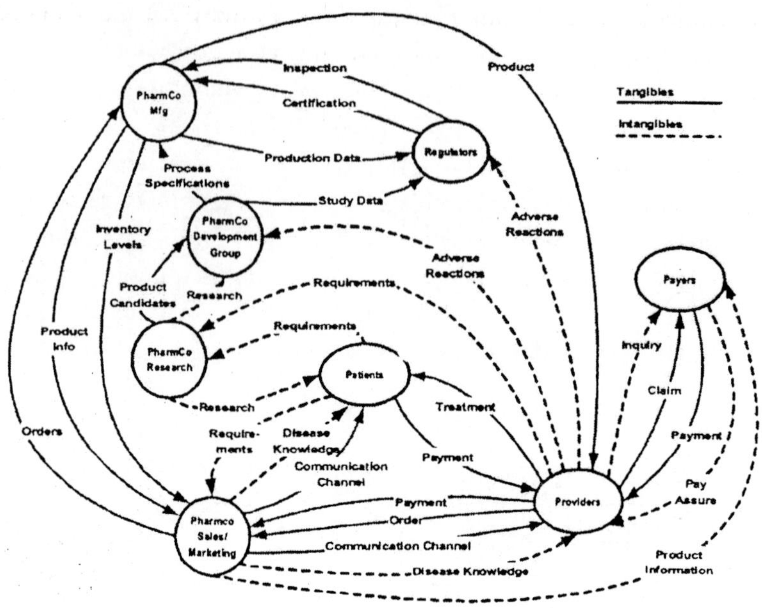

Fig. 7.5. PharmCo Value Network

With this type of modeling technique, tangible and intangible scorecards can be linked directly to real business activities. Whole system views provide a visually compelling way to surface the logic and reasoning behind performance metrics. The knowledge contributions to the business are specific, measurable and more manageable.

7.3.2. Value Network Principles

A value network perspective reveals powerful new principles and fundamentals for success in the knowledge economy.

1. Value Networks and Organizations are Complex Adaptive Systems : Value networks are complex adaptive systems that learn, if they are successful and modify behaviours according to feedback. As in all systems, the system is greater than the sum of its parts. This means a single transaction is only meaningful in relation to the value network as a whole. A single participant is only meaningful in relation to the other participants. The removal or addition of a single participant or transaction can impact the whole system. By the same token breaking one operating principle, assumption, or agreement – implied or explicit, has implications for the whole value system. This is because organizations are also social systems, which are shaped by shared beliefs and guiding principles that influence decisions and behaviour.

2. Healthy Value Networks Generate both Economic Success and Intangible Value for Participants : It is entirely possible to have business relationships with almost no intangible value being exchanged or generated. It could be argued, of course, that every product or service provides some emotional or social benefit. But that aside, one finds that the most robust and healthy organizations and business webs have extensive exchanges of intangibles.

3. Everybody is Supported to Win and Succeed : Every participant contributes and receives value in ways that sustain both their own success and the value network as a whole. When this is not true, participants either withdraw or are expelled - or the overall system becomes unstable and may collapse or reconfigure. People want others to succeed because there is an appreciation that individual success is directly linked to the health and vitality of the entire network. In successful value networks one finds less competition and increased levels of cooperation.

4. There is New Appreciation of What Can and Cannot be Managed : One participant cannot manage a whole system. Not even all participants working together could really "manage" the system, even though agreed upon behaviours and values are essential. However, each participant does need to understand how the whole system is working, so he or she can fully participate and gain the greatest value. With that whole system understanding, participants can manage their own inputs and outputs in ways that support the vitality of the whole value network. Participants can identify ways to maximize the value gained from every single tangible or intangible they receive. Further, each participant can find ways to enhance or increase the value of what they are contributing to other participants and the value network as a whole. Everyone can make sure there is a "fair exchange" for all the participants and that everyone is making a valuable contribution in both tangible and intangible value.

5. It is All about Relationships : An important benefit to viewing organizations as value networks is an increased appreciation that success today is all about relationships. We sometimes are dazzled by technologies and what they can enable us to do. But the bottom line is that business is about exchanges and transactions that happen between real people. Even when people never see each other or speak directly, it is only real people that make decisions and initiate action. Technologies may fill the role of decision makers at times, but only based on what a person would do. Viewing business as a linear process or only as transactions tends to diminish the role of people. The value network focus puts people back into the business model in such a way that every individual can see who he or she needs to be in relationship with and what his or her responsibility is in that relationship. Once intangibles become visible, people more fully appreciate their importance and it becomes easier to justify investing resources in producing and delivering them.

6. Intangibles build the Relationships : Enduring business relationships are rarely built solely on tangible transactions, especially when dealing with sophisticated or complex products and services. Although people have long made jokes about "the old boy networks," there is a great deal of truth there. Business relationships are human relationships and we do connect to new people and resources through people we trust and respect. The value network view demonstrates that knowledge and intangibles build the critical business relationships and create the environment for business success. We do not so much build a business, but rather grow or "weave" a web of trusted relationships. Companies and organizations that build healthy and rewarding relationships usually find they have engaged in intangible exchanges for months, or even years, before the tangible activities kick off with an order or request for service.

7. Trust is the Foundation : Knowledge and other intangible exchanges become very rich where there is trust. If people do not trust each other, they do not exchange knowledge and ideas and are reluctant to extend favours. People must feel that they are treated fairly and can trust the other members of their networks and organizations before they will fully participate and make their greatest contributions. Thus, the value network economy is driving business leaders to higher levels of integrity and fairness than were ever required in the past. While many business executives continue to operate by the industrial age competitive values, we can anticipate that the most successful companies will be those that embrace the new ethics. In the old, competitive environment a business could treat one partner badly and still be successful. In a value network such behaviours erode the entire web of relationships. Value networks thrive on trusting relationships, integrity, and transparency on the part of all participants.

7.3.3. Value Network Modeling to evolve Business Forms

Applying this approach to business issues and challenges offers insights that simply cannot be gained through other methods. For example, in a few hours of work a product team was able to reduce launch time by two months and better prepare the organization to support group for a global telecom firm was quickly able to see how it could completely reorganize to reduce head count, when nine months of working with process diagrams had not produced a breakthrough. Using the method to address a key business process, a training group may able to design a better process for gaining participant feedback.

As a business strategy tool, this method has supported developing innovative strategies in companies trying to reconfigure their business to leverage e-commerce. For example, by using the method strategically, a technology start-up developed a whole new strategy for funding instead of going to a venture capitalist. Another company mapped out the key business partnerships that would allow it to enter a rapidly expanding market.

Every company and organization is unique. Competitive advantage and branding are built not on the ways companies are alike, but on how they are different. Intangibles offer important clues to the unique characteristics and aspects of an organization. Business analysts are finding that this view helps them to identify sources of competitive advantage. A study of fast growing companies showed a much higher degree of knowledge and intangible exchanges than other companies in their industries. By using this analysis method, the real business models of companies like Cisco and eBay become visible at a glance. Long before both of these companies had received media attention, a study showed that they were operating from very different assumptions than traditional business or their competitors. Both of these companies had multiple, rich exchanges of knowledge and intangibles built on a foundation of trust and business integrity.

This modeling technique can be used at multiple levels for a wide variety of companies and organizations. Non-profits can also model the intangible exchanges that are especially dominant in organizations devoted to having a social impact.

The following value network model of a clothing manufacturer shows how knowledge and intangibles can be leveraged in an Internet strategy. The manufacturer moved into e-commerce by providing free marketing Web sites to its distributors. In this case, the manufacturer also allowed competing manufacturers to sell products via the same Web site. Selling competitors' products on the Web site only makes sense if we understand the flow of knowledge and intangible benefits that the manufacturer gains. The very savvy company focuses on these flows of knowledge and intangibles to build closer relationships with its end users. In the process it gains market intelligence, customer feedback and competitive intelligence. See Figure Fig. 7.6.

It is good news that traditional businesses are also evolving into value networks, even when they are not e-commerce based. Organizational boundaries are becoming more permeable. Work is organized more by contracts and projects than by employees and functions. Hierarchies are yielding to flatter organizations with cultures and processes that support self-managing individuals and teams. Technology is enabling people to work from anyplace at anytime. In this type of business environment, it is critical for everyone to understand how they contributing to the value networks they are participating in and supporting.

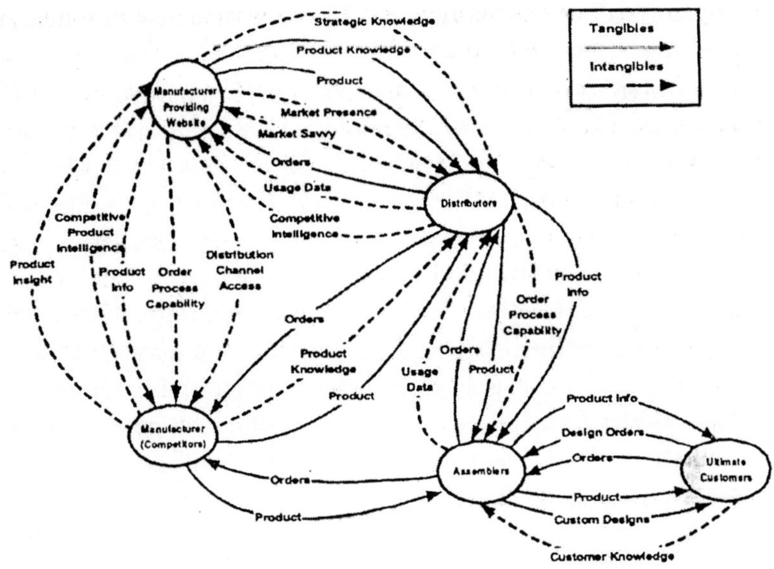

Fig. 7.6. Internet Enabled Value Network

In addition to above, there is evolving another networks in web service environment, i.e.,. NET concept.

7.4. .NET CONCEPT

A key point is the need to link knowledge management system with other applications relating to the management of intellectual capital, such as human resource management and learning. The word link is emphasized to point out that even hinting at rebuilding or replacing these infrastructure applications would be fiscally and practically unwise for most companies. Your technology team can use many techniques to accomplish this task; Microsoft advocates the use of its .NET technology to link and integrate existing intellectual capital processes with KM. In a three-tier architecture, the second tier calls for the implementation of business rules, metadata and the integration of diverse sources of data to present to the client (tier 1). Tier 2 of this architecture is where the benefits of the .NET approach can best be realized. .NET was designed to encapsulate diverse applications and present them in a uniform fashion to the client (tier 1) layer. The .NET approach is composed of unique services and languages that make application and user connectivity simple and customizable.

Before presenting a KM Expert Finder example of a .NET service, we take you quickly through the .NET platform includes a comprehensive family of products, built on industry Extensible Markup Language (XML) and Internet standards, that provides for each aspect of developing (tools), managing (servers), using (building block services and smart clients), and experiencing (rich user experiences) XML Web services. Potentially, .NET will integrate the applications, tools and servers you may already use today. Figure 7.7 is a graphical representation of a potential KM Expert Finder function developed with .NET components. Once again, we remind that this is a very high-level and simplistic representation of the technology. As we discuss the various .NET components in Table 7.1, we refer to this diagram to help you visualize how .NET could work within a KM environment.

Table 7.1. .NET Components

NET Term	Description
Web Services	A Web service is a module of application logic that can be published, discovered and executed over the Web (or intranet) using XML-based standards. These XML-based Web services (the numbered items in Figure 7.7), which developers can customize for use in any Web environment, are a part of the Microsoft. NET programming model. The NET platform enables the creation and use of XML-based applications, processes, and Web sites as Web services Web services share and combine information and functionality with each other by design, on any platform or smart device (such as a Web phone or palm computer), to provide tailored solutions for organizations and individuals. Building on a common programming model and drawing on a wealth of prebuilt components and service lets developers devote more time to creating reusable business logic components and less time to working on the underlying maintenance code necessary for all applications. In Microsoft NET, the infrastructure is built on the idea that computing is moving away from the era of isolated PCs and servers, packaged software, and disconnected "islands" of data in databases and on Web sites.
XML	XML, or Extensible Markup Language, is a format for

	structuring data on the Web. XML implements rules for formatting data in such a way that it is easy for a computer to read created files.
SOAP	Simple Object Access Protocol (SOAP) is built on XML. It makes it possible for applications to call each other in a standard, loosely coupled way, which makes it possible to build applications that are distributed across the Internet. If you think of the interactions between XML Web services as a phone call. XML describes the things that applications say to each other in their conversations; SOAP describes how they call each other on the phone. How do you greet the service at the other end? ("Hello?") How do you ask for something? For example, in Figure 7.7 the Locating Service (#2) uses SOAP as a standardized method for getting location information (on the registered or available services) from the Registry (of information) based on the request made by the user.
UDDI	If XML is the conversation and SOAP describes the rules on how you call someone. Universal Description, Discovery and Integration (UDDI) is the phone book. UDDI provides a directory of XML Web services, which allows you to find applications (or external businesses) that offer XML Web services.

Fig. 7.7 shows five Web services connecting the user request to the registry of services (UDDI) and the applications in a sample environment. These services are :

— Publishing service establishes that a Web entity – internal or external, is available. For example, a skills database from the learning organization may publish that it can identify experts.

— Locating service provides filtered connectivity — that is, it takes the search request to the UDDI to obtain a subset of data based on the request parameters. UDDI provides service calling information in SOAP format from the Publishing Service.

— Calling service provides to the requestor all known service options available (at this time) to satisfy the request.

— Invoke service allows the requestor to execute or actually find experts, based on the returned subset of information provided by the calling service.

— Execute service brings back the selected experts for review.

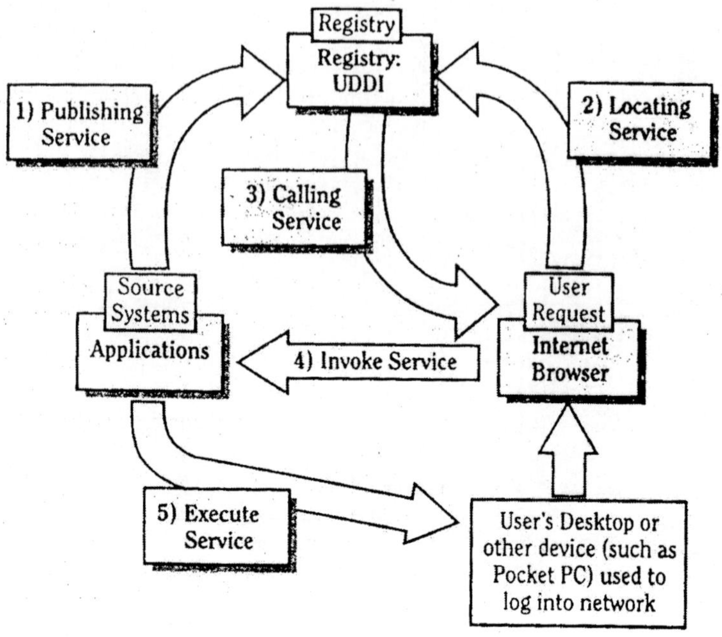

Fig. 7.7. .NET-KM View

Any systems across a company, from knowledge management to human resource or accounting databases, can be available as Web services that communicate and share data using common Internet standards such as XML and SOAP. These services can then be combined with other Web services – internally or externally. In the diagram shown in Figure 7.7, the KM system is using a .NET service to enhance its expert finding capabilities. Information regarding the participant's skills may be lodged in the training groups database, while the person's experience information may reside in the human resource database. The knowledge management system may know what topics the participant has contributed against (as either in the KA repository or in a persistent electronic conversation) and the rated value (by other users) of that content. Combining all this information through a .NET service would allow the knowledge management system to build a true picture of the participant's expertise.

These aspects, when integrated into the programmable logic

of a KM system, can clearly provide benefits by integrating external source information dynamically with internal KM information. This approach transforms the logic into reusable components that can be published and consumed through secure interactions across secured boundaries. .NET effectively allows systems to "talk" to one another, thus removing application layer barriers and facilitating the flow of knowledge within an enterprise.

Summing up we can say that networks are important tools in any organization which form the basis for increasing capital and ultimate the knowledge through the resources derived from relationships in the organization. Among the discussed networks, neurons networks are basically aim at classification problems and value network generate tangible and intangible values between two or more individuals, groups or the organizations. Where as, the .NET concept is a new concept which has been evolving in Web-environment.

8

Data And Web Mining

Traditional data analysis methods often involve manual work and interpretation of data that is slow, expensive and highly subjective. For example, if an HR professional is interested in analyzing the cost of turnover, he or she might have to extract data from several different sources, such as accounting records, termination reports and personnel hiring records. That data is then combined, reconciled and evaluated. As business databases have grown in size, the traditional approach has grown more impractical. Data mining has been evolved as the process of extracting information from really large data sets through the use of algorithms and techniques drawn from the fields of statistics, machine learning, and database management.

Data mining is the process of analyzing data from different perspective and summarizing it into useful information. It is regarded as an evolving approach to data analysis in very large databases that could become a useful tool to HR professionals. Data mining involves extracting knowledge based on patterns of data in very large databases. Yet, data mining goes beyond simply performing data analysis on large data sets. Organizations that employ thousands of employees and track a multimedia of employement-related information might find valuable information patterns contained within their databases to provide insights in such areas as employee retention and compensation planning.

Data mining has been used successfully in many functional areas such as finance and marketing. Its applications in many organizations provide an as yet unexplored opportunity to apply data-mining techniques. These systems typically hold a large amount of data — a requirement for data mining. While most applications provide opportunities to generate adhoc or standardized reports from specific sets of data, the relationships between the data sets are rarely explored. It is this type of relationship that data mining seeks to discover.

8.1. DEVELOPMENT OF DATA MINING

The current evolution of data mining functions and proudcts is the results of years of influence from many disciplines, including databases, information retrieval, statistics, algorithms and machine learning (Figure 8.1). Another computer science area that has had a major impact on the Knowledge Discovery in Databases or KDD process is multimedia and graphics. A major goal of KDD is to be able to describe the results of the KDD process in a meaningful manner. Because many different results are often produced, this is a nontrivial problem. Visualization techniques often involve sophisticated multimedia and graphies presentations. In addition, data mining techniques can be applied to multimedia applications.

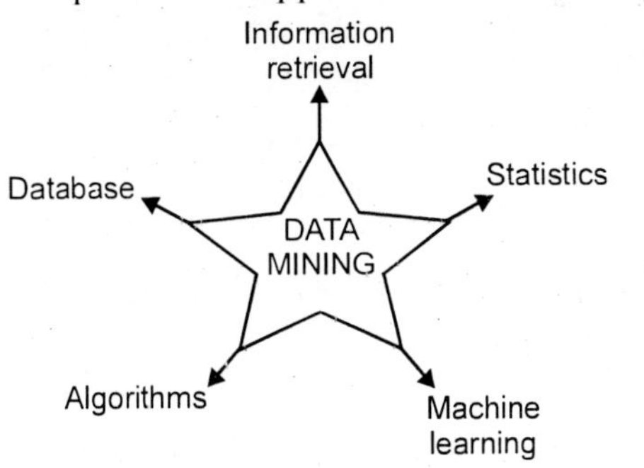

Fig. 8.1. Historical Perspective of Data Mining

Unlike previous research in these disparate areas, a major trend in the database community is to combine results from these seemingly different disciplines into one unifying data or algorithmic approach. Although in its infancy, the ultimate goal of this evolution is to develop a "big picture" view of the area that will facilitate integration of the various types of applications into real-world user domains.

Table 8.1 shows developments in the areas of artificial intelligence (AI), information retrieval (IR), database (DB), and statistics (Stat) leading to the current view of data mining. These different historical influences, which have led to the development of the total data mining area, have given rise to different views of what data mining functions actually are :

Table 8.1. Time Line of Data Mining Development

Time	Area	Contribution
Late 1700s	Stat	Bayes theorem of probability
Early 1900s	Stat	Regression analysis
Early 1920s	Stat	Maximum likelihood estimate
Early 1940s	AI	Neural networks
Early 1950s		Nearest neighbour
Early 1950s		Single link
Late 1950s	AI	Perceptron
Late 1950s	Stat	Resampling, bias reduction, jackfine estimator
Early 1960s	AI	ML started
Early 1960s	DB	Batch reports
Mid 1960s		Decision trees
Mid 1960s	Stat	Linear models for classification
	IR	Clustering
	Stat	Exploratory data analysis (EDA)
Late 1960s	DB	Relational data model
Early 1970s	IR	SMART IR sytems
Mid 1970s	AI	Genetic algorithims
Late 1970s	Stat	K-means clustering
Early 1980s	AI	Kohonen self-organizing map
Mid 1980s	AI	Decision tree algorthims
Early 1990s	DB	Association rule algorthims
		Web and search engines
1990s	DB	Data warehousing
1990s	DB	Online analytic processing (OLAP)

- Induction that is used to proceed from very specific knowledge to more general information. This type of technique is often found in AI applications.

- Because the primary objective of data mining is to describe some characteristics of a set of data by a general model, this approach can be viewed as a type of compression. Here the detailed data within the database are abstracted and compressed to a smaller description of the data characteristics that are found in the model.
- Data mining process itself can be viewed as a type of querying the underlying database. Indeed, an ongoing direction of data mining research is how to define a data query and whether a query language (like SQL) can be developed to capture the many different types of data mining queries.
- Describing a large databases, the impact of size and efficiency of developing an abstract model can be thought of as a type of search problem.
- It is interesting to think about the various data mining problems and how each may be viewed in several different perspective based on the viewpoint and background of the researcher or developer.

8.2. CONTINUOUS INNOVATION

Although data mining is a relatively new term, the technology is not. Companies have used powerful computers to sift through volumes of supermarket scanner data and analyze market research reports for years. However, continuos innovations in computer processing power, disk storage, and statistical software are dramatically increasing the accuracy of analysis while reducing the cost.

It is worth mentioning here the connections and differences between data mining and the more familiar activities of reports, queries and routine statistical studies applied to a database. Queries and reports are structured questions submitted to a database. For example, if an organization wanted to compare information on two different groups of employees, queries would be needed to extract the specific employees assigned to each group for further analysis.Thus, queries are typically an essential step in extracting data from the database. Data warehouses and datamarts greatly facilitate queries involving a time dimension. For example, trend analysis and forecasts require historical data that would be hard to obtain without such comprehensive databases. Such analysis might be applied to individual employee histories as part of performance analysis. Trends in statistics relating to Equal Employment Opportunity (EEO) could also be monitored in this way. In some respects, data mining can be regarded as a set of very sophisticated queries that involve sampling and statistical modeling. In any case, the additional query capabilities and uses should be factored into the decisions on implementation of a data warehouse or datamart for data mining use.

Decision-support system applications may also be regarded as predecessors to data-mining applications. Decision-support system applications are tools that allow users to collect data from databases, analyze the data and represent the analysis in many forms, such as graphs and reports. These systems may use statistical modeling packages to analyze data leading to information to support decisions organizations. These systems can combine information from other functional areas within the firm, such as customer service and marketing, to help to support human resource management decisions. For example, a user might build a statistical model to analyze data such as time to fill service requests and time to delivery as they relate to customer satisfaction levels. Information obtained from this analysis may then be used to establish performance goals for employees. While decision-support system applications may provide useful information for decision-makers in organizations, very specific analysis plans must be established. Essentially, the user must know what relationships exist before analyzing the data. Further, several iterations of the models may have to be tested before useful information can be identified.

For example, a university office of institutional research and studies (OIRS), may be responsible for certain decision-support and data-analysis studies that often involved university personnel. There was no datamart at the time. It was necessary to create special files from current databases and retain these year afer year in order to do any kinds of longitudinal analyses. Special statistical studies were sometimes possible if the right data had been collected. An example was historical trends in Equal Opportunity Employment practices. Flexibility and usefulness depended on the foresight of office analysts. If they had collected the right data, then they would be able to respond to new requests from management, state and federal agencies, and so on. If that foresight had not been in effect, it was necessary to approximate or decline the information request, or to labouriously go through old files to reconstrruct a usable database. while this permitted some statistical studies to be carried out, such limited access made data mining all but impossible. For specific statistical studies, on focuses on a specific set of variables and questions. For data mining, one essentially needs all the data to be accessible in a reasonably easy environment and the specific questions may not always be known precisely.

Descriptive statistics were often reported, especially those based on the current state of the system. Thus, it was possible for the OIRS to readily answer such questions as the age distribution of current faculty, its ethnic distribution, and gender distribution. However, to answer questions about trends in these data would require retaining the corresponding data from year to year. Ordinarily, only a small number of such yearly data sets might be retained. However, to make reasonable forecasts, for instance, a much longer series of data is required. More importantly, data-mining questions aimed at explaining the relationship of such trends to other variables in the system were practically impossible. Thus, data mining seeks to go beyond the old days of ordinary statistical reports showing only what is. It aims to find out more of the *how* and *why*.

Traditional database queries (Figure 8.2) access a database using a well-defined query stated in a language such as SQL. The output of the query consists of the data from the database that satisfies the query. The output is usually a subset of the database, but it may also be an extracted view or may contain aggregations. Data mining access of a database differs from this traditional access in several ways :

- **Query :** The query might not be well formed or precisely stated. The data miner might not even be exactly sure of what he wants to see.
- **Data :** The data accessed is usually a different version from that of the original operational database. The data have been

cleansed and modified to better support the mining process.

- **Output :** The output of the data mining query probably is not a subset of the database. Instead it is the output of some analysis of the contents of the database.

The current state of the art of data mining is similar to that of database query processing in the late 1960s and early 1970s. Over the next decade there undoubtedly will be great strides in extending the state of the art with respect to data mining. We probably will see the development of "query processing" models, standards and algorithms targeting the data mining applications. We probably will also see new data structures designed for the storage of databases being used for data mining applications. Although data mining is currently in its infancy, over the last decade we have seen a proliferation of mining algorithms, applications, and algorithms approaches.

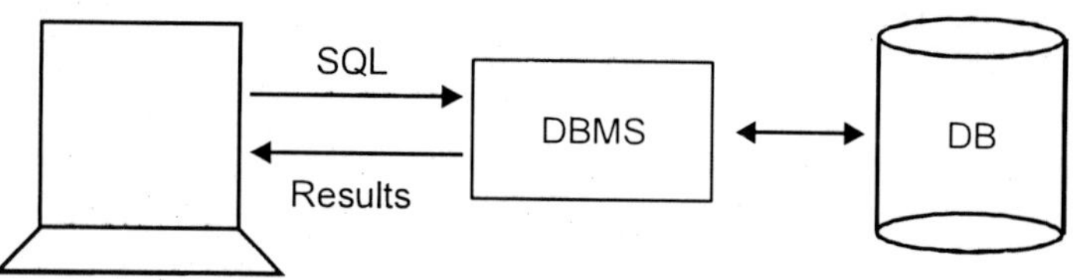

Fig. 8.2. Database Access

8.3. DATA MINING MODELS AND TASKS

Data mining comprises of three basic units namely Data, Information and Knowledge. All the three concepts are not independent but occurs in a continuous process in any investigation or a mental activity. The sequence of them is in ascending order. At every stage, each gets promoted to the other.

Data are any facts, numbers, or text that can be processed by a computer. Today, organizations are accumulating vast and growing amounts of data in different formats and different databases. This includes different kinds of data such as :

- operational or transactional data such as, sales, cost, inventory, payroll and accounting,
- nonoperational data, such as industry sales, forecast data, and macro economic data, and

- meta data — data about the data itself, such as Bibliographical Databases, logical database design or data dictioary definitions.

Finally, it enables them to "drill down" into summary information to view detail transactional data.

With data mining, a librarian could use point-of-reference and reading records of reader preference to achieve targeted promotions based on an individual's information seeking behaviour pattern history. By mining demographic data from use statistics, the librarian could procure reading materials and effect service promotions to appeal to specific subject specialists. For example, a University Library mines its Internet Usage history or the search history to identify the information seeking behaviour of scholars.

We can create two models for data mining. These are predective and descriptive models.

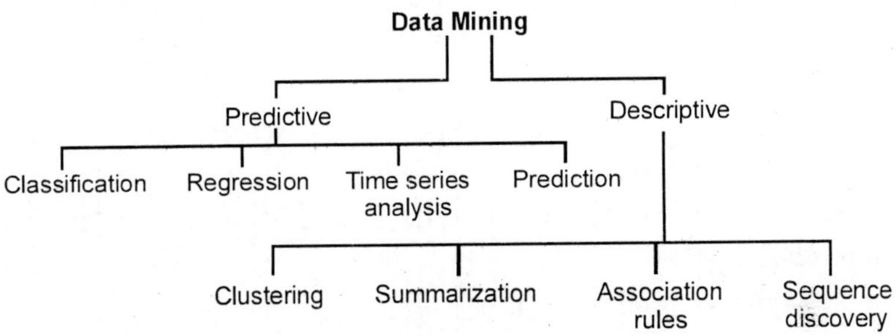

Fig. 8.3. Data Mining Models and Tasks

A *predictive model* makes a prediction about values of data using known results found from different data. Predictive modeling may be made based on the use of other historical data. For example, a credit card use might be refused not because of the user's own credit history, but because the current purchase is similar to earlier purchases that were subsequently found to be made with stolen cards. Predictive model data mining tasks include classification, regression, time series analysis, and prediction. Prediction may also be used to indicate a specific type of data mining function.

A *descriptive model* identifies patterns or relationships in data. Unlike the predictive model, serves as a way to explore the properties of the data examined, not to predict new properties. Clustering, summarization, association rules, and sequence discovery are usually viewed as descriptive in nature.

Data mining provides the link between transaction and analytical systems. Data mining software analyzes relationships and patterns in stored transaction data based on open-ended user queries. Several types of analytical software are available – statistical, machine learning, and neural networks. There are generally eight types of tasks associated with data minings they are :

8.3.1. Classification

Classification maps data into predefined groups or classes. It is often referred to as supervised learning because the classes are determined before examining the data. Two examples of classification applications are – determining whether to make a bank loan and identifying credit risks. Classification algorithms require that the classes be defined based on data attribute values. They often describe these classes by looking at the characteristics of data already known to belong to the classes. Pattern reconition is a type of classification where an input pattern is classified into one of several classes based on its similarity to these predefined classes.

For example in a University Library scholars are using the internet for various purposes like sending e-mail, information search and downloading and information exchange etc. The library could do a mining regarding the clientele visit to various websites. The Library could use the data to determine when clientele visit? and what they typically search? This information could be used to increase traffic by proving a portal.

8.3.2. Regression

Regression is used to map a data item to a real valued prediction variable. In actuality, regression involves the learning of the function that does this mapping. Regression assumes that the target data fit into some known type of function (e.g., linear, logistic, etc.) and then determines the best function of this type that models the given data. Some type of error analysis is used to determine which function is "best."

For example, A college professor wishes to reach a certain level of savings before her retirement. Periodically, he predicts what his retirement savings will be based on its current value and several past values. He uses a simple linear regression formula to predict this value by fitting past behaviour to a linear function and then using this function to predict the values at points in the future. Based on these values, he then alters his investment portfolio.

8.3.3. Time Series Analysis

With time series analysis, the value of an attribute is examined as it varies over time. The values usually are obtained as evenly spaced time points (daily, weekly, hourly etc.). A time series plot (Fig. 8.4), is used to visualize the time series. In this figure you can easily see that the plots for Y and Z have similar behaviour, while X appears to have less volatility. There are three basic functions performed in time series analysis. In one case, distance measures are used to determine the similarity between different time series. In the second case, the structure of the line is examined to determine (and perhaps classify) its behaviour. A third application would be to use the historical time series plot to predict future values. A time series example is given below.

Mr. Gupta is trying to determine whether to purchase stock from Companies X, Y, or Z. For a period of one month he charts the daily stock price for each company. Fig. 8.4 shows the time series plot that Mr. Gupta has generated. Using this and similar information available from his stockbroker, Mr. Gupta decides to purchase stock X because it is less volatile while overall showing a slightly larger relative amount of growth than either of the other stocks. As a matter of fact, the stocks for Y and Z have a similar behaviour. The behaviour of Y between days 6 and 20 is identical to that for Z between days 13 and 27.

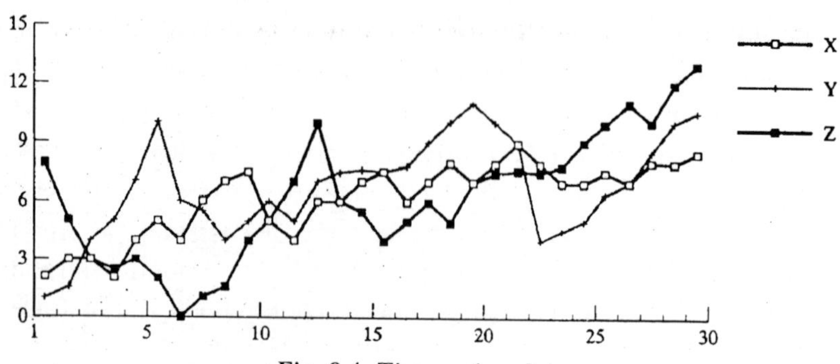

Fig. 8.4. Time series plots

8.3.4. Prediction

Many real-world data mining applications can be seen as predicting future data states based on past and current data. Prediction can be viewed as a type of classification. This is a data mining task that is different form the prediction model, although the prediction task is a type of prediction model. The difference is that prediction is predicting a future state rather than a current state. Here we are reffering to a type of application rather than to a type of data mining modeling approach, as discussed earlier. Prediction applications include flooding, speech recognition, machine learning, and pattern recognition. Although future values may be predicted using time series analysis or regression techniques, other approaches may be used as well. This can be explained in below given example.

Predicting flooding is a difficult problem. One approach uses monitors placed at various points in the river. These monitors collect data relevant to flood prediction water level, rain amount, time, humidity and so on. Then the water level at a potential flooding point in the river can be predicted based on the data collected by the sensors upriver from this point. The prediction must be made with respect to the time the data were collected.

8.3.5. Clustering

Clustering is similar to classification except that the groups are not predefined, but rather defined by the data alone. Clustering is alternatively referred to as unsupervised learning or segmentation. It can be thought of as partitioning or segmenting the data into groups that might or might not be disjointed. The clustering is usually accomplished by determining the similarity among the data on predefined attributes. The most similar data are grouped into clusters. For example, data can be mined to identify subject segments or reader affinities in libraries. Since the clusters are not predefined, a domain expert is often required to interpret the meaning of the created clusters.

A special type of clustering is called segmentation.With segmentation a database is partitioned into disjointed groupings of similar tuples called segments. Segmentation is often viewed as being identical to clustering. In other circles segmentation is viewed as a specific type of clustering applied to a database itself. Thus we can use the two terms, clustering and segmentation, interchangeably.

8.3.6. Summarization

Summarization is also called characterization or generalization. Summarization maps data into subsets with associated simple descriptions. It extracts or derives representative information about the database. This may be accomplished by actually retrieving portions of the data. Alternatviely, summary type information, such as the mean of some numeric attribute, can be derived from the data. The summarization succinctly characterizes the contents of the database.

The example may include the criteria used to compare universities on the basis of NAAC reports and All India survey by some body. This will be the summarization used to obtain the universities' rank.

8.3.7. Association Rules

Link analysis, alternatively referred to as affinity analysis or association, refers to the data mining task of uncovering relationships among the data. The best example of this type of application is to determine association rules. An association rule is a model that identifies specific types of data associations. These associations are often used in the retail sales community to identify items that are frequently purchased together. Associations are also used in many other applications such as predicting the failure of telecommunication switches.

For example scholars concerned with socio-economic survey

are sure to look for price index as well as population statistics. Another example may be as under.

A grocery store retailer is trying to decide whether to put bread on sale. To help determine the impact of this decision, the retailer generates association rules that show what other products are frequently purchased with bread. He finds that 60 percent of the time that bread is sold so are pretzels and that 70 percent of the time jelly is also sold. Based on these facts, he tries to capitalize on the association between bread, pretzels and jelly by placing some pretzels and jelly at the end of the aisle where the bread is placed. In addition, he decides not to place either of these items on sale at the same time.

Users of association rules must be cautioned that these are not causal relationships. They do not represent any relationship inherent in the actual data or in the real world. There probably is no relationship between bread and pretzels that causes them to be purchased together. And there is no guarantee that this association will apply in the future. However, association rules can be used to assist retail store management in effective advertising, marketing and inventory control.

8.3.8. Sequence Discovery

Sequence discovery is used to determine sequential patterns in data. These patterns are based on a time sequence of actions. These patterns are similar to associations in that data (or events) are found to be related, but the relationship is based on time. Unlike a market basket analysis, which requires the items to be purchased at the same time, in sequence discovery the items are purchased over the time in some order. For example, most people who purchase CD players may be found to purchase CDs within one week. As we will see, temporal association rules really fall into this category. This can be understood by below given example.

The Webmaster at the XYZ Corporation periodically analyzes the Web log data to determine how users of the XYZ's Web pages access them. He is interested in determining what sequences of pages are frequently accessed. He determines that 70 percent of the users of page A follow one of the following patterns of behaviour:

(A, B, C) or (A, D, B, C) or (A, E, B,C). He then determines to add a link directly from page A to page C.

In addition, Data are mined to anticipate behaviour patterns and trends. For example, scholars in Biological sciences who use Biosis shall definitely look for Web of Science. Biosis is a secondary service while Webof Science is a primary full text journal package.

8.4. LEVELS OF ANALYSIS IN DATA MINING

Different levels of analysis are available. These are :

- *Artificial Neural Networks* : Non-linear predictive models that learn through training and resemble biological neural networks in structures.
- *Genetic Algorithims* : Optimization techniques that use processes such as genetic combination, mutation and natural selection in a design based on the concepts of natural evolution.
- *Decision Trees* : Tree-shaped structures that represent sets of decisions. These decisions generate rules for the classification of a dataset. Specific decision tree methods include Classification and Regression Trees (CART) and Chi Square Automatic Interaction Detection (CHAID). CART and CHAID are decision tree techniques used for classification of a dataset. They provide a set of rules that you can apply to a new unclassified dataset by creating 2-way splits while CHAID segments using chi squares tests to create multi-way splits. CART typically requires less data preparation than CHAID.
- *Nearest Neighbour Method* : A technique that classifies each record in a dataset based on a combination of the classes of the K record (s) most similar to it in a historical dataset (where K 1). Sometimes called the k-nearest neighbour technique.
- *Rule Induction* : The extraction of useful if-then rules from data based on statistical significance.
- *Data Visualization* : The visual interpretion of complex relationships in multimensional data. Graphics tools are used to illustrate data relationships.

8.5. DATA MINING ISSUES

There are many important implementation issues associated with data mining :

1. Human Interactions : Since data mining problems are often not precisely stated, interfaces may be needed with both domain and technical experts. Technical experts are used to formulate the queries and assist in interpreting the results. Users are needed to identify training data and the desired results.

2. Overfitting : When a model is generated that is associated with a given database state, it is desirable that the model also fit future database states. Overfitting occurs when the model does not fit in future states. This may be caused by assumptions that are made about the data or may simply be caused by the small size of the training database. For example, a classification model for an employee database may be developed to classify employees as short, medium or tall. If the training database is quite small, the model might erroneously indicate that a short person is anyone under five feet eight inches because there is only one entry in the training database under five feet eight inches. In this case, many future employees would be erroneously classified as short. Overfitting can arise under other circumstances as well, even though the data are not changing.

3. Outliers : There are often many data entries that do not fit nicely into the derived model. This becomes even more of an issue with very large databases. If a model is developed that includes these outliers, then the model may not behave well for data that are not outliers.

4. Interpretation of Results : Currently, data mining output may require experts to correctly interpret the results, which might otherwise be meaningless to the average database user.

5. Visualization of Results : To easily view and understand the output of data mining algorithms, visualization of the results is helpful.

6. Large Datasets : The massive datasets associated with data mining create problems when applying algorithms designed for small datasets. Many modeling applications grow exponentially on the dataset size and thus are too inefficient for larger datasets. *Sampling* and *Parallelization* are effective tools to attack this scalability problem.

7. High Dimensionality : A conventional database scheme may be composed of many different attributes. The problem here is that not all attributes may be needed to solve a given data mining problem. Infact, the use of some attributes may interfere with the correct completion of a data mining task. The use of other attributes may simply increase the overall complexity and decrease the efficiency of an algorithm. This problem is sometimes referred to as the dimensionality curse, meaning that there are many attributes–dimensions involved and it is difficult to determine which one should be used. One solution to this high dimensionality problem is to reduce the number of attributes, which is known as dimensionality reduction.

8. Multimedia Data : Most previous data mining algorithms are targeted to traditional data types — numeric, character, text, etc. The use of multimedia data such as is found in GIS databases complicates or invalidates many proposed algorithms.

9. Missing Data : During the preprocessing phase of KDD, missing data may be replaced with estimates. This and other approaches to handling missing data can lead to invalid results in the data mining step.

10. Irrelevant Data : Some attributes in the databases might not be of interest to the data mining task being developed.

11. Noisy Data : Some attribute values might be invalid or incorrect. These values are often corrected before running data mining applications.

12. Changing Data : Databases cannot be assumed to be static. However, most data mining algorithms do assume a static database. This requires that the algorithms be completly rerun anytime the database changes.

13. Integration : The KDD process is not currently integrated into normal data processing activities. KDD requests may be treated as special, unusual, or one-time needs. This makes them inefficient, ineffective, and not general enough to be used on an ongoing basis. Integration of data mining functions into traditional database management systems is certainly a desirable goal.

14. Application : Determining the intended use for the information obtained from the data mining function is a challenge. Indeed, how business executives can effectively use the output is sometimes considered the more difficult part, not the running of the algorithms themselves. Because the data are of a type that has not previously been known, business practices may have to be modified to determine how to effectively use the information uncovered.

These issues should be addressed by data mining algorithms and products.

8.6. DATA MINING METRICS

Measuring the effectiveness or usefulness of a data mining approach is not always straightforward. Infact, different metrics can be used for different techniques and also based on the interest level. From an overall business or usefulness perspective, a measure such as Return on Investment (ROI) could be used. ROI examines the difference between what the data mining technique costs and what the savings or benefits from its use are. Of course, this would be difficult to measure because the return is hard to quantify. It could be measured as increased sales, reduced advertising expenditure, or both. In a specific advertising campaign implemented via targeted catalogue mailings, the percentage of catalogue recipients and the amount of purchase per recipient would provide one means to measure the effectiveness of the mailings.

The metrics use also include the traditional metrics of space and time based on complexity analysis. In some cases, such as accuracy in classification, more specific metrics targeted to a data mining task may be used.

8.7. TEMPORAL MINING

There is an another type of mining which is known as *Temporal mining*. This is the mining in temporal databases.

Databases traditionally do not contain temporal data. Instead, the data that are stored reflect data at a single point in time. Thus, it may be called a snapshot database. For example, an employee database normally contains only the current company employees rather than all employees who have ever worked for the company. However, many questions cannot be answered by this snapshot data. A company CEO might wish to determine trends in the hiring and firing of employees, or he might wish to obtain information about the ethnic diversity of employees and how it has changed over time. These types of data mining questions require temporal data. In a temporal database, data are maintained for multiple time points, not just one time point. The mining from these databases is known as *Temporal Mining*. This can be explained with following example.

XYZ Corporation, uses a temporal database to store employee information. It maintains the Social Security number (SSN), employee name, address, and salary for each employee. When a new tuple is stored in the database, the current data is added to this information. Anup Sharma is hired on 2/12/08 at a salary of 50,000. On his six month performance evaluation, he is given a raise and a promotion. On 12/12/2008, he moves to a new address. At the end of 2008, there are three tuples in the database for Anup Sharma.

Dats	Name	SSN	Address	Salary
2/12/2008	Anup Sharma	123456789	10, Vidya Vihar, Haridwar	50,000
8/12/2008	Anup Sharma	123456789	10, Vidya Vihar, Haridwar	52,000
12/12/2008	Anup Sharma	123456789	129, Vidya Vihar, Haridwar	52,000

Analysis of temporal (or time-vaying) data presents many interesting challenges. For example, there may be many different interpretions for time. In above example, the date stored in the record is the date representing when that information becomes current. This is often called the valid time. The valid time for information is the time during which the information is true in the modeled world. This usually consists of a start time and an end time. The end time in the example is implied by the start time of the next temporal record for the same employee. Another time that could have been used is the transaction time. The transaction time is the timestamp associated with the transaction that inserted this record. This could be different from the start time for the valid time interval. The transaction time interval is the time the tuple actually existed in the database. For example, Anup Sharma may have indicated on 15/11/08 that he would have the new address effective 12/12/08. The start valid time for the new address was 12/12/08, but the transaction time was 15/11/08. Other types of times may be used as well. When the employee information changes, a new tuple is inserted. Changes and deletes may occur only to change data that was incorrectly inserted.

Many different examples for temporal data exist. Satellites continually collect images and sensory data. This information is temporal and is associated with specific points in time. In a hospital, printouts of heartbeats may be kept for patients. This represents a continuous view of temporal data. When EEG is taken for a patients, several different brain waves are measured in parallel. Each wave represents a continuous set of data over time.

Temporal databases usually do not accept the same types of updates and queries as traditional snapshot databases. The only updates that are allowed are corrections and versions. Actual modifications of tuples usually are not allowed. Instead, a new tuple with a different valid time would be added. Temporal queries may involves fairly complicated temporal selection criteria.

As with spatial mining, several specialized data structures have been proposed to assist in temporal mining. There are many specialized data structures that have been proposed to index temporal databases that we do not discuss here. These usually are generalizations of B^+ trees and are similar to those structures we saw with spatial databases. One difference, of course, is that time is usually one dimension where as space may be two or three dimensions. These structures usually assume that a valid time range is associated with each tuple. One complicating factor is the use of the current time. Unlike spatial data, the temporal dimension keeps expanding. Thus, for items that are currently valid, it is not possible to have the current end time for the range. One solution to this problem is to use a special time value called now, which is the current time. Thus, a range that ends in "now" means that it is valid up to the current time. The resulting effect is that time ranges that end in "now" actually keep expanding in size.

Mining of temporal data involves many of the conventional data mining activities but, of course, is complicated by the temporal aspect and the more complicated types of queries. For example, time series data may be clustered based on similarities found. However, determining the similarity between two different sets of time series data is difficult, Given a time series, a future value also may be predicted. Association rules may involve temporal aspects and relationships.

8.8. TEXT MINING

Unlike the above mentioned data mining techniques that deal with structured data, text mining is to extract patterns from textual documents. A text mining technique typically involves text parsing and analysis to transform each unstructured document into an appropriate set of features and subsequently applies one or more above mentioned data mining techniques for extracting patterns from the feature space. Research in text mining has its roots in information retrieval. Text mining has grown form its origin to encompass text categorization, document clustering, term association discovery, routing and filtering, information extraction, document summarization, etc.

8.9. DATA VISUALIZATION

Data visualization takes advantage of human perception as a method for analysis. It allows decision makers to view complex patterns in the data as visual objects in three dimensions and colors, and supports advanced manipulation capabilities to slice, rotate or zoom the objects to provide varying levels of details of the patterns observed. The primary goals of data visualization could be exploration or confirmation. Data visualization for exploration is usually performed during early stages of data analysis when initial hypothesis about the data characteristics is not available. The ideal outcome is a set of hypotheses on the distribution of data along various dimensions as well as any interaction effects that may be visible. Visualization can also be used to identify outliers clusters, frequencies, relationships, and general patterns in the data. On the other hand, data visualization for confirmation is usually used to confirm hypotheses that are suspected from previous data analyses using other means. Visualizing the hypotheses provides yet another evidence for the confirmation of the hypotheses of interest.

Visualization techniques include:

- *Graphical* : Traditional graph structures including bar charts, pie charts, histograms, and line graphs may be used.
- *Geometric* : Geometric techniques include the box plot and scatter diagram techniques.
- *Icon-based* : Using figures, colors, or other icons can improve the presentation of the results.
- *Pixel-based* : With these techniques each data value is shown as a uniquely coloured pixel.
- *Hierarchical* : These techniques hierarchically divide the display area (screen) into regions based on data values.
- *Hybrid* : The preceding approaches can be combined into one display.

Any of these approaches may be two-dimensional or three-dimensional.

Keim and Kriegel has provided an elaborate analysis of visualization techniques for mining large databases and classified data visualization techniques into pixel-oriented, geometric projection, icon-based, hierarchical, and graph-based. A *pixel-oriented* technique maps each data value to a colored pixel and presents the data values belonging to each attribute in separate windows. *Geomatric projection* techniques aim at finding "interesting" projections of multimensional data sets. The class of geometric projection techniques includes principal component analysis, factor analysis, multimensional scaling etc. The idea to icon, e.g., a face icon in the Chernoff face visualization a stick figure in the stick figure technique. In an *icon-based technique*, two dimensions are mapped to the display dimensions and the remaining dimensions are mapped to the properties of an icon, e.g., the shape of nose, mouth and eyes of a face icon or the angles and/or limb lengths of a stick figure icon. If the data items are relatively dense with respect to the display dimensions, the resulting visualization presents texture patterns that are very according to the characteristics of the data and are, thus, detectable by preattentive perception. The *hierarchical visualization* techniques subdivide the k-dimensional space and present the subspaces in a hierarchical fashion. For example, the dimensional stacking technique subdivides the k-dimensional subspaces. Finally, the basic idea of a *graph-based technique* is to effectively present a large graph using specific layout algorithims, query languages, and abstraction techniques.

Today's Data Warehonsing and knowledge Discovery in Databases are also used along with Data mining; sometimes synonymously but they are different. Both are described below in brief.

8.10. DATA WAREHOUSING

Data warehousing is defined as a process of centralized data management and retrieval. Data warehousing, like data mining, is a relatively new term although the concept itself has been around for years. It represents an ideal vision of maintaining a central repository of all organizational data. Centralization of data is needed to maximize user access and analysis. Dramatic technological advances are making this vision a reality for many companies. And, equally dramatic advances in data analysis software are allowing users to access this data freely. The data analysis software is what supports data mining.

The term data warehouse was first used by William Inmon in the early 1980s. He defined data warehouse to be a set of data that supports DSS and is "subject-oriented, integrated, time-variant and nonvolatile." With data warehousing, corporate-wide data (current and historical) are merged into a single repository. Traditional databases contain operational data that represent the day-to-day needs of a Company. Traditional business data processing (such as billing, inventory control, payroll, and manufacturing support) support online transaction processing and batch reporting applications. A data warehouse, however, contains informational data, which are used to support other functions such as planing and forecasting. Although much of the content is similar between the operational and informational data, much is different As a matter of fact, the operational data are transformed into the informational data. Following example illustrates the difference between these two.

ACME Manufacturing Company maintains several operational databases – sales, billing, employee, manufacturing, and warehousing. These are used to support the day-to-day functions such as writing paychecks, placing orders for supplies needed in the manufacturing process, billing customers, and so on. The president of ACME, wishes to streamline manufacturing to concentrate production on the most profitable products. To perform this task, she asks several "what if" questions, does a projection of current sales into the future, and examines data at different geographic and time dimensions. All the data that she needs to perform this task can be found in one or more of the existing databases. However, it is not easily retrieved in the exact format that she desires. A data warehouse is created with exactly the sales information she needs bylocation and time. OLAP retrieval tools are provided to facilitate quick response to her questions at any and all dimension granularities.

The data warehouse market supports such diverse industries as manufacturing, retail, telecommunications, and health care. Think of a personnel database for a company that is continually modified as personnel are added and deleted. A personnel database that contains information about the current set of employees is sufficient. However, if management wishes to analyze trends with respect to employment history, more data are needed. They may wish to determine if there is a problem with too many employees quitting. To analyze this problem, they would need to know which employees have left, when they left, why they left, and other information about their employment. For management to make these types of high-level business analyses, more historical data– not just the current snapshot that is typically stored; and data from other sources – perhaps employment applications and results of exit interviews, are required. In addition, some of the data in the personnel database, such as address, may not be needed. A data warehouse provides just this information. In a nutshell, a data warehouse is a data repository used to support decision support systems.

The basic motivation for this shift to the strategic use of data is to increase business profitability. Traditional data processing applications support the day-to-day clerical and administrative decisions, while data warehousing supports long-term strategic decisions. A 1996 report by International Data Corporation (IDC) stated that an average return on investment (ROI) in data warehousing reached 401percent.

Figure 8.5 shows a simple view of a data warehouse. The basic components of a data warehousing system include data migration, the warehouse, and access tools. The data are extracted from operational systems, but must be reformatted, cleanzed, integrated, and summarized before being placed in the warehouse. Much of the operational data are not needed in the warehouse and are removed during this conversion process. This migration process is similar to that needed for data mining applications except that data mining applications need not necessarily be performed on summarized or business-wide data. The applications that are shown in Figure 8.5 access a warehouse include traditional querying, OLAP, and data mining. Since the warehouse is stored as a database, it can be accessed by traditional query languages.

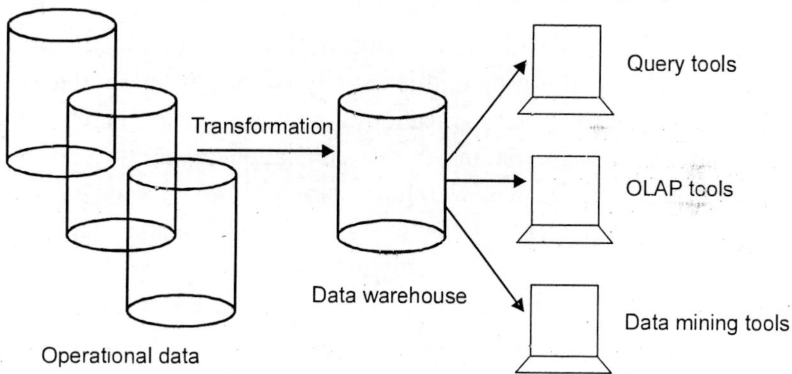

Fig. 8.5. Data warehouse

Table 8.2 summarizes the differences between operational data stored in traditional databases and the data stored in a data warehouse. The traditional database applications are related to OLTP where the users' requests are stated in a high-level query language (such as SQL) and the results are subsets of the relationships. Data warehouse applications are directly related to business decisions and analysis of the data, OLAP. While operational data usually

Table 8.2. Comparing Operational Database to Data Warehouse

	Operational Data	Data Warehouse
Application	OLTP	OLAP
Use	Precise queries	Ad hoc
Temporal	Snapshot	Historical
Modification	Dynamic	Static
Orientation	Application	Business
Data	Operational values	Integrated
Size	Gigabits	Terabits
Level	Detailed	Summarized
Access	Often	Less often
Response	Few seconds	Minutes
Data schema	Relational	Star/snowflake

represent facts concerning a snapshot in time (the current time), a warehouse has historical data as well. Data in the warehouse are not modified as frequently as data in a conventional database. Updates are batched and merged into the warehouse at weekly or monthly intervals. Although this means that the warehouse data are not completely up-to-date, this usually is not a problem with the normal decision support applications. A conventional database usually is related to one application type. This is a fallout of the normalization design process used. The warehouse is associated with the business enterprise, not with an application. Traditional databases may be on the order of megabytes or gigabytes, whereas a warehouse may be terabytes in size. The fact that conventional data are stored in many diverse formats and locations makes it inefficient to support decision support applications. OLTP users expect to get a response in a few seconds. As a result of the complexity of OLAP application, their users may have to wait minutes for a response to their query.

The data transformation process required to convert operational data to informational involves many functions including:

- Unwanted data must be removed.
- Converting heterogeneous sources into one common schema. This problem is the same as that found when accessing data from multiple heterogeneous sources. Each operational

database may contain the same data with different attribute names. For example, one system may use "Employee ID," while another uses "EID" for the same attribute. In addition, there may be multiple data types for the same attribute.

- As the operational data is probably a snapshot of the data, multiple snapshots may need to be merged to create the historical view.
- Summarizing data is performed to provide a higher level view of the data. This summarization may be done at multiple granularities and for different dimensions.
- New derived data, e.g., using age rather than birth date, may be added to better facilitate decision support functions.
- Handling missing and erroneous data must be performed. This could entail replacing them with predicted or default values or simply removing these entries.

The portion of the transformation that deals with ensuring valid and consistent data is sometimes referred to as *data scrubbing* or *data staging.*

There are many benefits to the use of a data warehouse. As it provides an integration of data from multiple sources, its use can provide more efficient access of the data. The data that are stored often provide different levels of summarization. For example, sales data may be found at a low level (purchase order), at a city level (total of sales for a city), or at higher levels (county, state, country, world). The summary can be provided for different types of granularity. The sales data could be summarized by both salesman and department. These summarizations are provided by the conversion process instead of being calculated when the data are accessed. Thus, this also speeds up the processing of the data for decision support applications.

The data warehouse may appear to increase the complexity of database management because it is a replica of the operational data. But keep in mind that much of the data in the warehouse are not simply a replication but an extension to or aggregation of the data. In addition, because the data warehouse contains historical data, data stored there probably will have a longer life span than the snapshot data found in the operational databases. The fact that the data in the warehouse need not be kept consistent with the current operational data also simplifies its maintenance. The benefits obtained by the capabilities (e.g., DSS support) provided usually are deemed to outweigh any disadvantages.

A subset of the complete data warehouse, data mart, may be stored and accessed separately. The level is at a departmental, regional, or functional level. These separate data marts are much smaller, and they more efficiently support narrower analytical types of applications.

A virtual warehouse is a warehouse implemented as a view from the operational data. While some of this view may actually be materialized for efficiency, it need not all be. There are several ways to improve the performance of data warehouse applications.

- *Summarization* : As many applications require summary-type information, data that are known to be needed for consolidation queries should be presummarized before storage. Different levels of summarization should be included to improve performance. With a 20 to 100 percent increase in storage space, an increase in performance of 2 to 10 times can be achieved
- *Denormalization* : Traditional normalization reduces such problems as redundancy as well as insert, update, and deletion anomalies. However, these improvements are achieved at the cost of increased processing time due to joins. With a data warehouse, improved performance can be achieved by storing denormalized data. Since data warehouses are not usually updated as frequently as operational data are, the negatives associated with update operations are not an issue.
- *Partitioning* : Dividing the data warehouse into smaller fragments may reduce processing time by allowing queries to access small data sets.

The relationship between data mining and data warehousing can be viewed as symbiotic. Data used in data mining applications are often slightly modified from that in the databases where the data permanently reside. The same is true for data in a data warehouse. When data are placed in a warehouse, they are extracted from the database, cleanzed, and reformatted. The fact that the data are derived from multiple sources with heterogeneous formats complicates the problem. In addition, the fact that the source databases are updated requires that the warehouse be updated periodically or work with stale data. These issues are identical to many of those associated with data mining and KDD (see Figure 8.6). While data mining and data warehousing are actually orthogonal issues, they are complementary. Due to the types of applications and massive amount of data in a data warehouse, data mining applications can be used to provide meaningful information needed for decision support systems. For example, management may use the results of classification or association rule applications to help determine the target population for an advertising campaign. In addition, data mining activities can benefit from the use of data in a data warehouse. However, its use is not required. *Data warehousing* and *data mining* are sometimes thought of as the same thing. Even though they are related, they are different and each can be used without the other.

8.11. KNOWLEDGE DISCOVERY IN DATABASES

The terms knowledge discovery in databases (KDD) and data mining are often also used interchangeably. In fact, there have been many other names given to this process of discovering useful (hidden) patterns in data – knowledge extraction, information discovery, exploratory data analysis, information harvesting, and unsupervised pattern recognition. Over the last few years KDD has been used to refer to a process consisting of many steps, while data mining is only one of these steps. The following definitions are modified from available literature.

Definition 1 : Knowledge discovery in databases (KDD) is the process of finding useful information and patterns in data.

Definition 2 : Data mining is the use of algorithms to extract the information and patterns derived by the KDD process.

The KDD process is often said to be nontrivial; however, we take the larger view that KDD is an all-encompassing concept. A traditional SQL database query can be viewed as the data mining part of a KDD process. Indeed, this may be viewed as somewhat simple and trivial. However, this was not the case 30 years ago. If we were to advance 30 years into the future, we might find that processes thought of today as nontrivial and complex will be viewed as equally simple. The definition of KDD includes the keyword useful. Although some definitions have included the term "potentially useful," we believe that if the information found in the process is not useful, then it really is not information. Of course, the idea of being useful is relative and depends on the individuals involved. KDD is a process that involves many different steps. The input to this process is the data, and the output is the useful information desired by the users. However, the objective may be unclear or inexact. The process itself is interactive and may require much elapsed time. To ensure the usefulness and accuracy of the results of the process, interaction throughout the process with both domain experts and technical experts might be needed. Figure 8.6 illustrates the overall KDD process.

The KDD process consists of the following five steps

- *Selection* : The data needed for the data mining process may be obtained from many different and heterogeneous data sources. This first step obtains the data from various databases, files, and nonelectronic sources.
- *Preprocessing* : The data to be used by the process may have incorrect or missing data. There may be anomalous data from multiple sources involving different data types and metrics. There may be many different activities performed at this time. Erroneous data may be corrected or removed, whereas missing data must be supplied or predicted.
- *Transformation* : Data from different sources must be converted into a common format for processing. Some data may be encoded or transformed into more usable formats. Data reduction may be used to reduce the number of possible data values being considered.
- *Data Mining* : Based on the data mining task being performed, this step applies algorithms to the transformed data to generate the desired results.

- *Interpretation/Evaluation* : How the data mining results are presented to the users is extremely important because the usefulness of the results is dependent on it. Various visualization and GUI strategies are used at this last step.

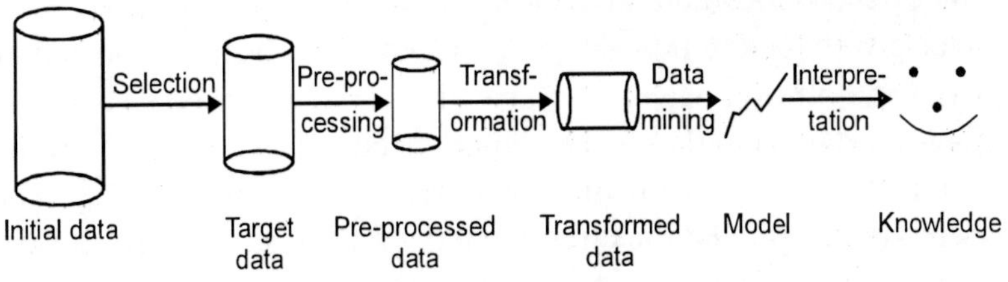

Fig. 8.6. KDD Process

Transformation techniques are used to make the data easier to mine and more useful, and to provide more meaningful results. The actual distribution of the data may be modified to facilitate the use by techniques that require specific types of data distributions. Some attribute values may be combined to provide new values, thus reducing the complexity of the data. For example, current date and birth date could be replaced by age. One attribute could be substituted for another. An example would be replacing a sequence of actual attribute values with the differences between consecutive values. Real valued attributes may be more easily handled by partitioning the values into ranges and using these discrete range values. Some data values may actually be removed. Outliers, extreme values that occur infrequently, may actually be removed. The data may be transformed by applying a function to the values. A common transformation function is to use the log of the value rather than the value itself. These techniques make the mining task easier by reducing the dimensionality or by reducing the variability of the data values. The removal of outliers can actually improve the quality of the results. As with all steps in the KDD process, however, care must be used in performing transformation. If used incorrectly, the transformation could actually change the data such that the results of the data mining step are inaccurate.

8.12. WEB MINING

Everyday, enormous amounts of information are generated

from all sectors, whether it be business, education, the scientific community, the World Wide Web (WWW), or one of many readily available off-line and online data sources. The Web can be viewed as the largest database available and presents a challenging task for effective design and access. The determining the size of the World Web is extremely difficult. In 1999 it was estimated to contain over 350 million pages with growth at the rate of about 1 million pages a day. Google recently announced that it indexes 5 billion Web documents. Web mining is used to understand customer behaviour, evaluate the effectiveness of a particular Web site, and help to quantify the success of marketing campaign.

Web mining is one of the most promising areas in data mining, because the Internet and WWW are dynamic sources of information. Web mining is the extraction of interesting and potentially useful patterns and implicit information from artifacts or activity related to the WWW. The main tasks that comprise Web mining include retrieving Web documents, selection and processing of Web information, pattern discovery in sites and across sites, and analysis of the patterns found there in.

Web mining can be categorized into three separate areas–Web-content mining, Web-structure mining, and Web-usage mining. A general classification of Web mining is shown in following figure.

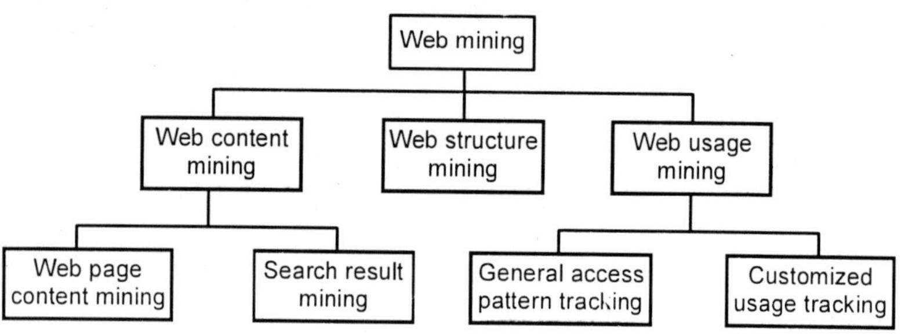

Fig. 8.7. Types of Web Mining

Web Content Mining : Web content mining examines the content of Web pages as well as results of Web searching. The content includes text as well as graphics data. Web content mining is further divided into *Web page content mining* and *search results mining*. The first is traditional searching of Web pages via content, while the second is a further search of pages found from a previous search. Thus, some mining activities have been built on top of traditional search engines, using their result as the data to be mined. Web content mining can be thought of as extending the work performed by basic search engines. There are many different techniques that can be used to search the Internet. Most search engines are keyword-based. Web content mining goes beyond this basic Information Retrieval or IR technology. It can improve on traditional search engines through such techniques as concept hierarchies and synonyms user profiles, and analyzing the links between pages.

Web-content mining is concerned with the discovery of new information and knowledge from web-based data, documents, and pages. There are two main approaches to Web-content mining– an information retrieval view and a database (DB) view. The information retrieval view is designed to work with both unstructured (free text, such as news stories) or semistructured documents (with both HTML and hyperlinked data), and attempts to identify patterns and models based on an analysis of the documents, using such techniques as clustering, classification, finding text patterns, and extraction rules. The other main approach, which is to content mine semi-structured documents, uses many of the same techniques as used for unstructured documents, but with the added complexity and challenge of analyzing documents containing a variety of media elements.

There are also applications that focus on the design of languages, which provide better querying of DBs containing web-based data. Researchers have developed many web-oriented query languages that attempt to extend standard DB query languages such as SQL to collect data from the WWW, e.g., WebLog and WebSQL. The TS1MMIS system extracts data from heterogeneous and semistructured information sources and correlates them to generate an integrated DB representation of the extracted information. Other applications focus on the building and management of multilevel or multi-layered DBs. This suggests a multilevel-DB approach to organizing web-based information. The main idea behind this method is that the lowest level of the DB contains primitive semistructured information stored in various Web repositories, such as hypertext documents. At the higher level(s), metadata or generalizations are extracted from lower levels and organized in structured collections such as relational or object-oriented DBs.

Web-structure Mining instead of looking at the text and data on the pages themselves, has as its goal the mining of knowledge from the structure of websites. More specificially, it attempts to examine the structures that exist between documents on a website, such as hyperlinks and other linkages. for instances, links pointing to a document indicate the popularity of the document, while links coming out of a document indicate the richness or perhaps the variety of topics covered in the document. The Page Rank and CLEVER method, take the advantages of the information conveyed by the links to find pertinent web pages.

The PageRank technique was designed to both increase the effectiveness of search engines and improve their efficiency. PageRank is used to measure the importance of a page and to prioritize pages returned from a traditional search engine using keyword searching. The effectiveness of this measure has been demonstrated by the success of Google. The PageRank value for a page is calculated based on the number of pages that point to it. This is actually a measure based on the number of backlinks to a page. A backlink is a link pointing to a page rather than pointing out from a page. The measure is not simply a count of the number of backlinks because a weighting is used to provide more importance to backlinks coming from important pages. Given a page p, we use B_p to be the set of pages that point to p, and F_p to be the set of links out of p. The PageRank of a page p is defined as [PBMW98]

$$\text{PR}(P) = c \sum_{q \in B_p} \frac{PR(q)}{N_q}$$

Here $N_q = |F_q|$. The constant c is a value between 0 and 1 and is used for normalization. A problem, called *rank sink*, that exists with this PageRank calculation is that when a cyclic reference occurs (page A points to page B and page B points to page A), the PR value for these pages increases. This problem is solved by adding an additional term to the formula:

$$\text{PR}(P) = c \sum_{q \in B_p} \frac{PR(q)}{N_q} + cE(v)$$

where c is maximized. Here E(v) is a vector that adds an artificial link. This simulates a random surfer who periodically decides to stop following links and jumps to a new page. E(v) adds links of small probabilities between every pair of nodes.

The PageRank technique is different from other approaches that look at links. It does not count all links the same. The values are normalized by the number of links in the page.

CLEVER, is the sytem developed at IBM and is aimed at finding both authoritative pages and hubs. This is defined as the "best source" for the requested information. In addition, a hub is a page that contains links to authoritative pages. The Clever system identifies authoritative pages and hub pages by creating weights. A search can be viewed as having a goal of finding the best hubs and authorities.

Because of the distributed and unsupervised development of sites, a user has no way of knowing whether the information contained within a Web page is accurate. Currently, there is nothing to prevent someone from producing a page that contains not only errors, but also blatant lies. In addition, some pages might be of a higher quality than others. These pages are often referred to as being the most authoritative. This is different from relevant. A page may be extremely relevant, but if it contains factual errors, users certainly do not want to retrieve it. The issue of authority usually does not surface in traditional information retrieval.

Web-usageMining is another major area in the broad spectrum of Web mining is Web-usage mining. Rather than looking at the content pages or the underlying structure, Web-usage mining is focused on Web user behaviour or, more specifically, modeling and predicting how a user will use and interact with the Web. In general, this form of mining examines secondary data, or the data that are derived from the interaction of users.

There are two main thrusts in Web-usage mining–*general access-pattern tracking* and *customized-usage tracking*. General access-pattern tracking analyzes Web logs in order to better understand access patterns and trends. Customized-usage tracking analyzes individual trends. Its purpose is to customize websites to users. The information displayed, the depth of the site structure, and the format of the resources can all be dynamically customized for each user over time, based on their patterns of access.

Srivastava, etc., have produced a taxonomy of different Web-mining applications and have categorized them into the following types:

- *Personalization* : The goal here is to produce a more "individualized" experience for a Web visitor, including making recommendations about other pages to visit based on the pages he/she has visited previously.
- *System Improvement* : Performance and speed have always been important factors when it comes to computing systems, and through Web-usage data, it is possible to improve system performance by creating policies and using such methods as load-balancing, Web caching and network transmission.
- *Site Modification* : It is also possible to modify aspects of a site based on user patterns and behavior. After a detailed analysis of a user's activities on a site, it is possible to make design changes and structural modifications to site to enhance a user's satisfaction and the site's usability.
- *Business Intelligence* : Another important application of Web-usage mining is the ability to mine for marketing intelligence information. Buchner and Mulvenna, used a data hypercube to consolidate Web-usage data together with marketing data to obtain insights with regards to e-commerce.
- *Usage Characterization* : There is a close relationship between data mining of Web-usage data and Web-usage characterization research. This area is focused more on such topics as interaction with the browser interface, navigational strategies, the occurrence of certain types of activities, and models of Web usage.

Yet another area that has been gaining interest is *agent-based approaches*. Agents are intelligent software components that "crawl through" the Internet and collect useful information, much like the way a virus-like worm moves through systems wreaking havoc.

Generally, agent-based Web-mining systems can be placed into three main categories– information categorization and filtering, intelligent search agents, and personal agents.

Information filtering/categorization agents try to automatically retrieve, filter, and categorize discovered information by using various information-retrieval techniques. Agents that can be classified in this category include HyPursuit and Bookmark Organizer. *Intelligent search agents* search the Internet for relevant information and use characteristics of a particular domain to organize and interpret the discovered information. Some of the better known include ParaSite, and FAQ-Finder. *Personalized Web agents* try to obtain or learn user preferences and discover Web information sources that correspond to these preferences, and possibly those of other individuals with similar interests, using collaborative filtering. Systems in this class include Netperceptions, Web Watcher.

There are some more new concepts in data mining have been evolving. These include – UDM, Hypertext and Hyper-media data mining, visual data mining and multimedia data mining.

8.13. UBIQUITOUS DATA MINING (UDM)

The advent of laptops, palmtops, cell phones, and wearable computers is making ubiquitous access to large quantity of data possible. Advanced analysis of data for extracting useful knowledge in the next natural step in the world of ubiquitous computing. However, there are challenges that exist for UDM. Human-computer interaction and data management are challenges that exist for UDM. Human-computer interaction and data managment are challenging issues. Moreover, the sociological and psycholigcal aspects of the integration between data mining technology and our lifestyle are yet to be explored. The key issues to consider include theories of UDM, advanced algorithms for mobile and distributed applications, data management issues, markup languages, and other data representation techniques; integration with database applications for mobile environments, architectural issues (architecture, control, security, and communication issues), specialized mobile devices for UDM, software agents and UDM (agent-based approaches in UDM, agent interaction-cooperation, collaboration, negotiation, organizational behaviour), applications of UDM (in business, science, engineering, medicine, and other disciplines), location management issues in UDM, and technology for web-based applications of UDM.

8.14. HYPERTEXT AND HYPERMEDIA DATA MINING

Hypertext and hypermedia data mining can be characterized as mining data that includes text, hyperlinks, text markups, and various other forms of hypermedia information. As such, it is closely related to both Web mining and multimedia mining, but in reality are quite close in terms of content and applications. While the WWW is substantially composed of hypertext and hypermedia elements, there are other kinds of hypertext/hypermedia data sources, including online catalogues, digital libraries, online information DBs, and hyperlink and inter-document structures.

Some of the important data mining techniques used for hypertext and hypermedia data mining include – classification (supervised learning), clustering (unsupervised learning), semistructured learning, and social network analysis. In the case of *classification*, or *supervised learning*, the process starts off by reviewing training data in which items are marked as being part of a certain class or group. This data are the basis from which the algorithm is trained. *Unsupervised learning*, or *clustering*, differs from classification in that while classification involves the use of training data, clustering is concerned with the creation of hierarchies of documents based on similarity and organizes the documents based on that hierarchy. *Semi-supervised learning* and *social network analysis* are other methods that are important to hypermedia-based data mining. *Semisupervised learning* is the case where there are both labeled and unlabeled documents and there is a need to learn from both types of documents. *Social network analysis* is also applicable because the Web is considered a social network that examines networks formed through collaborative association. Other research conducted in the area of hypertext data mining includes work on distributed hypertext resource discovery.

8.15. VISUAL DATA MINING

Visual data mining is an emerging area of explorative and intelligent data analysis and mining, based on the integration of concepts from computer graphics, visualization metaphors and methods, information and scientific data visualization, visual perception, cognitive psychology, diagrammatic reasoning, visual data formatting, and 3-D collaborative virtual environments. Research and developments in the methods and techniques for visual data mining have helped to identify many of the research directions in the field, including visual methods for data analysis, visual data mining process models, visual reasoning and uncertainty management, visual explanations, algorithmic animation methods, perceptual and cognitive aspects, and interactivity in visual data mining. Other key areas include the study of domain knowledge in visual reasoning, virtual environments, visual analysis of large DBs, collaborative exploration and model building, metrics for evaluation, generic system architectures and prototypes, and methods for visualizing semantic content.

8.16. MULTIMEDIA DATA MINING

Multimedia data mining is the mining and analysis of various types of data, including images, video, audio and animation. The idea of mining data that contains different kinds of information is the main objective of multimedia data mining. As multimedia data mining incorporates the areas of text mining as well as hypertext/ hypermedia mining, these fields are closely related. Much of the information describing these other areas also applies to multimedia data mining is that of audio data mining (mining music). The idea is basically to use audio signals to indicate the patterns of data or to represent the features of data mining results. It is possible not only to summarize melodies based on the approxmate patterns that repeatedly occur in the segment, but also to summariaze style based on tone, tempo or the major musical instruments played.

Whatever the techniques may be but the integration of data mining techniques into normal day-to-day activities has become commonplace. We are confronted daily with targeted advertising, and businesses have become more efficient through the use of data mining activities to reduce costs. *Data mining adversaries*, however, are concerned that this information is being obtained at the cost of reduced privacy. *Data mining applications* can derive much demographic informaing concerning customers that was preiously not known or hidden in the data. The unauthorized use of such data could result in the disclosure of information that is deemed to be confidential.

Summing up, we can say only data mining and/or web mining provides an attractive opportunity that has not been thoroughly explored for human resource information systems. The application of data-mining techniques to human resource information systems requires organizational expertize and work at prepare the system for mining. In particular, a datamart for human resource is a useful first step. Further, organizations must be aware of legal implications of decision making based on personal employee information. With proper preparation and consideration, human resource database together with data mining create an opportunity for organizations to develop their competitive advantage through using that information for strategic decisionmaking.

It would not be overly optimistic to say that data mining has a bright and promising future, and that the years to come will bring many new developments, methods, and technologies. While some analysts and experts in the field caution that data mining may go the way of artificial intelligence (AI) and end up not having the commercial success which was predicted, the field of data mining is still young enough that the possibilities are still limitless. By expanding applications that can use it, integrating technologies and methods, broadening its applicability to mainstream business applications, and making programs and interfaces easier for end-users to use, it is quite possible and likely that data mining will rapidly become one of the most important and key areas of research and technology.

In Libraries and Information centres, data mining/web mining can be primarily be used with a strong client focus — use and usage, choice of materials, budget commitments, communication and marketing of information and promoting library information services.

It enables libraries to determine relationships among "Internal" factors such as areas of subjects product positioning, or staff skills, and "external" factors such as economic indicators, comparative performance of various subjects, and customer demographics. It also enables them to determine the impact on usage, customer satisfaction, and overall performance of Library and Information services.

9

Leadership in Knowledge Management and KM Implementation

Knowledge management is the systematic process of creating, maintain and nurturing an organization to make the best use of its individual and collective knowledge to achieve the corporate mission, broadly viewed as sustainable competitive advantage or achieving high performance. The goal is for an organization to become aware of its knowledge, individually and collectively and to shape itself so that it makes the most effective and efficient use of the knowledge it has or can obtain.

Knowledge management is also a social activity; whether it is mediated knowledge involves people working together. Creation of intellectual capital can be facilitated through action learning and use of communities of learning or practice. It is important to note that there has been little empirical research on the effectiveness of action learning and communities of practice, although case studies suggest they are effective in developing intellectual capital. There are three social activities, action learning, creativity behaviour and adaptation which are described below.

Action learning involves giving teams a real business problem or issue to work on, havng them work on solving it and commit to an constructive controversy construct is similar to Jehn's notion of task-based rather than relationship-based conflict. She round that task-based conflict had negative effects for teams doing routine work but could actually be beneficial for teams, performing nonroutine tasks. This offers some support for the beneficial effects of constructive controversy in knowledge work contexts.

Constructive controversy should improve the creation of intellectual capital in teams in a number of ways. Most simply, the more discussion that occurs in teams, the greater the chance that new knowledge will be shared and disseminated among the members. More importantly, the discussion of opposing viewpoints should enhance the voicing of compatible or synergistic views and opinions. Intellectual capital should be hindered to the extent that the knowledge voiced by individual members is redundant. Constructive controversy should enhance the extent to which the team captures the full set of its members' information, thereby promoting the building of intellectual capital.

Teams have long been viewed as a means of enhancing the creation of new ideas though empirical evidence for this view has been found lacking. Too often process loss, in the form of social loafing and production blocking, prevents team members from producing more new ideas than they would have had they worked alone. Paulus et al., describe certain process behaviours that can be used to improve creativity in teams, thereby bringing their actual performance closer to their potential performance. These behaviours include brainstorming behaviours, such as discouraging evaluation of ideas and building on each other's ideas, and process management behaviours, such as setting goals, taking breaks, and scheduling iterative team and individual idea sessions.

Like constructive controversy, these types of *creativity-enhancing behaviours* should enhance intellectual capital creation in a number of ways. If evaluation of others' ideas is discouraged, that should prevent self-censoring of views that could help to build the team's intellectual capital. The practice of idea building should lead to the complementary, synergistic knowledge that emerges from the member interaction. It is these instances of knowledge that are truly possessed by the team, as opposed to any individual member. Finally, process management behaviours like goal setting should discourage the types of process losses that can dampen the creation of intellectual capital.

Adaptation can be defined as a beneficial change in task behaviours that comes in response to shifting task demands active set of behaviours that allow the individual or team to remain successful even in unstable task environments. Such behaviours include noticing the shift in task demands, formulating a new approach, and successfully implementing the new approach. Thus individuals or teams who fail to adapt may not have noticed the need for it, or they may have implemented an ineffective response to the change in task demands.

Adaptation behaviours are critical to the creation of intellectual capital because they act to replace outdated or outmoded capital. Unless a team adapts, its intellectual capital will—at best—remain stagnant. At worst, it will actually decrease as the current repertoire of information goes from knowledge to misconception. Thus, whereas constructive controversy and creativity behaviours create intellectual capital, adaptation replaces, replenishes, and builds on existing intellectual capital.

9.1. KNOWLEDGE MANAGEMENT ROLES

Knowledge management cannot be centralized in an organization e.g., in analogy to the management of capital. The role of a centralized unit is only a coordinating and administrating one. Generally, the most important knowledge management-related instruments have to be applied as close to where the knowledge is needed as possible, which is directly in the functional departments or projects. Thus, many organizations, especially the professional services firms, have established knowledge management-related roles which are distributed throughout the organization.

In the top area of the figure the Chief Knowledge Officer, or Knowledge Manager is responsible for knowledge management leadership. He or she might share responsibility with knowledge partners and/or stakeholders from the business units which knowledge management serves. In the upper middle part of the figure there are specific knowledge management roles that can be assigned in order to guarantee the efficient and effective performing of important knowledge management tasks and processes. The knowledge management diamond in the center of the figure denotes those four knowledge management roles that act as a kind of exchange platform for knowledge in an organization, a knowledge hub.

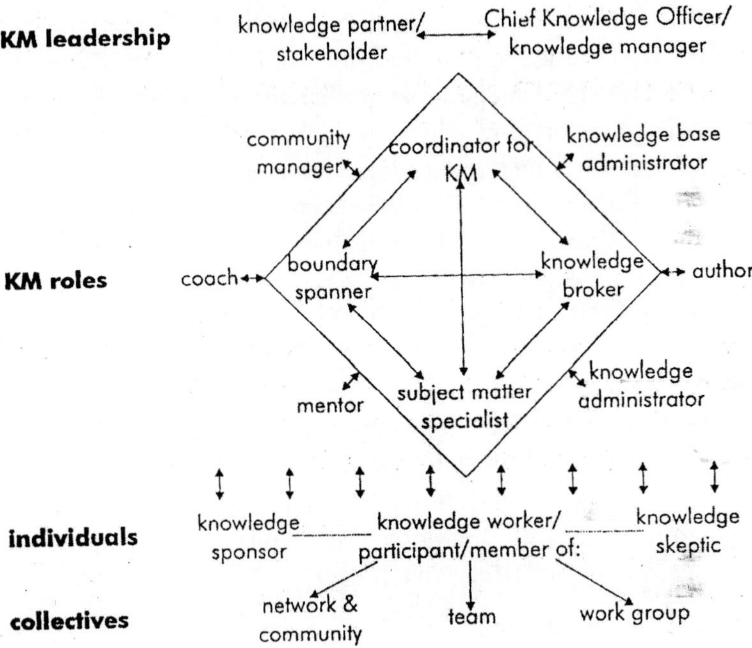

Fig. 9.1. Model of Knowledge Management Roles and Collectives

The basis of the model is formed by the knowledge workers which participate in the knowledge management initiative. From an IT point of view, these are called participants rather than users in order to stress the active role that they have with respect to the ICT-systems in place. The knowledge workers are more or less enthusiastic about knowledge management putting them somewhere on the dimension between the two poles knowledge sponsor and knowledge skeptic. Knowledge workers are grouped in work groups, teams and communities which have been identified as the most important unit of analysis and intervention in knowledge management initiatives. That is why the collectives form the basis of the knowledge management roles on which the whole knowledge management initiative is founded.

9.1.1. Knowledge Manager (CKO)

The highest ranked role in knowledge management is called the Chief Knowledge Officer (CKO), a term coined in analogy to other executive positions, such as the chief information officer (CIO). Other terms used to describe a similar role to the one held by a CKO are knowledge strategist director intellectual capital (e.g., Skandia), director knowledge transfer (e.g., Buckman Laboratories), knowledge asset manager or intellectual asset manager The term CKO has been in use to denote the head of knowledge management for quite a while, even though in the beginning it was more, connected to AI and expert systems and its relation to executives. Today, in many organizations, CKO and Knowledge Manager refer to the same position. However, especially in multinational professional services companies there are also examples where one CKO supervises several knowledge managers which are responsible for knowledge management, e.g., in one particular business unit.

According to the interviews and the knowledge management cases reported in the literature, the primary responsibilities of a Chief Knowledge Officer (CKO) are :

- to build a knowledge culture, to raise awareness, to get commitment of business leaders and to motivate employees to share knowledge,
- to design a knowledge management strategy aligned to the business strategy of the organization,
- to design, implement and oversee schemes and processes for knowledge codification and transfer,
- to lead a separate organizational unit which is designed to e.g., broker knowledge or to research and develop new knowledge,
- to get a knowledge (best practice) data base up and its running,
- to globalize knowledge management and thus coordinate

several existing knowledge management initiatives,

- to measure the value of intangible assets.

As an individual member of the organization, a CKO has to represent many of the positive connotations that knowledge management approaches have. The CKO acts as a symbol and promoter for extensive knowledge sharing, a trustful organizational culture, the use of new methods in training and education for employees, teams, and communities, the application of knowledge management-related ICT systems and last but not least the integration of knowledge management-related measures into corporate accounting and leadership systems. Various others related categories are briefly discussed below :

9.1.2. Subject Matter Specialist

A subject matter specialist, subject matter expert, knowledge integrator or knowledge editor or person responsible for a field of competence is an important role in knowledge management that is responsible for a multitude of tasks. Subject matter specialists have expertise in one particular area and serve as :

- *Gatekeeper of information and knowledge* : In this function, they formally approve contributions made by participants before they are entered into an organization's knowledge base.
- *Quality assurer* : Subject matter specialists review documents, provide additional links, improve the document's quality in terms of readability, understandability, use of a common language etc.
- *Expert in one or more topics* : In this function, a subject matter specialist might answer questions concerning his or her topic(s) if they remain unanswered within a certain amount of time.
- *Linking pin to agencies and research institutions* : A subject matter specialist might be responsible for keeping track of new developments in his or her topic(s), periodically provide reports about the newest developments, etc.

9.1.3. Knowledge Administrator

Knowledge administrators are also called *knowledge engineers* or *knowledge editors*. As opposed to subject matter specialists who are responsible for one specific domain or topic, knowledge administrators are responsible to help authors to capture, store and maintain knowledge independent of the domain in which they are working. If subject matter specialists are experts in the semantics and the contents, knowledge administrators are experts in the way knowledge elements have to be documented, linked, structured and organized. They help participants externalize and document their knowledge.

9.1.4. Knowledge Base Administrator

In analogy to data base administrators, knowledge base administrators are responsible for the development and maintenance of the technological infrastructure of KM, the knowledge management systems. At accenture, there are three different roles responsible for the administration of their knowledge management system, Knowledge Xchange– knowledge base sponsors, knowledge base integrators and knowledge base developers. The knowledge base sponsor develops policies, standards and procedures for the knowledge management system and develops the knowledge management system architecture. The knowledge base integrator provides overall coordination of structure and content for one knowledge base and ensures that security and ownership specifications are implemented. The knowledge base developer finally develops, supports and maintains the technical implementations of the knowledge base, ensures that it conforms with general IT standards set forth by the CIO, executes and administers the security and ownership specifications and implements modifications to a knowledge base structure.

9.1.5. Knowledge Broker

A knowledge broker is a person helping participants to locate the knowledge or experts needed. These are also called knowledge connectors, knowledge navigators, knowledge translators and knowledge stewards or, in a more focused setting, best practice sharing facilitator. Ernst & Young distinguishes between the following three levels of orders for their knowledge brokers can get:

- *Navigate* : to support people in navigating the organization-wide knowledge management system or KMS,
- *Research* : to collect documents and locate experts to a given topic by accessing the KMS,
- *Analyze* : to create a formal report on a topic which includes valuing, summarizing and relating documents and experts found in the KMS.

The role of knowledge brokers might involve participation in several communities in order to broker knowledge from one community to another. They argue that knowledge brokers work best in the context of overlapping communities. They call persons that "broker" knowledge between mutually exclusive communities "translators". A translator can frame the knowledge and interests of one community in terms of a different community's practice. In this respect, the knowledge broker also takes on the role of a *boundary spanner*. Thus, knowledge broker is a key role in organizational knowledge management.

9.1.6. Boundary Spanner

A boundary spanner has to network fields of competencies and broker contacts between experts in different fields needed to realize new business ideas or between communities. This might involve e.g., the organization of theme-centered workshops the primary goal of which is networking experts from different fields of competencies, the identification, refinement and distribution of boundary objects between communities, expert networks and knowledge repositories. They are responsible for the development of an inter-functional and inter-disciplinary network of relationships and thus are contact persons for the brokering of contacts both, within and outside the organization.

9.1.7. Knowledge Sponsor

Knowledge sponsors and knowledge champions are the people who are excited about the idea of knowledge management, commit themselves to this effort and want to help to make the effort a success without taking on a formal role or responsibility as knowledge management staff.

A knowledge sponsor is a senior executive of the organization implementing knowledge management who identifies with the knowledge management concepts, publicly shows enthusiasm about the project and is likely to invest in or support knowledge management projects. The knowledge sponsor secures the budget for knowledge management initiatives, networks with other knowledge sponsors and might even encourage employees to take on formal knowledge management roles, e.g., subject matter specialists or knowledge integrators. In the same category fall so-called network chairs, senior managers who facilitate the knowledge management process. The term network chair points to the support that is expected from the sponsor which is to help knowledge workers to network.

9.1.8. Community or Network Manager

There are a number of roles that have been suggested with respect to virtual communities or networks of experts in organizations. Examples are :

- *Greeter:* welcomes new members and introduces them to the community,
- *Host/facilitator*: encourages and moderates discussions,
- *Editor/cybrarian*: responsible for topics and contents,
- *Cop*: enforces the community rules,
- *Teacher*: educates the members of the community,
- *Recognized expert*: also called thought leader who upholds and dispenses the community's knowledge,
- *Event-coordinator*: plans and organizes events,
- *Supporter*: answers questions about the system(s),
- *Boundary spanner*: connects the community to other communities and acts as broker and translator,
- *Keeper of organizational ties*: maintains links with other organizational units, in particular the official hierarchy,
- *Care-taker*: cultivates social relationships,

- *System administrator*: responsible for hardware, software and security of the community server,
- *Account administrator*: administrates accounts, privileges and authentication of the members of the community,
- *Architect*: starts social relationships, develops social networks and optimizes the community structure considering the feedback.

Although these roles might be assigned to a number of members, it is likely that a small core group of approximately two to six members who initiated the community take on all of these roles so that each of the members of the core group is responsible for a number of roles. There are also several roles responsible for the management of the community which are distinguished in analogy to the roles defined for the management of business processes.

Community/network owner : A community owner is a senior manager or even a member of the board of directors who is responsible for the communities. As communities per definition are not directly goal-oriented collectives of people, the role of the community owner is to sponsor the community, provide budgets and support for time, travel and technologies (e.g., storage capacity for community homespaces) and promote the community topic.

Community/Network manager : This is regularly a role that is attributed to the originator of a community, sometimes split to a small group of people who initiated the community. This person or this core group is responsible for the functioning of the community, has the "last word" in the set up of policies and norms, e.g., about participation in the community, its organization, about themes and topics, the discussion style etc. Sometimes the community manager is supported by one or more community assistant(s) who e.g., answer questions about the community, its topics or the ICT used to support the community. A community manager coordinates the activities in a community, however, he or she is not responsible for all types of leadership that are necessary in a community, such as networking, facilitation, documentation, retention of expertise, learning, inquiry, management of boundaries or organizational ties.

Community/Network Moderator : A moderator supports discussions in communities, e.g., provides summaries about threads of discussions, links and organizes contributions or encourages contributions from experts outside the community. Often, community moderators are responsible for many communities so that they can cross-post contributions from one community to another one that might stimulate discussions elsewhere.

Within the group of the members of the community or network, experts, active or key members on the one hand and passive members on the other hand can be distinguished. The key members are the organization's experts in the community's topic and thus are responsible for answering the questions which are posed by the members of the community. This distinction, however, introduces a quasi-hierarchy in the community which can be counter-productive to the free flow of ideas.

The formal definition of roles with respect to communities changes the informal nature of these collectives of people and sometimes turns communities into official networks of experts. These might even get tasks assigned which temporally changes them into a team. However, members of a team might stick together after the team assignment was finished as a community showing once again that the boundaries between teams and communities are vague.

9.1.9. Mentor

Mentors are persons responsible for the development of new talent and for instilling their own tacit knowledge in new employees through a kind of "informal apprenticeship". *Mentoring* is based on the Greek mythology and can be defined as a deliberate pairing of a more skilled or experienced person with a lesser skilled or experienced one, with the agreed-upon goal of having the lesser skilled person grow and develop specific competencies. Generally, relationships between younger and older adults that contribute to career development are also called sponsor, patron or godfather relationships. Mentoring can be an interesting addition to other human resource development programs and are valuable for both, the mentor and the mentee.

In Japan, this kind of relationship has got a long tradition as the *sempai-kohai* principle. Every newly recruited employee in Japanese organizations, the younger so-called *kohai*, is assigned to a mentor, an older, teaching *sempai.* Many Western organizations and also Universities have taken over this principle that is used to reduce the time needed for the young recruited to take over all the tricks and know-how from the older employees. Mentoring functions can be divided into career functions, such as sponsorship, exposure, visibility, coaching, protection and challenging assignments, as well as psychosocial functions, such as role modeling, acceptance-and-confirmation, counseling and friendship, which enhance sense of competence, identity and effectiveness in a professional role. Mentoring also faces major obstacles, e.g., due to an unsupportive organizational culture, work design or incentive and reward systems. The complexity of cross-gender and/or cross-cultural mentoring relationships requires special attention. International mentoring might play an active role in developing cross-cultural competencies in international networks, e.g., in multi-national organizations.

9.1.10. Coach

A different form of a paired relationship is coaching. The coach, an internal or external consultant especially trained in psychology, interacts with a member of the organization in order to improve the performance or motivation of the latter. Coaching is a form of consulting in between psychotherapy - therapeutic interventions and training and often extends beyond work-related aspects to a more holistic "consulting for living" but nevertheless can be a useful instrument to remove or at least make visible knowledge barriers that can be attributed to individual employees.

9.1.11. Knowledge Skeptic

A knowledge skeptic is a person hostile to knowledge management in general and or the implementation of a knowledge management effort in particular. As many knowledge management efforts need a "critical mass" of participants who buy in the idea and on the other hand knowledge skeptics might jeopardize the success of the efforts, it is important to identify doubters in order to convince them so that they participate in or at least do not oppose the effort.

9.1.12. Knowledge Management Coordinator

Many organizations might employ their formal organizational structure and assign responsibility to their—line and project—managers or one particular employee within each organizational unit in order to roll out knowledge management initiatives. Thus, a coordinator for knowledge management is assigned responsibility to coordinate the implementation of knowledge management within one particular organizational unit. Typical responsibilities are:

- to ensure that knowledge processes are carried out within their area of responsibility, and
- to oversee that the knowledge created within their unit is harnessed and spread across organizational units.

Typical organizational units that might be assigned responsibility for knowledge management are a business or service process, a functional unit or a project. For example, Ernst & Young appoints one professional per larger assignment (= contract between Ernst & Young and a customer) as the assignment knowledge manager who is responsible for the knowledge process and the capturing of knowledge generated in the assignment.

9.1.13. Knowledge Worker and Participant

As knowledge work requires that knowledge is continuously revised, considered permanently improvable, not as truth, but as a resource. As opposed to traditional professional work, the expertize required for knowledge work is not basically acquired during one single and long-lasting learning period, but has to be constantly revised, extended, reflected and adapted. Knowledge workers require a distinctly different management style than more traditional professions– little direction and supervision, instead more protection and support by "covert leadership". Knowledge workers are the primary target group for a knowledge management initiative.

Generally, participants are all persons that are affected by knowledge management initiatives. Participants are distinguished from users with respect to the application of knowledge management system because of their active involvement into the functioning of knowledge management system. Thus, participants actively play roles such as knowledge creators, developers, providers or authors, as active members of work groups, teams or communities, contributors in newsgroups, commentators, refiners and evaluators of organization-internal and external knowledge elements, knowledge brokers and distributors etc.

Knowledge workers as well as participants can be classified according to their level of expertize. Many authors in the realm of knowledge management differentiate between knowledge providers and knowledge seekers or knowers and not knowers. As most of them do not refer to a theoretical basis, it remains unclear according to what criteria a participant could be selected as "knowing" versus "not knowing". It is also unclear to what extent the classification of "knowing" is topic-and context-dependent, especially concerning the granularity of such classifications. Moreover, a mere two-fold distinction seems to be too crude to guide knowledge management activities.

Thus, in the following five levels of expertize are distinguished which are based on a model on the development of expertize well-received in the literature. The model describes the development of expertize as applied to unstructured situations for which there is no set of facts and factors which fully determine the problem, the possible actions and the goal of the activity, e.g., patient care, business forecasts, social interactions. It stresses the importance of implicit knowledge for expert problem solving. The central hypothesis is that in the step-wise course of becoming an expert thinking is reorganized qualitatively which means that expert knowledge is organized differently from explicit knowledge about facts and rules. Thus, teaching means to subsequently lead the learning person from an analytic via a planning to an intuitive way of problem solving. A central concept is "power of judgement" as a holistic way of pattern recognition which is highly adapted to contexts. Thus, the qualitative adaptation of the person's organization of knowledge means a replacement of knowledge about facts and rules with a number of practical cases which are used as patterns to intuitively judge the adequate actions required in a specific situation. The five steps are briefly described in the following :

1. Novice : When novices observe an expert they are overwhelmed by the complexity of a situation so that they are not able to imitate an expert. In the first stage of learning, novices are provided with non-situational or context-free attributes and rules. These do not reflect the total situation, they ignore the total context and they do not require the novice to understand the total structure of the situation. The novice analyzes a situation by spotting single attributes and selects actions according to the rules remembered. The attributes are not implicitly integrated, but explicitly focused and summed up.

2. Advanced beginner : The advanced beginner has extensive practical experience in the domain. Thus, he or she can use more context-free attributes in his or her judgement of the situation and uses more complex rules to determine actions. The most important difference to the novice's problem solving is the use of so-called aspects. These are situational or context-specific attributes that the advanced beginner has encountered in a greater number of "similar" practical cases. The selection of actions is now not only based on context-free rules, but also on context-specific guidelines. However, the problem solving can still be characterized as not integrated as there is no conscious examination of configurations of attributes. The single attributes and aspects are considered as being of equal value and the advanced beginner should take into account as many attributes and aspects as possible. The number of attributes and aspects increase to a point where the learner is confronted with an overwhelming number of elements to be considered.

3. Competence : The central skill differentiating the level of competence from the two levels before is the potential to analyze a situation with the help of a perspective. The person is able to plan consciously and thoughtfully. Goals and plans increase the complexity of the analysis, but reduce the complexity of the situation because not all attributes and aspects have to be considered anymore. Conscious, analytical problem solving is maximized on this level of expertize. Actions are selected with the help of a perspective which the actor decides on. As a consequence of the subjective selection of a plan, he or she will feel responsible for his or her actions. This is different from the two levels before as actions were taken by strictly applying rules and guidelines and unwanted results could be attributed to inadequate rules or guidelines. Learning is supported by the analysis of situational case studies which require the selection of a perspective and the decisions derived by the application of the corresponding rules and guidelines.

4. Skillful Master : The central new skill in this stage is the ability to perceive situations as a whole as opposed to observing single attributes and aspects of a situation. This means a holistic recognition of similarities of the current situations with situations the master encountered before. The master has a "mental library" of typical situations perceived using a specific perspective. New situations are perceived from a specific perspective without consciously selecting it. The relative importance of attributes and aspects in the problem domain is not analyzed consciously anymore. The situation rather presents itself accentuated to the master, he or she intuitively expects which situations could follow the current situation. Actions are still selected consciously on the basis of maxims. These maxims are heuristic principles that relate a certain action to a configuration of attributes and aspects. The master consciously selects those actions that have proven successful in the type of situation in the past. Thus, the master perceives the problem character of a situation and the general direction in which he or she has to act without conscious efforts. The detailed planning of actions is still a conscious effort.

5. Expert : At this stage, every specific situation the expert encounters will automatically trigger the intuitively appropriate action(s). Experts not only store perspective-based types of situations, but associations of types of situations with corresponding actions. Situations are grouped in a way so that they require the same decisions and actions. They are stored in such a number that they cannot be verbally described. Thus, the expert does not process atomic facts logically, but perceives holistic similarities between the current situation and situations encountered before without having to take into account isolated single elements. Strategic planning does not occur anymore at this stage. The expert can handle situation after situation without strategic planning in a way that can be described as "goal-oriented without conscious goal-setting". The experts' knowledge is best analyzed with the help of story-telling. The expert should report critical situations holistically together with the context in which they occurred, the subjective assessments of the situations and the actions taken.

Table 9.1 shows the complete model with those elements of problem-solving highlighted which determine the central shifts between the stages.

Experts differ from novices substantially with respect to problem-solving. Experts not only have more profound area-specific knowledge, but also apply so-called schemes to analyze situations which allow them to consider more information about a problem quicker than novices. Experts are also quicker in deciding between relevant and irrelevant information than novices due to the automation of a large number of cognitive processes. This automation might also be disadvantageous, though, if experts experience difficulties to adapt to new problem settings or to accept new and revolutionary ideas or ways of problem solving. Experts spend more time to analyze the situation in difficult problem settings, are different from novices in their selection of problem solving strategies and are more able to control their cognitive processes than novices.

The application of this model and the consideration of the differences between experts and novices in particular has substantial consequences for the design of knowledge management system. This is especially true for knowledge management system functions such as personalization, system-supported recommendations and collaboration. Novices not only require a different presentation of knowledge elements than experts which means that personalization of knowledge management system should not only reflect a participant's role, but also his or her skill level with respect to the topic - dynamic, context-dependent personalization.

Table 9.1. Model of the Acquisition of Expertize

Skill level.	Components	Perspective	Decision	Commitment
1. Novice	context-free	none	analytical	detached
2. Advanced beginner	*context-free and situational*	none	analytical	detached
3. Competent	context-free and situational	*chosen*	analytical	detached understanding and deciding; *involved in outcome*
4. Proficient/ skillful master	context-free & situational	experienced	analytical	*involved under-standing* detached deciding.
5. Expert	context-free & situational	experienced	*intuitive*	*involved*

The various skill levels also suggest that in some cases novices who search the knowledge management system for information on whom they could ask personally for help might need support by intermediates—participants just one or two skill levels above their own, not experts who would require much more effort to reflect their decisions so that novices could learn from them. Knowledge management system in that case should present knowledge elements developed by intermediates as well as links to intermediates rather than experts.

Experts on the other hand might be best "teachers" for knowledge workers at the skill level *proficient* and *possibly competent*. Accordingly, tutorials and peer-to-peer learning deserves much more attention than the single-minded focus on experts teaching and answering questions of the rest of the employees. Also, communities might be designed with skill levels in mind. Some communities might intend to bring together people with skill levels not to far from each other so that perspective, decision and commitment are not too different. Other communities might intend to bridge the various skill levels and focus a topic independent of the experiences a person has made up to that point.

9.1.14. Knowledge Partner and Stakeholder

As knowledge management is a cross-functional effort, the

knowledge management team needs partners or allies in the implementation of such an effort. Earl and Scott identify HR professionals and IS executives as the main partners of CKOs in their survey of 20 CKOs in the US.

Stakeholders are those individuals, groups and networks of individuals in the environment of an organization who influence the organization's operations directly or might influence them in the future. In a study, 11 percent of the organizations reported to systematically manage relationships to stakeholders in order to improve the handling of knowledge. Examples for stakeholders of knowledge management are:

Functional Departments : Functional departments are the primary customers in many knowledge management initiatives. Participation of representatives of functional departments in design and implementation of knowledge management system is considered crucial as a positive attitude towards the knowledge management initiative, a supportive organizational culture, is the most important success factor for knowledge management.

Business Partners : In a time when organizations more and more integrate their value chains with suppliers, wholesalers and retailers to provide better services to customers, these business partners supposedly hold extensive knowledge which is of interest to the organization. Thus, business partners may also become knowledge partners that jointly innovate and develop ideas for products and services.

Senior Management : Senior management has to support the knowledge management initiative not only with sufficient funding, but also by giving a good example, by "living knowledge management" and by acting as knowledge champions coordinating KM-related issues throughout the organization and eventually by helping to reduce cross-functional knowledge management barriers.

Human Resource Management : Personnel training and education remains an important promoter for organizational learning. Many authors suggest that an apprentice watching a skillful master is the best way to transfer implicit knowledge. However, only 45.5 percent of the organizations surveyed by the

APQC considered themselves as effectively using apprenticing for knowledge sharing whereas 22.7 percent said they were ineffective in this respect. Apprenticing in fact was the least effective instrument for knowledge sharing as perceived by these organizations. The more e-learning and knowledge management grow together, the more learning will be decentralized and traditional personnel training and education will be integrated in the organization's knowledge management initiative.

IT Department : The organization's IT unit is responsible for the organization's ICT infrastructure and thus also for the implementation of ICT to support the KM initiative, the knowledge management platforms and KMS. Even though knowledge management units and the CKO are usually separated from the IT department, they have to work closely together in order to develop an integrated ICT solution that supports the intended organizational instruments to improve an organization's way of handling knowledge.

Data Management : Data management handles a substantial portion of the infrastructure on which knowledge management system or KMS are built. Data management is responsible for the quantitative portion of the enterprise knowledge base. Data-related tasks, such as data warehousing, data analysis, management of interfaces or data management for the Web are closely connected to the technical administration of KMS.

Public Relations : This group handles the organization's official communication to stakeholders and the public, e.g., the organization's Web presence. Thus, the knowledge management system appearance—and access to contents—has to be coordinated with the official communication, e.g., the organization's corporate identity. Public relations also often maintains a large network of experts in all kinds of fields potentially relevant for knowledge-related tasks.

Research and Development : R & D as well as technology and innovation management are often the core groups in an organization that apply knowledge management instruments and technologies first. They handle the bulk of organizational innovation. On the one hand, they are a major knowledge provider for the rest of the organization, but on the other hand they also need to be connected to the knowledge flows generated in the operative business processes. A knowledge management initiative has to consider the R & D processes and KMS have to be integrated with the ICT systems that are used by this organizational unit.

Universities and Research Institutions : Universities and partly state-funded, research institutions are important external sources for innovations, ideas, prototypes and concepts that might be turned into successful products and services, but also for new ground-breaking theories and approaches that might substantially influence organizations. Thus, universities can be important knowledge partners for organizations and many cooperations between universities and private organizations have already proven successful. However, in the Fraunhofer study cooperations with universities were ranked last of a list of instruments used for knowledge acquisition. Thus, it seems that there is potential for universities to play significantly enhanced roles in knowledge management. Some examples are:

- *Moderation of communities* : Universities might provide a platform for the exchange of ideas, moderate discussions and networking of experts in the field, periodically distill trend reports out of community interaction, evaluate and assess developments. Communities of innovation not necessarily have to be tied to traditional research disciplines. Interdisciplinary communities might be more successful in the assessment of trends and developments. As Universities usually have a good network infrastructure, it might be a good idea for them to provide such services with the help of ICT systems supporting electronic communities.
- *Incubator for start-ups* : Universities might act as an incubator for start-up organizations turning good ideas into products and services profiting from the geographical vicinity to research labs and students.
- *Translation and explanation of new ideas* : Universities might install interdisciplinary groups or teams, e.g., linguists and natural scientists that take on the linguistic re-formulation of ideas and concepts so that a broader community, e.g., of

organizations, but also of customers; can understand them, provide theme-oriented ontologies, structures and glossaries and visualize networks of terms, definitions and examples which could help organizations to organize their knowledge,

- *Educating talent* : The education of talent not necessarily has to be restricted to students of more or less one age group. In a society postulating life-long learning, universities might also engage in executive education. Distance education and telelearning might provide a technological basis on which such programs could be built without excessive costs.

Strategic Alliances and Relationships : In recent years, it has become popular for organizations in need of knowledge to look for strategic alliances and relationships or even to take over other organizations that promise to hold the competencies needed instead of developing them on their own.

This list shows that knowledge management is not only a true cross-functional initiative in an organization that has relations to many other organization-internal units, but is also an important initiative spanning the boundaries of organizations that has relations to organization-external units. As these units have their own initiatives to improve knowledge-related goals as well, coordination between all these initiatives is often quite a challenging task. Thus, it seems appropriate that in many organizations it is not an individual that is solely responsible for this coordination task, for example, a knowledge manager, but a community of interested stakeholders from various organizational units who can act as linking pins thus easing the burden on the head of the knowledge management initiative.

9.2. SEVEN C'S OF KNOWLEDGE LEADERSHIP

Leadership is a key influence on the conduct and outcomes of knowledge management in organizations and economies. 21st century leadership demands more vision and visibility. It is not only a function of learned behaviours, but also how those behaviours demonstrate impact. With global communications, there will be a perceived levelling of competence. Knowledge obsolesce will accelerate. The 'Digital Divide' could exacerbate the gap between the haves and have nots; but the human (vs. the information or technology) agenda will place the emphasis on all people and all cultures - where it belongs! Real-time learning will become the critical success factor for prosperity in both the public and private sectors. Leaders used to focus on 'leading' the organization. Tomorrow's leaders will be perceived more of local, national, regional and international statesmen who are able to effectively balance economics, education and the environment.

We live in a world of kaleidoscopic change. It is not the speed of change of a variable, or the speed of change of multiple variables. It is the compounding effect of the speed of change of multiple variables creating a landscape for innovation that challenges even the most adept manager. There is a new Knowledge Value Proposition. Cost, quality, and time are no longer the differentiators for market positioning. It is a far more complex relationship between economics, technology, and behaviour - sociological, psychological, managerial - that constitutes the "social capital" of an organization.

Here, we identify seven domains where we might consider the implications for knowledge leadership. These are matter of context, competence, culture, communities, conversation & common language, communication & coaching. Combindly, these are called seven Cs.

9.2.1. Matter of Context

In the new Human Capital orientation, performance metrics are dynamic and based on measuring the intangibles. Table 9.2 contrasts this with the traditional orientation. Organizational structures are networked with self-managing knowledge workers. The processes transcend organization boundaries, linking all stakeholders (e.g., suppliers, alliance partners, distributors, customers, and even competitors) into a strategic innovation system. Information technology is used for knowledge processing - monitoring the flow of knowledge, i.e., how ideas are generated and commercialized.

Most important, it is not one orientation - Financial or Human - at the expense of another. Both are necessary to ensure optimal flexibility, adaptability, and agility.

Effective Knowledge Leadership is also a function of vision and will increasingly be more so. Yet, according to Albert Hochleitner, Director General, Siemens Osterrich, "Less than 2 percent of our time is spent on the future perspective. Some companies are even lower than 1 percent. Although the urgent business of everyday life is important, it is not as important as the future." The reality is that executives know that visioning is important; but they have not a clue how to effectively implement it, given such accelerating uncertainty.

It may not be that the 'Knowledge Leader' is the one to create the vision - far from it. He must, however, create the frame within which the vision can be created by a critical mass of organization stakeholders. The leader manages the innovation infrastructure within which ideas are generated and applied. It is a function of listening, guiding thought and cross-leveraging insights. Once created, the vision must be articulated broadly both inside and outside the firm.

Table 9.2. Contrast in Management Styles

	Traditional/Industrial (Financial Capital)	**Knowledge/Innovation (Human Capital)**
Performance Measures	• Financial	• Comprehensive
	• Static	• Dynamic
	• Assets	• Relationship as assets
	• Competitive	• Collaborative
	• Market share	• Sets of alliances
Sturcture/Culture	• Distrust of borders	• Value-adding
	• Cost/expense	• Revenue/investment
People/Leadership	• Profitability	• Sustained growth
	• Independence	• Interdependence
Process	• Cause-effect	• Value system
	• Information processing	• Knowledge processing
	• Data/information	• Tacit/explicit knowledge
Technology	• Things/warehouse	• Flow/process

Today's leaders must inspire passion for the work. They need to ensure that teams are stable enough to meet the high frequency burst of information and complex demands on decision-making. They must have an ability to help others maintain focus and balanced as they establish priorities. They lead by example, walk-the-talk, and understand fundamentally the 'whole.' They are able to convey context and meaning in ways that enable others to leverage their own talents.

9.2.2. Matter of Competence

Peter F. Drucker suggested that innovation is the one competence needed to manage into the future, but we know there are several sub-competencies that come into play. For the last few years, the Banff Centre for Management has been researching and developing a competency-profiling system to assist managers in measuring the impact of their investment in the residential, experiential executive programs. So far, it has been tested with 5,000 executives from 500 organizations. 70 percent of organization competencies are generic and 30 percent are specific to the organization, its industry, and regional presence. Through customization, an organization can tailor and monitor its desired proficiency.

A Competency Map is an assessment tool that outlines the skills and behaviours required to successfully undertake a position or role. There are 35 identified competencies organized with the following categories– Direction Setting; Change Leadership; Critical Thinking; Organizational Development and Diversity; Personal/Organization Balance; Quality, Knowledge and Innovation. Each includes four levels of aptitude - an example of which is illustrated in Table 9.3.

Through the profiles and learning contract, the process provides for (a) Evaluation of a leader's competencies against researched standards, (b) Agreement between the participant, their supervisor and the instructor (i.e., the learning triad) and (c) Measurement of successful changes in behaviour.

Table 9.3. Competency Map

Under-Pining	Level 1	Level 2	Level 3	Level 4
A Sales/marketing customer service	• "Pushes Product" • provides information in format they use	• listens for needs • provides solution options	• builds relationships • proactive idea and solution generation	• builds partnerships • focus on customers customer or strategic goals
B Personal/ Team Leadership	• personally competent	• able to get immediate teamfunctioning competently	• works effectively interdepartmentally • can successfully lead an inter-departmental team	• works effectively inter-organizationally • often seen as an industry leader
C Adult Development	• focussed on "what's in it for me:"	• works well in defined parameters • employs cause & effect thinking/analysis • traditional approaches	• 'Systems' thinker • analyzer • initiates new ideas, projects • takes responesibility for own carrer and activities	• self directed • multi-systems thinker/analyzer • systematizes external/internal input and creative processes

It is almost impossible to be taught leadership. We have to learn it, experience it and be supported in the process. Too often, we sign-up for courses and expect to become a better leader. The truth is that the process can hardly be left to serendipity. The Banff Centre outlines a five-step learning process:

Step One – The Competency Profile: Assess the learner's competence in several aspects related to their role. Peers and colleagues can offer observation and feedback. Some organizations, such as Canadian Occidental Petroleum, CP Rail and Alberta Agriculture Food and Rural Development have created such Maps as a basis for performance management. The more specific and discrete you can be, the more relevance you can create with a prospective learner.

Step Two – The Learning Contract: Identify what is of most importance for the learner and focus. Capable individuals can generally only work on 4-5 major attributes at a time. By bringing together the learner, supervisor, and instructor, priorities can be established - identifying strengths, particular areas of focus, and strategies for testing learned competencies.

Step Three – The Learning Process: Whether pre-course, on-course or post-course, the Profile and Learning Contract provide focus. However, if the learning environment is simply academic or knowledge-transfer in design, results are sub-optimal. Learning must be hands-on. It must provide participants with opportunities to experiment with new behaviours, receive feedback, and (re)focus their learning. The learning environment must support creativity, critical inquiry, and practical application - the same criteria necessary for successful implementation of new concepts.

Step Four – Re-entry Planning: Careful consideration of the return to the workplace is essential. Individuals who have experienced intense remote learning environments cannot be expected to return to their organizations and 'teach' others. Re-entry is far more of a listening exercise - identifying language, motivation and talent in others ready to be nurtured.

Step Five – Measurement of Impact: Successful demonstration of desired skills and learning competencies is essential. You cannot learn about management and leadership by 'talking' about it. These knowledge concepts seem new at first. The good news is that they are intuitively obvious and clarify many 'fuzzy, soft' management concepts by illustrating how they contribute to the bottom line when put into practice.

There are new competencies also emerging. There are now position titles as knowledge architect, knowledge engineer, knowledge editor, knowledge analyst, knowledge navigator, knowledge gatekeeper, and knowledge brokers. There is considerable debate among knowledge professionals as to the relative merit of having a Chief Knowledge Officer (CKO). Regardless of your adoption of the knowledge nomenclature, it is essential that someone be designated to oversee the innovation process - how knowledge is created, exchanged, and applied in your organization for future sustainability.

9.3.3. Matter of Culture

Leadership training may be vested in the individual; but impactful leadership must start at the top and become an integral part of the organizational culture. Oftentimes, we see organizations investing in leadership development at he individual level, while the corporation values and culture remain unchanged.

Although in a survey conducted in 1997, innovation was defined as the number-one advantage of a knowledge program, developing a culture of knowledge-sharing is unquestionably the greatest obstacle.

Over the long-term, culture does more to influence the impact of corporate leadership than any other factor. It determines how individuals react and perform on a daily basis. Culture includes years of history - including successes and failures, good and bad decisions, individual and collective stories. All of these create a set of values - explicit and implicit - that constitute the underpinnings of the enterprise culture. The culture is what determines how leadership is or is not manifested in an organization.

The two greatest obstacles to successful knowledge leadership are a lack of trust and inadequate communications - specifically regarding values, mission and critical success factors. These two elements, combined with a lack of vision, appear to be at the root of leadership duress.

Trust is a multi-faceted and elusive concept that pervades everything we do. It includes other attributes, such as accountability, integrity, honesty and ethics. Nothing erodes or destroys corporate leadership than mis-trust. Distrustful leaders may achieve mediocre improvements, but they will never effectively harness the passion for outstanding business results.

Poor communications - both human and technical - may be the greatest leadership weakness. It leads to the ineffective performance, poor morale, and internal confusion. With continuous downsizing, constructive knowledge-sharing ceases. Worse, organizations become paralyzed with a lack of responsible risk-taking - an essential criteria for innovation.

Without vision, the organization and its constituency - are at a loss for a sense of direction. Usually, visions are actually only missions. They do not provide an articulation of an organization's uniqueness, or its aspirations. They do not articulate stretch goals that fire the imagination of employees and customers.

Creating and sustaining a culture where knowledge is valued is one of the most difficult challenges in practice. Appropriate cultures are those that engender change, innovation, openness, and trust. People are recognized and rewarded for their knowledge contribution. Conditions for effective knowledge creation and sharing require more flexible, networked organizational structures, multiple teams, and a climate of intensive and purposeful networking.

Several factors help create the conditions that encourage knowledge-sharing -systems for moving people, e.g., job rotation, appropriate learning events, effective teaming, and a comprehensive technology infrastructure.

9.3.4. Matter of Communities

Over the years, various disciplines or schools of thought - and even functions have begun to converge in scope of responsibility and practice. Each area has been broadening its theories and integrating core principles from the domains of others. There is a convergence of functional perspectives and a common agenda is emerging.

For instance, human resource professionals seek to develop more relevant performance measures as well as new ways to use information technology. Chief Information Officers, in order to justify investments in technology, are having to understand the organization structure, motivations of people, and cross-boundary processes. Quality experts are building training infrastructures for the transfer of knowledge and best practices. R&D managers are taking on new responsibilities for business development and reducing cycle time with increased customer interaction. Finance professionals are exploring ways to expand their audit capabilities to influence the business strategy of their clients. All are relying on emerging computer and communications technology advancements to do so.

There is a realization of - and respect for - alternative paradigms that did not exist a decade ago. Value is being created in the organization interfaces - the white space - the connections between individuals, organizations, and companies in the same industries and nations within regions of the world.

This notion of Communities of Practice has originated. Likely an outgrowth of quality circles and networked organizations, when made explicit - help to harness the creativity and promote cross-fertilization of ideas necessary for prosperous innovation. "At the simplest level, there are a small group of people who have worked together over a period of time ... not a team, not a task force, not necessarily an authorized or identified group ..; perform the same, tasks ... or collaborate on a shared task ... or work together on a product. They are peers in the execution of real work. What holds them together is a common sense of purpose and a real need to know what each other knows".

Even the best strategic planning process often does not provide for an understanding of such natural connections. However, modern managers must take notice of these streams of activity to optimize the innovation process. This is where knowledge leadership resides - where ideas originate, are exchanged, and eventually result in marketable products and services. Observing this convergence of competencies provides insights into how the entire operation may be effectively led.

Innovation becomes the glue that bonds together diverse constituencies. Knowledge and intellectual capital become the mechanisms to build synergy. Such a redefined focus on knowledge and innovation is not the latest consulting fad. It is the essence of sustainable organizations and economies of the future. Instead of operating from the pure perspective of competition, leaders will learn to collaborate and contribute to the success of one another.

9.3.5. Matter of Conversations and Common Language

Innovation language - a language that transcends the paradigm and biases of one particular function. Ideally, such a language would also encompass industries, sectors and regions of the world and, therefore, be universal in scope. There are several attempts to define the knowledge language with a glossary of terms- one such effort initiated by Skandia and Ericsson in Sweden - includes an on-line capability to add to the existing 400 terms. Of course, whatever terms or language is adopted must apply to the heritage, purpose, mission and strategy of the enterprise. Such language must pervade all operations and planning efforts.

Once connections are made among internal and external constituencies - with an explicit understanding of potential spheres of influence - attention should be given to purposeful conversations. Mastering the art of structured conversation and dialogue has been the focus of many academic consultants. Furthermore, there are many successful CEOs beginning to manage according to the quality and level of conversations. It is discovered that learning and improvement are really two sides of the same coin. Through a weeklong course for senior executive team, researcher realized the value of conversations - the flow of meaning, if you will - among and between his senior management. The common bond was the quest for highly effective learning.

Stata's style is to encourage his employees to become a community of inquirer's, not advocates. With such a mindset, managers are encouraged to understand and leverage the diversity of knowledge, skills, experiences of one another.

9.3.6. Matter of Communications

With the dramatic increases in the functionality of computer and communications technology - including the explosion of the World Wide Web and e-commerce - companies must develop a strategy of how best to leverage the technology. There must be a take of full advantage of both internal and external mechanisms (e.g., group-ware, multi-media, cyberspace) to optimize results. Further, communications is not always technical. Keeping the organization and stakeholders apprised of priorities, changes in direction, success stories, and more is not only difficult, it is essential.

"You do not get a second chance to make a first impression." These days, with companies being managed by chaos theory and the degree of complexity, simple but not simplistic communications should be the order of the day. A communication strategy must be fully integrated with any plans to leverage human capital - more specifically knowledge - of all stakeholders in the innovation process.

External messages must be consistent with interrial culture, values, and vision. How companies are perceived in the marketplace - branding, ethics, direction, success stories, etc. - must be conveyed skillfully and on a regular basis. More and more companies around the world are using the platform of knowledge-type advertising campaigns:

"*Knowledge is powerful medicine.* " - Eli Lilly (Fortune, July 1995)

"*Understanding comes with Time.*"- Time Magazine (Fortune, July 1995)

"*Prepare to have that idea shattered.*" - Hewlett-Packard (Fortune July 1995)

"*A brilliant deduction.*" - Gifts in Kind America (Fortune, June 1995)

"*Knowledge of the world on-line.*" - Oracle (CNN ad, November 28, 1995)

"*Old tradition, new thinking*" - Harvard Funds (Fortune, June 1995)

"*Travel provides the power of knowledge*" - American Express (CNN ad, Feb. 1996)

In the Knowledge Economy, taglines have taken on a deeper significance. Not only are they designed for marketing products and services, they serve as a concise vehicle to present a timely image to external stakeholders and a motivational tool for employees. Sometimes, we forget how important might be the right words in the right context.

Communication strategy may be as much of a learning-process as a dissemination tool - perhaps even more so. We need to envision the innovation activity as a value-system, not a value-chain of events. For example, we may have more to gain from tapping into customer knowledge, i.e., what customers know; than approaching them as the end of a delivery chain. Communications may be more a function of operating a distributed learning network of expertize. It can be the source of an intelligence service as well as a business development function. Leadership is a function of listening - and acting upon insights - not merely a receptacle doe stakeholder contact.

9.3.7. Matter of Coaching

Coaching is a guided relationship process established between two parties. The process is forward looking, change-oriented, and developmental. It is a tool to enable client success, productivity, revenue growth, and stakeholder value. Coaching is more about 'being' than 'doing.' Effective coaches engage in a process that involves trust, support and shared values.

The coach's main role deals with expanding the ability to see contexts, rather than supplying content. The coaching process affirms the person, seeks to clarify choices, and acts as a catalyst for achieving both individual and organizational purposes. The coaching task connects the inner person, e.g., confidence, values, purpose, with the external manifestation of leadership, e.g., articulating vision, reaching targets, and achieving goals.

Coaching is the opposite of judging and the need for control. This is why its essence is congruent with the fundamental precepts of the Knowledge- Economy. The coaching relationship enables people to work out issues and find answers through their own effective discovery process.

Effective leaders know they do not have all the answers. However, they do generally have a healthy curiosity, sense of direction, standards of excellence and a track record of success. They genuinely value others and have a need to 'know what the others know.' They are constantly learning, not afraid to experiment with new ideas, nor afraid to make mistakes. They know that facilitating a process is almost always preferable to claiming answers and dictating action. Knowledge leaders will coach as well as be coached. They will navigate through uncharted territory with full confidence in the value of mutual talent.

With the shift to on-the-job learning, it is important to have others - not neces-sarilv managers - guide them through their own innovation process.

9.4. LEARNING OBJECTIVES AND ABILITIES FOR KNOWLEDGE MANAGER

In the course of history, and as the world moved into a new era of global connectivity, we have to focus on the importance of intellectual capital, and the opportunity offered by knowledge management to help achieve e-Government. E-Government is government of the people, by the people and for the people in a virtual world, a collaborative government where technology meets human creativity, and where government manages and shares its vast stores of knowledge with, and for the benefit of, the citizen.

Out of the growing chaos engendered by the Internet and the nearly exponential increase in data and information, emerged a government-wide Knowledge Management Working Group dedicated to fostering interagency collaboration, inter-agency communities of practice, and the sharing of knowledge throughout the government. This group, starting from small beginnings, began to grow as more and more government agencies and organizations realized the potential knowledge management holds. But even though each member realized and agreed on this potential, they all had different ways of defining knowledge management, and different ideas about what it could do for their organizations.

At first this appeared confusing, but finally it began to dawn upon this learning community that the true value of knowledge management was both what it held for each of their organizations and that it was bringing them together to build a connected and sharing government. Still, there was the realization that if knowledge management was defined as everything, knowledge management would, of course, fall short. Nothing can be everything. So the government-wide knowledge management group devised a plan. They would partner with not only each other, but also with academia and industry associations, to figure out what those things were in knowledge management that made sense for government knowledge workers - like Knowledge Managers and Chief Knowledge Officers - to know.

Now a great cry went up throughout the land to find those partners who already offered knowledge management certification programs, those partners who had knowledge of and an interest in what a government knowledge management certification program might look like. And lo and behold, they were found, and they agreed to participate in this important endeavor. Together, government, industry associations and academic organizations began to define a conceptual framework for knowledge management through developing criteria for accredited government certification programs.

9.4.1. Knowledge and Understanding

The learning objectives developed by the government-wide Knowledge Management Working Group cover the breadth of what is needed to implement knowledge management successfully in the federal sector. The depth of knowledge and ability needed in each area is highly dependent on the specific job that needs to be done. Half of the learning objectives identified through the above process are concerned with the specific knowledge an individual needs in order to work effectively in the area of Knowledge Management.

Have knowledge of the value added by Knowledge Management to the business proposition, including the return on investment, performance measures, and the ability to develop a business case : Although Knowledge Management is capitalized, we often speak to knowledge management as having a small "k" and a small "m." The intent is that knowledge management is not an initiative in and of itself, but supports the mission and business objectives of the organization. This objective positions knowledge management as a strategic enabler at the enterprise level. Fundamental in this objective is tie-in to strategic business planning. Knowledge management is an extremely broad discipline and using metrics brings solid management practices to the forefront of decision makers, thereby enabling choices. As knowledge management matches corresponding effort with metrics in other domains of the firm, it will be recognized as a viable management practice.

Performance measures are the essence of good management practices. The progress of knowledge management initiatives needs to be continually monitored to ensure progress toward their objectives. Given the complex and dynamic nature of modern organizations, knowledge management - or any other organizational initiative - cannot guarantee that plans and strategies will succeed. Well-designed performance measures provide indications of the efficiency and effectiveness of people, processes, and programs, which in turn help the managers to understand and adapt their organizations. Indeed, performance measures are so integral to organizational success that the Federal Government In United States has passed several pieces of legislation that specifically call for formal metrics. Legislation during the last ten years includes the Government Performance and Results Act (GPRA) of 1993, the Government Management Reform Act of 1994, and the Information Technology Management Reform Act of 1996.

Have knowledge of the strategies and processes to transfer explicit and tacit knowledge across time, space and organizational boundaries, including retrieval of critical archived information enabling ideas to build upon ideas : Since Nonaka and Takeuchi first explored the interaction between tacit and explicit knowledge, there has been a steady growth of interest on the capture of tacit knowledge. Aging workforce issues in the public sector have served as a catalyst for the development of processes and systems that facilitate understanding the role and importance of context in decision-making.

But this objective goes even farther. Transfer is the focus, not just understanding the nature of tacit and explicit knowledge. Increasing the dynamics of transfer by itself moves knowledge through the organization at an increased rate. The more knowledge is being transferred, the more it is available to the organization as a resource.

Understanding the relationship between tacit and explicit

knowledge and its impact on the organization leads to informed decisions on an organization's knowledge management approach. A high ratio of tacit knowledge leads to a strong dependence on the individual and reliance on the connectivity between individuals for knowledge flow. The loss of that individual and his/her knowledge can have a serious effect on the organization. A high ratio of explicit knowledge requires an investment in the transfer of knowledge from tacit to explicit and may present issues regarding context, currency, and authoritative source. However, a high ratio of explicit knowledge leads to less dependence on the individual, and explicit knowledge can be stored and easily moved around.

Have knowledge of state-of-the-art and evolving technology solutions that promote KM, including portals and collaborative and distributed learning technologies : We live in a world of technology. Knowledge repositories, automated libraries, computer services, databases, etc. offer the capability for not only storing large amounts of data and information, but also efficient and intelligent retrieval and assemblage capability. Powerful search algorithms, intelligent agents and semantic interpreters allow employees to rapidly retrieve information needed for problem solving and decision-making. Knowledge managers need to be aware of these capabilities, how they are used and how to integrate their operation with people to ensure knowledge availability and application.

In many organizations, portals are the principle delivery mechanism for an enterprise's knowledge sharing. Collaborative systems range from intranets to video teleconferencing to whiteboards. Their purpose is to aid groups of individuals, either co-located or dispersed, to work more effectively together to foster innovations, solve problems and make decisions. For example, distributed learning uses information technology to facilitate learning without having the instructor co-located. Individuals at different locations, using their own computers, can learn via the Internet or computer-based training. The increasing rate of change necessitates the need for faster learning, forcing us to change our traditional concepts. Class-room-based learning may be supplemented or complemented with new virtual capabilities.

Have knowledge of and the ability to facilitate knowledge creation, sharing and reuse including developing partnerships and alliances, designing creative knowledge spaces, and using incentive structures : Knowledge creation, sharing and reuse are the heart of knowledge management programs, and indeed these behaviours are intricately tied to each other. As people share knowledge within an organization, and others use it and find new ways to improve on it and innovate, the value of that knowledge increases for the entire organization. This process also provides the opportunity to identify integrators-knowledge leaders, who connect people and ideas together and subject matter experts, who provide a depth of thinking in specific areas. In turn, those involved in exchanges benefit from the exchange through a more complete understanding of the area addressed, thereby becoming a more valuable resource to the organization.

Three examples of facilitating knowledge creation, sharing and reuse are included in this objective to facilitate an understanding of the eclectic nature of knowledge management. Partnerships and Alliances are means by which organizations can share information and knowledge while working together toward mutual goals. Knowledge spaces build on the concept of "open space," providing space and time for people to mentally explore events or thoughts and formulate ways in which to proceed. Open space, whether physical or virtual, provides a place to brainstorm and be creative. It comes in many forms–online chat rooms, threaded e-mail discussions, weekly in-person discussion forums, communities, discussion groups, coffee rooms, and water cooler encounters. Here knowledge workers can sort out complexities and receive feedback from others, hopefully resulting in new ideas and improved decision-making capabilities.

Senior leaders and managers may need to revamp incentive and reward structures and performance measures to help to promote the creation, sharing and reuse of knowledge. Some organizations provide bonuses and other rewards to individuals who go out of their way to share knowledge with others. Event intermediations such as Knowledge Fairs have been successfully held in such organizations as the World Bank.

Have knowledge of learning styles and behaviours, strive for continuous improvement and be actively engaged in exploring new ideas and concepts : People learn differently. Some learn through reading, others through lectures or visual or graphic representations while still others learn by doing. Effective transfer of information requires understanding different learning styles and how people learn. Adults learn best from direct experience with real-world problems. How can this be extrapolated across a virtual environment? As learning becomes the mutual responsibility of leaders and workers, knowledge professionals must be constant learners, seeking new information and exhibiting behaviour for others to model by continuously striving to improve the organization's use of information and knowledge.

This objective also sets the stage for capitalizing on new learning approaches including broadband web-based multi-media. As new concepts unfold, models and theories for learning will evolve. A foundation in this area will prepare Knowledge Managers for the future.

Have working knowledge of state-of-the-art research and implementation strategies for knowledge management, information management, document and records management, and data management. This includes project management of knowledge initiatives and retrieval of critical archived information : Knowledge leaders and workers need to understand the conceptual linkages between Knowledge Management, Information Management and Data and Records Management. Knowledge management is part of a larger movement enabled by information technology, a movement that has brought us into the Information Age and is rapidly propelling us toward an age of increasing complexity where knowledge appears to be the only thing that can deal with complexity. There are continuing advances in data management, document and records management, and information management that will make information technology infrastructures more effective in supporting knowledge workers as they strive to make their organization more effective through the intelligent management of knowledge.

Have understanding of the global and economic importance

of developing knowledge-based organizations to meet the challenges of the knowledge era : We live in an omni-linked world. Anyone in the world can talk to almost anyone else in the world real-time. Technology has provided totally new ways of moving and transferring data, information and knowledge among individuals, organizations and governments. The results of these interactions are increased communication, and a corresponding increase in the flow of ideas and the making of decisions. Organizations are forced to scan, select and quickly respond to the increased flow of web-based exchanges and actions. Moreover, as the number of nodes in networks increase, the number of links increase, and as the links and their consequent relationships increase, so does the complexity. Critical thinking, the possession of deep knowledge and the ability to work collaboratively with others who think differently may help address issues of increasing complexity. Knowledge-based organizations need to provide time and space for critical thinking.

9.4.2. Abilities

The second half of the KM learning objectives deals with abilities, or skills. These are discussed briefly below.

Have the ability to use systems thinking in implementing solutions : KM addresses powerful activities throughout environments, organizations, cultures and economies. Systems Thinking provides a means for looking at the "big" picture while examining the component parts. Systems Thinking assumes that almost everything is a system, made up of connecting elements. Systems have boundaries and behaviors that are different from their individual elements. Systems Thinking emphasizes on the importance of relationships and structure within the organization and makes individuals aware of the effects of their efforts on others in the organization, permitting them to understand and perform their roles more effectively.

Systems thinking helps to manage complexity by providing a tool for decision-makers to map and understand cause and effect relationships among data, information and events in an organization. This is done through a process of identifying patterns that repeat themselves over and over again in decision-making and organizational life. This process forces decision-makers to consider the consequences of their actions and their impact on and relationship to other organizational functions. Systems thinking not only helps increase an individual's critical thinking skills, but also enhances collaboration and serves as a basis for collective inquiry by providing a common language and perspective for dialogue and understanding.

Have the ability to design, develop and sustain communities of interest and practice : Communities are social constructs. In a primarily virtual world, communities provide a fundamental capability for developing and sharing expertise throughout the workforce. Communities of practice share a domain of practice, crossing operational, functional and organizational boundaries, and defining themselves by knowledge areas, not tasks. In like manner, communities of interest share a domain of interest. Communities are managed by establishing and developing connections between individuals and organizations, and focusing on value added, mutual exchange and continuous learning. Communities have an evolving agenda as participant knowledge builds and related areas of exchange emerge.

Collaboration, innovation, learning and knowledge sharing are at the core of communities of practice and interest. Communities increase information flows in order to maximize knowledge and exploit existing competencies to achieve maximum return. They also facilitate the transfer of best practices and lessons learned between organizational content centers, thus creating efficiencies while improving effectiveness. And Communities fill in the gaps where organizational knowledge falls short and where enterprise information is under exploited. In short, sometimes we do not know what we do not know. Communities encourage personnel to access key resources and build new knowledge to complete tasks faster, better and easier.

Have the ability to create, develop and sustain the flow of knowledge : The flow of data, information and knowledge moves around in the networks of systems and people. It is shared through team interaction, communities and events and is facilitated through knowledge repositories and portals. This flow is both horizontal and vertical, including the continuous, rapid two-way communication between key components of the organization and top-level decision-makers.

With increased connectivity, we reach further and further across organizations, communities, industries and the globe to tap resources. Virtual teamwork requires new skills of leadership, management and facilitation to create and maintain the trust, open communication and interdependencies needed for physically separated individuals to collaborate effectively.

Many companies and organizations invest a considerable amount of money in restructuring organizational charts and re-engineering business processes only to be disappointed with the results. That is because much of the work happens outside the formal organizational structure. Often what needs attention is the informal organization, the networks of relationships that employees form across functions and divisions need to quickly accomplish tasks. These informal relationships can cut through formal reporting procedures to jump-start stalled initiatives and meet extraordinary deadlines. However, information networks can just as easily sabotage the best laid plans of companies by blocking communication and fomenting opposition to change unless leaders know how to identify and direct them. Learning how to map these social links can help harness the real power of organizations.

Have the ability to perform cultural and ethnographic analyses, develop knowledge taxonomies, facilitate knowledge audits, and perform knowledge mapping and needs assessments : As the amount of information and knowledge increases, tools such as taxonomies, audits and maps help to organize information for decision-making. While search engines and agents keep improving, the bottom line is that the human brain is the final arbiter of effective relationships and patterns. Analytic techniques such as cultural and ethnographic analyses help leaders understand organizational cultures and their characteristics. Culture is often cited as one of the main barriers to successful implementation of knowledge management.

A taxonomy is a framework for arranging or categorizing information and knowledge so that people can find and use it effectively. This is applicable when designing a knowledge base, but also applies to the wider knowledge system. For example, if knowledge is organized into groupings based upon a community of interest or practice on a web-site or knowledge base, then mentoring programs, training and other knowledge transfer processes should support these same groupings to facilitate knowledge flow. It is not necessary to pick just one way of arranging information and knowledge, but it is important to evaluate the many different ways before beginning any kind of knowledge base design.

Conducting a "knowledge audit" to find out how information is collected, stored and reported, and how the reports are used, can be beneficial in streamlining the information flow within an organization, saving time and effort. A knowledge audit examines what information is available and whether it is used. Simply put, the purpose of a knowledge audit is to help the organization "know what it knows" and then measure the quantity and usefulness of that knowledge base.

Have the ability to capture, evaluate and use best-known practices : The use of best practices across industry and government can provide efficiencies and increase effectiveness, if they are indeed best practices for the organization implementing them. How is the applicability of a best practice determined? How do you understand the context of the best practice, the simple rules that made it successful in some organizations?

Storytelling, the construction of examples to illustrate a point, can be used to effectively transfer knowledge, and best practices. An organizational story is a detailed narrative of management actions, employee interactions, or other intra-organizational events that are communicated informally within the organization. A variety of story forms exist and will arise naturally throughout organizations, including scenarios and anecdotes. Scenarios are the articulation of possible future states, constructed within the imaginative limits of the author. While scenarios provide an awareness of alternatives - of value in and of itself- they are often used as planning tools for possible future situations. The plan becomes a vehicle to respond to recognized key elements in each scenario. An anecdote is a brief sequence experienced in the field or arising from a brainstorming session. To reinforce positive behaviour, sensitive managers can seek out and disseminate anecdotes that embody the value desired in the organization. The capture and distribution of anecdotes across organizations carries high value. Dave Snowden, a consultant in Great Britain who has investigated the use of storytelling in organizations for the past dozen years, has discovered that once a critical number of anecdotes are captured from a community, the value set or rules underlying the behavior of that community can be determined. Understanding these values allows the use of informal as well as formal aspects of the organization.

Conveying information in a story provides a rich context. Context remains in memory longer and creates more memory traces than random information bites. Therefore, a story is more likely to be acted upon than other means of communication. Storytelling connects people, develops creativity, and increases confidence. The appeal of stories in organizations helps to build descriptive capabilities, increase organizational learning, convey complex meaning and communicate common values and rule sets.

Have the ability to manage change and complex knowledge projects : Management concepts, whether old or new, are about change management. And in today's world where complexity is increasing, according to Ashby's Law of Requisite Variety there must be as many or more ways to change a system as those things in a system that need to be changed.

Cultural change of any kind is a long, slow process. Accomplishing change requires daily support of sharing knowledge openly throughout the entire organization. Knowledge management initiatives are particularly challenging to change agents because of the uncertainty of outcome. Most managers like to change only one or two things at a time to mitigate against unintended consequences. When many factors within the organization are simultaneously changed, communicating, coordination and leadership become important in reducing resistance to change and maintaining motivation.

Have the ability to identify customers and stakeholders and tie organizational goals to the needs and requirements of those customers and stakeholders : Total Quality Management brought to the forefront the tried and true values successful organizations have used for years, a focus on customers and stakeholders. No matter what new approach or initiative is popular, we must keep a focused eye on the needs of our constituents, and ensure all efforts underway contribute to fulfilling their needs. This makes good business sense.

9.5. KNOWLEDGE MANAGEMENT STRATEGY FORMULATION

The main purpose of knowledge management is to enhance knowledge processing at an organizational level. Then, how would we formulate a knowledge management strategy in order to do so? What would its dimensions be? Its targets of impact? How can the KLC or Knowledge Life Cycle inform us of how best to articulate and express knowledge management strategy?

Confine the responses to these questions to the notion of knowledge management strategy in terms of its own externally aimed business processes. In other words, we are not discussing strategy for the knowledge management function itself, or for its own internally aimed operations. Rather, we are talking about the expression of what a knowledge management function would do in terms of the initiatives it would undertake as it interacts with the target knowledge processing environment of interest to it.

This last statement, then, already begins to illustrate the application and value of the KLC to the development of a knowledge management strategy. That is, the new knowledge management brings a conception of knowledge processing as a social process to the table, a vision that in a very material way gives knowledge management something to work with. It is not about enhancing business-use transactions directly. It is about enhancing an end-to-end social value network called knowledge processing that is described by a model we call the KLC. The beneficial influence of the KLC on strategy, then, is that it helps us to focus on and frame the boundaries of the environment that is the target of our strategies.

Next, consider the distinction we make between the

knowledge production side of the KLC and the knowledge integration side, see Fig. 9.2.

To put a more purposeful spin on this, we can also say that the knowledge integration side of the KLC is "supply-side" in scope, since its purpose is to enhance the supply of evaluated knowledge claims to its constituents. And the knowledgeproduction side is, in turn, "demand-side," in the sense that its activities and subprocesses make it possible for people in organizations to satisfy their demands for new knowledge. So we have supply-side knowledge processing (KP) on the one hand, and demand-side KP on the other.

With this characterization of the KLC now firmly in mind, we can begin to formulate many different kinds of knowledge management interventions that would be targeted at enhancing supply-side KP or, alternatively, demand-side KP. Let us say, then, that some knowledge management interventions might be supply-side in scope while others would be demand-side in scope. So we can have supply-side knowledge management and demand-side knowledge management, just as we have supply-side KP and demand-side KP. The purpose of supply-side knowledge management is to enhance supply-side KP; and the purpose of demand-side knowledge management is to enhance demand-side KP. Here again, we can attribute the beginnings of a knowledge management strategy to the insights we receive from our understanding of the KLC, because in some organizations enhancements to demand-side knowledge processing may be more urgently needed than enhancements to supply-side knowledge processing or vice versa. Depending on what the priority is, our knowledge management strategy is impacted accordingly.

Next in analysis of the application of the KLC to formulating knowledge management strategy, is the recognition that the tools and methods we use to make interventions can be of two kinds– social and technological, the latter being IT-based. Some of interventions, therefore, could consist of the implementation of IT-based systems to enhance supply or demand-side knowledge processing. Other interventions may have nothing to do with technology and may be comprised, instead, of the implementation of new social technologies or operating models, such as

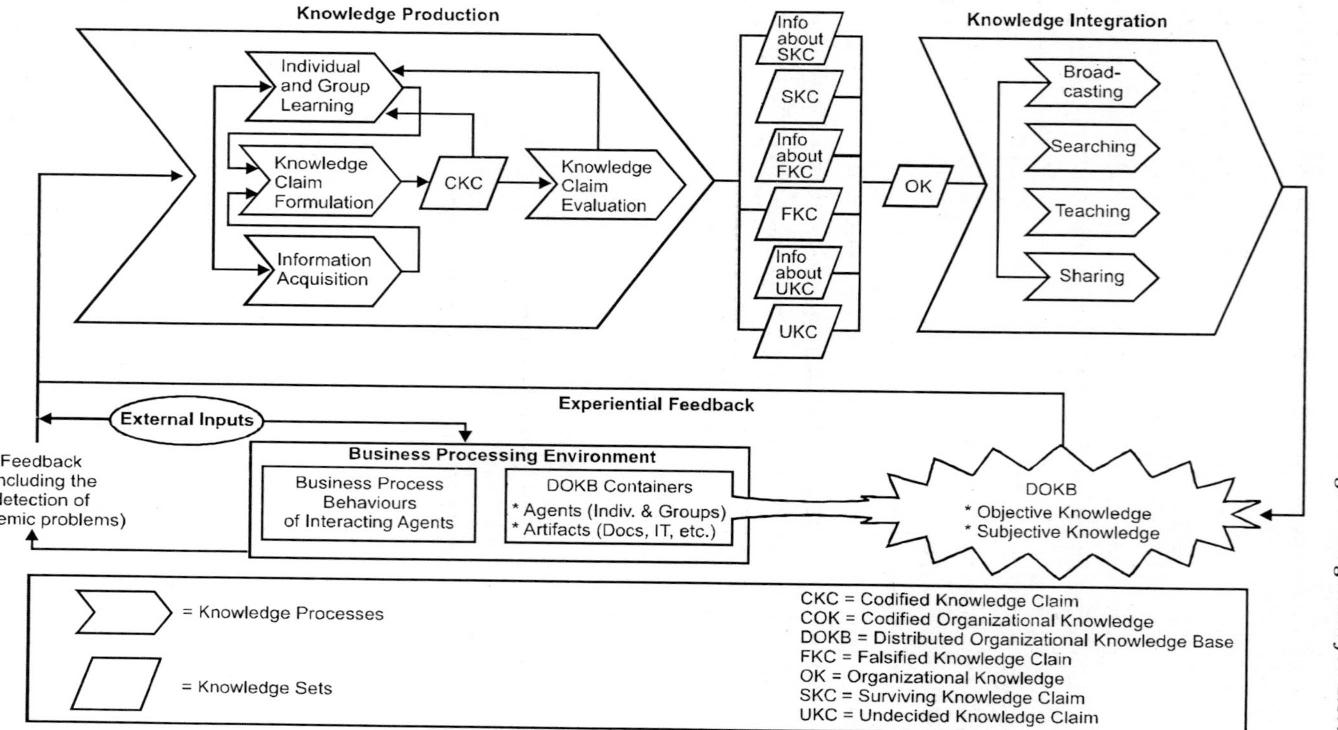

Fig. 9.2.Knowledge Life Cycle

communities of practice programs, training, group decision-making processes, or what have you. This last option, in particular, i.e., social interventions, rises to our attention thanks largely to the influence of the KLC on our thinking. Social interventions make sense, we can see, because the KLC makes it clear to us that knowledge processing, above all, involves social processes. We can also support it in many ways using technology, but knowledge management is, first and foremost, a social science, not a technological one.

When we combine the supply and demand-side KM orientations with the potential use of social versus technological tools and interventions, we get a strategic framework that shows us what the possibilities are in terms of how we might structure a very high-level plan to, in fact, make interventions, see Fig. 9.3 &) 9.4.

By formulating and expressing knowledge management strategies in this way, we can clearly establish the relevance of our individual knowledge management initiatives (within a particular planning period) to their individual and collective impact on knowledge processing as a whole. Today's knowledge management strategies would be largely defined and carried out like yesterday's– very business-use transactional, and very means-oriented, with little or no capability for determining what the overall impact on knowledge processing will be at the level of the whole organization, much less its further impact on business outcomes.

Knowledge Processing / Interventions	**Demand-Side KP**	**Supply-Side KP**	**Supply/Demand-Side KP**
Social Interventions	Demand-Side Social Interventions	Supply-Side Social Interventions	S/DS Social Social Interventions
Technological Interventions	Demand-Side Technological Interventions	Supply-Side Technological Interventions	S/DS Technological Interventions
Socio/Techno Interventions Interventions	Demand-Side Integrated Interventions	Supply-Side Integrated Interventions	S/DS Socio/Techno Interventions

Fig. 9.4. A Framework for KM Strategy

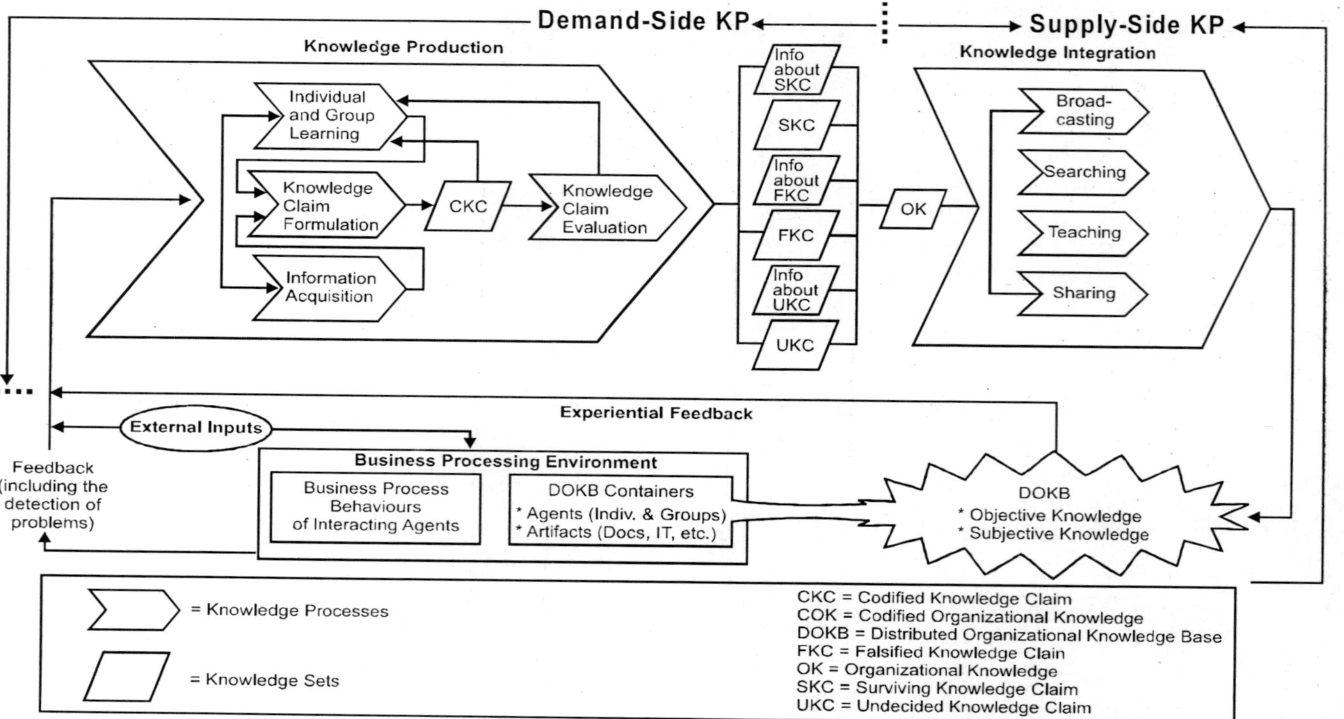

Fig. 9.3. Supply and Demand-Side Knowledge Processing

9.6. IMPLEMENTING KNOWLEDGE MANAGEMENT

Organizations implementing knowledge management must draw their expertise from several different sources :

- Internal, centralized IT departments,
- Team-based local experts,
- External vendors, contractors, partners, and consultants, and
- End users and front-line staff,

Although we cannot undermine the importance of IT staff who will actually build as tem, the most important part of this team member set is the set of local team-based expert. The burden of balancing counteracting requirements falls on the shoulders of the knowledge management team (see Fig. 9.5). Drawing participant from variety or functional groups within and outside your company is essential. If do properly, this approach will become the strength of your knowledge management team and major contributor to the success of such an endeavor.

Active end-user involvement throughout the knowledge management project is critical to its success. In most companies or organizations there are the early adopters of technology—the gurus within your company. These are the people who come in early or stay late to new tools that become available. Even though many of these folks tend to be non–technologists, they are the best people to gauge the possible usefulness of each feature that your system has. These local experts are often the first to notice the limitations of existing systems, and to think of possible upgrades and changes to meet the evolving needs of their group. Examples of such workers include marketing people who realize that existing technology could possibly be used to deliver the latest sales figures and data needed by traveling salespeople in remote locations.Relying solely on local experts, of course, has its limitations. Even though local experts might possess a fairly high degree of technical knowledge besides knowledge of their own job, they might lack an understanding of the interdependencies between complex systems, networks, and technology that pure technologists like the IT staff might be able to bring in. While the local experts will bring in the business case and ideas, it is IT staff who will bring in knowledge of:

- Infrastructural capabilities and limitations,
- Connectivity and compatibility among the team-based systems and the overall organizational technology infrastructure,
- Standardization issues across different platforms, applications, and tools, and
- Technicalities underlying the adaptation of these tools by various knowledge worker groups within the company.

When you are selecting team members from the internal IT department within your company, it is critical that you select personnel with credibility in the eventual user group. This help to ensure that the relevant set of stakeholder needs are adequately represented. With increase emphasis on customer service, it is easy for internal customers to outsource their development services to external consultants. Therefore, delegates selected from the IT department might have a more expansive view of who the customer is. This must include the internal custom at the same level of significance as they would view an external customer or buyer. The skills, of course, are a priority in making these decisions.

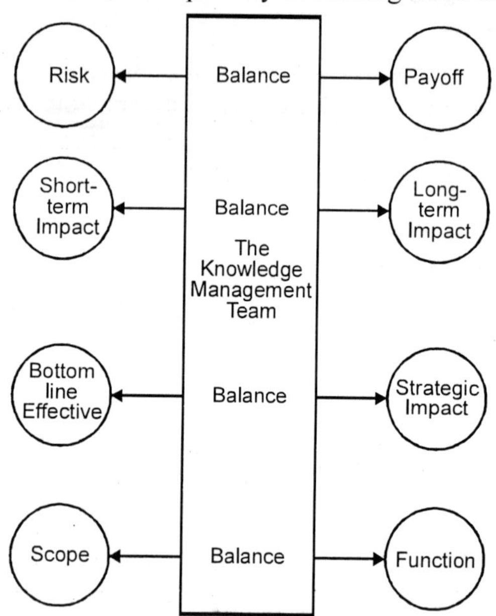

Fig. 9.5. KM Team must strike the Right Balance

Nonlocal experts and extra-departmental proponents promote team laterality. *Laterality* is the ability to cut across functional boundaries and relate to people from different points. People who exhibit this characteristic are best suited to be on a knowledge management system. Such members can:

- Act as a bridge and as interpreters between people from different backgrounds, areas, and specializations.
- Learn faster than the average person in your company and are not defensive about their lack of understanding or knowledge in areas other than thier own.
- Bring value to the overall team synergy as they tend to be confident but not egoistically constrained.
- Learn the basic things and understand the frameworks that their colaborators refer to.
- Have the ability to deal creatively and rationally with the problems that the aforementioned differences can, and often do, lead to. Groups of such people have also been referred to as community of practice; they are characterized by:
    - Multifunctional groups that incorporate diverse viewpoints, training, ages, and roles
    - Enacting a common purpose by engaging in real work, building tilings, solving problems, delivering service, and using real tools.
    - Developing intellectual property, knowledge, firm culture, internal language, and new skills.
    - Making lasting changes in the people and the competency that they embody.

Even though most of the technical, design, and soft skills needed for the knowledge man agement project might be available in-house, there might be some areas that are no one's strength within the company. These shortcomings can often be overcome by bringing in external consultants. Internal participants might have slight cultural differences owing to their differing departmental and functional affiliations, but they are still tied together by a common frame of reference built around the overall company culture, dominant values, and image. However, external consultants do not always fit into this frame of reference. Because external participants often lack this common frame of reference, it is essential that other binding mechanisms, such as their personal characteristics, be strongly matched with those of internal team members.

Nevertheless, this lack of shared culture can often be turned from a liability into an asset. These external participants can bring a balanced, unbiased outsider perspective into the entire design process.

In such cases, trust becomes another significant issue. Given the nature of the consulting business, it should come as no surprise if the consultant is developing exactly the same type of system for your competitor a few months down the road. Selecting a consultant should therefore be partially based on the extent to which the person or consulting company, is willing to transfer existing skills to your company's employees. Some of the other issues that must be considered while selecting a consultant include:

- The consultants reputation for integrity.
- The consultants history that demonstrates the ability to maintain confidentiality about past projects.
- Whether the consultant has worked successfully for your own company on earlier projects.
- Whether the consultant or consulting company, is working, on a similar project for a competitor.
- Whether your internal team trusts and has confidence in the consulting company.

In any case, highly specialized and capable consultants are often hard to find. Since knowledge management projects are strategically oriented, the level of confidentiality must backed up with specific, legal nondisclosure agreements. Where highly confidential material is involved, it might he a better idea to have an employee trained in the deficient area rather than bringing in a consultant. An option that is always open, budgets permitting, is to let consultant from the consulting position to a permanent job within your company. However corporate budgets can often restrict this option.

KM stakeholders should typify the group that they represent. For example, the person representing your company's human resources department should be one who is typically of the HR department, and has had sufficient level of experience within your own company.

9.6.1. Team Construction

For formulation and implementation of knowledge management we have to construct a team. This may be reavled in following table.

Table 9.4. Structuring the Knowledge Management Team

Focus	Share holder Group	Role in Knowledge Management Project	Characteristics Strongly Desired
Teams	User teams	• Provide functional expertise.	• Must understand work processes in their area.
	Finance Marketing	• Provide business expertize in their specific area.	• Must have good inter-personal and team skill.
	Other functional areas with which the knowledge management initive is concerned.	• Participate in the process design stage.	• Must have a certain degree of credibility within other participating groups. • Must be willing to see from other functional view points.
Techn-ology	IT experts/information systems	• Provide technology expertise	• Must understand technology in depth.
	Internal IT staff	• Participate in the actual implementation and design.	• Must have good inter-personal skills.
	External consultants	• Represent the internal and internally proficient technologists. • Actually write the code. • Bring in a perspective on functional capabilities and limitations of existing systems.	• Must have strong team skills. • Must be willing to understand the perspectives brought in by other team members and actually incorporate them into the design. • Must be willing to learn.

			• Must be credible. • Must have an expansive customer orientation.
Organizational	Senior management sponsors/knowledge champion (s) CKO	• Support the legitmacy of the project.	• Must understand management and strategic process.
		• Bring in vision that correlates with the overall company-wide vision.	• Must be credible.
		• Serve on steering committees (if needed).	• Must have a strong leadership position that almost everyone on the team accepts.
		• Commit the resources needed.	• Must themselves believe what they say. • Need to be thoroughly convinced of the worth of the project.

9.6.2. Team Composition and Selection Criteria

As with most other technologically driven enterprise-wide teams, functional diversity in knowledge management teams should be taken as a given characteristic. Teams need designed for effectiveness. While there is no straightforward formula for designing a good knowledge management team, the team's design has much to do with the nature of the project itself. Functional diversity can lead to only two possible outcomes depending on how it is handled. The first, and very common, outcome is destructive conflict and tension. The second, more desirable, outcome is characterized by synergy, creativity and innovation. This happens only when laterality among team members is high and there is sufficient room to accomodate different backgrounds, values, skills, perspectives, and assumptions that the members bring into the team. Table 9.5 summarizes the major team design considerations.

9.6.3. Temporary Versus Permanent Team Members

Knowledge management is not like a typical business

restructuring or technology introduction project. Those projects are temporary and depend on temporary teams, whereas a knowledge management project needs at least a small portion of the group to be permanent. A knowledge management project is not over once a knowledge management system is implemented; it must go on and continually improve and change with changing external and internal environments. While some members might be needed on the team only during the initial stages, others are not as temporary. Team members can be dedicated to the project either full time or part time. The size of the core team must be kept to the smallest size possible—the smallest member count that can actually do the work. Temporary team members often belong to specific user groups. The core team should consist of only the following participants:

- Knowledge champion or a senior manager.
- IT staff.

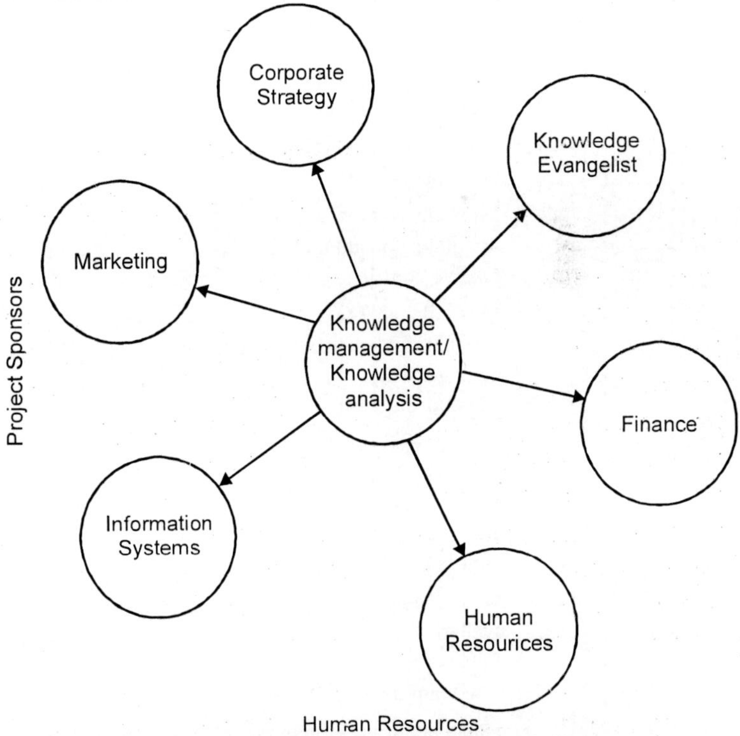

Fig. 9.6. KM Team Structure

- User delegates representing the core business area that is going to depend on the knowledge management system. This could be engineering staff in case the knowledge management system is built to support research and development; it could be marketing if the KM system is for sales force enablement, etc.

The remaining participants, in most cases, should be involved in the startup phases of the project and can be called in later for further input as and when needed.

Table 9.5. Designing the Knowledge Management Project Team

Team Design Element	Characteristics of the Knowledge Management Team Members Selected	Notes
Defining the knowledge management project leader's role	The leader of the team: • Must be credible. • Must have a sufficient level of authority and resource capability. • Should not change; must be stable. • Must know how to facilitate, consult and resolve conflicts. • Must take charge of the conventional project management, scheduling and coordination duties. • Must have direct reporting capability to upper management or should be drawn from within upper middle management. • Must manage the life cycle of the team, as well as selection of the core team members. • Must encourage structured decision making.	These criteria can be also used for selecting the project leader.

	• Must be experienced in both complex projects and in various roles within the company.	
Defining the team composition and selection criteria for team members	Knowledge management project team members must be drawn from different functional areas and departments of the firm. As expected, they will have different areas of specialization and back-grounds. The following common characteristics must be shared by members selected for the team: • Must have specialized expertize. • Must have had sufficient experience within the company or working with the company as an external consultant. • Must have the required competencies that truly represent the concerns of the department or functional area that the team member represents. • Might work full time or part time on this project. • Might be a member of the core team or the temporary startup team. • Must demonstrate laterality. • Must believe in the project and must have a clear vision for what improved knowledge flows can and should do for this unit or department.	All groups that will be affected by the knowledge management project and, conversely, all group that are expected to use and contributeto this knowledge and knowledge management efforts must be adequately & accurately represented in the team.

9.6.4. Team Life Span and Sizing Issues

There are two schools ol thought on the future of knowledge management: One school believes that knowledge management will continue to depend on people to manage knowledge throughout the lirerime of the organization; the second and more convincing school believes that knowledge management is a *self-eliminating* field. This means that as a company begins to accept knowledge management practices, they should, over several years, become so second nature to employees as the company evolves that eventually there should be no need for a knowledge manager or CKO to manage knowledge. Knowledge workers themselves should be able to handle all knowledge management tasks once knowledge management becomes embedded in the company culture or organization and in work practices.

One would argue why the knowledge management team would, in the first place, do their job so well that would eliminate their very need! That is a hard question to answer. Though there is a lot of ongoing research to find an answer to this question, there is little other than very strong financial and promotional incentives that can help here. For that matter, team members on the knowledge management team should be promised strong rewards and promotions should the knowledge management initiative truly succeed. A team that sets out to work with the fear of losing their job by performing too well is bound to be undermotivated, if not unmotivated.

Once the team is constructed we have to move on to implementation of knowledge management.

9.7. ROAD MAP FOR IMPLEMENTATION

Tiwana has given a 10 - step road map for knowledge management. Broadly we can view these 10 steps into four phases in Fig. 9.7.

— Infrastructural evaluation
— KM system analysis, design and development
— System deployment
— Evaluation

Table 9.6 describes how each of these steps of logically can be arranged.

9.7.1. Phase 1 : Infrastructural Evaluation

The first phase of the 10-step technique involves two steps. In the first step you analyze your existing infrastructure, then you identify concrete steps that you can take to leverage and build your knowledge management system upon. In the second step you analyze knowledge gaps by creaLing knowledgc maps lor your company. You further use these knowledge maps to creait a high-level strategic link between business strategy and knowledge management. You then use this link develop both the knowledge management strategy and system in a manner that aligns them with business performance and objectives.

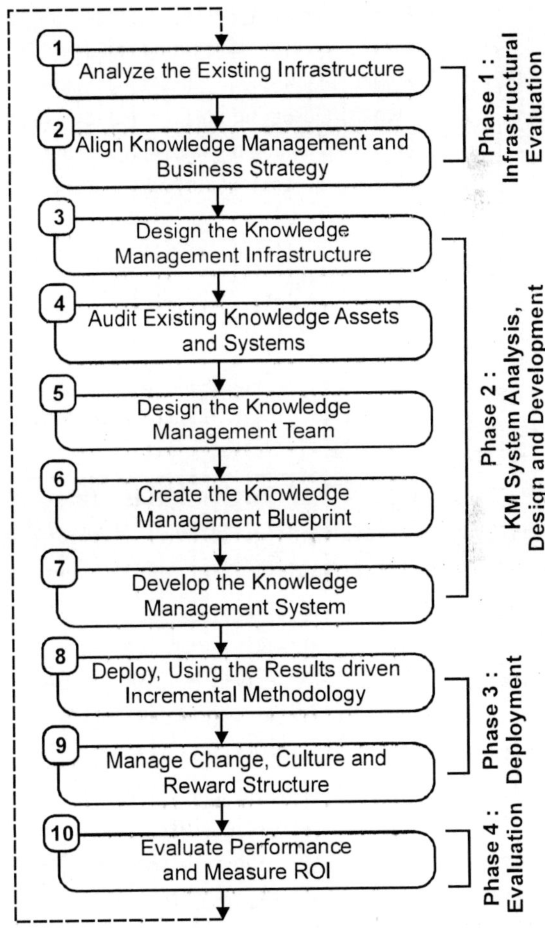

Fig. 9.7. 10-step Knowledge Management Roadmap

Table 9.6. Organization of the Four Phases of the 10-Step KM Roadmap

Part	Chapter	Step
Phase 1 : Infrastructural Evaluation		
		Step 1 : Analyzing existing infrastructure
		Step 2 : Aligning knowledge management & business strategy.
Phase 2 : KM System Analysis, Design and Development		
		Step 3 : Designing the knowledge mangement architecture and integrating existing infrastructure
		Step 4 : Auditing and analyzing existing knowledge
		Step 5 : Designing the knowledge managment team
		Step 6 : Creating the knowledge management blueprint
		Step 7 : Developing the knowledge management system
Phase 3 : Deployment		
		Step 8 : Deploying with RDI methodology
		Step 9 : Change management, culture, reward structure design, and choice of the CKO
Phase 4 : Performance Evaluation		
		Step 10: Measuring results of knowledge management, devising ROI metrics, and evaluating system performance

Step 1 : Analysis of Existing Infrastructure : In this first step, you gain an understanding of various components that constitute the knowledge management strategy and technology framework. By analyzing and accounting for what is already in place in your company, you can identity critical gaps in the existing infrastructure. Consequently, you will be able to build upon what already exists. The key lies in accurately identifying and fixing what will work as a part of the knowledge management system and what will not. There is no silver bullet for knowledge management– anything making that claim is fraught with immense risk. Although leveraging existing infrastructure is the logically, scientifically, rationally, theoretically, commonsensically, and financially right approach, it also stands a better chance of generating stronger management support for your knowledge management project because of the perception that you are not completely abandoning the "old" existing investments.

Specifically, as a part of this first step, we should focus on the following:

– Understanding the role ol your company's existing networks, intranet, and extranets in knowledge management. You will analyze, leverage, and build upon data mining, data warehousing, project management, and decision support system (DSS) tools that might already be in place.
– Understanding the knowledge management technology framework and its components.
– Considering the option of using knowledge servers for enterprise integration, and performing a preliminary analysis of business needs that match up with relevant knowledge server choices.
– Integrating existing intranets, extranets, and GroupWare into your knowledge management system.
– Understanding the limitations of implemented tools and identifying existing gaps in your company's existing technology infrastructure.
– Taking concrete steps to leverage and build upon existing infrastructural investments.

Step 2: Aligning KM and Business Strategy : Knowledge drives strategy, and strategy drives knowledge management. Without a clearly articulated link between knowledge management and business strategy, even the world's best knowledge management system will deliver zilch. Business strategy is usually at a high level, and lofty goals. Developing systems is always at a low level-- specifications and features are needed, not abstractions, visions, or business ideas. The second step in the 10-step road map allows you to make the connection between these two. Raise knowledge management system design to the level of business strategy and pull strategy down to the level of systems design. As a part of the process of creating this alignment between knowledge management and business strategy, do the following :

– Shift your company from strategic programming to strategic planning.
– Move your systems design practices and business decisions

away from the seemingly right orous, fallacious notion of making predictions using extrapolations from past data. You must shift this critical decision-making dependency on knowledge thai is both within and outside your company.

- Perform a knowledge-based SWOT (srrengths, weaknesses, opportunities and threats) analysis and create knowledge maps for your own company, your main competitors, and your industry or organization as a whole.
- Analyze knowledge gaps and identify how knowledge management can fill. Do a cost-benefit analysis to prioritize filling such gaps.
- Determine whether a codification or personalization focus is better suited for your company or organization.
- Balance exploitation, exploration, and just-in-time and just-in-case delivery supported by your knowledge management system.
- Before you can design your knowledge management system, determine the right diagnostic questions to ask.
- Translate your strategy-KM link to knowledge management system design characteristics. You must articulate a clear strategy-KM link and incorporate the 24 critical success factors in knowledge management design that we have learned from some exemplary knowledge management projects worldwide.
- Mobilize initiatives to help you "sell" your knowledge management project internally.
- Diagnose and validate your strategy-KM link, and use it to drive the resr of the design process.

When such alignment between your knowledge management and business strategy is clearly established from the outset, you can be sure that your knowledge management system is moving in a direction that holds promise for long-lasting competitive advantage and that it will *actually* benefit both your company's employees and its bottom line.

9.7.2. Knowledge Management System Analysis Design and Development

The second phase of knowledge management implementation involves analysis, design and development of the knowledge management system. The five steps that constitute this phase area

- Knowledge management architecture design and component selection,
- Knowledge audit and analysis,
- Knowledge management team design,
- Creation a knowledge management blueprint, and
- Actual systems development.

Let us briefly examine each of these steps and understand the key tasks that need to be accomplished at each step.

Step 3: Knowledge Management Architecture and Design: As the third step toward deploying knowledge management, you must select the infrastructural components that constitute the knowledge management system architecture. Knowledge management systems use a seven-layer architecture, and the technology required to build each layer is readily available. Integrating these components to create the knowledge management system model requires thinking in terms of an infostructure rather than an infrastructure.

Your first big choice is the collaborative platform. You can choose to use an open standard, such as the Web, or opt for a packaged solution such as Lotus Notes or a similar proprietary group support platform. You must also create profiling mechanisms for push-and pull-based knowledge delivery while balancing cost versus value-added for each additional enabling component. Specifically, as a part of this third step, you must:

- Comprehend various components of the knowledge infostructure,
- Identify internal and external knowledge source feeds that must be integrated,
- Choose IT components to find, create, assemble and apply knowledge,

- Identify elements of the interface layer– clients, server, gateways, and the platform,
- Decide on the collaborative platform– Web or Notes?
- Identify and understand components of the collaborative intelligence layer– artificial intelligence, data warehouses, genetic algorithms, neural networks, expert reasoning systems, rule bases, and case-based reasoning,
- Optimize knowledge object molecularity with your own company in mind,
- Balance cost against value-added for each enabling component,
- Balance push- and pull-based mechanisms for knowledge delivery,
- Identify the right mix of components for searching, indexing, and retrieval,
- Create knowledge tags and attributes– domain, form, type, product/service, time, and location tags,
- Create profiling mechanisms for knowledge delivery, and
- Retrofit IT on the SECI knowledge management model to validate your choices.

You do this after considering the ways in which work is done in your own company. The choice of these componenets will vary according to the different corporate cultures and work norms that exists in different companies.

Step 4 : Knowledge Audit and Analysis : A knowledge management pro|ect must begin with what your company already knows. In the fourth step, you audit and analyze knowledge, but first you must understand why a knowledge audit is needed. Then you assemble an audit team representing various organizational units. This team performs a preliminary assessment of knowledge assets within your company to identify those that are both critical and the weakest.

As a part of this step you will :

- Use Bohn's Stages of Knowledge Growth framework to measure process knowledge.

- Identify, evaluate, and rate critical process knowledge on an 8-point scale.
- Select an audit method out of several possible options.
- Assemble a preliminary knowledge audit team.
- Audit and analyze your company's existing knowledge.
- Identify your company's knowledge-spot.
- Choose a strategic position for your knowledge management system that is in line with the strategic gaps identified in step 2.

Step 5: Designing the Knowledge Management Team : In the fifth step on the knowledge management road map, you design the knowledge management team that design, build, implement, and deploy your company's knowledge management system, design an effective knowledge management team, you must identify key stakeholders b within and outside your company and identify sources of expertize that are needed to s cessfully design, build, and deploy the system while balancing the technical and manage requirements.

We examine the issues of correctly sizing the knowledge management team, managing diverse and often divergent stakeholder expectations and applying techniques for both identifying and avoiding critical failure points in such teams. Specifically, you must take the following steps to designs an effective team for implementing knowledge management:

- Identify key stakeholders – IT, management, and end users; and manage their expectation.
- Identify sources of requisite expertize.
- Identify critical points of failure in terms or unmet requirements, control, manageme buy-in, and end user buy-in.
- Balance the knowledge management team's constitution—organizationally, strategically and technologically.
- Balance technical and managerial expemse that forms a part of this team.
- Resolve team-sizing issues.

Step 6 : Creating the Knowledge Management System Blueprint : The knowledge management team identified in step 5 builds upon a knowledge management system blueprint that provides a plan for building and incrementally improving a knowledge management system. As you work towards designing a knowledge management architecture, you must understand its seven layers specifically in the context of your company and determine how each of these can be optimized for performance and scalability as well as high levels of interoperability.

Specifically, you will address the following issues in this step:

- Customize the details of the seven layers of the knowledge management architecture to your own company.
- Understand and select the components required by your company– integrative repositories, content centers, knowledge aggregation and mining tools, the collaborative platform, knowledge directories, the user interface options, push delivery mechanisms, and integrative elements.
- Design the system for high levels of interoperability with existing IT investments; optimize for performance and scalability.
- Understand and execute repository life-cycle management.
- Understand and incorporate the seven key user interface (UI) considerations.
- Position and scope the knowledge management system to a feasible level where benefits exceed costs.
- Make the build-or-buy decision and understand the trade offs.
- *Future proof* the knowledge management system so that it does not "run out of gas" when the next wave of fancy technology hits the market.

This step integrates work from all preceding steps so that it culminates in a strategically oriented knowledge management system design.

Step 7 : Developing the Knowledge Management System: Once you have created a blueprint for your knowledge management system, the next step is that of actually putting together a working system.

It you choose the Internet rather than depend on a properietary collaborative platform, you can convert your company intranet to a front end for your system.

Web-friendly document standards such as DMA (Document Management Alliance) and Web DMA provide a great opportunity to build collaborative document systems to industry standards. Even though users will see a familiar intranet interface that they are probably already used to, the fundamental shift caused by the knowledge management system at the back end is the reorientation from a client/server architecture to an agent-computing architecture.

We will look at occasionally feasible approaches to integrate an array of hardware including copiers, printers and scanners, built arround these standards into the knowledge management system itself. In this step, you will specifically :

- Develop the interface layer. Create platform independence, leverage the intranet, enable universal authorship, and optimize video and audio streaming.
- Develop the access and authentication layer. Secure data, control access, and distribute control.
- Develop the collaborative filtering and intelligence layer, using intelligent agents and collaborative filtering systems. Look at options to buy intelligent agents versus easy and free tools that can be used to build your own.
- Develop and integrate the application layer with the intelligence layer and the transport layer.
- Leverage the extant transport layer to take advantage of existing networks that already in place in your company.
- Develop the middleware and legacy integration layer to connect the knowledge management system both to true legacy data and "recent," inconsistent legacy data repositories and databases left behind by custom systems that your company needs to retire for reasons of cost or lack of functionality.
- Integrate and enhance the repository layer.

9.7.3. Phase 3 : Deployment

The third phase in the 10-step road map involves the process of deploying the knowledge management system that you built in the preceding stages. This phase involves two steps:

1. Deployment of the system with a results-driven incremental technique, more commonly known as the RDI method. This step also involves the selection and implementation of a pilot project to precede the introduction of a full-fledged knowledge management system.
2. Cultural change, revised reward structures, and the choice of using (or not using) a Chief Knowledge Officer (CKO) to make knowledge management produce results. This is perhaps the most important complementary step that is critical to the acceptance and the consequent success, or a knowledge management system in any company.

Step 8: Pilot Testing and Deployment Using the RDI Methodology : A large-scale project such as a typical knowledge management system must take into account the *actual* needs of its users. Although a cross-functional knowledge management team can help to uncover many of these needs, a pilot deployment is the ultimate reality check. In the eighth step on the knowledge management road map, you must decide how you can select knowledge management at least with the highest payoffs first.

Specifically, the deployment step requires you to:

- Understand the need for a pilot knowledge management system deployment, and evaluate the need to run one; if it is needed, select the right, nontrivial and representative pilot project.
- Identify and isolate failure points in pilot projects.
- Understand the knowledge management system life cycle and us implications for knowledge management system deployment.
- Eliminate the "big-bang" information packaging methodology, the waterfall methodology, and systems development life cycle (SDLC) orientation.

- Understand the scope of knowledge management system deployment.
- Use the RDI methodology to deploy the system, using cumulative results-driven business releases.
- Decide when to use prototypes, and when not to use them.
- Convert factors to processes.
- Create cumulative results-driven business releases by selecting releases with the highest payoffs first, and
- Identify and avoid the traps in the RDI methodology.

Well-executed deployment will ensure that the knowledge management system is well received by the users for whom it is built.

Step 9: CKO, Reward Structures, Technology and Change Management : The most erroneous assumption that many companies make is that the intrinsic value of an innovation such as a knowledge management system will lead to its enthusiastic adoption and use by their employees. Knowledge sharing cannot be mandated– your employees are not like troops; they are like volunteers. Encouraging use and gaining employee support require intel granon of business processes with knowledge management system use, and new reward structures that motivate employees to use the system and contribute to its infusion, championing and training. Above all, it requires enthusiastic leadership that sets an example to follow.

As part of this one but last step on the knowledge management road map, you need to:

- Understand the role of a chief knowledge officer and decide whether your company—big or small—needs to formally have a CKO at all. This decision further requires an understanding ol how a CKO relates to the CIO, CFO, and CEO. If you decide not to appoint a CKO, who else can best play that evangelist's role?
- Organize the four broad categories of the CKO's or knowledge manager's responsibilities. To do so, you must understand the CKO's technological and organizational

functions. We examine the backgrounds most successful CKOs come from.

- Enable process triggers for knowledge management system success.
- Plan for knowledge management success using the knowledge evangelist as an agent for selling foresight. Selling foresight is as hard as selling oxygen, but not as hard as selling the Brooklyn Bridge. It is difficult, but it can be done.
- Manage and implement cultural and process changes to make your knowledge management system as well as your knowledge management strategy succeed.

Many companies hastily appointed CKOs out of a fear of being left behind, only to realize later that they did not really need one.

9.7.4. Performance Evaluation

The last phase involves one step that most companies have been struggling with– measuring business value of knowledge management. When pushed for hard data, managers have often resorted to ill-suited and easily misused approaches, such as cost-benefit analysis, net present value (NPV) evaluation, vague ROI measures, or at best Tobin's *q*.

Step 10: Metrics for Knowledge Work : The tenth step—measuring return on knowledge investment —must account for both financial and competitive impacts of knowledge management on your business. This step guides you through the process of selecting an appropriate set of metrics and arriving at a lean but powerful composite.

In this last iterative step on the 10-step knowledge management road map, you will do the following:

- Understand how to measure the business impact of knowledge management, using a set of lean metrics.
- Calculate returns-on-investment (ROI) for knowledge management investments.
- Decide when to use benchmarking as a comparative knowledge metric.

– Evaluate knowledge management ROI using the Balanced Scorecard method.
– Use quality function deployment for creating strategic knowledge metrics.
– Identify and stay clear of the seven common measurement pitfalls, and identify what not to measure.

APQC's Road Map to Knowledge Management

Each stage illustrated in Figure 9.8 is described as if it were distinct from the others. In reality, the stages flow into each other, as different parts of the organization move at different speeds and various elements fall into place. For example, not all organizations begin their journey with Stage 1. Sometimes, Stage 2 marks the beginning of the KM journey because a manager simply wants to share knowledge in his or her business unit and sees KM as the solution to a problem.

Some firms move through the stages very quickly, learning from early adopters and barely stopping to notice they have moved to a whole new level of implementation. It is important to remember that the stages are a composite of the experiences of many companies.

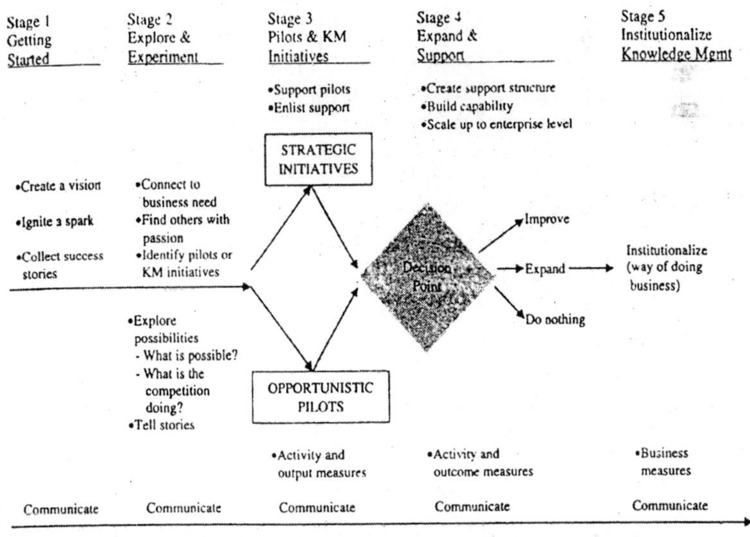

Fig. 9.8. APQC Road Map to Knowledge Management Results

- Review and select software tools for tracking complex metrics, QFDs, and BSCs.

We can also classify and evaluate processes using The *APQC Process Classification Framework.*

Being able to measure returns serves two purposes– It arms you with hard data and dollar figures that you can use to prove the impact of effective knowledge management, and it lets you refine knowledge management design through subsequent iterations.

This is all about knowledge management and its implmementation. Knowledge management is not solely a technology problem; it is partly a management problem. Only by aligning the two can you build knowledge management technology thai will truly enable effective knowledge management. Knowledge management can enhance an organization's performance but at the same time we should not forget that :

- *Knowledge management is not knowledge engineering*: Knowledge engineering has been a vital part of computer science but is barely even related to knowledge management. Knowledge management is a business problem and falls in the domain of information systems and management, not in computer science. Knowledge management needs to meld information systems and people in ways that knowledge engineering has never been able to.
- *Knowledge management is about process, not just digital networks*: Management of knowledge has to encompass and improve business processes. Agreed that *IT* is the biggest enabler for effective knowledge management if used correctly. However, Drucker warns that focusing on the Tand not the *I* in *IT* will deliver little. The *T* will never be used effectively if the people who are supposed to use it are not in the equation right from the start.

"Without a way of capturing and integrating past knowledge, any development process can quickly dissolve into chaos." Evidence from companies "loudly" suggests one thing–KM needs a knowledge culture driven by a performance-linked-to-reward system that encourages these knowledge workers to both pass along what they know and says "it's okay to admit that you do not know something."

- *Knowledge management is not about building a "smarter" intranet*: A knowledge management system can use your company's intranet, as its front end, but one should never be mistaken for the other. Saying that your intranet is your knowledge management system is something as senseless as saying that jetliner in the cockpit. The "just-add-water" approach traditionally used with packaged intranets collapses face down when used ior knowledge management. The internet is, however, a part of the equation that provides a stable messaging and collaboration platform.
- *Knowledge management is not about a one-time investment*: Knowledge management, like any other future-oriented investment, requires consistent attention over a substantial period of time even after it begins lo delivet results. KM critically requires metrics that allow businesses to measure its impact, provide room for improvement, and to provide a robust basis for resource allocation.
- *Knowledge management is not about enterprise-wide lnfobabns*: While enterprise integration helps, the primary focus of KM is on creating, getting, importing, delivering, and most importantly helping the right people apply the right knowledge at the right time. Knowledge management solutions must, therefore, reflect the way individuals and organizations have managed and shared information, albeit more effectively.
- *Knowledge management is not about "capture"*: Document management vendors would have you believe otherwise, bill knowledge management is not about capturing "knowledge." An inevitable loss of context occurs when documents are "sanitized" for use across the company. While a document management system lacks context, experience and insight, it still has a marginal place in knowledge management technology. Knowledge, in its entirety, cannot be captured. Overall, the understanding of the interplay between

knowledge management and business process redesign will continue to develop as enterprises seek new ways of redesigning their business processes in a world of rapid learning and constant change. Knowledge management will increasingly be seen as an activity that can be intimately linked and grounded in the execution of business processes, and business processes will increasingly be seen as a nexus of enterprise knowledge.

10

Ethical and Legal Issues in Knowledge Management

Knowledge management is a discipline that promotes an integrated approach to identifying, managing and sharing all of an enterprise's information assets. This discipline discusses the managerial implications of this evolving concept. However there are other issues that arise at each and every stage of knowledge development.

These can be broadly categorized into-ethical issues and legal issues.

10.1. ETHICAL ISSUES

You cannot separale technology and its uses and still be ethically and socially responsible. As a professional, you must explore how the technology you create will be used. Ethics are standards of conduct that are agreed upon by cultures and organizations. Potter Stewart defines ethics as knowing the difference between what you have a right to do and what is right to do. It is important that information professionals act according to the highest ethical standards or else face increased governmental intervention.

Often, when professionals in the data industry are asked what they think of their ethical obligation concerning databases and data mining, their response is that they are obligated to follow the letter of the law. Of course, they must adhere to the law. But ethics are often times more restrictive than what is called for by the law. Sadly, there are a number of information professionals who either lack an awareness of what their companies actually do with data, or purposely come to the conclusion that it is not their business. They are enablers in the sense that they solve management's problems. What management does with that data is not their concern.

Are there guidelines or an ethical code to help database experts as they grapple with ethical dilemmas? Should there be such guidelines? Many people in the IS arena say no. They argue it is not their place to decide how data is used, but rather up to others in the organization to make that determination. But what is the ethical obligation of an IS professional who, through whatever means, finds out that the data that he or she has been asked to gather or "mine" is going to be used in a manner that they believe is unethical. The answer to that question, of course, has to be addressed individually, based on one's own ethical standards. But as data mining becomes more commonplace and as companies push for even greater profits and marketshare, IS professionals will increasingly encounter ethical dilemmas.

Article 31 of *The Direct Marketing Association 's Guidelines for Ethical Business Practice* states that "Marketers should be sensitive to the issue of consumer privacy and should only collect, combine, rent, sell, exchange, or use marketing data. Marketing data should be used only for marketing purposes". Essentially, what is of the utmost importance to consumers is that information collected for one purpose should not be analyzed for an unrelated secondary purpose unless it is clearly compatible with the original purpose. Michael Turner, Executive Director of the Information Services Executive Council, a New York-based affiliate of the Direct Marketing Association, states, "For instance, detailed consumer information lets apparel retailers market their products to consumers with more precision. But if privacy rules impose restrictions and barriers to data collection, those limitations could increase the prices consumers pay when they buy from catalogue or online apparel retailers by 3.5 percent to 11 percent". Obviously, if retailers cannot target their advertising, then their only option is to mass advertise, which drives up costs. Technological advances make it possible to track in great detail what a person does in his or her personal life. With this profile of personal details comes a substantial ethical obligation to safeguard this data from disclosure to unauthorized individuals. Ignoring any legal ramifications, the ethical responsibility is firmly placed on information professionals and businesses whether they like it or not. Otherwise, they risk lawsuits and harm individuals in the process.

The data industry has come under harsh review. There is a raft of federal and local laws under consideration to control the collection, sale and use of data. American companies have yet to match the tougher privacy regulations already in place in Europe, while personal and class-action litigation against businesses over data privacy issues is increasing.

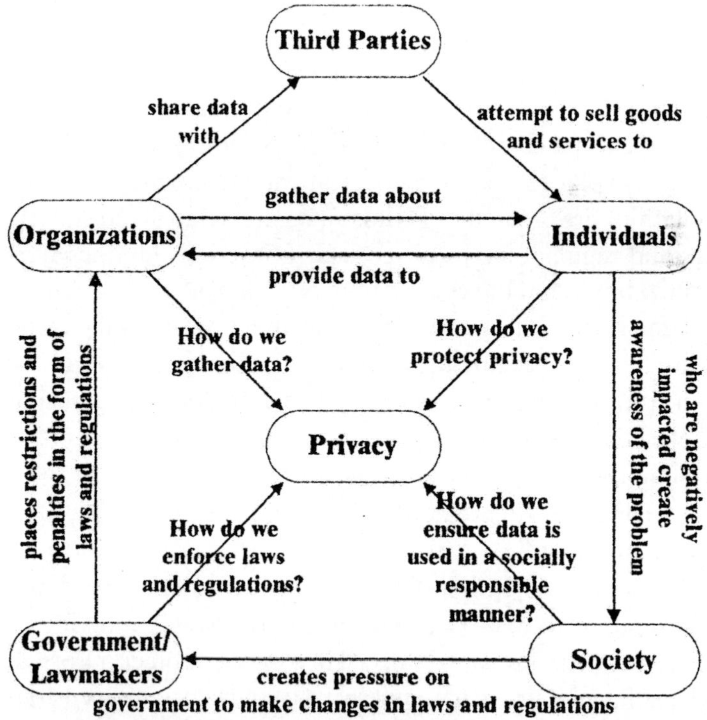

Fig. 10.1. Ethical Violations often fuel the creation of Laws and Regulations

Figure 10.1 demonstrates the iterative nature of how business practices create ethical dilemmas that harm individuals who assert pressure on society to create laws and regulations that change business practices. In following the outer loop of the diagram starting at the top-left, what often happens is that organizations, through some unethical activity, ultimately harm one or more individuals. In addition to gathering data about purchases, businesses oftentimes share information with others who are required to process the order. For example, payment credit card clearing houses and package delivery companies must be informed of the order, where to pick it up, who to deliver it to, and sometimes the contents of the shipment as well. These third party providers also must adhere to the highest ethical standards, but sometimes, based on this shared data, these third parties attempt to sell goods and services directly to individuals – the consumers or sell the data to others. Following the top-right-hand side of Figure 10.1, individuals who are negatively impacted by this experience create an awareness of the problem in society and help build pressure within society for lawmakers to address the issue. As illustrated by the bottom part of Figure 10.1, society creates pressure on the government and lawmakers to create laws and regulations; if enough pressure is placed upon the government and lawmakers, laws and regulations are created. It is illustrated at the left-hand side. These laws and regulations, in turn, place restrictions and penalties on organizations, and the cycle continues. Like all cycles, sometimes laws and regulations go too far in one direction or another, whether we are talking about being too restrictive for businesses or too lax in terms of protecting consumers. The situation where businesses are placed under too many restrictions ultimately harms consumers through, for example, inflated marketing costs.

The inner square deals with social and ethical implications that are presented. Organizations are concerned with the question of "How do we gather data?" without posing problems for individuals with respect to their right to privacy. Individuals are concerned with the question of "How do we protect ourprivacy?" while still maintaining national security and consuming customized goods and services? Sadly, many consumers have become accustomed or, more accurately, resigned to the fact that businesses gather personal information about them, often surreptitiously. With enough individuals concerned about privacy, society is concerned with the question of "How do we ensure data is used in a socially responsible manner?"

Lawmakers and the government must then be charged with the task of answering the question of "How do we enforce these laws and regulations?" Oftentimes, laws and regulations are created by society - not to protect the individual, but rather to protect society itself. Consider what would happen if such laws and regulations did not exist. In that case, consumers might stop giving information, at least accurate information, if they were concerned about privacy. Then, information about purchasing behaviour and all other aspects of society would become limited and unavailable to those who need to make decisions. So, although laws and regulations are often in response to abuses perpetrated by organizations on individuals, in reality, society is acting in its own self-interest. Those who make laws and regulations understand the importance, in this case, of information in our economy. Even privacy advocates concede there are benefits to society when personal data is shared. Privacy advocates do not argue that consumer information should not be shared, but rather that consumers themselves should be given the option of how much information is shared and with whom.

Businesses are correct when they complain that much of the regulatory initiatives are driven by unusual cases of misuse of information. However, society is predisposed to believe the worst. These stories of misuse only confirm its pre-existing fears. Therefore, businesses must be sensitive to how the public perceives their business practices, which include data mining. In an attempt to elevate data privacy to the level of importance that it should have within an organization, some organizations have created a management position known as ihe chief privacy officer, who attempts to limit liabilities or issues surrounding data collection, data storage and data mining.

This cycle is best illustrated with an example. Suppose, based on your participation in a chat room or mailing lisl or your surfing behaviour, someone deduces that either you or someone close to you has a terminal illness. First, what if you wanted this information to remain private? Second, how could such information be used in an unethical manner. May be you would start receiving solicitations for donation from organizations that are seeking cures for this illness. Even worse, what if you began to receive otters for cures that at best, have questionable chances of success? Data-mining and profiling techniques that allow companies to identify their best customers could just as easily be used by unscrupulous businesses to zero in on vulnerable customers - the elderly the poor the sick, and the unsophisticated - offering them inferior or predatory deals.

This is the time when we should have some code of ethics. Some model codes are given use for consideration.

10.1.2. Corporate Codes of Ethics

Regulations now require a firm to have a code of ethics, though many firms have had such a code for a long time. It is interesting to note that Enron has a code of ethics, and that the board agreed to suspend it to allow some of Enron's executives to participate in the partnerships that removed debt from the balance sheet. A code is only useful if it is followed. Raytheon, a large defense contractor, has an extensive Web site devoted to ethics. Its comprehensive ethics statement follows:

"Our Reputation—A Foundation Built on Personal Integrity and Ethical Principles"

Throughout its history, Raytheon has been a global leader in technology and systems development. Our continued growth, profitability and prosperity are linked to our employees' ability to make decisions that are consistent with Raytheon's business values and core ethical principles. By embedding these business values and principles in our policies and practices, Raytheon has established an ethical business culture that is accepted by its employees and woven into the fabric of the ways in which we work. We are an exceptional company, committed to:

Integrity : We are honest and forthright in our dealings with employees, customers, suppliers, teammates, competitors, shareholders and the community. We conduct our business with respect for laws and regulations and we promote individual responsibility to ensure that all actions are based on the highest ethical standards.

Respect : We treat others as we would want to be treated—attentive to personal dignity and receptive to diversity of ideas. We recognize the value that comes from respecting individuality, personal experience and varied heritages.

Teamwork : We value teams because they promote trust, openness, challenge, opportunity and growth. We join with each other, our customers and our suppliers to provide high-value solutions to complex problems, requirements and demands.

Quality : We believe that quality and continuous process improvement are fundamental to the way we develop, manufacture, and support our products and services. We are customer-driven—striving to meet and exceed expectations in all that we do.

Innovation : We build on our heritage of technological excellence through creative thinking, novel ideas and practical solutions. Customer success is enhanced through our technology leadership and program execution. We encourage, recognize and reward our employees for being creative, resourceful and productive.

Citizenship : We give back to the communities where we live and work. We serve as stewards of the environment and strive to leave the world better for having been a good corporate citizen in the global marketplace.

These principles support and guide our leadership in establishing the strategic direction of the company. Our employees, representatives, and suppliers are expected to conduct their business in accordance with these ethical principles. We must do more than be compliant with laws, regulations and policies; we must work according to our ethical principles and endeavour to conduct ourselves in a manner beyond reproach. Raytheon's reputation is based on the personal integrity of each of its employees and those with whom we do business. Sound judgment must be exercised in the service of our reputation as a global business leader, employer of choice and good corporate citizen.

Many corporations have codes of ethical conduct and some

are quite extensive. A statement of corporate ethics provides guidelines for managers and is a valuable part of corporate governance.

10.1.3. Ethics For Information Technology Professionals

A professional code of conduct for computer professionals was developed by the Association for Computing Machinery, a society of individuals who teach and work in the field. This code applies peripherally to users and managers who may work with technology, but who do not consider themselves professionals. Ethical considerations include the following concerns:

- Data in the organization are used for their intended purpose and the intended purpose is legitimate.
- Monitoring of workers is undertaken with their consent and the data are used to help rather than punish the workers involved.
- Systems and services made available to individuals external to the firm behave as specified and cause no harm to others.
- Systems within the firm are not guilty of harassment.
- Appropriate privacy is maintained, for example, e-mail files are not read by individuals not involved in the exchange of messages.
- Appropriate software copyrights are observed and intellectual property is respected.
- Systems are secured and well controlled.

Ethical decisions arise frequently when dealing with information technology. Mason suggested how to identify and approach a situation where ethical considerations arise.

The crucial point occurs when a moral agent—one that by definition has choices— decides to change the state of information or information technology in a human system.Changes in hardware, software, information content, information flow, knowledge-based jobs and the rules and regulations affecting information are among the many things that agents do that affect others. We must use our moral imagination to guide our choices so that we can contribute positively toward making the kind of ethical world in which we want to live and want to bequeath to our future generations. How can we do this? Fundamental is our conscience, aided by our understanding and expertize in information technology. If we have an inkling our behaviour . . . might in some way harm others, we probably should examine our decisions a tittle more carefully and from an ethical point-of-view.

The facts of an ethical situation can be summarized by four factors. The first factor is to clearly identify the moral agent. Whose actions will bring about the technology-induced change? The next factor is the set of alternative courses-of-action available to the agent. These are the real world acts that will have an effect on the human system under consideration. Acts have consequences, hence the third factor is delineation of the results that are expected to occur if each act is taken. Finally, it is essential to identify the stakeholders who will be affected by the consequences of the acts, stakeholders have an interest in what the agent does.

It is easy to choose ethical behaviour in a classroom setting when discussing a case study. It is much more difficult when working in an organization and facing budgetary constraints and pressure from peers, customers, top management and stockholders. Kallman and Grillo suggest several informal guidelines for ethical behaviour:

- *The family test*: Would you be comfortable telling your closest family members about your decision or action?
- *The investigative reporter test*: How would your actions look if reported in a newspaper or on a television news program?
- *The feeling test*: How does the decision feel to you? If you are uneasy about a decision or action but cannot understand why, your intuition is telling you it is not the right thing to do.
- *The empathy test*: How does this decision look if you put yourself in someone else's position? How would it look to another party affected by your actions?

Significant lapses in business ethics in the United States and around the world create a new awareness of the need for ethical behaviour in highly interdependent societies and economies. The ethical issues surrounding technology are probably easier than most and knowledge helps you make the right decisions.

10.1.4. Ethical Use of Technology

A number of ethical issues are concerned with information technology. These issues are related to privacy, data collected online, especially from individuals visiting different Web sites, the piracy of digital content, workplace monitoring, security and spam.

Privacy : The present basis of personal privacy protection is the U.S. Constitution, various Supreme Court rulings, and laws such as the 1971 Fair Credit Reporting Act, the 1978 Right of Financial Privacy Act, and the 1974 Privacy Act, which deals with the release of government records. More recently the Children's Online Privacy Act of 1998 was passed; it prohibits collection of children's information from those thirteen years and younger from Web sites without permission from their parents. Certain Web sites must obtain parental consent before collecting personal information from children. With some exceptions, sites also must obtain parental consent before collecting, using, or disclosing personal information from children.

The United States and Europe have quite different views of privacy. The European Union has a law that prohibits the purchase and sale of personal data, something quite common in the United States. The law basically makes it illegal to use information about a customer in ways the customer never intended, which means that a firm cannot sell data to another company to use for marketing purposes. A key provision of the law is a prohibition for any company doing business in the European Union from transmitting personal data to a country that does not guarantee comparable privacy protection—namely the United States. The United States has a much more relaxed policy, relying primarily on industry self-regulation. One fear is that this legislation could have a chilling effect on electronic commerce.

The difficulty is in determining at what point the right to privacy conflicts with other rights. Society certainly has the need and the right to have certain kinds of information that contributes to the general welfare. Demographic information and information on income levels are vitally important in establishing national policy. Information on wages and financial conditions, however, is considered to be extremely sensitive by most individuals. Individuals should have the right to ascertain whether information held about them is correct and to enforce the correction of errors. However, less agreement surrounds the issue of penalties imposed for misuse of private information maintained in some type of data bank. Other questions arise as to whether individuals should have the right to know who requested information about them from a data bank because this requirement forces a great deal of costly record keeping on the part of the owner of the data.

Some legislators in the United States are concerned about the practice of state governments selling data. A number of states sell access to automobile registration data. Direct-mail marketing organizations use auto registration information to target mailings. In other instances, individuals obtain the license plate numbers of a group attending a meeting and use that information to harass the attendees.

The Web introduces another privacy concern – companies collecting information about people who visit their Web site without the visitor's knowledge. The Federal Trade Commission (FTC) conducted a recent survey; a group of agency lawyers surfed the Web for two weeks, visiting some 1,400 sites. Of these sites, more than 90 percent collected personal information from visitors, but only 14 percent of them disclosed how the information would be used. The FTC concluded that some form of formal regulation is needed and that self-regulation of the Internet had largely failed.

A Japanese committee studied privacy issues in Japan and suggested the following guidelines:

- Personal data may only be collected with the consent of the individuals concerned. For example, the recommendation applies to the use of cookies, because using cookies to gather historical information on personal Web access patterns is "possible without the consent of the individuals concerned."
- An individual should have the right to veto the use of personal data, so that personal data already available to an online

service provider cannot be used or transferred to a third party without the consent of the individual concerned.

– To ensure the proper management of personal data, a manager within the organization who understands the objectives of the guidelines and who is capable of implementing them should be appointed to manage the personal data.

A number of suggested ethical codes of conduct concerns privacy. The Computer Professionals for Social Responsibility offer the following guidelines from the Code of Fair Information Practices.

- *Promote Information Privacy* : Computer Professionals- for Social Responsibility (CPSR) and Privacy International.
- *Stop Data Misuse* : Personal information obtained for one purpose should not be used for another purpose without informed consent.
- *Encourage Data Minimization* : Collect only the information necessary for a particular purpose. Dispose of personally identifiable information where possible.
- *Promote Data Integrity* : Ensure the accuracy, reliability, completeness and timeliness of personal information.
- *Allow Data Inspection* : Notify record subjects about record-keeping practices and data use. Allow individuals to inspect and correct personal information. Do not create secret record-keeping systems.
- *Establish Privacy Policies* : Establish and enforce an information privacy policy. Make the policy publicly available.

As a manager you may be in a position to either collect or purchase data from customers or suppliers. In such a position, you will be concerned about privacy and any other ethical issues involved. You may want to ask how the data you collect could be misused, and how it could damage the customer and your company.

10.2. LEGAL ISSUES

Every legitimate business operates in a legal environment. Contracts, taxataion and copyrights are among the issues that fall under the legal system. Many questions that arise from knowledge ownership are not settled. But new laws can change the rules and plug loopholes in this emerging areas. In an age of prolific litigation, library professionals should be aware of the legal ramifications arising from knowledge sharing. The legal issues are concerned with

— The Liability question
— Liability of the knowledge developer
— Liability of the expert
— Liability of the user

Knowledge - a product or a service? This is also a serious question.

Librarians deal with knowledge in the present technological environment. In terms of legal ownership of knowledge, the question of whether knowledge is a product or service attracts varied opinions.

One legal opinion suggests that if knowledge is codified in a package and sold as a mass marketed item, then it is a product. If the package is custom designed, then it is viewed as a service.

Hence, knowledge can be a product as well as a service depending upon the situation and dimension how it is dispensed with. Knowledge, is concerned with certain products when a discussion of legal and ethical issues are discussed. They are :

— Copyright
— Trademark and
— Tradenames

All the above three items fall under the Intellectual Property Law. As Librarians, the information professionals are concerned with copyright with which information and documents are rightly concerned.

10.2.1. Copyright

Copyright is the ownership of an intellectual property within the limits prescribed by a particular nation's or international law. Copyright is the legal right granted to an author, composer, playwriter, publisher, or distributor to exclusive publication, production, sale, or distribution of a literary, musical, dramatic, or artistic work. The legal ownership of a work can take any of the following forms: written text, program source code, graphics images, sculpture, music, sound recording, motion picture, pantomime, choreograph and architecture.

In general the copyright law provides that the owner of a property has the exclusive right to print, distribute and copy the work and permission must be obtained by anyone else to reuse the work in these ways. Copyright is provided automatically to the author of any original work covered by the law as soon as the work is created. The author does not have to formally register the work, although registration makes the copyright more visible. Copyright extends to unpublished as well as published works. The law extends copyright for 50 years beyond the life of the author. For works by an anonymous author or an author who uses a fictitious name–pseudonymous, as well as works "made for hire," such as a publication written by an employee of a company, the copyright lasts 120 years from date of creation or 95 years from date of publication, whichever is shorter. For reviews and certain other purposes, the "fair use" of a work, typically a quotation or paragraph, is allowed without permission of the author.

10.2.2. Internet and Copyright

The Internet, one of the most remarkable developments in international communication and information access, is fastly becoming a home of copyright accuse. The notion of freedom of information and the ease of posting, copying and distributing messages on the Internet may have created a false impression that text and graphic materials on World Wide Web sites, postings in "usenet" news groups and messages distributed through e-mail lists and other electronic channels are exempt from copyright statutes. Generally speaking, facts may not be copyrighted; but content related to presentation, organization and conclusions derived from facts certainly can be.

10.2.3. Copyrights, Patents and Trademarks

Copyright is distinct from other forms of author protection such as *patents*, which give inventors exclusive rights over use of their inventions, and *trademarks*, which are legally protected words or symbols that represent products or services. Whereas a patent protects the application of an idea and a trademark protect a device that indicates the provider of particular services or goods, copyright protects the expression of an idea. And whereas the operative notion in patents is novetly, so that a patent represents some invention that is new and has never been made before, the basic concept behind copyright is originality, so that a copyright represents something that has originated from a particular author and not from another. Copyrights, patents and trademarks are all examples of what is known in the law as intellectual property.

10.3. INTELLECTUAL PROPERTY RIGHTS

Intellectual property rights or IPR has been called a subtle and esoteric area of the law that evolves in response to technological change. It connotes the right to literary, artistic and scientific work; performances of performing artists; phonographs and broadcast; inventions in all fields of human endeavour; scientific discoveries; industrial design, trademarks; service marks and commercial names and designations and all other products resulting from intellectual activity in the industrial, scientific, literary and artistic fields. It is a generic term covering patents, registered design, trademarks, copyright, layout of integrated circuits, trade secretes, geographical indicators and anticompetitive practices in contractual licenses.

The developments of information and communication have brought major changes in the working of libraries and information centers working. Now a days, information is being produced, processed, stored and distributed in digital form through electronic networks, i.e., CD-ROM network, LAN, WAN and Internet globally. Web-based information can be accessed within a fraction of minutes anywhere at anytime. On one hand, it facilitates fast accessing on the similar time, it has created many problems; of which, IPR is the one.

The copyright law, which was framed in printing era by and large being force on the existing electronic/digital environment so there is a need to modify IPR, which confers exclusive right to the author to exploit the work created by him and the author should not make exercise profit and should not become barrier in the free flow of information. Currently, the issue of copyright in the networked digital environment is being debated all over the world. As communications and the exchange of information cross borders rapidly and easily, the impact of domestic copyright laws has become muted. In a number of developed nations, including Canada, the United Kingdom, other members of the European Union (EU) and the United States, copyright is a form of protection provided by laws to the authors of original works of authorship. These include literary, dramatic, musical, artistic, and other intellectual works. This protection is available to both published and unpublished works.

As far as our country India, is concerned, first legislation on copyright was framed in 1914 that was based on the UK copyright act of 1911. After independence, some changes were made into it and it was known as Indian copyright act 1957. Later, it has been revised so many times in 1983, 1984, 1992, 1994 and 1999 to incorporate further advancement yet is silent on the status of electronic publications. IT Act 2000 has defined cyber law as a 'term which refers to all the legal and regulatory aspects of Internet and the World Wide Web'. Anything that concerns with or related to or to emanating from any legal aspects or issues concerning any activity of netizens and other, on Internet in Cyber Space comes within the ambit of Cyber Law besides, IPR and copyright.

The genius of United States copyright law is that it balances the intellectual property rights of authors, publishers and copyright owners with society's need for the free exchange of ideas. Taken together, fair use and other public rights to utilize copyrighted works, as established in the Copyright Act of 1976, constitute indispensable legal doctrines for promoting the dissemination of knowledge, while ensuring authors, publishers and copyright owners protection of their creative works and economic investments. The preservation and continuation of these balanced rights in an electronic environment are essential to the free flow of information and to the development of an information infrastructure that serves the public interest. Although the emerging information infrastructure is raising awareness of technological changes that pose challenges to copyright systems, the potential impact of technology was anticipated by the passage of the Copyright Act of 1976. Congress expressly intended that the revised copyright law would apply to all types of media. With few exceptions, the protections and provisions of the copyright statute are as relevant and applicable to an electronic environment as they are to a print and broadcast environment.

The U.S. and Canada have adopted very different approaches to intellectual property and copyright issues. For example, the Canadian Copyright Act does not contain the special considerations for library and educational use found in the U.S. Copyright Act of 1976, nor does it place federal or provincial government works in the public domain. Because of these differences, this statement addresses these issues from the U.S. perspective.

Only in the last 50 years have many nations begun to realize the massive cultural, social and economic benefits of protecting intellectual property. With technology beginning to pose new dilemmas for both content owners and users, the library community should be eminently qualified to maintain a balance in the law.

10.3.1. Factors to be considerered

It is a fact that much abuse of intellectual property rights is taking place on the web. Most of the contents of many 'adult' sites for example are digitized without the knowledge or consent of the copyright owners or indeed the subject(s). The modern copyright law is completelyinadequate to the task of dealing with computers or networks in any reasonable manner. In particular the interpretations of what constitutes copying of a work have been alternately both liberal and harsh in the recent past. In some sense, the Web is a publishing medium and the owners of intellectual property must recognize that once published, many people will make lots of uses of their intellectual property in ways they have anticipated and some that are unforeseen. The key is where you may deprive the owner/author of income, which they might expect to receive.

The libraries as a service provider, have allowed their users to read a document, to browse the whole document, to browse whole collection, to search their catalogues, to supply xerox copy for individual use, to procure other's library material on inter-library loan either in whole or xerox of particular page, a clearing centers, to distribute reproduced copies of documents requiring public awareness etc. whether these activities will continue in digital era?

Today we have a lot of information in digital format and with the advancement in information and communication technologies this is being increasingly adopted in our lives. Digital information is being generated in two ways– by converting the existing documents in to digital form or the contents which are 'born digital' In the later case, there is no need of conversion because they are born originally as digital. Digital resources are the set of electronic sources enabled by technical capabilities to create, search and use enormous amount of information. They are the excellent complementary addition to the maximum use of information. Digital resources manipulate digital data in any medium like text, images, sounds, and static or dynamic images.

There should be a *digital preservation policy* for the digital preservation. A policy can be defined as a course or general plan of action adopted by a governmental body, party or person. It gives general direction for the whole of an organization, and as such it remains on a reasonably high level. A digital preservation policy would state the principles and long-term direction that would guide preservation strategies and actions. The primary aims of a policy should be to provide guidance and authorization on the preservation of digital materials and to ensure the authenticity, reliability and long-term accessibility of them. Moreover, a policy should explain how digital preservation can serve major needs of an institution and state some principles and rules on specific aspects which then laid the basis of implementation.

1. General Principles : Digital preservation is crucial as part of a series of other issues which effect the creation, storage and use of a resource. These issues are all inter-dependent and have suggested the need for an integrated policy framework to develop a cost-effective approach resource creation, preservation and use. An integrated policy framework may also assist funding agencies in maximizing their scholarly and financial investment in the creation of primary and secondary data resources, and data creators in maximizing the cost effectiveness, fitness for purpose, and design, of their digitization programmes.

There should be some principles to be followed; some of them for qualifying this activity are :

— A policy needs to induce a common understanding of the objectives, of whether each collection item should be preserved with maximum effort possibly applying multiple preservation paths, or whether a certain pragmatism should be pursued;

— A digital policy should facilitate the sustainability of an institution's present and future digital holdings;

— A digital preservation policy has to demonstrate its benefits, its effectiveness;

— A digital policy should be connected and integrated with a risk assessment document;

— Every policy should be practicable, not definitive, capable of being put into practice by institutions with varying resources and needs, and, especially, flexible to adapt itself to changing administrative and technological circumstances;

— A policy should be characterized by clarity, adequacy, transparency, efficiently, effectiveness and logical organization of contents;

— A digital preservation policy should be written in a simple and suitable language, without redundancies and, at the same time, without lowering the level of quality contained in its contents; and

— Once a digital preservation policy is operative, it should be re-thorough, reviewed or newly conceived on a regular basis to take into account changes in the organizational, legal and technical environment and to make rules and guidelines more precise and explicit where there is any ambiguity about implementation.

Besides, a digital policy should offer achievable solutions, provide for the management training and, finally, be maintained through time.

2. Benefits of Digital Preservation Policy : The challenges posed by digital information have increasingly led to recognition of the inter-dependence between the stages of creation, use and preservation of digital resources and the importance of the legal and economic environments in which they operate. The potential volume of information which could be acquired or digitized, and the need to make the most cost-effective use of limited resources, have emphasized the need for selection, standards and co-operation between different organizations. Organizations are developing internal policies for the creation, management, and preservation of digital resources and increasingly are sharing their experience in this field.

A digital preservation policy could guarantee many benefits at each institutional level, such as ensuring digital materials available for current and future use, providing a comprehensive statement on this theme and planning coherent digital preservation programmes. Besides, the formulation of a policy allows to deal with difficult subjects as the short-lasting life span and small capacities of digital materials, the obsolescence of the hardware required to access them, the obsolescence of software for reading the data and file formats and, finally, the structural and technical heterogeneity of the different types of digital materials.

3. Scope and Objectives of Digital Preservation Policy : The main scope of a digital preservation policy is to achieve the following objectives:

— Preserving and providing continued access to digital material, both born digital and digitized material;

— Ensuring that preserved digital materials are authentic;

— Preserving damage and deterioration of the physical media by ensuring an environmental control;

— Reversing damage, if it is possible; and

— Changing the format of digital materials to preserve their intellectual content, if it is necessary.

In a digital environment, the framework and preservation may include institutions with a traditional interest in long-term preservation but also extend to a wider range of individuals and institutions which have a short-term or even indirect interest in this process.

The digital information covered by the framework can be the primary form of the data, surrogate versions of primary information held in digital or physical form, or the metadata for collection management of these objects. The framework recognizes that digital media are new, distinctive and require new approaches to their preservation. At the same time it recognizes that these approaches may need to be integrated with those for other media and, where relevant, should draw on the existing and extensive professional experience in managing them. It recognizes that individuals and organizations may be responsible for hybrid resources consisting of a mixture ot digital and other media, or solely focused on information in a digital form. The framework will therefore be applicable to those seeking to extend and modify existing policies for traditional collections to include digital information and for those developing data policies for purely digital collections.

People who has responsibility in the developing and implementation of a digital preservation policy should carry out the following functions:

- making decisions of retention, use and preservation of digital materials at the acquisition or creation stage, not later;
- establishing maintenance procedures and quality control within monitoring processes and programmes;
- establishing and implementing strategies for digital preservation, such as migration, emulation or technology preservation;
- developing a disaster recovery programme;
- ensuring security of access to digital materials.

In additions, the following are some points, which are to be solved while we talk about the intellectual property rights:

— In case of the digitization, can the transmission of digitized text through Internet be considered as commercial distribution or public communication?

— Is database, a collective work to be protected by copyright law? What can be considered fair use in Internet environment?

— Whether libraries should be prevented from employing digital technology to preserve the work?

— In general, when the data are collected for personal use only, you may claim protection under the fair use provisions of copyright law but to what extent do you have a copy of the data from a site constitute an infringement is unclear. For example, were you to collect the daily strip each day, it could be argued you were about to deprive the author of some of his anthology book income from you. Will proving you own a complete set of such books constitute rebuttal? Certainly collecting such information and making it available in its collected form is likely to draw the attention of the owners and quite rightly so.

— The storing of other people's data is also a burning point. Web sites effectively give away their data for free as part of their publishing process. It is in fact what this paper is relying on as a mechanism underlying its operations. Nevertheless, the idea that some surfers are making more permanent copies of this data sits uncomfortably with some information providers. Some sites will never even realize that they have been mined. Others may well be keeping careful watch. Some will simply notice in their agent log files that a 'Python-agent visited their site. If you visit often enough to annoy, you may also expect to be noticed.

— The other problem is of linking other people's data. In fact, the web refers to the connectivity from one site to another. Without such links between disparate places, the web would not be a web at all so much as a collection of little islands. The now ubiquitous advertising banners serve to take up a lot of slack here and are tacitly approved by both parties to the link but it will still be severe blow to the web if such links are found to breach intellectual property rights. The last word has yet to be written on this issue but it bodes poorly for the existence of search engines at all if it is allowed to stand. The question of jurisdiction when links are transnational will also be a challenge.

The exporting of other people's data constitutes other problem. This is clearly an infringement of the law as it stands and in fact you are unlikely to find anyone supporting the position that you should be allowed to take his or her data and make commercial use of it. In this sense web publishing will remain like all other forms of publishing. Having said this, the web like traditional paper publishing features a number of data sources which are effectively free for all. These include, open public records, data that the owner wants to have widely disseminated and data, which is otherwise clearly marked as for public use.

10.3.2. Suggestions

The Copyright should be existed for the public goodness and to promote the progress of Science and Useful Arts. The fundamental purpose of copyright is to serve the public interest by encouraging the advancement of knowledge through a system of exclusive but limited rights for authors and copyright owners. So, there is a need to revise the present national laws as suggested by IFLA or to make a universal copyright law, which must be accepted by all nations of the world. IFLA has suggested various points in relation to digital information and libraries as under:

(i) IFLA believes that the benefits of new technologies should be available to all and the information should be accessed regardless of format. In national copyright legislations exceptions, allowed in the Beme conventions and other similar right convention, should be revised if necessary to assume that permitted uses apply equally to information in electronic form and to information in print.

(ii) The lending of published electronic resources by libraries for cultural and educational purposes should not be restricted by legislation.

— Fair use and other relevant provisions are the essential means by which teachers teach, students learn, and researchers advance knowledge. So, fair use, the library, and other relevant provisions of the Copyright must be preserved in the development of the emerging information infrastructure.

— The digital works of enduring value need to be preserved just as research libraries have long preserved printed works. Libraries have traditionally undertaken archival responsibilities because publishers and database producers have generally preserved particular knowledge only as long as it has economic value in the marketplace. As with other formats, the preservation of electronic information will be the responsibility of libraries and they will continue to perform this important societal role. So, the policy framework of the emerging information infrastructure must provide for the archiving of electronic materials by research libraries to maintain permanent collections and environments for public access. Accomplishing this goal will require strengthening the library provisions of the copyright law to allow preservation activities that use electronic or other appropriate technologies as they emerge.

— The library community has recognized that there will be a variety of payment methods for the purchase of copyrighted materials in electronic formats, just as there are differing contractual agreements for acquiring printed information. The research library community is committed to working with publishers and database producers to develop model agreements that deploy licenses that do not contract around fair use or other copyright provisions. But, the licensing agreements should not be allowed to abrogate the fair use and library provisions authorized in the copyright statute.

— Institutions of learning must continue to employ policies and procedures that encourage copyright compliance. Here, the librarians and educators should have an obligation to educate information users about their rights and responsibilities under intellectual property law. The librarians should continue to work as catalyst for the fee flow of information between users and creators of information.

— Copyright should not be applied to government information. This is the fundamental principle of democratic government — that the open exchange of public information is essential to the functioning of a free and open society. The government information should remain in the public domain free of copyright or copyright-like restrictions. Only under selected circumstances, it should be made restricted for public use.

— The research library community affirms that the distribution of copyrighted information, which exceeds fair use, and the enumerated limitations of the law require the permission of and/or compensation to authors, publishers and copyright owners. The continuation of library provisions and fair use in an electronic environment has far greater potential to promote the sale of copyrighted materials than to substitute for purchase. There is every reason to believe that the increasing demand for and use of copyrighted works fostered by new information technologies will result in the equivalent or even greater compensation for authors, publishers and copyright owners. But, the information infrastructure must permit authors to be compensated for the success of their creative works, and copyright owners must have an opportunity for a fair return on their investment. The information infrastructure however, must be based on an underlying ethos of abundance rather than scarcity. With such an approach, authors, copyright owners and publishers will have a full range of new opportunities in an electronic information environment and libraries will be able to perform their roles as partners in promoting science and the useful arts.

10.4. INTELLECTUAL PROPERTY RIGHTS IN INDIA

The protection of intellectual property rights in India continues to be strengthened. There is a well-established statutory, administrative and judicial framework to safeguard rights, whether they relate to patents, trademarks, copyright or industrial designs. Well-known international trademarks have been protected in India even when they were not registered in India. The Indian Trademarks Law has been extended through court decisions to service marks in addition to trademarks for goods. Computer software companies have successfully curtailed piracy through court orders. Computer databases have been protected. The courts, under the doctrine of breach of confidentiality, accorded an extensive protection of trade secrets. Right to privacy, which is not protected even in all developed countries, has been recognized in India.

With Specific reference to the obligations under Article 70.8 and 70.9 of the TRIPS Agreement, where India was required to provide a means for receipts of applications for product patents for pharmaceuticals and agricultural chemicals and to grant exclusive marketing rights on fulfilment of certain conditions, the Embassy would like to state the following:

10.4.1. Comments on the Submission of International Intellectual Property Association

India is availing of the transition period available under Article 65 of the TRIPs Agreement to meet her obligations under the seven areas covered by the Agreement. India's achievements in this field have been in the passing of TRIPs plus legislation in the tield of Copyright Law. The 1994 amendment to the-Act of 1957 provides protection to all original literary, dramatic, musical and artistic works, cinematography films and sound recordings. The most recent changes bring sectors such as satellite broadcasting, computer software and digital technology under Indian copyright protection.

The submission of the IIPA to USTR has raised four issues, namely, extent of piracy in different sectors, observations on the Copyright Law of India, the enforcement of the Copyright Law, and points relating to judicial processes and reforms.

10.4.2. Copyright Law and Related Issues

The IIPA has been appreciative of the Copyright Act of 1957 as amended in 1994. It has observed that overall, the new law is Trade Related Aspects of Intellectual Property (TRIPS) compatible from the stand point of substantive rights, except that the term of protection for performers should be increased from 25 to 50 years. International Intellectual Property Association or IIPA has also observed that the criminal provisions in the Act are among the toughest in the world. It, however, suggested that the level of fines should be increased. At present the minimum fine for the first offence is Rs.50, 000 and the maximum Rs. 200,000. In dollar terms this comes to 1,400 and 5,500. The amount of fines, decided in 1994, on the basis of the per capita income in India are satisfactory, even if they should appear to be low when one considers them in US dollars and in the context of the US per capita income. For making the Copyright Act TRIPS-compatible, India has time till January 1, 2000, as per Article 65.2 of the TRIPS Agreement.

IIPA has also suggested that the lack of presumptions with respect to ownership and subsistence of rights, and the need to prove actual knowledge must be remedied in amendments to the Copyright Act to make the law fully TRIPs-compatible, and bring it into conformity with the WIPO Copyright Treaty and the Performances and Phonograms Treaty.

In regard to the presumption of ownership of copyright issue, it is observed that in 1996 the Supreme Court of India, in a major ruling aimed at curbing piracy in audio and video cassettes in the country, said that ownership evidence of the original work was not required to prove the charge of copyright violation. Thus, even if there is no explicit provision in the Act, the case law makes the presumption of ownership of copyright. In fact the IIPA has also referred to the Supreme Court ruling.

Justifying suggested amendments to the Copyright Act in regard to the need to prove actual knowledge for raising/confiscating equipment for piracy, the IIPA has stated, "while raids on cable systems have been successful to date, it has been necessary to catch the pirate in the act of broadcasting a particular film without a licence in order for the police to be able to seize the pirate's broadcasting equipment." In this connection it may be mentioned that, in Section 64(l) of the Copyright Act, it has been clearly provided as under:

"Any police officer not below the rank of a sub-inspector, may, if he is satisfied that an offence under Section 63 in respect of the infringement of copyright in any work has been, is being, or is likely to be committed, seize without warrant, all copies of the work, and all plates used for the purpose of making infringing copies of the work, wherever found, and all copies and plates so seized shall, as soon as practicable, be produced before a Magistrate".

It will thus be seen that law does not require that the police witness the act of infringement in order to seize the goods involved. The law only requires that the police officer be satisfied that an offence "in respect of the infringement of copyright in any work has been, is being, or is likely to be committed for the purpose of seizing, without warrant, all copies of the work and the plates used for making the infringing copies. This can further be adduced from the fact that he has the power to seize an infringing work even when he is satisfied that an offence is likely to be committed"thereby ruling out the essentiality of witnessing use of the goods to be seized in an act of infringement. Thus, the powers vested with the police take care of not only the past and present cases of infringement but also future cases where there is a likelihood of infringement of copyright provisions.

The WIPO Copyright Treaty, 1996 and the WIPO Performances and Phonograms Treaty, 1996 have not yet come into force as the requisite number of countries have not yet ratified or acceded to the treaties. India has also not yet acceded to the treaties.

The IIPA has also observed that as cable-showing of pirated products has begun to diminish, there has been an increase in unauthorized showing of US films in student unions in universities. The Copyright Act provides an exception "to the performance, in the course of the activities of an education institution, of a cinematography film,...if the audience is limited to ... staff and students, the parents and guardians of the students and persons directly connected with the activities of the institution..." (Section 52 (1)). IIPA has suggested that this provision should be interpreted narrowly to make such showings an infringement. If not, the provision must be amended and narrowed to be Berne and TRIPS-compatible. It may be observed that the Indian Copyright Act is fully compatible with the Berne and the Berne provisions included in the TRIPS. As such, no amendment is needed in the Act. However, the enforcement agencies may ensure that the exemption provisions for educational purposes are not misused for copyright infringement.

IIPA in their submissions have also stated, "on the recording side, RIAA is concerned about an apparently over board provision in section 33 which may limit the ability of authors, and composers, as well as producers, to licence their works individually, rather than through a registered collection society." IIPA has suggested that this should be clarified in favour of full rights of all right holders to licence their rights individually. Section 33 of the Copyright Act, which provides for copyright societies, does not take away the rights of individual copyright owners. As per provison to Section 33 "an owner of copyright shall, in his individual capacity, continue to have the right to grant licences in respect of his own works consistent with his obligations as a member of the registered, copyright society."

IIPA have also demanded a narrower interpretation of provisions relating to educational use of copyrighted work. First of all, no such instance has been brought lo the notice of the Department of Education, Ministry of Human Resource Development, Government of India, which is the nodal Ministry for copyright. Further, it is quite likely that instances, if any, do not involve any commercial losses.

10.4.3. Enforcement of Copyright Law

IIPA has mentioned about the number of raids against pirates. It, however, has also mentioned a number of enforcement problems, including the increase in mobility of pirate wholesalers and retailers as enforcement has increased, occasional leaks of information from enforcement authorities to pirate operators, and the slow progress of cases through the courts. The Embassy would like to highlight that the Government of India has also greatly intensified anti-piracy operations.

The Government has also taken a number of measures to strengthen the enforcement of copyright law. A summary of these measures is given below:

Measures taken by the Department of Education, Ministry of Human resource Development, Government of India for strengthening the enforcement of the copyright and neighbouring rights include constitution of a Copyright Enforcement Advisory Council (CEAC), creation of separate cells in state police headquarters, encouraging setting up of collective administration societies and organization of seminars and workshops to create greater awareness about copyright law among the enforcement personnel and the general public.

The CEAC is reconstituted from time to time to review periodically the progress of enforcement of the Copyright Act and to advise the government on measures for improving the enforcement. The present CEAC was constituted for a period of three years with effect from November 6, 1997. Additional Secretary, Department of Education is the chairman of the CEAC. The CEAC members include representatives of copyright industry organizations and chiefs of state police forces. The CEAC meets at least twice every year. The reconstituted CEAC has already met twice. The CEAC discusses in detail issues of enforcement, piracy, etc.

Special cells for copyright enforcement have so far been set up in the 23 States and Union Territories: These are the States / Union Territories of Andhra Pradesh, Assam, A &N Islands, Chandigarh, Dadra & Nagar Haveli, Daman & Diu, Delhi, Goa, Gujarat, Haryana, Himachal Pradesh, Jammu & Kashmir, Karnataka, Kerala, Madhya Pradesh, Meghalaya, Orissa, Pondicherry, Punjab, Sikkim, Tamil Nadu, Tripura and West Bengal. States have also been advised to designate a nodal officer for copyright enforcement to facilitate easy interaction by copyright industry organizations and copyright owners.

For collective administration of copyright, copyright societies are set up for different classes of works. At present there are three registered copyright societies.These are the Society for Copyright Regulations of Indian Producers of Films & Television (SCRIPT) for cinematography films, Indian Performing Rights Society Limited (IPRS) for musical works and Phonographic Performance Limited (PPL) for sound recordings. These societies, particularly the PPL and the IPRS, have been quite active in anti-piracy work. The PPL has even set up a special anti-piracy cell under a retired Director General of Police and this cell has been working in tandem with the police.

The Government also initiates a number of seminars/ workshops on copyright issues. The participants in these seminars include enforcement personnel like the police as well as representatives of industry organizations. The Ministry had also proposed a few new schemes during the Ninth Five-Year Plan. These new schemes provide for extending financial assistance to the States for setting up/strengthening the special copyright enforcement cells in the State police, giving financial assistance for organizing training seminars and workshops for enforcement personnel, organizing seminars and workshops to create general awareness about copyright and for encouraging study of intellectual property rights in the educational system, besides modernizing the Copyright Office. A scheme is also on the anvil for extending financial assistance to Collective Administration Societies.

The IIPA has also suggested that a central body be set up at the federal level to coordinate enforcement. For the time being, the Government of India is working on strengthening the copyright enforcement cells at the State level.

10.4.4. Modernization of Intellectual Property Administration System

Government of India has taken several measures to streamline and strengthen the intellectual property administration systems in the country. Two projects were implemented with the help of WIPO/UNDP for the modernization of patent information services and trademarks registry, details of which are given below:

(*a*) *Modernization of Patent Information Services*

1. The Office of Patent Information System (PIS) was set up in 1980 with a view to provide scientific and technological information contained in patents documents to the users, namely scientists, researchers, universities, Indian Institutes of Technology and others for taking up further research and development. It is estimated that about 80 percent of the world's knowledge of viable and adaptable technology are contained in about 30 million patent documents. One million documents are being added every year, covering 400,000 inventions. If the information contained in these documents is made available to industry, it can provide information for further research, facilitate evaluation of technology to be purchased under licensing arrangements, and identify worldwide developments in specific fields.
2. It was, therefore, felt necessary to establish a modernized patent information service centre through upgrading and mechanization of procedures relating to collection, retrieval and dissemination of patent information, using state-of-the-art technology and trained personnel.
3. Accordingly, a project for modernization of PIS was taken up with the financial assistance of UPDP and Government of India (at a cost of US$1.22 million of which $0.69 million provided by LTNDP) and technical assistance of World Intellectual Property Organisation (WIPO) in January, 1992. This project had been completed in June 1996.
4. As a part of activities, several awareness/training programs were organized in India for the benefit of scientific and industrial communities. Additional manpower to PIS was provided along with modem office equipment such as computers, CD-ROMs and on-line access to external and internal databases. Computerized Indian patent databases have also been established. All these activities are expected to result in better and improved services to the users.

(*b*) *Modernization of Trade Marks Registry*

1. The use and promotion of trademarks helps to inform

consumers about goods and services available in the market. The use of trademarks facilitates identifying those responsible for putting those goods in the market. An effective trademarks system would help to protect consumers against misleading practices. Therefore, it was recognized that in the interest of consumers, the Government of India should promote the use and provide effective protection for trademarks.

2. Accordingly, a project for modernization of trademarks registry was taken up in April 1993 at a cost of US$1.24 million, out of which US$ 0.58 million were provided by the UNDP. The project had been implemented in May 1996 with the technical assistance of WIPO.
3. Under the project, the capability of the Registry has been enhanced by modernizing and streamlining trade marks registration procedures; posts of electronic data processing personnel have been created; awareness programs organized; Registry has been strengthened in terms, of modern office equipment; networking established between Head and Branch Offices, etc. It would now be possible to issue registration certificate in a shorter period than before.
4. Further strengthening of the capabilities of the trademark registry is also being taken up.

(c) ***Modernization of Patent Offices***

1. A proposal is now under consideration for taking up modernization of Patent Offices.
2. The Patent Offices, apart from grant of patent, perform other functions like public information and guidance, maintenance of public library and search room production of journals, publication of official gazette etc.
3. In view of the economic initiatives and liberalization measures taken by the Government since mid-1991, the number of applications for patents are expected to increase significantly. From a level of 3552 in 1991-92, it was increased to 8562 in 1996-97 and might have rise further in last years. Accordingly, a proposal is under consideration

for modernization of patent offices incorporating the following elements:-

- Human Resource Development;
- Infrastructure Support and Strengthening;
- Computerization and Modernization; and
- Elimination of backlog of patent applications.

It is worthy to mention that IT Act 2000 has been implemented by Indian government for protecting intellectual properties to a great extent in electronic is great extent in electronic and computer environment.

10.5. INTERNATIONAL SCENARIO

Many nations have data protection laws that attempt to ensure an individual's privacy rights. These include but are not limited to:

- The Russian Federation Law on Information, Informalization, and Information Protection of 1995;
- The U.K. Data Protection Act of 1998;
- The New Zealand Privacy Act of 1993 ;
- The 1995 EU Data Protection Directive;
- The Hong Kong Personal Data (Privacy) Ordinance of 1996;
- The Estonia Personal Data Protection Act in June 1996.

The Electronic Privacy Information Center (EPIC) and Privacy International reviewed the state of privacy in over fifty countries around the world. The report found many countries around the world are enacting comprehensive data protection iaws.

Other nations, such as China have no general data protection laws enacted, although data privacy is referred to in a few regulations in both countries. Interestingly, however, the Chinese Constitution proclaims citizens have limited rights to privacy even though few laws limit government actions. For example, Article 37 of its constitution provides that the freedom of citizens of the People's Republic of China is inviolable, and Article 40 states: "Freedom and privacy of correspondence of citizens of the People's Republic of China are protected by law." However, whenever technological advancements seem on the brink of loosening the government's grip over its citizens, the Chinese government uses all its power to either suppress the technology or mold it to fit its own political agenda.

Summing up, technology offers options for designing new organization structures, especially networked organizations that concentrate on core competencies and outsource other activities. These organizations have the potential for great efficiencies, but they must coordinate with other companies in their network that provide them with goods and services.

The combination of computers, databases, and telecommunications, especially the Internet, provide the manager with an incredible number of options for improving the way organizations function. Your challenge is to innovate, to develop strategies in which technology will contribute to the firm's competitive advantage. Then you must choose appropriate technology, implement it successfully, and continually manage change. It is likely that technology will play a major role in the design of your organization and the way in which it does business including the library services, but we should not forget the ethical and legal issues of knowledge management. We must pay regards to them.

11

Knowledge Management in Libraries

Knowledge Management in Libraries is earlier to the thoughts and contributions falling outside the Information Science domain. Libraries originated with the basics of the concept knowledge Management Classification and cataloguing — the fundamental principles for the library practice is the concrete evidence to the origin of knowledge management.The advent of the internet and related technological developments in the last 3-4 decades has not only increased but stocks and flows of information, which now have a significant digital dimension, but also have transformed the nature of library and information services. In the midst of these changes, knowledge management has emerged as a further significant influence on library practice as reflected in the creation of new products and services and in new knowledge-linked titles for those (hitherto known as librarians) involved in their delivery. Although not everyone within the community approves of this development the challenges and opportunities it presents. Typical of this latter viewpoint is the argument that since the organisation of knowledge has always been the strong suite of librarians, they must not only engage in, but also actively spearhead knowledge management initiatives.

There is little doubt that as a term 'knowledge management'

leaves a fair amount to be desired. It implies a measure of control that is not always realistic and in a way reflects the management philosophies of the Industrial rather than the Information Age. There is also the issue as to whether or not knowledge can be managed. Arguably this is not so much a matter of knowledge management, as of changing entire business cultures and strategies in favour of those that value learning and sharing the resulting knowledge. Although some aspects of knowledge such as culture, organizational structure, communication processes and information can be managed, knowledge itself, arguably, cannot. Nonetheless, for all its perceived terminological and conceptual limitations, knowledge management has become part of the organisational landscape. This is true of so-called 'old economy' companies such as hotel chains, banks and the oil and petroleum industries as well as the 'new economy' firms in information and financial services and the large management consultancies and their boutique counterparts. It also applies to industries such as automobile and aircraft manufacture that have made the transition to new economy status along with such diverse entities as the World Bank and a growing number of national and international governments. Among the reasons why this is the case are that knowledge is now regarded as the fundamental basis of wealth creation, of innovation and productivity and the only sustainable source of competitive advantage.

But where do libraries and information centres fit into this highly business-intensive, not to say commercial portrayal of knowledge management?

Not only are library and information professionals expert in content management, something that is often central to successful knowledge management, but individual professionals have demonstrated their management potential by transferring to careers in consultancy and other forms of business. On the whole, however, the LIS professions may still labour under a dual, self-imposed handicap in seeking to exploit opportunities in knowledge management. The first is a traditional reluctance to move beyond the information container towards analysis and interpretation of its contents, and the second is that information professionals continue to be promoted themselves as service-oriented, rather than value-oriented. The perpetuation of such attitudes may well help to explain the general absence of an LIS component within the mainstream knowledge management.

11.1. ROLE OF LIS PROFESSIONALS IN KNOWLEDGE MANAGEMENT

To survive in a world of global competition, organisations increasingly depend on their ability to transform information into knowledge as the basis of competitiveness, decision-making and the production of new products and services. In an LIS context, the term information overload could also be added here, with the clear implication that libraries and information centres will continue to perform access and intermediary roles which embrace not just information but also knowledge management. The difference today is that these traditional roles could be expanded if not transformed, by the promotion and facilitation of information literacy, and through activities aimed at helping to capture tacit knowledge and by turning personal knowledge into corporate knowledge that can be widely shared throughout the library and applied appropriately. These knowledge management activities can help to transform the library into a more efficient, knowledge-sharing organization which promotes relationships in and between libraries, and between libraries and users, in order to strengthen knowledge networking and to quicken knowledge flow. This mixture of traditional and emerging professional responses is motivated by responses to both threats and opportunities, for example new roles and possibilities through knowledge management and the combined challenges of library budget shortfalls and higher user expectations.

There is a general acknowledgement within the literature that since information management is an important part of each knowledge management program, LIS professionals with the relevant information management skills have the potential to be significant players in knowledge management programs. Typical of such views is that whereas information management is not knowledge management, knowledge is communicated through information, and hence information professionals have the theoretical basis and practical skills to provide an essential element of knowledge management. The promotion of information literacy is another way in which librarians can make a contribution to knowledge management, with the. ability to identify, access, evaluate, organize and communicate information and knowledge constituting a core capability for the knowledge society.

To this, Dewe adds a further role for librarians in the knowledge distribution process through the development of open access publishing via institutional research repositories. At a more general level, with fundamental values encapsulated in knowledge sharing and customer service, the library and information community clearly fits within the knowledge management environment, a fit which is enhanced by core skills in information acquisition, organization and use.

Marianne Broadbent was among the early advocates of potential LIS involvement in knowledge management. However, she perceived such involvement as conditional upon the nature of the work performed by individual LIS professionals and the extent to which they were able to look beyond the confines of professional values and perceptions. Broadbent applied an earlier categorization of knowledge workers to the library profession, arguing that those engaged in activities such as the creation, packaging and re-use of knowledge might be described as knowledge workers. On the other hand, librarians engaged in routine work or in organising things for others, were as likely to be administrative rather than knowledge workers. All such categorizations tend to be (paradoxically) both generic and highly subjective (in that one person's interpretation of job content can be very different from another's), while in any case focusing on a relatively narrow, if important, aspect of knowledge management. More useful in addressing fundamental questions about the potential role and place of the LIS professions within knowledge management are issues to do with the understanding of business values and objectives, and of organisational politics and the need for LIS professionals to be able to demonstrate credibility in a highly competitive field.

Broadbents own record in demonstrating such credibility in highly competitive academic and business consulting environments speaks for itself, and her role in initiating debate on the LIS-knowledge management relationship marks a further significant contribution. Unfortunately, not a lot seems to have happened since 1998, either in the general sense of a clarification of this relationship, or with regard to the specifics of how the LIS professions might prepare for, engage in and exploit the opportunities presented by knowledge management. Certainly there are plenty of articles and lots of motherhood statements of the 'librarians have always been engaged in knowledge management' type, a genre by no means confined to the LIS literature. In the wider literature, moreover, there are plenty of papers providing often detailed descriptions of successful knowledge management projects, complete with listings of stages of development, and the enunciation of knowledge management methodologies. The problem is that most of these are set in business environments and/or are organizationally contextual, with few links either to the LIS environment or to how and where these professions might become involved.

Broadbent herself has used the IBM example which categorized an approach to knowledge management in terms of– making knowledge visible, building knowledge intensity, developing a knowledge culture and building knowledge infrastructure. There is little point at this stage going into the detail behind these headings because for many practising LIS professionals they would raise potentially insurmountable obstacles in terms of competence and authority. Clearly in knowledge-based organizations, a variety of professionals have opportunities to contribute to the development and reinforcement of knowledge processes and infrastructures and even to knowledge cultures. The problem is that the LIS professions appear to have made very slow progress in identifying and then enunciating in any kind of detail what this means for them, and how their expertise, education and training and cultural traits must develop and interface with those of others if they are to become serious players in the knowledge management space.

Some would of course argue that LIS professionals are already making their mark in the knowledge management space and particularly in specialist new roles such as information architects, taxonomy development or content management for organizational intranets. They are also prominent in specific sectors such as health and law, often through expertise in the management of new technologies. Nevertheless, a few heroic examples may not necessarily constitute a long-term trend, and often this appears to involve LIS professionals in doing more of the same, and in standing still in terms of career progression, with accession to more senior knowledge management roles being more a matter of aspiration than of achievement and this despite notable exceptions including librarians.

There is also a point of view that LIS professionals should stick to what they know and resist being drawn into futile attempts to serve other professional masters. In seeking to exercise this kind of choice, LIS professionals would be well advised to consider the potential risks involved in non-participation, not least those of being seen to be irrelevant in their organisations and losing out to others. Should the LIS professions opt to buy into the knowledge management game in search of new opportunities and improved status, they must however, be prepared to take a holistic view and focus on organizational rather than simply personal or professional object. They must also be prepared to take the risk of self-promotion in competitive markets for higher-level jobs. In order to prepare for such risk-taking activities as well as to ready themselves for a range of roles across the knowledge management spectrum, LIS professionals must also address any existing and potential gaps between their current and future needs for education.

11.2. ROLE OF KM IN LIBRARIES

The role of knowledge management in libraries today, has become more vital along with the development of knowledge economy. It is a new management mode with unique characteristics that distinguish it from conventional management. The major components of Knowledge Management in libraries are :

- Human Resource Management
- Knowledge Innovation
- Information Technology and
- Knowledge Dissemination

11.2.1. Human Resource Management

The most important resource in the knowledge economy system is the talents of the personnel. The libraries should attach importance to vocational training and lifelong education of library staff to raise their scientific knowledge level and ability of acquiring and innovating knowledge. An all-round improvement of library staff's quality and positioning of the human value will become important objectives of knowledge management in libraries.

11.2.2. Knowledge Innovation

Knowledge innovation is the core of the knowledge economy society. Knowledge innovation management in libraries refers to the management of the production, diffusion and transfer of knowledge as well as of the network systems constructed by related institutions and organizations. It includes three aspects, namely,

- theoretical innovation management of knowledge,
- technical innovation management, and
- organizational innovation management.

Theoretical innovation management is to enrich and enlarge the theoretical and practical research fields of library and information science.

Technical innovation management is to manage the network systems so that libraries build up technical facilities to support knowledge management.

Organizational innovation management is to create a set of effective organizational management systems adaptable to the requirements in the electronic and digital library era to support and strengthen knowledge management activities.

It has been rightly said that "libraries are laboratories for any research". Hence libraries represent an indispensable link in the scientific system chain, an important link in the knowledge innovation. The library work is a component of knowledge innovation.

Libraries act as bridges for turning the results of knowledge innovation into realistic productive forces. Knowledge management in libraries is to promote relationship in and between libraries, between library and user, to strengthen knowledge internetworking and to quicken knowledge flow, in the knowledge economy era, libraries will carry out researches on development and application of information resources, construction of virtual libraries, protection of intellectual property rights in the electronic era etc.

11.2.3. Information Technology

Knowledge acquisition is the starting point of knowledge management in libraries. The application of information technologies enlarges the scope of knowledge acquisition, rises knowledge acquisition speed and reduces knowledge acquisition cost. It is possible to link closely knowledge sources and knowledge workers by computer networks, thus constructing knowledge networks in libraries. The knowledge acquired must be accumulated and converged into knowledge warehouses of libraries. Information technology functions as a source and tool for knowledge innovation.

The right definition for information technology can be that– "It is an ensemblage of Communication Technology, Computer Technology and Information Science". Of the three components of Information Technology, Information Science is more vital as it is fundamental to any form of communication.

11.2.4. Knowledge Dissemination

The objective of Knowledge innovation is knowledge dissemination. Knowledge creators do not have much time and energy to look for knowledge users. It is very difficult for the users to acquire knowledge that already exists in the minds of knowledge creators. Libraries play the part of knowledge disseminator using diverse media and channels to disseminate various new knowledge. Therefore, it is necessary to strengthen knowledge dissemination management in libraries in the following ways:

- uninterruptedly strengthening the creation of libraries' own document resources and deepening the development of document information resources;
- continuously raising the quality of libraries stairs and strengthening continuous engineering education of working stalls;

- giving full play to the special role of the expert system in knowledge dissemination; and
- making a comprehensive utilization of all media to ensure security of operation of networks, and prevent online criminal activities and online dissemination of inapropriate information.

11.3. TYPOLOGY OF ORGANIZATIONAL KNOWLEDGE

Rob Cross and Lloyd Baird have identified five kinds of knowledge in organizations. The most important is the knowledge embedded in the minds of workers. This tacit and explicit knowledge is gained through everyday experience on the job. It is shared most commonly in social interactions with other workers. This knowledge can be withheld on a whim, and it can leave the organization with the worker. We all can recall times when the absence of an individual has arrested an organizational initiative in its tracks.

Second, organizational knowledge is explicit and tacit knowledge shared in work groups. As with individuals, this knowledge is subject to loss with the elimination or restructuring of a work group. At one point during corporate downsizing, for example, one of the Big Three automakers had eliminated so many employees that management found it lacked the knowledge required to design a new car and bring it into production. People had to be brought back onto the payroll, now as expensive consultants, to get new designs out the door.

Third, organizations can create knowledge repositories composed of explicit knowledge that has been documented and organized for access. Often these are called data warehouses or data malls. Frequently, they resemble libraries or archives in some respects. The knowledge is collected and organized in some symbolic form, such as a catalogue or a bibliography. Authorized users may access the knowledge. To continue the saga of the automaker, a "big book" of auto design was created with all the knowledge considered critical for designing and producing a new-model vehicle. By documenting this knowledge, the automaker is less susceptible to loss of knowledge through downsizing or turnover. However, knowledge repositories also have limitations. They can include only a fraction of the most important data to an organization. Unless updated constantly, repositories quickly go out of date. In addition, they always will be consulted second, after colleagues and coworkers.

Sometimes the fact that organizational processes themselves contain a great deal of embedded knowledge is overlooked. This is the fourth type of organizational knowledge. The way that work is organized and carried out incorporates a great deal of knowledge. For example, current cataloguing practice is based on the knowledge that OCLC can provide acceptable cataloguing information for more than 90 percent of the items that a typical academic library adds to its collection. This one piece of knowledge has been embedded in the radical redesign of cataloguing operations in recent years.

Finally, knowledge is embedded in products and services. The libraries focus on delivering scholarly information and support services. In the past, this involved printed, and sometimes recorded, media almost exclusively. Like IBM ignoring the emerging personal computer market in the 1980s, libraries risk losing their role as the primary academic information provider if they do not address the knowledge that most users are requesting electronic formats in the provision of resources and services.

The collection, processing and dissemination of organizational knowledge will seem familiar to most librarians. Frequently, it mimics the process that academic libraries use to process scholarly knowledge. Good selection is paramount. In the case of organizational knowledge, librarians need to select and use the knowledge that is most critical to achieving library goals. For example, if a library is committed to increasing the effectiveness of its internet portal and catalogue, it would need to create knowledge from usage data, including user behaviour such as databases accessed, failure rates, persistence rates, and so forth. The library then can benchmark against other libraries to identify areas of comparative strength and weakness. In addition, it can collect best practices to share with staff and users to generate more effective desired use. On the other hand, some knowledge, such as hour or day of use or major, might be considered less important for reaching goals and not be included in the knowledge system.

Organization of knowledge also is critical for improving library operations. Knowledge must be structured in ways that are intuitive for the intended community of practice. Knowledge that is intuitive for cataloguers may not be immediately intuitive for an archivist or reference librarian, and vice versa. Implicit knowledge must be divided into broad groups of similar knowledge with excellent transferal capability. Explicit knowledge must use structured subject descriptors to maintain order and accessibility. Descriptors are dynamic and must be updated constantly to represent changes in the field. Librarians excel at this type of work. Organizing library operational knowledge needs only the organizational will and resources to occur.

Librarians are learning to be proactive in their delivery of scholarly knowledge and will need to use many of the same techniques to share operational knowledge within the library. Commitment, training and support are key factors in the transfer of knowledge. If library personnel are not committed to achieving library goals, or if they are not well trained in the use of organizational knowledge, it is likely that efforts to manage knowledge will fail. Both are necessary prerequisites. Should a selector, for example, fail to be familiar with or use available knowledge about collection use or implicit knowledge about faculty interests and goals in making access and selection decisions, it is unlikely that the library will have the information that meets scholars' needs. For this purpose, the person responsible for collection development needs to ensure that appropriate knowledge and the opportunities to learn it are available to each selector. Continuing support also is important. Librarians need to be encouraged and rewarded constantly for applying useful knowledge to achieve organizational goals. The intent of this area is to expand and support the use of knowledge-based judgments to achieve library goals.

Finally, as with all management processes, knowledge management efforts need to be evaluated and updated. Knowledge that improves effectiveness needs to be identified and supported.

Other knowledge needs to be revised or eliminated. In the dynamic world of libraries, no library will succeed for very long when it is not managing its most valuable resource, its knowledge, as effectively as possible.

11.4. KNOWLEDGE MANAGEMENT PROCESSES

Thomas H. Davenport, David W. De Long and Michael C. Beers identified four types, each of which focuses on a broad objective: (1) to create knowledge repositories; (2) to improve knowledge access; (3) to enhance the knowledge environment; and (4) to manage knowledge as an asset. The following subsections describe how each of these types of projects can be applied in libraries.

11.4.1. Create Knowledge Repositories

Librarians are familiar with knowledge repositories. In terms of library operational information, most integrated library systems contain a component intended to provide useful information about library operation and user activity. This kind of information can be used to create explicit organizational knowledge, to inform services, to guide operations, and to measure goal attainment. Data about new monographs, for example, are created routinely when these items are added to the collection. These data could be combined with circulation data and online reviews to create notices for distribution to prospective readers. Or, usage data from an electronic reserve service could be aggregated and sent to the instructor or other staff in time to modify activities to take advantage of what has been used. In each of these cases, data that are collected routinely as part of the operation of the integrated library system can be used to create and share knowledge that contributes to the improvement of teaching and research. By creating knowledge from existing data, libraries add value to integrated library systems.

External knowledge repositories also can be used to achieve organizational objectives. Several years ago, faculty in the College of Engineering at New Mexico State University adopted the goal of quality, rather than quantity, in scholarly publishing. Working with the library, faculty used information from the Institute for Scientific Information and other resources as tools for determining where to publish their scholarly research. The result has been that the School of Electrical Engineering ranked in the top ten for publication impact as measured by the Institute of Scientific Information.

11.4.2. Improve Knowledge Access

A second type of knowledge management project is one that improves access to and transfer of organizational knowledge. This often takes place by creating expert networks where individuals with desired expertise are organized formally into a network and put into contact with others, creating a community of interest. An example might be a network of subject specialists, perhaps from several institutions, who come together to share experiences and learn from each other. Another method is to create yellow pages, classifying individuals by different areas of expertize into a logical whole. Internal cross-training and exchange with other organizations also are used.

National Institute of Standards and Technology (NIST), Australis has created a virtual library to complement and reinforce existing library services and to encourage increased knowledge transfer. The virtual library emphasizes services that are proactive, such as selective dissemination of information and document delivery. In addition, research consultants combine tacit knowledge drawn from working directly on research teams with knowledge of the virtual library to identify and transfer useful research information directly to users. The result is more highly focused provision of appropriate scholarly information in formats and at times convenient to the users. INFLIBNET Centre, Ahemdabad in India is also doing alomst the same thing for information dissemination.

Often technological innovations can enhance the knowledge process. Lotus Notes and Intranets are popular in private organizations; electronic mail and hosted listservs are popular in public organizations. British Petroleum has had great success in using videoconferencing to speed up repairs by eliminating repair crew travel. The library at New Mexico State University approached e-mail as a strategic knowledge resource in the early 1990s. The result has been the creation and application of organizational knowledge to optimize the effectiveness of e-mail in organizational activities.

11.4.3. Enhance the Knowledge Environment

Enhancing the knowledge environment is the third type of knowledge management process. It focuses on creating an environment that encourages the creation and transfer of knowledge. If the tacit knowledge about users held by a reference librarian could be shared with systems personnel, for example, a more effective library home page would result. To create an environment supporting this kind of knowledge, management must generate meaningful contacts among the staff, provide resources and incentives, and praise progress. NIST virtual library also can serve as a useful example for enhancing knowledge environments. In addition to providing an integrated library system and connectivity to other electronic resources, it supports the Electronic Information and Publications Programs as the access portal for the NIST publication database and for delivering electronic documents for the entire organization. Both the library and the electronic publication program benefit from this cooperative environment. The library gains additional information resources of high internal value, and the electronic program does not have to support the distribution of the information.

11.4.4. Manage Knowledge as an Asset

Managing knowledge as an asset is the last type of knowledge management project and perhaps the least familiar to librarians. Although some companies audit their intellectual resources internally each year, libraries tend to simply list their physical holdings and easily quantifiable activities, assuming that each item or activity measured is equally valuable and goal related. Some firms manage their intellectual capital to achieve maximum return, something most librarians have not considered. What would happen if librarians began to manage the library's assets explicitly to achieve maximum return? How would libraries value the operations knowledge in the heads of library workers? How should libraries value the knowledge embedded in their processes and products?

How should they value the growing amount of information to which they have electronic access? It is no longer enough for library leaders to make intuitive decisions. To achieve quality, commitment, and acceptability, these decisions must be based on organizational knowledge and made collaboratively. The cross-organizational committee systems developed by the Kao and Sharp Corporations in Japan provide a way to create and manage organizational knowledge. In both companies, opportunities for innovation are presented on a regular basis, reallocation of resources is argued, and decisions are made to support the promising initiatives on a temporary, but corporation-wide, basis. After evaluation, the best initiatives are implemented.

The Association of Research Libraries (ARL) and the Big Twelve Plus Research Library Consortium both have projects intended to manage scholarly information as an asset. In these collaboratives, libraries are directly cosponsoring the publication of journals in high-cost fields of scholarship. In so doing, they are working with authors and publishers to achieve reduced costs and improve the quality of scholarly information. In time, operational information will be used to create knowledge on the effectiveness of these efforts to manage scholarly information as an asset. What has done by these two organization in, is being achieved by UGC-INFONET and INDEST constortia in India.

11.5. KNOWLEDGE MANAGEMENT IN ACADEMIC LIBRARIES

Libraries are human organisations, so they are subject to the same sort of influences that many other organizations must deal with. The changing environment of academic life demands new competencies in academic librarians. As a result, the knowledge and expertize of academic librarians needs to be seen as the library's greatest asset.

The following section is divided into three main parts. The first part highlights a number of important issues facing academic libraries. The second part looks at how knowledge management practices could be applied in academic libraries. The final part explores the skills and competencies needed to carry out knowledge management activities within academic libraries.

11.5.1. Changing Environment and Issues Facing Academic Libraries

1. Multiple Formats of Information : The rapid growth of information and communication technologies (ICTs) are said to be changing the way academic libraries operate today. Academic library collections are no longer collections comprised almost entirely of printed materials but collections comprised almost of materials in multiple formats and media. Information technologies such as computers, multimedia and CD-ROMs are bringing unprecedented abilities to academic libraries in providing services and resources to the university community. Over the past few years, the Web has had a tremendous effect on the growth of information and the speed of transmission. But the problem with the Web is that, there is no real organization of information like in the case of libraries. New means to deliver information over the Web places a challenge to academic librarians in terms of helping students make sense of information found on websites.

Another challenge facing academic libraries in the networked online environment is to exploit all forms of digital and telecommunication technologies and find new ways and means to provide feasible forms of collections, services and access to library materials. These technologies however, require greater responsibility to academic librarians. The challenge for academic librarians is to manage services, which offer users a carefully selected mix of multiple formats and media. Academic libraries should rethink their role in the whole university community. There is a need to support the needs of the users since the teaching and learning patterns in universities have changed.

As information and research resources become more varied, this places a challenge to academic libraries. It is argued that the changes in the nature of information, in research strategies and in the structure of higher education are affecting academic libraries. These changes define much of the shifting context within which academic libraries must operate. The changes brought by electronicmedia necessitate transformation in the way librarians think about their jobs, the users of information and communication process of which they are part of. Academic librarians must strive to remain competent navigators of each medium on order to assist the library users.

2. Changing User Needs : As universities' market demands are changing in terms of improving students learning outcomes, this has a direct impact on academic libraries and their delivery of services. Due to societal and technological developments, traditional teaching changes increasingly in creating learning environments. Students participate in flexible learning processes via more 'indirect' contacts with teachers and facilities, including scientific information. In addition, the teaching and learning patterns have developed towards greater modularization and place an emphasis on self-directed, independent study and student-centred learning. This places greater demands on the library, which is increasingly being used for group work and librarians face increased pressure on the enquiry service and a greater need for user support and education.

Academic libraries have to provide information services for users acting in the changing academic environment. Academic librarians need to liaise with library users, faculties and schools to support the effective teaching, learning and research in universities. Liaison is particularly important in a world of resource-based learning where students are encouraged to carry out more independent work and make wider use of a range of learning resources including electronic information resources. The challenges require academic libraries to offer user-friendly ICT oriented facilities like remote access to information and services, analyse the changing user needs and give support to users in new academic environments.

3. Organizational Structures : As a result of rapid environmental changes, academic libraries need to rethink their organizational structures in an attempt to provide quality service to the university community. The question to ask is– are academic libraries organizationally capable of addressing the challenges and issues facing them? Hazen pointed out that the structures that define academic libraries vary between countries, between institutions and between types of the institutions. In other words, the type of organizational structure existing in academic libraries is determined by their readiness to deal with current challenges. It is also suggested that "we must flatten our organizations and eliminate the bureaucracies that make us inflexible and slow in our response to our environment and the opportunities that are constantly presented". Flatter organisational structures are more conducive to innovation than are rigid hierarchies. They promote the creation of ideas.

There is a need to reshape the structure of academic libraries so that they will be able to improve the services they provide to both today's and tomorrow's users. Wilson urged university librarians to make their organizations more client-centred, to redesign work processes in light of organizational goals, and restructure in order to support front-line performance. The emphasis is more on the needs of the library user than the needs of the library. It is argued that the hallmark of a learning organisation is information sharing, team-based structure, empowered employees, decentralised decision making and participative strategy. Like other organizations, academic libraries need to reshape their structures to better serve their users.

4. Changing Role of Academic Librarians : In an age of great change in information formats, delivery models and technologies, an important new role emerges for the academic librarian. Bertnes argued that knowledge workers will be the most important profession in this century. There is no doubt that they are librarians. One of the major roles of academic librarians in the knowledge economy is that of knowledge managers. It is evident that academic librarians can no longer meet the information needs of the university community through the traditional avenue of simply adding to their library collections. Academic librarians need to go an extra mile. They need to understand the information and knowledge needs of users. They should be in a position to map internal and external knowledge that would assist them in increasing their efficiency. In other words, academic librarians should extend their information management roles and enhance their knowledge management competencies. It is pointed out that academic librarians as knowledge workers, need to play active roles insearching for innovative solutions to the issues involved in adapting to new environments.

11.5.2. Applying Knowledge Management Practices in Academic Libraries

The basic goal of knowledge management within libraries is to leverage the available knowledge that may help academic librarians to carry out their tasks more efficiently and effectively. Knowledge management is also aimed at extending the role of librarians to manage all types of information and tacit knowledge for the benefit of the library. Knowledge management can help to transform the library into a more efficient, knowledge sharing organization. Kim pointed out that knowledge management practices aim to draw out the tacit knowledge people have, what they carry around with them, what they observe and learn from experience, rather than what is usually explicitly stated. It is important for academic libraries to determine and manage their knowledge assets to avoid duplication of efforts. Knowledge management process involves the creation, capturing, sharing and utilization of knowledge.

1. Knowledge Creation : Whether the key objective of academic libraries is to provide resources and information services to support the university community, the key resource that is required is knowledge. That is, the knowledge of the library's operation, the knowledge of library users and their needs, knowledge of the library collection and knowledge of library facilities and technologies available. These types of knowledge must be put together so that new knowledge is created which leads to the improvement and development of service to the users and functioning of the academic library. However, this diverse knowledge is rather dispersed across all library sections and up the library hierarchy. The knowledge is not held by one individual only but by a number of individuals. Newell *et al.*,pointed out that:

"*Knowledge creation is typically the outcome of an interactive process that will involve a number of individuals who are brought together in a project team or some other collaborative arrangement.*"

Only where there is interaction and communication can be a comparison of each person's ideas and experiences with those of others. Knowledge creation is a particularly important process of knowledge management. It focuses on the development of new skills, new products, better ideas and more efficient processes. In addition, knowledge creation refers to the ability to originate novel and useful ideas and solutions. As a result, when an organization knows what it knows, values and prioritizes that knowledge, and develops systems for leveraging and sharing, it leads directly to the creation of new knowledge.

Knowledge in the context of academic libraries can be created through understanding the user needs and requirements as well as understanding the university's curricula. It is pointed out that from the library's perspective, knowledge creation implies participating more in user's reading and studying by identifying information needs. In order to succeed, academic library services must link with the university's academic programme or curricula. Academic librarians can become part of the knowledge creation process through participating in the teaching and research activities of the university. Knowledge creation in this context should involve all the management effort through which the academic library consciously strives to acquire competencies that it does not have both internally and externally.

2. Knowledge Capturing and Acquisition : Capturing and acquiring knowledge is crucial to the success and development of a knowledge-based organization. Organizations often suffer permanent loss of valuable experts through dismissals, redundancies, retirement and death. The reason for this is that much knowledge is stored in the heads of the people and it is often lost if not captured elsewhere. The surest way to avoid collective loss of organizational memory is to identify the expertize and the skills of staff and capture it.

Academic libraries need to develop ways of capturing its internal knowledge, devise systems to identify people's expertize and develop ways of sharing it. Formal processes of capturing knowledge can include collating internal profiles of academic librarians and also standardizing routine information-update reports.

In addition, successful libraries are those that are user-centred and are able to respond to users' needs. As users became more sophisticated, academic libraries need to develop innovative ways to respond - to add value to their services. Academic libraries need to be aware and to aim at capturing the knowledge that exists within them. The type of enquiries, for example, that are most commonly received at the reference desk should be captured and placed within easy reach to better serve users in the shortest time possible. It is important to create a folder of frequently asked questions to enable academic librarians to not only provide an in-depth customized reference service but also to become knowledgeable about handling different enquiries.

Huseman and Goodman pointed out that there are times when an organization does not possess certain knowledge internally and does not have the skills to find it. As a result, academic libraries find themselves unable to develop the know-how that they need. Extra knowledge must therefore be acquired somehow if it is felt it will be useful to the goals of the academic library. The academic library as an organization may want to look outside its own boundaries to outsource or acquire new knowledge. From the point of view of knowledge management, outsourcing may be described as substituting external know-how for internal know-how.

In addition, as work practices change and people work more flexibly, it is important to provide ways to allow them to access external information. Librarians have been dealing with building and searching online databases for a longtime. This kind of experience can be very helpful in building knowledge bases and repositories, a crucial area of knowledge management for managing organizational memory.

Knowledge acquisition is the starting point of knowledge management in libraries. Knowledge in academic libraries can be acquired through:

- Establishing knowledge links or networking with other libraries and with institutions of all kinds;

- Attending training programmes, conferences, seminars and workshops;
- Subscribing to listservs and online or virtual communities of practice; and
- Buying knowledge products or resources in the form of manuals, blueprints, reports and research reports.

Academic libraries need to gear up to equip academic librarians with the know-how they need to cope with the rapid changes of the 21st century, which is more information driven and knowledge-generated than any other area.

3. Knowledge Sharing : The expertize exists in people and much of this kind of knowledge is tacit rather than explicit, which makes it difficult to be shared. At its most basic, knowledge sharing is simply about transferring the dispersed know-how of organizational members more effectively. It is based on the experiences gained internally and externally in the organization. Making this know-how available to other organizational members will eliminate or reduce duplication of efforts and form the basis for problem solving and decision-making.

In the context of academic libraries, it can be noted that a great deal of knowledge sharing is entirely uncoordinated and any sharing of information and knowledge has been on an informal basis and usually based on conversation. Although knowledge has always been present in organizations and to some extent shared, this has been very much on an *ad hoc* basis, until recently it was certainly not overtly managed or promoted as the key to organizational success. More emphasis is placed on formalizing knowledge sharing.

It is pointed out that in many library settings, there is no systematic approach to organize the knowledge of the enterprise, and making it available to other librarians and staff in order to improve the operation of the library. For academic libraries to utilize their know-how, it is necessary that they become knowledge-based organizations. Academic libraries need to prepare themselves for using and sharing knowledge. To determine if there is any practice of knowledge sharing in academic libraries, we need to ask ourselves these questions– are academic librarians encouraged to share knowledge? Are the skills and competencies in the academic library identified and shared? How is the knowledge shared? Is knowledge sharing the norm?

The expertize, and know-how of organisational members should be valued and shared. It is vital that knowledge should be shared and distributed within an organization, so that isolated information or experience can be used by the whole company. In reality, distribution and sharing knowledge is not easy task. However, it is important for organizations to motivate why knowledge is being shared. The importance of knowledge sharing should be based on the capability of academic librarians to identify, integrate and acquire external knowledge. This should include knowledge denoting library practices, users and operational capabilities.

11.5.3. Skills and Competencies needed for Knowledge Management

As knowledge management activities are aimed at facilitating the creation, capturing and acquisition, sharing and utilization of knowledge, the successful implementation of such knowledge-enabling initiatives in the workplace requires the knowledge manager to apply several skills-sets. In the perspective of academic libraries, there is a need for academic librarians to extend their expertize. The transformation from librarian to knowledge manager is clearly underway. However, this impending shift of incorporating knowledge management in the library activities requires a great deal of preparation. The challenge for the information professional lies in applying competencies used in 'managing information' to the broader picture of 'managing knowledge'. The greater challenge is managing the know-how of organisational members, which they acquire through years of experience.

The success of academic libraries depends on the capabilities and skills of its staff to serve the needs of the academic community more efficiently and effectively. To be successful in this environment, individuals need to acquire new combination of skills. It is argued that managing knowledge requires a mix of technical, organizational and interpersonal skills. In making knowledge more accessible, it useful to have knowledge of the organization, customer service orientation and training skills.

Teng and Hawamdeh summed up the skills needed by the information professional in a knowledge-based environment:

- IT literacy, that is knowing how to use the appropriate technology to capture, catalogue and disseminate information and knowledge to the target audience and knowing how to translate that knowledge into a central database for employees of the organization to access;
- A sharp and analytical mind;
- Innovation and inquiring;
- Enables knowledge creation, flow and communication within the organization and between staff and public.

Besides, it is important for academic libraries to encourage librarians to constantly update their skills and competencies in this changing environment.

11.6. KNOWLEDGE MANAGEMENT IN PUBLIC LIBRARIES

Knowledge management in public libraries in its infact age. It has been applied in National Library Board, Singapore. It is being applied with success to cope up with the mission of the board expanding the learning capacity of the nation and enhancing the nation's competitiveness and promoting a gracions society.

11.6.1. Knowledge Management in the National Library Board

The National Library Board, Singapore began its humble beginnings in the 1960s. During the post-war years, the role of the National Library then was to function as a repository of information materials consisting of mainly print forms. The main objective was to serve as an institution to nurture a reading society and to provide book loans freely to the masses as part of the nation-wide campaign to promote reading and literacy. With the information explosion and the need to remain competitive, it was necessary to restructure the National Library to meet the needs of Singaporeans in the twenty-first century and beyond. The National Library Board (NLB) was formed on 1 September 1995 to spearhead the formulation of new policies, strategies and implementation of the recommendations outlined in the Library 2000 Report. Six strategic thrusts were outlined for the NLB to accomplish:

1. Establish an adaptive public library system, consisting of a network of national reference libraries, a three-tier public library system of regional, community and neighbourhood libraries; assist in the setting-up of school libraries and develop specialized libraries for specific sectors.
2. Create a network of borderless libraries linking all publicly funded libraries within Singapore to overseas libraries and information services through computer networking.
3. Put in place a co-ordinated national collection strategy.
4. Offer quality service through market orientation.
5. Create symbiotic linkages with government, business and the general public.
6. Help to shape Singapore into a global knowledge hub, offering information on regional business and culture.

The NLB has made significant strides since its inception. With the $6 billion in grants given by the government, the NLB has initiated and rolled out many prototyped services and value-added facilities in the bid to anticipate and keep pace with the changing informational needs of its readers. The direction for the present and future is towards equipping and preparing staff and users to meet the challenges of a knowledge-based economy and to instil a corporate culture in line with that of the Singapore government's directive, of the philosophy of lifelong learning.

11.6.2. Current Knowledge Management Practices

NLB has put in place several knowledge management initiatives started in the last few years and is continually seeking ways to excel in customer service and information provision. O'Delland Grayson, in a book titled *If Only We Knew What We Know*, postulates that the key in risking knowledge transfer of best practices a success is to approach it in terms of the core value propositions of the company. That is, to focus on the basic and fundamental goals for the existence and continuance of the corporation. They identify three categories into which value propositions tend to fall:

- customer intimacy;
- product-to-market excellence;
- operational excellence.

Customer intimacy focuses on capturing and using knowledge across the company about how to market, sell and service customers more efficiently and effectively. By sharing knowledge about customer needs and behaviour these companies hope to sharpen their sales and marketing edge, retain more valuable clients, and provide higher-value products and services with better profit margins. Product-to-market excellence involves using the best standards in product development to achieve the time-to-market strategy. Operational excellence transfers best practices from one location to another throughout the global organization.

O'Dell and Grayson also believe that the presence of various factors is crucial to the success of knowledge management. These factors or enablers involve:

- a culture which is supportive of knowledge management;
- necessary technology to facilitate and aid knowledge management;
- support systems and infrastructure that are equipped to handle knowledge sharing and information transfer;
- measurements in place to gauge the benefits of the KM process.

Customer satisfaction and *retention* are the primary focus of the NLB, whose existence relies upon the public's patronage of the library. This means therefore that the NLB must seek to understand and cater to the varying needs of the public. This is being done through the transfer of knowledge and best practices through both formal and informal communication. Front-line performance and service are of paramount importance in presenting and preserving the corporate image of the statutory board, to inspire confidence and to win satisfaction from the public. Both formal and informal surveys are frequently being commissioned by the NLB to be conducted in public libraries. Feedback is collected from readers about customer service, opinions of the collection and facilities of the library and new services on trial. This feedback is taken seriously and used as a gauge to measure, staff performance and as input for further enhancements and improvements.

NLB has also recently established a focus group feedback mechanism, which actively recruits individuals from all sectors of the population to give inputs on the current level of service and contribute suggestions on further improvements to be made. It is by constant solicitation of feedback from customers that the NLB can tailor its services and collections to be relevant to the overall population.

The knowledge of users' behavioural patterns, for example that most readers tend to visit the library to browse books according to subject categories, has led to the revamp of the library's collection classification system. First prototyped in the Tampines Regional Library, the arrangement of books according to the ten broad subject categories (Arts, Business and Management, Computers and IT, Cookery, Home and Garden, Parenting, Pets and Animals, Recreation, Singapore Collection and Travel Guides) has resulted in very positive feedback from the public.

This system is currently being rolled out to the other community libraries and feedback has been encouraging. Based also on the type of enquiries most commonly received at the information counter, frequently requested materials are placed within easy reach at the counters to better serve customers in the shortest possible time. Resource files consisting of information from various print and non-print sources on a popularly requested topic, were also compiled in the past, on topics of common and recurring interest to students and placed at the counters for fast and convenient access to information.

The formation of the NLB Web site was a necessity to keep up with the Internet as an emerging tool for communication among the masses. The Web site functions as a one-stop centre, where information on its public libraries and collection, together with the provision of the online catalogue and traditional borrowing services such as renewal and reservation functions, are housed together.

The aggressive introduction of multimedia terminals in libraries serves a twofold purpose:

- to expose the public to information stored in databases and the Internet; and
- to provide affordable and convenient access to these non-print information sources to the public.

As the NLB is moving away from "spoonfeeding" readers, students in particular are heading towards a self-help or self-reliant culture. These efforts not only help readers to obtain information they need faster, but also provide good training for them to learn about the way information is organized and to educate them on how research should be conducted. User education sessions, information literacy programmes and Internet talks have also been implemented to aid in these efforts.

As a further attempt to play a more involved and critical role in education, the student virtual community (SVC) was launched to serve the needs of students, teachers and parents. SVC serves as a one-stop collection of information to aid students in the project-based environment with online resources and project tips tailored to the schools' curriculum. The business virtual community and the Chinese virtual community have similar approaches and aims– to serve the needs of the business community and the Chinese-speaking community respectively.

These efforts are comparable with the marketing strategies adopted by commercial corporations, with the aim to garner customer loyalty and boost sales. NLB serves a different clientele altogether and the ultimate goal is not commercial profitability but customer satisfaction and an accelerating exponential increase in loans. By anticipating the needs of readers and by careful selection and packaging of information sources, together with a staff dedicated to providing quality customer service, the NLB is in the process of capturing knowledge about its customers to serve them better.

Improving services means shorter queues at the counter and faster processing time for materials to be made available for borrowing. From past surveys conducted in libraries, the common feedback obtained was that readers were most unhappy with having to queue for close to half an hour or longer to borrow and return books during peak periods. This perennial problem arose from the limited number of computer terminals available and a shortage of manpower. Solutions had to be devised to enable readers to borrow and return books without having to queue. The solution arrived in the form of self-check machines from 3M, which allowed readers to perform do-it-yourself borrowing and returning. Queuing time was cut to less than ten minutes even during peak periods and staff were freed from performing manual and routine stamping of book duties to provide informational assistance to readers.

The process for book returning has been refined even further with the introduction of infrared technology (RFID), which automatically "returns" a book which is slotted into the bookdrop. Initially prototyped at the Bukit Batok and Toa Payoh Community Libraries, this service is an improvement over the bookdrop system, which still required staff to be stationed in the backroom to return books manually for readers. This latest technology for returning books has since been rolled out to the Library @ Orchard and the Marine Parade Community Library.

The introduction of Borrower Enquiry (BNQ) stations was also a step towards enhancing the self-help culture and a way to cut queues forming at the counter. These terminals enable readers to check their loan records and to make payment for any fines or charges incurred. Thus, readers no longer had to queue at the counter to perform these services.

The NLB's eight-year plan, since its formation as a statutory board in 1995, was to ensure that a community library was sited within easy and convenient access of the various constituencies in Singapore and had to be located near the bus terminals or the Mass Rapid Transit stations. This directive saw the formation of the Library Development Group, which was formed to oversee the planning and the setting-up of new libraries. In the past, the planning for a new library could take up to a year. With this group, a library could be set up within three to six months, as the experiences and lessons learned from one library project could be refined and then transferred to the next. This means a significant reduction in time, more efficient work process and a speedier development of new libraries across the island.

A team of staff solely dedicated to planning and implementing new projects and prototype services was also set up to facilitate the process of project management. A business process re-engineering unit at the NLB's headquarter looks into how current practices can be improved on and how the most efficient methods of performing a semce can be rolled out.

The time taken by staff at the warehouse to process new items has also been shortened significantly, as most of the processing is currently outsourced to publishers and vendors. These "shelf-ready books" thus arrive at the warehouse already barcoded, labelled with the call number and security stripped and are ready to be transferred to the various libraries quicker, compared with the past when books had to undergo many processing steps and staff had to be deployed to perform them. Selection of new items has also been made easier with outsourced vendors, who regularly recommend items on subjects of interest to the library and librarians are on hand to either approve or reject their recommendations.

NLB is not interested in reinventing the wheel that is, tackling each problem as it comes along or engaging in constant firefighting, but is constantly under pressure to be faster, better and bigger. This means understanding the customer base and using that knowledge to ensure the fast delivery and development of services. Feedback from staff is also crucial in making sure that "ideas and practices flow throughout the organisation". This is done through the Work Improvement Teams suggestion scheme, which awards staff monetary rewards for each suggestion rendered. By sharing their creativity and best practices with one another, performance can be boosted and standards drawn to ensure uniformity of service and operational policies. Thus, through the transfer of best practices, whether informally among staff or formally through official briefings and seminars, the NLB can shorten the time taken to produce results by ensuring that ideas and comments flow to the right place and development of products are warranted and successfully launched.

Operational excellence translates to higher productivity and higher efficiency in staff performance. Under the lifelong learning plan, staff have recently been inducted into a "Learning not enough" seminar, which propounds the necessity of constant upgrading of skills and knowledge to keep up with changes in the information age. A number of experts in their various fields have also been invited on a regular basis to share with the NLB the "secrets" of lemaining competitive and overcoming obstacles amidst the "permanent white-water" situation of the twenty-first century.

With seventeen community libraries across the island and more being built each year, it is important to ensure that even-one practices the same standards and that best practices are shared among the branches for consistent and efficient operations. This is done through regular fortnightly meetings among the managers of all the public libraries with the directors, as well as formal briefings and communications by the manager of each branch to her branch staff. With the NLB's propensity for policy revisions and implementation of new services, it is especially important for staff to be kept informed and in-the-know about new projects in the pipeline and those that are currently in existence. Product demonstrations and briefings are thus a regular feature to encourage staff participation and involvement in projects and to ensure that staff are equipped with the right knowledge to assist readers in using these services and facilities. Operational excellence also means sharing knowledge about what works best and ensuring that everyone has that same knowledge and experience to implement that practice in their individual tasks. This prevents duplication of effort and is a time-saving device, especially for staff facing the pressures of front-line service. This is partly the reason for the creation of the InfoXpress, which is a database for capturing frequently asked questions from the public. Staff having access to this database can use it to quickly satisfy readers' queries, as answers and reference sources have been indexed by topics. This enables staff not only to provide an in-depth customized reference service but also to become knowledgeable about handling different enquiries. A similar database using Lotus Notes as a platform for consolidating and sharing best practices is also in place at the Tampines Regional Library.

NLB has also recently been admitted to the Singapore Service Quality Class (SQC). It was launched by the Singapore Productivity and Standards Board in July 1997 and recognizes organizations that have achieved a high standard of performance. The NLB has already established and put into practice documented Service Standards over the last few years for various aspects of work performance, such as in the areas of customer service, collection development, administration and finance, grooming, programmes, staff development and human resource management. These measures ensure that:

- workflows are consistent across departments;
- the efficiency and effectiveness of services delivered can be systematically accessed; and
- output for all divisions is maintained at a high level.

The recent formation of the Programme Development Group in 1999 has also contributed to efficient operations in libraries. This group acts as a co-ordinating body for all programmes to be hosted at each of the 17 community libraries. As a result duplication efforts are eliminated, as the librarians at each library are no longer required to source for speakers and programmes on their own. With a central programming unit overseeing and managing the planning, sourcing and organising of various large-scale as well as bimonthly programmes, the programme workflow for branches is shortened and has become less operationally intensive. Staff at the libraries are thus freed from such administrative duties and can focus on serving the needs of the public more concertedly.

The roles and expectations of paraprofessionals in the NLB have expanded in scope and depth. Traditionally, they have handled routine and unchallenging tasks such as the processing of books for borrowing and returning. Now, they are expected to provide basic reference information service and receiving both structured and on-the-job training is essential to their job requirements. Databases like the above are thus vital tools to enable paraprofessionals and professionals alike to share their experience, knowledge and expertise with one another, so that the NLB's information service as a whole is raised to a new level of competence.

In view of the numerous comments about the user-unfriendliness of the OPAC system, the NLB has spent a total of $6 million to upgrade its computer systems. With the Everybody's Catalogue replacing OPAC, users no longer need to type-in commands, but can click on the displayed tool bar menu to navigate their searches. Thus, knowledge gained from usability studies has helped the NLB to design an interface that is windows-based and is easy to use. This simple yet powerful online cataloguing system thus makes it more conducive for readers to perform do-it-yourself searches.

Best practices, operational procedures and policies in general are regularly circulated among staff and are also posted to the NLB's intranet to ensure that staff actively acquire the knowledge essential to perform their duties as well as they can. The Project Broadcast database, as part of the Lotus Notes platform, was also implemented to record team members' contributions and accomplishments for projects to which they have been assigned. This is valuable in accessing staff performance and also for tracking the success and failures of various initiatives and gives a good guide to how successful ideas and work processes from one project can be applied to the next.

Above are just some examples of knowledge management efforts in which the NLB is currently engaged. There is a strong corporate culture within the NLB, which allows ideas and expertize to be shared among staff of all grades and across time and space. This pro-sharing environment is also strongly supported by very advanced technology and infrastructure, in the form of the best PCs available, the fastest connections possible, the best facilities for the newer libraries and the recruitment of the best staff for top key management positions. What is perhaps lacking is the glaring absence of a knowledge audit system to record the expertize of staff and to keep a record of the best practices of branches or divisions, which can be transferred across departments.

The challenges faced by librarians in this knowledge-based environment and how the corporate culture is essential in helping staff to internalise the knowledge-seeking, sharing and lifelong learning process are discussed further.

11.6.3. Roles and Expectations of Librarians in the Knowledge Management Environment of the NLB

The traditional role played by the librarian was passive and he or she was engaged in routine and mundane tasks, such as shelf-reading of books, processing of books for borrowing and returning and, in general, performed duties which did not require much mental stimulation. In continuous information explosion and expansion era, librarians are increasingly valued and remunerated for their analytical skills and "professional" judgements. These are skills that are deemed to have been picked up by librarians from their constant exposure to all forms of media and other information sources in their working environment.

The current trend in the NLB is to employ people with varied educational and working backgrounds in order to tap into their areas of specialization and knowledge. There is also a need for librarians to be open to changes and to be willing to acquire and apply IT knowledge in their daily work - two vital characteristics essential to working in the knowledge-based environment of the NLB. The NLB has recently set up an institute to look into the continuous upgrading of the skills and knowledge of its staff. Courses, seminars and workshops are run for the benefit of staff to expose them to current information-processing trends and the information technology skills necessary to cope with new and emerging formats and databases acquired by the NLB for the public.

1. Librarian as Information Manager : Librarians' core duties now include information packaging and information customization. The initiative falls on the libraries to reach out to the community by targeting, anticipating and then meeting their informational requirements. Thus, various virtual communities have been set up student, business and Chinese virtual community - to cater to the interests and needs of the specific groups within society. Continuous review, evaluation and revision of packaged information would be an important task for librarians to perform and to remain relevant to their audience.

Often, knowing where to obtain information is the key to being able to give readers the information they need. This involves active sourcing and extensive reading on the part of librarians. The reference point enquiry service provided by the National Reference Library is a good example, which aims to provide phone-in, e-mailed-in or faxed-in customized answers to enquirers. Owing to the nature of the enquiries received, often only pointers to specific Web sites or books or journals are necessary to satisfy the requests.

The three-tier library system envisaged in the Library 2000 report also aims to support this structure, which clearlv differentiates the roles played by staff in the three levels of information dissemination, based on the type of clientele they attract. In a Children's Community Library, for instance, the information needs of children below the age of ten years are not as sophisticated as those of adults and tertiary students, who visit the regional library in search of information.

This means that staff at the regional library would need more specialized reference training to be equipped to provide a more in-depth reference service to their readers.

2. Librarian as Teacher : User education, information literacy packages and class visits now assume, a core responsibility on the part of librarians to educate readers on how to search for information, how to conduct research, how to use electronic databases and the Internet to obtain information they need, and finally how to evaluate information obtained from print and non-print formats.

Librarians' roles have evolved from being mere disseminators of information to taking on the responsibility of "teaching" the public to acquire the basic reference skills necessary to conduct research on their own, with additional guidance from staff.

The core role that librarians need to play in general is active, involving research to be conducted, information to be packaged and knowledge to be passed on to the public. Some of the skills needed by the information professional in a knowledge-based environment can be summed up in the following:

- IT literacy, that is knowing how to use the appropriate technology to capture, catalogue and disseminate information and knowledge to the target audience and knowing how to translate that knowledge into a centralised database for employees of the organisation to access;
- a sharp and analytical mind;
- innovative and inquiring; and
- enables knowledge creation, flow and communication within the organisation and between staff and public.

The future directions for the NLB, as it moves rapidly into the knowledge management arena are discussed below.

11.6.4. Practical Methods

O'Dell and Grayson advocate that the first step towards creating a successful knowledge management system is being able to identify the core values of the organization that will keep customers happy and satisfied. Once the core values have been identified, the focus should turn to the key enablers that are important in supporting the knowledge management system. The NLB's focus has always been on its customers, sometimes to the extent of bending rules and regulations to satisfy their demands. Much has been done to probe and record the customer profiles of the NLB and a great deal of knowledge has been put to good use in the design and customization of databases and collections for users. Attention must now be turned to two key enablers discussed earlier-corporate culture and measurement for further improvements and for systematic knowledge management efforts to be accomplished on a larger scale in the NLB.

Knowledge auditing is one way to measure the success of the knowledge management efforts. This involves the identification and audit of intellectual assets and tagging a non-monetary value to them. As knowledge audit is undertaken to validate the organization's ability to achieve its goals and to monitor development of strategic capabilities, this can be measured in terms of compliments from customers, an increase in loans and attendance at public talks and workshops held at the libraries. Push technology and alert services can also be implemented to customize even further the information needs of its customer base.

Knowledge mapping is another practical method used. This involves a visual representation of intangible assets in an organization in the form of a tree or map. An NLB directory can be created, which details staffs expertize and knowledge, and this can be a useful tool for people seeking specific types of information. Recognition is also given to the "expert" for making known his or her area of specialization. The reputation of the individual is also garnered from this "free publicity" of the person's inherent knowledge. A scenario-planning tool such as TANGO is a third method used to measure the success of the knowledge management efforts. This helps managers to learn how to manage a knowledge organization. Perhaps the creation of a Knowledge Management Centre and the appointment of a Chief Knowledge Officer in the NLB can give credence and backing to the knowledge management efforts. This centre can look into ways of measuring the intellectual capital and knowledge transfer in tangible terms, such as implementing a monetary reward system to create an environment for the free flow of knowledge sharing and transfer.

Ultimately, however, the success of the knowledge management process is measured by both internal and external satisfaction from the NLB's employees and their customers. Visible signs are a low turnover rate, loyalty to the organization and a high morale among staff, who are able to keep up with the tremendous changes in the information rat race. Increased customer patronage and positive feedback from readers, together with increased loans and usage of library facilities, are healthy signs that the organization is meeting the customers' needs and expectations.

Thus, the NLB as a statutory board is only now slowly adopting parts of the knowledge-based management concepts in its operations. Many improvements have been made and, also there have been many behind-the-scene failures. What is encouraging is that staff and the public are being equipped with the knowledge necessary to cope with the rapid changes of the twenty-first century, which is more information-driven and knowledge-generated than any other era.

What the NLB needs to focus on next is a way to encourage more informal sharing and transfer of knowledge among staff and to devise a financial system to motivate and cultivate this sharing process. The knowledge management process must ultimately become a self-running and employee-driven system. More can be done to make the voices of its rank and file employees heard and be counted. Just as customers are the driving force for the NLB's existence, its staff are those who make the organisation work and function. Simply transplanting outside consultants to assume key management positions in the NLB and inviting them to give talks and seminars would not make the knowledge-sharing process effective and open. More employees can be groomed and encouraged to share the knowledge they have acquired through many years of experience. The NLB must touch base with it1 ground level statt tor the KM process to be a success. Only when knowledge-sharing efforts become truly effortless can the NLB lay claim to being an aspiring lifelong learning organization.

Such efforts can also be made to improve the conditions of public libraries in India.

11.7. KNOWLEDGE MANAGEMENT IN SPECIAL LIBRARIES

Librarians effectively create, locate, capture and share their organization's knowledge and expertize whilst they argue necessitates to make explicit and store for distribution and reuse and a Special/Corporate Library is a Centre with a special mission to fulfill the information needs of the parent organization. Libraries are repositories of information with documentary sources, centers of storing and organizations for information and knowledge. The Special Librarians are Information resource experts who collect, analyze, evaluate, package and disseminate information to facilitate accurate decision making in corporate, academic and government settings. The Special Librarian's job involves apart from providing traditional services through an operational documentary base and online searching the access, organization, sorting, repackaging, synthesizing, finding answers and understanding members' specializations.

Librarians who are experienced in the information field are constantly working closely with the user who is a member of the organization, and it is easy for the promotion of interaction between the users. Librarians have an interaction with other libraries. They are an important knowledge base for the organization.

It is pertinent to say that Special Libraries and the Librarians are in the best position to be key players in the knowledge management of their organization.

11.7.1. Challenges for the Special Librarian

Knowledge Management is of growing importance in organizational development as a dynamic process. It is also most important to the financial services sector. The banking industry has become very competitive, and customer focus, addressing issues on financial regulations, trade and globalization are foremost in the banking agenda.

In the Sri Lankan financial services sector, commercial banking is a dominant services industry, facing an aggressive competitive environment. This sector comprises of 22 Commercial banks out of which there are 11 domestic banks. A study of domestic banks' libraries conducted to find out the Library and information work done in the knowledge management field for organizational development, reveals that out of the 11 banks, 8 have libraries with an objective of delivering library and Information Services (LIS) for organizational work and decision-making, professional development and acting as an organization for learning.

The study also revealed that most libraries are working towards or have an approach to knowledge management, but mainly through Information Management practices. All libraries apart from providing traditional library services and explicit knowledge, are involved in tracing organizational information and history, done by collecting organizational information from Annual Reports and organizational reports, internal reports, conference, seminar and workshop proceedings, circulars, and by discussions with people. Interactions with organizational members for deriving knowledge and interactions between members for sharing knowledge according to their specializations are carried out by 5 libraries. 5 libraries are involved in networking. Creating knowledge through information gathered by providing information products are practiced by 5 libraries and 7 are using information technology tools such as e-mail, internet and the intranet to deliver the information for creation and practices of knowledge management.

However these information behaviour practices in the context of knowledge practices is done almost in an informal manner, other than the explicitly transferred knowledge through traditional library services. Information is a central need for organizations, but the main practice of information management is the acquisition and management of external information, with little interest in methodical acquiring and effective management and organization of internal information for knowledge sharing. Therefore important functions are lost without due recognition of the special libraries and librarians in the knowledge management processes, leaving the library to be perceived as a passive entity delivering routine and conventional services. This is the main contributory factor cited in the literature about the librarians been regarded only as part of the support staff of the organization, working quietly in the background, often uninvolved in any of the critical functions of the organization. Information professionals have to recast their roles as knowledge professionals and function as knowledge workers.

Therefore the special librarian will have to address the challenges before them and reposition LIS to suit current management thinking.

Improving the image of the Special Librarian is a major challenge to overcome and another is to work with limited resources such as financial, human and technological resources.

It would be difficult to convince the management to increase budget allocations or funds for the library with such perceptions of the library, where as funds are needed to go into new projects. This could be addressed by joining a network with similar institutions for effective sharing of knowledge. If the Internet connection is available then the intranet is a powerful technological and a marketing tool to disseminate information and interact with the organizational users. Make effective e-mail and the library software based internal flow of information. Thus with the professional experience and skills these endeavors can facilitate the access of information without being worried about the expenses for commercial software.

Working with the available staff is essential. Thus lead the team and use the skills of other members for effective services and provide training and development opportunities for them.

It is necessary to have a deep understanding of the information needs of the users as well as to obtain their expertize knowledge for direction to others needing them. Interact with the users and employees at strategic levels to transfer knowledge about the rest of the organization. This requires a database of persons. Usually provision of Selective Dissemination of Information services helps in knowing what is required by individual users. This needs to be developed to acquire knowledge of what they are specialized in.

To interact it is necessary to develop teams. Teams play a central part in the knowledge creating company as they provide a shared context where individuals can interact with each other and have a constant dialogue. Since converting tacit knowledge of individuals to explicitness is vital to generate organizational knowledge it requires a shared context through interaction to create new perspectives. This also requires to maintain a good relationship with the Senior Management.

Effective information management is a major concern. This can be accomplished by the management and organization of information and providing related and needs based services. The librarian must acquire the relevant information, organize it for effective access by the users and transfer knowledge to decision makers. Establish cost effective user oriented and value added information services that are aligned with the organizational strategies. Continue to improve accessibility of information by evaluating the transmitting processes.

Promotion, innovation, creation and generation of knowledge are critical targets of organizational knowledge. Research, analyze, repackage and product and competitor information to be made available in a proactive manner for effective awareness. Compile databases based on the software available. It must be continuous to reflect the firm's changing context. Deliver specific information packages and alerting services such as competitive intelligence, business intelligence and Industry monitors for proper representation of knowledge.

11.7.2. Other Efforts

Other efforts for knowledge management may be alike thsoe have discussed in academic/public libraries case.

11.8. LIS EDUCATION FOR KNOWLEDGE MANAGEMENT

There is a growing acknowledgement within the literature that the LIS professions have a serious contribution to make to the success of knowledge management, but also that in the process Library & Information Science (LIS) education needs to undergo substantial change. However, the broad interdisciplinary nature of the subject has complicated such matters as curriculum design and the additional capabilities accruing to students and sources of provision, while not enough is known about the educational needs of future students or skill sets demanded by the market for knowledge-literate library and information professionals. Nor, in seeking to respond to such challenges and others more specific to knowledge management, have educators and other stakeholders had much to go on in terms of relevant research findings. This situation is improving in Australia. The Australian Library and Information Association has launched a project called Library and information science education for the knowledge age [LISEKA]. Its purpose is 'to develop an education framework to underpin the career-long education of future generations of library and information workers, to sustain them throughout their careers'. There are examples of similar projects that are being undertaken elsewhere by LIS bodies.

LIS schools have responded in different ways to the need to educate professionals and provide them with the appropriate knowledge-related skills and capabilities. However, this response has appeared at times to be somewhat haphazard and often a reaction to perceived threats, either of a technological nature or from other professional groups. The interdisciplinary nature of knowledge management and the presence of a range of general management-type programs, along with those aimed at specific professional groups, has militated against any broad consensus on curriculum content or vehicles for provision. There is a need for in-depth research that sets the knowledge management education process for LIS professionals firmly within the wider educational environment, which identifies current trends and, on the basis of feedback from key knowledge management players including educators, employers and professional bodies, investigates the options and alternatives available to LIS educators and provides a framework for future action.

As can be seen from an online search of LIS databases, there is already an emerging literature on the knowledge management dimension to LIS education. However much of this literature is descriptive rather than research-based, depicting different approaches to knowledge management education in practical situations. Three notable themes emerging in the literature which are reviewed briefly here are: educational requisites and market demands, the different approaches taken towards knowledge management education and new job opportunities.

11.8.1. New Job Opportunities

In view of the links between information and knowledge, the LIS community can be seen to have an early involvement in aspects of what would now be called knowledge management. This has particularly been the case in the organization and retrieval of information, something that has found new impetus under the guise of content management, a major element of knowledge management practice. Not surprisingly, therefore, the literature is rich in calls for information professionals to expand their horizons and use their special skills in the management of information to become key contributors to the development of knowledge management.

As recognition of these new career opportunities for LIS professionals has dawned, the education sector has begun to respond with additions and in some cases quite radical reforms to their curricula. In 1998, Reardon reviewed developments in LIS education from the 1940s to the 1990s, and traced the path from bibliographic management to information management and its segmentation into specialisms along with the emerging demands of the private sector. He identified the presence of networked contacts within the profession as a substantial basis for LIS involvement with knowledge management initiatives.

Reardon argued that LIS courses needed to focus more on the theoretical elements of knowledge, as well as on human behaviour as a generator of knowledge. He provided a framework for developing knowledge management courses which reflected the importance of different skills and studies in this context and promoted the idea of a central role for LIS professionals, along with the need for them to have faith in their own abilities and to have the confidence for self-promotion. A paper by Martin Knowledge management and the US professions entitled 'New directions in education for LIS' was also a clear illustration of this kind of response. In it Martin described the fundamental changes in mission and objectives of one education provider, the School of Business Information Technology at RMIT University. There he attributed to the challenges of a changing job market and the need among other things, for the department to amend its recruitment strategies in order to recruit students who were more commercially and technically oriented, in comparison with its traditional LIS entrants.

Although recommendations of this kind were a step in the right direction and led to genuine changes in both the LIS curriculum and in perceptions of professional roles, they failed to generate any consensus on the place of knowledge management in LIS education, let alone a coherent response by either educators or professional bodies. However, the literature does reflect a growing interest in markets for knowledge management staff and in the related education and skills of the people competing for employment in those markets.

11.8.2. Educational Requisites and Market Demands

To evaluate market demands and identify the skills of knowledge managers as required by their employers, Morris analysed knowledge management job advertisements in the UK over a six-month period, and then asked knowledge management employers and agencies to confirm their perceptions of both the required skills and likely growth in the job market. She concluded that the UK market for knowledge management roles was still relatively small, but was growing. She pointed out that the key skills of knowledge management could vary from post to post, but could nevertheless, be divided into the following general categories: experience and general skills, educational requirements, personal attributes, knowledge management skills, LIS/information management skills and IT skills.

Additionally, to identify the core perceptions of information professionals about knowledge management and the skill sets it required. Todd and Southon conducted a two-year study, based on their experience at the Department of Information Studies at the University of Technology, Sydney, they assessed the opinions of 56 leading information professionals across Australia by means of a questionnaire and focus group discussions. The questionnaire highlighted the changing role of the information industry with trends and developments in services, markets, technology and professional roles, which demanded that more attention should be paid to the human element in knowledge management in organizations.

A number of themes emerged from this research, leading to certain assumptions about the nature of information and knowledge, the differences between knowledge management and information management and the understanding of organizational culture. The themes were the knowledge management phenomenon, the place of knowledge management in information science, organization structure and performance, intuition and technology, communication and culture, techniques and solutions, the corporate knowledge base, and knowledge management strategies.

They also reported some challenges that they faced in evaluating the first cycle of their own knowledge management program. These included creating enough confidence among students, providing a defined role for them in knowledge management, promoting the business awareness of students and creating organisational links to situate their learning and using internet more effectively.

In a similar study, Breen et al., conducted three separate surveys covering the United Kingdom and Ireland, embracing not only the desired skills, but also the personality characteristics deemed necessary if LIS graduates were to take full advantage of new opportunities in the private sector. The first questionnaire sought to identify the requisite skills of information specialists in human resource departments in the information management industry. It revealed that companies did not intend to use librarians for the subject organisation of digital information. The second survey aimed to explore how well LIS educational programs equipped students with the necessary skills identified in the first study. Supplemented by data from departmental websites, it revealed that in addition to courses that prepared students for employment in the library sector, LIS schools also offered some courses that would be helpful for working in the broader information management sector. The third survey, of LIS graduate perceptions of the extent to which their studies had been helpful in the workplace revealed that while LIS graduates had appropriate skills to become information or knowledge managers, there remained a need to change the stereotypical view of the librarian, and to highlight their competence and capabilities in this field. The survey also revealed a need for LIS schools to think not just in terms of skills, but also of the personality traits of graduates.

Milne on the other hand, reviewed the literature on the role of information professionals in knowledge-based organizations in order to specify the essential skills and attitudes of knowledge workers that had to be considered by LIS schools in planning their educational programs. She emphasized the ability to work in multi-disciplinary teams as essential to the process and practice of knowledge management, and suggested that LIS educators promote the generic skills of their students by adopting creative learning/teaching styles. She also concluded, however, that most information graduates already possessed the skills and attributes that they needed for success in a knowledge management environment. However, to find their place in this new environment, information professionals needed to work to change a current mindset outside the profession, whereby librarians were seen as being merely service providers. They also needed to work to increase the understanding of their key role in the development of business within their organizations and to apply their information management skills to meet current challenges.

11.8.3. Different Approaches to Knowledge Management Education

Not only is knowledge management multidisciplinary in nature: other professional areas and disciplines have an interest in it. As a consequence, multiple perspectives, initiatives, procedures and strategies have been implemented in the knowledge management field. Knowledge management discourses have occurred within the educational programs of many disciplines, including computer and business schools as well as library and information science departments. Accordingly, various approaches have been proposed for designing and conducting knowledge management education programs.

Chaudhry and Higgins studied different approaches to knowledge management education in various academic disciplines by examining a sample of 37 courses offered in the USA, the UK, Australia, Canada and Singapore. They concluded that in the delivery of these programs, information systems departments gave more emphasis to the information technology component of the program, while information studies departments were more disposed to an emphasis on information organisation and retrieval. Business schools were found to put more emphasis on business strategies. Hence, the authors suggested the need for a collaborative approach to knowledge management education to avoid the danger of unevenness in content.

Researchers at the School of Computer and Information Science at Edith Cowan University developed a provisional model for a knowledge management course. In doing so, they sought to measure the preferences of information professionals in relation to course content and course options, industry demand for knowledge management qualified personnel, and attitudes toward knowledge management. The results of this survey showed that there was ambivalence among information professionals regarding the inclusion of information science subjects, including information organization and information retrieval, in the curriculum. The results also revealed strong support for the provision of intensive short courses, as well as ongoing market demands for trained knowledge management personnel. In undertaking this study, Brogan et al., suggested that LIS course designers consider the multi-disciplinary character of knowledge management and the competitive nature of the marketplace, while noting that information science subjects were not enough by themselves.

As most authors acknowledge, this variety in content and emphasis in knowledge management courses has created competition for knowledge management graduates. Arguably, since LIS courses equip students with sufficient skills for participating in key knowledge management processes, they should be competitive in this market, provided the LIS schools apply rational education and training strategies.

So, it seems clear that there is much of relevance to the future prospects of the LIS professions. It is relatively easy to demonstrate a role for LIS professionals in knowledge management that is basically a continuation of the find, organise and disseminate junction that has long been fulfilled by the information professions. This role is already apparent within the content management area of knowledge management. What is not so simple is to understand and then articulate how LIS professionals can migrate to other knowledge management roles within organizations, especially those of a strategic or policy-making nature. Broadbent has written about two foundations for knowledge management: the management of information flows and, the application of peoples' competencies, skills, talents, thoughts, ideas, intuitions, commitments, motivations and imagination. It is not clear how either the work experience or educational background of most LIS professionals would equip them to operate within this area of the organizational knowledge management domain.

However, the problems, and the associated need for more research, begin further back than the point at which things begin to happen in library and information centres. The essential problem is to do with the nature of knowledge and its management, and with the challenges of separating the generic elements of knowledge management from those that are organizationally, professionally or disciplinarily contextual. It is only when we fully understand the nature of the overall domain that we can begin to address issues around the application of knowledge management within an LIS context.

Within the literature of LIS, two points are emerging with some clarity. The first is that information professionals have the potential to make a serious contribution to the practice of knowledge management and the second is that knowledge management has much to offer to the management of libraries and advancement of the professions. Knowledge management is a wide, interdisciplinary field and it goes beyond individual skills and qualifications to embrace the many aspects of management of a key resource. This suggests that rather more is needed than for LIS professionals to promote their expertise more widely if they to aspire to involvement at the strategic and policy-making level. For many in the information professions this is likely to entail the cultivation of new attitudes and the learning of different kinds of skills; and opening up to new ways of thinking. However, this is not a challenge faced by the LIS profession alone and several traditional areas, such as human resources management, find themselves with the same challenge. If the LIS professions are to respond effectively they will be better able to do so if informed by empirical research into past and current practices, with emerging lessons learned and an understanding of potential methodologies and strategic options.

Knowledge management education in Library & Information Science (LIS) yet to be started in Indian Library Schools. There are very few universities which have included knowledge management in research level programmes. But we can hope that it will soon be included in the curriculum at under graduate and Post graduate levels for future benefits.

11.9. BARRIERS TO THE MIGRATION OF LIS PROFESSIONALS

There is a general acknowledgement within the literature that although LIS professionals may have excellent information management skills, they need to gain additional skills and cross existing boundaries in order to become significant players in knowledge management. The obstacles might be personal, organizational and/or professional; some may arise from the personal characteristics of LIS graduates and some from their inappropriate type of education. Abell and Oxbrow state that from the employer's point of view the specific obstacles are as follows:

- lack of business knowledge,
- lack of understanding of the interplay between information and organizational objectives,
- poor team and leadership skills, and
- lack of management skills.

A general focus on external information lack of business understanding and lack of visibility of the discipline itself have resulted in hampering the impact of LIS skills in knowledge management environments. Schwarzwalder claims that the major disadvantage of librarians as knowledge management players is that they have little or no influence in terms of changing organizational culture. Librarians are poorly placed as change agents but, as already suggested, they can expand their influence by partnering with other groups within their organizations.

A review of the literature, establishes that for many commentators the principal barriers for LIS professionals are their:

- concern with external information resources rather than internal organizational knowledge assets,
- lack of business knowledge,
- content ignorance,
- image problem,
- name problem,
- lack of visibility,
- personality issues, and

- lack of the required management skills.

11.9.1. Concern with External Information Resources

It has been claimed that librarians limit themselves to external and published information. In 1998, having conducted some case studies of knowledge management in practice, Cooper reported that some of the former researchers were hesitant about involvement in the management of internal information, partly because in their professional education and previous experience they had concentrated on external sources of information and partly because involvement in the management of internal information was perceived to offer little of value in terms of their own career development. TFPL Limited, London study conducted in 1999 mentioned supports the view that librarians were more concerned with external information and to some extent the management of records and documents. Tom Davenport and Lawrence Prusak went so far as to blame information professionals for preferring books to people, although the comment is outdated and may have lost some validity. Writing from a higher educational perspective, Townley states that librarians do not manage knowledge about their organizations as they manage their other resources and claims that they have done little to use organizational information to create knowledge that could be used to improve the functionality of library and higher education processes.

These and many other commentators refer to librarians' strong focus on external sources of knowledge as a barrier to their fuller engagement with knowledge management practice but, in sharp contrast, some research suggests that anything between eighty and ninety-five percent of the information used in an organization is generated internally - an important point for LIS professionals seeking to contribute to knowledge management, according to Abell and Oxbrow. Michael Koenig, however, sees this barrier beginning to crumble, arguing that knowledge management is moving into a new stage of recognition for the importance and incorporation of information and knowledge external to the parent organization. Although the knowledge management "mindset" for years has focused on organizations' internal information and knowledge assets, he claims that the "narrow emphasis of knowledge management is now broadening", believing this "phenomenon" to be driven by the "extension of Intranet based KM systems to Extranet based systems". "Concern about the knowledge about to be lost as post war baby-boomers are beginning to hit retirement age" and a "repeat of the same broadening phenomenon that occurred with MIS, Management Information Systems".

According to Koenig, such information and knowledge has always been the province of the librarian and the information professional, and this apparent "broadening" of the knowledge management domain presents obvious and important opportunities for the field of librarianship, particularly in the area of the organization's knowledge management system design. If he is correct, LIS professionals need to take into account both external and internal knowledge sources, and learn to manage both forms of resource. It remains to be seem, however, whether he is correct. His paper cites the argument that is a rather abstract one, especially the notion that the "broadening phenomenon that occurred with MIS" might act as a driver of current attitudes towards knowledge management. Those in the LIS community who are interested in professional engagement with knowledge management will no doubt watch with interest for more empirical evidence of a shift in "mindset" but until such a shift actually happens the continuing focus of the LIS profession on external information resources is likely to be seen as a significant barrier to its knowledge management credentials.

11.9.2. Ignorance of Business Goals

The second main point noted in this review is that knowledge management is an integrated approach to the achievement of organizational goals and that the potential contribution of LIS professionals to knowledge management initiatives might be inhibited by a general ignorance of business goals. Those working in the special libraries sector are accustomed to hearing and reading that their efforts need to become more closely aligned to business goals and practice, and many do indeed take pride in their level of corporate involvement. It is clear that such engagement is essential if LIS professionals are to have any impact on their organizations' knowledge management. A study of knowledge management job advertisements in Australia over a three month period in 2005, for instance, found that, while it was difficult to draw hard-and-fast distinctions between operational and strategic functions, a large percentage of the advertisements were strategically focused and required, amongst their leading attributes, a strong background in business analysis. However, there is found very little evidence of involvement of information professionals in knowledge management implementation at a strategic level and suggested that the graduates of LIS schools "lacked business understanding" and "commitment to organizational goals". St. Claire, DiMattia and Oder addressed similar obstacles, including a lack of organizational and political understanding, unwillingness to address issues of return on investment, insufficient understanding of business practices and limited access to high-level decision-making.

There is nothing new about these claims. Davenport and Prusak in their paper call for information professionals to get out of the library and into the business, an exhortation that has been repeated many times. Many in the profession, especially those working in special libraries, would argue that is precisely what they have been doing. Nonetheless, the view that LIS professionals need to engage more with core business persists. Doug Church suggests that information professionals should think in terms of benefits to their organizations. In a similar vein, Pearlstein claims that librarians need to "understand that they do not work in a vacuum, their library's services must be tied directly to the corporate mission". Schwarzwalder states:

"Unfortunately, many library efforts focus on projects with very little payback. Often these projects are focused on making the operation of the library more efficient. While this is a laudable goal, these efforts typically yield small incremental gains that are invisible to the customer base. Such efforts do little to convince sponsors that the library is capable of engineering-or even recognizing-worthwhile knowledge management applications."

Southon and Todd were blaming librarians for not considering overall goals in their activities. They state that: "the focus was on the technical processes of gathering and organizing information to enable access, with little engagement with what is done with that information or the overall impact of the service on the organization" and that all LIS activities should be conducted in the light of overall organizational objectives. Davenport and Cronin found that much information science literature places knowledge management essentially within traditional information science frameworks with little extension to the conceptual and organizational dimensions. As Butler puts it :

Librarians have been actively involved in knowledge management for many years - but in their libraries, not in relation to the organization as a whole. And here in lies the key. As previously outlined, knowledge management is holistic. It affects the whole of the organization and most of its elements. Senior management in many public and private sector organizations, therefore sometimes do not automatically think of involving their libraries in their knowledge initiatives. Because libraries tend not to be aligned with the goals of the business, they are still not viewed as integral to the business.

This is a point that LIS educators would do well to note.

11.9.3. Content Ignorance

Business knowledge lack is the third main barrier identified here as content ignorance. Davenport and Prusak blame information professionals for their distance from the information content and usage of information. It is suggested that "librarians' traditional reluctance to move beyond the information container towards analysis and interpretation of its contents has resulted in organizations overlooking their potential contribution, even in areas where their competence should be obvious. Information professionals are seen as service-oriented, but not value-oriented - they do not understand the impact they can have on the business. Van House and Sutton stated: "the traditional focus of LIS has not been on information at all but rather on its containers - books, journals, maps and so on. It acquires, describes, stores and disseminates them without much concern for how their intellectual content is used". As Barlow put it so aptly: "We thought for many years that we were in the wine business. In fact, we were in the bottling business. And we do not know a damned thing about wine."

While these criticisms might suggest poor linkage between libraries and the overall goals of their parent organizations, they also highlight the potential contribution for libraries to leverage knowledge management initiatives within their organizations, provided they see the implications of knowledge management activities for the success of their parent organizations and start working to expand a more business-oriented perspective within the profession.

11.9.4. Image Problem

The image problem facing some LIS professionals is a barrier to knowledge management engagement that hardly needs laboring - the old stereotypes and reputation that attach themselves to the profession, including hair in buns, sensible shoes and the stern bespectacled, cardigan-clad "shushing" controller of books, do not encourage employers to employ LIS professionals at high levels of management. As Breen et. al., state: "Few people, if asked to describe a librarian, would include the adjectives – risk-taking or ambitious. Neither are librarians perceived as being creative". Research a few years ago suggested that while LIS graduates are being equipped with the necessary skills, the image of "the librarian" was significantly impeding the entry of LIS graduates into the knowledge management employment sector. Graduates with LIS skills need to market themselves more effectively in the information technology workplace.

While LIS graduates may have many of the qualities required in a knowledge manager, a survey of companies in the business sector revealed that human resource managers do not think of LIS graduates when they recruit information specialists. Furthermore, even LIS departments do not perceive their graduates as "ambitious" or "risk-takers" or, in many cases, as having the requisite "business acumen". There would seem to be a two-fold problem - the image of librarians and the perceived characteristics of candidates versus the desired ones. While librarians are still being taught the basic skills of classification and information organization, their common barrier to entering this employment field, it is suggested, is the stereotypical view of the librarian. There is an implication that the librarian's skill in creating order indicates a lack of creativity and a disinterest in how the information is used.

One of the hopes is that, with developments in LIS education and in the range of professional and personal development undertaken by many in the profession, employers' perceptions may change. Such a change is suggested by Anne Morris's report which refers to signs that employers' perceptions are changing, based on the increasing number of advertisements for knowledge management positions stipulating the desirability of an LIS degree. Nonetheless, expectations on both sides still need to improve.

Numerous websites document attempts to change the old stereotypes under which librarians have suffered. "Progressive Librarian", "The Shifted librarian", "New Breed Librarian", Information Officer, Information Scientist and "Anarchist Librarian" are all examples of these efforts although the last may not appeal to employers anxious to maximize management of their organization's intellectual assets.

11.9.5. Name Problem

Name Problem is generally accepted that the external perception of the profession has greatly improved, but it still has a long way to go if the profession's qualifications and career paths are to be regarded in the same esteem as those of other professional groups, such as engineers, doctors, lawyers and so on. Closely linked to the problem of image is the name, librarian, which, although simple and functional, is seen to serve the profession as a whole rather poorly in the third millennium. "According to *The American Heritage Dictionary of the English Language*, a librarian is a person who is a specialist in library work". Shamel asks whether that describes what all LIS professionals do? Terminology does make a difference although Abell and Oxbrow suggest that the title librarian should not necessarily determine the role librarians play or how they are perceived. A title should not be constraining. They need to think in terms of what they can achieve rather than in terms of their nomenclature. To suggest, however, that position titles should not necessarily affect how librarians are perceived is a purely normative statement and does not reflect the realities of organizational politics.

11.9.6. Visibility

This brings one to the issue of visibility. For years some commentators have reported a general lack of awareness among managers about the real contributions made by libraries and information centers. Shamel asks "Why do we not make ourselves known to these people? How can the Harvard Business Review write a book on knowledge management and not include the role of librarians? Who among us can reach the authors and publishers of such business books so that they carry our message to managers and decision-makers?". This problem may stem from education. As Shamel puts it, "The business literature does not communicate the value of librarians and information management skills. The business schools do not teach the value of librarians and information managers along with the role of technology. It is a wonder any business today employs any librarians at all...I interviewed the president of a pharmaceutical company which employs over 700 people. It has two drugs on the market, many more in the pipeline, and not one librarian."

11.9.7. Personal Attributes

Some commentators believe that one of the main barriers for LIS professionals to engagement in knowledge management at a high level is their personal attributes, which are based in a specific educational culture. Sue Myburgh believes that the most dangerous threat to the profession is the "librarian mindset". In a key passage, Abell and Oxbrow put it this way.

"People in senior positions were not born with an innate understanding of their industry or organization. They acquired it throughout their career, just as information professionals do - or do they? Is that the difference - that those reaching top management positions never saw any barriers to doing so? Their training as an accountant, engineer or HR professional did not somehow set them apart from the business of their organization. They expected that

there would be opportunities for them and they were ready to take them."

How many information professionals set out with the same attitude, or are ready to look for opportunities to extend their experience and influence? How many expect that they could and should succeed at senior management level?

One could add, how many university librarians even attempt to move into promoted positions outside the library?

Davenport and Cano, said that – knowledge work is about the acquisition, creation, packaging, application or reuse of knowledge. They point to the need to take a process approach to knowledge work, maintaining, moreover, that people involved in knowledge management initiatives typically showed attributes of ambition and risk taking. These are not, by general consensus, the characteristics of many people currently in the LIS profession. Another general criticism of LIS professionals is that they are reluctant and/or slow to change even when the need to do so is apparent, with the result that they fail to seize the opportunities. For this reason, Loughridge suggests, more attention should be paid to the personality, motivation and career aspirations of the students recruited. This is an area that may repay some study because it is by no means clear that LIS schools and departments are attracting students who are significantly different from those recruited in the days when most LIS students were self-confessed bibliophiles. Indeed, while many might disagree, there is anecdotal evidence from educators that nothing much has changed in terms of student recruitment.

11.9.8. Lack of Management Skills

Lack of management skills is one of the main reasons given in the literature for librarians' low status and image amongst employers. It is worth noting that, although the British studies suggested that LIS students were graduating with the skills and understandings to work in the knowledge management environment, there is also some indication that LIS professionals are not generally involved in knowledge management implementation at a strategic level. Earlier it was suggested that there is a distinction between managing knowledge and being a knowledge manager, and that the latter involves effecting significant change in organizational culture. Todd and Southon make a similar distinction between knowledge management, "which involves the co-ordination of a broad range of professionals and disciplines, *led by a professional of very high-level skills*", and what they call "the enriched role of the information professional within a broader knowledge management program".

The study of Australian knowledge management job advertisements mentioned earlier found that a substantial proportion of the positions advertised required a high degree of strategic *nous* and were geared to objectives such as the fostering of knowledge sharing, leveraging of corporate knowledge, development of knowledge management strategies and the organization of cultural change. Characteristics looked for by the organizations or their recruitment agencies included "a strong background in business analysis, previous consultancy experience, experience of a wide variety technologies, high-level conceptual skills, project and change management skills, and of course a significant track record in knowledge management initiatives". Lack of these high level management skills constitutes a significant barrier to greater engagement by LIS professionals in knowledge management.

Summing up, it can be said that knowledge management has emerged as a key concern of management. And, on one thing most of the knowledge management literature is agreed - knowledge management is a multi-faceted discipline or area of practice, which requires a wide range of capabilities. It is therefore unavoidable that LIS professionals would demonstrate deficiencies as well as proficiencies were they to attempt to take full advantage of emerging knowledge management opportunities. Of course, the same might be said to apply to any of the other professional groups with a stake in knowledge management, but if LIS professionals are to engage successfully in knowledge management, they not only need to reinforce their knowledge management-enabling competencies- they must also take a holistic view, cross boundaries and go beyond the narrow scope of their profession. As Abell and Oxbrow say, moving out of a specific information role for a while does not necessarily mean leaving the profession. It could be the opportunity to acquire experience that enables professional expertise to be applied with more obvious benefit. It is worth recalling a point put by CW Choo :

"*To reinvent their roles, information professionals need to move from being information custodians to knowledge partners who have the entrepreneurial energy, the business knowledge, and the specialized skills to lever the power of information. This attitudinal shift and role redefinition must take place in a framework of a deeper and more complete understanding of how organizations create, share, and use knowledge. Knowledge management is not the domain of a single profession but is the result of collaboration across multiple streams of expertize.*"

There is considerable consensus along the lines, however, that the LIS profession faces significant barriers if its members are to become major players in the knowledge management domain. Part of the problem stems from the profession's long-standing focus on published information resources as distinct from information resources and knowledge generated within organizations. According to Koenig, knowledge management is broadening to include external information resources - which would remove one of the barriers to greater LIS engagement in knowledge management - but that broadening remains to be demonstrated, and in the meantime the profession also continues to be hindered by its traditional focus on the information "container", as distinct from the content. Linked to this is the continuing view - right or wrong - that members of the profession lack the business knowledge required to be a serious contributor to the leveraging of corporate knowledge. There are also the related barriers of image, nomenclature and visibility, two of which may be beyond the control of the profession, the personality traits of librarians - if, indeed, one can generalize about these - and finally the management skills.

On this last issue there is not a clear consensus. The British studies suggest that LIS professionals are graduating with the required skills for the knowledge management environment, yet it is widely agreed that knowledge management requires a multi-disciplinary approach and, if job advertisements are a worthwhile guide, organizations are looking for people with very high level management skills and experience to effect the required changes in organizational structure and culture. Not all positions in the knowledge management sector require a strategic focus like those considered here. There is a significant proportion of positions advertised that require operational expertise. Whether or not one accepts Koenig's proposition that we are entering a fourth phase of knowledge management implementation in which there is greater focus on external sources of information, there is no doubt, judging by job advertisements and the many advertisements for conferences, workshops and seminars, that we have been going through a period of greater focus on specific areas of knowledge management - such as the development of corporate taxonomies - some of which may call on the kinds of information management expertize LIS graduates have.

What is clear is that, if they are to negotiate the barriers outlined here and contribute to their organizations' knowledge management development, LIS professionals need to be able to map out the contributions that the profession is already making to knowledge management and its potential contribution. There appears to be little attempt in the growing body of literature on LIS professionals and knowledge management to do so but there is a growing number of case studies that may provide useful indicators. Such an exercise would be useful both for the profession itself and for its educators. Knowledge management programs tend to vary according to the academic department providing the program, and there may be a danger that the focus on information "containers" at the expense of content is perpetuated by educational programs. Of course, this may be unavoidable where LIS educators attempt to add knowledge management to already full LIS programs instead of providing separate knowledge management programs, thus preparing LIS graduates for the potential job market in knowledge management.

For LIS researchers, there is a considerable amount to be done, not simply in terms of the mapping exercise referred to here. If it is the case that librarians still suffer in terms of image and visibility then there is a clear need to undertake some market research and establish just what senior managers think they want in their knowledge managers and how they perceive the LIS profession. For the professional associations, too, there may be some work ahead. Breen and her colleagues suggest that LIS graduates need to market themselves more effectively. This is a role that they share with their professional associations. If some of the external perceptions about the profession are unfounded, such as the view that LIS professionals are insufficiently engaged in and knowledgeable about business goals - and it is assumed here that these are misconceptions - then our professional bodies need to help persuade employers and employers' associations that the profession has changed, that it continues to change and that its contribution to organizational knowledge sharing and generation can contribute to organizational performance.

University librarians have made significant attempts in recent years to move beyond their library walls and engage more with their parent institutions. The most obvious example is the development of institutional repositories, typically projects that have been led by university librarians. Such developments see university libraries transform themselves from collecting agencies, responsible for the development and management of collections of published information resources, to publishers, with a focus on providing access to their universities' research output. Earlier five broad roles for librarians in knowledge management were identified– facilitating an environment conducive to knowledge sharing; managing the corporate memory; transfer of information management and related skills to a new context that is linked to business processes and core operations; development of corporate information literacy; and management of information in a digital/ electronic environment. The development of institutional repositories and supporting metadata engages roles third and fifth.

The fourth role is another in which there are interesting developments, with an increasing emphasis in recent years on embedding information literacy instruction in the curriculum, but here too there is a challenge. Librarians need to move beyond the notion that information literacy is concerned primarily with teaching library users about the library's information tools-catalogues, databases and so on, and to see it in broader terms of furthering their universities' mission to foster lifelong learning in its students and of engaging with organizational learning to develop an information literate workforce. They need to convince themselves, not just senior management, that they have a contribution to make.

Thus, Knowledge management is a wide, interdisciplinary field and it goes beyond individual skills and qualifications to embrace the many aspects of management of a key resource. If LIS professionals are to play more prominent roles in knowledge management, they will in all likelihood have to promote their expertise more widely, and also aspire to different roles of a more strategic and policy-making nature. For many in the information professions this is likely to entail learning different kinds of skills and opening up to new ways of thinking. However, this is not a challenge faced by the LIS professions alone, and several traditional areas such as human resources management find themselves faced with the same challenge. Underlying such perspectives in a library context however, is recognition that the practice of knowledge management has much to offer to the management of libraries and for advancement of the LIS profession.

12

EPILOGUE

Knowledge management has had a difficult gestation, but now is emerging as an important element of enterprise strategies. It is enabled by technology tools, but encompasses far more than technology.

The old knowledge management—still widely practiced in many circles—is not entirely free of theoretical foundations itself. And it may even qualify, for some, as a science. But on both fronts, it is quite different from the new knowledge management and considerably narrower. While mostly unspoken, we could say, for example, that the theory of first-generation knowledge management goes something like this — that we can assume the existence of pre-existing knowledge and that knowledge management is about getting that "knowledge" (actually "information") to the right people at the right time. The scope of first-generation knowledge management's interests, therefore, is (and has been) the delivery of existing information. We say "information" and not "knowledge" because no persuasive distinction between the two has ever been made in the conventional practice of (old) knowledge management, and the rerm "information" is used in the knowledge management literature at least as often, it seems, as the term "knowledge" is.

Thus, the old knowledge management is largely predicated on the view that valuable knowledge simply exists and that the purpose of knowledge management, therefore, is to enhance its delivery to people who need it. But since no meaningful distinction between knowledge and information has ever been made in the practice of first-generation knowledge management, we feel safe in concluding that the old knowledge management has not been about "knowledge" management at all— has been about "information" management.

Further, the assumption that knowledge (information) simply exists and that knowledge management's role should merely be to aid in its capture and delivery.is also unfounded, or at least arbitrary. While it may be convenient for some to ignore the means by which knowledge is produced—and not just shared or delivered—that still leaves the rest of us, who actually from time to time have a need to learn, innovate, and adapt, dissatisfied. More important still, *the essence of life, and of individuals and human organizations, is adaptation to changes in the environment. The old knowledge management is not about such adaptation, and therefore it is basically incrementalist in orientation and not focused on the most essential of organizational functions. Compared to the new knowledge management, then, it is unimportant, a mere diversion from the fundamental questions of organizational existence and development.*

The new knowledge management, then, is aimed at enhancing the whole cycle of knowledge production and integration, not just the easier and more convenient tasks of rounding up documents and other artifacts for access and distribution in computer-based repositories. Its scope of attention is, therefore, considerably broader and deeper than its first-generation cousin, as are its value propositions. Moreover, the distinction it makes between knowledge and information takes it into utterly new areas of insight and opportunity. There is a difference between knowledge and information, and the new knowledge management opens our eyes to it for the first time in the practice of knowledge management.

Perhaps the most dramatic example of this new perspective is the connection we have drawn between knowledge management and corporate malfeasance. We can interpret such behaviours as *error-ridden knowledge in practice*, employed by unscrupulous corporate executives, whose knowledge in use is not only faulty, but whose knowledge in use somehow managed to get a great deal farther along than it should have. Thus, such knowledge in use is riddled with errors, and the processes in place that produced and validated it, i.e., the knowledge processing processes; are dysfunctional, as well.

By focusing on enhancing the quality and integrity of organizational knowledge processing, the new knowledge management can play an extremely valuable role in helping to reduce corporate malfeasance. Indeed, by calling attention to the dimensions of errors in our knowledge and to the importance of the processes used to produce and evaluate ir, we can have a material impact on improving the quality of the business processing outcomes that follow. But since the old, first-generation knowledge management makes no distinction between knowledge processing and business processing—much less between knowledge and information in terms of errors, validity, or anything else—no such role for knowledge management could possibly come out of it. Its sole purpose is to enhance the delivery of information.

Deep in the heart of the new knowledge management are two principal claims that perhaps underlie its practice more than anything else. The first, taken from Popper and from Peirce is that *there can he no certainty of truth and therefore no certain knowledge. All human knowledge is fallible.* We can, however, endeavour to get closer to the truth, and the way we can do it by seeking to find and eliminate the errors in our thinking. This approach to learning is what Popper referred to as fallibilism.

The second insight follows closely on the heels of the first in the sense that *what people, in fact, seem to do as they go about the process of making decisions and learning is problem recognition, solution formulation and error elimination through trial and error.*

When we combine these two ideas, what we get is a fundamental dynamic found in all humans– the need to solve problems by reaching tentative solutions and then eliminating the errors in them through trial-end-error processes of testing and evaluation as a precursor to decisions and action. Thus, the difference between knowledge and information is that while both consist of claims about the world, beauty and truth, only knowledge consists of claims that have survived our tests and evaluations of whether they are in error. This does not make them necessarily true, but it does make them preferable to us as a basis for decisions and action, and that is why we pay so much attention to the idea of metaclaims and the role that they play in knowledge processing in the new knowledge management.

12.1. SOME LATEST DEVELOPMENT

With the advancement of technologies some new concepts are emerging in the field of knowledge management. A few one described below.

12.1.1. Knowledge Commercialisation

The essence of knowledge commercialization has emerged as the challenge of turning organizational knowledge into commercially viable products and services. Much of today's economy in developed countries already has a large knowledge component. This may be in the form of knowledge that has been used to create a product (e.g. scientific and engineering knowledge), in added-value services (e.g. training and support) or even in the sale of intellectual property, such as licensing patents. There are also industries whose core product is knowledge. Examples include education, scientific publishing and management consultancy. These industries offer useful insights for those who follow them in the knowledge productization route, although followers must be careful not to copy blindly but take account of the changing global business landscape and developments in the Internet.

For most organizations, there are three main ways of commercializing knowledge.

- *Knowledge enriched products and services* : An example is Zurich Financial Insurance's risk knowledge that has been packaged as its Risk Intelligence service.
- *Advisory services* : An example is that of British Telecom who sells knowledge management consultancy services based on its own internal experience.
- *Publishing* : An example is that of Best Practices LLC, a North Carolina consultancy that now makes significant

revenues from selling best practice information globally over the Internet.

There are, of course, many variants on these three main approaches. The process of commercialization involves these stages:

— Identification of knowledge assets with commercial potential.
— Understanding customers' needs and expectations.
— Creating product and service packages.
— Marketing the product, and
— Continual adaptation of the product /service offering based on feedback.

The first of these should pose little problem in that some good principles of information audits and information mapping have been available for a decade or more. With slight modification to include all forms of knowledge, including that of people's expertize, they form a good basis for preparing a knowledge inventory. Unfortunately, although identifying "what you know" is usually touted as the first activity in a knowledge management initiative, few organizations do this thoroughly in practice. The part of the problem is the time and effort needed to do a comprehensive audit. Yet the same organizations find little difficulty in allocating resources to monitor their financial and physical assets, generating monthly financial reports and putting asset number stickers on physical equipment. It is all a question of what's seen as important. As long as formal balance sheets require detailed asset information on the tangible assets an organization has, yet give little or no regard to the more valuable intangible ones, then this situation is likely to prevail.

To complete step 1, some assessment of commercial potential is needed. This must take account of likely demand (step 2) but also of how much additional development is needed to make it a viable offering (step 3). Too frequently, knowledge is developed in the context of immediate need without considering how it might be better codified and stored for later packaging. This causes unnecessary additional effort later on. For example, a best practice case written for internal use is likely to interweave individual names, situation specific material with general lessons. Some thinking about the potential future uses might mean that its structure is split into generic and specific components, in the same way that today more computer programs are developed by separating data and procedural layers.

Step 2 is adaptation of what is often part of an information audit or a user requirements exercise in the scoping of new information systems. The difference is that it is done with external potential customers in mind, rather than internal staff. As with conventional knowledge audits, the starting point should not be "what knowledge do you need", but it should be on the tasks that people perform and the outcomes they require. This helps to reveal the vital question that knowledge manages should pose more often–"knowledge for what?" This step also uses many of the tools of market research, such as surveys of perceptions of various challenges and solutions, and focus groups to discuss potential offerings. With the Internet, the process of competitor analysis also becomes easier. Again, what is frequently found is that although the processes of competitor and business intelligence are well developed, many organizations have not yet made them part of their core knowledge management tool-kit.

Step 3 is concerned with developing a product. While it is possible, and frequently practiced, simply to offer expertize in the form of an advisory service, a little more thought given to packaging will reap economies of scale and increase profitability. A good example of this is in the computer software systems business. If each assignment is simply regarded as a one-off, then the systems house will simply deploy a team with the appropriate skills mix and develop the software. If, on the other hand, it is viewed as a repeat business, the software house will seek to reuse software code, and take more care in creating an architecture and a library of modules. Each assignment adds to and improves the product modules in the warehouse, as well as adding to individual expertize. Their marketing strategy is to portray to the customer that they are getting a customized solution, and thus command a premium price, while at the same time using off-the-shelf components, whose development costs have largely been paid. This is the approach that a sustainable knowledge business should adapt.

Any product - not just a knowledge product - is the result of the gradual refinement of knowledge. Initial ideas get generated and shared, often in very informal and ad-hoc situations - think of the number of businesses that have emerged from the notes written on the back of a napkin in a bar or restaurant. Over time, structure is added, product scoping documents are created, designs are validated, prototypes are developed, and manufacturing processes documented or programmed. Sometimes the knowledge is tacit, as in the designer's head. At other times it is explicit, as in design drawings. Every stage of the product development life cycle is an opportunity for a knowledge business.

Fig. 12.1 shows the generic types of products and services that can be produced, not just from product knowledge gained during a product development cycle, but from any knowledge that resides in an organization. These have been divided into object-based knowledge for example in documents and databases, and people-based. Each of an organization's knowledge assets, whether explicit (object-based) or tacit (people-based), is capable of commercializing in one way or another. Let's look briefly at each opportunity:

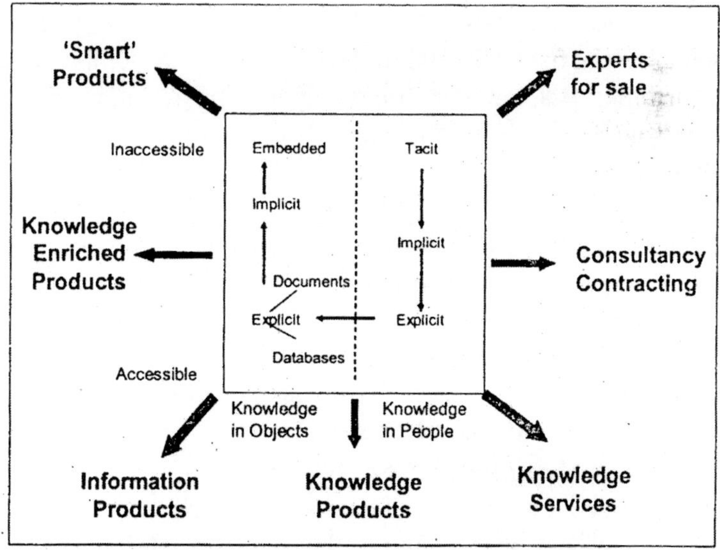

Fig. 12.1. Types of Knowledge Product and Service

Experts for Sale : Which of your staff or which team is recognized as world-class in their field? Could they generate more revenue for your company if their expertize was sold externally? Today, Porsche designers spend much of their time designing products other than Porsche cars, For example the Fuji Finepix 6800 Digital Camera is an example.

Consultancy and Contracting : Could you actually develop a consultancy business from one of your business units? ITNet, a UK software house, emerged from the IT department of drinks manufacturer Cadbury-Schweppes.

Knowledge Services : Could you add value to your products by providing ancillary higher value services, rather than simply compete on price for the basic product? Computer suppliers, like IBM and Unisys, now have services businesses that deal with computer hardware of all makes and are bigger revenue earners than their original core businesses.

Knowledge Products : Are there processes or procedures that are 'best-in-class' which could be turned into methodologies for resale? For example, Ford Motor Company now licenses its 62 point methodology for developing and sharing best practices.

Information Products : Are there documents, reports or databases that have external marketability? Many companies sell on customer lists, but more are seeing the opportunities in selling related analyses. Others package some of their know-how as publications.

Knowledge-enriched Products : Could your products be enhanced, not just by additional services, but by knowledge sold as part of the product? Fertilizers and agricultural chemicals are sold with detailed instructions, but they could also be sold with real-time services that monitor ground conditions from satellites and integrate this information with weather forecasts to optimize application times and dosage amounts.

Smart Products : Could your product have built-in intelligence? Today, cars have many built in sensors and management systems. In future, they will be able to select best routes to avoid traffic jams, and automatically book services when potential mechanical problems are identified.

There is wide overlap between these categories. For example, people who deliver training can also deliver consultancy, while training workbooks could be sold as publications. The interesting packaging challenge is this. The more structured and packaged that knowledge is, the easier it is to replicate, sell and deliver over electronic networks. However, knowledge that is in people's heads generally has higher value because it can be made specific to context and draw on deep personal knowledge and experience. How can a knowledge supplier get the best of both worlds - ease of packaging combined with high value?

The answer is to follow a hybrid route. What was previously premium knowledge becomes less so as it becomes diffused - inevitably in today's 'knowledge-leaky' world. It is therefore packaged into documents, methodologies or computer software. Accompanying this, the human expert remains at the forefront of knowledge, as well as having deep experience of how best to use the methodology. Thus, Ernst & Young introduced in 1996 an online advice system ERNIE. Subscribers can get both immediate packaged knowledge, yet have their questions emailed to appropriate advisers to give a more customized response. In turn, existing knowledge base records are improved and updated. Already such hybrid approaches are widely used in the field of customer support. Some suppliers use artificial intelligence techniques to scan an email and send the most appropriate response. In some cases automated responses to 80 per cent of enquires have been reported. It does not take much imagination to turn these techniques into a paid-for knowledge service, where packaged information is augmented by human expertise.

Step 4 of the commercialization process is marketing. Although organizations who commercialize their knowledge may well use conventional channels, the cost of developing sales and distribution channels can be high for the new entrant. In contrast, the benefits of Internet marketing are well established - round the clock service, global reach, lower cost per transaction and so on. Despite the demise of several ambitious dot.com start-up companies, the Internet remains a hot-bed of innovation for marketing and other business activities, and is probably a necessity for any knowledge-based company that wants to leverage their knowledge assets quickly before they become outdated. For object-based knowledge products, in particular, it is a cost-effective medium for marketing and delivery.

The basic principles of marketing revolve around the 3Cs (Customers, Company, Competitors) and 4Ps (Product, Price, Promotion, Place). What's the same and what's different in the online environment?

Customers : You must know their needs, expectations and what they feel about your products and services. In the online environment, the opportunities for data collection about their behaviours are enormous. What needs to be added are some good analysis of online click patterns and some more human 1-to-1 interaction e.g. via email.

Competitors : You must know who they are? In an online environment they are often not who you think they are. Amazon.com, for example, is not now merely a bookseller. It gathers and exploits customer knowledge remorselessly and has created a business model that it has now taken into products as diverse as kitchen gadgets and toys.

Company : You really must know your strengths and weaknesses, since on the Web there are thousands of other companies doing similar things to you. Most organizations have failed to link their front-office (the Web store) to their back-office effectively.

Products : Information products can be tailored very cost-effectively, e.g.– through content management software. Information on the Internet has a different structure to that in traditional publications - more chunky, hyperlinks and more up to date. What will you offer online? Some or your entire portfolio? What can you deliver online? For example, will you have a team of experts around the world who are *au fait* with the environment and culture of the customer; on call 24 hours-a-day? You will need to if you want to offer a people-based service that is time and location independent. Will you develop separate brands for online and offline products?

Pricing : Know what your customers value. On the Internet there is a general expectation that things will cost much less – if you do not price appropriately, they will quickly find someone who does. The good news is that more people are gradually recognizing the benefit of paying for quality information - well organized, relevant, actionable, accurate etc.

Place : Although the Internet provides one single place to do business globally, you may have to address specific trading laws, taxes and import procedures or restrict your geographic coverage. You will also need to take account of local custom and habit.

Promotion : Internet does not readily lend itself to 'brochureware' i.e., simply putting existing hard-copy material on line. A new array of marketing tools such as email, online communities and affiliate marketing comes into play.

The main commonality with conventional marketing is the overall approach. You need to identify and target specific customer groups and individuals. You need to understand their intentions motivations, needs and level of spending authority. You need to guide them through a buying process that matches their needs with your products so that they can be more successful.

Based on several years analysis of successful and less successful websites, especially those selling specialist knowledge, the lOPs of Internet marketing have been proposed. In summary, they are:

Positioning : This is presenting your website such that a new reader can ascertain within a few seconds how the information on the site helps them. Compelling content relevant to user needs is much more effective than product promotional literature.

Packaging : Internet offers innovative ways of packaging information and services. For example on-line training is a fast growth area. For physical products, consideration must be given as to how to convey their characteristics virtually, such as through application notes or short video clips showing satisfied customers.

Portals : Every industry or profession has its well known 'portal' sites or starting points. If your website is not one of these, then potential customers must find you quickly from them.

Pathways : Visitors reach your site from many other places, both offline and online. There are proven techniques to raise the position in search engine results. It is also helpful to have reciprocal links with complementary websites.

Page Impressions : A website must attract and retain attention and guide people easily to the required knowledge or information on how to purchase it!. The style must reinforce your positioning and branding. Too many sites are overloaded with irrelevant graphics at the expense of quality information.

Personalization : Visitors, particular returning ones, should be shown pages that relate to their interests or even their most recent mouse clicks. E-commerce personalization packages can do this, although there is an overhead in tagging content according to different market segments.

Progression : It is difficult to sell expensive knowledge, such as a Rs.1,00,000 consultancy assignment, directly from a web page (though not impossible!). Everyone expects something for nothing! So have a free offering, and then a range of products priced at Rs. 500, Rs. 5000, Rs. 10,000 and so on. Buyers can proceed a step at a time, gaining familiarity and confidence in your products as they progress.

Payments : It must be easy to do business. Third party payment service providers that process credit card transactions within seconds, now make it easy for users to download information products when they need them.

Processes : Many dot.coms have suffered through not having an existing business process infrastructure to work with. On the other hand this has been an Achilles heel for many traditional companies. Generally, an Internet business should use the resources of the parent company when it helps, but retain its independence and flexibility where the parent company would get in the way.

Performance : As with other areas of business, the bottom line is what will ultimately count for most businesses. Performance needs to be measured in several areas - from the customer experience, the effectiveness of business processes, benefits to the business, both financial and non-financial. A good starting point, and one often neglected, is to conduct random tests as a customer. Can you find what you want quickly?

Were your questions promptly answered? Did you get what you expect-quickly and accurately?

Although Internet marketing is a fast-growing means of selling knowledge. It is important not to overlook the use of established marketing channels. The more that the knowledge is tacit, the greater the importance of personal relationships. While so much can be done virtually, using email, video–conferencing and telephone, occasional face-to-face meetings are reassuring for many customers.

There are some challenges. Organizations that have knowledge assets to sell can learn much from the experience of other companies selling knowledge products, from management consultancies to patent attorneys, or even from other departments within their own firm. Typical of the challenges that must be addressed, particularly for those organizations where knowledge is not their core product are:

- Getting the knowledge business opportunity on the investment and management agenda. At a time when many knowledge managers already have their work cut out to create a knowledge sharing culture, and business development managers are more *au fait* with current lines of business, it is most likely that a champion will emerge elsewhere in the business, for example from an e-business area. However, knowledge managers should augment this enthusiasm with their knowledge about knowledge.
- Overcoming the often perceived notion that selling internally beneficial knowledge externally will damage the core business. However, Pilkington has made more money from licensing its float glass process to competitors than it would have done if it had kept it as internal knowledge.
- Recognizing the gap between having the knowledge and the idea, and packaging it into a viable product or service. Even management consultancies spend considerable resources on developing capability profiles, writing proposals and

marketing. Packaged knowledge needs even more product development to create products that are easily reproducible at low cost.

- Conveying the depth and quality of knowledge. Until a customer experiences a knowledge product, they cannot fully appreciate it. The use of good product descriptions and samples help. Even better are ways in which the potential customer can sample the product and testimonials from satisfied customers in similar situations.
- A particular problem of knowledge product or service is that it is not easy to return for a refund if the customer is not satisfied. The mere act of receiving the product or service transfers knowledge that cannot be unlearnt. This also highlights the need for building confidence measures around the product marketing and considering different pricing mechanisms.

Perhaps the biggest challenge, is that involving personal relationships. Transferring knowledge is very personal. Two qualified engineers may be able to solve a customer problem effectively. But from the customer's perception, it may be the one who solves it more slowly, but who keeps the customer informed that is deemed of higher quality. This human interface and relationship aspect - the social capital element of the knowledge product - is one that will distinguish a leader. Customers' emotional and social needs are different and an advantage of personal selling is that the sales message can be adjusted in real-time to accommodate the feedback. It is therefore particularly important, when selling online, that as much of the human element as possible is introduced into the transaction, including access to phone, 1-to-1 emails and instant messaging.

12.1.2. Peer to Peer Network

The term "peer-to-peer computing" gained currency after the widely publicized Napster case. Napster, the best-known example of a P2P network, was set up as a network of PCs with a central server acting as a clearinghouse. Users could download Napster client software and install it to make selected folders on their PCs available for sharing, as well as searching for and downloading files from other nodes on the network. The central server acted as a lookup service that would direct a user to a particular node where the requested file was available. Thus, the lookup function was a client-server interaction, followed by the file transfer that was peer-to-peer. Though attacked initially as a medium for piracy, industry has now woken up to exploring possible positive uses of P2P for information sharing, and electronic commerce in general.

Peer-to-peer technology is a decentralized mechanism of file transfer and relies on group norms for its survival. Instead of creating a vast repository of knowledge, P2P offers a way of managing distributed repositories of knowledge, where the repositories can be individuals in the organization or processes in the organization (see Figure 12.2). By allowing for transfer of heterogeneous document formats and with its highly scalable architecture, a P2P network can create a dynamic method for transfer of knowledge as opposed to a static model of knowledge transfer. Search processes in a P2P setting can be more flexible than in a server based knowledge management system or KMS,

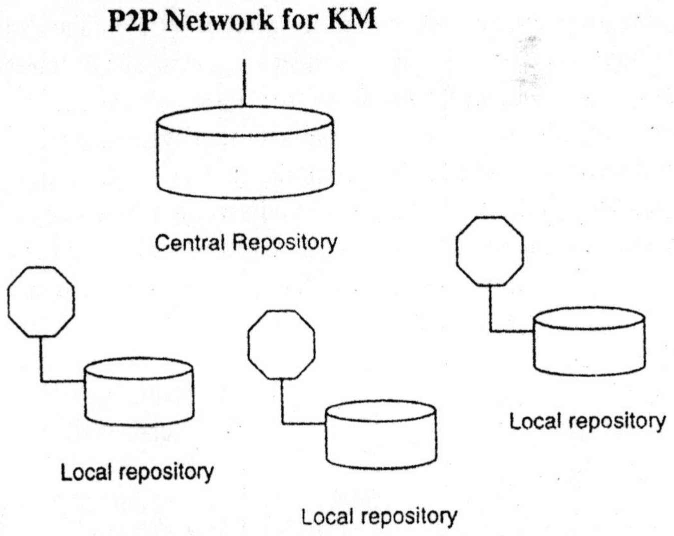

P2P Network for KM

Central Repository

Local repository

Local repository

Local repository

Fig. 12.2. Conceptual Framework of Peer-to-Peer Network for KM

with different systems interacting with each other regardless of access mode. With a minimum interoperability between the Corba/ DCOM/ Java/ XML standards, there could be a wealth of information that is missing in the traditional KMS setting.

To take the Napster example, it would be extremely difficult to create a super repository with up-to-date listings of MP3 collections of various users. A P2P search mechanism on the other hand does not need an expensive central repository, but relies on the ability of nodes within the network to query other nodes about the availability of the required files. Similarly, when a user at one of the nodes in a P2P, KMS needs knowledge about a process or seeks access to specific organizational resources, he sends out a query to other nodes, which in turn can ensure the search is relevant and up to date. There is, thus, an interactive aspect to knowledge search in a P2P environment so that the search technology can be complemented by a 'human' intelligence component. A database search can only reveal encoded knowledge; P2P search mechanisms for knowledge can reveal the presence of knowledge residing at user nodes and thus can help in the discovery of hidden knowledge. P2P knowledge management systems can therefore mediate a decentralized collaboration of various individuals in the organization. Further, the dynamic nature of knowledge exchange facilitates the dissemination of up-to-date and as yet unrecorded knowledge through the organization.

Peer-to-peer knowledge management systems enable richer communication between participants and can contribute to the propagation of hidden and implicit knowledge, which needs a great amount of organizational effort to be transferred through a centralized system of knowledge management. P2P technology can ensure search is up to date and fosters an organization's ability to tap vital organizational intelligence. P2P technology also does away with the limitations posed by storing data at a central server, creating a strategic point of failure. Current client-server-based knowledge management initiatives typically provide little privacy for their users, and P2P networks can address the privacy concerns of users.

Knowledge management theorists posit that knowledge is created through a continuous and dynamic interpersonal interaction between tacit and explicit knowledge. P2P embodies the spirit of dynamic interaction and is therefore an ideal knowledge management vehicle. Successful P2P initiatives such as Freenet have demonstrated that the individuals who provide content on a P2P network can monitor the access and usage of the resources they contribute. The peer-to-peer technology can therefore be structured to provide selective incentives to some members for enhancing organizational knowledge and further reinforce the reward system by excluding access to the non-cooperators. Thus, P2P transfer of knowledge can solve the incentive problems plaguing knowledge transfer systems by ensuring that the right knowledge is created and distributed.

Additionally, P2P can address the issues of recombination of knowledge with which conventional KMS cannot deal. For example, if the users in the manufacturing department have access to product designs from marketing, they would be able to combine the new product ideas with their own knowledge about design. With a client-server-based KMS, there is a problem of who does the updating on the server, without protecting the privacy of the individuals who are recombining the knowledge. The users in manufacturing could be apprehensive of too many individuals viewing their plans, and would like to control access to their knowledge. P2P systems such as Freenet can solve this problem by providing for inserted files to be placed selectively on nodes already possessing.files with similar

12.1.3. Measuring Knowledge - Alternatives to the Status Quo

Considerable effort has been devoted to alternative accounting models that capture the value-creating activities of KM before their financial realization. These efforts began with the recognition that financial statements focus on value realization, not value creation. For example, a Wharton School symposium on financial reporting and standard setting concluded that "continuing on the present course, we believe, will lead to the growing irrelevance of conventional financial reporting in the new age of information". Here, we briefly describe six alternative approaches to knowledge alternative. These alternatives are summarized in

Table 12.1. Knowledge Accounting Approaches

Approach	Characteristics
Total Value Creation (TVC®)	• Discounted Cash Model of Value Creating Activities • Financial and Non-Financial Information • Supplements Existing Financial Reporting Systems
Accounting For The Future (AFTF)	• Discounted Cash Model of Value Creating Activities • Physical & Intangible Assets Valued at Present Value of Future Cash Flows • Replaces Existing Financial Reporting System • Financial but no Non-financial Information
Balanced Scorecard	• Customerized: Measured Derive from Management's Strategic Objectives • Supplements Existing Financial Reporting Systems • Focuses on Performance in Four Areas: Financial, Customer, Internal Processes and Innovation and Learning • Financial and Non-Financial Information
Skandia Navigator	• Very Simialar to the Balanced Score card Approach • Focuses on Performance in Five Areas: Financial, Customer, Human process and Renewal and Development • Supplements Exisiting Finnancial Reporting Systems • Customized: Measures Derive from Management's Strategic Objectives • Financial and Non-Financial Information
Intangible Asset Monitor	• Builds upon Skandia AFS Approach • Very Similar to the Balanced Scorecard Model • Supplements Existing Financial Reporting Systems • Financial and Non-Financial Information
Value Chain Score -board	• Ten Step Model of the Process by which Innovation Creates Value • Criteria for Choosing among Measures • Supplements Existing Financial Reporting
Systems	• Financial and Non-Financial Information

Table 12.1. Following this, we compare the alternative approaches to knowledge alternative and consider the future of knowledge alternative.

1. Total Value Creation (TVC) : Total Value Creation (TVC), designed by a consortium headed by the Canadian Institute of Chartered Accountants (C1CA), attempts to capture an organization's value-creating activities, instead of the value-realizing activities that are the focus of existing financial accounting efforts. Traditional financial reporting focuses on realized economic transactions. In contrast, TVC provides a means for reporting value-creating activities before they are realized through transactions. The basic TVC model is a discounted cash flow framework within which managers can disclose their planned value-creating activities and the anticipated consequences of these activities. TVC's authors argue that it is a supplement to, not a replacement of, existing financial reporting approaches. Currently, the consortium of developers provides two case studies that illustrate reporting using the TVC model. Proponents argue that TVC may initially be most valuable as an internal reporting system for management to assess plans for value-creating activities. After extensive testing as an internal reporting system, the CICA argues that TVC may also be a useful supplement to existing financial reports.

2. Accounting for the Future (AFTF) : Nash uses the discounted cash flow approach advocated by the TVC to propose a replacement for existing financial reporting. Accounting for the Future (AFTF) redefines assets, liability, and equities using present values instead of purchase costs. For example, consider a company that purchases a Rs.200,000 computer system to use in constructing a knowledge system that has an expected present value of future cash flows of Rs.1,000,000. Using traditional financial reporting, the computer system would be valued as a Rs.200,000 asset. Using AFTF, the computer system would be a Rs.1,000,000 asset. In AFTF, physical and intangible assets, as well as acquired and internally developed assets are all valued at the present value of their expected future cash flows.

3. Kaplan's Balanced Scorecard : Kaplan & co-authors

propose the Balanced Scorecard as a method for better capturing the value-creating activities that derive from intangible assets. Managers establish balanced scorecards that reflect the specific measurable objectives that derive from their corporate strategy. Typically, managers identify measures in each of four strategic areas– financial performance, customers, internal processes and, learning and growth. Since no single measure or area completely captures a company's value-creating activities, companies and managers should be evaluated across all four areas of strategic focus.

Kaplan proposes the balanced scorecard as an internal supplement to existing reporting systems. Consequently, using the balanced scorecard approach would not affect existing financial statement reporting. Instead, a balanced scorecard reporting approach would provide supplemental information about intangible assets that would otherwise go unreported. In addition, because balanced scorecard measures derive from corporate strategies, such measures are unique to individual companies. As a result, knowledge management initiatives reported under a balanced score would be incomparable across companies.

4. Skandia Navigator : Skandia AFS, a Swedish insurance and banking company is an innovator in financial reporting on intellectual capital. Skandia's Navigator is a business-planning model that is strikingly similar to the balanced scorecard approach of identifying critical business areas and developing related measures. Navigator includes five focus areas– financial, customer, human, process and renewal and development. Skandia's subdivisions report 18 to 20 measures across each of the five Navigator categories. Skandia AFS currently uses the model for both internal and external reporting.

Consistent with concerns about the comparability of balanced scorecard style reporting approaches, existing Skandia financial reports suggest that comparability across units is not present in Skandia's own application of the Navigator model. For example, The American Skandia Variable Annuities group uses the number of contracts as its measure of customer success, while the Skandia Banken Distance Banking group has chosen the number of customers as its key customer success measure.

5. Intangible Assets Monitor Model : In 1988, a small group of Swedish service companies and accountants, called the Konrad Group, published "The Invisible Balance Sheet", which called for supplementing annual reports with information about organizational intangible assets. Parts of this report, such as its distinction between individual capital, structural capital, and customer capital, are now well integrated into the knowledge management literature (e.g., included in Skandia's intellectual capital reporting initiatives). The report defined key indicators of each type of capital, and discussed the annual reports of Swedish company innovators in reporting on intangible assets.

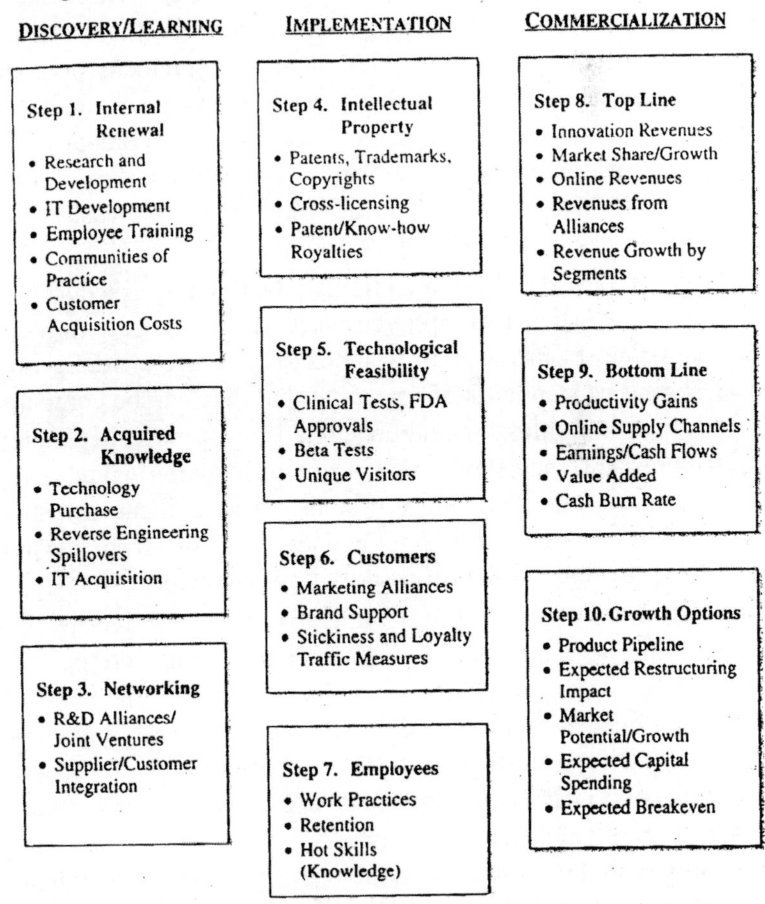

Fig. 12.3. Value Chain Scoreboard

Karl-Erik Sveiby has continued the development of the model by proposing an "intangible assets monitor" a reporting system that is quite similar to a business scorecard approach. The similarities between the business score-card and intangible assets monitor approaches are sufficiently similar that Sveiby has a Web site devoted to discussing their similarities and differences.

Lev has recently proposed the Value Chain Scorecard in an attempt to capture the economic processes by which intangible assets create company financial value. Value Chain Scoreboard model consists of ten economic processes that attempt a comprehensive representation of the innovation process (See Figure 12.3). He categorizes these ten processes into the three broader categories of: (1) discovery and learning, (2) implementation, and (3) commercialization. For each process in the value chain model, he provides example measures for a biotechnology company. Lev also proposes three criteria for firms' choices of measures within the processes that are quite helpful in insuring that measures are objective, measurable, relevant and auditable.

First, they should be quantitative. Qualitative aspects of the value chain – such as employee work practices, patent cross-licensing; may be provided in an annex to the Scoreboard. Second, they should be standardized, meaning that they can be compared across firms for valuation and benchmarking purposes. Third and most important, they should be confirmed by empirical evidence as relevant to users– generally by establishing a significant statistical association between the measures and indicators of corporate value such as stock return and productivity improvement.

Coming to a the Future and Prospects for Knowledge Accounting, we can say the unique economic characteristics of knowledge include its non-scarcity, i.e., that one person's consumption of knowledge does not diminish its supply, high fixed and low marginal costs, increasing returns to scale, net benefits but not costs, to increasing numbers of users, difficulty in excluding other's use, and high development risks. Accounting for knowledge is tightly bound with the economic characteristics of knowledge. And these economic characteristics result in imperfect solutions to the problem of knowledge alternatives.

12.1.4. Risk Management in QM

Today, Organizations are facing with continual technology evolution and new business models including virtual networks and the Internet, applications integrated with business partners, new business operations including e-business and mobile-business, and knowledge management. Concerns have continuously increased about the ability to keep this new environment aligned with business objectives. IT governance is key to facilitating and encouraging the business side of the company to work closely with technology managers and in line with board directions. One aspect of IT governance should involve the governance of knowledge

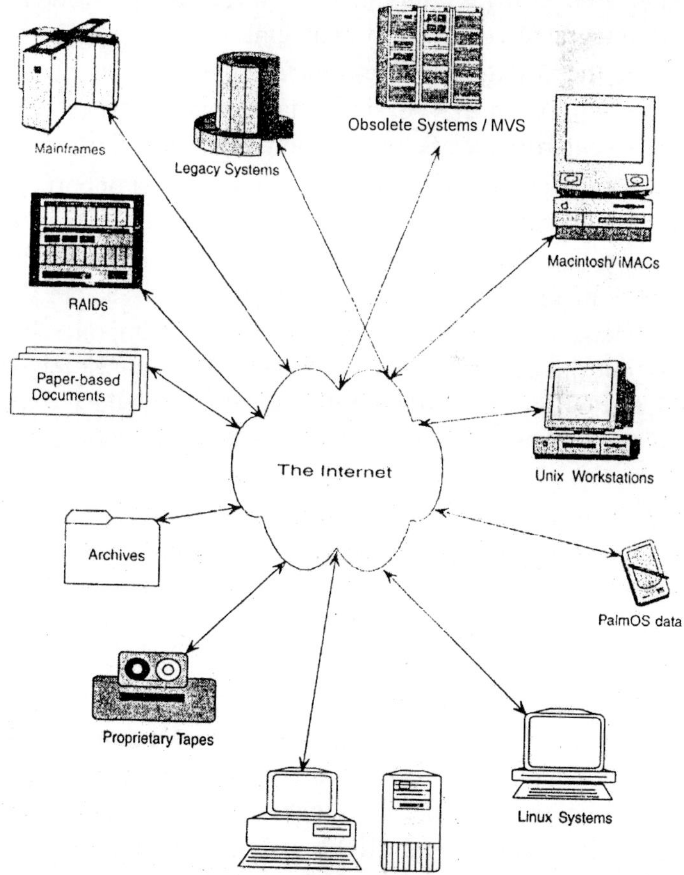

Fig. 12.4. Data in Electronic Environment

management to ensure that knowledge management strategies, knowledge infrastructure and technologies are in line with both IT strategies and organizational board directions.

Elecironic data, as shown in Figure 12.4 exists on PCs, UNIX work proprietary systems, linux machines, Apple Macintosh systems, iMacs, and Pal, OS devices. As organizations grapple with technology decision chains, increasing attention comes to bear on identifying an integrated solution that can met current and emerging user needs. Business information no longer comes from or resides in a single place; it is derived from disparate information streams—collaborative documents, Web pages, newsfeeds, e-mail, etc. At the same time as firms, enterprises, and knowledge workers are seeking integrated solutions to managing and using information resources, the emergence of intranet technology has presented enormous opportunities for information sharing and content delivery to enterprise workers and collaborative audiences.

At one hand, technology is providing us better opportunities, at the same time it is posining problems for us. Risk management is a board process which identifies risks, security and controls for knowledge management infrastructure and systems.There should be Risk Management Committee, which needs to appoint persons to carry out this risk management process. We suggest the Chief Knowledge Officer of the organization together with the IT internal auditor and security managers are appropriate persons to carry out this task.

The risk management team should first identify the knowledge management assets – including personnel, systems, infrastructure and networks, locations; and then identify risks associated with these assets. The next phase involves identifying existing controls and security measures over these assets and then analysing the risks by determining the likelihood, consequence, and level of the risks. The risks are then evaluated and prioritized, and an action plan drawn up to implement the recommendations for additional knowledge management security and control measures to counter or mitigate the identified knowledge management risks. For some knowledge management risks, management may accept the risk, thereby self-insuring against that risk. During this process, it is important to communicate with management and staff involved in knowledge management about the findings from the risk management process, and solicit from them suggestions for improving knowledge management security and controls. This process is not just carried out once and then forgotten, but should be monitored and reviewed on a continuing basis by the knowledge management governance committee.

The knowledge management governance committee will also need to consider which knowledge management technologies will be employed throughout the organization.

Examples of knowledge management technologies include:

- Retrieval engines;
- Content management;
- Document and records management;
- Learning systems;
- Automatic classification systems such as neural networks, linguistic, or semantic processing systems;
- Intelligent technologies including AI, intelligent agents, regression and correlation, expert systems, case-based reasoning, data and text mining, and rule-based systems;
- Communication systems including email, discussion forums, groupware; and
- Archiving.

Table 12.2. Selection of Risks in the KM Environment

Approaches	Possible Actions
Strategic/Planning	• Mismatch of KM strategy to corporate and ITstrategies
	• Unidentified or excessive costs especially maintenance and support
	• Overlooked essential KM functionality
Accidental or Intentional	• Damage
	• Loss
	• Modification
	• Destruction
	• Use :

Approaches	Possible Actions
	to/of specialized KM or traditional IT hardware used to run KM systems, KM software, knowledge repositories as well as feeder software and associated data bases. Loss or incapaciation of key KM experts, knowledge engineers, programmers, or knowledge maintenance personal is also of concern
Fraud and Abuse	• Substitution/deletion of knowledge repositories • Obscure placement of forward chaining demons in a knowledge base if expert systems or knowledge based systems are an integral part of the KM systems • Unauthorized access to KM systems or KM management/audit trails • Modification, deletion or insertion of KM information when passing through a network, communications or other layers of operating or support software such as data warehousing. This includes other application software when linked or integrated with KM systems
Other Exposures	• Inability of imbedded KM software to recover/restart • KM hardware, infrastructure or software failure — especially real-time monitoring or imbedded systems • Lack of knowledge use histories (audit trails) in hardcopy and/or magnetic/optical form • Inadequate trace facilities in KM/KB software for degbugging and KM/KB testing • KM systems knowledge not based on best expert's knowledge, reasoning, and explanations • Inadequate control of and access to KM repositories • Poor quantity or quality of KM personnel • poor management, supervision and control of the KM application and repositories if held elsewhere to IT department (e.g., under R & D) • Inadequate training and supervision of KM personnel

Approaches	Possible Actions
	• Inadequate KM hardware/software maintenance • Legal liability for reliance on KM opinion when that opinion caused loss of life, damage, or monetary loss • Inadequate KM documentation of tools, environment and applications

Each of these technologies has its own risks and associated security and controls mechanisms. However, these technologies need to be considered in light of a knowledge management framework and are just one part of the knowledge foundations required to support the knowledge processes within an organization.

1. Security and Controls in the KM Environment : Holsapple and Joshi provide an investigation of factors that influence the management of knowledge in organizations. One of the managerial influences on knowledge management is control, which involves two critical issues of protection and quality of the knowledge resources. They believe that the protection of knowledge resources from "... *loss, obsolescence, unauthorized exposure, unauthorized modification, and erroneous assimilation is crucial for the effective management of knowledge*". They argue that management needs to consider knowledge validity (accuracy, consistency and certainty) and knowledge utility (clarity, meaning, relevance and importance) when establishing sufficient controls to govern knowledge quality. The security and controls discussed here are concerned with knowledge validity. Knowledge management systems are presented below and are summarized in Table 12.3.

In some organizations the trustees for knowledge management systems are end user departments such as Research and Development (R&D) departments. This may be done order to qualify for tax deduction incentives in this area. One emerging issue concerns the appropriateness of the trusteeship, control and maintenance of the knowledge management resting with R&D. In certain organizations this department is known for its flexibility of approach, creativity and informality - not great attributes for implementing and enforcing strict internal controls.

As with traditional information systems processing, systems access security is vitally important for knowledge management systems. knowledge management tools and environments need to be reviewed to determine the extensiveness of security features as some may be deficient in security and reliability. Management and auditors working in these environments will need to specify additional security features for their clients' knowledge management systems and then pressure knowledge management tool vendors to incorporate these features into their products. Knowledge management software houses may also want their products certified by major consulting/accounting firms, as to the provision of adequate security, control, and auditability features.

Table 12.3. Selection of Security and Controls in the KM Environment

Selection of Security	Controls in the KM Environment
KM Hardware	Sensitive knowledge access: • key locked equipment • restricted/controlled boot up procedures • biometric access controls • encryption provisions Up-to-date documentation Regular audits of KM equipment Logging and follow-up of all reported faults KM back-up: • strategy • equipment • KM maintenance: • diagnostic aids • documentation KM environmental considerations: • uninterrupted power supplies or voltage regulators • air conditioners • physical protection barriers to restrict physical acess Security infrastructure
KM Software	Automated procedures for KM access control

Selection of Security	Controls in the KM Environment
	Valid software license agreements
	Up-to-date documentation
	KM software integrity checks
	Appropriate KM maintenance strategy
	KM software upgrade controls
	Logging and follow-up of all reported software faults
	KM repository encryption
	KM explanation facilities if using expert systems or KBS: • HOW facilities • WHY facilities
	Help facilities
	KM repository integrity checking
	Restricted screen/report output and knowledge document delivery
	Separate development and run time versions
	Graphical layouts of KM repository
	Cross reference listings
	Knowledge dictionary or thesaurus maintenance access and controls
	Knowledge use trace facilities
	Knowledge use or consultation case history maintenance if KBS
	Audit trail logging of all activity
	Certified by major con sulting/accounting firm
KM Systems Development	KM systems development methodology followed
	Separate KM systems development from production KM
	Appropriate design documentation
	Validation and testing of KM systems
	Quality assurance/control review
	Auditor involvement in KM systems development reviews
	Separate development and production KM source libraries
	Separate development and run time versions of KM software
KM Applications	Systems access security & strong authentication

Selection of Security	Controls in the KM Environment
	Smart Cards Secure Client Digital Certificates Correct option setting for run time versions Edit facilities for data input Knowledge repositories/KB encryption Reasonableness checks Output review by competent personnel Hardcopy or magnetic/optical collection of case histories Management/audit review of audit trails Good application documentation Unauthorized copying protection Back-up and recovery
KM Network Controls	Internet, Extranet or Intranet access controls Virtual Private networks (VPN's) - site to site VPN Gateway Transmission encryption of Knowledge in transit Public Key Infrastructure (PKI) Dedicated connections Firewalls
KM Human Resources	Management commitment to KM strategy Assign responsibility for: • KM systems development • KM production operations • KM disaster planning Adequate training of KM personnel Supervision and management of KM personnel KM Information Centre Segregation of duties Mandatory vacations Personnel security checks Maintenance supplier vetting

Traditional input controls such as appropriate edits, accuracy, completeness, and reasonableness checking will need to be refined in the knowledge management environment. Input data validation may be simple, for example a range check from numeric 1 to 20, or context-sensitive, where the validation of the input data is dependent on other information already entered into the knowledge management system. Most knowledge management tools provide facilities for simple data editing but fall short on context-sensitive validation, especially of textual data in documents. For knowledge management systems that included Knowledge Based Systems (KBS), such facilities as '*Whenever Modified*' slots (in object-based knowledge management/knowledge based tools) provide for the context-sensitive style to be programmed into the knowledge management systems more easily. Other control features include ability to retract and backtrack in a consultation to enable corrections to be made. Care is required when programming these facilities, as practitioners comment that it is an area where many programming errors can be made. Also, facilities such as repeated data requests and using 'Are you sure?' type of questions. Many KBS provide the facilities for entering 'unknown' as an answer to certain questions. These KBS require rules to deal with unknowns, although with mature KBS unknowns would be infrequently used. From a management/audit perspective, we are concerned that these KBS receive a proper set of facts for the consultation under consideration, in order for it to arrive at an appropriate decision. Most interactions with knowledge management are via workstations where the user answers system queries by supplying numeric and symbolic facts and perhaps opinions. It is important that proper management and audit trails exist of the user-supplied input, which should be logged to a usage/case history file. Currently these facilities are provided by many KBS systems and may be used at the designer's or user's discretion. More sophisticated facilities are required to mandatory log all interactions with the Knowledge Management/Knowledge Based system into a proper management/audit trail.

During knowledge processing, the inference engine will usually provide a combination of forward and backward chaining control mechanisms to solve the goal state and provide a decision or judgment. For both management and auditors, the importance of having adequate trace facilities provided by the KM/KBS or processing environment is very important. These trace facilities show the consultation's questions and answers as well as the rule firing or instantiations, and the conclusions reached by the KM/KBS. This then provides a very detailed audit trail of the inferencing process and knowledge used to obtain to a decision or recommendation.

For knowledge management outputs, which are usually in the form of documents or a report of the consultation and recommendation, there should be some form of reasonableness checking and knowledgeable user review prior to making decisions. Jamieson points out that there is a potential high risk of inadvertent reliance on the KM/KBS results by users, where after a period of time users may not question the systems judgments. This highlights the importance of continual validation and review of knowledge, especially in high risk applications.

If knowledge bases and repositories are of strategic importance to the organization then encryption of the knowledge management repository may be considered.

Legal liability may arise from the use of a KM/KBS. Care is required to caveat the decisions made by the knowledge management system so that the organization may not be litigated against for loss of assets or life as a result of someone acting on the system's decisions. The final responsibility must fall on a person in the organization, not on the system.

In a similar way to *controlling the amendments to source programs* for an application, alterations to knowledge, or KB system rule changes should also be approved, correctly updated and validated, and the knowledge management repository maintained in such a form that unauthorized amendments to it are prevented. This involves maintaining a secure knowledge management systems development library with versions of the knowledge management system held that are equivalent to the released production versions. This also presupposes some sort of knowledge management systems development section with abilities to modify copies of the knowledge management systems source, fix errors and release new versions when appropriate.

Documentation is, and always will be, a perennial problem and knowledge management systems are no exception. However, with these systems there is an ever greater need to correctly document the expertize that is encapsulated in the knowledge management repository and its associated design. While systems design, KM systems in operation should have, at the minimum, adequate on-line help facilities which are context-sensitive. An exception to this guideline is for knowledge management systems embedded within other information systems where these types of facilities may never be required. In this case, system evaluation is performed during development and at periodic intervals by quality assurance or audit. A knowledge worker's or user's guide is useful as an introduction to the knowledge management system, which could also be on-line. For KBS, when the operational version is used for consultations, then adequate documentation of the consultation, usually in hardcopy format is required, perhaps to give to the customer and to keep for statutory records purposes as proof of the business transaction or event. Optical or magnetic records may also be used to document case histories for later management or audit review. Adequate documentation of the operator's responsibilities at the end of the day is also required. This may include procedures for appropriate retention of magnetic, optical or hardcopy files and back-ups for the knowledge management systems.

Contingency planning for knowledge management is just as important as for traditional IT systems. Alternative locations and equipment, especially for specialized KM/AI hardware, must be found if KM systems requiring this equipment are critical to the organization. Regular off-site storage of development versions and knowledge management production source is important for recovery purposes. Important requirements such as knowledge management repository consultation, case histories and documentation should also be stored off-site on a regular basis.

These security and controls are examples of the types of controls needed to be considered by organizations establishing knowledge management systems.

2. Security and Control Concerns with Knowledge Repositories : There are a number problems associated with knowledge repositories. One of problems involves where the knowledge repositories are located and who is responsible for them and their security. If the knowledge repositories are controlled in the same way as corporate databases, then they may fall under the security that is given to all other major IT systems. However, if the knowledge repositories are located within an end user environment on a knowledge server then these systems may be inadequately controlled. As a result, knowledge management systems may have no systems access security, inadequate monitoring, and lack adequate backup and recovery procedures and facilities. If this is the case then management may need to review the security over these knowledge management systems and apply the same procedures as they would over their corporate IT systems. With knowledge repositories we need to ask questions as to who is responsible for placing documents within the repository, how is access to these documents controlled, and who is responsible for the disposal of the documents.

Some organizations have setup knowledge centres within the various divisions of their organization. Knowledge centres are responsible for the addition, maintenance and review of documents placed within the knowledge repositories. These knowledge centres should also be responsible for the security and accuracy of information and knowledge that is placed within the repositories. Personnel in these knowledge centres need be responsible for the setting up and maintenance of the knowledge dictionary or thesaurus for the organization. The knowledge dictionary may also relate to knowledge maps or taxonomies that may be purchased off the shelf, manually constructed, automatically generated or even a combination of all three. The knowledge dictionary is very important as it holds the key to accessing the many documents held within knowledge repositories. Knowledge held in documents within the knowledge repository is indexed and accessed by the terms set out in the knowledge dictionary. Therefore, protection over the knowledge dictionary is as vital as security over knowledge repositories. A person having access to the knowledge dictionary in a covert or incompetent manner may intentionally or accidentally destroy or corrupt key terms within the knowledge dictionary, or may in fact destroy the whole knowledge dictionary or substitute another in its place. Rebuilding of the knowledge dictionary may take many person days of effort and may even be impossible to reconstruct, thereby causing the organization significant losses due to an inability to access documents within the knowledge repositories.

Another concern is with the knowledge held within the knowledge repositories. Firstly, how are documents held within the knowledge repositories, are they encrypted or held in a clear text form? Secondly, are all documents held in a form that cannot be altered, or are these documents in an open form so that many people within the organization may have access to substitute, modify or delete them. If the documents are held in an Acrobat PDF form, then document security features may be enabled that provides protection on features such as content accessibility, print, change, extract or copy, altering author comments and fields, and document assembly. Adobe Acrobat also provides password protection and encryption over the document and over the document security features.

Important concerns relating to security include confidentiality, integrity, monitoring and availability. *Confidentiality* involves ensuring that the knowledge held remains confidential and is only used for the purposes to which that knowledge was collected. It also implies that there may be degrees of confidentiality associated with a document. For example, there may be three levels of confidentiality namely, open access, commercially in confidence, or for senior management only. These levels of confidentiality need to be carefully thought through by an organization so that they formulate their own method of grading information, and access control information use, so that for example, only authorized personnel within the organization with appropriate security clearance will have access to the knowledge held at that security level. Confidentiality relates closely to privacy concerns.

Integrity is an issue that may be overlooked by those responsible for the knowledge management system. Integrity implies that the knowledge in the knowledge repository will remain current and correct, overtime. This embodies the ideas of accuracy and currency of knowledge. In the knowledge management system a lack of accuracy or currency of knowledge may involve the organization in serious loss, damage to reputation, or severe financial exposure as a result of decisions made on the basis of that knowledge. Thus, it is important to audit the knowledge held within the knowledge repositories to ensure that that knowledge is current and correct overtime. *Integrity* also relates to the security of the knowledge held. If an unauthorised person has access to knowledge held within a document, then they may substitute, modify or delete knowledge and therefore compromized the accuracy and integrity of the knowledge incorporated within the document.

Monitoring of knowledge use is also an important concern. An organization needs to be able to track who has accessed the knowledge from documents in the repository, identify when that document was accessed, what was done to the document during the access, and if tracked, what use was made of the knowledge. Knowledge management systems may not yet have the monitoring and auditing facilities to allow this use to be tracked and captured. Others may have the facility within the knowledge management system but this facility may not have been enabled. In other cases, the logs from the monitoring system may not be kept for an appropriate length of time.

Availability of the knowledge repository is also an issue that needs to be addressed. It is of no use to have a knowledge repository that is unavailable to knowledge workers around the globe. This may arise through some unfortunate incident which may have destroyed the knowledge repository or prevented access to it. Examples include acts of cyber-terrorism or actual terrorism, accidental mishaps leading to the deletion of key knowledge repositories, or an attack that may render communication lines to the repository inoperative. Availability requires that an organization's knowledge infrastructure including communication lines, knowledge servers and knowledge systems are all operational and are securely protected from penetration. Should a disaster occur, it is important that a fallback facility is pre-arranged so that the organization may keep operating as usual following the disaster, by switching to those fallback facilities. It is a must that key knowledge systems and associated knowledge repositories are backed up and held securely off-site. Many organizations are using electronic vaulting as one of their backup and recovery strategies.

3. Knowledge Management Audit and Assurance : As well as identifying risks and putting in place security and control mechanisms to mitigate or control these risks, knowledge management should also consider audit assurance of its systems and environments. knowledge management monitoring of knowledge flows, online alerting mechanisms and audit of knowledge systems to provide assurance to knowledge management are explained here.

(i) *Knowledge Audit and Monitoring* : Knowledge audit has traditionally involved the review of an organization to determine where knowledge is located within the organization and then look at the best methods of being able to retrieve, extract, capture, store, and disseminate the knowledge to others. Doyle proposes a knowledge audit that involves a readiness assessment, then a gap analysis, followed by benchmarking to best knowledge management practices. Knowledge auditing also has a different connotation which is to monitor the usage of knowledge within the organization. If the knowledge management systems do not have monitoring and auditing systems included, then these need to be specified and programmed into the knowledge management systems. Knowledge management auditing subsystems will provide continuous monitoring and auditing facilities to personnel in the knowledge centres, who have been allocated the responsibility for reviewing knowledge auditing reports. When a knowledge worker accesses a knowledge document in the repository the knowledge auditing system will record the date and time of access, which knowledge worker accessed the document, what document was accessed, and the use for which that knowledge access was put, if this feature was incorporated into the knowledge auditing system. This knowledge access record then becomes part of an audit trail which knowledge centre management may review and the follow up at their discretion. Part of the continuous monitoring knowledge management auditing system may involve an alerting component. There may be some access control specified on certain documents, for example, any access to a particular document or any change to a particular document. If such an access or change occurs to a document so marked, then not only will an alerting record be written to the knowledge auditing database, but an immediate alert will be sent to the knowledge centre's alert console for immediate follow-up by knowledge centre personnel. Such an auditing system may be named a KSCARF (knowledge System Control Audit Review File). KSCARF will also need to provide the facility for knowledge centre management to maintain the KSCARF system, that is the ability to print auditing reports, maintain the alerting and auditing parameters, and archive knowledge auditing reports. These reports may be called on by management, police or other government agencies in the case of serious crime, abuse or other criminal acts. These knowledge reports need to be secured and held in a secure area as they may be called on as evidence. It.is recommended that knowledge auditing reports should be held for a minimum period of seven years.

(ii) *Knowledge Assurance* : Knowledge assurance refers to a review of the knowledge management systems and infrastructure to ensure that these systems are adequately secured, controllable and auditable so that those who use the systems can rely on the results produced by those systems. This will involve having qualified knowledge auditors to perform quality assurance checks on the knowledge management systems. This function may be carried out by an organization's quality assurance department or section if they have the required knowledge and abilities to carry out these audits. Knowledge assurance work may also be undertaken by many of the major audit/consultancy firms that operate globally. These reviews will consider not just the technology involved but also a review of the security and control structures that have been built in and around the knowledge management systems. Technical aspects will also be considered including security, backup and recovery facilities, a review of the knowledge management system itself, and a review of knowledge centre activities such as knowledge dictionary maintenance and control of the allocation of thesaurus/dictionary terms to documents.

4. Privacy Concerns for KM : Privacy is an important issue to address when discussing knowledge repositories. In many countries, there exists privacy legislation for both public and private sectors. Privacy legislation usually requires that an organization informs all persons, from whom the organization is soliciting knowledge or information which is going to end in a knowledge repository, of certain key privacy tenets affecting how the information or knowledge solicited from them will be used and retained in the knowledge repository. Contributors need to be informed of what information or knowledge is being captured in the first place and then informed as the use for which that information or knowledge will be used in the future. It is then the organization's responsibility to monitor who has access to that knowledge, who maintains the knowledge, and how that knowledge is used a within the organization. If there is open access to knowledge documents within the knowledge repository, this may seriously compromise the organization in meeting the set criteria from privacy legislation. For example, even when an organization is capturing knowledge from persons using the World Wide Web, they may need to have a privacy statement on the Web for their knowledge management system that informs the users/contributors of the privacy conditions that will apply to knowledge being given. Breaches of privacy in knowledge management systems may cause lack of trust by customers/contributors and may even leave the organization open to legal liability.

Many countries either have privacy legislation or are currently implementing such legislation. In Australia, new national privacy laws came into effect on December 21, 2001 under the Privacy Amendment (Private Sector) Act 2000. The privacy legislation is based on 10 key National Privacy Principles (NPPs). The following explanations and implications of the NPPs are based on Braue's interpretations for organizations with websites and have been modified to show the implications for knowledge management:

(i) *Collection* : Only collect information relevant to the organization by fair means and not in an unreasonable intrusive way. For knowledge management, this means having a clear, coherent and specific privacy policy stating the identity of the organization and how to contact it, what knowledge will be collected, who will see the knowledge, why the organization needs the knowledge and what will happen if it does not have that knowledge.

(ii) *Use and Disclosure* : The organization cannot disclose personal information unless it is for a specific need and customers/contributors would reasonably expect that disclosure. Knowledge users/contributors trust an organization when they give it personal information, and it is in the organization's best interest not to abuse that trust in any way. Any questionable ideas on use and disclosure should be run past the organization's privacy officer, legal representative or a privacy consultant.

(iii) *Data Quality* : Make sure any personal information collected, used or disclosed by the organization is accurate, complete and up-to-date. For knowledge management systems, this involves ensuring that personal information or knowledge captured in knowledge repositories remains current and correct. This may involve offering a Web self-service portal to the knowledge repository so that customers/contributors can notify the organization of any changes or make changes themselves to their personal information or knowledge stored in the knowledge repository.

(iv) *Data Security* : An organization needs to take reasonable steps to protect personal information from misuse and loss from unauthorised access, modification or disclosure. There is need to destroy or eliminate identifying details from information no longer needed for a specific purpose. For knowledge management, this means implementing appropriate security measures that both protect personal data and knowledge stored in knowledge repositories, e.g., by encryption; and prevent unauthorized access to the repositories and/or use of that knowledge, e.g., by authentication, systems access control, and activity logging.

(v) *Openness* : Information management policy and make this policy available to anyone who asks for it. For knowledge management, this entails publishing the knowledge management personal information management policy on a web page prior to customers/users entering the knowledge management site, and including links to the organization's privacy policy on its web site. An organization may also consider auditing and certification of the privacy policy, for example through such organizations as the Australian Privacy Compliance Centre (www.privacycompliance.org), and eTick - administrator of the Australian Privacy Seal Audit and Certification (APSAC) program.

(vi) *Access and Correction* : Organizations are to allow customers to see information held on them and must be able to correct any incorrect information held. For knowledge management, this involves either an online self-service portal or a K-Centre providing procedures for customers/contributors to update incorrect or changed information/knowledge via email, fax or via a call Centre.

(vii) *Identifiers* : Organizations cannot use the same identification number or code that another organization has assigned to a particular customer. This is in order to prevent aggregation of customer or client data from multiple sources. For knowledge management, this means that the organization should develop its own process for identifying customers/contributors and ensure that they do not communicate customer/contributors identifiers when sharing this information with other organizations, including multiple divisions of a company.

(viii) *Anonymity* : Where practicable individuals must have the option of not identifying themselves when entering into transactions with an organization. For knowledge management, this entails that an organization must not demand personal information just to allow customers/

contributors to enter their knowledge repositories site. Knowledge management systems should be built with basic level functionality available to all and then present a second tier offering extra value addons if a customer/contributor offers more knowledge/information about themselves.

(ix) *Transborder Data Flows* : Organizations should not transfer information out of Australia unless the recipient is in a jurisdiction where privacy is at least equal to the NPP standards and the recipient is likely to uphold customer/contributor's privacy. Organizations should get approval for these transfers wherever possible. For knowledge management, this means great care should be taken with whom knowledge and personal information is to be communicated outside national borders. Compromising customers'/contributors' privacy may seriously damage an organization's reputation and may even lead to legal liability.

(x) *Sensitive Information* : Organizations should not collect sensitive information about any persons unless they have provided authorisation, or would authorize it but cannot, or the organization needs the information to benefit public health or safety. Although the law does not define 'sensitive', this principle is intended to protect medical records and other health-care related information. So for knowledge management systems holding personal information and knowledge about customers'/contributors' medical or health records, the organization should seek legal advice before implementing knowledge systems dealing with this type of information and knowledge.

Many knowledge management systems interact or form a key component of customer relation management (CRM) systems. The privacy principles and implications outlined above should be seriously taken into account by knowledge management when developing and implementing these systems.

Thus, the use of continuous monitoring audit techniques can help to ensure that the use of knowledge in the repositories is tracked to the users of that knowledge, and if possible, how that knowledge was used. It is important that knowledge management also consider the important issue of privacy to personal information and knowledge held in the repositories. The privacy principles discussed above should present knowledge management with suggestions how knowledge management can deal with the implications of privacy for knowledge management systems and repositories. The framework and guidelines presented here should provide knowledge managers with the ability to secure their knowledge management systems, repositories, and infrastructure, and to address the risks associated with knowledge management.

12.2. FUTURE TECHNOLOGIES FOR KM

What does Knowledge Management need from technology? Ways to reduce manual labor to collect, organize, and disseminate knowledge. Collecting knowledge is not the same as collecting information. It is insufficient to merely gather and bundle together interesting and related pieces of information. Rather, the information must be filtered, analyzed, validated, and fused with contextually related sources, and prioritized. Automating any portion of the knowledge processes will be valuable, although help is especially needed with organizing and sorting the vast quantity of information.

Knowledge Management is one of several fields (e.g., logistics, financial planning) needing more intelligent applications that can decide among many possible scenarios using uncertain data. This overlapping requirement will continue to drive advances in search engines, text and multimedia analysis and human-computer interactions.

In particular, text understanding is an extremely difficult challenge to overcome because humans do more than analyze the semantics, syntax, and word relationships to deduce concepts. In fact, a sentence's concept is only part of the paragraph's theme, which is only part of the overall thesis of the document. People have been taught how to mentally hold and wait as they read in order to connect concepts throughout the document to determine the meaning. Thus, a search engine that correctly identifies the meaning of a sentence, or even paragraph, can still not deliver a pertinent response to a user who is interested in finding a document about a topic. For example, the following excerpt might be returned for a query on salaries for workers with MBAs.

"This circular reasoning is sufficiently vague that it seems to confirm the view that everyone in the U.S. is getting smarter because the stock market says so. It appeals to newly minted MBAs because it justifies high salaries and stock options. Gurus, pundits and intellectuals can then make claims about the priceless value of their knowledge capital despite the fact that it is not feasible to determine a valuation that can be verified independently."

Yet, the document is actually about the value of knowledge capital and not salary levels, as is evident from additional passages.

"The value of knowledge capital has become the financial community's favourite rationalization for the current stratospheric prices of some stocks. If you probe further and ask a broker to define "knowledge capital." You are likely to hear that it is the difference between what investors are willing to pay and the book value of a firm.

This circular reasoning is sufficiently vague that it seems to confirm the view that everyone in the U.S. is getting smarter because the stock market says so. It appeals to newly minted MBAs because it justifies high salaries and stock options. Gurus, pundits and intellectuals can then make claims about the priceless value of their knowledge capital despite the fact that it is not feasible to determine a valuation that can be verified independently.

There are, however, those who detest the flimsy rationale of self-serving knowledge capital claimants. It is the job of CFOs, auditors and accountants to come up with assessments of the worth of a firm's intangible assets. This is critically important when explaining the price paid for an acquisition, in granting stock options and in paying sign-up bonuses for unique talent. It is up to the financial scorekeepers to rein in exaggerated claims of intangible wealth and juxtapose reality against fantasy."

This is an important distinction that exemplifies the ability of people to discern meaning from context and not just from mechanical language constructs. Information systems must capture the broader contextually influence on meaning to be able to accurately match stored information to user's interests.

One of the key areas that must be improved is the representation of concepts. *Ontologies* are frameworks of conceptual relationships that define how to structure the meaning of information. These relationships cannot be distilled into a single connecting term or phrase, but must be embodied by describing the multiple ways words are grouped and used to convey meaning among people.

There is no single conceptual basis for ontologies, even at a general level. The conceptual relationships and attributes that form an ontology framework depend on culture as well as the knowledge domain. Consequently, there are innumerable ontological organization schemes, which is a major hurdle to overcome before automated reasoning systems can truly comprehend information. The first step is to have sophisticated knowledge representation languages pervade information repositories. Several projects are addressing this, including:

- *Ontolingua* - An ontology development system from Stanford University that uses object-oriented functions and an axiom base for ontology design and specification. It has a set of APIs to enable interoperability for distributed ontology servers.
- *WebKB* - A knowledge based language that uses Conceptual Graphs. It can be embedded within HTML documents for use on the Web.
- *Semantic Web* - It is a concept proposed by Tim Berners-Lee for World Wide Web consortium. It uses the Resource Description Framework to embed semantic assertions into the Web to allow automated reasoning.

These representations must be coupled to specific knowledge of the context of how the information was created and how it is being used. This type of information is captured and contained in large Knowledge Bases (KB) that provide specific facts necessary to disambiguate several possible meanings from grammatically correct sentences, and to identify when a proper noun refers to particular objects by related information in the document. One example is a KB created from the CIA's World Fact Book using automatic knowledge extraction and refinement, based in part on the Ontolingua representation language. Also, the Rapid Knowledge Formation program at DARPA is building the technology to greatly increase both the creation speed and size of large-scale Knowledge Bases.

While we would like IT tools to be able to accurately comprehend text and reason about the user's intent, it would also be valuable to automatically extract important topics and produce a succinct summary. Clearly, producing a summary that captures the conceptual essence of a document requires full text understanding capabilities. However, even mediocre text analysis algorithms can generate highly useful summaries because they allow people to quickly discern whether the document is worth spending time on to explore further. There are commercial summarizers currently available, although their limited capabilities have restricted their wide-scale adoption. Examples of existing programs are:

- InXight's commercial tool Summarizer which extracts sentences and supports multiple languages.
- IBM's Summarization module for the Intelligent Miner for Text system.
- USC's Summarist system that uses symbolic knowledge from WordNet and other semantic sources with NLP processing to perform topic identification, interpretation and generation.
- DARPA's Translingual Identification, Detection, Extraction, and Summarization (TIDES) program which is working "to develop the technology to enable individuals working in English to locate, access, and utilize network-accessible text documents in multiple languages, without requiring any knowledge of the target languages. The accomplishment of this will require advances in component technologies of information retrieval, machine translation, document understanding, information extraction and summarization, as well as the integration technologies which fuse these components into an end-to-end capability yielding substantially more value than the serial staging of the component functions. The mission extends to the rapid development of retrieval and translation capability for a new

language of interest."

Other important technologies that have the potential to significantly improve knowledge management systems are:

- *Intelligent Agents*: these small software components can roam networks performing tasks proactively such as personalized information retrieval, database replication and coordination for distributed groups, and tracking of information dissemination and use to improve system effectiveness. In order to enable this capability, a pervasive framework is required similar to the discussion of embedding semantics throughout the network. DARPA Agent Markup Language program is building such an infrastructure.
- *Improved Human-Computer Interfaces (HCI)*: This is a particularly important area that needs substantial scientific and technical advances. Scientifically, we need to understand the influence of various HCI methods and tools on the transfer of information from a machine to a human's cognitive processes. Indeed, we have yet to design our IT systems to account for the multiple perspectives people use to view the same information at different times. New HCI tools are being developed and tested heuristically, such as web presentation on cellular phones and personal digital assistants. In addition, DARPA's Small Unit Operation Situational Awareness Program is working on automated distributed information fusion, adjudication, and dissemination to enable validated and fused information to be presented on a handheld device to individuals.
- *Distributed Computational Devices*: The level of text understanding required for an IT system to be able.to automate knowledge capture, organization and distribution is very high. This will require a combination of computationally intensive algorithms and large knowledge bases. Although these can be hosted on a server centrally located in an organization, people's mobility and real-time need for knowledge introduces the desire to empower distributed handheld devices with as much of this computational power as possible, as described for the

DARPA Small Unit Operation Situational Awareness Program. In addition, DARPA's Fundamental Research Interface Program is developing technology to combine biological, Micro-electromechanical, and IT systems to build revolutionary miniature IT devices with biologically inspired architectures.

12.3. HAS KM ARRIVED

Inspite of Above Latest Development, the question is sometimes asked Has KM Arrived? Recent journalistic reports have uncovered increasing numbers of companies exploring or embracing the practice of knowledge management. A number of certification programs in knowledge management are being developed and marketed. At last report, several dozen college and university programs in knowledge management had been established, with reports of additional programs arriving regularly.

Virtually every research report on knowledge management or one of its component processes finds growth and potential in the market. To cite recent ones:

According to a 14-year study conducted by the Center for Effective Organizations in the Marshall School of Business at the University of Southern California, there is a growing trend among major American corporations to devote more time and resources to the management of knowledge and to creating incentive systems that tie pay to performance. According to the USC study, companies are using these programs to replace the seniority-based reward practices and loyalty relationships that existed when the study began in 1987.

Knowledge Management magazine published a report on "The State of KM" in its May 2001 issue. It was prepared in cooperation with Greg Dyer, senior research analyst for IDC's Knowledge Management Services program. Survey respondents indicated that their companies do understand the value of deploying knowledge management solutions, and that their knowledge efforts are strategic in nature, with substantial involvement by executive managers.

Among the results was some data that suggests the relevance

of knowledge management in times of a weak economy-- When asked the reasons for respondents' companies adopting knowledge management, 51.9 percent said it was to retain the expertize of personnel - more than 8 percentage points higher than the second-ranking answer, which was to increase customer satisfaction.

When those being surveyed were asked about business uses of the knowledge management initiatives under way, more than three-quarters said it was to capture and share best practices, while five-eighths said it was to provide training and learning.

The Knowledge Management survey results also echoed other analyses of corporate knowledge management deployments with regard to management and leadership – senior corporate management leads almost half of all initiatives, with a cross-functional team being the most common approach.

Finally, the survey revealed that there is no illusion about the major challenges facing executives interested in knowledge-enabling their companies: they are lack of employee time, the absence of a sharing culture, a lack of understanding of the benefits of knowledge management - and, fourth on the list, that persistent bugaboo, the ROI challenge. Despite the incessant drumbeat in recent years, "Lack of appropriate technology" ranked only 10th on the list.

12.3.1. Early Drivers

There are some core functions that have been found to be the early drivers toward knowledge management. One is a felt need for improved messaging and collaboration support, whether that be robust e-mail, instant messaging among employees, or real-time groupware tools. Another is the challenge of document management, which is evolving to become much more a process concern and far less about specific pieces of paper or office files.

There is no question that the availability of technology tools is an enabler. The abilities these tools offer to the aggressively competing company or organization can make a difference. They are, to use an off-heard phrase, necessary though not sufficient to drive and support knowledge management.

Three categories of tools are likely to play central roles in the strategic deployment of knowledge management systems.

1. The first category is tools to facilitate access to expertize that exists within the company. Basex, a New York-based consultancy and analyst firm, issued a report in mid-2001 in which it suggested that software systems that facilitate the process of locating expertise within a company could be KM's killer application. It is a nuanced argument; the author, Charles Canning-Smith, takes pains to point out that the nature of the corporate culture plays a key role in determining the success of the deployment of such a tool in speeding time to market, reducing costs and improving the bottom line.

2. Knowledge is useless unless it is shared with those for whom it has business benefit. Knowledge in a repository, a knowledge base, is a potential asset, but its value will not be realized until it makes a difference. Hence the importance of the just-now-developing category of what we call "just-in-time knowledge" tools. These are delivery tools rooted in the e-learning space but focused not on training but on the injunction oft voiced by Carla O'Dell, the Executive Director of the American Productivity and Quality Council, that the essence of knowledge management must be getting the right knowledge to the right people at the right time.

3. The identity of the technology tool that in the short- to mid-term is likely to be the glue that holds knowledge processes together will come as no surprise. It is, of course, the enterprise information portal. Particularly, it is the second-generation portal - personalized, of course, but also offering data access to legacy back-end systems, transactional capabilities and support for real-time collaboration. The label "portal" is particularly well chosen to describe these tools, which have such a tremendous capacity to empower by eliminating tedious processes and heterogeneous interfaces, integrating the unique blend of information and knowledge required by any given employee and putting it at his or her fingertips.

Corporate portal deployment is still in an early stage. Hummingbird in 2000 queried 1,000 companies about their plans, and reported that 60 percent of them were in the "conceptual" phase while only 15 percent had deployments underway or completed. Another survey, done by Delphi Group, indicated that only one-quarter of the companies it questioned had already invested in portal technology, but companies amounting to half the sample said they had make a significant investment in portals within the following year.

How they pursue that investment will make a difference. A portal ought not to be a shrink-wrapped buy. It is a complex tool for knowledge access and sharing that will deliver value only if designed to meet specific business needs.

The developments in communications technology promise to impact companies' ability to migrate to knowledge-centric approaches. In particular, the recent announcements about the interoperability of instant messaging tools offer great promise for expanding the potential for useful collaboration within the enterprise and adding functionality to those expertise-accessing systems.

In addition, in the wireless environment, faster and more robust wide-area wireless data access has changed the entire face of knowledge empowerment. As carriers lurch unevenly toward 3G and 4G networks, Customer Related Management or CRM tools and handhelds suggests where we may well be headed.

Improved real-time availability is not merely an enabler, though - it is likely to be a harsh taskmistress as well. As John Jordan of Cap Gemini Ernst & Young noted in an edition of the Business Innovation Newsletter, "Increased connectivity challenges organizations to shorten strategy and operational cycles." The opportunities for profiting from better information and decision-making capability are almost endless, but the difficulties are numerous as well, and extend well beyond the technical and process hurdles to include organizational and behavioural gaps.

There are indications that the marketplace for knowledge management tools and strategic and deployment advice may well be considerably stronger in the rest of the world. Some of those indications are anecdotal, but there are numbers as well.

12.3.2. The Paradox

Despite all these positive indicators, the future of knowledge management is a bit confused, for a number of reasons.

One is because, like all loosely defined undertakings, knowledge management is a moving target. Despite the many attempts to define it, and despite the existence of official-sounding bodies like IBM's Institute for Knowledge Management and the Knowledge Management Consortium International, knowledge management remains very much in the eye of the beholder. It means different things to different people. As Tom Davenport, the Director of the Accenture Institute for Strategic Change, pointed out in CIO a while ago, knowledge management is "an ever-growing collection of stuff."

Where once it was about the creation and use of technology-based repositories and about developing a knowledge-oriented culture and structure, today it is about e-learning, and business rules, and business intelligence, and lots more.

To quote Davenport, "The drift and accretion of knowledge management surely has a downside. In referring to so many different ideas, the concept will probably lose focus, and knowledge management initiatives may try to do too much."

What Davenport describes, and what a number of companies have experienced of late, is characteristic of the middle period in the adoption of a new strategic methodology. It is, in Tom Kuhn's terms, the period of the establishment of a new paradigm, the return to a "normal" that is in fact different from what went before. The definitional confusion will pass. For now, though, we must be careful to define our terms to be sure that we are discussing the same processes.

The relation of the business discipline of knowledge management to the vendors of technology tools has been much discussed of late. Eric Berkman writes that "knowledge management has fallen in victim to a mixture of bad implementation practices and software vendors eager to turn a complex process into a pure technology play. The result–like many a business concept, knowledge management has evolved from a hot buzzword to a phrase that now evokes more skepticism than enthusiasm." To drive the point home, he evokes the image of the vendor feeding frenzy that was the trade show floor at the annual knowledge management World conference in Silicon Valley. It is a scene many of us have seen.

It is mean here to re-plow old ground, but the fact remains that despite the best efforts of many practitioners, analysts, journalists, and commentators, there remain senior corporate executives who believe that knowledge management is a technology-driven, rather than technology-enabled, undertaking. And so they hand the pilot project to an IT executive, who goes looking for a vendor to deliver the goods. And there are plenty of vendors eager to deliver knowledge management solutions.

The scene on the knowledge management World show floor in the near future promises to be very different from a couple of years ago. In addition, the endeavour of knowledge management is challenging, as is anything in the business world that involves people. It is with good reason that the human resources function is emerging as a strategic role that deserves a seat on the executive committee. Knowledge management is about what people know, what they need to know, and how they can help to each other and their employers to work well and prosper.

For those corporations and other large organizations that are clear about the need to knowledge-enable their operations and processes, the road has not been a simple one - again. Cultural change not only does not come easily, the need for it is often not obvious to the old-school business executive. Success requires dogged determination on the part of senior management, clear-sighted project and practice leaders, and buy-in from the knowledge workers themselves. The fact remains that deploying knowledge management is not a guaranteed success. It is certainly not in the same ballpark as deploying a new relational database, or even deploying an ERP or CRM system.

The building and nurturing of communities illustrate the challenge of committing to knowledge as a corporate tool for competitive advantage. As organic, somewhat amorphous entities, communities need to be nurtured and managed, but they can not really be directed. In other words, you can not directly make them succeed, but you can and should support them nonetheless. As Sun Tzu wrote in *The Art of War*, "In all fighting, the direct method may be used for joining battle, but indirect methods will be needed to secure victory."

These are economic times that reward the far-sighted in corporate leadership who understood there would be competitive value in knowledge-enabling their companies. Forward-thinking companies view periods of turmoil as opportunities to refresh their strategies, challenge their assumptions and innovate to gain market share. Even cutbacks—if handled deftly and with an eye toward conserving knowledge and expertize and improving efficiencies—can yield positive results. In particular, layoffs have far less impact if unique knowledge does not walk out the door with ex-employees.

But the identification, harvesting and central storage of company knowledge is not something that can be deployed in a few months. Knowledge management is a key component of an affirmative corporate response to an economic downturn, but the deployment needs to have been planned and begun long before the GNP growth starts to shrink.

Yet even that is challenging, for knowledge-enabling a large organization relies on the loyalty of employees. Employees need to trust that to the extent possible companies will take care of them, or else they will not share their knowledge. And without that shared knowledge, companies run a real risk of harming themselves, of losing their way amidst the high waves and torrential downpours of a rapidly-changing business and economic climate.

A thoroughgoing knowledge strategy is proactive and long-term. It needs to in place and working, like the patch to a leaky boat, long before the skies turn gray. Because if it is not, if senior managers suddenly set about gathering employee knowledge in response to a sales downturn, sirens will sound, storm warnings will be run up, and employee trust will be hidden away with that knowledge. After all, who will willingly help rig the ladder that is likely to lead him or her over the side?

Knowledge management is too often understood as purely a conservative mechanism - as a way of retaining unique expertize so as to avoid the time and costs associated with developing that knowledge again. But knowledge management ought also to be understood as being about the process of creating new corporate knowledge. This extends it to encompass the set of business endeavors often referred to as innovation. And those are, if anything, even more frightening to the uninitiated or insufficiently motivated than is the term knowledge management.

Finally, a key link in the knowledge management chain remains unforged. Despite the earnest efforts of a number of creative and original thinkers and scholars, we cannot yet show how and to what extent knowledge management impacts a company's bottom line. For senior corporate managers to embrace knowledge management processes, particularly in hard times, they must be able to show to their boards why it is worth it, in terms that matter. We therefore are badly in need of a subtle but revolutionary shift in how companies are valued.

Ultimately, metrics must be developed that quantify the contribution of knowledge developed and used within the company to that company's value. We need to be able to show, and the accountancy and capital markets standards bodies must be willing to accept, that intangible assets not acquired through a market transaction nonetheless have market value, have exchange value. It is only then that we will be able truly to cost-justify knowledge management. And, we are moving in that direction.

12.3.4. The Burden of Success

To the extent that knowledge management is in fact an approach that contributes to a company's competitive advantage, it is disappearing as a distinct business process. Instead, it is being incorporated as a component of other business processes. Increasingly, rather than speaking of a knowledge management deployment, we are hearing references to a knowledge-enabled call center, an R&D unit that uses knowledge and expertize tools, an HR department that's knowledge oriented.

Analysts from the Basex consultancy in mid-2001 surveyed

the Web sites of a number of companies that generate what Basex considers knowledge management news to ascertain whether the Web site actually used the term "knowledge management" and whether it described what it does in knowledge management terms. Based on what it found, Basex assigned each company a grade, ranging from an *A* if the company uses the term "knowledge management," relates it to sharing and describes what it does in knowledge management terms, through *B* for use of terms equivalent to knowledge management, to a low grade of *C* if the company plays in the KM marketplace but does not use KM terminology.

The result? Very few of the 32 companies surveyed, all of which in Basex's judgment were knowledge management companies, identified themselves that way. Only 9 percent got an *A* grade. 19 percent got an *A*-, which required using the term knowledge management and relating it to sharing. This avoidance of the term "knowledge management" is not likely to be much of a problem for end users - for large enterprises seeking to embrace knowledge approaches to competitiveness and cost-effectiveness. In fact, given the ambiguity and confusion that has surrounded the term, the absence of the knowledge management label may be a positive factor in getting sign-off on the project.

It certainly may prove to be a problem tor a self-defined knowledge management marketplace. Knowledge management is a multi-billion dollar industry. But it is a stealthy one, and one lacking broad, compelling rhetorical appeal, if you are selling knowledge management services - consulting services, portals, collaboration tools, expertize software or any of the other categories-you know that knowledge management as a marketing tag is not performing very well, and may not be the most effective label for you.

12.3.5. Where Should We Go with KM?

Is this then the beginning of the end for knowledge management as a distinct endeavour? Will knowledge management go the way, for example, of the quality movement?

When we rolled out *Knowledge Management* in 1998, we

characterized knowledge management as risk management for the enterprise. If anything, the risks to competitive organizations have increased in the ensuing three years.

"To take advantage of this shift," "organizations have to change in ways large and small. They have to jettison many of the old assumptions, while embracing new forms of organization and business methods that may be utterly alien."

That is happening. *But knowledge management* is proving not to be the best label for that phenomenon.

The name has been challenged repeatedly since Karl-Erik Sveiby wrote, "Personally I dislike the notion 'Knowledge Management.' Knowledge is a human faculty, not something that can be 'managed,' except by the individual him/herself. A better guidance for our thinking is therefore phrases such as 'to be Knowledge Focused' or to 'see' the world from a 'Knowledge Perspective.'

Lars Johansen, the President and CEO of IT Factory, has recently been delivering a presentation in which he declares that knowledge management is a technology in the process of moving from the "hype" stage to the stage of really providing value for companies. "By the time knowledge management really becomes widely used in organizations," says Johansen, "we would not call it knowledge management anymore, because it will be in everything we do. It will be both transparent and pervasive. In other words, its use is so widespread that essentially everyone is using it, and they do not even know that they are using it."

Knowledge management functionality will be seamlessly embedded into the business application user interface. But at this point, users are not really thinking of it as knowledge management anymore, they are just thinking in terms of answers they need to pressing questions right now.

So in the end, as says Johansen, we would not think of knowledge management as knowledge management anymore. We will simply think of it as the right answers at the right time in the right context.

APPENDICES

APPENDIX–A

ALTERNATIVE SCHEMES FOR STRUCTURING KM SYSTEMS

This appendix provides examples of several alternative arrangement schemes both for site content and maps. Most styles are followed by an example and a location URL that can be investigated further.

Alternate Structures

The key point is that there are many other ways of organizing content when you are creating a Web-based front end fot your knowledge management system, so do not just limit your choices without taking a look at these alternatives. The structures are presented in the order of popularity of use and perceived usefulness.

Alphabetical

The alphabetical approach does not work well if content is not referred to consistently by everyone. It is a bad idea when cross-functional teams arc involved in your company, and a good one when every one shares the same vocabulary. The sample site can be found at http://www.moIndaJ.se/bibl/subject.htm.

Alphanumeric

Alphanumeric style is very similar to the alphabetical structure, except that content under each alphabetical category is arranged by the numeric code. This works only when you can have some kind or numeric codes assigned to each content item. This style seems to have very low applicability to knowledge management design. The sample site can be found at http://www.dvjb.kvl.dk/dvjbfag/umnetO2.htm.

Dewey Decimal Codes

Dewey Decimal Coding (DDC) is a classification scheme used in libraries. If your content can be neatly categorized in such categories, this might be an equal to consider. ADAM helps you to find the relevant information by providing a searchable online catalogue describing Internet resources such as Websites or electronic mailing lists, in much the same way as a library- catalogue describes bibliographic resources such as books and journals. This site can be found at http://adam.ac.uk/adam/index.html.

Another example can be found on the Web at http://bized.ac.uk/ roads /htdocs/subjectlisting/Default/numlist.html.

Classification Schemes for Public Libraries

A number of library classification schemes exist. One such site based on public library classification schemes is the Finnish site Suomabzisia linkkejii aianmukaisrsti jilrjeitettynii. This site can be found at http:// www.kirjasto.sci.fi/lindex.htm.

Universal Decimal Classification

Another mechanism to organize and structure content, as seen through the system front end, is the Universal Decimal Classification scheme. A sample site, the NISS Directory of Networked Resources use this scheme. As you might guess, this is appropriate only for content that is highly structured. Rarely do companies—even those that follow a deep structured codification strategy for knowledge management—have content so highly structured. This scheme is much used in special libraries to arrange their contents. This site can be found at http://www.niss.ac.uk/subject/ index.html.

ACM Computing Classification System

The Computing Research Repository (CoRR), which is sponsored by ACM, the Los Alamos e-Print archive and NCSTRL (Networked Computer Science Technics Reference Library), uses the ACM computing classification system for driving its structure. This method might be useful for organizing content and driving structure for highly organized explicated documents and artifacts that exist in electronic form. The site can be found on Web at http://xxx.lanl.gov/archive/cs/intro.html.

The Library of Congress Classification Scheme

A promising method for classification and categorization of general content is that based on the Library of Congress (LOC) classification scheme. An example of such a site is Cyberstacks at Iowa State University. This site, can be found on the Web on http://www.public.iastate.edu/-CYBERSTACKS/narrow.htm.

Predicast -Revised Event Codes

Bay Networks Int., uses this set of codes for figuring out ways in which people looked for information. Since one artifact can fall under multiple categories, clustering .schemes need to be consistent. This scheme is based on the Predicasi Revised Event Code, Event Name List; and a readers guide to business press. Detailed information can he found in the expensive book (over $600) Predicasti Basebook, available in many libraries.

The schemes described above are excellent for highly structured content. They could be used if content within your system is highly structured and can be fitted into a limited number of categories. If this is not the case, which is most likely to be true, you must not try using such scheme.

However, if some of the content in your system could (due to the nature of your organization) neatly fit into one of the above categories, you can use category codes such as LOC or ACM codes, to assign meta tags to content. These tags can be used to retrieve and find content based on standardized codes even when they are not explicitly used. It is unlikely that any knowledge management system can manage with such a limited set of classification categories, but these could be used or combined to transparently add one more level of tagging to your knowledge management system's content—both formal and informal.

APPENDIX–B

SOFTWARE TOOLS FOR KNOWLEDGE MANAGEMENT

Ascent

Ascent develops custom database mining software, using a spectrum of techniques developed in artifical intelligence and allied fields. These techniques include decision tree construction neural-net training, genetic evolution, clustering, derived-attribute discover, and visualisation with the characteristics of the application always driving the technique-selection process. Ascent also develops the sophisticated infrastructure needed to support database mining applications, with a special expertise in database system management, database conditioning client/server computing, knowledge engineering and the construction of regularity-exposing graphical user interface. Ascent's database mining and visualization are very expensive. For further information, visit Ascent's Web site at www.ascent.com

BrainForest Professional for Palm Pilot PDAs

BrainForest Professional for your hand-held PDA and your desktop is an action item, checklist manager, idea keeper and project planner for mobile users. For knowledge management systems that support mobile users, this application can be used as a component for linking personal digital assistants, desktops and shared systems. BrainForest displays information on a hand-held device or desktop computer using an intuitive trees, branches and leaves analogy, similar to the Outline function in Microsoft Word.

BrainForest groups related ideas, action items, checklists, to-dos, Internet URLs, electronic mail addresses, etc., together. Users can keep track of teams and projects, recurring items, due dates and priorities. BrainForest is sold in two versions: a mobile PDA-only version and an extended version that includes a desktop client. For further information, visit Aportis' Website at www.aportis.com.

Business Vue 2.0

BusinessVue is a corporate intelligence software that is also included in AlphaCONNECT's StockVue 99 program. This program allows you to retrieve corporate profiles via Market Guide, query the DR-LINK™ database, and get access to thousands of news stories link to Dun &C Bradstreet for business-to-business credit information on companies worldwide, get stock quotes and news articles from PC Quote, gain access to analyzation with Zack's Investment Research and research SEC filings with Edgar Online can also configure it to automatically send important information to key contacts via e-mail pager, or fax and export information to leading business applications like Excel and ACT!

BusinessVue an excellent example of intelligent filtering technology is used to gather corporate intelligence from the Internet. Further details can be found on AlphaCONNECT's home page at www.alphaconect. com.

CBR Content Navigator

Inference Corporation's CBR Content Navigator provides "conversation-based access to multiple sources of knowledge." Access to the knowledge can be via the Web, CD-ROM, or call center representative. CBR knowledge management technology captures the diagnostic process of solving problems and allows a knowledge base to be built. Users can then type in descriptions of queries in everyday language. An intelligent analysis of this query provides the parameters to define a search of the knowledge base by means of case-based retrieval techniques. The search results are used to generate a set of questions to diagnose customer problems and recommend solutions. More information on this product can be found at www.inference.com.

Concept Explorer

Concept Lxplorer is a family of visual, knowledge-based tools for searching Web content. Users can explore relationships between search terms to build effective search queries without needing to understand details of search engine query syntax. The program analyzes sample ASCII documents or HTML Web pages and identifies semantic relationships among the most useful words and phrases to represent their subject matter. The result is a web of connections between key concepts, which is stored in a knowledge base. A graphical visualizer enables users to explore this knowledge base and build queries that can improve the accuracy of standard search engines. For further details, visit Knowledge Discovery Systems on the Web at http://www.kdsystems.com/.

DataWare Knowledge Management Suite

DataWare knowledge management suite unifies access to disparate corporate knowledge repositories such as document management systems, RDBMS, Group Ware applications, electronic mail systems and external news feeds. It seamlessly integrates material from all of these sources into a central information repository while allowing users to continue working in familiar formats. The suite uses natural language querying, an ANSI-compliant thesaurus, concept-clustered results and relevance ranking to facilitate linking between related materials and on request, notifies users of updates or changes to specific topics of interest. For further details, visit DataWare Technologies on the Web at www.dataware.com.

DeltaMiner

MIS-AG's DeltaMiner integrates new search techniques and business intelligence methodologies into an OLAP front end that embraces the concept of active information management. MIS suggests that such an approach can maximize returns from tremendous amounts of little-used data collected in data marts assembled by many companies.

Finding useful information using traditional "passive" search techniques can be slow and cumbersome and usually leaves a large amount of important trends and variance sources hidden, especially when they lie outside of the normally examined controlling paths. By integrating standard OLAP analysis techniques, this tool makes it possible to pivot and cross-tabulate data for analyzing OLAP hypercubes. DeltaMiner automatically seeks the views that will be most meaningful, thereby increasing analysis effjcieficy. DeltaMiner further highlights the most significant exceptions by reorganizing cross-tabulations to magnify the 10 best or 10 worst results from the given data set. This tool also provides extensive graphic visualization features that help users graphically interpret significant exceptions.

DeltaMiner also automates ranking and portfolio analysis techniques and automatically suggests classifications for data sets. Further, by employing chain analysis techniques, this tool lets users ask new and more relevant questions of their data. All these techniques can be cross-linked to create powerful analysis chains. This analysis path is visually recorded in analysis tree, as MIS describes it. Via a data-driven drill down that does not follow any preset paths, DeltaMmer guides you rapidly to the main causes exceptions in your data.

A feature that makes this tool an excellent candidate for an expansive knowledge management system is its open database connectivity. DeltaMiner can directly be connected to various data sources including MIS ALFA TM/1, Microsoft OLA I Service and Oracle Express. For further information, visit MIS AG on the Web at www.mis.de.

Email Ferret

Email Ferret is a small utility for finding electronic mail addresses of people on rhe Web. Unlike most e-mail directories, it runs as a client on your desktop rather than in a browser. Email Ferret seeks out e-mail addresses by simultaneously querying multiple Web-based e-mail directories. Addresses can then be added to an electronic address book, copied or mailed to, using a standard electronic mail client.

Like most other Ferret Soft utilities, this tool automatically updates itself every time it is run as it automatically checks the Ferret Soft configuration server for any updates. Updates and new search engine configurations are extremely small, and the entire update process is last and unnoticeable. For more information, FerretSoft's home page at http://www.ferretsoft.com can be seen.

Employee Appraiser 4.0

Employee Appraiser 4.0 includes hundreds of professionally written phrases and paragraphs that you use to get started. When you have got the right combinations of paragraphs that you want, you can choose the Writing Tuner buttons and adjust tone or intensity.

Forms in Microsoft Word, Corel WordPerfect, Lotus Word Pro, and other programs can be imported into Employee Appraiser. Its word-scanning glossary feature checks for inappropriate or illegal language.

The Employee Folder helps managers track performance against objectives all year. When it comes time to write the review, Employee Appraiser shows you the key events and lets you easily put them into the appraisal form. Using this feature ensures that appropriate credit is given to each employee and that evaluations are truly evaluations rather than last-minute perceptions. For further information visit Austin Hayne's Website at http://www.austin-hayne.com.

File, Phone, and News Ferrets

File Ferret Phone Ferret, and New Ferret are three additional utilities from File Ferret. File Ferret searches both Web-based file databases and the Archie protocol databases for Shareware, public domain software and other files. Retrieved files can then be downloaded by built-in file transfer protocol (FTP) support.

Phone Ferret retrieves information from white pages and locates United States telephone numbers by searching the most popular phone number directories. For users with dialer software installed, numbers can be directly dialed from the search results.

News Ferret searches multiple newsgroups to locate Usenet articles, automatically joining multipart messages and decoding binary attachments. The articles can then be retrieved and displayed, or saved for latet review. Search results can be sorted according to different criteria such as source, etc. For more information, visit FerretSoft's home page at http://www.ferrersoft.com.

G2 WebMiner

G2 WebMiner enables applications created with G2 to access and reason about data available over the Internet to provide inrelligent decision support solutions. It can be used to mine data from an organization's Internet Website or intranet, perform rule-based analysis and then make intelligent decisions. For further details, visit Gensym Corporation's Web site at www.gensym.com.

HyperKnowledge

It is a knowledge modeling tool which assists in tasks such as knowledge capture, process design, team building, training and education, and information systems definition. One epository of knowledge can be exploited in multiple ways. HyperKnowledge models provide a means of prototyping business logic, since they can be executed as they are being built. The HyperKnowledge approach is to regard all knowledge as knowledge of processes. Specifically, knowledge is represented in terms of the what, how and why of processes. A HyperKnowledge model consists of reuseable components of knowledge and because it inherently contains all the processes from which any concept is made, an appropriate component or class structure can be automatically derived. When used for information systems design, the model can be exported into an information systems development environment using the industry standards. For further details, visit HyperKnowledge on the Web at www.hyperknowledge.com.

Hyperwave

Hyperwave Information Server is a flexible and feature-rich platform that can provide your portal solution "out of the box," or can be easily customized to meet specific needs. Built upon the Hyperwave Information Server, Hyperwave Information Portal provides a secure and single point of integration, access and navigation through the myriad enterprise systems and information sources facing by workers in today's middle office. The middle office is where organizations unstructured data resides, where the front office and the back office collide, where negotiation, product differentiation and competitive advantage thrive.

The Hyperwave Information Portal provides a searchable repository that aggregates key information sources by automatically and dynamically creating and maintaining hyperlinks your organization's unstructured data including documents, e-mail, PowerPoint presentation videos, images, etc., as well as giving access to structured data. User access is directly from browser. Browser-based access provides ease of use for users and administrators alike plus the integrity of accurately hyperlinked information.

Displaying information in a familiar and easy-to-navigate hierarchical structure, the system seamlessly integrates access to information stored in a variety of native formats. Users can be set up to receive e-mail notifications of new or changed information so they are always up to date with the information that is most relevant to them.

Fully automated hyperlink generation and management coupled with sophisticated document management capabilities ensure information context, consistency and accessibility.

Extensive security and personalization mechanisms are built into Hyperwave. For further details, visit Hyperwave on the Web at www.hyperwave. com.

Info Ferret

Info Ferret is a powerful search utility lor finding information on the Net. It queries Web-based databases including online newspapers and magazines results of probable interest to the user. This tool automatically updates itself everytime it is run. Updates and new search engine configurations are extremely small and the enure update process is fast and unnoticeable.

For more information, visit KnetSoft's home page at http:// www.ferretsoft.com.

Inspiration Professional

Inspiration Professional is a powerful visual thinking tool that helps to clarify and organize ideas and information. Inspiration's Diagram view makes it easy to brainstorm, plan and explain the interrelationships between processes, variables and events. A powerful feature that makes Inspiration stand out against competing products is its ability to convert visual diagrams and mind maps to outlines readable by any word processor. It can create concept maps, process flows, knowledge maps and flowcharts. Inspiration also comes with an extensive set of symbols, templates specifically suited for diagramming, outlining, flowcharting, knowledge mapping, brainstorming, and multimedia design. For more information, visit Inspiration Software's Website at www.inspiration.com.

Intranetics

Intranetics 2.0 is a suite of 20 intranet applications and is a highly recommended route for basing your knowledge management system's front end using an intranet. Each application can be customized to meet your specific business needs. Intranetics is created for businesses and departments with up to 500 users. The software also provides a flexible application framework that allows you to easily integrate existing or custom applications. Through its secure extranet capabilities, your customers, business partners and remote offices can have access to specific applications with either password-protected or anonymous access. A key strength of this suite comes from its ability to integrate existing applications currently in use within your company.

Intranetics 2.0 security provisions build on those provided by the network operating system and Web server, greatly easing administration requirements. Intranetics 2.0 allows companies to define their own security scheme and set levels of access for individual users, including access to specific applications and information fields within an application. Intranerics 2.0 works with a Web server and so is integrated into the server's own security mechanisms.

Two versions of Intranetics are currently available– the standard version and the Microsoft Back Office Small Business Server version. The standard edition, can support up to 500 users, while the smaller version is optimized for Microsoft Back Office Small Business Server. This version is capable of supporting up to 50 users. Both version support most 4.0 version browsers. The company also offers reasonably priced technical support programs. Intranetics is more highly recommended than any other competing tools in its target market because it offers good value and powerful functions. For detailed information, visit the company's home page at http://www.intranetics.com/.

KA^2 Knowledge Agents

Knowledge agents gather, filter and disseminate information from external and internal sources–such as electronic mail, GroupWare, databases, document management systems, intranets, business intelligence applications and external news feeds; and automatically profile and distribute it against individual requirements. They are designed to provide a centralized corporate knowledge base that acts as the main storage repository and broker for the corporate memory.

Knowledge agents includes a full text search engine capable of indexing more than 200 file formats. Using automatic profiling and knowledge mapping technology, the system constantly queries the knowledge base and responds the instant a relevant piece of material is identified. This technology is based on what is described as a vocabulary of interest, which is compiled for each individual, group or organization. For more details, visit AppliedNet Ltd., on the Web at www.appliednet.co.uk.

KeyFlow

KeyFlow is a dynamic workflow management tool that enables users to easily visualize and automate existing business processes, monitor their progress and modify them in real rime to improve efficiency and respond rapidly to changing business needs.

With KeyFlow, documents can be automatically circulated through a business process according to predetermined criteria, ensuring that established policies and procedures are observed. KeyFlow allows knowledge workers to apply their knowledge of the business design efficient business processes that can be used by anyone within a department of the enterprise.

KeyFlow integrates seamlessly into the Microsoft: Exchange environment, taking advantage of client user interface, standard active messaging, user addressing and public folder and replication facilities. KeyFlow's graphical user interface allows users to select the steps needed to build a business process and to link several steps to create a workflow map. It also provides a full suite of controls, such as voting and conditional prerequisites that enable you to automate business processes. For further information, visit KeyFile Corporation's product site at http://www.keyflow.com.

KnowledgeSEEKER

KnowledgeSEEKER is a data mining software tool that employs a unique cross-referencing process that enables businesses to draw conclusions from varied and disparate databases. The application of KnowledgeSEEKER can be tailored to suit the specific needs of any number of different business tasks, from customer profiling and segmentation to fraud detection and risk analysis. The conclusions that can be drawn from the data are often surprising, since the software works independent of any user but putting less importance on pre-conceived ideas.

Angoss, the developer, claims that KnowledgeSEEKFR is faster and easier to use and interpret than both traditional statistical models and new technologies such as neural networks. Analysis results are rapidly displayed in the form of a clear and interactive decision tree or for more advanced users, as Prolog source code. Both the sensitivity of the correlation finding and the volume of the information displayed are easily user defined. For further details visit Angoss Internationals Website at www.angoss.com.

MarketFirst

MarketFirst, although developed for electronic commerce marketing applications, can be a powerful tool to build into a knowledge management system design. A simple drag-and-drop interface utilizes a flowchart meraphor based on business rules, audience segmentation. The feature of most interest in KM applications is its automatic profiling and segmentation capability. MarketFirst's extensible database features automatic incremental profiling, a capability that allows you to easily customize profile attributes and extend the database to reflect specific needs. Workgroup collaboration through e-mail messaging is enabled by its support for popular e-mail servers. All MarketFirst reports can be published tor review to a corporate intranet or Internet Website and viewed through a Web browser. For more information, visit MarketFirst's Website at www.marketfirst.com.

Microsoft FrontPage 2000

The Microsoft FrontPage 2000 Website creation and management tool is very well integrated with Microsoft Office 2000. A relatively low cost tool, FrontPage can be a very good intranet front-end development tool. The multiple views in FrontPage 2000 allow you to see all the files in your Web, run reports to find slow pages and older files, set up your site's navigational structure and keep track of Web tasks. For example, you can create and edit Web, pages in Page View, use Folders View to see all the content on your Web, then set up how your pages link to one another in Navigation View. FrontPage 2000 features extensive summary report capabilities and can help you to identify changed or broken links. When you are consid ering remote access through dial-up connections, its "Find Slow Pages" option lets you local pages that take too long to load based on the modem speed you have specified.

You can create Websites in a folder on your hard disk without installing a Web serve. This makes getting started with FrontPage 2000 as simple as getting started with Microsol Office. FrontPage also supports nested sub-Webs and document check-in/check-out capabilities. Flexible security in FrontPage 2000 allows you to turn a folder in your Web into a sub Web, complete with unique permissions by group or user. FrontPage also supports collaborative development that, in effect, almost duplicates a light version of its project management tool. This feature can be very useful if multiple people are involved in the development of your knowledge management system front end.

The only downside of this tool is that it inserts a lot of Microsoft-specific HTML that can make manual editing both confusing and tedious.

This additional code inserted into Web pages also bloats their file sizes. If your Web server supports FrontPage extensions (on UNIX or NT), its FrontPage components can simplify the task of building interactive pages. This tool is strongly recommended if your servers support FrontPage extensions and if you use Microsoft Office 2000 as your company's official work suite. However, if you need extensive manual editing for your Web pages, other good alternatives, such as Macromedia Dream Weaver, are worth considering. Further information, templates and sample sites can be found at www.microsoft.com/frontpage/.

Microsoft Project

Microsoft Project is a popular project management tool that can help you plan and track your projects effectively and identify and respond to conflicts before they happen. It allows scheduling and tracking of project information by hour, day, week or month. Collaborative features in this tool let you consolidate multiple projects to view cross-project dependencies and multiple-project reports. MS Project features custom time-period tracking to pinpoint how long team members spend on each task, each day.

It further allows efficient time allocation using multiple critical paths that allow you to identity groups of tasks that could jeopardize your project's completion date. Through extensive cross-project linking, you can track changes and links between separate projects with new placeholder tasks that represent dependencies on other project plans. Through tight integration with e-mail systems and browsers, which makes it an attractive choice for integrating in knowledge management systems, you can assign tasks and then get status updates from team members.

Integration with your local intranet means that you can post project information and Gantt charts to your intranet, where they can be viewed easily in a Web browser by those involved with the project. It further allows for sharing information across other Microsoft Office applications such as Microsoft Excel spreadsheets and the Microsoft PowerPoint presentation graphics program. Through its full open database connectivity (ODBC) support, you can directly save and retrieve Microsoft Project 98 data from ODBC-compliant databases, such as Microsoft SQL Server and Oracle, to facilitate enterprise-level analysis, reporting and data integration. For further details and templates, visit the Microsoft site at http://www.microsoft.com/office/project/.

Mind Manager

Mind Manager, based on Tony Buzans book on Mind Mapping,

supports extensive collaboration via the Internet. It is perhaps the best mind mapping tool.

Mind Manager does what hardly any software tools directly help with—supporting independent tacit thought. Its full version supports Internet-based conferencing and provides an extensive symbol library, extensive cross-linking functionality and numerous other features that make it a worthy investment.

Although Mindjet, the development details that it is an organization tool, that statement underestimates its true value for knowledge management applications. For further information, sample mind maps, user guides, and extensive links to mind mapping concept sites, visit Mindject LLC on the Web at www.mindman.com.

MIS Alea

MIS Alea, developed by MIS AG of Germany and distributed by its subsidiaries in the United States and several other countries, allows easy multidimensional analysis of data and brings in capabilities far beyond those possible by using conventional multilevel database queries. In fact complex queries and relationships can be analyzed using existing data in databases and data warehouses.

MIS Alea lets you define the relationships that you are interested in and make comparisons instantaneously by building hierarchies to view data from the highest level to the lowest. An excellent drag-and-drop support is provided by this tool. Creating hierarchies and new relationships is as simple as dragging and dropping the elements of your model under each other.

Expandability and scalability are key. If your company, for example, opens another ket or launches a new product, MIS Alea allows you to add these elements by using a dimension editor feature and without rebuilding your tables or database, such updates are immediately reflected in ever, aspect of your model.

For further information, visit MIS AC, on the Web at www.mis.de.

MIS InterfaceBuilder

MIS InterfaceBuilder is a powerful development tool for the construction, maintenance and refinement of professional planning and information systems applications created with MIS InterfaceBuilder are made available to a wide circle of users through MIS Interface Viewer.

The critical stages of development and prototyping can be earned out by skilled users-quick results are guaranteed by involving people with expert knowledge, thus avoiding unnecessary friction. This development tool integrates seamlessly into existing Excel installations so the designer can often build on existing know-how especially in the sensitive areas of formats and layouts.

The "assistants" and "wizards" in MIS InterfaceBuilder support the links between reports and the MIS Solutions 01 AP-Base. This support enables features such as drop-down lists, check boxes and scrolling to be integrated easily and helps users to gain quick access later.

The large number of ready-to-use standard functions often enables the developer to create complex functionalities, using what the company describes as point and dick programming. Drill-down sensitivities, QDBC-Drill-Through, signals, printing files, comment sheet functions, and user-specific system behaviour are examples of the man standard functions available on demand.

The extensive graphics capabilities of Excel can be used in conjunction with OLAP data and control elements of the Builder. Typical EIS (Enterprise Information System) tools such as drill-down or signal functions can be added to expand the functionality of reports.

Its universal alias administator makes it possible to use a variety of aliases, so for instance, a product could be offered under a product number or under a name in a selection of languages. For further information, visit MIS AG on the Web at www.mis.de.

Opentext Livelink

Livelink developed by Opentext Corporation, is a Web-based application that provides a comprehensive, off-the-shelf collaborative platform for organizations. Aptly, Opentext claims that "Livelink enables companies to speed their metabolism and bubble up vital corporate information across functional across functional, organizational and geographic boundaries." Livelink is easy to implement, use and maintain. Its server enables companies to scale up content sharing to enterprise-wide levels through extensive use of dynamic hyperlinks. This product also provides an Intranet solution that seamlessly integrates with many products and existing technologies.

Hundreds of Global 2000 companies such as AT & T, ISO, OSRAM, Oracle, Swiss Bank Corporation, and Union Bank of Switzerland use Livelink as their mission-critical collaborative application. For further information, visit Opentext Corporation on the Web at http://www.opentext.com/livelink/.

PalmPilot AportisDoc

AportisDoc is an unofficial industry standard tor displaying and interchanging electronic tcext across enterprise systems on 3Com Palm computing devices. The program itself lets you read search through and annotate Palm.Doc documents in an efficient, compressed form enabling users to carry more documents that are larger. This program also supports teleprompting and book marking of portions of large documents. Thousands of electronic books and useful materials are available today in AportisDoc format, including reference works, weather reports, HTML codes, the Bible, postal and country codes, bus and subway schedules, travel guides, and sports schedules.

More significantly, documents of any nature can be made accessible to your employees in this format. This means that some of the essential reference information that is made available to your employees through your company's intranet can then be made available to these users even when they do not have access to the Web in order to get to the intranet.

AportisDoc is distributed in three editions, AportisDoc Mobile Edition, AportisDoc Professional, and the free AportisDoc Reader. Besides including all of the functionality of the AportisDoc Mobile Edition, AportisDoc Professional includes the "Make AportisDoc" drag-and-drop desktop applications for Windows 95/98/NT and Macintosh users, and desktop-based readers. AportisDoc Professional offers drag-and-drop creation of AportisDoc documents from Microsoft Word, TEXT, HTML, and other documents. For further details, visit Aportis on the Web at www.aportis.com.

PalmPilot BrainForest Mobile Edition

BrainForest is a desktop-to-PalmOS linked tool for visualizing textual information. BrainForest displays information on a hand-held computing device such as a PalmPilot or, desktop computer using an intuitive trees analog. It groups related ideas, action items, checklists, to-dos, Internet URLs, e-mail addresses, etc., together. Items can be rearranged via simple dragging of an item from one location to another. Trees may be copied and pasted, shown or hidden. On an enterprise-wide shared knowledge management system, it can be used to keep track of teams and projects, recurring items, due dates, and priorities, so that projects can be kept under control.

BrainForest is distributed in two editions, BrainForest Mobile Edition and BrainForest Professional. BrainForest and AportisDoc are useful tool worth considering if your employees use PalmPilots extensively. Wireless connectivity of the Palm VII, built-in TCP/IP support that allows users to reach intranets and easily available, and inexpensive customization tools make the PalmPilots a viable alternative to on-the-field, connected knowledge workers. For further details, visit Aportis on the Web at www.aportis.com.

PalmPilot Datebk3

PalmPilot Datebk3 is a replacement shell for PalmOS devices that allows users to create graphically oriented visual displays of information about scheduling and project management activities. Using the PalmPilot-to-Web connectivity supported by many commercially available group scheduling and activity management software tools, this application can create a potent weapon in the efficiency-oriented arsenal.

This Web-Palm linkage not only creates an excellent link to the rest of the enterprise but also arguably smooths the introduction of a knowledge management system with a "sweet reward," that is, Palm computers for employees.

Performance Now

Performance Now Enterprise Edition is based on the thesis that good, solid performance management is the key to retaining and developing the most valuable knowledge asset in your company and its people. Performance Now, developed by Knowledge Point Inc., is a total performance management solution for organizations of all sizes.

The tool supplies the framework for implementing a comprehensive performance management system that aligns employee focus with corporate objectives. It includes support for providing valuable day-to-day feedback, for writing meaningful performance reviews, and providing effective coaching to knowledge workers.

Such a tool can be extremely helpful in objectively tying employee compensation to their contribution to your company's knowledge assets. It also streamlines the process and put human resource in control while giving managers powerful tools to track performance, provide valuable feedback and write the kind of employee reviews that help maximize potential.

Performance Now Enterprise Edition is made up of four core modules. The Form Designer and Application Administrator supply powerful tools for designing, implementing and monitoring your performance management system. The Performance Manager and Performance Appraiser give managers valuable tools and just-in-time training to help them better to manage and develop their people. The result is an integrated approach to performance management that results in consistency and focus throughout your company.

Additional modules allow you to further customize performance and modify competencies and customize the associated review text and coaching ideas. Other modules can be industry-specific competency information to create versions for manufacturing, health a finance and state and local government. Further information can be obtained from KnowledgePoint's Website at http://www.performancenow.com/.

Perspecta

Perspecta allows users to query databases using conceptual navigation without needing to understand the schema and idiosyncrasies of the underlying databases, it provides users with the right queries to the given context and set of interests and suggests alternatives as the dialog progresses. It is equivalent to providing each of your users with trained expert librarian who intimately understands the form and content of your information. Perspecta uses knowledge-based, statistical and linguistic techniques to integrate database meta data into an overall conceptual network. This is done by using a Concept Editor to build a Concept Database—a collection of linked concepts and relationships that define the domain of the database. More tnformarion can be found on Perspecta's Website at www.perspecta.com.

Profiler

Profiler is an intelligent employee-screening package that enables employers to select job applicants who are like their company's proven performers. If enough data is collected, information on current employees can help to determine which applicants for the same job would, or would not, meet the criteria for that job. Evaluating these complex patterns within large amounts of data is a very difficult job for a person, but quite easy for the computer when given the task.

Profiler brings complex pattern recognition technology down to the user's level, allowing the HR manager to determine what is important to measure in an employee and what is important to screen for in an applicant. Further information can be found on American Heuristics Corporation's web site at http://www.heuristics.com.

Remote Control Toolbar

Remote Control Toolbar is a complement to the FerretSoft family of utilities. It launches with your browser and resides in the system tray so installed Ferrets can quickly and easily be initialized and put to work. Visit FerretSoft's home page at http://www.ferretsoft.com for further information.

RetrievalWare

RetrievalWare and its associated products constitute a set of tools for building text-based knowledge retrieval solutions. RetrievalWare uses Semantic Networks and adaptive pattern recognition processing (APRP) technologies to do "fuzzy" searching for producing accurate matches even if queries or terms in the documents are misspelled or the documents have been poorly scanned. It also employs an embedded, full semantic dictionary—available in English, French, Spanish and German—of more than 400,000 word meanings, 50,000 language idioms and 1.6 million word associations. This dictionary is used to expand queries and produce results based on word meanings, related words, and concept analysis. For further details visit Excalibur, Inc. on the Web at www.excalib.com.

SemioMap

SemioMap performs text mining rather than data mining. Instead of exploring relationships within structured data, it explores relationships within text, a form of unstructured data. It does this by building concept maps of large, dynamic text collections, using sophisticated linguistic semiotic analysis to identify the linkages of concepts in different documents.

SemioMap uses lexical extraction software that automatically extracts the concepts from a text collection. The list of concepts, the lexicon, is used to identify clusters of related concepts within the documents. The SemioMap lexical extractor is based on research in "linguistic semiotics". It extracts phrases instead of keywords from text and tracks the co-occurrencts of extracted phrases. The extractor can be customized to improve its performance in different environments.

SmartDraw

SmartDraw is an excellent graphics tool that can be used to create and process diagrams and models. Its extensive set of graphics libraries include UML and process modeling. SmartDraw sells in two versions–standard and professional. This is an extremely good value and with extensive integration with Microsoft Office, it is perhaps one of the best choices in its category of tools for Windows-based collaborative enterprises.

For further information, visit SmartDraw on the Web at www.smartdraw.com.

SolutionSeries

SolutionSeries is "problem resolution" software for capturing, diagnosing, solving and distributing resolutions to problems. Users describe problems in natural language. Knowledge in external documents and third-party knowledge bases can also be used. A "solution" is a collection of statements that describe a problem in terms of its cause, symptoms, and fix. Primus, the developer, describes its search method as associative problem-solving technology. A customizable dictionary is used to recognize synonyms. For further details, visit Primus, Inc. at www.primus.com.

ThoughtFlow

ThoughtFlow is a goal-oriented collaboration framework. It can assist in tasks such as goal setting, strategic planning, problem solving, decision making and performance management. It provides a method of organizing information and sharing knowledge during such tasks. ThoughtFlow has a "goal-oriented language definition" ftamework that gives users a shared verbal and visual language about the domain under discussion. Key issues and the connections between them are shown visually and knowledge elements are made explicit and indexed, allowing context-specific retrieval. Further details can be found at Vidya Technologies' home page at www.vidyainc.com.

Web-Enabled ART Enterprise

ART "Enterprise is the development tool for building high-performance Web-enablcd intelligent applications. The product builds on a combination of artificial intelligence (AI) techniques for representing and automating knowledge, with a highly scalable inference engine ART Enterprise provides a rich environment lor rapid prototyping, object-oriented programming and quick development ot intelligent applications using CBR and pattern matching rules. Further details can be found on Brightwares home page at www.brightware.com.

Wee Ferret

Web Ferret is a desktop-based, meta search Web client utility for finding Web pages on the Net. This tool automatically updates itself everytime it is run. Updates and new search engine configurations are extremely small and the entire update process is fast and unnoticeable.

This utility and its other counterparts, such as e-mail Ferret and Info Ferret, make extensive use of the multithreading capabilities of Windows98, Windows XP, and Windows NT etc., to query multiple databases or search engines simultaneously. Query results are made available immediately and can be acted upon by a simple double-click on the result of interest. This opens up the user's default browser or tool associated with the URL, while the query can continue in the background.

For more information, visit FerretSoft's home page at http://www.ferretsoft.com.

Suggested Readings

Abell, A., and Oxbrow, N. 2001. Competing with Knowledge: the Information Professionals in tlie Knowledge Management Age. Library Association Publishing, London.

Ahuja, G. and Katila, R. 2001. Technological Acquisition and the Innovation Performance of Acquiring Firms: A Longitudinal Study. *Strategic Management Journal*. 22 : 197-220.

Allee, V, 1997. The Knowledge Evolution: Expanding Organizational Intelligence. Butterworth-Heinemann, Boston.

Bhatt, G. D. 2002. Management Strategies for Individual Knowledge and Organizational Knowledge. *Journal of Knowledge Management.* 6 (1) : 31-39.

Brophy, P. 2001. The Library in the Twenty-first Century: New Services for the Information Age. Library Association Publishing, London.

Bukdwitz, W.R. and Williams, R.L. 2000. The Field Book of Knowledge Management. Addison Wesley, Singapore.

Davenport, E. 2004. Organizations, Knowledge Management and Libraries: Issues, Opportunities and Challenges. In H.C. Hobohm edited 'Knowledge Management: Libraries and Librarians taking up the Challenge'. K.G Saur, Munchen.

Davenport, T. H. and Prusak, L. 1993. Blow up the Corporate Library. *International Journal of Information Management*. 16 (6) : 405-12.

Davenport, T. and Prusak, L. 1997. Working Knowledge. Havard Business School Press, Boston, Massachusetts.

Davenport, T.H. and Prusak, L. 1998. Information Ecology:

Mastering the Information and Knowledge Environment. Oxford University Press, New York.

Dhiman, A.K.2001. Role of Library Professionals in the Era of Information Technology. *Indian Journal of Information, Library & Society*. 14 (1-2) : 81-85.

Dhiman, A.K. 2001. Impact of Information Technology (IT) on Library Management. In Kalpana Dasgupta edited 'Library Practices for Effective Management' (47th All India Library Conference Papers). Indian Library Association, Delhi.Pp. 191-202.

Dhiman, A.K. 2003. Internet Based Library Services. In Pandey S.K. Sharma edited "Electronic Information Environment and Library Services: A Paradigm' (48th All India Library Conference Papers). Indian Library Association, New Delhi. Pp. 99-106.

Dhiman, A.K. 2003. Data Mining and its Use in Libraries. In TAV Murthy edited "Mapping Technology on Libraries and People (CALIBER-2003)'. INFLIBNET, Ahemdabad. Pp. 568-74.

Dhiman, A.K. and Arya, C. 2003. Leadership Qualities for Information Professionals. *International Library Movement*. 25 (1): 25-32.

Dhiman, A.K. 2003. Knowledge Management System for Knowledge Management in IT Era. *Indian Journal of Information, Library & Society*. 16 (1-2): 1-8.

Dhiman, A.K. 2003. Intellectual Property Rights in Digital Environment. In Y. Singh et al., edited 'New Challenges in Information Management and E-learning in the Age of Globalization (SIS - 2003 Papers)'. IIT, Roorkee. Pp. 292-98.

Dhiman, A.K. 2003. Basics of Information Technology for Librarians and Information Scientists. 2 Vols. Ess Ess Publications, New Delhi.

Dhiman, A.K. 2006. Information Technology and Marketing of Library Services. *Library Progress*. 26 (1) : 29-38.

Dhiman, A.K. 2007. L'enseignement de la bibliotheconomie et des sciences de l'information (French Language Article)-(Trends in Library & Information Science Education and Profession in India). *Bibliotheque*(s). 31 (March) : 34-36.

Dhiman, A. K. 2007. Information & Communication Technology Development and Changing Faces of Library & Information Science Education in India. *PEARL : A Journal of Library Science*. 1 (3) : 3-10.

Dhiman, A.K. 2007. Library 2.0: Emerging Trend in Library Services. In Jagtar Singh edited "Developing Library and Information Resources and Services in the Internet Era (53rd All India Library Conference Papers)." Indian Library Association, New Delhi. Pp. 274-85.

Dhiman, A.K. 2007. Dynamics of Library Science and Future Librarianship.In K. Amudhavalli edited "Dynamics of Digital Information Systems : Prof. M. Bavakutty Festschrift Voluime". Ess Ess Publication, New Delhi. Pp. 124-39.

Dhiman, A.K. 2008. Educating Library Professionals: An Essentiality in Digital Era. *PEARL : A Journal of Library Science*. 2 (1): 11-15.

Dhiman, A.K. 2008. Hand Book of Special Libraries and Librarianship. Ess Ess Publications, New Delhi.

Dhiman, A.K. 2008. Intellectual Property Rights in Digital Environment: Some Issues. In R. Chandra et al., edited "National Workshop on Digital Library Proceedings". ILA, New Delhi. Pp. 104-11.

Dhiman, A.K. 2009. Ontology and Ontological Systems for Semantic Webs in Digital Libraries. In Jagdish Arora edited 'E-Content Management: Challenges and Strategies (CALIBER-09 Papers)'. INFLIBNET, Ahemdabad. Pp. 202-10.

Dhiman, A.K. and Gupta, R.K. 2008. Managing Libraries through Knowledge Management. *SRELS Journal of Information Studies*. 45 (3): 271-78.

Dhiman, A.K. and Gupta, Rajkishore. 2008. Digital Resources and Digital Preservation Policy. In R.U. Meshram, D.H. Vairagare and V.K. Saxena edited "Recent Advances in Library Technology and Innovatives (3rd All India Library Conference

Papers of CGLA)." CGLA Nagpur Chapter, Nagpur. Pp. 105-15.

Dhiman, A.K. and Sharma, Hemant. 2007. Knowledge Management in Library & Information Centres. *Library Progress*. 27 (1): 37-43.

Dhiman, A.K. and Sharma, Hemant. 2008. Institutional Repositories: the Emerging Gateways of Accessing Knowledge in Networked Environment. *University News*. 46 (5): 100-03.

Dhiman, A.K. and Sharma, Hemant. 2008. Blogging and Uses of Blogs in Libraries. In Jagdish Arora edited 'Automation to Transformation (6th International CALIBER-08 Papers)'. Pp. 437-45.

Dhiman, A.K. and Sharma, Hemant. 2008. Access of Scholarly Publications through Institutional Repositories. *Pakistan Journal of Library Science*. 9 : 97-111.

Dhiman, A.K. and Sinha, S.C. 2002. Academic Libraries. Ess Ess Publications, New Delhi.

Dhiman, A.K. and Rani, Yashoda. 2004. Library Management: A Manual Book for Effective Management. Ess Ess Publications, New Delhi.

Dhiman, A.K. and Rani, Yashoda. 2005. Learn - Library Management. Ess Ess Publications, New Delhi.

Dhiman, A.K. and Rani, Yashoda. 2005. Learn - Computer Basics and its Application in Libraries. Ess Ess Publications, New Delhi.

Dhiman, A.K. and Rani, Yashoda. 2007. Resource Sharing, Networking and Library & Information Networks. Ess Ess Publications, New Delhi.

Dhiman, A.K. and Rani, Y. 2008. Library & Information Science Education and Profession in India. Trends and Prospects. *Indian Journal of Information, Library & Society*. 21(1-2) : 1-27.

DiMattia, S. and Oder, N. 1997. Knowledge Management: Hope, Hype or Harbinger. *Library Journal*. 122 (15): 33-35.

Firestone, J. M. and McElroy, M. W. 2003. Key Issues in the New Knowledge Management. Butterworth-Heinemann, Amsterdam.

Gandhi, S. 2004. Knowledge Management and Reference Services. *The Journal of Academic Librarianship*. 30 (5) : 368-381.

Gupta, B., Iyer, L. S. and Aronson, J. E. 2000. Knowledge Management: Practices and Challenges. *Industrial Management and Data Systems*. 100 (1): 17-21.

Hobohm, H. C. (Editor). 2004. Knowledge Management: Libraries and Librarians taking up the Challenge. Saur, Munich.

Khanna, J.K.I981. Personnel Management in Libraries. Ess Ess Publications, New Delhi.

Koina, C. 2003. Librarians are the Ultimate Knowledge Managers?. *The Australian Library Journal*. 52 (3): 269-72.

Leonard-Barton, D. 1995. Wellsprings of Knowledge. Harvard Business School Press, Boston, MA.

Malhotra, Y. 1998. Compilation of Definitions of Knowledge Management. Available at www.brint.com.

Martin, W. 1999. New Directions in Education for LIS: Knowledge Management Programs at RMIT. *Journal of Education for Library and Information Science*. 40 (3): 142-50.

Materska, K. 2004. Librarians in the Knowledge Age. *New Library World*. 105 (1198/9): 142-48.

Milne, P. 1999. Knowledge Management and LIS Education. *Education for Library and Information Services: Australia*. 16 (3) : 31-38.

Nohria, M. 2000. Knowledge Management : Enabling Business Growth. Tata McGraw Hill, New Delhi.

Nonaka, I. and Takeuchi, H. 1995. The Knowledge Creating Company, New York. Oxford University Press, New York.

Parker, K. R. and Nitse, P. S. 2005. Libraries as Knowledge Management Centers. *Library Management*. 26 (4/5): 176-89.

Perez, E .1999. Knowledge Management in the Library — Not. *Database Magazine*. 22 (2): 75-78.

Polanyi, M. 1958. Personal Knowledge. University of Chicago Press, Chicago, IL.

Polanyi, M. 1966. The Tacit Knowledge. Routledge and Kegan Paul, London, UK.

Polanyi, M.I966. The Tacit Dimension. Doubleday, Garden City, New York.

Schwarzwalder, R. 1999. Librarians as Knowledge Management Agents. *EContent*. 22 (4) :63-65.

Sharma, C.K. 1983. Library Management and Organisation. 2 Vols, Sharma Publications, Delhi.

Sharma, C.K. and Sharma, Hemant 2007. Suchna Sanchar Prodyogiki. Atlantic Publishers, Delhi.

Shinde, K.J. and Dhiman, A.K. 2008. ICTs in Agricultural Sector: Status, Uses and Some Issues. *Green Farming*. 1(12): 61-64.

Sinha, S.C. and Dhiman, A.K. 2002. Research Methodology. 2 Vols. Ess Ess Publications, New Delhi.

Sinha, S.C. and Dhiman, A.K. 2002. Special Libraries: Technical and Research Libraries. Ess Ess Publications, New Delhi.

Snowden, D. 2000. Cynefin : a Sense of Time and Space, the Social Ecology of Knowledge Management. IN C. Despres and D. Chauvel edited 'Knowledge Horizon : the Present and the Promise of Knowledge Management.' Butterworth Heinemann, USA.

Snowden, D. 2002. Complex Acts in Knowledge, Paradox and Descriptive Self-awareness. *Journal of Knowledge Management*. 6 (2) : 1-14.

Teng, S. and Hawamdeh, S. 2002. Knowledge Management in Public Libraries. *Aslib Proceeding*. 54 (3): 188 - 97.

Townley, C. T. 2001. Knowledge Management and Academic Libraries. *College and Research Libraries*. 62 (1): 44-55.

Tiwana, A. 2001. The Essential Guide to Knowledge Management. Pearson Education Asia, Delhi.

Von Krogh, G., Ichijo, K and Nonaka, I. 2000. Enabling Knowledge Creation. Oxford University Press, New York.

Warrier, S.E. 2003. Knowledge Management. Vikas Publishing House, New Delhi.

White, T. 2004. Knowledge Management in an Academic Library: Based on the Case Study 'KM within OULS'. Paper presented at the 70th IFLA General Conference and Council, Buenos Aires, Argentina.

Wigg, K. 1993. Knowledge Management Foundations - Thinking about Thinking - How People and Organizations Create, Represent and Use Knowledge. Schema Press, Arlington, TX.

Wigg, K. 1994. Knowledge Management : the Central Focus for Intelligent Acting Organization. Schema Press, Arlington, TX.

Wigg, K. 1995. Knowledge Management Methods : Practical Approaches to Managing Knowledge. Schema Press, Arlington, TX.

Wilson, T.D. 2002. The Nonsense of Knowledge Management. *Information Research.* 8 (1): 39.

Index

L

M

N

O

P

R

S

T

U

V

W